MATHEMATICS FOR BUSINESS AND CONSUMERS

Mathematics for Business and Consumers

REVISED EDITION

Robert D. Mason
Walter H. Lange
Temoleon G. Rousos

all of
The University of Toledo
Toledo, Ohio

1980

BUSINESS PUBLICATIONS, INC.
Plano, Texas 75075

ISBN 0-256-02307-7
Library of Congress Catalog Card No. 79-54421

Printed in the United States of America

4 5 6 7 8 9 0 ML 7 6 5 4 3

To our wives:
Dorothy, Donna, and Irene

Preface

Mathematics for Business and Consumers is a text-workbook designed primarily for a one-semester course in business mathematics offered in community colleges, technical colleges, junior colleges, and four-year colleges. It can also be used in courses stressing both business and consumer mathematics, or only consumer mathematics.

As in the first edition, to exemplify the broad applications of mathematics in business a large number of actual illustrations have been drawn from wholesale and retail establishments, banks, consumer finance companies, insurance firms, and manufacturers.

The textbook is basically student oriented. Its purpose is to actively involve the student in the learning process.

Consumer mathematics is introduced early because in class testing the book the authors discovered that students were highly motivated by such topics as consumer spending and installment credit. There is no reason, however, why the chapters cannot be covered in any sequence.

HIGHLIGHTS OF THIS EDITION

Behavorial Objectives. Each section has an objective indicating what the student will be able to do after completing the section.

Clear Explanations. Each section begins with a clear explanation of the topic. The topic is approached from a "real-world" point of view. This makes the material relevant for the student.

Problem-Solution. Each section has one or more sample problems followed by detailed solutions.

Calculators. As an added feature in this revised edition, the student is shown how to solve many of the sample problems using a calculator. These calculator solutions appear in the margin adjacent to the solutions given in the text.

Self-Review Problems. At various points in each section there are self-review problems which are designed to give students an opportunity to work problems similar to the sample problems. They serve to reinforce the student's understanding of the preceding material. Answers and methods of solution are given in the margin adjacent to the self-review problems.

Section Assignments. To further reinforce comprehension, there is an assignment set after each section. The answers and methods of solution for selected problems are given in Appendix B. There is a large number of problems, to allow the instructor a wide latitude when assigning them. Space is provided to show the method of solution. These sections are perforated and can be assigned by the instructor to be completed outside of class.

Chapter Review Assignment. There is a chapter review assignment at the end of each chapter. A wide assortment of problems covers all of the material in the chapter. These sections are also perforated. No answers are given.

Chapter Self-Review Test. A chapter self-review test for every chapter is provided in Appendix A. These allow students to evaluate their overall comprehension of the subject matter. Answers and methods of solution are given for all problems in Appendix C.

Additional Problems. Numerous problems have been added to all sections. They use current data.

New Topics.

- *Chapter 4:* Consumer Spending, including unit pricing, cost of transportation, cost of renting or owning a home, and budgeting.
- A section on checking accounts.
- *Chapter 14:* Business Expenses, including payroll registers, advertising expenses, and other business expenses (workers' compensation, unemployment insurance, and freight costs).
- *Chapter 20:* The Metric System.

Other Changes. The first four chapters on reviewing basic operations have been consolidated into three chapters. The chapters on simple and compound interest have been combined into a single chapter on banking services.

Acknowledgments

We are indebted to the reviewers for their helpful comments and suggestions. For the first edition these include Professors Robert J. Bishop, Macomb County Community College; John S. Campbell, San Jose City College; Robert Ochs, Miami Dade Community College, South Campus; Richard D. Godfrey, Grand Rapids Junior College; Steven C. Lawlor, Foothill College; Esther H. Highland, Queensborough Community College; Vik Shah, Lansing Community College; Charles Nichols, University of Toledo; and Dr. Murray P. Leavitt, De Anza College.

Many of the changes in this new edition resulted from suggestions by students and professors too numerous to mention. However, we would particularly like to thank Paul Londrigan and the staff at C. S. Mott Community College, Arthur DeManty at Fresno City College, and Helen G. Scoon at Madison Area Tech College for their helpful suggestions based on their experience with the first edition. Special thanks to Alec Beaudoin (Triton College), John S. Campbell (San Jose City College), Frederick H. Janke (Tompkins-Cortland Community College), and Charles Nichols who read the entire manuscript and whose invaluable critique is reflected in this edition.

A special thanks is due to colleague Charles Nichols for his detailed critique. We are also grateful to many insurance underwriters, bankers, retailers, and colleagues for their assistance in preparing specific portions of the manuscript. Our appreciation to Donna T. Lange for her assistance.

February 1980

Robert D. Mason
Walter H. Lange
Temoleon G. Rousos

A Note to the Student

This is not an ordinary textbook. It is constructed to aid you in your study by presenting the subject matter in small, easy-to-take steps with frequent checks to determine whether you fully understood the preceding material.

As you progress through each chapter you will be asked to fill in blanks or solve a problem. The answer to each **self-review** is always given. Following is an example.

SELF-REVIEW

Cover the answers in the left margin.

Susan and Kevin Carr are sales representatives. They receive a commission of \$0.55 for each box of greeting cards sold, \$1.15 for each set of memo pads, and \$0.85 for each child's deluxe coloring book. Complete the following:

Answers					
A. 32 × \$0.55 = \$17.60	A. Commission for 32 boxes of cards is:	32	× \$______	=	\$______
B. 50 × \$1.15 = \$57.50	B. Commission for 50 sets of memo pads is:	______	× \$______	=	\$______
C. 564 × \$0.85 = \$479.40	C. Commission for 564 coloring books is:	______	× \$______	=	\$______
D. Total = \$554.50	D. Total commission is:				\$______

Now verify your answers against those given in the margin.

There are **section assignments** after each section, if you need additional practice. The answers to selected problems, and the method of solution, are given in Appendix B.

Another distinctive feature of this text is the **Chapter Self-Review Test** with answers and method of solution. By completing this test you can better evaluate your comprehension of all of the material in the chapter.

Your instructor will probably assign the **review assignment** at the end of each chapter. The combination of (1) the many self-reviews in the chapter, (2) the section assignments, (3) the Chapter Self-Review Test, and (4) the chapter review assignments should aid you in mastering the subject matter.

R. D. M.
W. H. L.
T. G. R.

Contents

1

A Brief Review of Basic Computations

SECTION 1-1: COMPUTATIONS WITH WHOLE NUMBERS AND DECIMALS

Objective: To add, subtract, multiply, and divide, and to round whole numbers and decimal numbers.

ADDITION

The operation of combining two or more numbers to give one number is called **addition.** The usual practice when adding is to align the numbers vertically.

Problem

Several deposits to a checking account at the First National Bank were: \$242.39, \$3.08, \$94.98, and \$1,357.00. What is the total amount deposited?

Solution

Write the numbers vertically; note that the decimal points must be aligned.

Using a calculator:

Enter	Press	Display
242.39	+	242.39
3.08	+	245.47
94.98	+	340.45
1357	=	1697.45

Deposit Date	*Amount Deposited*
	1 1 1 2
January 3	\$ 242.39
January 8	3.08
February 27	94.98
April 9	1,357.00
Total of deposits . . .	\$1,697.45

The numbers in the extreme right column are summed first: That is, 9 + 8 + 8 + 0 = 25.

The 5 is entered in the total and the 2 is *carried over* to the column to the left. The sum of that column, 2 + 3 + 0 + 9 + 0, is 14.

The 4 is entered in the total and the 1 is carried over to the next column to the left.

This process is continued until all the columns have been totaled. The sum of the deposits is \$1,697.45.

"Albert Einstein didn't do too badly, and he never had a pocket calculator!"

A NOTE TO THE STUDENT: As you progress through each chapter, there are self-review problems for you to solve. By actually doing each problem, you can determine *immediately* whether you have understood the preceding material. The answers to the problems are in the left margin. *Cover them before solving the problems.*

1 SELF-REVIEW

A. 18,000
42,000
386,000
365,000
811,000

A. There were 18,000 murders, 42,000 forcible rapes, 386,000 robberies, and 365,000 aggravated assaults committed in the United States during one year, according to the Federal Bureau of Investigation. The total number of these violent crimes is ____________.

B. $103.97

B. The Florida Power and Light Company estimated these typical monthly costs for electricity for selected appliances, comfort conditioning, and home entertainment. Determine the total monthly cost: $__________

Dishwasher	$ 1.35
Range with oven	2.61
Egg cooker	0.05
Toaster	0.14
Microwave oven	0.72
Dryer	3.38
3-ton central air conditioning	94.50
Color television	1.22

Now uncover the answers in the left margin and check your answers.

SUBTRACTION

The procedure for determining the difference between two amounts is called **subtraction.** The difference can be positive or negative.

Problems

A. A Burger King Whopper costs $1.19. A 30¢ off coupon is used. What is the price of the Whopper?

B. The balance in a checking account is $121.18. A check for $129.37 is written. What is the new balance?

Using a calculator:

Enter	Press	Display
1.19	−	1.19
.3	=	0.89

Enter	Press	Display
121.18	−	121.18
129.37	=	−8.19

Solutions

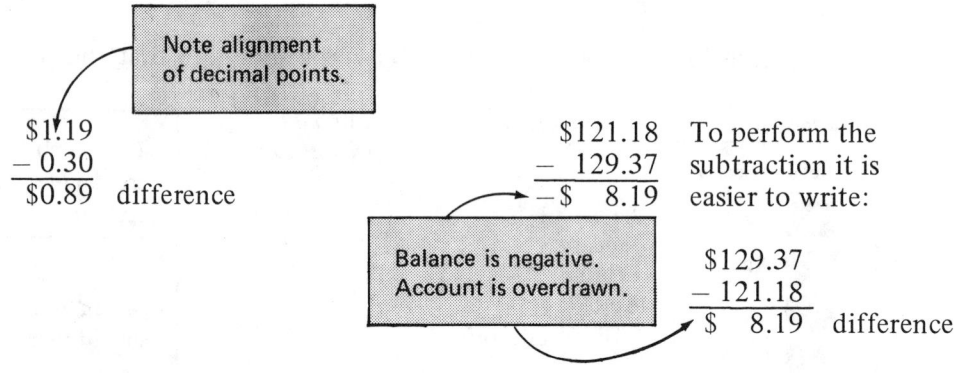

Note alignment of decimal points.

$1.19
− 0.30
$0.89 difference

$121.18
− 129.37
−$ 8.19

Balance is negative. Account is overdrawn.

To perform the subtraction it is easier to write:

$129.37
− 121.18
$ 8.19 difference

2 SELF-REVIEW

Cover the answers in the left margin before solving the following problems.

A. $53,091,000
− 20,643,000
$32,448,000 earnings after taxes

A. Merrill Lynch & Company, Inc., had earnings of $53,091,000 before income taxes for the third quarter. Income taxes were $20,643,000. The earnings after paying the income taxes were $____________.

B. $329.88
− 268.00
$ 61.88

B. K mart has the XG 7 Minolta camera with a f1.7 lens on sale for $268.00. The regular price is $329.88, according to an advertisement in the Sarasota (Florida) *Herald-Tribune.* What is the difference between the regular price of the XG 7 and the sale price? $__________.

Now uncover the answers in the left margin and check your answers.

Certain problems require that some numbers be added and others be subtracted to arrive at the total. To determine the total, the numbers to be added and subtracted are separated. Then:

Step 1. Find the total of the numbers to be added.
Step 2. Find the total of the numbers to be subtracted.
Step 3. Subtract the two totals. The answer can be positive or negative.

Problem Deposits and withdrawals in a new checking account at the City National Bank were: July 6, deposit $500.00; July 11, withdrawal $241.72; July 18, withdrawal $80.16; July 27, deposit $291.86; July 31, withdrawal $42.75. What is the total (called the *balance*) in the account at the end of July?

Solution

Deposits		*Withdrawals*		*End-of-Month Balance*	
$500.00		$241.72		$791.86	deposits
291.86		80.16		– 364.63	withdrawals
$791.86	total	42.75		$427.23	balance at end of July
		$364.63	total		

An alternate solution using a calculator:

Enter	Press	Display
500	–	500
241.72	–	258.28
80.16	+	178.12
291.86	–	469.98
42.75	=	427.23

3 SELF-REVIEW

Northside Ford had 243 automobiles on the sales lot March 1. During March, 18 were received from the factory, and 52 were sold. In April, no automobiles were received from the factory, and 60 were sold. In May, 43 were received from the factory; 65 were sold. In June, 121 were received from the factory; 103 were sold. What was the total number of automobiles on the sales lot on June 30?

Separating the number received from the factory from the number sold to customers:

	On Hand and Received from the Factory		*Number Sold*		
On hand March 1	______				
Received in March	______	March	______		
Received in April	______	April	______		
Received in May	______	May	______	Total at end of June and on hand from factory	______
Received in June	______	June	______	Total sold to customers	______
Total	______	Total	______	End-of-month balance	______

	On Hand	*Sold*
March 1	243	
March	18	52
April	0	60
May	43	65
June	121	103
Total	425	280

End-of-month balance:
425 – 280 = 145

MULTIPLICATION

Multiplication can be viewed as repeated addition. For example, 3 × 7 is the same as 7 + 7 + 7 = 21. And 6 × 8 is the same as 8 + 8 + 8 + 8 + 8 + 8 = 48.

The answer to the multiplication of two numbers is called the **product.**

$$\begin{array}{r} 7 \\ \text{multiply sign} \rightarrow \underline{\times 3} \\ 21 \leftarrow \text{product} \end{array}$$

Obviously, if the problem involved multiplying 36 × 487, adding 487 + 487 + 487 . . . a total of 36 times would be very time-consuming. The alternative is to multiply the two numbers. (The smaller of the two numbers is usually placed underneath.)

Problem Find the product of 487 and 36.

Solution

Using a calculator:

Enter	Press	Display
487	×	487
36	=	17532

```
  487
X  36
 2922  ←  6 X 487
14610  ←  30 X 487
17532  ←  the product
```

It should be noted that in multiplying 487 by 30, the 0 is usually omitted:

```
  487
X  36
 2922
1461   ←  0 was omitted
17532
```

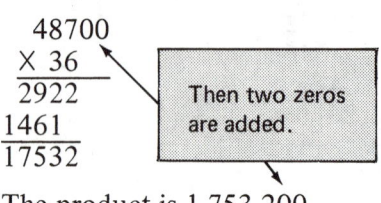

If the multiplicand or multiplier (or both) *end* in zeros, the zeros may be ignored during the multiplication process. Then they are added on to the product. Examples:

```
 48700
X   36
  2922
 1461
 17532
```

Then two zeros are added.

The product is 1,753,200.

```
 48700
X  360
  2922
 1461
 17532
```

Then three zeros are added.

The product is 17,532,000.

In multiplying two numbers containing decimals, the *product must have as many decimal places as found in the numbers being multiplied.*

Problems A. Determine the product of 1.035 and 2.61.

B. Determine the product of 2.013 and 6.7.

Solutions

Using a calculator:

Enter	Press	Display
1.035	×	1.035
2.61	=	2.70135

A.

```
Multiplicand    1.035  ← has three decimal places
Multiplier    X 2.61   ← has two decimal places
                1035
               6210
              2070
Product       2.70135
```

Has five decimal places counting from the right.

B.

```
  2.013
  X 6.7
  14091
 12078
13.4871
```

Has four decimal places counting from the right.

4 SELF-REVIEW

A. Standard Oil of California common stock is selling on the New York Stock Exchange at $46.25 a share. An investor purchases 1,200 shares. Disregarding the commission paid, what is the total amount paid for the shares?

$________________

A.

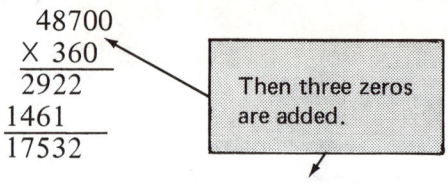

```
  $46.25
 X 1200
   9250
  4625
 $55500
```

The product is is $55,500.00.

B. Dacron voile is priced at $4.88 a yard. The total cost of 26.5 yards is:

$________________

B.

```
   $4.88
  X 26.5
    2440
   2928
   976
 $129320
```

The product is $129.32.

DIVISION

In a sense, **division** is the opposite of multiplication. Since 3 X 7 = 21, then 21 ÷ 7 = 3, or 21 ÷ 3 = 7. The answer to a division problem is called the **quotient.** Division can be shown several ways:

$$\frac{48}{6} \quad \text{or} \quad 48 \div 6 \quad \text{or} \quad 6\overline{)48}$$

6-6-86 Horn + Hardart 13
Dr Larkin 2 5½ High was 9
F.D.A. aproved new Drug
For lukemica
(ZnTeX) Cancer Drug
Tran - 11.37
uTilities - 1.45

...ually dividing 48 by 6 to arrive at the quo-
...e that the first number (4) cannot be divided
...e 6, however, will go into 48 eight times. The
...ioned above the 8, as shown.

```
  8
6)48
  48
   0
```

...tate amounting to $4,950 is to be divided
... among 75 cousins. How much will each
...eceive?

...rive at the quotient, note that the first num-
... cannot be divided by 75. Nor does 75 go into
...t two numbers (49). The 75 will, however, go
...e first three digits (495) six times. The six is
...ned above the 5, as shown, and multiplied by
...e 450 is then subtracted from 495 to give 45.

```
    6
75)4950
   450
    45
```

75	=	66

Next, the zero is brought down to give 450. Six times 75 gives exactly 450. The quotient is 66. Each cousin will receive exactly $66. To verify: $66 × 75 = $4,950. If there is a remainder, it may be expressed as a fraction, or as a decimal.

```
   66 ← quotient
75)4950
   450
    450
    450
      0
```

Problem Divide 14 by 4.

Solution Remainder expressed as a fraction:

```
  3
4)14
  12
   2
```

Answer: $3\frac{2}{4}$ or $3\frac{1}{2}$

Remainder expressed as a decimal:

```
  3.5
4)14.0
  12
   20
   20
    0
```

Note placement of decimal point.

Answer: 3.5

Using a calculator:

Enter	Press	Display
14	÷	14
4	=	3.5

There may be a decimal in the numbers being divided. Examples are 27 divided by 4.5, and 24.9 divided by 6.237.

Problem Divide 16 by 0.125.

Solution Step 1. The decimal point in 0.125 is moved to the right until a whole number is obtained: 0.125.)16.

Step 2. The decimal point in the number being divided is moved to the right the same number of places as in Step 1. (It may be necessary to add zeros to the number being divided.)

125.)16000. (In this problem the decimal point after 16 was moved three places to the right.)

Step 3. The decimal point in the quotient is positioned directly above the decimal point in the number being divided:

125)16000. — Decimal points

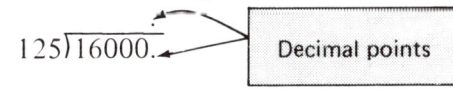

Step 4. Divide as usual.

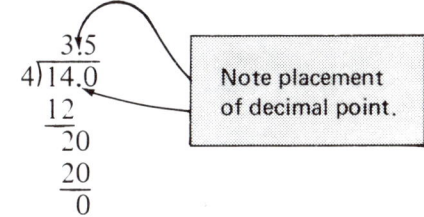

```
      128.
125)16000.
```

5 SELF-REVIEW

A. Complete the division of $104 \div 40$.

$$\begin{array}{r} 2 \\ 40\overline{)104} \\ - \\ \hline 24 \end{array}$$

Leaving the remainder as a fraction, the quotient is ________.

Continue the division. The quotient as a decimal number is ____.

B. Divide 88 by 1.25.

$1.25\overline{)88}$

Leaving the remainder as a fraction, the quotient is ________.

Continue the division. The quotient as a decimal number is ________.

Answers:

A. $\begin{array}{r} 2.6 \\ 40\overline{)104.0} \\ -80 \\ \hline 240 \end{array}$ B. $\begin{array}{r} 70. \\ 1.25\overline{)8800.} \\ 875 \\ \hline 50 \end{array}$

$2\frac{24}{40} = 2\frac{3}{5}$ $70\frac{50}{125} = 70\frac{2}{5}$

2.6 70.4

ROUNDING It is frequently necessary to round off an answer which makes it less accurate but perhaps more meaningful or useful. As an illustration, suppose \$47.29 is to be rounded to the nearest 10 cents. Is it closer to \$47.20 or \$47.30? Note in the drawing it is closer to \$47.30 than to \$47.20. Thus, \$47.29 rounded to the nearest 10 cents is \$47.30.

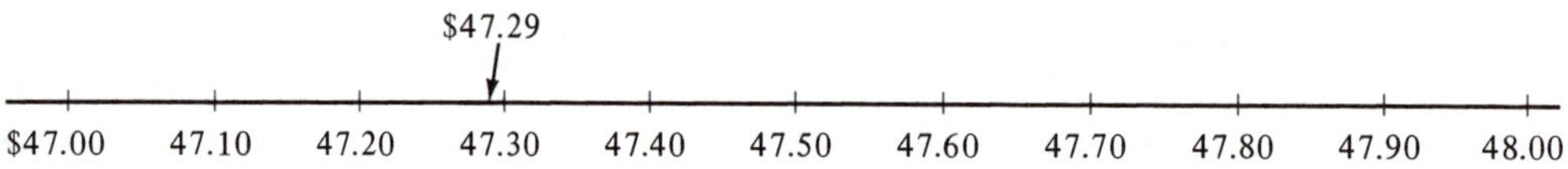

Rounded to the nearest \$1, \$47.29 is closer to \$47 than to \$48. Thus, \$47.29 rounded to the nearest dollar would be \$47.

Suppose \$47.50, which is exactly half way between \$47 and \$48, is to be rounded to the nearest dollar. It is generally rounded up to \$48.

Problems

A. Round \$48,596,324,123 to the nearest million dollars.

B. Round 12.65 ounces to the nearest tenth of an ounce.

Solutions

A. \$48,596,324,123 is closer to \$48,596,000,000 than to \$48,597,000,000. Thus it rounds to \$48,596,000,000.

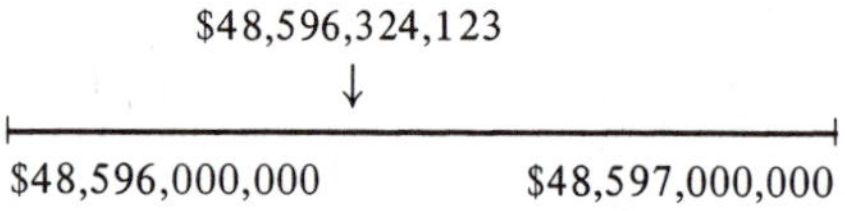

B. 12.65 is half way between 12.60 and 12.70. Thus it is rounded up to 12.7.

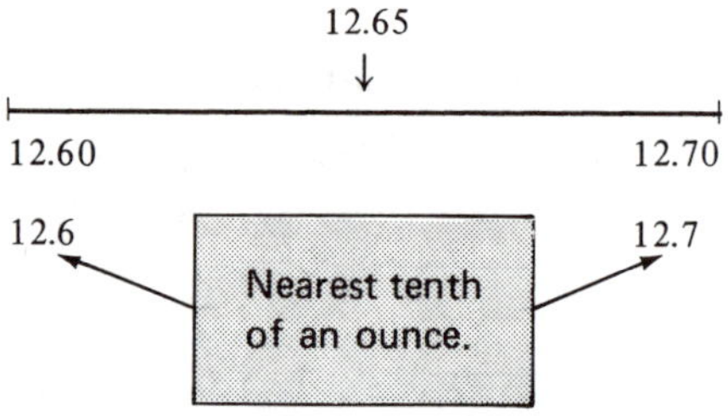

6 SELF-REVIEW

A. Round 4.47392 ounces to the nearest hundredth ounce. ____________

B. Round \$43,702 to the nearest thousand dollars. \$__________

C. Round 112.5 tons to the nearest ton. __________

D. Round \$465.842 to the nearest ten cents. \$__________

Answers:

A. 4.47 ounces

B. \$44,000

C. 113 tons

D. \$465.80

ASSIGNMENT 1-1
COMPUTATIONS WITH WHOLE NUMBERS AND DECIMALS

Name ______________________ **Date Due** ____________ **Grade** ______

Answers to selected problems are given in Appendix B.

Find the total:

1. $803.01
   19.27
   84.67
   1.00
   327.99

2. 0.009
   1.003
   6.971
   0.762
   6.199
   4.582

3. 176 + 14.03 + 192.1 + 846.19 + 1.10 = ____________

4. 0.0012 + 0.00319 + 2.01 + 0.00007 = ____________

Find the difference:

5. $6,071.15
   − 842.98

6. 4.0012
   − 0.1912

7. $846.17 minus $45.69 = ____________

8. $567.89 − $832.98 = ____________

Find the product:

9. 767
   X 28

10. 1.324
    X 1.7

11. 22.3 X 9.003 = ____________

12. Multiply 822 by 0.006: ____________

Find the quotient (round to the nearest tenth, such as 61.6):

13. $8.4\overline{)14.6}$

14. $0.17\overline{)8.4}$

15. Divide 18 by 40: ______

16. 0.245 ÷ 0.6 = ______

17. Round $32,467.55 to the nearest $10: $________

18. Round 44,567.8255 to the nearest tenth: ________

19. Multiply 26 by 18.291 and round the answer to the nearest hundredth: ____________

20. Divide 49 by 0.12 and round the answer to the nearest whole number: ____________

For problems 21 through 24, determine the balance:

		21.	22.	23.	24.
6/1	Balance	$662.46	$814.14	$1,000.00	$500.00
6/10	Deposit	87.19	629.16	426.88	46.14
6/10	Withdrawal	429.68	729.25	86.03	400.00
6/19	Withdrawal	58.17	876.08	129.16	200.00
6/26	Deposit	10.00	62.03	375.00	0.00
6/29	Deposit	81.00	100.00	87.00	0.00
6/30	Balance	$________	$________	$________	$________

25. Find the savings on the two items advertised by Radio Shack.

A. $_______, found by

B. $_______, found by

Cable Kit
SAVE 21%
Reg. 2.39 1⁸⁹
Pkg. of 3
278-014
6′ cables terminated with sub-mini and mini phone plug, co-axial power plug.

Screw Strips
SAVE 25%
Reg. 1.19 89¢ Pkg. of 3
274-657
3 screw terminals. Barrier prevents shorts. Base, 7/8″ wide x 13/32″ high.

26. Find the savings on each size shade based on this advertisement from the *Toronto Globe and Mail.*

Scalloped Hem
with silk-look fringe

Approximate size, tip-to-tip Width, Length	Simpsons Regular Price,	Now, each
D. 28¼" x 58"	11.98	**10.18**
D1. 31¼" x 70"	13.98	**11.88**
D2. 37¼" x 70"	14.98	**12.73**
D3. 43¼" x 70"	17.98	**15.28**
D4. 49¼" x 70"	21.98	**18.68**
D5. 55¼" x 70"	24.49	**20.81**
D6. 64¼" x 70"	37.98	**32.28**
D7. 73¼" x 70"	41.98	**35.68**

Savings

D. _______

D1. _______

D2. _______

D3. _______

D4. _______

D5. _______

D6. _______

D7. _______

27. The following purchases were made: toothpaste, $1.29; aspirin, $1.49; Jergens skin lotion, $1.19; and Sure deodorant, $0.99. The sales tax was $0.30. A $10 bill was given to the clerk. What change was received?

$_______, found by

28. These items were purchased: a half-gallon of ice cream at $1.79, a can of chocolate syrup at $0.79, a gallon of milk at $1.89, breakfast rolls at $0.67, hot dog buns at $0.59, and 2 loaves of bread totaling $1.38. There was no sales tax. What was the change from a $20 bill?

$_______, found by

29. Based on this advertisement from the *London Sunday Times,* how much can be saved per pillow by taking advantage of the sale?

A. Luxury £_______, found by

B. Supreme £_______, found by

Luxury Curled/Goose Feather Pillows Normally £6.50, ONLY **£3.45**

Supreme Feather/Duck Down Pillows Worth £20, ONLY **£11.95**

30. Copper wire is priced at 4.1 cents per foot. What would 15.7 feet cost (nearest cent)?

$_______, found by

31. Kroger advertised a turkey for $0.79/lb. One was purchased for $15.86. To the nearest tenth of a pound, what did the turkey weigh?

______ lb., found by

32. A VW Rabbit Diesel averages 43.2 miles per gallon. If a gallon of diesel fuel costs 98.9 cents, how much would it cost to drive approximately 850 miles from New York City to Chicago (nearest cent)?

$_______, found by

SECTION 1-2: COMPUTATIONS WITH FRACTIONS

Objective: To add, subtract, multiply, and divide fractions.

In addition to encountering whole numbers and decimals in daily business transactions, one also encounters **fractions.** As illustrations, the price of a share of IBM stock is \$312¼, a select group of Haggar slacks are ⅓ off, and it takes 1½ yards of material to make a blouse.

A fraction can be considered as part of the whole, such as 3 parts out of 4. It can also be thought of as a ratio, such as the ratio of 3 to 4. A fraction can also be considered as indicating division, such as ¾. It means 3 divided by 4. The number 3 is called the **numerator** (upper number), and 4 is called the **denominator** (lower number).

ADDING FRACTIONS

If all the fractions to be added have the **same** denominator, then (1) the numerators are added, and (2) the total is placed over the denominator.

Problem Add: $\frac{4}{8} + \frac{1}{8} + \frac{2}{8}$

Solution $\frac{4}{8} + \frac{1}{8} + \frac{2}{8} = \frac{7}{8}$ ← total of the numerators; ← the denominator

1 — SELF-REVIEW

A. Add: $\frac{3}{8} + \frac{1}{8} + \frac{1}{8} + \frac{5}{8} =$ _____ B. Add: $\frac{4}{10} + \frac{1}{10} + \frac{5}{10} =$ _____

A. $\frac{10}{8}$ B. $\frac{10}{10}$

Fractions not having the same denominator are encountered in business. For example, net changes in the price of stock are shown in the financial pages of daily newspapers as: Exxon up ⅛, NCR down ¾, Boise Cascade up 1½.

Fractions having unlike denominators must be converted to fractions with the same denominator in order to add them. This denominator is called the **common denominator** and is a number into which each denominator divides evenly. For example, the common denominator for ½ and ¾ is 4 because both 2 and 4 divide evenly into 4. Another illustration: The common denominator for ⅜, $\frac{5}{16}$, and ¼ is 16 because all the denominators will divide evenly into 16.

Most fractions encountered in business are such that the common denominator can be determined easily. If not, a simple technique to arrive at a common denominator is to *find the product of the denominators of the fractions.* Example: The common denominator for the fractions ⅗ and ⅝ is 40, computed by 5 × 8.

> *Technical note:* A more complex method of converting fractions to a common denominator requires that the *least common denominator* be found. This method will not be discussed because rarely in business is it necessary to add fractions with unlike denominators, such as $\frac{13}{29} + \frac{1}{15} + \frac{53}{87}$.

Fractions to be added having **unlike** denominators are changed to fractions with the same common denominator by this procedure:

Step 1. Determine the common denominator by finding the product of the denominators. Example: The common denominator for ⅜ + ⅗ + ½ is 80, calculated by 8 × 5 × 2.

Step 2. Divide the common denominator (80) by the denominator of the first fraction (8): 80 ÷ 8 = 10.

Step 3. Multiply this quotient (10) by both the numerator and denominator of the first fraction: $\frac{3}{8} \times \frac{10}{10} = \frac{30}{80}$. Thus, $\frac{3}{8}$ converts to $\frac{30}{80}$.

Step 4. Convert the remaining fractions to fractions having the common denominator (80), using the same procedure. Then add the fractions.

2 SELF-REVIEW

A. $80 \div 5 = 16$

$\frac{3}{5} \times \frac{16}{16} = \frac{48}{80}$

$\frac{1}{2} \times \frac{40}{40} = \frac{40}{80}$

Adding:

$\frac{30}{80} + \frac{48}{80} + \frac{40}{80} = \frac{118}{80}$

B. $\frac{10}{40} + \frac{32}{40} + \frac{20}{40} = \frac{62}{40}$

A. Convert the second fraction ($\frac{3}{5}$) to the common denominator of 80 by first dividing 80 by 5 = _____. Multiply the quotient (16) by both the numerator and denominator of the fraction: $\frac{3}{5} \times \frac{16}{16} =$ _____. Converting $\frac{1}{2}$ to a fraction having the common denominator of 80 gives _____. Adding

$$\frac{3}{8} + \frac{3}{5} + \frac{1}{2} = \frac{30}{80} + \frac{\quad}{80} + \frac{\quad}{\quad} = \frac{\quad}{80}.$$

B. Add: $\frac{1}{4} + \frac{4}{5} + \frac{1}{2} = \_\_ + \_\_ + \_\_ = \_\_.$

SUBTRACTING FRACTIONS

A problem involving the **subtraction** of fractions is solved using a procedure similar to that for adding fractions.

For fractions having the **same** denominator: Subtract the numerators and place the difference over the denominator.

Problem What does $\frac{6}{10} - \frac{2}{10}$ equal?

Solution Since the denominators are the same, the numerators are subtracted, and the difference is placed over the denominator.

$$\frac{6}{10} - \frac{2}{10} = \frac{4}{10} \begin{array}{l} \leftarrow \text{difference} \\ \leftarrow \text{denominator} \end{array}$$

For fractions having **unlike** denominators: Convert each fraction to a common denominator. Then subtract the numerators and place the difference over the common denominator.

Problem What does $\frac{5}{16} - \frac{1}{4}$ equal?

Solution The common denominator is 64, computed by 16 × 4. $\frac{5}{16}$ converts to $\frac{20}{64}$, and $\frac{1}{4}$ converts to $\frac{16}{64}$.

Subtracting: $\frac{20}{64} - \frac{16}{64} = \frac{4}{64}$ ← difference ← common denominator

REDUCING FRACTIONS

The fraction $\frac{4}{64}$ in the previous problem can be reduced to its **lowest terms** by dividing both the numerator (4) and the denominator (64) by one number which will divide equally into the two numbers and not result in remainders. The number 4 will divide into both 4 and 64 and not result in remainders.

Dividing: $\frac{4 \div 4}{64 \div 4} = \frac{1}{16}$ ← The usual practice is to reduce fractions where possible.

Some fractions cannot be reduced. Examples: $\frac{1}{2}$, $\frac{3}{16}$, $\frac{7}{10}$, $\frac{5}{8}$, and $\frac{15}{19}$.

3 SELF-REVIEW

A. $\frac{6}{8}$, 2, $\frac{3}{4}$

A. $\frac{3}{8} + \frac{1}{8} + \frac{2}{8} = \frac{\quad}{8}$. To reduce $\frac{6}{8}$ to its lowest terms, the numerator and the denominator are divided by ——. The resulting fraction is ——.

B. $\frac{2}{8}$, $\frac{1}{4}$

B. $\frac{3}{8} + \frac{1}{8} - \frac{2}{8} = \frac{\quad}{8}$. This fraction reduced to its lowest terms is ——.

C. $\frac{40}{80} - \frac{60}{80} + \frac{32}{80} = \frac{12}{80}$

$\frac{3}{20}$

C. $\frac{1}{2} - \frac{3}{4} + \frac{4}{10} = \frac{\quad}{\quad} - \frac{\quad}{\quad} + \frac{\quad}{\quad} = \frac{\quad}{\quad}$. Reduced to its lowest terms: ——

MORE ON ADDING AND SUBTRACTING FRACTIONS

There are many instances in business where whole numbers and fractions are combined. The price of Pepsi stock ($23\frac{1}{4}$) and the California state sales tax of $4\frac{3}{4}\%$ are two illustrations. These are called **mixed numbers.**

To add or subtract mixed numbers:

Step 1. Add or subtract the fractions.
Step 2. Add or subtract the whole numbers.
Step 3. Combine the two.

Problem Pepsi opened at $23\frac{1}{4}$. What is the closing price if:

A. The price increased $\frac{7}{8}$?
B. The price decreased $1\frac{1}{2}$?

Solution A. Adding

$$23\frac{1}{4} = 23\frac{2}{8}$$
$$+\frac{7}{8} = \frac{7}{8}$$
$$23\frac{9}{8} = 24\frac{1}{8} \text{ closing price}$$

$$\frac{9}{8} = \frac{8}{8} + \frac{1}{8}$$
$$= 1 + \frac{1}{8}$$
$$= 1\frac{1}{8}$$
$$\text{Then: } 23\frac{9}{8} = 23 + 1\frac{1}{8}$$

B. Subtracting

$$23\frac{1}{4} = 23\frac{2}{8} = 22\frac{10}{8}$$
$$-1\frac{1}{2} = -1\frac{4}{8} = -1\frac{4}{8}$$
$$21\frac{6}{8}$$
$$= 21\frac{3}{4} \text{ closing price}$$

If the fractions cannot be subtracted it is necessary to "borrow" 1 from 23 in the form of $\frac{8}{8}$.

4 SELF-REVIEW

A. $56\frac{3}{8} = 56\frac{3}{8}$

$+1\frac{3}{4} = 1\frac{6}{8}$

$57\frac{9}{8} = 58\frac{1}{8}$

B. $56\frac{3}{8} = 56\frac{3}{8} = 55\frac{11}{8}$

$-2\frac{1}{2} = -2\frac{4}{8} = -2\frac{4}{8}$

$53\frac{7}{8}$

The opening price of Standard Oil of California stock is 56⅜. What is the closing price at the end of the day if:

A. It went up 1¾?

Adding

$56\frac{3}{8} =$ _____

$+1\frac{3}{4} =$ _____

Total = _____

B. It went down 2½?

Subtracting

$56\frac{3}{8} =$ _____

$-2\frac{1}{2} = -$ _____

Total = _____

MULTIPLYING FRACTIONS

The **product** of two or more fractions is accomplished by this procedure:

Step 1. Multiply the numerators.
Step 2. Multiply the denominators.
Step 3. The product of the numerators is placed over the product of the denominators to give the answer in the form of a fraction.

Problems A. Multiply: $\frac{2}{3} \times \frac{4}{7}$ B. Multiply: $\frac{4}{5} \times 300$

Solutions

$\frac{2}{3} \times \frac{4}{7} = \frac{8}{21}$ ← product of the numerators / ← product of the denominators

$\frac{4}{5} \times \frac{300}{1} = \frac{1200}{5} = 240$

Every whole number has a denominator of 1.

It should be noted that the multiplication of two or more fractions can be indicated by using parentheses.

$$\left(\frac{2}{3}\right)\left(\frac{5}{6}\right)\left(\frac{3}{4}\right) = \frac{30}{72} \text{ or } \frac{5}{12}$$

5 SELF-REVIEW

A. $\frac{15}{224}$ B. $\frac{28}{45}$

C. $\frac{3}{8} \times \frac{160}{1} = \frac{480}{8} = 60$

A. $\frac{1}{8} \times \frac{3}{4} \times \frac{5}{7} =$ _____ B. $\left(\frac{4}{5}\right)\left(\frac{7}{9}\right) =$ _____ C. $\frac{3}{8} \times 160 =$ _____

DIVIDING FRACTIONS

Problem Divide: $\frac{2}{5}$ by $\frac{3}{4}$

Solution $\frac{2}{5} \div \frac{3}{4}$ can be written: $\dfrac{\frac{2}{5}}{\frac{3}{4}}$ $\frac{2}{5}$ (the numerator), $\frac{3}{4}$ (the denominator)

To solve, invert the denominator. The denominator is the fraction the numerator is being divided by. ¾ inverted is $\frac{4}{3}$. Then multiply the two fractions: $\frac{2}{5} \times \frac{4}{3} = \frac{8}{15}$.

A. $\frac{3}{8} \times \frac{4}{3} = \frac{12}{24} = \frac{1}{2}$

B. $\frac{15}{7} \times \frac{7}{2} = \frac{105}{14} = \frac{15}{2}$

6 SELF-REVIEW

A. $\frac{3}{8} \div \frac{3}{4} =$ ____

B. $\frac{15}{7} \div \frac{2}{7} =$ ____

MORE ON MULTIPLICATION AND DIVISION OF FRACTIONS

There are many instances in business where **mixed numbers** need to be multiplied or divided.

To multiply or divide mixed numbers:

Step 1. Convert the mixed number to an **improper fraction.** *An improper fraction is a fraction where the numerator of the fraction is equal to or larger than the denominator.*

Step 2. Multiply or divide the improper fractions.

Illustration: $2\frac{1}{4} = 2 + \frac{1}{4}$

$= \frac{8}{4} + \frac{1}{4}$

$= \frac{9}{4}$, an improper fraction

Problems

A. *Multiplying:* The sales manager wants to increase this month's sales of \$30,000 by $1\frac{1}{2}$ times by the end of July. What will sales be at the end of July?

B. *Dividing:* The profit on a construction job amounted to \$50,000. It is to be divided among two and one-half partners (two full partners and one half partner). What will each receive?

Solutions

A. $\$30{,}000 \times 1\frac{1}{2}$

$= \frac{\$30{,}000}{1} \times \frac{3}{2}$ ← $1\frac{1}{2} = \frac{2}{2} + \frac{1}{2}$

$= \$45{,}000$

B. $\$50{,}000 \div 2\frac{1}{2}$

$= \frac{\$50{,}000}{1} \div \frac{5}{2}$ ← $2\frac{1}{2} = \frac{4}{2} + \frac{1}{2}$

$= \frac{\$50{,}000}{1} \times \frac{2}{5}$ ← Fraction is inverted

= \$20,000 per share, meaning two partners each receive \$20,000 and the half partner receives \$10,000.

A. Cost $= 2\frac{1}{3} \times \$6$

$= \frac{7}{3} \times \frac{\$6}{1}$

$= \frac{42}{3}$ or \$14

B. $\$65{,}000 \div 10\frac{5}{6}$

$\frac{\$65{,}000}{1} \div \frac{65}{6}$

$\frac{\$65{,}000}{1} \times \frac{6}{65}$

$\frac{\$390{,}000}{65}$ or \$6,000

7 SELF-REVIEW

A. A brass towel bar 2 feet 4 inches ($2\frac{1}{3}$ feet) long is purchased for \$6 a foot. What is the cost?

Cost = ____ × \$6

$= \frac{\_\_\_}{3} \times \frac{\$6}{1}$

= \$____

B. A share of \$65,000 is to be distributed among an NBA team of ten players (full share each), a coach ($\frac{1}{2}$ share), and a trainer ($\frac{1}{3}$ share). There are $10\frac{5}{6}$ shares in all ($10 + \frac{1}{2} + \frac{1}{3}$). How much does each player receive?

\$65,000 ÷ ____

$\frac{\$65{,}000}{1} \div \frac{\_\_\_}{6}$

$\frac{\$65{,}000}{1} \times$ ____

\$____

ASSIGNMENT 1-2
COMPUTATIONS WITH FRACTIONS

Name ______________________ Date Due ____________ Grade _____

Answers to selected problems are given in Appendix B.

For problems 1 through 6, perform these operations:

Operation	*Fractions*	*Answer*	*Answer Reduced to Lowest Terms*
Example. Add	$\frac{1}{4} + \frac{3}{8} + \frac{1}{8}$	$\frac{6}{8}$	$\frac{3}{4}$
1. Add	$1\frac{5}{16} + \frac{3}{8}$	______	______
2. Add and subtract	$\frac{5}{8} + 1\frac{1}{4} - \frac{1}{2}$	______	______
3. Multiply	$\frac{1}{3} \times \frac{3}{10}$	______	______
4. Multiply	$1\frac{3}{4} \times 10{,}000$	______	______
5. Divide	$\frac{7}{8} \div \frac{1}{2}$	______	______
6. Divide	$14{,}000 \div 3\frac{1}{2}$	______	______

7. What is the total of the changes in these 13 stocks? (The net change is the last figure in each row.)

   ______, found by

AllegCp	wt	....	36	$21\frac{1}{4}$	$-\frac{1}{8}$
AllegA	wtO	....	30	$6\frac{3}{4}$	$-\frac{1}{4}$
AllegA	wtN	....	21	$1\frac{3}{8}$	$+\frac{1}{8}$
AllgA pf	3	....	2	$40\frac{3}{4}$	$-\frac{3}{4}$
AlldArt		....	1048	$6\frac{7}{8}$	$+\frac{3}{8}$
AlmySt	.20e	8	11	$7\frac{1}{8}$	$-\frac{1}{4}$
Alphain	.05e	12	64	$8\frac{5}{8}$	$-\frac{1}{8}$
Altamil	.32e	5	21	$10\frac{3}{4}$	$-\frac{1}{4}$
AltecCp		....	114	$1\frac{5}{8}$	$+\frac{1}{8}$
Altec pf		....	1	$7\frac{3}{8}$	$-\frac{1}{8}$
AlterFd	.50	7	13	$16\frac{5}{8}$	$+\frac{3}{8}$
Alcoa pf	3.75	....	z100	$46\frac{1}{4}$	$-\frac{5}{8}$
Amdhl	.40	24	1054	$51\frac{5}{8}$	$+\frac{1}{2}$

8. Hook Drugs stock is sold over-the-counter. On a recent day $\$17\frac{3}{4}$ was bid, and $\$18\frac{1}{2}$ was asked. As a fraction, what is the difference between the bid price and the asking price?

   ______, found by

9. When Ringling Bros. and Barnum and Bailey Circus played Cleveland, Ohio, the *Plain Dealer* offered opening-night tickets at half price. What was the *Plain Dealer* price for a:

   A. $7 ticket — $______, found by

   B. $6 ticket — $______, found by

   C. $5 ticket — $______, found by

   D. $4 ticket — $______, found by

10. Wards advertised one third off their six-cylinder tune-up kit, which regularly sells at $1.77. What is the sale price?

    $____, found by

11. Sears' "value of the week" is an 88¢ quart of oil for 66¢. The reduction is what fractional part of the original?

    ____, found by

12. A dozen jelly donuts cost \$0.60 to make. They are sold for \$2.00 a dozen. The cost is what fractional part of the selling price?

__________, found by

13. A recipe in *Good Housekeeping* which makes 6 servings of almond dessert buns calls for $3\frac{3}{4}$ ounces of vanilla pudding mix. How many ounces of vanilla pudding mix would be needed for 8 servings?

__________ oz., found by

14. Anne Collins designed a $1\frac{3}{4}$-ounce tank suit for Bobbie Brooks (a clothing manufacturer) which sells for \$25. If cost depended on weight, how much would a 4-ounce suit cost (nearest cent)?

\$__________, found by

15. The 155 acres of landscaped grounds surrounding the Capitol in Washington, D.C., and nearby congressional offices are kept green with 40 tons of fertilizer a year. How many tons of fertilizer per acre are used?

______ tons, found by

16. Referring to Problem 15, records in the Architect's Office in the Capitol indicated that the cost of fertilizer last year was \$160 a ton. This year the price was $1\frac{1}{2}$ times last year's price. Find the cost of fertilizing the Capitol grounds and nearby congressional lawns:

A. Last year. \$__________, found by

B. This year. \$__________, found by

17. Based on the quotation, wheat closed in December at $\$3.43\frac{3}{4}$ per bushel. At the given closing prices, find the cost to the nearest cent of 7,243 bushels for:

WHEAT	Open	High	Low	Close	Chg
Dec	3.49	3.49	3.43¼	3.43¾	—.02¾
Mar	3.43	3.43½	3.38¾	3.39	—.02¾
May	3.37½	3.38¼	3.33¾	3.34½	—.01¾
Jul	3.23¾	3.25	3.21	3.21¼	—.01¾

A. December

\$___________, found by

B. March

\$___________, found by

C. May

\$___________, found by

D. July

\$___________, found by

18. A few years ago the New York Yankees voted the team manager a half share of World Series money. In all there were $27\frac{1}{4}$ shares. The Yankees' World Series money totaled \$940,125. What did each full share equal?

\$__________, found by

REVIEW ASSIGNMENT FOR CHAPTER 1
A BRIEF REVIEW OF BASIC COMPUTATIONS

Name ______________________ Date Due ______________ Grade _____

1. Add: $\begin{array}{r} 4{,}217 \\ 964 \\ \underline{1{,}516} \end{array}$

2. Add: $\begin{array}{r} 12{,}961 \\ 1{,}437 \\ \underline{23{,}119} \end{array}$

3. Subtract: $\begin{array}{r} 4{,}117 \\ \underline{-\ 968} \end{array}$

4. Subtract: $\begin{array}{r} 671 \\ \underline{-\ 493} \end{array}$

5. Multiply: $\begin{array}{r} 74 \\ \underline{\times\ 23} \end{array}$

6. Multiply: $\begin{array}{r} 176 \\ \underline{\times\ 18} \end{array}$

7. Divide: $4{,}161 \div 73 =$ ________

8. Divide: $5{,}022 \div 62 =$ ________

9. Add: $147.15 + $73.60 + $1,962.03 = $__________

10. Add: $4{,}231.7 + 961.812 + 431.82 =$ __________

11. Subtract: $431.71 – $97.84 = $__________

12. Subtract: $96.071 - 83.9784 =$ __________

13. Multiply: $4.31 × 2.071 = $__________ (nearest cent)

14. Multiply: $1.82 \times 13.7 =$ __________

15. Divide and round to the nearest tenth: $4.71\overline{)17.8}$

16. Divide and round to the nearest hundredth: $41.6\overline{)40.81}$

For Problems 17 through 24, perform the operation indicated. Reduce answers to their lowest terms.

17. Add: $\frac{1}{8} + \frac{3}{16} + \frac{1}{2} =$ ________

18. Add: $\frac{3}{10} + \frac{2}{10} + \frac{1}{10} =$ ________

19. Subtract: $13\frac{1}{8} - \frac{3}{4} =$ ________

20. Subtract: $37\frac{3}{8} - 2\frac{11}{16} =$ ________

21. Multiply: $\frac{7}{8} \times 24 =$ ________

22. Multiply: $\frac{3}{4} \times \frac{16}{21} =$ ________

23. Divide: $2\frac{1}{2} \div \frac{1}{2} =$ ________

24. Divide: $\frac{7}{10} \div 3\frac{1}{2} =$ ________

25. Determine the total amount deposited if these sums were deposited: $17.89, $171.49, and $97.91.

    $__________, found by

26. Complete the deposit slip by determining the total and net deposits.

    Total ________

    Net ________

CASH	CURRENCY	3	00
	COIN		75
LIST CHECKS SINGLY		194	73
		19	16
TOTAL FROM OTHER SIDE			
TOTAL			
LESS CASH RECEIVED		25	00
NET DEPOSIT			

27. If $293.47 had been deposited and $116.47 withdrawn from a beginning balance of $471.53, what is the new balance?

$____________, found by

28. According to the *Toledo Blade,* James Alloway, City Manager of Dayton, Ohio, quit that $47,500 job to accept a similar position with San Jose, California, at $55,000 per year. How much more will he earn in San Jose?

$____________, found by

29. Calculate the difference in percent between the "old net rate" and the "new net rate" from this *London Sunday Times* advertisement for The Leeds Permanent Building Society.

	Old Net Rate	New Net Rate	*Difference*
	Basic rate income tax paid by Society		
SUBSCRIPTION SHARES (For regular monthly savings)	6.75%	7.95%	_______%
HIGH RETURN SHARES (Fixed term investment)	3-year: 6.50%	7.70%	_______%
	2-year: 6.00%	7.20%	_______%
PAID-UP SHARES (For ordinary savings)	5.50%	6.70%	_______%
DEPOSIT ACCOUNTS	5.25%	6.45%	_______%

30. Mahler's advertised a Columbus Day carpet sale in the *Washington Post.* One carpet sells for $10.88 per square yard complete. The Johnsons need 22.5 square yards. How much will it cost them?

$____________, found by

31. How much will be saved by buying four bastiste tailored panels from the Lion Store during the sale?

$_________,

found by

Sale! Bastiste Tailored Panels

Reg. 2.99 Now **2/$5**

45" wide and 63" or 84" long. Assorted colors. DRAPERIES.

32. The *Los Angeles Times* reports that David Rockefeller, Jr., traveled 100,000 miles while visiting 25 states in 18 months to promote the arts in education. What is the average number of miles traveled per month? (nearest mile)

________________, found by

33. Singer, in the *New York Times,* advertised $30 off its $149.95 zig-zag machine. Approximately, what fractional part of the regular price could be saved by buying the machine on sale?

________, found by

TO THE STUDENT: There is a SELF-REVIEW TEST for this chapter in Appendix A, *with answers* in Appendix C.

2

Percents

SECTION 2-1: CONVERTING A PERCENT TO A FRACTION OR A DECIMAL

Objective: To perform conversions between percents, decimals, and fractions.

A **percent** is often used to advertise the interest a bank pays on its savings accounts or certificates, a reduction in the price of retail goods, or changes in earnings and production. As examples, Coast Federal Savings pays 8.0% on its eight-year certificates; the Sarasota Health and Fitness Center has reduced the price of its three-month beauty course by 40%; and the earnings of the Standard Oil Company of California increased 112% during the third quarter.

Percent, symbolized by %, is an abbreviation of the Latin word **per centum** which means *by the hundred.* Thus, percent may be literally translated as *divided by 100.*

A dollar, or any quantity, can be subdivided into 100 equal parts. The 8% Coast Federal Savings pays on its certificates, therefore, is the same as 8 parts of 100, or $^{8}/_{100}$. Instead of announcing that the certificate will earn $^{8}/_{100}$, the common usage is 8%.

A quantity, such as 8%, must be changed to either a *fraction* or *a decimal* in order to perform any mathematical calculations.

CONVERTING A PERCENT TO A FRACTION

A percent can be converted to a **fraction** by placing it over 100. The resulting fraction should be reduced whenever possible.

For example: $40\% = {}^{40}/_{100} = {}^{2}/_{5}$.

Problems Convert to fractions: A. 8% B. 20% C. 93%

Solutions A. $8\% = \frac{8}{100} = \frac{2}{25}$ B. $20\% = \frac{20}{100} = \frac{1}{5}$ C. $93\% = \frac{93}{100}$ ← This fraction cannot be reduced.

1 SELF-REVIEW

A reminder: Cover the answers in the margin.

A. $\frac{10}{100}$ B. $\frac{35}{100}$

$\frac{1}{10}$ $\frac{7}{20}$

C. $\frac{13}{100}$

Convert the following percents to fractions (reduce where possible).

A. 10% = _____ B. 35% = _____ C. 13% = _____

Reduced = _____ Reduced = _____

An alternate approach to converting a percent to a fraction is to multiply the numerical part of the percent times 1%. For illustration:

$$20\% = 20 \times 1\%$$
$$= 20 \times \frac{1}{100} = \frac{20}{100} = \frac{1}{5}$$

This approach is very useful in converting percents which contain fractions.

Problem Convert $12\frac{1}{2}\%$ to a fraction.

Solution

$$12\tfrac{1}{2}\% = 12\tfrac{1}{2} \times 1\%$$
$$= \frac{25}{2} \times \frac{1}{100} = \frac{25}{200} = \frac{1}{8}$$

A. $5\frac{1}{2}\% = 5\frac{1}{2} \times 1\% = \frac{11}{2} \times \frac{1}{100} = \frac{11}{200}$

B. $\frac{1}{2}\% = \frac{1}{2} \times 1\% = \frac{1}{2} \times \frac{1}{100} = \frac{1}{200}$

2 SELF-REVIEW

A. Convert $5\frac{1}{2}\%$ to a fraction.

$5\frac{1}{2}\%$ = _____ X 1%
= _____ X _____
= _____

B. Convert $\frac{1}{2}\%$ to a fraction.

$\frac{1}{2}\%$ = _____ X 1%
= _____ X $\frac{1}{100}$
= _____

CONVERTING A PERCENT TO A DECIMAL

A percent, such as 21%, can be converted to a **decimal** by:

Step 1. Deleting the % symbol.
Step 2. Dividing the resulting number by 100. The quotient is a decimal.

Problem Convert 21% to a decimal.

Solution Step 1. Deleting the % symbol gives 21.
Step 2. Dividing 21 by 100 gives the decimal 0.21.

Using a calculator:

Enter	Press	Display
21	÷	21
100	=	0.21

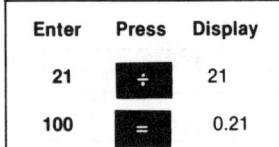

A somewhat simpler approach is to (1) delete the % sign and then (2) multiply the resulting quantity by the decimal 0.01. (Note: 0.01 is the same as $\frac{1}{100}$). That is, 21% = 21(0.01) = 0.21.

In essence, multiplying the number 21 by 0.01 merely moves the decimal point *two* places to the *left*. The original decimal point is after the number 21, that is, (21.). Other examples: 95% = 0.95; 138% = 1.38; and 0.12% = 0.0012.

If a **mixed number,** such as $62\frac{1}{2}\%$, is to be converted to a decimal, it can be written 62.5%. Then moving the decimal two places to the left gives 0.625, or $0.62\frac{1}{2}$. Thus, $236\frac{1}{4}\%$ written as a decimal is 2.3625, or $2.36\frac{1}{4}$.

A. 0.87 B. 6.19

C. $0.33\frac{1}{3}$ D. 0.001

3 SELF-REVIEW

Change each of the following percents to a decimal:

A. 87% = _____ as a decimal.

B. 619% = _____ as a decimal.

C. J. C. Penney marked down a group of sweaters $33\frac{1}{3}\%$. As a decimal:

_____

D. Food prices declined 0.1% during the month. As a decimal:

_____

ASSIGNMENT 2-1
CONVERTING A PERCENT TO A FRACTION OR TO A DECIMAL

Name ______________________ **Date Due** ____________ **Grade** _____

Answers to selected problems are given in Appendix B.

In Problems 1 through 6, convert each percent to a fraction and to a decimal.

	Percent	Converted to a Fraction	Fraction Reduced to Lowest Terms	Converted to a Decimal
Ex.	81%	$\frac{81}{100}$	$\frac{81}{100}$	0.81
1.	16%	________	________	________
2.	$8\frac{1}{2}\%$	________	________	________
3.	$66\frac{2}{3}\%$	________	________	________
4.	125%	________	________	________
5.	$1\frac{3}{4}\%$	________	________	________
6.	0.073%	________	________	________

In Problems 7 through 16, convert each percent to a fraction reduced to lowest terms and to a decimal.

7. *Time* reported that ground-combat units were involved in 20% of the incidents where the United States has seriously threatened to unleash some of its military might.

   A. As a fraction: ________ B. As a decimal: ________

8. *Newsweek* reported that Rupert Murdoch of Australia purchased 23.8% interest in the New York Magazine Company.

   A. As a fraction: ________ B. As a decimal: ________

9. Sixty-five percent of the air controllers at Chicago's O'Hare Field either have ulcers or show ulcer symptoms, according to *Psychology Today*.

   A. As a fraction: ________ B. As a decimal: ________

10. Sunset Shutters advertised in the *Los Angeles Times* 25% off on all styles of custom shutters.

    A. As a fraction: ________ B. As a decimal: ________

11. First Federal Savings and Loan Association pays 5% interest on regular savings accounts.

    A. As a fraction: ________ B. As a decimal: ________

12. The *Atlanta Constitution* reported that the trade agreement talks between the United States and the U.S.S.R. were 95% complete.

    A. As a fraction: ________ B. As a decimal: ________

13. From Paul Weingarten, of the *Chicago Tribune,* writing about corporate names:

A. As a fraction: ______ or ______

B. As a decimal: ______ or ______

> **Then there was a run on initials. "They all wanted to be IBM or RCA, but they didn't realize that thousands of companies had initials, and maybe the top 1 or 2 per cent were recognizable to most people. After a while, many abandoned initials."**

14. The misses' sweaters advertisement calls for savings of 50% to 75%.

A. As fractions: ______

B. As decimals: ______

> **50%-75% off**
> **misses' sweaters**

15. The Cape Cod curtains are 30% off.

A. As a fraction: ______

B As a decimal: ______

> **30% off**
> **crisp Cape Cod curtains**

16. The ad promises 15% saved:

A. As a fraction: ______

B. As a decimal: ______

> SAVE 15%

In Problems 17 through 25, explain what the percents mean.

17. The *Dallas Morning News* carried the weather forecast for Texarkana.

> **TEXARKANA — Partly cloudy through Sunday with a 20 percent chance of thundershowers Saturday. High Saturday and Sunday upper 80s. Low early Sunday mid-60s.**

______

18. *Time* magazine reported that approximately 40% of the population of the United States watched the last episode of *Roots* on television.

______

19. New York City has an 8% sales tax.

______

20. The *Perrysbury Messenger-Journal* reported that 90% of all the homes in Wood County had television sets.

______

21. First Federal Savings and Loan Association pays an interest rate of 6% on passbook savings accounts.

______

22. During one stretch of last season's NBA schedule, Joe Carpenter made 85% of his free throws.

______

23. The average American family spends 25% of its net income for shelter.

______

24. John Jones earned a grade of 80% on his first business mathematics test.

______

25. Harriet's of Philadelphia is marking down everything in the store 30%.

______

SECTION 2-2: CONVERTING DECIMALS AND FRACTIONS TO PERCENTS

Objective: To perform conversions between decimals, fractions, and percents.

CONVERTING A DECIMAL TO A PERCENT

Logically, the procedure for converting a **decimal to a percent** is the reverse of that described in Section 2-1. The most direct way is to move the decimal point *two* places to the *right* and attach the % symbol.

Problems

A. Convert the decimal 0.25 to a percent.
B. Convert the decimal 0.125 to a percent.
C. Convert the decimal 0.08 to a percent.

Solutions

	Decimal	*Move Decimal and Attach %*	*Usually Written*
A.	0.25	0.25.%	25%
B.	0.125	0.12.5%	12.5%
C.	0.08	0.08.%	8%

1 — SELF-REVIEW

Express each decimal as a percent:

A. 0.40 = ______%   B. 0.625 = ______%   C. 1.08 = ______%
D. 0.015 = ______%   E. 0.0005 = ______%   F. 11.4 = ______%

A. 40% B. 62.5%
C. 108% D. 1.5%
E. 0.05% F. 1,140%

G. Dave Parker of the Pittsburgh Pirates is leading the league with a batting average of .384. This means that he has a hit what percent of the time he comes to bat? ______%

G. 38.4%

H. The annual return on a selected group of electronic stocks is .0968. What is the percent return? ______%

H. 9.68%

CONVERTING A FRACTION TO A PERCENT

A **fraction** is first changed to a **decimal** by:

Step 1. Dividing the numerator of the fraction by the denominator, which gives a decimal.

Step 2. The decimal is then converted to a percent by moving the decimal point *two* places to the *right* and attaching the % symbol.

Problems

Convert these fractions to percents: A. $\frac{1}{4}$; B. $\frac{3}{8}$; C. $1\frac{1}{4}$.

Solutions

A. To convert $\frac{1}{4}$:

Dividing 1 by 4 = 0.25
Moving point = 25%

B. To convert $\frac{3}{8}$:

Dividing 3 by 8 = 0.375
Moving point = 37.5%

C. To convert $1\frac{1}{4}$:

$1\frac{1}{4} = \frac{5}{4}$
= 1.25
= 125%

Using a calculator:

Enter	Press	Display
3	÷	3
8	=	0.375

2 SELF-REVIEW

A. $3 \div 4 = 0.75$
$= 75\%$

B. $13 \div 20 = 0.65$
$= 65\%$

C. $\frac{17}{5} = 17 \div 5$
$= 3.4$
$= 340\%$

D. $\frac{300}{12000} = \frac{1}{40} = 0.025$
$= 2.5\%$

Convert the following fractions to percents.

A. $\frac{3}{4}$ B. $\frac{13}{20}$ C. $3\frac{2}{5}$

$3 \div 4 = 0.$____ $= $____%

$13 \div 20 = $____ $= $____%

$3\frac{2}{5} = \frac{17}{5} = $____ $\div$ ____ $=$ ____ $=$ ____%

D. The camera department occupies 300 square feet of the total 12,000 square feet in a department store. What percent of the total square footage is occupied by the camera department? ____%

FRACTIONAL PERCENTS

Is ½ the same as ½%? It is not! The first, ½, is a **fraction,** and the second, ½%, is a **fractional percent.** As noted previously, the fraction ½ equals $^{50}/_{100}$, or 50%. The fractional percent ½%, however, means ½ of 1%. This could be written ½ of $^{1}/_{100}$ which equals $^{1}/_{200}$. As a decimal, $^{1}/_{200} = 0.005$. Therefore, ½% $= {}^{1}/_{200} = 0.005$.

Another way to consider the conversion of the fractional percent ½% to a decimal is: The decimal equivalent of the fraction ½ is 0.5. Thus, ½% is the same as 0.5%. Again, a percent may be converted to a decimal by moving the decimal point two places to the left, that is, 0.5% = 0.005.

3 SELF-REVIEW

	Interpret	*Decimal*
A.	$\frac{3}{4}$ of 1%	0.0075
B.	$\frac{2}{5}$ of 1%	0.004
C.	$\frac{1}{4}$ of 1%	0.0025

	Percent	*Interpretation*	*Converted to a Decimal*
A.	$\frac{3}{4}\%$	____ of 1%	____
B.	$\frac{2}{5}\%$	____	____

C. The First National Bank of New York announced an increase in its prime rate from 11½% to 11¾%. This means that the bank raised its prime rate ____ of 1%. The increase expressed as a decimal is ____.

ASSIGNMENT 2-2
CONVERTING DECIMALS AND FRACTIONS TO PERCENTS

Name ______________________ Date Due ______________ Grade _____

Answers to selected problems are given in Appendix B.

In Problems 1 through 8, convert to percents these decimals and fractions:

	Decimal	*Percent*		*Fraction*	*Percent*
Ex.	0.10	10%			
1.	0.06	________	5.	$\frac{37}{40}$	________
2.	0.81	________	6.	$\frac{5}{8}$	________
3.	2.39	________	7.	$4\frac{1}{8}$	________
4.	23.9	________	8.	$1\frac{1}{10}$	________

In Problems 9 to 18, convert the fraction or decimal to a percent.

9. Convert the ratio (fraction) taken from a Merit advertisement to a percent.

   ________%

Confirmed: **9 out of 10 MERIT smokers not considering other brands.**

10. The Office of Institutional Research at a major midwestern university estimated that, based on past experience, out of 100 who enroll as freshmen, only 53 will ever reach the senior year. $^{53}/_{100}$ converted to a percent is _____%.

11. There is a midwinter sale on misses' coordinates. Convert the fractions to percents.

    1/4 to 1/2 off misses' coordinates

    A. $\frac{1}{4}$ = _____%   B. $\frac{1}{2}$ = _____%

12. The U.S. Public Health Service reported in *Vital Statistics of the United States* that the number of illegitimate live births compared to total births is in the ratio of 9.7 to 100.

    _______% of the births are illegitimate.

13. The *Federal Reserve Bulletin* reports the bank rate charged on short-term business loans in selected cities rose from 0.095 to 0.105.

    0.095 converts to _____%, 0.105 to _____%.

14. The dropout rate at Benton Harbor (Michigan) High School was 19.87 per 100 students. Statewide, 10.11 out of every 100 male 11th-graders dropped out. Cite these dropout rates as percents.

    A. 19.87 per 100 = ______%   B. 10.11 out of every 100 = ______%

15. Note that these property tax rates are dollars and cents per thousand dollars. Convert the ten rates (A-J) to percents.

RATES OF TAXATION IN WOOD COUNTY

In pursuance of Section 323.08 Revised Code, I, Edward N. Nietz, Treasurer of Wood County, do hereby give notice that the amount of taxes levied on the Tax Duplicate expressed in Dollars and Cents on each One Thousand Dollars of Valuation for the tax year is as follows:

			Countywide Purposes*	Township Purposes	Local School Purposes	Vocational School Purposes	Total Tax Rate
Total Countywide Rate*							
County General Fund	(A)	$2.35					
County Park	(B)	0.05					
Community Mental Health	(C)	0.80					
Retarded School Levy	(D)	0.80					
Total Countywide Purposes*	(E)	$4.00					
Bloom Township			(F)	(G)	(H)	(I)	(J)
A01 Elmwood LSD			$4.00	$3.30	$30.50	$1.50	$39.30

A. ________%

B. ________%

C. ________%

D. ________%

E. ________%

F. ________%

G. ________%

H. ________%

I. ________%

J. ________%

16. Convert the ratio (fraction) 2 to 1 to a percent.

_______%

> **Declines outstripped gainers by more than 2-1 on the New York Stock Exchange, with nearly 1,100 issues losing ground.**

17. Convert the fractions of "Your Cost" to "Normal Retail" to percents for England, Germany, France, and Italy. Carry the percents to the nearest hundredth percent.

A. England _______%

B. Germany _______%

C. France _______%

D. Italy _______%

Compare what you'd normally pay for an Andrew Pallack No. 4 plus make suit (hand-sewn on all but the straight seams, hand-basted canvases, 32 separate pressings, hand-sewn buttons and hand-finished buttonholes) at normal retail prices and your direct wholesale price for the same suit at our factory.

YOUR HOME	NORMAL RETAIL*	YOUR COST
England	184 Pounds	84 Pounds
Germany	671 Marks	306 Marks
France	1665 Francs	759 Francs
Italy	309,734 Lira	141,150 Lira
Brazil	6717 Cruzeiros	3061 Cruzeiros
Japan	72163 Yen	32,886 Yen
San Diego. USA	350 Dollars	159.50 Dollars
Switzerland	584 Francs	266 Francs
Mexico	8751 Pesos	3988 Pesos

Other Suits $159.50-$189.50

Andrew Pallack is the only name menswear designer selling direct to the public at wholesale prices.

18. Referring to the Andrew Pallack advertisement in Problem 17, perform the same conversions, to the nearest hundredth percent, for Brazil; Japan; San Diego, California; Switzerland; and Mexico.

A. Brazil _______% B. Japan _______% C. San Diego _______%

D. Switzerland _______% E. Mexico _______%

19. Compare $\frac{1}{4}$ to $\frac{1}{4}\%$. A. $\frac{1}{4}$ as a decimal is _______ B. $\frac{1}{4}\%$ as a decimal is __________

20. Given the quantities $\frac{1}{50}$, $\frac{1}{5}\%$, and 0.002:

A. Of the three, which is the largest? ______________

B. Of the three, which is the smallest? ______________

REVIEW ASSIGNMENT FOR CHAPTER 2
PERCENTS

Name ______________________ **Date Due** ____________ **Grade** ______

1. The word "percent" means per ____________.
2. The ratio 14.6 to 100 expressed as a percent is ______.
3. Since the percent symbol (%) and the word "percent" do not lend themselves to mathematical calculations, they must be changed to either a ____________ or a ____________ before doing any calculations.

For Problems 4 through 12, complete the table:

	% (nearest tenth)	*Decimal (nearest hundredth)*	*Fraction (reduced)*
4.	15.0%	______	______
5.	______	0.240	______
6.	______	______	$\frac{9}{20}$
7.	260.0%	______	______
8.	______	0.008	______
9.	______	______	$5\frac{1}{3}$
10.	$\frac{1}{10}$%	______	______
11.	______	47	______
12.	______	______	$\frac{7}{300}$

13. How do you convert a percent to a decimal?

____

____

14. How do you convert a fraction to a decimal?

____

____

15. How do you convert a decimal to a percent? ______________________________

16. A department store advertised 100% cotton shirts.

   A. As a decimal, 100% is ______

   B. As a fraction, 100% is ______

   C. What does 100% cotton mean? ____________

100% cotton . . . soft, long-wearing, absorbent. Full-cut T-shirts

17. Convert the percents dealing with income tax estimates to decimals and fractions.

A. Write 7% as: A decimal ______ A fraction ______

B. Write 5% as: A decimal ______ A fraction ______

> **Overall, income tax estimates now are expected to rise by 7 per cent next year, rather than the 5 per cent projected earlier.**

18. Sportfame advertised "¼ off" on all tennis shoes. What percent are the tennis shoes being reduced? ______________________ %

19. In Problem 18, what percent of the regular price do you pay for tennis shoes which are on sale? ______________________ %

20. From the stock market section of *The New York Times,* convert the Salomon Brothers' Key Rates (in percents) to decimals.

Key Rates In percent

	Yesterday	
FEDERAL FUNDS	9.56	________
3-MONTH TREASURY BILLS	8.84	________
TREASURY NOTES	8.81	________
TREASURY BONDS	8.71	________
BELL SYSTEM BONDS	9.04	________
MUNICIPAL BONDS	6.59	________
6-MONTH SAVINGS CERTIFICATES	9.29	________

Salomon Brothers estimates for bellwether issues

Percents	*Decimals*
9.56	______
8.84	______
8.81	______
8.71	______
9.04	______
6.59	______
9.29	______

21. Refering to the Sears advertisement:

A. Convert 25% to: A decimal __________

A fraction __________

B. Convert 40% to: A decimal __________

A fraction __________

C. Convert ⅓ to: A decimal __________

A percent __________

> Dishwashers and Compactors 25% to 40% OFF Reg. Prices | Sears | Gas Water Heaters 1/3 OFF Reg. Prices

22. Convert the percents in the ad to fractions (reduced) and to decimals.

A. 15% as: A fraction __________

A decimal __________

B. 50% as: A fraction __________

A decimal __________

> **15%–50% OFF**
> *on selected items*

23. The annual rate of return on the invested assets of life insurance was 0.0738. This number written as a percent is ________%.

24. A senator charged that the Pentagon allowed a company to make a 34,000% profit on an item. Change 34,000% to a decimal. ____________

25. Change all the percents in the paragraph from the entertainment section of the *Toledo Blade* to their decimal equivalents.

A. Channel 13's gain of 2% ________

B. Channel 11's loss of 7% ________

> **But as compared with the February survey, Ch. 13 posted a gain of 2 per cent and Ch. 11 lost 7 per cent.**

TO THE STUDENT: There is a SELF-REVIEW TEST for this chapter in Appendix A, *with answers* in Appendix C.

3

Percentages

SECTION 3-1: PERCENTAGE, RATE, AND BASE

Objective: To compute the percentage, rate, or base.

Chapter 2 dealt with percents. It was pointed out that a percent, such as 8%, can be converted to a decimal (0.08) or the fraction $^{8}/_{100}$, or $^{2}/_{25}$ reduced. This conversion is necessary in order to answer such queries as:

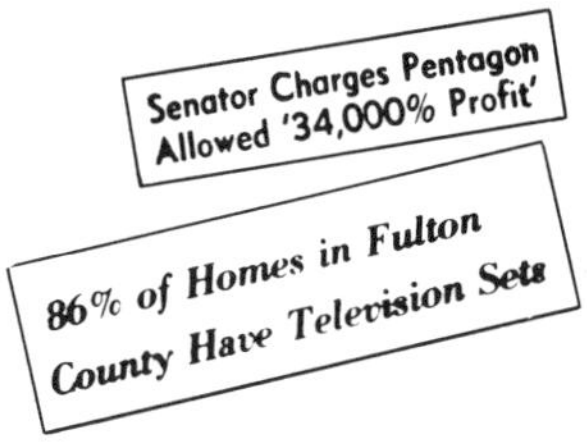
Senator Charges Pentagon Allowed '34,000% Profit'
86% of Homes in Fulton County Have Television Sets

1. What is 80% of the goal of $800,000 for the new church?
2. A $55 profit is what percent of the selling price of a $350 sofa?
3. If the $4\frac{1}{2}$% sales tax added to the price of a new car amounted to $252, what was the total purchase price of the car?

Virtually every problem encountered involving percents can be reduced to one of the three types just cited. Note that in each problem *two* figures are given and there is *one* unknown. In the church building fund problem, for example, 80% of the goal of $800,000 was reached, but the amount already collected for the new church is unknown. The solution to each of these three types of problems is examined in this chapter.

BASE, RATE, AND PERCENTAGE

Most of the problems dealing with percents revolve around three terms—the **base**, designated by B; the **rate**, designated by R; and the **percentage**, designated by P.

The **base**, B, can be loosely defined as the *total*, or 100 percent, of any quantity. It may be the total number covered by Medicare health insurance (23.5 million) or the initial deposit of $200 in a Wachovia Bank & Trust savings account.

The **rate**, R, is defined as the *percent* or *fractional part* under consideration. Some examples are: 17.2% of the households in Shreveport, Louisiana, lack some or all plumbing; Zambia is assessed 0.04% of the total cost of operating the United Nations.

The word **"percentage,"** designated by P, is a rather inappropriate one. It is not the same as the accepted concept of percent. Instead, P might be the *amount* of interest earned during a one-year period on $1,000, given an interest rate of 7%. In another problem, P might be the *amount* of money assessed Zambia as its share of U.N. expenses.

CALCULATING THE PERCENTAGE

In essence, the percentage, P, is the product of the base and the rate.

Percentage = Base × Rate or $P = B \times R$

Problem

A study at a state university of 2,992 freshmen (the base, B) showed that only 46.46% (the rate, R) were on hand the senior year. The question is: How many students (the percentage) reached the senior year?

Solution

Using a calculator:

Enter	Press	Display
2992	×	2992
.4646	=	1390.0832

or

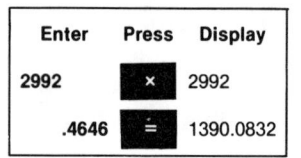

Using a calculator with a percent key %:

Enter	Press	Display
2992	×	2992
46.46	%	1390.0832

$$\begin{aligned} \text{Percentage} &= \text{Base} \times \text{Rate} \\ \text{In letters: } P &= B \times R \\ &= 2{,}992 \times 46.46\% \\ &= 2{,}992 \times 0.4646 \\ &= 1{,}390 \text{ students reached the senior year} \end{aligned}$$

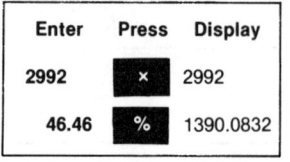

Note that to perform the calculations, the rate of 46.46% had to be changed to a decimal. Also note that the percentage, P, and the base, B, are in the *same* units. In this problem, P and B represent the *number* of students enrolled.

If the rate (percent), R, is over 100% of the base, the *percentage, P, will be greater than the base.* For illustration, suppose that a team of assembly-line workers has a quota of 200 electronic panels which it must assemble during the eight-hour workday. B is the total quantity of 200. If the team produces 100% of its quota, this obviously means that it assembled 200 panels.

Problem

The team produced 150% of its quota on Thursday. How many panels did the team assemble?

Solution

$$\begin{aligned} \text{Percentage} &= \text{Base} \times \text{Rate} \\ P &= B \times R \\ &= 200 \times 150\% \\ &= 200 \times 1.50 \\ &= 300 \text{ electronic panels assembled} \end{aligned}$$

1 SELF-REVIEW

A reminder: Cover the answers in the margin.

A. A church has a building fund goal of $800,000. It has collected 80% of its goal. How much money has been collected?

In words: Percentage = ________ × ________
= $__________ × ________%
= $__________ × 0.______
= $__________

Base × Rate
= $800,000 × 80%
= $800,000 × 0.80
= $640,000

B. Many life insurance companies set an annual level of sales for each of their underwriters. The goal set for Anne Lopez was $2 million in new policies. It was announced at the end of the year that she actually had written 110% of her goal. What was the value of the new policies she wrote?

In letters: ____ = ____ × ____
= $__________ × ______%
= $__________ million

$P = B \times R$
= $2 million × 110%
= $2.2 million

CALCULATING THE RATE

Suppose that the percentage, P, and base, B, are given, but the **rate**, R, is unknown. Solving the equation $P = B \times R$ for R:

$$\text{Rate (percent)}, R = \frac{\text{Percentage}, P}{\text{Base}, B}, \quad \text{or} \quad \text{Rate} = \frac{\text{Part}}{\text{Whole}}$$

$$\text{or} \quad R = \frac{P}{B}$$

Problem There are 65.6 million homes in the United States wired for electricity, according to *Merchandising Week.* The numbers of homes having blenders, coffeemakers, color television sets, and other selected electrical appliances are shown in the table.

Item	*No. of Homes (in millions)*
Blender	26.2
Coffeemaker	59.7
Color television set	33.5
Toaster	61.7
Washer, clothes	61.8

What percent of the homes have color television sets?

Solution In order to apply the formula $R = \frac{P}{B}$, one must decide whether 33.5 million or 65.6 million is the base. Recall that the base is defined as the *total,* or 100%, of any quantity. The total number of homes, or 65.6 million, is the base.

Using a calculator:

Enter	Press	Display
33.5	÷	33.5
65.6	=	0.5106707

$$R = \frac{\text{Percentage}, P}{\text{Base}, B}, \quad \text{or} \quad \frac{\text{Part}}{\text{Whole}}$$

$$= \frac{P}{B}$$

$$= \frac{33.5}{65.6}$$

$$= 0.5107, \quad \text{or} \quad 51.1\% \text{ have color TV sets}$$

2 SELF-REVIEW

A sofa is marked to sell for \$350. The profit on the sofa is \$55. The \$55 profit is what percent (%) of the selling price of \$350?

$$\text{Rate (percent)}, R = \frac{\text{Percentage}, P}{\text{Base}, B}$$

In letters: R = ——

= ———

= ________ (decimal) or ______% (round to nearest tenth)

$R = \frac{P}{B}$

$= \frac{\$55}{\$350}$

$= 0.1571$ or 15.7%

CALCULATING THE BASE

As noted previously, the **base**, B, is the whole, or total, quantity. If it is unknown, the rate, R, and the percentage, P, must be known. Recall that $P = B \times R$.

Solving the equation $P = B \times R$ for B:

$$\text{Base, } B = \frac{\text{Percentage, } P}{\text{Rate, } R}, \quad \text{or} \quad B = \frac{P}{R}$$

Problem

The U.S. Civil Service Commission reported that a minority group of about 502,000 persons was included in the total number employed in the federal government. This minority group accounted for 20% of the total number employed.

What is the total number of persons employed by the federal government?

Solution

$$\text{Base} = \frac{\text{Percentage}}{\text{Rate}}$$

$$B = \frac{P}{R}$$

$$= \frac{502{,}000}{0.20}$$

$$= 2{,}510{,}000$$ (total number of persons employed by the federal government)

Using a calculator:

Enter	Press	Display
502000	÷	502000
.2	=	2510000

or

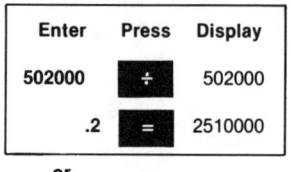

Using a calculator with a percent key %:

Enter	Press	Display
502000	÷	502000
20	%	2510000

3 SELF-REVIEW

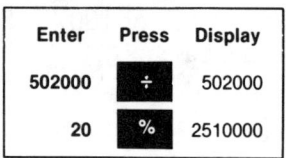

The sales tax on a new car amounted to \$252. The sales tax rate is $4\frac{1}{2}\%$. Thus, the \$252 is $4\frac{1}{2}\%$ of the selling price. What is the selling price of the car?

In words: Base = ____________

B = $ ________ / ______ %

= ________

= $ ____________

$$\text{Base} = \frac{\text{Percentage}}{\text{Rate}}$$

$$B = \frac{\$252}{4\frac{1}{2}\%}$$

$$= \frac{\$252}{0.045}$$

$$= \$5{,}600.00$$

The total purchase price of the car is the selling price plus the tax, or \$5,600 + \$252 = \$5,852.

ASSIGNMENT 3-1
PERCENTAGE, RATE, AND BASE

Name ____________________ Date Due ____________ Grade ______

Answers to selected problems are given in Appendix B.

For Problems 1 through 6, find the percentage, or rate, or base (nearest tenth).

	Percentage	*Rate*	*Base*
Ex.	\$23.40	14.2%	\$164.80
1.	________ tons	74%	461 tons
2.	\$__________	12½%	\$3,147.20
3.	237 million	______%	711 million
4.	1,099.6 miles	______%	12,563 miles
5.	7.1 hours	14%	______ hours
6.	8,147 persons	43.8%	__________ persons

7. What is 35% of \$95 (nearest hundredth)?

   \$_________, found by

8. Find 15% of \$300.

   \$_________, found by

9. 132.6 is what percent of 4,216.72 (nearest tenth percent)?

   _________%, found by

10. \$12,000 is what percent of \$76,000 (nearest percent)?

    _________%, found by

11. 617 is 62.5% of what number (nearest tenth)?

    _________, found by

12. If 6% of a number is 141, what is the number?

    _________, found by

13. *Consumer Reports* indicates that dealer cost for a Mercedes 300D is 80% of the sticker price. Betty Steinberg wants to offer the dealer \$100 over dealer cost. The sticker price on a Mercedes 300D at Vin Devers Mercedes is \$15,791. How much should she offer?

    \$______________, found by

14. *The New York Times* reports, "The consumer price increase in the metropolitan area from last year to this year is 4.8%."

    A. At that rate, what is the increase (nearest cent) on a record album priced at \$7.98 last year?

       \$_______, found by

    B. What is this year's price?

       \$_______, found by

15. *Time,* in an article entitled "Striking Back at the Super Snoops," stated that Senator Minnetle Dodere pays property taxes of $1,252.94 per year on her home. Her home has a market value of $47,110. The property taxes are what percent of the market value of her home (nearest hundredth percent)?

__________%, found by

16. The President intended to reduce the White House staff by as many as 88 out of the 250 White House jobs. What percent of the White House jobs did the President intend to eliminate?

__________%, found by

17. *Newsweek* reported: "Deep beneath the tundra of Alaska's North Slope is a vast reservoir of natural gas, estimated at 26 trillion cubic feet—nearly 11% of the nation's known reserves." What are the nation's known reserves (nearest tenth of a trillion)?

__________ trillion, found by

18. In a recent year 6.2 million barrels of oil were imported into the United States daily. This accounted for about 38% of the oil consumed. What was the total daily consumption of oil in the United States (nearest tenth of a million)?

__________ million barrels, found by

19. The Edison Company has recently requested a 22.6% increase in electricity rates from the Public Utilities Commission. If the increase is approved, a family now paying $170 per month would pay how much per month?

$__________, found by

20. Michigan Blue Cross-Blue Shield announced a need to increase the present monthly premium of some 247,000 Michigan senior citizens by 16%, or about $2 a month.

A. What is the present monthly premium?

$__________, found by

B. What will the new monthly premium be?

$__________, found by

21. The social security rate increased from 6.05% in 1978 to 6.13% in 1979, an increase of 0.08%. The increase is what percent of the 1978 rate (nearest tenth percent)?

__________%, found by

SECTION 3-2: RATE OF INCREASE OR DECREASE

Objective: To calculate the percent increase and percent decrease.

New York Stock Exchange Average DOWN **8.5 %**	3% Price-Boost

The terms "rate of increase" and "percent increase" are often used interchangeably. As illustrations of the use of percents to report an increase or decrease:

The average price of a new home on the West Coast is \$68,000, an increase of 20.5% over last year. If inflation continues at that pace, the Federal Home Loan Bank Board estimates that the average price of a new home will be up to \$200,000 by 1988—an increase of 194% over this year.

Standard Oil of California reported that foreign petroleum earnings were \$113 million during the third quarter, down 10% from the earnings of \$126 million last year.

RATE OF INCREASE

The **rate of increase** is computed by:

$$\text{Rate of increase} = \frac{\text{Amount of increase}}{\text{Original (base) value}}$$

Problem NCR reported that the rentals of its computers, electronic cash registers, and other equipment for the first nine months of this year amounted to \$754 million, compared with only \$659 million last year. What is the percent increase in rental income this year over last year?

Solution The original (base) value was last year's rental amount of \$659 million.

Using a calculator:

Enter	Press	Display
754	−	754
659	= ÷	95
659	=	0.1441578

$$\text{Rate of increase} = \frac{\text{Amount of increase}}{\text{Original (base) value}}$$

$$= \frac{\$754 - \$659}{\$659}$$

$$= \frac{\$95}{\$659}$$

$$= 0.1441578, \quad \text{or} \quad 14.4\% \text{ (nearest tenth \%)}$$

1 SELF-REVIEW

Last year the American Electric Power Company, Inc., paid \$1.2 million in state income taxes. This year it paid \$1.6 million. What was the percent increase from last year to this year?

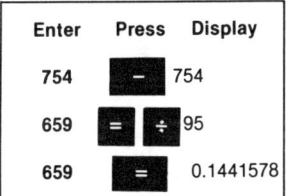

In words: Rate of increase = ____________________

$= \dfrac{(\$\_\_\_ - \$\_\_\_)}{\$\_\_\_}$

$= \dfrac{\$\_\_\_}{\$\_\_\_}$

= 0.__________ or ______% (nearest tenth %)

$$\frac{\text{Amount of increase}}{\text{Original (base) value}}$$

$$= \frac{(\$1.6 - \$1.2)}{\$1.2}$$

$$= \frac{\$0.4}{\$1.2}$$

$= 0.3333333$ or 33.3% (nearest tenth %)

RATE OF DECREASE

The **rate of decrease** is computed similarly to the rate of increase.

$$\text{Rate of decrease} = \frac{\text{Amount of decrease}}{\text{Original (base) value}}$$

Problem Last month a Tonkyo speaker, Model TM5, sold for \$50. The price was just reduced to \$40 to celebrate the firm's tenth anniversary. What was the percent reduction in the price of the speaker?

Solution

$$\begin{aligned}\text{Rate of decrease} &= \frac{\text{Amount of decrease}}{\text{Original (base) value}}\\ &= \frac{\$50 - \$40}{\$50}\\ &= \frac{\$10}{\$50}\\ &= 0.20, \quad \text{or} \quad 20\%\end{aligned}$$

2 SELF-REVIEW

$$\frac{\text{Amount of decrease}}{\text{Original (base) value}}$$

$$= \frac{(200 - 80)}{200}$$

$$= \frac{120}{200}$$

$$= 0.60 \quad \text{or} \quad 60\%$$

A. Production dropped from 200 units the first six months of last year to 80 units the last six months. What was the percent decrease in production from the first six months to the last six months of the year?

In words: Rate of decrease = ____________________

= (______ – ______) / ______

= ______

= 0.____, or ____%

11.1%, found by

$$\frac{\$54 - \$48}{\$54} = \frac{\$6}{\$54} = 0.1111111$$

B. Sears reduced the price of its Die Hard battery from \$54 to \$48. What was the percent reduction in price?

_______%, found by

ASSIGNMENT 3-2
RATE OF INCREASE OR DECREASE

Name ________________ Date Due ________ Grade ____

Answers to selected problems are given in Appendix B.

For Problems 1 through 6, find the percent increase or decrease from last year to this year (nearest tenth percent).

	Item	*Last Year*	*This Year*	*Amount of Increase or Decrease*	*Percent of Increase or Decrease*
Ex.	Graphite sales	\$50,000,000.00	\$80,000,000.00	\$30,000,000.00	60.0% increase
Ex.	TV set	\$400.00	\$275.00	−\$125.00	31.3% decrease
1.	Lettuce (box)	\$8.00	\$11.00	______	______
2.	Football ticket	\$4.50	\$5.00	______	______
3.	Red snapper (lb.)	\$2.50	\$2.25	______	______
4.	Production (units)	325 units	310 units	______	______
5.	Latex paint (gal.)	\$14.99	\$18.99	______	______
6.	City population	78,320	74,250	______	______

7. The price of a loaf of bread increased from \$0.59 to \$0.89.

   A. What is the amount of increase?

   \$_______, found by

   B. What is the rate of increase (nearest tenth percent)?

   _______%, found by

8. Unemployment rates increased from 5.4% to 6.0%. To the nearest tenth percent, what is the percent increase?

   _______%, found by

9. Several years ago the legal speed limit for most highways was decreased from 70 mph to 55 mph.

   A. What was the amount of decrease?

   _______ mph, found by

   B. What was the percent decrease (nearest percent)?

   _______%, found by

10. Enrollment at an eastern university decreased from 10,173 to 8,987. To the nearest percent, what was the percent decrease?

    _______%, found by

11. The *Williamsport Sun-Gazette* carried an advertisement reducing the \$7.49 little boys' embossed cowboy boots to \$5.88. What percent reduction is this (nearest tenth percent)?

    _______%, found by

12. J. C. Penney's summer sale catalog indicates that flared-leg chino slacks, regularly priced at $12.00 per pair, are on sale for $10.20 a pair. What is the percent reduction?

_______%, found by

13. With respect to energy problems and natural gas prices: "The Senate is considering a deregulation plan which would allow the ceiling to rise from its present $1.46 per thousand cubic feet to about $2.48 for two years." What percent increase is this (nearest tenth percent)?

_______%, found by

14. A home illustrated in *Time* increased in price from $39,000 five years ago to $65,000 today. What is the percent increase (nearest percent)?

_______%, found by

15. In celebration of the Chinese New Year (year 4675), LaChoy reduced the regular price of its 42-ounce bi-pack from $1.89 to $1.39. What percent reduction is this (nearest tenth percent)?

_______%, found by

16. Referring to the 1979 article on social security, what is the percent increase in the:

A. Wage base subject to tax in 1978 and 1979?

_______%, found by

B. Tax rate in 1978 to 1979?

_______%, found by

C. Wage base subject to tax in 1980 and 1987?

_______%, found by

D. Tax rate in 1981 and 1987?

_______%, found by

Under Social Security revisions enacted in 1977, the amount of a worker's wage base subjected to tax rises from $17,700 in 1978 to $22,900 this year and the tax rate goes from 6.05 per cent to 6.13 per cent.

The wage base goes up to $25,900 in 1980 but the tax rate remains stable. In 1981, the base will rise to $29,700 and the rate to 6.65 per cent. By 1987, the wage base will be $42,600 and the tax rate will be 7.15 per cent.

17. Referring to the 1979 article in the *Toledo Blade:*

A. What is the percent increase (nearest tenth percent) in United Airlines passengers from December 1977 to December 1978 at Toledo Express Airport?

_______%, found by

B. How does the percent increase compare to United's national figures?

____

United Airlines Notes Increase In Passengers

A total of 17,160 passengers boarded United Airlines flights at Toledo Express Airport during December, compared to 16,588 in December, 1977.

Nationally, the airline had a 24.9 per cent increase in business during December and record traffic for the entire year.

18. *The New York Times* reported that Newark, due to a severe budget crisis, had reduced the number of city employees, including policemen, from 5,000 to 4,550. What percent reduction, to the nearest percent, does this represent?

_______%, found by

19. Hughes Airwest, advertising in the *Los Angeles Times,* reduced the cost of its Tuesday, Wednesday, or Saturday fight to Las Vegas from $41.50 to $29.00. What percent (nearest percent) reduction is this?

_______%, found by

20. John Bulloch, tailor, advertising in the *Toronto Globe and Mail,* marked down men's suits from $250 to $155. What percent reduction is this?

_______%, found by

REVIEW ASSIGNMENT FOR CHAPTER 3
PERCENTAGES

Name ______________________ **Date Due** ____________ **Grade** _____

For problems 1 through 6, the sales tax is equal to the sales tax *rate* times the selling price.

	Item	*Base: Selling Price*	*Rate: Sales Tax Rate*	*Percentage: Sales Tax*
1.	Phono turntable	$100.00	4%	______
2.	Sweater	19.00	5%	______
3.	Saw	12.00	______	$ 0.54
4.	Rare stamp	50.00	______	4.00
5.	Sofa	________	6%	30.00
6.	Roll of film	________	6.25%	0.22

7. Pete Rose of the Philadelphia Phillies had a batting average of .312 one year. That means that he got a hit 31.2% of the times he came to bat. How many hits would Pete Rose have if he came to bat 700 times?

   __________, found by

8. Many utilities offer senior citizens discounts. Frank Garcia, age 74, paid a $94 electric bill last month after receiving a 14% discount. What was Garcia's bill before the discount (nearest cent)?

   $__________, found by

9. Toyota Motors, Ltd., increased the average price of its 1979 autos by $357, or 7% over the average price of its 1978 autos.

   A. What was the average price of its 1978 autos?

   $__________, found by

   B. What is the average price of its 1979 autos?

   $__________, found by

10. A smoke alarm is listed in a wholesale catalog for $14.95. Shipping costs increased 0.9%, and the price of the alarm was increased accordingly. What is the new price (nearest cent)?

    $__________, found by

11. The average hourly wage for the U.S. worker in September was $6.80, up 10 cents from the August average. What was the percent increase in average hourly wages from August to September (nearest tenth percent)?

    __________%, found by

12. A 16% increase in Michigan Blue Cross-Blue Shield premiums includes 11% to cover higher deductibles and 5% for administrative costs. What percent of the 16% increase is for administrative costs (nearest hundredth percent)?

    __________%, found by

13. Thomas "Lud" Ashley, Democrat from Ohio's 9th Congressional District, received 87,810 votes to his opponent's 70,635 in a recent election. What percent of the total vote did Rep. Ashley receive (nearest tenth percent)?

    __________%, found by

14. The *London Times* reports on a "shrinking man." If Emmanuel Vitria was 5 feet 10 inches before the heart transplant:

A. How tall is he now?

____ feet ____ inches, found by

B. What percent reduction in his height has occurred since the transplant?

____%, found by

Shrinking man

MARSEILLES, France (CP) — Emmanuel Vitria, the world's longest-surviving heart transplant patient, has shrunk seven inches since the transplant operation about nine years ago. Doctors say the loss of height is due to the side effects of the drug used to prevent Mr. Vitria's body from rejecting the new heart.

15. A family receiving $526 per month pension from social security two years ago is now receiving $600, according to *Family Circle.* Find the percent increase in the pension payment (nearest tenth percent).

__________%, found by

16. Avco stock dipped to $13.50 from a high of $20.50. What is the percent decrease (nearest tenth percent)?

__________%, found by

17. Prior to the 1979 Super Bowl, the Pittsburgh Steelers had won about 88% of their 17 games. What was their won-loss record?

____ won ____ lost, found by

18. *Time* reports that during a recent water shortage, residents of Marin County, California, reduced their daily consumption of water to 10.4 million gallons, or 66⅔% of their previous consumption. What was their previous consumption (nearest tenth million)?

__________ million gallons, found by

19. Guntersville, Alabama, is accustomed to winter temperatures averaging 63° F *(Newsweek).* This year, according to one observer, "on one of the warmest mornings we've had in five weeks, it was 26° F." This extremely low temperature represents what percent decrease from the average winter temperature (nearest tenth percent)?

__________%, found by

20. A sales person informed a customer that the price of an electronic calculator was $52.20, including the sales tax of 4.5%. What was the selling price of the calculator before the sales tax was added?

$__________, found by

TO THE STUDENT: There is a SELF-REVIEW TEST for this chapter in Appendix A, *with answers* in Appendix C.

4

Consumer Spending

SECTION 4-1: UNIT PRICING—COMPARISON SHOPPING

Objective: To compute the unit price and to determine the "best buy" based on a comparison of unit prices.

The price paid for an item is one factor which influences a consumer's choice while shopping in supermarkets, drugstores, and discount stores.

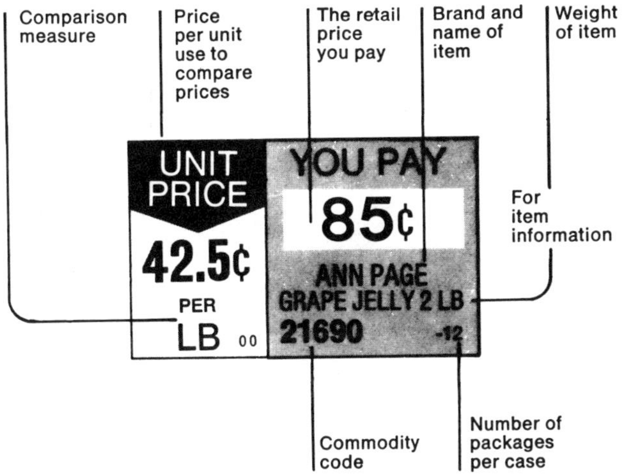

The many different weights, sizes, and numbers of items per package make it difficult for a shopper to make price and value comparisons.

Numerous studies reveal that about 40% of the time shoppers make the wrong choice when selecting the package with the most quantity for the least amount of money.

Unit pricing is a system which allows a shopper to compare the prices of various items quickly and easily. Investigations have shown that 94% of the shoppers who understood unit pricing changed from one package size to another of the same brand.

The **unit price** of an item is the *price per unit* of weight, measure, or count. Unit price of an item is determined by dividing the price by the weight, measure, or count of the item.

$$\text{Unit price} = \frac{\text{Price}}{\text{Weight, measure, or count}}$$

Problems Determine the unit price of each of the following products:

A. Unit price by weight:

What is the price per ounce?

B. Unit price by measure:

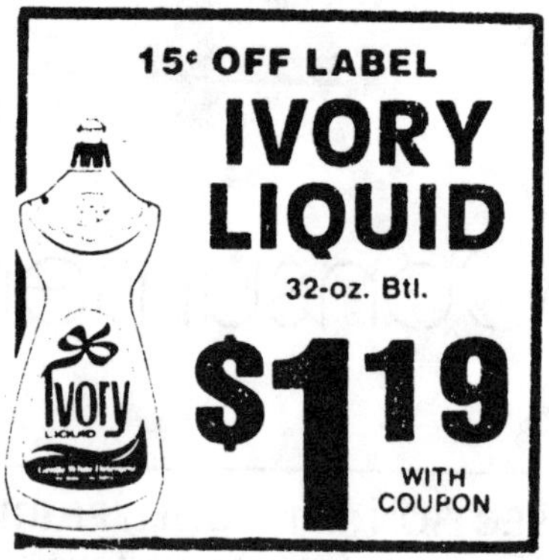

What is the price per ounce?

C. Unit price by count:

What is the price per Q-tip?

Solutions

A. $\text{Unit price} = \dfrac{\text{Price}}{\text{Weight}} = \dfrac{\$2.79}{6} = \$0.47$ per ounce

B. $\text{Unit price} = \dfrac{\text{Price}}{\text{Measure}} = \dfrac{\$1.19}{32} = \$0.037$ per fluid ounce

C. $\text{Unit price} = \dfrac{\text{Price}}{\text{Count}} = \dfrac{\$1.08}{400} = \$0.003$ per item (Q-tip)

A reminder: Cover the answers in the margin.

Determine the unit price of the following products:

A.

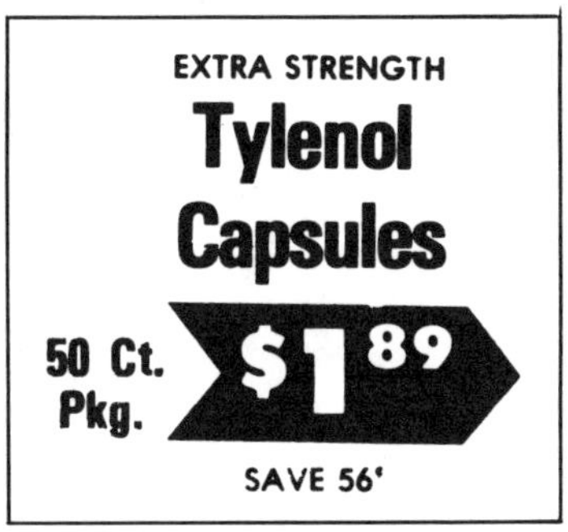

B.

A. Unit price $= \frac{\$1.29}{4.5}$

$= \$0.2866$

B. Unit price $= \frac{\$1.89}{50}$

$= \$0.0378$ per capsule

A. Unit price $= \frac{\text{Price}}{\text{Weight}}$

= \$______

= \$__________ per pound

B. Unit price $= \frac{\text{Price}}{\text{Count}}$

= \$______

= \$__________ per ________

To compare costs of products in various sizes of packages of the *same* brand, compute the unit price of each size package. The size package with the lowest unit price is the best buy.

Be careful! Compare only *like* items to determine the best buy. Do not compare grape jam with raspberry jam or Smucker's jelly with brand XYZ. Also compare ounces with ounces, and liters with liters, *not* ounces with liters or pounds with ounces.

Problem A supermarket sells Minute Maid orange juice in 12-ounce, 16-ounce, and 24-ounce cans. Using the unit price, determine the best buy for the Minute Maid orange juice.

Solution A. 12-oz. can for \$1.15. B. 16-oz. can for \$1.52. C. 24-oz. can for \$1.72.

A. Unit price $= \frac{\text{Price}}{\text{Measure}} = \frac{\$1.15}{12} = \$0.096$

B. Unit price $= \frac{\text{Price}}{\text{Measure}} = \frac{\$1.52}{16} = \$0.095$

C. Unit price $= \frac{\text{Price}}{\text{Measure}} = \frac{\$1.72}{24} = \$0.072$

The best buy is the 24-ounce can for \$1.72.

While the price of a product is a key factor in a consumer's decision to buy, such things as quality, taste, personal preference, convenience, and size of package must also be considered.

2 SELF-REVIEW

A supermarket sells Wisk detergent as advertised. Determine the unit price and the best buy.

A. Unit price $= \frac{\$4.99}{128}$

$= \$0.03898$

B. Unit price $= \frac{\$1.99}{64}$

$= \$0.03109$

Best buy: 64-ounce bottle for $1.99

A. Unit price $= \dfrac{\text{Price}}{\text{Measure}}$

$= \dfrac{\$\_\_\_\_\_}{128}$

$= \$$__________ per ounce

B. Unit price $= \dfrac{\text{Price}}{\text{Measure}}$

$= \dfrac{\$\_\_\_\_\_}{64}$

$= \$$__________ per ounce

The best buy is the ____-ounce bottle for $_______.

ASSIGNMENT 4-1
UNIT PRICING—COMPARISON SHOPPING

Name ______________________ **Date Due** ____________ **Grade** _____

Answers to selected problems are given in Appendix B.

For Problems 1 through 6, find the unit price of each item.

	Item	*Price*	*Weight, Measure or Count*	*Unit Price*
Ex.	Hot dog buns	\$0.79	8 count	\$0.09875 per bun
1.	Hellman's mayonnaise	2.19	48 ounces	____________
2.	Del Monte's sliced carrots	0.37	16 ounces	____________
3.	Storage bags	0.59	25 count	____________
4.	Wilson tennis balls	2.28	Can of 3 balls	____________
5.	Northern white bathroom tissue	0.89	4 rolls	____________
6.	Dixie 5-ounce kitchen cups	0.59	50 count	____________

7. Tom Mills purchased a $10\frac{3}{4}$-ounce can of Campbell's vegtable beef soup for 32 cents. What was the unit price of the soup?

   \$__________ per ounce, found by

8. A $4\frac{1}{2}$-ounce tube of Pillsbury buttermilk biscuits sells for 17 cents. What is the unit price?

   \$__________ per ounce, found by

In Problems 9 through 19, determine the unit price, then select the "best buy," assuming price is the only consideration.

9. Kroger carried SOS cleaner pads in these sizes:

   A. 4-pack: 29 cents — \$__________ per pad, found by

   B. 10-pack: 63 cents — \$__________ per pad, found by

   C. 18-pack: \$1.03 — \$__________, per pad, found by

   Best buy: ______________________

10. Del's carried Stock Italian Vermouth in these sizes:

    A. 375 milliliter: \$1.69 — \$______________ per milliliter, found by

    B. 750 milliliter: \$3.44 — \$______________ per milliliter, found by

    Best buy: ______________________

11. Churchill's sold Durkee's whole cloves in these sizes:

    A. 28.3 grams: \$1.13 — \$______________ per gram, found by

    B. 45 grams: \$2.59 — \$______________ per gram, found by

    Best buy: ______________________

12. Food Fair sold Realemon reconstituted lemon juice in the sizes shown:

    A. 8 fluid ounces: 53 cents — \$__________ per fluid ounce, found by

    B. 16 fluid ounces: 83 cents — \$__________ per fluid ounce, found by

    C. 32 fluid ounces: \$1.15 — \$__________ per fluid ounce, found by

    Best buy: ______________________

13. A&P had three sizes of Maxwell House regular-grind coffee:

A. 3-pound tin: $7.79

$__________ per __________, found by

B. 2-pound tin: $4.99

$__________ per __________, found by

C. 1-pound tin: $2.69

$__________ per __________, found by

Best buy: ______________________________

14. Kazmaier's Five-Star stocked Shurfine granulated sugar in these sizes:

A. 5-pound bag: $1.19

$__________ per __________, found by

B. 10-pound bag: $2.37

$__________ per __________, found by

C. 25-pound bag: $5.99

$__________ per __________, found by

Best buy: ______________________________

15. Giant Food Stores stocked Kellogg's cornflakes in several different packages:

A. 340-gram box: 65 cents

$__________ per __________, found by

B. 510-gram box: 89 cents

$__________ per __________, found by

C. Variety Pak, 255 grams: 99 cents

$__________ per __________, found by

D. Request Pak, 142-gram box: 75 cents

$__________ per __________, found by

Best buy: ______________________________

16. Big Bear stocked Wesson Oil in three sizes:

A. 16 fluid ounces: $1.03

$__________ per __________, found by

B. 24 fluid ounces: $1.25

$__________ per __________, found by

C. 38 fluid ounces: $1.93

$__________ per __________, found by

Best buy: ______________________________

17. Edward's Food Warehouse had Gerber's bananas with pineapple in two sizes:

A. 220 grams: 32 cents

$__________ per gram, found by

B. 135 grams: 22 cents

$__________ per __________, found by

Best buy: ______________________________

18. Foodtown stocked Coca-Cola in four different ways (1 liter = 33.6 ounces):

A. 2-liter throwaway plastic bottle: 99 cents

$__________ per ounce, found by

B. Eight 16-ounce returnable bottles: $1.65

$__________ per ounce, found by

C. 1-liter nonreturnable bottles: two for 88 cents

$__________ per __________, found by

D. 12-ounce cans: six for $1.29

$__________ per __________, found by

Best buy: ______________________________

19. Farmer Jack's had Heinz tomato ketchup available in three sizes (16 ounces = 1 pound; 1 gram = .0022 pounds):

A. 2 pounds: $1.09

$__________ per pound, found by

B. 1 pound, 8 ounces: 85 cents

$__________ per pound, found by

C. 397 grams: 53 cents

$__________ per pound, found by

Best buy: ______________________________

SECTION 4-2: COST OF TRANSPORTATION

Objective: To determine the cost and the per-mile cost of owning and maintaining an automobile, renting an automobile, taking a taxicab, and traveling by air and railroad.

COST OF OPERATING AN AUTOMOBILE

A typical car owner spends nearly $3,000 a year to operate and maintain an automobile, according to the AAA. Two factors influencing the cost are the number of miles driven during the year and the age of the automobile. The total cost can be subdivided into **variable costs** and **fixed costs.**

Variable Costs: These include the cost of gasoline, oil, filters, or a new battery, tire, or headlight. The total cost for gasoline and oil increases as the number of miles driven increases. The need for a new headlight or tire usually cannot be determined in advance.

Fixed Costs: These costs remain about the same year after year. Included are such items as depreciation, insurance, and license fees.

$$\text{Total cost} = \text{Variable costs} + \text{Fixed costs}$$

The cost per mile of operating an automobile is determined by adding the annual variable and fixed costs and then dividing the total by the number of miles traveled during the year.

$$\text{Cost per mile} = \frac{\text{Total cost}}{\text{Number of miles traveled}}$$

Problem

A used automobile was purchased three years ago for $3,500. A record of the expenses during the past year were as shown below:

Item	*Annual Cost*
Variable costs:	
Gasoline	$ 720
(traveled 9,000 miles; car averages 12.5 miles per gallon)	
Oil changes, lubrication	50
Repair and new parts	247
(new headlight, $4; battery, $48; 2 tires, $110; fender repair, $47; tune-up, $38)	
Miscellaneous	40
(car washes, turnpike fees, etc.)	
Total variable costs	$1,057
Fixed costs:	
Annual depreciation	$ 767
(The car, purchased for $3,500 three years ago is now worth only $1,200. It depreciated $2,300 in three years, or $767 a year.)	
Insurance	620
(bodily injury and property damage, $305; comprehensive, $82; collision, $203; medical, $30)	
License ($37) and inspection ($3)	40
Total fixed costs	$1,427

Using a calculator with memory:

Enter	Press	Display
3500	−	3500
1200	= ÷	2300
3	= m+	766.66666
305	+	305
82	+	387
203	+	590
30	= m+	620
37	+	87
3	= m+	40
	RM	1426.66666

The car was driven 9,000 miles during the year. What are the total cost and the cost per mile of operating and maintaining this used automobile?

Solution Total cost = Variable costs + Fixed costs
= \$1,057 + \$1,427
= \$2,484

$$\text{Cost per mile} = \frac{\text{Total cost}}{\text{Number of miles traveled}} = \frac{\$2,484}{9,000} = \$.276 \text{ or } 27.6 \text{ cents a mile}$$

1 SELF-REVIEW

A large Chrysler was purchased two years ago for \$8,800. It is now worth \$4,500. During the past year it was driven 10,500 miles and averaged 15 miles a gallon. Determine the total cost of operating the car last year, and the cost per mile.

Answers	*Items*	*Annual Cost (nearest dollar)*
	Variable costs	
700 gallons; \$763.	Gasoline (10,500 miles ÷ 15 mpg) = _____ gallons × \$1.09 a gallon	\$________
	Oil change/lube	60
\$154	Repairs and parts: tire, \$78; tune-up, \$49; radiator leak, \$27	________
	Miscellaneous: toll fees, parking, etc.	80
\$1,057	Total variable costs	\$________
	Fixed costs	
\$2,150	Annual depreciation (\$8,800 – \$4,500) ÷ 2	\$________
	Insurance	421
\$45	License \$42; state inspection \$3	________
\$2,616	Total fixed costs	\$________

Total cost = Variable cost + Fixed cost
= \$______ + \$________
= \$________

Cost per mile = Total cost / Number of miles traveled
= \$________ / ______ miles
= ______ cents per mile

Total cost:
= \$1,057 + \$2,616
= \$3,673

Cost per mile:
$= \frac{\$3,673}{10,500}$
= .3498 or
35¢ per mile

RENTING AN AUTOMOBILE Hertz Rent a Car and Avis Rent a Car are two well-known automobile rental agencies. One agency determines the total cost of a rental by adding these charges:

1. A *daily rate,* ranging from \$14.95 a day for a compact to \$23.95 for a deluxe automobile.

Plus 2. A *mileage charge,* ranging from 14 cents a mile for a compact to 24 cents a mile for a deluxe automobile.

Plus 3. The *cost of the gasoline* used.

The **cost per day** is computed by dividing the total cost by the number of days the car was rented. The **cost per mile** equals total cost divided by number of miles.

$$\text{Cost per day} = \frac{\text{Total cost}}{\text{Number of days}}$$

$$\text{Cost per mile} = \frac{\text{Total cost}}{\text{Number of miles}}$$

Problem A midsize automobile is rented for three days at $17.95 a day. The mileage charge is 18 cents a mile. The gasoline cost $22.50 for the 500 miles traveled. What are the cost per day and the cost per mile?

Solution

Total Cost

1. Daily: 3 days × $17.95	=	$ 53.85
2. Mileage: 18 cents a mile × 500	=	90.00
3. Cost of gasoline	=	22.50
Total	=	$166.35

$$\text{Cost per day} = \frac{\text{Total cost}}{\text{Number of days}} = \frac{\$166.35}{3} = \$55.45$$

$$\text{Cost per mile} = \frac{\text{Total cost}}{\text{Number of miles}} = \frac{\$166.35}{500} = \$0.33$$

2 SELF-REVIEW

An agency rents a deluxe car for five days at $21.95 a day. The mileage charge is 22 cents a mile. The cost of gasoline for a 800-mile trip was $54. What are the cost per day and the cost per mile?

Total Cost

A. Daily: ____ days × ________ = $__________

B. Mileage: _____ cents × _______ = __________

C. Cost of gasoline = __________

Total = $__________

Cost per day = $__________ = $________

Cost per mile = $__________ = $________

Total cost:

A. 5 × $21.95	=	$109.75
B. $.22 × 800	=	176.00
C. Gasoline	=	54.00
Total	=	$339.75

$$\text{Cost per day} = \frac{\$339.75}{5} = \$67.95$$

$$\text{Cost per mile} = \frac{\$339.75}{800} = \$0.42$$

TRAVELING BY TAXICAB

Taxicab fares vary from city to city and even within a city. The actual charges by two cab companies in a large city are:

Veteran Cab:

$1.40 first mile or less
$0.70 for each additional mile or fraction of a mile

Checkered Cab:

$1.25 for first mile or less
$0.80 next ½ mile
$0.70 next ½ mile
$0.60 thereafter for each mile or fraction

Cost:	\$1.40	\$0.70	\$0.70	\$0.70
Mile:	First	Second	Third	Fourth

Cost:	\$1.25	\$0.80	\$0.70	\$0.60	\$0.60
Mile:	First	½	½	Third	Fourth
		Second			

Problem Susan Rothfus is considering taking a taxicab to work every day (2¼ miles from her home). What would the Veteran and Checkered cab companies charge for a one-way trip? What is the cost per mile?

Solution *Veteran Cab:*

First mile	\$1.40
Second mile:	0.70
Next ¼ mile:	0.70
Total	\$2.80

$$\text{Cost per mile} = \frac{\text{Total cost}}{\text{Number of miles}} = \frac{\$2.80}{2.25} = \$1.24$$

Checkered Cab:

First mile:	\$1.25
Second mile:	1.50 ← \$0.80 + \$0.70
Next ¼ mile:	0.60
Total	\$3.35

$$\text{Cost per mile} = \frac{\text{Total cost}}{\text{Number of miles}} = \frac{\$3.35}{2.25} = \$1.49$$

3 SELF-REVIEW

Tom Johnson is considering taking either a Veteran or a Checkered Cab to his job located 1¼ miles from his home. What is the cost for a one-way trip? What is the cost per mile?

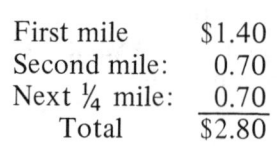

Veteran	*Checkered*
\$1.40	\$1.25
0.70	0.80
\$2.10	\$2.05

Cost per mile:

$\frac{\$2.10}{1.25}$	$\frac{\$2.05}{1.25}$
\$1.68	\$1.64

Veteran Cab:

First mile: \$________

Next ¼ mile: ________

Total \$________

Cost per mile = \$________ / miles

= \$________

Checkered Cab:

First mile: \$________

Next ¼ mile: ________

Total \$________

Cost per mile = \$________ / miles

= \$________

TRAVELING BY AIR AND BY RAILROAD

The airlines and railroads publish informative **timetables** (also called **schedules**) which list one-way and round-trip fares and departure and arrival times. Airline fares have become very complex. Delta, for example, has 15 different fares, including first class, deluxe night coach, weekday SuperSaver, children's Super-Saver, weekend Freedom Fare night coach, and senior citizens' coach.

Table 4-1 is a typical railroad rate schedule. Table 4-2 is for air travel.

TABLE 4-1
Amtrak's One-Way Coach Fare (double for round trip)

CHICAGO - FLORIDA LINE*

BETWEEN \ AND	Chicago	Bloomington	Louisville	Nashville	Birmingham	Jacksonville	Orlando	St. Petersburg	Miami
	$	$	$	$	$	$	$	$	$
Chicago	—	18.50	23.50	34.00	45.00	64.00	73.00	77.00	85.00
Lafayette	9.75	8.25	15.50	27.50	38.50	61.00	68.00	75.00	81.00
Bloomington	18.50	—	8.25	20.00	31.00	54.00	63.00	67.00	76.00
Louisville	23.50	8.25	—	11.75	24.50	47.50	56.00	60.00	67.00
Bowl'ng Green	29.50	14.75	7.75	5.25	18.50	43.50	52.00	57.00	64.00
Nashville	34.00	20.00	11.75	—	13.25	39.50	46.50	53.00	59.00
Decatur	40.50	27.50	20.50	8.00	5.75	32.00	40.50	45.00	54.00
Birmingham	45.00	31.00	24.50	13.25	—	28.00	35.00	40.50	47.00
Montgomery	51.00	36.00	30.00	20.50	6.75	24.50	32.50	38.00	45.00
Dothan	58.00	43.50	36.00	26.50	14.25	18.00	26.50	30.50	38.50
Valdosta	64.00	52.00	44.50	34.00	22.50	9.75	18.50	24.00	30 50
Jacksonville	64.00	54.00	47.50	39.50	28.00	—	10.25	17.50	25.00

TABLE 4-2
Air Fares from Los Angeles to Boston and Chicago

Leave	Arrive	Flight No.	Stops or Via	Freq.	Service
From: **LOS ANGELES** (PST)					
For Reservations Please Call: 380-1511					
To:					
BOSTON (EST)					F $365.00 Y $224.00 FN $224.00 YN $179.00
11 00a	8 46p	**166/286**	Mpls.-St. Paul	Daily	M
12 45a	12 34p	**172/282**	Mpls.-St. Paul	Daily	M ★
CHICAGO (CST)					F $258.00 Y $161.00 FN $161.00 YN $129.00
All Flights Serve Chicago's O'Hare Airport					
11 00a	6 05p	**166/382**	Mpls.-St. Paul	Daily	M
5 05p	1 57a ♦	**22/222**	Mpls.-St. Paul	Daily	M **747**
12 45a	8 09a	**172/700**	Mpls.-St. Paul	Daily	M ★ **DC10**

F – First class
Y – Coach class
FN – First class, night
YN – Coach class, night

Problems

A. What is the cost of a one-way coach fare on Amtrak's Chicago-Florida line from Louisville, Kentucky, to Miami, Florida? What is the cost per mile?

B. What is the cost of one-way air fare, coach class, from Los Angeles to Boston? What is the cost per mile?

Solutions

A. Read down the left column of Amtrak's schedule to Louisville. Then go across to the column headed by Miami and read the fare. It is \$67. The distance from Louisville to Miami is 1,059 miles.

$$\text{Cost per mile} = \frac{\$67}{1{,}059}$$
$$= \$0.06$$

B. The coach class fare (labeled Y) from Los Angeles to Boston is \$224. The distance from Los Angeles to Boston is 3,052 miles.

$$\text{Cost per mile} = \frac{\$224}{3{,}052}$$
$$= \$0.07$$

4 SELF-REVIEW

Use Tables 4-1 and 4-2.

A. What is the cost of a one-way coach fare on Amtrak's Chicago-Florida Line from Chicago to Miami? $_____. The distance between Chicago and Miami is 1,360 miles. The cost per mile is $__________, found by

B. What is the cost of a one-way, first class night air fare from Los Angeles to Chicago? $________. The mileage from Los Angeles to Chicago is 2,095. The cost per mile is $__________, found by

A. Amtrak: $85

Cost per mile: $0.06, found by

$$\frac{\$85}{1{,}360} = \$0.0625$$

B. Air fare: $161

Cost per mile: $0.08, found by

$$\frac{\$161}{2{,}095} = \$0.0768$$

ASSIGNMENT 4-2
COST OF TRANSPORTATION

Name ______________________ Date Due ______________ Grade _____

Answers to selected problems are given in Appendix B.

For problems 1 through 6, find the total annual cost and cost per mile for operating each automobile.

	Annual Mileage	*Variable Cost*	*Fixed Cost*	*Total Annual Cost*	*Cost per Mile*
Ex.	14,600	$1,478.00	$2,756.00	$4,234.00	$0.29
1.	12,000	925.00	1,835.00	________	______
2.	15,620	1,416.50	1,551.30	________	______
3.	9,840	1,022.90	2,125.90	________	______
4.	5,910	781.65	1,286.85	________	______
5.	21,435	2,416.58	798.67	________	______
6.	19,725	868.75	1,498.25	________	______

7. A foreign subcompact car was purchased two years ago for $4,750. It is now worth $2,800. Last year it was driven 11,400 miles and averaged 23 mpg. The average cost of regular gasoline for the year (1979) was 87.9 cents a gallon. Variable costs consisted of: gasoline; $37.50 for oil changes and lubrication; $115 for repairs and parts; and $35 for miscellaneous expenses. Fixed costs consisted of: annual depreciation; insurance costing $516 annually; and license fees amounting to $32.50. Find the:

   A. Total variable cost.

   $____________, found by

   B. Total fixed costs.

   $____________, found by

   C. Total cost.

   $____________, found by

   D. Cost per mile.

   $____________, found by

8. A Chevrolet Caprice was purchased three years ago for $6,800. It is now worth $2,300. Last year it was driven 15,600 miles and averaged 16 miles per gallon. The average cost of unleaded gasoline (1979) was 94.9 cents a gallon. Oil changes, lubes, and so on amounted to $55. Four new tires were purchased, at a total cost of $204.50. A major tune-up cost $59.95, and two new shock absorbers cost $38.40. Parking fees, tolls, and so on cost $72.40 during the year. Aside from the annual depreciation, other fixed costs included an annual insurance premium of $472 and license fees of $32.70. Find the:

   A. Total variable cost.

   $____________, found by

   B. Total fixed cost.

   $____________, found by

   C. Total cost.

   $____________, found by

   D. Cost per mile.

   $____________, found by

9. Tom Paulino and Nick Austin rented a luxury limousine for one day for the college's Spring Frolic. The rental charge was $23.95 per day, plus 27 cents per mile, plus gasoline. The gasoline cost $27.80 for the 210 miles traveled.

   A. What was the total cost?

   $____________, found by

   B. What was the cost per mile?

   $____________, found by

10. Mary Dunhill, Pat Auglaize, and Amy Cottrell are flying to Miami and renting a car during their spring break. They plan to rent the car for six days and estimate driving 50 miles per day. The car they want rents for $16.35 a day, plus 17 cents a mile, plus the cost of gasoline. They estimate they will get 15 mpg, with gas costing $0.849 a gallon.

A. What is the estimated total cost of renting a car?

$____________, found by

B. What is the estimated cost per mile?

$____________, found by

C. What is the estimated cost per day?

$____________, found by

11. Refer to the Checkered Cab fares given in this section. William and Grace Adams took a Checkered Cab from their hotel to the restaurant-theater while they were on vacation. The one-way trip was 3.4 miles.

A. What was the cost for the one-way trip?

$________, found by

B. What would cab fare for the evening cost if they also went back to the hotel by Checkered Cab?

$________, found by

C. What is the cost per mile?

$________, found by

12. Refer to the taxicab fares given in this section. Tom, Dick, and Harry take a Veteran Cab to work and back home five days a week. They live 1.8 miles from work. Find the:

A. Total cost of a one-way trip.

$________, found by

B. Total cost for the five round trips.

$________, found by

C. Cost per person per week.

$________, found by

D. Cost per mile for each person.

$________, found by

13. The table gives one-way Amtrak rates. Cincinnati to Houston is via Chicago. It is 1,040 miles from Cincinnati to Houston. Buffalo to Houston is via Chicago. It is 1,470 miles from Buffalo to Houston. It is 1,085 miles from Chicago to Houston.

BETWEEN AND	DETROIT via	DETROIT Coach $	DETROIT Roomette $	HOUSTON via	HOUSTON Coach $	HOUSTON Roomette $
Atlanta	CB	80.50	ch133.00	E	71.00	110.00
Boston	N	70.50	kd78.50	C	143.00	243.50
Buffalo	—	20.00	—	C	111.50	189.00
Chicago	—	21.00	s32.00	—	75.00	119.50
Cincinnati	—	—	—	C	96.00	156.50

A. Find the cost per mile for coach fare between Cincinnati and Houston.

$________, found by

B. Find the cost per mile for coach fare between Buffalo and Houston.

$________, found by

C. Find the cost per mile for coach fare between Chicago and Houston.

$________, found by

D. Explain the difference in the answers to A, B, and C.

____

____

____

14. The regular rate is $144 round trip to fly American Airlines from New York City (LaGuardia) to Detroit, Michigan (Metro). If the flight is booked 30 days in advance, the rate is $72 for weekday service (called a SuperSaver rate). It is 667 miles from New York City to Detroit.

A. What is the cost per mile at the regular rate?

$________, found by

B. What is the cost per mile at the SuperSaver rate?

$________, found by

SECTION 4-3: COST OF OWNING OR RENTING A HOME

Objective: To determine the total annual cost and the average monthly cost of owning or renting a home.

There are many factors to be considered in making a decision to buy or to rent a home. To mention a few: Homeowners have pride of ownership and the possibility of a substantial increase in the value of their homes after several years. Interest paid on mortgages and real estate taxes can be deducted from the homeowners' federal income taxes. However, homeowners have a higher maintenance cost for plumbing repairs, painting, and remodeling, compared to renters.

Renters have the advantage of low maintenance costs (or none), and the freedom to move on short notice. However, since renters do not own their houses or apartments, there is no possible investment gain, meaning that they cannot sell them for a profit after several years. Renters do not pay interest on mortgages and real estate taxes; therefore, these items cannot be deducted from their federal income taxes.

The total cost of **owning** and maintaining a home includes such items as homeowners' insurance, real estate taxes, utilities, and mortgage payments. The total cost of *renting* includes such items as the amount paid for a renters' insurance policy (which usually consists of insurance on household goods only), utilities, and rent payments.

The total annual cost of owning or renting is arrived at by adding all the expenses for the year. The average monthly cost is computed by dividing the total annual cost by 12.

$$\text{Average monthly cost} = \frac{\text{Total annual cost}}{12}$$

Problem Daisy and Don Murray are buying a $50,000 home. Jean and Peter Classen rent a $50,000 home. What are their annual expenses? What are their average monthly expenses?

	Annual Expense	
Type of Expense	*Owner*	*Renter*
Homeowner or renter insurance	$ 280	$ 110
Real estate taxes	1,300	0
Maintenance (plumbing repairs, etc.) .	410	0
Utilities (telephone, electric, etc.) . . .	820	820
Heating	1,280	0
Mortgage or rent payment	4,100	5,200
Total	$8,190	$6,130

Includes building and household goods (owner insurance)

Includes only household goods (renter insurance)

Heat included with the rent

The totals make it appear that there is a definite economic advantage in favor of renting. This is misleading for two reasons: First, homeowners receive a tax break when paying their federal income taxes because the interest on the mortgage loan and the real estate taxes can be deducted. Allowing for these deductions, the cost of owning a home or renting a home is approximately the same. Second, the homeowner is building up an investment and will, after a period of time, own the home.

Solution The average monthly costs of owning and renting a $50,000 home are:

Owning:

$$\text{Average monthly cost} = \frac{\text{Total annual cost}}{12} = \frac{\$8{,}190}{12} = \$682.50$$

Renting:

$$\text{Average monthly cost} = \frac{\text{Total annual cost}}{12} = \frac{\$6{,}130}{12} = \$510.83$$

1 SELF-REVIEW

The Kornaths are buying a $35,000 home. Their annual housing expenses are:

Homeowners' insurance	$ 200
Real estate taxes	940
Maintenance expenses (plumbing repairs, painting)	230
$915 Utilities (telephone, $160; electric, $480; water, $275)	______
Heating	620
Mortgage payments	1,440

A. $4,345

A. What are their total annual housing expenses? $________

B. $\frac{\$4{,}345}{12} = \$362.08$

B. What is their average monthly expense? $__________

BUYING A HOME

Many budget studies indicate that the maximum a family can comfortably afford to spend on housing, including maintenance, heat, and so on, is 35% of its net annual income. A family considering the purchase of a home should estimate the cost of living in that particular dwelling before making a decision to buy.

Problem

Mary and John Locker have two children and need a larger home. They are considering buying a $70,000 house in a Milwaukee, Wisconsin, suburb. They are wondering if they can afford to purchase and maintain the home on their $1,500 monthly income. The realtor has provided them with this list of probable annual expenses. Can they afford to buy this home?

Type of Expense	*Annual Amount*	*Type of Expense*	*Annual Amount*
Homeowners' insurance	$ 380	Heating	$ 1,200
Real estate taxes	1,950	Mortgage payment	5,850
Maintenance	600	Miscellaneous	100
Utilities	950	Total	$11,030

Solution

The Lockers' annual income is $18,000, found by 12 months × $1,500. Therefore, the maximum they can afford to pay for housing is 35% × $18,000 = $6,300.

The $6,300 is substantially less than the estimated $11,030 needed to purchase and maintain the home! The Lockers should consider a less expensive home.

2 SELF-REVIEW

Yes

35% × $25,300 = $8,855; $8,855 is greater than $7,960

The Johnstons have an annual net income of $25,300. They are considering purchasing a home having annual expenses of $7,960. Using the 35% maximum, can they afford this home? _____ Reason ______________________________

____

ASSIGNMENT 4-3
COST OF OWNING OR RENTING A HOME

Name ______________________ Date Due ____________ Grade _____

Answers to selected problems are given in Appendix B.

For problems 1 through 6, find the total annual cost and average monthly cost for owning or renting each home.

	Own/ Rent	*Monthly Mortgage or Rent Payment*	*Annual Taxes*	*Annual Insur-ance*	*Annual Mainte-nance*	*Annual Utilities*	*Total Annual Cost*	*Average Monthly Cost*
Ex.	Own	$476.17	$2,750	$201	$370	$2,080	$11,115.04	$926.25
1.	Own	359.81	2,200	111	344	1,840	________	________
2.	Own	285.70	1,650	105	395	1,625	________	________
3.	Rent	450.00	0	110	0	1,760	________	________
4.	Rent	350.00	0	95	0	820	________	________
5.	Own	438.79	2,000	287	430	1,910	________	________
6.	Rent	500.00	0	125	0	0	________	________

7. Mike and Pat Cheng are buying a $40,000 home. Their annual housing expenses are: mortgage payments, $4,704.60; real estate taxes, $1,183.00; annual insurance premium, $196.00; maintenance (plumbing repairs, painting, insulation, etc.), $365.00; and utilities (heating, electric, telephone, etc.), $1,720.00.

   A. What are their total annual housing expenses?

   $____________, found by

   B. What is their average monthly expense?

   $____________, found by

8. Charles and Lisa Park are buying a $45,000 home. Their annual housing expenses are: mortgage payments, $4,739.82; real estate taxes, $1,323.00; annual insurance premium, $230.00; maintenance, $279.00; and utilities, $1,435.00.

   A. What are their total annual housing expenses?

   $____________, found by

   B. What is their average monthly expense?

   $____________, found by

9. Joe and Allison Turski are renting a home for $425 a month. Their renters' insurance (contents only, not property) has an annual premium of $142. They pay no real estate taxes or utilities. Some minor remodeling they did cost $315.

   A. What are their total annual housing expenses?

   $____________, found by

   B. What is their average monthly expense?

   $____________, found by

10. Margaret and Louis Fairchild rent a condominium for $620 a month. They pay a monthly fee of $35 for all maintenance work. Their renters' insurance costs $235 annually. They pay no real estate taxes. Their utility bills totaled $785 during the year.

A. What are their total annual housing expenses?

$____________, found by

B. What is their average monthly expense?

$____________, found by

11. Wendy and Art Moore are considering the purchase of a $45,000 home. Their semimonthly (twice a month) net income is $815. They do not wish to spend more than 35% of their net annual income for housing. They estimate their housing expenses to be: mortgage payment, $428.55 per month; annual insurance premium, $128.00; semiannual (twice a year) real estate taxes, $900.00; utilities, $1,120.00 annually; and maintenance, $300.00 per year.

Should they buy? ________ Why or why not? ____________________

12. The Becker family is thinking of buying and moving into a $60,000 home. Their weekly net income is $425. They do not wish to spend more than 35% of their net annual income for housing. They have estimated their housing expenses to be: mortgage payment, $497.70 per month; annual insurance premium, $317.00; semiannual real estate taxes, $1,560.00; utilities, $1,860.00 annually; and maintenance, $500.00 per year.

A. Should the Becker family buy the $60,000 home? ________

Why or why not? ____________________

B. Assuming that a typical home rents for 1% of the purchase price per month, and further assuming that the Beckers would pay $500 a year for renters' insurance and maintenance, could they afford to rent the $60,000 home? ________ Why or why not? ____________________

SECTION 4-4: BUDGETING

Objective: To allocate net income and to analyze a budget.

A person, or family, spends money for food, clothing, transportation, and other expenses. Too much money often may be spent on one category, such as transportation. As a result, for example, if the monthly installment payments are not made, an expensive automobile might be repossessed and a substantial down payment lost.

A personalized plan, often referred to as a **budget**, helps to prevent such losses by allowing a person or family to chose between the more important and less important uses of the money earned. *A budget is an organized projection for spending money on a weekly, monthly, or yearly basis.* It helps people to control their spending in order to pay all their bills when due.

- Money management is the process of setting up, following, evaluating and when necessary, revising a plan for the use of income.

It has been estimated that many families could raise their level of living between 10 and 20% by using a family financial plan (budget). A number of budgets have been published by consumer groups, banks, finance companies, universities, and the federal government. It should be emphasized that these are only guidelines. Most of them, however, are based on surveys of how families in the United States actually spend their money. Individual plans vary depending on age of family members, whether they live in the city or the country, the region of the United States, their health, and so on.

The federal government published data on how a hypothetical family of four, living in an urban area, might spend their money for various expenses. Table 4-3 shows the percent of net income which typically might be spent by families with lower, intermediate, and higher incomes.

TABLE 4-3

	Expenses	Budget Level: Net Income, 4-Person Family		
		Lower (less than $10,900)	Intermediate (more than $10,900; less than $15,740)	Higher (over $15,740)
Food, beverages, lunches →	Food	35%	29%	27%
Mortgage payment or rent, utilities, home furnishings, insurance, maintenance →	Housing	23	29	32
Auto costs: gasoline, oil, insurance; subway, bus fare →	Transportation	9	11	10
Clothes, barber or beauty shops, health clubs, etc. →	Clothing and personal care	12	11	12
Physician, dentist, hospital, prescriptions →	Medical	10	7	5
Gifts, contributions, charity, churches, life insurance →	Gifts and contributions	6	7	8
Occupational expenses, tuition, savings, entertainment, recreation, tobacco →	Other items	5	6	6

ALLOCATIONS

A family with no budgeting experience may want to follow the percents indicated in Table 4-3 as a starting point for deciding how much to expend in each of the major categories.

Problem The Mostellars, a family of four, have a net income of $11,800 a year. They plan to set up a budget following the percents shown in Table 4-3. How much should they allocate annually and monthly for food, housing, and other expenses?

Solution

From Table 4-3 → Percent

Expenses	Percent	Net Income	Budget Allocation Annual	Budget Allocation Monthly
Food	29%	$11,800	$ 3,422	$285
Housing	29	11,800	3,422	285
Transportation	11	11,800	1,298	108
Clothing	11	11,800	1,298	108
Medical	7	11,800	826	69
Gifts	7	11,800	826	69
Other	6	11,800	708	59
Total	100%		$11,800	$983

Monthly = $\frac{\text{Annual}}{12}$

Rounded to nearest one dollar

BUDGET ANALYSIS *Analyzing a budget is the process of comparing the actual amounts spent with the amounts budgeted.* A budget is usually analyzed at the end of a time period, such as a month, a quarter, or a year.

Problem The Mostellars kept a record of their spending for two months, April and May. Each month they computed the difference between the amount actually spent and the amount budgeted. Were they over or under the amounts budgeted for the two-month period?

Solution

Expense	Budgeted Monthly	Actual for April	Difference	Actual for May	Difference	Two Months Combined
Food	$285	$295	$+10	$305	$+20	$+30 over
Housing	285	285	0	360	+75	+75 over
Transportation . .	108	185	+77	90	−18	+59 over
Clothing	108	98	−10	70	−28	−38 under
Medical	69	75	+ 6	65	− 4	+ 2 over
Gifts	69	40	−19	42	−27	−46 under
Other	59	50	− 9	35	−24	−33 under
Amount over or under						$+49 over

$10 + $20

−$18 + $77

$49 over total amounts budgeted for April and May

1 SELF-REVIEW

Complete the budget chart for the Urbanski family of four, with a net income of $16,000. They set up their original budget following the percents in Table 4-3. For the months of June and July combined, are they spending over or under their budget?

Item	Percent		Net Income		Annual Budget	Monthly Budget	Actual Spent for June	Difference	Actual Spent for July	Difference	Combined
Food	27	X	$16,000	=	$4,320	$360	$400	$+40	$350	$−10	$+30
Housing	32	X	16,000	=	______	______	420	______	400	______	______
Transportation . . .	10	X	16,000	=	______	______	130	______	150	______	______
Clothing	12	X	16,000	=	______	______	170	______	200	______	______
Medical	5	X	16,000	=	______	______	68	______	40	______	______
Gifts	8	X	16,000	=	______	______	104	______	155	______	______
Other	6	X	16,000	=	______	______	85	______	60	______	______
Amount over or under											______

Item	Annual	Monthly	June Difference	July Difference	Combined
Food	$4,320	$360	$+40	$−10	$+30
Housing	5,120	427	− 7	−27	−34
Trans.	1,600	133	− 3	+17	+14
Clothing	1,920	160	+10	+40	+50
Medical	800	67	+ 1	−27	−26
Gifts	1,280	107	− 3	+48	+45
Other	960	80	+ 5	−20	−15
					$+64

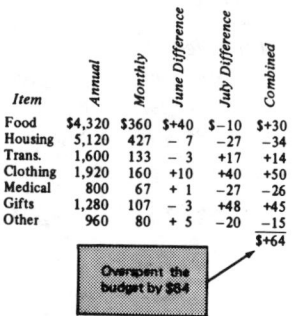

Overspent the budget by $64

ASSIGNMENT 4-4
BUDGETING

Name ______________________ Date Due ____________ Grade _____

Answers to selected problems are given in Appendix B.

For Problems 1 through 6: Using Table 4-3, determine the budgeted amount for each category for families with the given annual net incomes.

	Annual Net Income	*Food*	*Housing*	*Transportation*	*Clothing and Personal Care*	*Medical*	*Gifts and Contributions*	*Other Items*
Ex.	$14,750 (Inter.)	$4,277.50	$4,277.50	$1,622.50	$1,622.50	$1,032.50	$1,032.50	$885.00
1.	18,000 (Higher)	______	______	______	______	______	______	______
2.	9,800 (Lower)	______	______	______	______	______	______	______
3.	15,600	______	______	______	______	______	______	______
4.	10,500	______	______	______	______	______	______	______
5.	27,800	______	______	______	______	______	______	______
6.	44,300	______	______	______	______	______	______	______

7. Jim and Alice Ward have two children. Their annual net income is $10,800. Using Table 4-3, determine their monthly budget allocation for food, housing, and so on.

8. The Cartwrights, a family of four, have an annual net income of $29,800. Using Table 4-3, determine their monthly budget allocation for food, housing, and so on.

9. The Ward family of four (Problem 7) maintained a record of their expenditures for October and November. Analyze their budget with reference to Table 4-3.

Item	*Monthly Budget (Problem 7)*	*Actual for October*	*Difference*	*Actual for November*	*Difference*	*Two Months Combined*
Food		$350		$345		
Housing		200		200		
Transportation		105		112		
Clothing		97		103		
Medical		95		95		
Gifts		45		63		
Other		45		47		
Totals						

Are they spending over or under their budget? Any suggestions?

10. The Cartwright family of four (Problem 8) maintained a record of their expenditures for March and April. Analyze their budget with reference to Table 4-3.

Item	*Monthly Budget (Problem 8)*	*Actual for March*	*Difference*	*Actual for April*	*Difference*	*Two Months Combined*
Food		$470		$510		
Housing		665		665		
Transportation		279		279		
Clothing		195		213		
Medical		97		97		
Gifts		115		87		
Other		100		115		
Totals						

Are they spending over or under their budget? Any suggestions?

REVIEW ASSIGNMENT FOR CHAPTER 4
CONSUMER SPENDING

Name ______________________ Date Due ____________ Grade _____

1. Kelley's Five-Star supermarkets sell Van Camp pork and beans in five sizes. Compute the unit price for each size.

A. 8-ounce size, 32¢. Unit price $______________, found by

B. 16-ounce size, 45¢. Unit price $______________, found by

C. 21-ounce size, 57¢. Unit price $______________, found by

D. 31-ounce size, 82¢. Unit price $______________, found by

E. 53-ounce size, $1.35. Unit price $______________, found by

F. Best buy ______________ ______________

2. Betty Jensen purchased a VW Rabbit Diesel one year ago. She paid $6,000 for a car which could now be sold for $5,800. She drove 16,000 miles last year and averaged 48 mpg. The cost of diesel fuel averaged 84.9 cents a gallon. Oil changes, filters, and lube jobs cost her $48 during the year. All other work was done under warranty. She did spend $9.50 on washing and waxing. Her annual car insurance premium was $240. Find the:

A. Total variable cost, $__________, found by

B. Total fixed cost, $__________, found by

C. Total cost, $__________, found by

D. Cost per mile, $__________, found by

3. The Zenko family flew to Denver and rented a station wagon for six days. Their rental charge is $21.95 per day, plus 21 cents per mile, plus the cost of gasoline. If their station wagon gets 15 mpg and gas costs 89.9 cents per gallon, find the cost of renting the station wagon for six days, if they drive:

A. 300 miles, $__________ found by

B. 600 miles, $__________ found by

C. 900 miles, $__________ found by

4. The Browns are buying a $25,000 home. Their annual housing expenses are: mortgage payments, $2,632.68; real estate taxes, $978.00; annual insurance premium, $122.00; maintenance, $463.00; and utilities, $1,510.00.

A. What are their total annual housing expenses?

$__________, found by

B. What is their average monthly expense?

$__________, found by

5. The Grimaldis, a family of four, have an annual net income of $15,600. They maintained a record of their expenditures for June and July. Using Table 4-3, determine their monthly budget allocations, and analyze their budget.

Item	*Monthly Budget Allocations*	*Actual for June*	*Difference*	*Actual for July*	*Difference*	*Two Months Combined*
Food	________	$380	____	$375	____	____
Housing	________	375	____	375	____	____
Transportation	________	145	____	150	____	____
Clothing	________	137	____	140	____	____
Medical	________	90	____	90	____	____
Gifts	________	95	____	102	____	____
Other	________	78	____	68	____	____
Totals			____		____	____

Are they spending over or under their budget? ________ Any suggestions?

____

____

TO THE STUDENT: There is a SELF-REVIEW TEST for this chapter in Appendix A, *with answers* in Appendix C.

5

Consumer Credit—Charge Accounts

SECTION 5-1: THE PREVIOUS-BALANCE AND THE ADJUSTED-BALANCE METHODS OF DETERMINING THE FINANCE CHARGE

Objective: To compute the finance charge, new balance, and minimum payment using the previous-balance method and the adjusted-balance method.

INTRODUCTION

In recent years there has been a drastic change in the way consumers and businesses pay for such items as meals at restaurants, airline fares, gasoline and repairs at service stations, and purchases made at various retail stores. Stimulated by television commercials, newspaper advertisements, and the like, many consumers have developed an insatiable demand for new automobiles, clothing, cameras, blenders, dishwashers, color television sets, travel, and so on. To encourage immediate purchases, department stores, through charge accounts, urge "buy now, pay later," and travel agencies have charge plans whereby a vacationer can "fly now, pay later."

Shopping for Credit Can Save You Cash

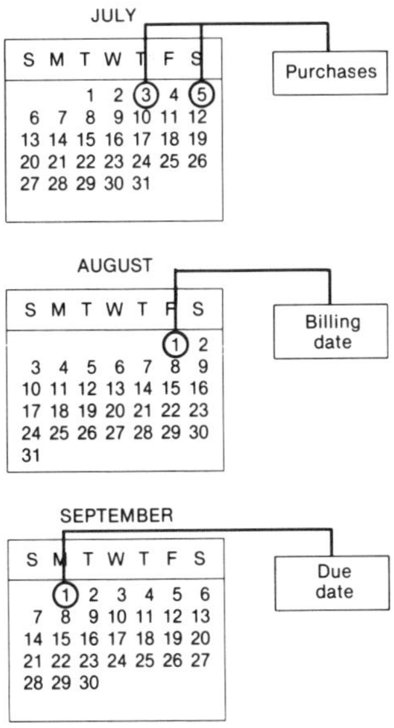

Prior to July 1, 1969, consumers who bought on credit were not always informed of the exact amount being charged for the use of credit. Now, Regulation Z of the Consumer Credit Protection Act, commonly referred to as the Truth-in-Lending Law, requires that the creditor inform the customer of the cost of credit. It should be noted, however, that Regulation Z does *not* fix the maximum, minimum, or any charges involving credit.

The two most important disclosures required by Regulation Z are the **finance charge** and the **annual percentage rate** (often abbreviated APR). The finance charge is the dollar amount the consumer pays for credit. The annual percentage rate is the "true" or "effective" annual interest rate. It can be considered as an index to the relative cost of using credit or borrowing money.

The Truth-in-Lending Law specifically separates the granting of credit into two categories—open-end credit, commonly referred to as **charge accounts**, and credit other than open end, commonly referred to as **installment credit.**

Credit cards issued by local department stores, other retail stores, oil companies, Master Charge, Visa, and others are used in granting what is commonly referred to as *open-end credit.* Instead of paying cash, the purchase is charged, using the card for identification and for billing purposes.

The customer is mailed a monthly bill which includes all purchases made on credit during the billing period. If the bill is paid in full before the next *billing date, there is no charge for credit.* If it is not, a *finance charge* is added.

For example, a man's suit was purchased July 3 and cosmetics were purchased July 5. If the customer's billing date is August 1, full payment is due by September 1 (the next billing date). No finance charge is added if full payment is received before September 1. If it is not received by September 1, a finance charge is added.

There are four methods used in determining the finance charge:

1. The previous-balance method.
2. The adjusted-balance method.
3. The average daily balance method—no new monthly purchases included.
4. The average daily balance method—new monthly purchases included.

The first two methods will be examined in this section.

PREVIOUS-BALANCE METHOD OF COMPUTING FINANCE CHARGES

To conform to the Truth-in-Lending Law, granters of credit must be very precise in stating their credit terms and printing the terms on their monthly statements, including the method for determining the finance charge.

Note in Exhibit 5-1 that the finance charge is computed by taking a percent of the previous balance. Note also that if the buyer does not pay in full each month, a minimum monthly payment is required.

Finance charge = Percent X Previous balance

EXHIBIT 5-1

WINKELMAN'S FLEXI-CHARGE AGREEMENT

Buyer agrees to pay to Winkelman Stores, Incorporated, for all purchases in full by the Payment Due Date which will be shown on the Monthly Statement (in which event there will be no **FINANCE CHARGE**) or, at Buyer's option, to pay in monthly payments (which shall be not less than the Minimum Monthly Payment shown on the chart below) and any portion of the New Balance which is delinquent or is in excess of the credit limit.

NEW BALANCE	Under $10	$10 - $150	$151 -$200	$201 - $250	$251 - $300	Over $300
Minimum Monthly Payment	Balance	$10	$15	$20	$25	10% of Balance

If the New Balance shown on any Statement is not paid or credited in full by the Payment Due Date, Buyer agrees to pay a **FINANCE CHARGE** computed by a Periodic Rate of 1½% per month, which is an **ANNUAL PERCENTAGE RATE** of **18%**, applied to the first **$600** (or a minimum charge of 50¢) and by a periodic rate of **1%** per month, which is an **ANNUAL PERCENTAGE RATE** of **12%**, applied to amounts over **$600** of the Previous Balance without deducting current Payments or Credits, but excluding unpaid **FINANCE CHARGE**. Each payment will be applied first to any unpaid **FINANCE CHARGE**. Winkelman's may change

Problems

Sally Walker has a charge account with Winkelman's, with credit terms as indicated in Exhibit 5-1. Determine the finance charge and minimum payment if her previous balance had been (A) $208 and (B) $720.

Solutions

A. Previous balance of $208. The finance charge (FC) is $3.12, found by:

FC = % X Previous balance
= 1.5% X $208
= 0.015 X $208
= $3.12

B. Previous balance of $720. The finance charge is $10.20, found by:

FC = 1.5% of $600 + 1% ($720 − $600)
= 0.015 X $600 + 0.01 X $120
= $9.00 + $1.20
= $10.20

Amounts charged by store for granting credit.

The minimum payment is $20, found by: Consult chart in Exhibit 5-1. $208 is between $201 and $250. Thus, the minimum payment is $20.

The minimum payment is $72, found by: Consult chart in Exhibit 5-1. $720 is over $300. Thus minimum payment is 10% of $720 = $72.

Using a calculator:

Enter	Press	Display	
600	×	600	
.015	=	9	(Record) 9
720	−	720	
600	= ×	120	
.01	= +	1.2	
9	=	10.2	(Reenter) 9

Using a calculator with memory:

Enter	Press	Display
600	×	600
.015	= m+	9
720	−	720
600	= ×	120
.01	= +	1.2
	RM	9
	=	10.2

After a payment is made and after any additional purchases, it is logical to determine the amount a buyer still owes at this point. This amount is called the **new balance.**

The new balance is found by subtracting the payments and credits from the previous balance, adding the finance charge, and adding the new purchases.

New balance	=	Previous balance	−	Payments and credits	+	Finance charge	+	New purchases

Problem Suppose that Sally Walker (in the above problem) has a previous balance of \$208, makes a payment of \$40, and purchases additional items worth \$18. What is her new balance?

Solution

New balance	=	Previous balance	−	Payments and credits	+	Finance charge	+	New purchases
	=	\$208.00	−	\$40.00	+	\$3.12	+	\$18.00
	=	\$189.12						

1 SELF-REVIEW

A reminder: Cover the answers in the margin.

Bruce Folger has a charge account with a store that has a finance charge of 1.25% of the first \$500 of previous balance and 1% on the portion of previous balance over \$500. Also, a minimum payment of \$10 is required on previous balances from \$10 to \$200. Over \$200, the minimum payment is 5% of the previous balance. Determine the finance charge and the minimum payment if he had:

A. A previous balance of \$190.

FC = ______% X Previous balance
= ______% X \$______
= 0.________ X \$______
= \$2.38 (rounded to nearest cent)

The minimum payment is \$________.

B. A previous balance of \$660.

FC = ______% X \$______ + 1% X \$______
= 0.0125 X \$______ + 0.01 X \$______
= \$______ + \$______
= \$______

The minimum payment is \$________, found by: _____% of \$660 = \$________.

Suppose Bruce Folger makes a payment of \$40 and purchases additional items for \$22. What is his "new balance"?

New balance	=	Previous balance	−	Payments and credits	+	Finance charge	+	New purchases

A. For previous balance of \$190:

New balance = \$______ − \$_____ + \$________ + \$_____
= \$174.38

B. For previous balance of \$660:

New balance = \$______ − \$_____ + \$________ + \$_____
= \$649.85

A.

FC = 1.25%
= 1.25% X \$190
= 0.0125 X \$190
= \$2.38

Minimum payment: \$10

B.

FC = 1.25% X 500 + 1% X 160
= 0.0125 X 500 + 0.01 X 160
= \$6.25 + \$1.60
= \$7.85

Minimum payment: \$33, found by: 5% of \$660

A.

New balance: \$190 − \$40 + \$2.38 + \$22

B.

New balance: \$660 − \$40 + \$7.85 + \$22

ADJUSTED-BALANCE METHOD OF COMPUTING FINANCE CHARGES

Exhibit 5-2 shows a portion of a typical charge account statement that uses the **adjusted-balance** method of computing finance charges. Note that the finance charge is determined by taking a percent of the previous balance *after deducting payments and credits.*

EXHIBIT 5-2
Portion of a Monthly Statement

LION STORE TOLEDO, OH. 43603 PHONE 255-9500	TYPE 1 ACCOUNTS - YOUR FINANCE CHARGE IS COMPUTED BY PERIODIC RATES OF 1.5% APPLIED TO THE FIRST $600 OF YOUR "PREVIOUS BALANCE" AND 1% APPLIED TO THE PORTION IN EXCESS OF $600, AFTER DEDUCTING CURRENT PAYMENTS AND/OR CREDITS APPEARING ON THIS STATEMENT. THESE PERIODIC RATES CORRESPOND TO ANNUAL PERCENTAGE RATES OF 18% AND 12% RESPECTIVELY.

The previous balance minus payments and credits is called the adjusted balance. Thus:

Adjusted balance = Previous balance − (Payments and credits)

It follows, then, that the finance charge is a percent of the adjusted balance.

Finance charge = Percent × Adjusted balance

When the finance charge is determined using the adjusted-balance method, the new balance is found by subtracting the payments and credits from the previous balance, adding the finance charge, and adding the new purchases.

New balance = Previous balance − Payments and credits + Finance charge + New purchases

Problems Keith Sweigart has a charge account with the Lion Store, with credit terms as indicated in Exhibit 5-2. Determine the adjusted balance, the finance charge, and the new balance if his previous balance had been (A) $160, with a $40 payment and new purchase of $16; (B) $740, with a $100 payment, $20 credit, and new purchases of $36.

Solutions A. Previous balance of $160, and $40 payment:

$$\begin{aligned}\text{Adjusted balance} &= \text{Previous balance} - (\text{Payments and credits})\\ &= \$160 - \$40\\ &= \$120\end{aligned}$$

$$\begin{aligned}\text{FC} &= \% \times \text{Adjusted balance}\\ &= 1.5\% \times \$120\\ &= 0.015 \times \$120\\ &= \$1.80\end{aligned}$$

$$\begin{aligned}\text{New balance} &= \$160 - \$40 + \$1.80 + \$16\\ &= \$137.80\end{aligned}$$

B. Previous balance of \$740, with \$100 payment and \$20 credit:

$$
\begin{aligned}
\text{Adjusted balance} &= \text{Previous balance} - (\text{Payments and credits}) \\
&= \$740 - (\$100 + \$20) \\
&= \$740 - \$120 \\
&= \$620 \\
FC &= 1.5\% \text{ of } \$600 + 1\% \text{ of } \$20 \\
&= 0.015 \times \$600 + 0.01 \times \$20 \\
&= \$9.00 + \$0.20 \\
&= \$9.20 \\
\text{New balance} &= \$740 - \$120 + \$9.20 + \$36 \\
&= \$665.20
\end{aligned}
$$

A typical monthly statement is shown in Exhibit 5-3. The customer had a previous balance of \$114.67 from the previous month (part of November and part of December). A \$40 payment was made, leaving a remaining previous balance of \$74.67. The finance charge of \$1.12, found by 1.5% of \$74.67, was added. Purchases totaling \$151.27 were made during part of December and part of January. The new balance is \$227.06.

EXHIBIT 5-3
Monthly Charge Account Statement

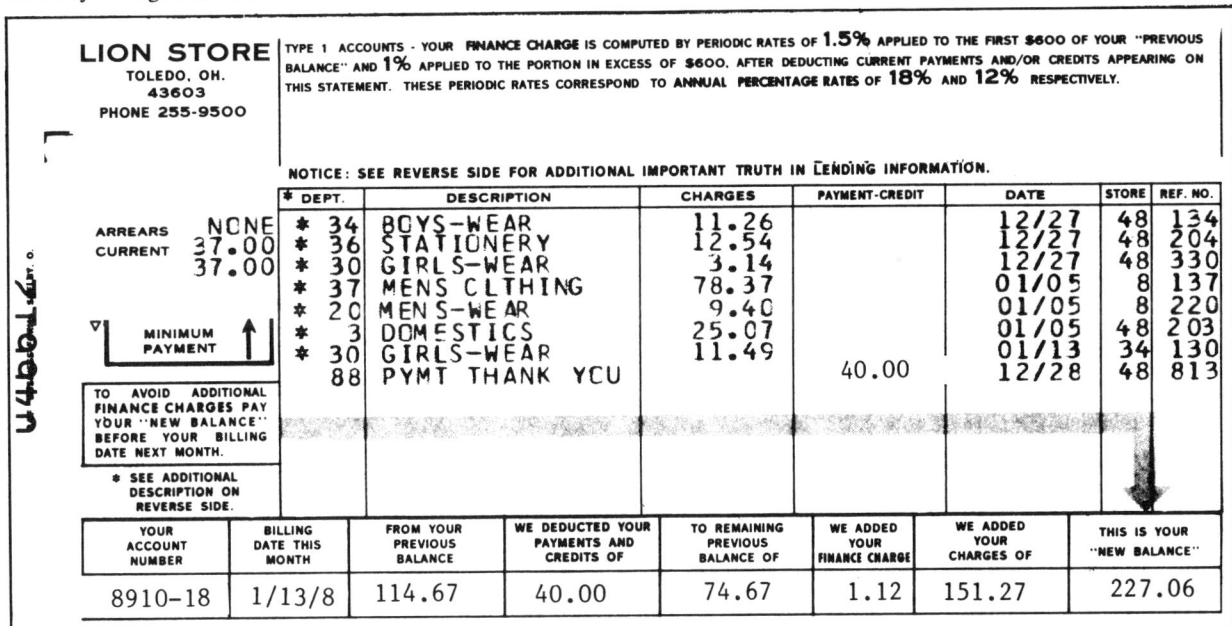

LION STORE
TOLEDO, OH.
43603
PHONE 255-9500

TYPE 1 ACCOUNTS - YOUR FINANCE CHARGE IS COMPUTED BY PERIODIC RATES OF 1.5% APPLIED TO THE FIRST \$600 OF YOUR "PREVIOUS BALANCE" AND 1% APPLIED TO THE PORTION IN EXCESS OF \$600, AFTER DEDUCTING CURRENT PAYMENTS AND/OR CREDITS APPEARING ON THIS STATEMENT. THESE PERIODIC RATES CORRESPOND TO ANNUAL PERCENTAGE RATES OF 18% AND 12% RESPECTIVELY.

NOTICE: SEE REVERSE SIDE FOR ADDITIONAL IMPORTANT TRUTH IN LENDING INFORMATION.

ARREARS NONE
CURRENT 37.00
37.00

MINIMUM PAYMENT

TO AVOID ADDITIONAL FINANCE CHARGES PAY YOUR "NEW BALANCE" BEFORE YOUR BILLING DATE NEXT MONTH.

* SEE ADDITIONAL DESCRIPTION ON REVERSE SIDE.

* DEPT.	DESCRIPTION	CHARGES	PAYMENT-CREDIT	DATE	STORE	REF. NO.
* 34	BOYS-WEAR	11.26		12/27	48	134
* 36	STATIONERY	12.54		12/27	48	204
* 30	GIRLS-WEAR	3.14		12/27	48	330
* 37	MENS CLTHING	78.37		01/05	8	137
* 20	MENS-WEAR	9.40		01/05	8	220
* 3	DOMESTICS	25.07		01/05	48	203
* 30	GIRLS-WEAR	11.49		01/13	34	130
88	PYMT THANK YOU		40.00	12/28	48	813

YOUR ACCOUNT NUMBER	BILLING DATE THIS MONTH	FROM YOUR PREVIOUS BALANCE	WE DEDUCTED YOUR PAYMENTS AND CREDITS OF	TO REMAINING PREVIOUS BALANCE OF	WE ADDED YOUR FINANCE CHARGE	WE ADDED YOUR CHARGES OF	THIS IS YOUR "NEW BALANCE"
8910-18	1/13/8	114.67	40.00	74.67	1.12	151.27	227.06

Remaining previous balance is the same as adjusted balance

2 SELF-REVIEW

Suppose the next month the customer in Exhibit 5-3 made a payment of $150 and had new charges of $15.36. Determine the:

A. $77.06
B. $1.16
C. $93.58

A. Adjusted balance. $__________

B. Finance charge. $__________

C. New balance. $__________

YOUR ACCOUNT NUMBER	BILLING DATE THIS MONTH	FROM YOUR PREVIOUS BALANCE	WE DEDUCTED YOUR PAYMENTS AND CREDITS OF	TO REMAINING PREVIOUS BALANCE OF	WE ADDED YOUR FINANCE CHARGE	WE ADDED YOUR CHARGES OF	THIS IS YOUR NEW BALANCE
8910-18	2/13/8	227.06	150.00	A.	B.	15.36	C.

Note: this month's previous balance is last month's new balance.

Exhibit 5-3A is from the J. C. Penney catalog and shows the monthly periodic rate, annual percentage rate, and portion of the average daily balance to which the monthly periodic rate is applied for selected states.

EXHIBIT 5-3A

State of Residence	Monthly Periodic Rate	Annual Percentage Rate	Portion of Average Daily Balance to Which Applied
AK, AZ, CA, DE, SC	1.5% 1.0%	18% 12%	$1,000 or less over $1,000
DC, KA, MD, MA, NB, NJ, NM, MS, NY, OH, TX, VT, WV, WI	1.5% 1.0%	18% 12%	$500 or less over $500
MO	1.5% .75%	18% 9%	$500 or less over $500
PA	1.25%	15%	entire
MN, SD, WA	1%	12%	entire
AR	.83%	10%	entire
IA	1.5% 1.25%	18% 15%	$500 or less over $500
CT	1.25% 1%	15% 12%	$250 or less over $250

ASSIGNMENT 5-1
THE PREVIOUS-BALANCE AND THE ADJUSTED-BALANCE METHODS OF DETERMINING THE FINANCE CHARGE

Name ______________________ Date Due ____________ Grade _____

Answers to selected problems are given in Appendix B.

For Problems 1 through 6, assume the finance charge is computed by applying periodic rates of $1\frac{1}{2}\%$ per month to the first $500 of the previous balance and 1% per month on such balances in excess of $500.

	Previous Balance	*Finance Charge*		*Previous Balance*	*Finance Charge*
Ex.	$735.50	$9.86			
1.	420.00	________	4.	$1,945.00	$________
2.	378.00	________	5.	692.63	________
3.	580.00	________	6.	471.58	________

7. Using Exhibit 5-1, determine the minimum payment on a new balance of:

   A. $190 $________

   B. $745.36 $________, found by

8. Using Exhibit 5-1, what is the minimum payment on a new balance of:

   A. $246.50 $________

   B. $478.65 $________, found by

9. Find the new balance for the holder of this Standard Oil Company credit card.

   $________, found by

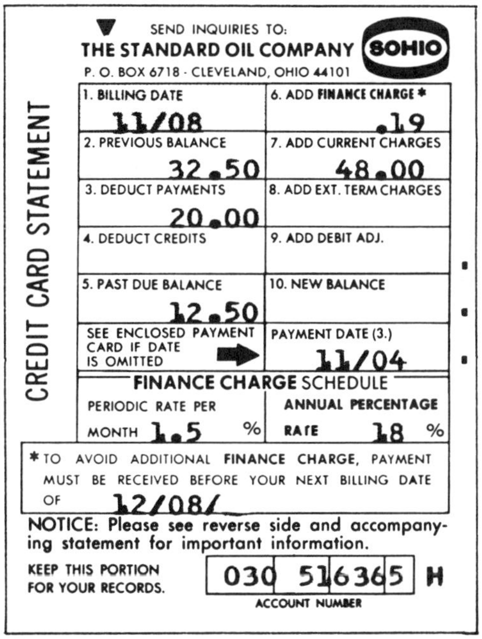

SEND INQUIRIES TO:
THE STANDARD OIL COMPANY SOHIO
P. O. BOX 6718 · CLEVELAND, OHIO 44101

CREDIT CARD STATEMENT

1. BILLING DATE 11/08	6. ADD FINANCE CHARGE * .19
2. PREVIOUS BALANCE 32.50	7. ADD CURRENT CHARGES 48.00
3. DEDUCT PAYMENTS 20.00	8. ADD EXT. TERM CHARGES
4. DEDUCT CREDITS	9. ADD DEBIT ADJ.
5. PAST DUE BALANCE 12.50	10. NEW BALANCE
SEE ENCLOSED PAYMENT CARD IF DATE IS OMITTED	PAYMENT DATE (3.) 11/04

FINANCE CHARGE SCHEDULE

PERIODIC RATE PER MONTH 1.5 %	ANNUAL PERCENTAGE RATE 18 %

* TO AVOID ADDITIONAL FINANCE CHARGE, PAYMENT MUST BE RECEIVED BEFORE YOUR NEXT BILLING DATE OF 12/08/

NOTICE: Please see reverse side and accompanying statement for important information.

KEEP THIS PORTION FOR YOUR RECORDS. 030 516365 H
ACCOUNT NUMBER

10. In Problem 9, suppose the payments totaled $32.50. What would the new balance be?

    $________, found by

11. What method is being used to calculate the finance charge in Problem 9? ____________________

12. In Problem 9, what would the finance charge have been if the previous-balance method was used?

$________, found by

13. Tammy Loring has a charge account with a Goodyear Store with terms as shown. Loring had a previous balance of $460; she made a $50 payment; and she had $37.50 in new purchases. Find the:

A. Finance charge, $________, found by B. New balance, $________, found by

METHODS OF COMPUTING FINANCE CHARGES

METHOD NO. 1 (PREVIOUS BALANCE METHOD): The FINANCE CHARGE is computed by multiplying the previous balance before application of any charges, payments or credits during the billing period, by the periodic rate(s) shown on the face of this Statement.*

IF YOUR BALANCE IS	PERIODIC RATE APPLIED	ANNUAL PERCENTAGE RATE APPLIED
UP TO $33	.50	
$33–$600	1.5%	18%
OVER $600	1.0%	12%

14. John Perez also has an account with the Goodyear Store (see Problem 13). He had a previous balance of $870; made a $200 payment; and had $32 in new purchases. Find the:

A. Finance charge, $________, found by B. New balance, $________, found by

15. In Problem 13, what would Loring's finance charge and new balance be if the store used the adjusted balance method?

A. $________ finance charge, found by B. $__________ new balance, found by

16. In Problem 14, what would Perez's finance charge and new balance be if the store used the adjusted balance method?

A. $________ finance charge, found by B. $__________ new balance, found by

17. Calculate A through E in the statement form.

The **FINANCE CHARGE** is determined by applying periodic rates of **1½%** per month to the first **$600** of the Adjusted ~~Balance and~~ **1%** on such balance in excess of **$600**, corresponding to **ANNUAL PERCENTAGE RATES** of **18%** and **12%**, respectively.

Minimum monthly Payment: **1/10th** of New Balance, but not less than **$10** (or balance if less).

Payment must be received before same closing date next month.

NOTICE: See reverse side and enclosed statement for important information.

* DEPT.	DESCRIPTION	CHARGES	PAYMENT-CREDIT	DATE	STORE	REF. NO.
24	LINGERIE	8.59		04/28	48	125
* 14	NOTIONS	3.66		05/04	48	101
* 35	DRESS	26.13		05/04	48	109
* 30	GIRLS-WEAR	8.36		05/04	48	330
78	SOX-SLIPPERS	4.17		05/11	48	115
88	PYMT THANK YOU		26.40	04/22	48	R1

PREVIOUS BALANCE	− PAYMENTS	AND CREDITS	= ADJUSTED BALANCE	+ FINANCE CHARGE	+ PURCHASES	= NEW BALANCE
126.40	A.		B.	C.	D.	E.

18. Suppose the next month the customer in Problem 17 made a payment of $102.41 and had new charges of $42.31. Determine the:

A. Finance charge, $________, found by B. New balance, $________, found by

SECTION 5-2: AVERAGE DAILY BALANCE METHOD—NO NEW MONTHLY PURCHASES INCLUDED

Objective: To compute the finance charge, new balance, and minimum payment using the average daily balance method—no new monthly purchases included.

Exhibit 5-4 is typical of a customer contract for determining the finance charge on an unpaid balance using the **average daily balance** method when new purchases are *not* included. This provision is specifically stated in Point 3*b*.

EXHIBIT 5-4

CUSTOMER COPY

RETAIL CHARGE AGREEMENT

The undersigned hereinafter referred to as Buyer, for the purpose of obtaining a BankAmericard from the ASSIGNEE BANK identified in the assignment section of this instrument, hereby agrees to the following terms and conditions:

1 The Buyer authorizes the Bank to obtain all information necessary to process Buyer's BankAmericard application
2 The Buyer requests and authorizes Bank to pay the account, to the member merchants of your plan, the amount of all credit purchases made by the use of my BankAmericard from time to time
3 To pay Bank amount advanced on charge slips together with applicable FINANCE CHARGES as follows
   a FINANCE CHARGES are imposed at a periodic rate of **1.5**% per month (an ANNUAL PERCENTAGE RATE OF **18**%) (1) on amounts advanced for purchases which are not paid within 25 days of the date of the billing statement on which they first appear, and (2) on cash advances from the date the advance is made or the check is paid by the Bank
   b FINANCE CHARGES for previous purchases are calculated by applying the above periodic rate to the previous purchases' Average Daily Balance The Average Daily Balance equals the total of the outstanding daily balances for previous purchases during the billing period (not including new purchases which appear on the statement) less payments and credits as made and allocated to purchases, divided by the number of days in the billing period NO FINANCE CHARGES WILL BE IMPOSED FOR PREVIOUS PURCHASES DURING THE CURRENT BILLING PERIOD IF THE NEW BALANCE IS PAID IN FULL ON OR BEFORE THE DUE DATE
   c FINANCE CHARGES for cash advances are calculated by applying the above periodic rate ... the Cash Advances' Ave... Balance The Average Daily ... the total of ... balances for ... the ...

Q I'm beginning to fear that I'm one of those credit card-oholics who can't stop charging. Can you tell me how much an average person owes, with what income, before he seeks help?

A Credit counselors, now doing a booming business, profile their average client as a 30-year-old man or woman with a family of four. He or she earns about $13,500 a year and owes approximately $7,000 to nine different creditors.

The **finance charge** is determined by taking a specified percent of the average daily balance.

> Finance charge = Percent X Average daily balance

The **average daily balance** is determined by totaling the balance for each day in the billing cycle and dividing the total by the number of days in the cycle.

$$\text{Average daily balance} = \frac{\text{Total of balances for each day in billing cycle}}{\text{Number of days in the cycle}}$$

Problem Suppose that A&J Department Store accepts Visa and determines the finance charge by taking 1.5% of the average daily balance—excluding new purchases. Sam Walker purchased clothing for $300 in January. On February 1 (the billing date) he was billed for $300. If he pays the $300 by March 1, no finance charge will be assessed.

He made a payment of $100 on February 10. On February 13 he made purchases totaling $400. On the March 1 bill, find (A) the average daily balance; (B) finance charge; (C) the new balance.

Solution

Dates	*Payments*	*Balance Each Day*	*No. of Days*	*Balance X No. of Days*
Feb. 1, 2, 3, ... 9		$300	9	$2,700
Feb. 10	−$100	200	1	200
Feb. 11, 12, ... 28		200	18	3,600
Totals			28	$6,500

A. Average daily balance $= \dfrac{\text{Total balance(s)}}{\text{Number of days}}$

$= \dfrac{\$6{,}500}{28}$

$= \$232.1428$
$= \$232.14$

B. Finance charge $= \% \times$ Average daily balance
$= 1.5\% \times \$232.14$
$= \$3.482$
$= \$3.48$

C. The new balance is found by:

$$\text{New balance} = \text{Previous balance} - \text{Payments and credits} + \text{Finance charge} + \text{New purchases}$$
$$= \$300.00 - \$100.00 + \$3.48 + \$400.00$$
$$= \$603.48$$

Problem Another example: Purchases on August 25 totaled \$400. The billing date was September 5. Payments of \$100 on September 11 and \$100 on September 21 were made. On the October 5 billing, find (A) the average daily balance; (B) the finance charge if the rate is 1.5% of the average daily balance; (C) the new balance.

Solution

Dates	*Payments*	*Balance Each Day*	*No. of of Days*	*Balance X No. of Days*
Sept. 5, 6 . . . 10		\$400	6	\$2,400
Sept. 11	\$100	300	1	300
Sept. 12, 13 . . . 20		300	9	2,700
Sept. 21	100	200	1	200
Sept. 22, 23 . . . Oct. 4		200	13	2,600
Totals			30	\$8,200

A. Average daily balance $= \dfrac{\text{Total balance(s)}}{\text{Number of days}}$

$= \dfrac{\$8{,}200}{30}$

$= \$273.33$

B. Finance charge $= \% \times$ Average daily balance
$= 1.5\% \times \$273.33$
$= \$4.099$
$= \$4.10$

C. The October 5 bill would show a previous balance of \$400.00, plus a finance charge of \$4.10, minus payments of \$200.00, plus no new charges, for a new balance of \$204.10.

1 SELF-REVIEW

Lasalle's finance charges are computed at a monthly rate of 1.25% of the average daily balance—no new purchases included. Sally Williamson had a previous balance amounting to $260. Her billing date is August 10. Payments of $60 on August 15 and $90 on August 25 were made. For the September 10 billing, what are the average daily balance, the finance charge, and the new balance?

	Dates	*Payments*	*Balance Each Day*	*No. of Days*	*Balance × No. of Days*
A.	Aug. 10, 11,... 14		$260	5	$______
B.	Aug. 15	$60	200	1	______
C.	Aug. 16, 17,... 24		______	______	______
D.	Aug. 25	90	______	______	______
E.	Aug. 26, 27... Sept. 9		110	15	______
	Totals			______	$______

F. Average daily balance $= \frac{\text{Total balance(s)}}{\text{Number of days}}$

$= \frac{\_\_\_\_\_\_}{31}$

$= \$163.23$

G. Finance charge = % × Average daily balance
= 1.25% × $163.23
= $______

H. New balance = Previous balance − Payments and credits + Finance charge + New purchases

= $______ − $150 + $______ + $______

= $______

	Bal.	*Days*	*Bal. × Days*
A.	$260	5	$1,300
B.	200	1	200
C.	200	9	1,800
D.	110	1	110
E.	110	15	1,650
Totals		31	$5,060

F. Average daily balance:

$= \frac{\$5{,}060}{31}$

$= \$163.23$

G. Finance charge = $2.04

H. New balance:

= $260 − $150 + $2.04 + 0

= $112.04

ASSIGNMENT 5-2
AVERAGE DAILY BALANCE METHOD—NO NEW MONTHLY PURCHASES INCLUDED

Name ______________________________ Date Due ____________ Grade _____

Answers to selected problems are given in Appendix B.

For Problems 1 and 2, determine the average daily balance for an account with transactions as shown in the table.

1.

Balance on Sept. 1	\$270
Payment on Sept. 11	70
Payment on Sept. 21	100

Next billing is October 1.

\$__________, found by

2.

Balance on May 10	\$1,119.63
Payment on May 24	125.00
Payment on June 2	650.00

Next billing is June 10.

\$__________, found by

A FINANCE CHARGE will be calculated by applying periodic rates of 1½% per month (ANNUAL PERCENTAGE RATE OF 18%) to the first \$500 of the average daily balance, and 1% per month (ANNUAL PERCENTAGE RATE OF 12%) to the average daily balance in excess of \$500. The average daily balance is determined by totaling the balance outstanding each day during the billing period and dividing this sum by the number of days in that period. The balance outstanding on any given day is the ending balance of the previous day, less any credits or payments received that day. It does not include any purchases made or miscellaneous debits incurred during the billing period.

3. Using the above description from Jacobsen's, find the finance charge for Problem 1.

\$__________, found by

4. Using the above description from Jacobsen's, find the finance charge for Problem 2.

\$__________, found by

PLEASE MENTION THIS ACCOUNT NUMBER WHEN ORDERING OR WRITING.	BILLING DATE	PREVIOUS BALANCE	NEW BALANCE
70 87123 03897 8	OCT 03	\$ 147.00	\$

If the *FINANCE CHARGE* exceeds 50¢, the *ANNUAL PERCENTAGE RATE* is 18% on the first \$600 of the AVERAGE DAILY BALANCE and 12% on that part of the AVERAGE DAILY BALANCE in excess of \$600. The AVERAGE DAILY BALANCE excludes any purchases added during the monthly billing period and any unpaid *FINANCE CHARGE.*

To avoid a *FINANCE CHARGE* next month, pay this amount within 30 days from Billing Date.

14351-409 Rev. 7/15/77

NOTICE: SEE REVERSE SIDE FOR IMPORTANT INFORMATION.

5. Joseph Barolo has a charge account with Sears. The average daily balance does not include new purchases. He had transactions as shown in the table at the right. Next billing is October 3. Find the:

Balance on Sept. 3	\$147.00
Payment on Sept. 23	47.00
Purchases on Sept. 30	37.90

A. Average daily balance.

\$__________, found by

B. Finance charge.

\$__________, found by

C. New balance.

\$__________, found by

6. J. C. Penney determines the finance charge as indicated. The average daily balance—no new purchases included method is used. Sue Khan has the following transactions:

Balance on Dec. 11	$767.50
Payment on Dec. 20	75.00
Purchase on Dec. 23	43.50
Payment on Dec. 29	75.00
Purchase on Jan. 8	17.13

Pay New Balance by ▶ to avoid FINANCE CHARGE | Next Billing Date 01–11 | ANNUAL PERCENTAGE RATE(S)

Balances | Periodic Rate(s)

UP TO $ 500 1.50 % 18.0 %

OVER $ 500 1.00 % 12.0 %

MINIMUM CHARGE .50

FINANCE CHARGE is computed on $ the AVERAGE DAILY BALANCE. (See Reverse Side for explanation)

Next billing is January 11. Find the:

A. Average daily balance.

$__________, found by

B. Finance charge.

$__________, found by

C. New balance.

$__________, found by

7. Suppose an account had the transactions shown at the right. The finance charge is computed using a rate of 1.5%. Next billing is August 1. Find the finance charge if the following methods are used:

Balance on July 1	$500
Payment on July 21	300

A. Previous-balance method.

$__________, found by

B. Adjusted-balance method.

$__________, found by

C. Average daily balance—no new purchases included method.

$__________, found by

8. In Problem 7, suppose the payment were made on July 2. Find the finance charge if the following methods are used:

A. Previous-balance method.

$__________, found by

B. Adjusted-balance method.

$__________, found by

C. Average daily balance—no new purchases included method.

$__________, found by

SECTION 5-3: AVERAGE DAILY BALANCE METHOD—NEW MONTHLY PURCHASES INCLUDED

Objective: To compute the finance charge, new balance, and minimum payment using the average daily balance method—new monthly purchases included.

More and more granters of credit are shifting to the **average daily balance method—new purchases included** for determining the finance charge. The reason is that it brings in more revenue than either the adjusted-balance method or the average daily balance method excluding new purchases.

If a customer does not pay an account *in full* by the due date, new purchases are immediately added to the previous balance and are subject to a finance charge.

As an example, the J. L. Hudson Company's retail charge agreement (Exhibit 5-5) states in Point 2*a*, "The outstanding balance for any given day is determined by *adding to the prior day's ending balance any purchases made* and subtracting any payments received and credits given."

EXHIBIT 5-5

HUDSON'S RETAIL CHARGE AGREEMENT

I agree that the following terms and conditions will govern this charge account established by Hudson's* for me. *Division of Dayton-Hudson Corporation

1. I can avoid incurring a **FINANCE CHARGE** by paying my account balance, "New Balance," in full, provided that such payment is received before the next closing date. If I elect not to pay the "New Balance" in full, my payment may be more than the minimum payment and up to the full amount due on the account "New Balance," but not less than 1/10 (10%) of the "New Balance." Whenever the "New Balance" is less than $100, the minimum monthly payment will be $10 or the "New Balance," whichever is less. Payments will be applied first to **FINANCE CHARGE** then to the remaining outstanding balance.

   No **FINANCE CHARGE** will be added for a billing cycle in which there is no previous balance or during which payments and credits equal or exceed the previous balance. I may pay the account balance, "New Balance," at any time without incurring additional **FINANCE CHARGE**.

2. a. The **FINANCE CHARGE**, if any, is to be computed by applying a periodic rate of 1.5% (18% **ANNUAL PERCENTAGE RATE**) to the Average Daily Balance. The Average Daily Balance is determined by totaling the balances outstanding for each day in the billing cycle and dividing that total by the number of days in the billing cycle. The outstanding balance for any given day is determined by adding to the prior day's ending balance any purchases made and subtracting any payments received and credits given. A minimum **FINANCE CHARGE** of 35¢ may be imposed if the Average Daily Balance does not exceed $25. **FINANCE CHARGES** in this agreement are agreed to be a Time Price Differential.

Problem Recall from the preceding problem that Walker purchased clothing for $300 in January. The billing date was February 1; $100 was paid on February 10; and on February 13 purchases totaling $400 were made. Suppose the finance charge is 1.5% of the average daily balance—new purchases included. On the March 1 bill, find (A) the average daily balance; (B) the finance charge; (C) the new balance.

Solution

Dates	*Purchases or Payments*	*Balance Each Day*	*No. of Days*	*Balance × No. of Days*
Feb. 1, 2, . . . 9		$300	9	$ 2,700
Feb. 10	−$100	200	1	200
Feb. 11, 12		200	2	400
Feb. 13	+ 400	600	1	600
Feb. 14, 15, . . . 28		600	15	9,000
Total			28	$12,900

A. Average daily balance $= \dfrac{\text{Total balance(s)}}{\text{Number of days}}$

$= \dfrac{\$12{,}900}{28}$

$= \$460.71$

B. Finance charge = % × Average daily balance
= 1.5% × $460.71
= $6.91

C. The new balance on March 1 is found by:

New balance	=	Previous balance	−	Payments and credits	+	Finance charge	+	New purchases
	=	$300.00	−	$100.00	+	$6.91	+	$400.00
	=	$606.91						

It is interesting to compare the four methods for computing the finance charge for the above problem, as in the table below.

Method	*Finance Charge*
Previous balance method (1.5% of $300)	$4.50
Adjusted balance method (1.5% of $200)	3.00
Average daily balance—no new purchases included	3.48
Average daily balance—new purchases included	6.91

1 SELF-REVIEW

On May 1 an account had a $600 balance. A $100 payment was made on May 6, and a $300 payment was made May 18. A purchase of $50 was made on May 10 and another purchase of $150 on May 22. The finance charge is 1.5% of the average daily balance—new purchases included. For the June 1 billing, determine the average daily balance, the finance charge, and the new balance.

	Dates	*Purchases or Payments*	*Balance Each Day*	*No. of Days*	*Balance × No. of Days*
A.	May 1, 2, . . . 5		$600	5	$________
B.	May 6	−$100	500	1	________
C.	May 7, 8, 9		500	3	________
D.	May 10	+ 50	550	1	________
E.	May 11, 12, . . . 17		550	7	________
F.	May 18	− 300	250	1	________
G.	May 19, 20, 21		250	3	________
H.	May 22	+ 150	400	1	________
I.	May 23, 24, . . . 31		400	9	________
J.	Totals			31	$________

K. Average daily balance $= \dfrac{\text{Total balance(s)}}{\text{Number of days}}$

$= \dfrac{\$14{,}400}{31}$

= $________

L. FC = % × Average daily balance

= ____% × $________

= $________

M. New balance:

New balance	=	Previous balance	−	Payments and credits	+	Finance charge	+	New purchases
	=	$600.00	−	$400.00	+	$6.97	+	$______
	=	$______						

	Balance × No. of Days
A.	$ 3,000
B.	500
C.	1,500
D.	550
E.	3,850
F.	250
G.	750
H.	400
I.	3,600
J. Totals	$14,400

K. Average daily balance: $464.52

L. Finance charge:
= 1.5% × $464.52
= $6.97

M. New balance:
= $600 − $400 + $6.97 + $200
= $406.97

ASSIGNMENT 5-3
AVERAGE DAILY BALANCE METHOD—NEW MONTHLY PURCHASES INCLUDED

Name ______________________________ **Date Due** ____________ **Grade** _____

Answers to selected problems are given in Appendix B.

For Problems 1 through 4, determine the average daily balance—new monthly purchases included for an account with the transactions as shown:

1. | | |
   |---|---|
   | Balance on April 1 . . . . | $415.50 |
   | Payment on April 16 . . . . | 150.00 |
   | Purchase on April 22 . . . . | 47.12 |

   Next billing is May 1.

   $__________, found by

2. | | |
   |---|---|
   | Balance on Oct. 9 . . . . | $712.73 |
   | Payment on Oct. 21 . . . . | 50.00 |
   | Purchase on Nov. 3 . . . . | 38.68 |

   Next billing is Nov. 9.

   $__________, found by

3. Use Exhibit 5-5 from the J. L. Hudson Company to determine the finance charge for Problem 1.

   $__________, found by

4. Use Exhibit 5-5 from the J. L. Hudson Company to determine the finance charge for Problem 2.

   $__________, found by

5. Kim Price received her charge statement from Lasalles Macy Store, with the transactions as shown. The average daily balance is computed with new purchases included. Compute A, B, C, D, E, and F for her statement dated 6/1. The balance on May 1 is $373.50.

DATE	DEPT NO	DESCRIPTION	PURCHASES	CREDITS	PAYMENTS	ITEM NO
5/9	148	Pre-teen Clothing	24.97			06-14222
5/13		Payment-Thank You			$50.00	
5/26	214	Jr. Sportswear	19.16			06-70828

BILL CLOSING DATE	PREVIOUS BALANCE	FINANCE CHARGE	TOTAL PURCHASES THIS MONTH	CREDITS	PAYMENTS	NEW BALANCE
6/1	$373.50	B.	C.	D.	E.	F.

PAY NEW BALANCE IN FULL WITHIN 25 DAYS OF BILL CLOSING DATE TO AVOID **FINANCE CHARGE** NEXT MONTH. **FINANCE CHARGE,** IF ANY, IS COMPUTED ON THE AVERAGE DAILY BALANCE OF $A. BY APPLYING MONTHLY PERIODIC RATES OF 1½% TO THE FIRST $600 ON THAT BALANCE AND 1% TO THE PORTION OVER $600, CORRESPONDING TO **ANNUAL PERCENTAGE RATES** OF 18% AND 12% RESPECTIVELY, SUBJECT TO A MINIMUM **FINANCE CHARGE** OF $.50.

ACCOUNT NUMBER	257-96-071
MIN. AMOUNT DUE ON NEW BALANCE	5.21
AMOUNT PAST DUE	
TOTAL MINIMUM AMOUNT NOW DUE	5.21

6. Pete Athens received the following Master Charge statement. The finance charge is computed on the average daily balance—new purchases included method. For the statement dated 10/06, compute A, B, C, D, E, F, G, and the totals line. The balance on Sept. 6 is $183.11.

Master Charge® Statement

FIRST NATL BANK OF TOLEDO

FINANCE CHARGES on your account are calculated under the following schedule:

Dollar Amount	(Monthly) Periodic Rates Purchases	(Monthly) Periodic Rates Cash Advances	Corresponding Nominal ANNUAL PERCENTAGE RATES Purchases	Corresponding Nominal ANNUAL PERCENTAGE RATES Cash Advances
FIRST $200.00	2.00%		24.00%	
$200.01 to $400.00	1.50%		18.00%	
$400.01 and above	1.00%		12.00%	

Reference Number	Date	Description of Transaction			Debits / Credits (—) Purchases Returns Advances Payments
24904063600909	0907	GRIFFS INC	MAUMEE	OH	51.21
24802409600922	0907	MINNESOTA FABRICS	MAUMEE	OH	26.73
25646806050914	0907	BARGAIN CITY	MAUMEE	OH	15.52
26116003210919	0913	THE ANDERSONS	MAUMEE	OH	77.52
2690080049	0926	PAYMENT—THANK YOU			83.11—
SEND INQUIRIES	TO	PO BOX 1629 TOLEDO OHIO 43603			

	B. ***FINANCE CHARGES***	A. Computed On Average Daily Balance Of:	***ANNUAL PERCENTAGE RATES***	Payment Due Date	Statement Closing Date
Purchases	$	$	24.00 %	10/31	10/06
Cash Advances	$	$	24.00 %	10/31	10/06

	Previous Balance	Payments	Credits	New Debits Purchases/Advances	***FINANCE CHARGES***	New Balance
Purchases	183.11	C.	D.	E.	F.	G.
Cash Advances						
Totals						

To avoid additional ***FINANCE CHARGES*** on your Purchases New Balance, pay at least the full amount thereof prior to your Payment Due Date. If not so paid, ***FINANCE CHARGES*** will be incurred on the principal portion thereof as of your Statement Closing Date and ***FINANCE CHARGES*** will be incurred on purchases posted during your next billing cycle (the one beginning with your Statement Closing Date) as of the date of posting of each. ***FINANCE CHARGES*** will accrue on the Principal of Cash Advances until payment is received.

BANK ABOVE NAMED IS IN ASSOCIATION WITH MEMBER(S) OF BANCSYSTEMS ASSOCIATION

Account Number 516 31010 040 Credit Line 900.00 Number of days in this billing cycle 30

5 *NOTICE: SEE REVERSE SIDE FOR IMPORTANT INFORMATION*

REVIEW ASSIGNMENT FOR CHAPTER 5
CONSUMER CREDIT—CHARGE ACCOUNTS

Name ______________________ Date Due ____________ Grade _____

For Problems 1 through 4, the finance charge is 1.25% on the first \$500 and 1% on that portion over \$500. Use the following transactions and minimum payment schedule.

Balance on Sept. 1	\$570
Payment on Sept. 6	170
Purchase on Sept. 11	70
Purchase on Sept. 21	90

Next billing is Oct. 1.

I agree to pay at least the minimum monthly payment shown on my statement upon receipt of each monthly statement. The amount of such minimum payment shall be in accordance with the following schedule:

If the New Balance Is:	\$.01 to \$10.00	\$10.01 to \$200.00	\$200.01 to \$300.00	\$300.01 to \$400.00	\$400.01 to \$500.00	\$500.01 to \$600.00	Over \$600.00
Your Scheduled Monthly Payment Will Be:	Balance	\$10.00	\$15.00	\$20.00	\$25.00	\$30.00	Add \$10.00 for Every \$100.00

1. Suppose the account is with a Goodyear Store which uses the *previous-balance method.* Find the:

   A. Previous balance, \$__________, found by

   B. Finance charge, \$______, found by

   C. New balance, \$__________, found by

   D. Minimum payment, \$_______, found by

2. Suppose the account is with Fleeger's Pro Hardware, which uses the *adjusted-balance method.* Find the:

   A. Adjusted balance, \$__________, found by

   B. Finance charge, \$______, found by

   C. New balance, \$__________, found by

   D. Minimum payment, \$_______, found by

3. Suppose the account is with Sears, which uses the *average daily balance—no new purchases included method.* Find the:

   A. Average daily balance, \$_________, found by

   B. Finance charge, \$______, found by

   C. New balance, \$__________, found by

   D. Minimum payment, \$_______, found by

4. Suppose the account is with Alden's, which uses the *average daily balance–new purchases included method.* Find the:

A. Average daily balance, $__________, found by B. Finance charge, $_______, found by

C. New balance, $__________, found by D. Minimum payment, $________, found by

Problems 5 through 8 are based on the data in the table below. A charge statement billed on the first of the month shows the following transactions:

Unpaid previous balance as of March 1 . . .	$200.00
Purchases on March 11	35.00
Payment on March 16	100.00
Purchases on March 21	45.00
Payment on March 26	50.00

5. Suppose that the account is in a department store in Connecticut or Minnesota, where the maximum rate which can be applied to the previous balance is 1.00%. What are the finance charge and the new balance on the April 1 billing if the department store uses the *previous-balance method?*

A. Finance charge, $__________, found by B. New balance, $__________, found by

6. Suppose that the account is in a department store in South Dakota or Washington, where the maximum rate which can be applied to the adjusted balance is 1.00%. What are the finance charge and the new balance on the April 1 billing if the department store uses the *adjusted-balance method?*

A. Finance charge, $__________, found by B. New balance, $__________, found by

7. Suppose that the account is in a department store in Arkansas, where the maximum rate which can be applied to the average daily balance is 0.83%. What are the finance charge and the new balance on the April 1 billing if the department store uses the *average daily balance–no new purchases included method?*

A. Finance charge, $__________, found by B. New balance, $__________, found by

8. Suppose that the account is in a department store in Pennsylvania, where the maximum rate which can be applied to the average daily balance is 1.25%. What are the finance charge and the new balance on the April 1 billing if the department store uses the *average daily balance–new purchases included method?*

A. Finance charge, $__________, found by B. New balance, $__________, found by

TO THE STUDENT: There is a SELF-REVIEW TEST for this chapter in Appendix A, *with answers* in Appendix C.

6

Consumer Credit—Installment Credit

SECTION 6-1: INSTALLMENT CREDIT

Objective: To determine the amount financed, the total amount paid, and the monthly payment on installment accounts.

Do you owe too much?

average income	average debt	ratio of debt to income
less than $3,000	$ 99	4.3%
$3,000—$4,999	328	8.1
$5,000—$5,999	659	12.0
$6,000—$7,499	796	11.6
$7,500—$8,499	963	11.9
$8,500—$9,999	1,140	12.3
$10,000—$12,499	1,229	10.9
$12,500—$14,999	1,247	9.2
$15,000—$19,999	1,137	6.8
$20,000 or more	917	3.2

The Truth-in-Lending Law deals with open-end credit (charge accounts) and *other than open-end credit.* Other than open-end credit is commonly referred to as **installment credit.** Durable goods, such as automobiles, stereos, refrigerators, dishwashers, and furniture are sold on installment terms. Installment credit is offered by banks, finance companies, automobile dealers, and some retailers.

In buying on installment credit, a consumer purchases the item for immediate use and pays for it in a series of weekly or monthly payments. A small portion of the total price, called the **down payment**, is usually required. A finance charge is added to the cash price in order to cover bookkeeping expenses, credit checks, computer operations, and the wages of persons handling the accounts.

DETERMINING THE AMOUNT OF EACH PAYMENT ON INSTALLMENT ACCOUNTS

To determine the amount of each payment:

Step 1. Find the *amount to be financed* by subtracting the down payment from the purchase price or cash price.

> Amount financed = Cash price − Down payment

Step 2. Find the *total amount paid in installments* by adding the finance charge to the amount financed.

> Total amount paid in installments = Amount financed + Finance charge

Step 3. The *monthly payment* is found by dividing the total amount paid in installments by the number of payments.

$$\text{Monthly payment} = \frac{\text{Total amount paid in installments}}{\text{Number of payments}}$$

Problem

A GE dishwasher is advertised for $450. It can be purchased either by paying cash, or making a $50 down payment and 12 monthly payments (installments). If the monthly payment plan is used, the finance charge is $44. What is the monthly payment?

Solution Step 1. Determine the amount financed.

Amount financed = Cash price – Down payment
= \$450 – \$50
= \$400

Step 2. Determine the total amount paid in installments.

Total amount paid in installments = Amount financed + Finance charge
= \$400 + \$44
= \$444

Step 3: Determine the monthly payment.

$$\text{Monthly payment} = \frac{\text{Total amount paid in installments}}{\text{Number of payments}} = \frac{\$444}{12} = \$37$$

1 SELF-REVIEW

A reminder: Cover the answers in the margin.

Consider the advertisement for a Volare. The finance charge is \$1,021.12. Complete the calculations below to verify that the monthly payment is \$94.19.

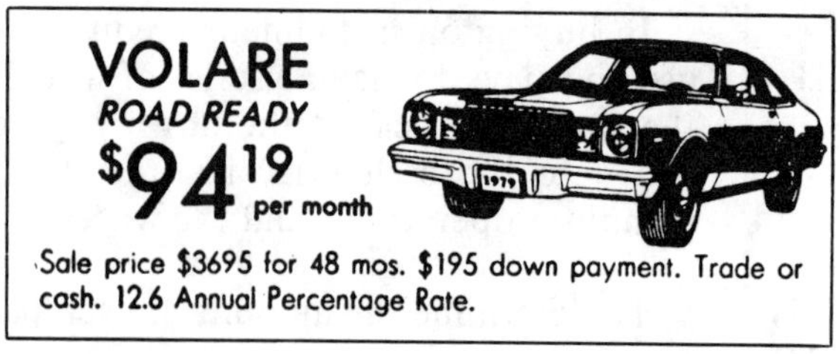

Amount financed:
= \$3,695 – \$195
= \$3,500

Step 1. Determine the amount financed.

Amount financed = Cash price – Down payment
= \$________ – \$______
= \$________

Total:
= \$3,500 + \$1,021.12
= \$4,521.12

Step 2. Determine the total amount paid in installments.

Total amount paid in installments = Amount financed + Finance charge
= \$________ + \$____________
= \$____________

Monthly payment:
$= \frac{\$4,521.12}{48}$
= \$94.19

Step 3. Determine the monthly payment.

$$\text{Monthly payment} = \frac{\text{Total amount paid in installments}}{\text{Number of payments}}$$

$= \frac{\$\_\_\_\_\_\_\_\_\_\_}{48}$

= \$________

ASSIGNMENT 6-1
INSTALLMENT CREDIT

Name ______________________ Date Due ______________ Grade _____

Answers to selected problems are given in Appendix B.

For Problems 1 through 6, determine the amount financed, total amount paid, and monthly payment.

	Cash Price	*Down Payment*	*Amount Financed*	*Finance Charge*	*Total Amount Paid in Installments*	*No. of Payments*	*Monthly Payment*
Ex.	$6,283	$ 283	$6,000	$1,200.00	$7,200.00	36	$200.00
1.	540	100	440	40.00	480.00	12	________
2.	175	25	150	20.25	170.25	15	________
3.	180	36	144	12.96	________	12	________
4.	300	60	240	24.00	________	10	________
5.	2,000	500	________	195.00	________	24	________
6.	4,240	1,240	________	360.00	________	18	________

7. A stereo-tape deck player is on sale for $275. The purchaser can either pay cash or make a down payment of $35 and pay off the installment account with 15 monthly payments. If the 15-month installment plan is used, a finance charge of $27 is added. What is the monthly payment?

   $__________, found by

8. Bernath Hi-Way Furniture advertised an Early American sofa for $289.98 cash, or $19.98 down and six easy monthly payments. If the six easy monthly payments are chosen, the finance charge is $24.30. What is each monthly payment?

   $__________, found by

9. A Buick Riviera two-door hardtop is offered at a cash price of $5,695. The dealer will accept a cash down payment of $895 and finance the remainder for 48 months, with a finance charge of $1,663.63. What is each monthly payment?

   $__________, found by

10. The finance charge for the 1977 Vega Wagon is $1,264.20 for 60-month financing. Find the monthly payment.

    1977 VEGA
    WAGON
    Stock No. 7005 Our Price 3806.48
    206.48 down

    $__________, found by

11. Home Furniture Company of Dallas has a special savings on a sofa and loveseat pair in Herculon for $399. If the buyer finances $300 of the cost, a finance charge of $30 would be added for six payments. How much would each monthly payment be?

$__________, found by

12. Trento Motors, Ltd., had a Fiat on sale for $1,299. The person purchasing the car made a down payment of $99 and financed the remainder through a finance company. If the finance charge is $155.76 and the agreement is for 12 monthly payments, what is the amount of each payment?

$__________, found by

13. Huntington Banks offer the following home improvement loans. Find the monthly payment for 24-, 36-, and 48-month loans.

	24 Monthly Payments			*36 Monthly Payments*			*48 Monthly Payments*		
Amount Financed	*Finance Charge*	*Total of Payments*	*Monthly Payment*	*Finance Charge*	*Total of Payments*	*Monthly Payment*	*Finance Charge*	*Total of Payments*	*Monthly Payment*
$1,500	$240.00	$1,740.00	A. ________	359.76	$1,859.76	C. ________	$480	$1,980	E. ________
2,000	319.84	2,319.84	B. ________	479.68	2,479.68	D. ________	640	2,640	F. ________

14. Determine the monthly payment in each case to pay off a $4,000 loan for 36 months.

A. Credit union, finance charge $709.52

$__________, found by

B. Sylvania Savings, finance charge $844.16

$__________, found by

C. Ohio Citizens, finance charge $892.76

$__________, found by

D. Mid-American, finance charge $893.12

$__________, found by

E. First National, finance charge $908.24

$__________, found by

F. Hobart Trust, finance charge $918.24

$__________, found by

15. A camping trailer can be purchased for $1,200 cash or by financing $900 for 15 months, with a finance charge of $106.88. What is each monthly payment if financing is chosen?

$__________, found by

SECTION 6-2: ANNUAL PERCENTAGE RATE (APR) ON INSTALLMENT ACCOUNTS

Objective: To determine the annual percentage rate (APR) on installment accounts.

> Just as consumer sense has taught you to shop for the lowest cost per pound on grocery items, economy dictates that you shop for money by looking for the lowest annual percentage rate.

The Truth-in-Lending Law (Section 226.5 b-1) specifies that the calculation of the **annual percentage rate**, abbreviated APR, on credit plans that involve periodic payments must be "in accordance with the actuarial method of computation so that it can be disclosed with an accuracy at least to the nearest quarter of one percent." Since the actuarial method of computation is somewhat complicated, tables have been prepared to assist in computing annual percentage rates. A portion of such a table is shown in Table 6-1.

To compute the annual percentage rate on installment accounts using Table 6-1, it is necessary to know:

1. The finance charge.
2. The amount financed.
3. The number of monthly payments.

To determine the annual percentage rate, using Table 6-1:

Step 1. Find the finance charge per $100 of amount financed by dividing the finance charge by the amount financed and multiplying by $100.

Type and Source of Credit	Annual Percentage Rate
Finance Companies:	
Personal property brokers	
First $200	30%
$200 to $500	24%
$500 to $1,500	18%
$1,500 to $10,000	12%
Industrial loan companies	
First $700	24%
$700 to $10,000	12%
Small loan companies	
First $100	30%
$100 to $300	24%
Pawnbrokers	
Small loans,	
up to 90 days	160–240%
$200 to $5,000	30–12%

$$\text{Finance charge per \$100} = \frac{\text{Finance charge}}{\text{Amount financed}} \times \$100$$

Step 2. Refer to Table 6-1.

a. Read down the left column entitled "Number of Payments" to the line for the indicated number of payments.

b. Read across–horizontally–to the number closest to the finance charge per $100 (computed in Step 1 above).

c. Read vertically to the top of the column to locate the annual percentage rate.

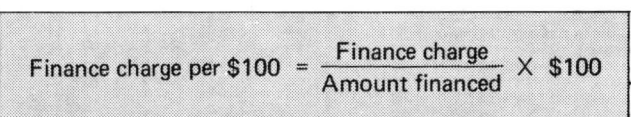

Problem A GE dishwasher priced at $450 can be purchased using installment credit. A $50 down payment is required, leaving an amount to be financed of $400. A finance charge of $44 is added, and the installment loan is repaid in 12 monthly installments. What is the annual percentage rate?

Solution Step 1. Determine the finance charge per $100.

$$\text{Finance charge per \$100} = \frac{\text{Finance charge}}{\text{Amount financed}} \times \$100$$

$$= \frac{\$44}{\$400} \times \$100$$

$$= 0.11 \times \$100$$

$$= \$11.00$$

Step 2. Refer to Table 6-1.

a. Read down the "Number of Payments" column to the line for 12 months.

b. Read across to the number closest to $11.00. It is $11.02.

c. Read vertically to the top of the column. The annual percentage rate (APR) is 19.75%.

TABLE 6-1. Annual Percentage Rate Table for Monthly Payment Plans

No. of Pmts.	Annual Percentage Rate															
	10.00%	10.25%	10.50%	10.75%	11.00%	11.25%	11.50%	11.75%	12.00%	12.25%	12.50%	12.75%	13.00%	13.25%	13.50%	13.75%
	(Finance Charge per $100 of Amount Financed)															
6	2.94	3.01	3.08	3.16	3.23	3.31	3.38	3.45	3.53	3.60	3.68	3.75	3.83	3.90	3.97	4.05
12	5.50	5.64	5.78	5.92	6.06	6.20	6.34	6.48	6.62	6.76	6.90	7.04	7.18	7.32	7.46	7.60
18	8.10	8.31	8.52	8.73	8.93	9.14	9.35	9.56	9.77	9.98	10.19	10.40	10.61	10.82	11.03	11.24
24	10.75	11.02	11.30	11.58	11.86	12.14	12.42	12.70	12.98	13.26	13.54	13.82	14.10	14.38	14.66	14.95
30	13.43	13.78	14.13	14.48	14.83	15.19	15.54	15.89	16.24	16.60	16.95	17.31	17.66	18.02	18.38	18.74
36	16.16	16.58	17.01	17.43	17.86	18.29	18.71	19.14	19.57	20.00	20.43	20.87	21.30	21.73	22.17	22.60
42	18.93	19.43	19.93	20.43	20.93	21.44	21.94	22.45	22.96	23.47	23.98	24.49	25.00	25.51	26.03	26.55
48	21.74	22.32	22.90	23.48	24.06	24.64	25.23	25.81	26.40	26.99	27.58	28.18	28.77	29.37	29.97	30.57
54	24.59	25.25	25.91	26.57	27.23	27.90	28.56	29.23	29.91	30.58	31.25	31.93	32.61	33.29	33.98	34.66
60	27.48	28.22	28.96	29.71	30.45	31.20	31.96	32.71	33.47	34.23	34.99	35.75	36.52	37.29	38.06	38.83

No. of Pmts.	Annual Percentage Rate															
	14.00%	14.25%	14.50%	14.75%	15.00%	15.25%	15.50%	15.75%	16.00%	16.25%	16.50%	16.75%	17.00%	17.25%	17.50%	17.75%
	(Finance Charge per $100 of Amount Financed)															
6	4.12	4.20	4.27	4.35	4.42	4.49	4.57	4.64	4.72	4.79	4.87	4.94	5.02	5.09	5.17	5.24
12	7.74	7.89	8.03	8.17	8.31	8.45	8.59	8.74	8.88	9.02	9.16	9.30	9.45	9.59	9.73	9.87
18	11.45	11.66	11.87	12.08	12.29	12.50	12.72	12.93	13.14	13.35	13.57	13.78	13.99	14.21	14.42	14.64
24	15.23	15.51	15.80	16.08	16.37	16.65	16.94	17.22	17.51	17.80	18.09	18.37	18.66	18.95	19.24	19.53
30	19.10	19.45	19.81	20.17	20.54	20.90	21.26	21.62	21.99	22.35	22.72	23.08	23.45	23.81	24.18	24.55
36	23.04	23.48	23.92	24.35	24.80	25.24	25.68	26.12	26.57	27.01	27.46	27.90	28.35	28.80	29.25	29.70
42	27.06	27.58	28.10	28.62	29.15	29.67	30.19	30.72	31.25	31.78	32.31	32.84	33.37	33.90	34.44	34.97
48	31.17	31.77	32.37	32.98	33.59	34.20	34.81	35.42	36.03	36.65	37.27	37.88	38.50	39.13	39.75	40.37
54	35.35	36.04	36.73	37.42	38.12	38.82	39.52	40.22	40.92	41.63	42.33	43.04	43.75	44.47	45.18	45.90
60	39.61	40.39	41.17	41.95	42.74	43.53	44.32	45.11	45.91	46.71	47.51	48.31	49.12	49.92	50.73	51.55

No. of Pmts.	Annual Percentage Rate															
	18.00%	18.25%	18.50%	18.75%	19.00%	19.25%	19.50%	19.75%	20.00%	20.25%	20.50%	20.75%	21.00%	21.25%	21.50%	21.75%
	(Finance Charge per $100 of Amount Financed)															
6	5.32	5.39	5.46	5.54	5.61	5.69	5.76	5.84	5.91	5.99	6.06	6.14	6.21	6.29	6.36	6.44
12	10.02	10.16	10.30	10.44	10.59	10.73	10.87	11.02	11.16	11.31	11.45	11.59	11.74	11.88	12.02	12.17
18	14.85	15.07	15.28	15.49	15.71	15.93	16.14	16.36	16.57	16.79	17.01	17.22	17.44	17.66	17.88	18.09
24	19.82	20.11	20.40	20.69	20.98	21.27	21.56	21.86	22.15	22.44	22.74	23.03	23.33	23.62	23.92	24.21
30	24.92	25.29	25.66	26.03	26.40	26.77	27.14	27.52	27.89	28.26	28.64	29.01	29.39	29.77	30.14	30.52
36	30.15	30.60	31.05	31.51	31.96	32.42	32.87	33.33	33.79	34.25	34.71	35.17	35.63	36.09	36.56	37.02
42	35.51	36.05	36.59	37.13	37.67	38.21	38.76	39.30	39.85	40.40	40.95	41.50	42.05	42.60	43.15	43.71
48	41.00	41.63	42.26	42.89	43.52	44.15	44.79	45.43	46.07	46.71	47.35	47.99	48.64	49.28	49.93	50.58
54	46.62	47.34	48.06	48.79	49.51	50.24	50.97	51.70	52.44	53.17	53.91	54.65	55.39	56.14	56.88	57.63
60	52.36	53.18	54.00	54.82	55.64	56.47	57.30	58.13	58.96	59.80	60.64	61.48	62.32	63.17	64.01	64.86

No. of Pmts.	Annual Percentage Rate															
	22.00%	22.25%	22.50%	22.75%	23.00%	23.25%	23.50%	23.75%	24.00%	24.25%	24.50%	24.75%	25.00%	25.25%	25.50%	25.75%
	(Finance Charge per $100 of Amount Financed)															
6	6.51	6.59	6.66	6.74	6.81	6.89	6.96	7.04	7.12	7.19	7.27	7.34	7.42	7.49	7.57	7.64
12	12.31	12.46	12.60	12.75	12.89	13.04	13.18	13.33	13.47	13.62	13.76	13.91	14.05	14.20	14.34	14.49
18	18.31	18.53	18.75	18.97	19.19	19.41	19.62	19.84	20.06	20.28	20.50	20.72	20.95	21.17	21.39	21.61
24	24.51	24.80	25.10	25.40	25.70	25.99	26.29	26.59	26.89	27.19	27.49	27.79	28.09	28.39	28.69	29.00
30	30.90	31.28	31.66	32.04	32.42	32.80	33.18	33.57	33.95	34.33	34.72	35.10	35.49	35.88	36.26	36.65
36	37.49	37.95	38.42	38.89	39.35	39.82	40.29	40.77	41.24	41.71	42.19	42.66	43.14	43.61	44.09	44.57
42	44.26	44.82	45.38	45.94	46.50	47.06	47.62	48.19	48.75	49.32	49.89	50.46	51.03	51.60	52.17	52.74
48	51.23	51.88	52.54	53.19	53.85	54.51	55.16	55.83	56.49	57.15	57.82	58.49	59.15	59.82	60.50	61.17
54	58.38	59.13	59.88	60.65	61.40	62.16	62.92	63.68	64.44	65.21	65.98	66.75	67.52	68.29	69.07	69.84
60	65.71	66.57	67.42	68.28	69.14	70.01	70.87	71.74	72.61	73.48	74.35	75.23	76.11	76.99	77.87	78.76

1 SELF-REVIEW

A Volare is advertised for $3,695 cash, a $195 down payment, a finance charge of $1,021.12, and 48 monthly payments of $94.19 each. What is the annual percentage rate?

Step 1. Determine the finance charge per $100.

$$\text{Finance charge per } \$100 = \frac{\text{Finance charge}}{\text{Amount financed}} \times \$100$$

$$= \frac{\$\_\_\_\_\_\_}{\$\_\_\_\_\_\_} \times \$100$$

$$= 0.2917485 \times \$100 = \$\_\_\_\_.\_\_\_\_$$

FC per $100:

$$= \frac{\$1{,}021.12}{\$3{,}500.00} \times \$100$$

$= \$29.17$

Step 2. Refer to Table 6-1.

a. Read down the left-hand column to ____ months.

b. Read across to the number closest to $29.17. It is $____.____.

c. Read vertically to the top of the column to locate the annual percentage rate. It is ____.____%.

a. 48 months
b. $29.37
c. 13.25%

ASSIGNMENT 6-2
ANNUAL PERCENTAGE RATE (APR) ON INSTALLMENT ACCOUNTS

Name ______________________ **Date Due** ____________ **Grade** _____

Answers to selected problems are given in Appendix B.

For Problems 1 through 4, find the finance charge per $100 and the annual percentage rate.

	Amount Financed	*Finance Charge*	*No. of Monthly Payments*	*Finance Charge per $100*	*Annual Percentage Rate*
Ex.	$6,000	$1,200.00	36	$20.00	12.25%
1.	440	52.00	12	11.82	________
2.	1,500	195.00	24	13.00	________
3.	3,000	360.00	18	________	________
4.	170	8.50	6	________	________

5. Marie and Bill Parker are given a home-improvement installment account from their local bank for $2,000 for three years. The finance charge is $390.

   A. What is the finance charge per $100?

   $________, found by

   B. What is the annual percentage rate?

   ________%, found by

6. A used Pontiac automobile is advertised for $2,295. A local bank will loan the Harrisons $2,000 to purchase the car. The loan would be for two years with a finance charge of $320.80.

   A. What is the finance charge per $100?

   $________, found by

   B. What is the annual percentage rate?

   ________%, found by

7. Home insulation program loans are available to help homeowners insulate their homes better and conserve energy. Find the annual percentage rate for these loans from American Finance Corp.:

	Loan Amount	*Term*	*Monthly Payment*	*Finance Charge*	*Total of Payments*
American Finance Corporation 1238 Sylvania (478-9522) 2223 Woodville, Oregon	$ 750 $1,000	36 mos. 48 mos.	$30.00 $34.00	$330.00 $632.00	$1,080.00 $1,632.00

   A. 36-month loan for $750

   ________%, found by

   B. 48-month loan for $1,000

   ________%, found by

8. Find the annual percentage rate for the home insulation program loans available from Mid-American National Bank & Trust.

	Loan Amount	Term	Monthly Payment	Finance Charge	Total of Payments
Mid-American National Bank & Trust All branches. Check the Yellow Pages for branch nearest you.	$ 400 $ 750 $1,000	12 mos. 24 mos. 36 mos.	$35.66 $35.62 $33.61	$ 27.92 $104.88 $209.96	$ 427.92 $ 854.88 $1,209.96

A. 12-month loan for $400

________%, found by

B. 24-month loan for $750

________%, found by

C. 36-month loan for $1,000

________%, found by

9. Find the:

A. Amount financed for the '77 Monza.

$____________, found by

B. Total amount paid in installments.

$____________, found by

C. Finance charge.

$__________, found by

D. Finance charge per $100.

$__________, found by

E. Annual percentage rate.

__________%, found by

10. A 1975 Honda motorcycle is for sale for a cash price of $897. The Honda can also be purchased for $32 down and $32 per month for 36 months. If the motorcycle is purchased on the installment plan, find the:

A. Amount financed.

$_________, found by

B. Total amount paid in installments.

$_________, found by

C. Finance charge.

$_________, found by

D. Finance charge per $100.

$_________, found by

E. Annual percentage rate.

_________%, found by

11. A "friend" sold a "friend" a used car worth $600 cash for $300 down and $60 per month for six months.

A. What is the annual percentage rate?

_________%, found by

B. Comment on the annual percentage rate.

____

____

12. Mr. and Mrs. Armitage loaned each of their children $5,000 for college, to be paid back at $111.11 per month for 54 months.

A. What is the APR?

_________%, found by

B. Comment on the annual percentage rate.

____

____

SECTION 6-3: INSTALLMENT ACCOUNTS—ADD-ON INTEREST

Objective: To determine the amount financed, the finance charge, the total amount paid in installments, the monthly payment, and the annual percentage rate (APR) on installment accounts.

> On the telephone, and across the desk, be sure to ask the lender specifically for "annual percentage rate." Some lenders might make loan rates sound lower by quoting some other rate.

Banks and finance companies, in granting installment loans for automobiles, boats, home improvements, recreational vehicles, and personal loans, use a method known as **add-on interest** to arrive at the finance charge. It is determined by computing a rate of interest on the amount to be financed for the **term** of the loan.

Essential to the discussion of add-on interest is **simple interest.** A brief summary of the concept of simple interest follows. A more detailed explanation is found in Chapter 11.

The charge for the use of money is known as **interest.** If a businessperson borrows money from a bank, the bank will charge **interest,** I, for the use of the money.

The original amount of money borrowed is called the **principal,** P.

The interest, I, is calculated for a specified period of **time,** t, always measured in years, at a specified **rate,** r. The rate is expressed as a *percent* per year of the principal that is to be charged for the length of time the money is borrowed.

The basic interest formula is:

Using a calculator:

Enter	Press	Display
2000	×	2000
.06	= ×	120
18	÷	2160
12	=	180

> Interest = Principal × Rate × Time, or $I = Prt$

Problems A. Calculate the interest charge on $2,000 borrowed for a period of one year at 6%. $P = \$2{,}000$, $r = 6\%$, $t = 1$.

B. Calculate the interest charge if the same loan were for a period of 18 months.

Solutions A.

$$\begin{aligned} I &= Prt \\ &= \$2{,}000 \times 0.06 \times 1 \\ &= \$120.00 \end{aligned}$$

B.

$$\begin{aligned} I &= Prt \\ &= \$2{,}000 \times 0.06 \times \frac{18}{12} \\ &= \$180.00 \end{aligned}$$

Problem Chris Dixon is buying a used Ford LTD with a cash price of $2,200. He has a $200 down payment. He is going to finance the car with a finance company that charges 10.94% add-on interest for 18 months. Determine: (A) the amount financed; (B) the finance charge; (C) the total amount paid in installments; (D) the monthly payment; and (E) the annual percentage rate.

Solution A. The amount financed is $2,000, found by

$$\begin{aligned} \text{Amount financed} &= \text{Cash price} - \text{Down payment} \\ &= \$2{,}200 - \$200 \\ &= \$2{,}000 \end{aligned}$$

B. The finance charge is $328.20, found by the simple-interest formula where the principal is the amount financed of $2,000. Thus:

$$\begin{aligned} I &= Prt \\ &= \$2{,}000 \times 10.94\% \times \frac{18}{12} \\ &= \$328.20 \end{aligned}$$

C. Total paid in installments is $2,328.20, found by

$$\begin{aligned} \text{Total paid in installments} &= \text{Amount financed} + \text{Finance charge} \\ &= \$2{,}000 + \$328.20 \\ &= \$2{,}328.20 \end{aligned}$$

D. The monthly payment is \$129.34, found by

$$\text{Monthly payment} = \frac{\text{Total paid in installments}}{\text{Number of payments}}$$
$$= \frac{\$2{,}328.20}{18}$$
$$= \$129.3444$$
$$= \$129.34 \text{ (nearest cent)}$$

E. The annual percentage rate is 19.75%, found by:

Step 1. $$\text{Finance charge per }\$100 = \frac{\text{Finance charge}}{\text{Amount financed}} \times \$100$$
$$= \frac{\$328.20}{\$2{,}000} \times \$100$$
$$= \$16.41$$

Step 2. Refer to Table 6-1.

a. Read down the left-hand column to 18.

b. Read across to the number closest to 16.41. It is 16.36.

c. Read vertically to the top of the column to locate the annual percentage rate. It is 19.75%.

1 SELF-REVIEW

The Texas Trust Company uses 7.5% add-on interest to determine the finance charge on home improvement loans. On a loan of \$3,000 for 30 months, calculate (A) the finance charge; (B) the monthly payment; (C) the annual percentage rate.

A. $I = \$3{,}000 \times 7.5\% \times \frac{30}{12}$
$= \$562.50$

A. The finance charge is determined using the simple-interest formula:

$$I = Prt$$
$$= \$\_\_\_\_\_ \times \_\_\_\% \times \frac{\_\_\_}{12}$$
$$= \$\_\_\_\_\_$$

B. Monthly payment:
$= \frac{\$3{,}000.00 + \$562.50}{30}$
$= \$118.75$

B. The monthly payment is found by:

$$\text{Monthly payment} = \frac{\text{Total paid in installments}}{\text{Number of payments}}$$
$$= \frac{\$\_\_\_\_\_ + \$\_\_\_\_\_}{30}$$
$$= \$\_\_\_\_\_$$

C. APR:
FC per \$100:
$= \frac{\text{Finance charge}}{\text{Amount financed}} \times \$100$
$= \frac{\$562.50}{\$3{,}000.00} \times \$100$
$= \$18.75$

C. The annual percentage rate is found by:

Step 1. $$\text{Finance charge per }\$100 = \frac{\text{Finance charge}}{\text{Amount financed}} \times \$\_\_\_\_\_$$
$$= \frac{\$\_\_\_\_\_}{\$\_\_\_\_\_} \times \$100$$
$$= \$\_\_\_\_\_$$

a. 30
b. \$18.74
c. 13.75%

Step 2. Refer to Table 6-1.

a. Read down the left-hand column to ____.

b. Read across to number closest to \$18.75. It is _______.

c. The annual percentage rate is _______%.

ASSIGNMENT 6-3
INSTALLMENT ACCOUNTS—ADD-ON INTEREST

Name ______________________ **Date Due** ____________ **Grade** _____

Answers to selected problems are given in Appendix B.

In Problems 1 through 6, find the finance charge.

	Amount Financed (Principal)	*Add-On Interest Rate*	*Term*	*Finance Charge (Interest)*
Ex.	$4,200.00	6.5%	36 months (3 years)	$819.00
1.	3,500.00	7%	1 year	________
2.	2,700.00	11%	12 months	________
3.	745.00	8.5%	18 months	________
4.	1,274.00	11.5%	30 months	________
5.	5,876.92	$8\frac{1}{4}$%	2.5 years	________
6.	961.54	$9\frac{1}{2}$%	1.5 years	________

7. Calculate the interest charge on $1,750 borrowed for a period of two years at 8% add-on interest.

   $__________, found by

8. Calculate the interest charge on $3,975 borrowed for a period of three years at 9% add-on interest.

   $__________, found by

9. Jean Pappas is buying a new Dodge that has a cash price of $6,495. She has a $495 down payment. Because of an excellent credit rating, she is able to finance the remainder with a local full-service bank at 6% add-on interest for three years. Find the:

   A. Amount financed.

   $________, found by

   B. Finance charge.

   $________, found by

   C. Total amount paid in installments.

   $________, found by

   D. Monthly payment.

   $________, found by

   E. Annual percentage rate.

   ________%, found by

10. Sam Jacobs needs to borrow $300 for tuition. He can get a six-month loan at 7% add-on interest. Find the:

A. Finance charge.

$_________, found by

B. Total amount paid in installments.

$_________, found by

C. Monthly payment.

$_________, found by

D. Annual percentage rate.

_________%, found by

11. A 48-month home improvement loan from Huntington Banks for $2,500 carries 8% add-on interest.

A. What is the monthly payment?

$_________, found by

B. What is the annual percentage rate?

_________%, found by

12. Amy Karras purchased a used automobile with a cash price of $2,065. After a down payment of $1,265, she financed $801.50 ($1.50 title fee included) at 11% add-on interest for two years.

A. What is the monthly payment?

$_________, found by

B. What is the annual percentage rate?

_________%, found by

13. Tom Lewis bought the 1979 Chevette advertised. After a 15% down payment, he financed the remainder at 9% add-on interest for four years. Find the:

> Stock No. 013
> **'79 CHEVETTE**
> 4 door, 4 speed, Bright Yellow, 4 cycle, AM radio, console, White sidewalls.
> List Price $4086
> WILL DENNIS PRICE
> **$3662**

A. Amount financed.

$___________, found by

B. Finance charge.

$___________, found by

C. Total amount paid in installments.

$___________, found by

D. Monthly payment.

$_________, found by

E. Annual percentage rate.

_________%, found by

14. The '79 Horizon advertised at the right was purchased with a 5% down payment and the remainder financed at 8.5% add-on interest for five years. Find the:

> **'79 HORIZON**
> **4 DOOR**
> **AS LOW AS**
> **$3899**
> **FRONT WHEEL DRIVE**

A. Amount financed.

$___________, found by

B. Finance charge.

$___________, found by

C. Total amount paid in installments.

$___________, found by

D. Monthly payment.

$_________, found by

E. Annual percentage rate.

_________%, found by

SECTION 6-4: REFUND OF FINANCE CHARGE—THE RULE OF 78

Objective: To determine the finance charge saved and the amount of the final payment, using the Rule of 78.

Section 226.8, b-7 of the Truth-in-Lending Law stipulates that when credit is granted to a consumer, the party granting the credit (retailers such as Macys or Montgomery Ward) must disclose the method of computing any *unearned* finance charge. Thus, if the consumer decides to pay an installment loan off before the final payment is due, the consumer will know exactly how much of the unearned finance charge will be rebated. Sears, Roebuck and Company's retail installment contract contains the following statement:

> I agree to pay the amount of each monthly installment on or before the due date thereof until the amount financed and the Finance Charge for each purchase is fully paid. If I pay in full in advance, any unearned Finance Charge will be rebated under the Rule of 78. I will receive a sales slip identifying each item of merchandise subject to this security agreement.

The **Rule of 78** mentioned in the Sears retail installment contract is one of the most commonly used methods to determine the amount of refund to be returned to the consumer should the debt be paid off earlier than stipulated in the contract. The rule derives its name from the fact that in a 12-month contract, when the digits corresponding to the number of installments are summed, the total is 78. That is, 1 + 2 + 3 + 4 + 5 + 6 + 7 + 8 + 9 + 10 + 11 + 12 = 78.

This method is often referred to as the **sum-of-the-digits** method. In a sense, this designation is more appropriate because the procedure can be applied to an installment contract having any number of payments. For a nine-month contract, the sum of 1, 2, 3, 4, 5, 6, 7, 8, and 9 is 45. For a ten-month installment contract the sum of the digits is 55, and for 24 months, the sum of the digits is 300.

The Rule of 78 is based on the premise that the total finance charge on a 12-month loan is divided into 78 parts. The 78 parts are distributed as shown in Exhibit 6-1.

EXHIBIT 6-1

Payment Number	*1*	*2*	*3*	*4*	*5*	*6*	*7*	*8*	*9*	*10*	*11*	*12*
Fraction of finance charge paid off	$\frac{12}{78}$	$\frac{11}{78}$	$\frac{10}{78}$	$\frac{9}{78}$	$\frac{8}{78}$	$\frac{7}{78}$	$\frac{6}{78}$	$\frac{5}{78}$	$\frac{4}{78}$	$\frac{3}{78}$	$\frac{2}{78}$	$\frac{1}{78}$

Each time a payment is made, the bank or lender earns the fraction of the finance charge paid off that month. When the first payment is made, the bank earns $^{12}/_{78}$ of the finance charge. If the loan is paid off with the first payment, $^{66}/_{78}$ of the finance charge is unearned by the lender and would be refunded to the consumer. The unearned $^{66}/_{78}$ of the finance charge is found by $^{78}/_{78} - {}^{12}/_{78}$.

For the second payment, the bank earns $^{11}/_{78}$ of the finance charge. The two-month total is $^{12}/_{78} + {}^{11}/_{78}$, or $^{23}/_{78}$. Thus if the loan is paid off with the second payment, the unearned finance charge is $^{78}/_{78} - {}^{23}/_{78}$, or $^{55}/_{78}$.

> 14. PREPAYMENT PENALTY: Unearned charges calculated by the Rule of 78's, less $10.00 acquisition charge.

> *"Who goeth a borrowing goeth a sorrowing."*
> Benjamin Franklin

A. $\frac{10}{78}$

B. $\frac{33}{78}$

C. $\frac{78}{78} - \frac{33}{78}$ or $\frac{45}{78}$

D. $\frac{4}{78}$

1 SELF-REVIEW

Use Exhibit 6-1 to complete these statements:

A. For the third payment, the bank would earn $\frac{\quad}{78}$ of the finance charge.

B. For the three months, the total earned by the bank is ——, found by $\frac{12}{78} + \frac{11}{78} + \frac{10}{78}$.

C. Thus, if the loan is paid off with the third payment, the unearned finance charge is $\frac{78}{78} - \frac{\quad}{78}$, or $\frac{\quad}{78}$.

D. For the ninth payment, the bank would earn $\frac{\quad}{78}$ of the finance charge. The remaining fractions of unearned finance charge are $\frac{3}{78} + \frac{2}{78} + \frac{1}{78}$, or $\frac{6}{78}$.

It is interesting to note that a much larger portion of the finance charge is paid off with the first few payments than for the last few payments. Obviously, the finance charge is not distributed evenly over the 12-month period.

DETERMINING THE AMOUNT OF THE REFUND (unearned finance charge)

The amount of the refund or unearned finance charge is computed by:

Step 1. Determine the fraction representing the portion of the finance charge to be refunded.

$$\text{Refund fraction} = \frac{\text{Sum of the digits of the number of remaining payments}}{\text{Sum of the digits of the total number of payments}}$$

Step 2. Multiply the refund fraction times the finance charge.

$$\text{Refund} = \text{Refund fraction} \times \text{Finance charge}$$

Problem Richard Heckler took out a one-year, $1,950 loan for a car with a finance charge of $156 and monthly payments of $175.50. If he decides to pay off the loan with the eighth payment, how much of a refund will he receive?

Solution Step 1. If the loan is paid off with the eighth payment, the refund is based on the four remaining payments. Thus:

$$\text{Refund fraction} = \frac{\text{Sum of the digits of the number of remaining payments}}{\text{Sum of the digits of the total number of payments}}$$

$$= \frac{4 + 3 + 2 + 1}{12 + 11 + 10 + 9 + 8 + 7 + 6 + 5 + 4 + 3 + 2 + 1}$$

$$= \frac{10}{78}$$

Step 2. $\text{Refund} = \text{Refund fraction} \times \text{Finance charge}$

$$= \frac{10}{78} \times \$156$$

$$= \$20$$

Using a calculator:

Enter	Press	Display
10	÷	10
78	= ×	0.1282051
156	=	19.999995

In the preceding problem, Heckler is going to make payments Nos. 8, 9, 10, 11, and 12. He will receive a refund of \$20. The final payment is \$857.50, found by

(5 payments of \$175.50) – \$20 refund = \$877.50 – \$20 = \$857.50

2 SELF-REVIEW

A 12-month installment contract, incorporating the Rule of 78, was signed for the purchase of a \$2,000 automobile. The finance charge is \$160 and the monthly payment is \$180. If the loan is paid off with the fifth payment, the buyer wants to know what the refund and the final payment would be.

A. If the loan is paid off with the fifth payment, the refund is based on the ____ remaining payments.

B. The refund fraction = $\dfrac{\text{Sum of digits of the number of remaining payments}}{\text{Sum of digits of the total number of payments}}$

$$= \frac{7 + \quad + \quad + \quad + \quad + \quad + 1}{78} = \frac{28}{78}$$

C. The refund = Refund fraction × ____________

$$= \frac{28}{78} \times \$\_\_\_\_$$

= \$________ (rounded to nearest cent)

D. The final payment is found by: Payment Nos. 5, 6, 7, 8, 9, 10, 11, and 12 must be made, for a total of ____ payments.

(8 payments × \$________) – Refund of \$________ = Final payment

\$____________ – \$57.44 = \$____________

Answers:

A. 7

B. $\dfrac{7 + 6 + 5 + 4 + 3 + 2 + 1}{78} = \dfrac{28}{78}$

C. Finance charge:
$= \dfrac{28}{78} \times \$160$
= \$57.44

D. 8 payments
(8 × \$180) – \$57.44
= \$1,440.00 – \$57.44
= \$1,382.56 final payment

The number of payments in the preceding examples was 12, and the sum of the digits 12, 11, 10, 9, 8, 7, 6, 5, 4, 3, 2, and 1 is 78. Instead of summing the digits, a formula can be used to find the sum of a series of consecutive numbers.

$$S = N\left(\frac{N+1}{2}\right)$$

Where S is the sum of the digits;
N is the total number of payments, or the number of remaining payments (depending on the problem).

For 12 payments, the sum of the digits using the formula is 78, found by:

$$S = N\left(\frac{N+1}{2}\right) = 12\left(\frac{12+1}{2}\right) = 12\left(\frac{13}{2}\right) = 78$$

Using a calculator:

Enter	Press	Display
12	+	12
1	= ×	13
12	= ÷	156
2	=	78

For 24 payments, the sum of the digits using the formula is 300, found by:

$$S = N\left(\frac{N+1}{2}\right) = 24\left(\frac{24+1}{2}\right) = 24\left(\frac{25}{2}\right) = 300$$

$15\left(\frac{15+1}{2}\right) = 120$

3 SELF-REVIEW

Using the formula for finding the sum of a series of consecutive numbers, what is the sum of the digits for an installment loan for the purchase of living room furniture, to be paid back in 15 equal installments?

4 SELF-REVIEW

A sizable down payment on a Ford Thunderbird reduced the amount to be paid to $1,500. The new owner took out an 18-month auto loan for that amount. The total finance charge, based on 8% add-on interest, was $180. Monthly payments were $93.33. The owner of the Thunderbird decided to pay off the loan at the end of one year (with the 12th payment). Under the Rule of 78, determine the amount of the final payment.

A. What is the sum of the digits for the total number of payments? ________

B. What is the sum of the digits for the number of remaining payments? ________

C. What is the unearned finance charge? ________

D. In order to pay off the loan the owner must pay the 12th payment and the six remaining payments. Thus the owner actually makes seven payments. What is the total amount of the seven payments? ________

E. The total amount of the seven payments minus the unearned finance charge gives what amount for the final payment? ________

A. $18\left(\frac{18+1}{2}\right) = 171$

B. $6\left(\frac{6+1}{2}\right) = 21$

C. $\frac{21}{171} \times \$180 = \$22.11$

D. 7 × $93.33 = $653.31

E. $653.31 – $22.11 = $631.20

ASSIGNMENT 6-4
REFUND OF FINANCE CHARGE—THE RULE OF 78

Name ______________________ Date Due ____________ Grade _____

Answers to selected problems are given in Appendix B.

Assume a 12-month installment contract for Problems 1 through 6. Find the:
A. Total portion of finance charge earned by the bank.
B. Total portion of finance charge refunded if loan is paid off.

	Loan Paid Off with Payment No.	*A.*	*B.*		*Loan Paid Off with Payment No.*	*A.*	*B.*
Ex.	6	$\frac{57}{78}$	$\frac{21}{78}$				
1.	4	____	$\frac{36}{78}$	4.	11	____	____
2.	5	____	____	5.	8	____	____
3.	10	____	____	6.	7	____	____

7. Kathy Lajewski has a $3,000, one-year auto loan with a finance charge of $240 (8% add-on interest) and monthly payments of $270. If she decides to pay off the loan with the sixth payment, how much of a refund will she receive?

   $________, found by

8. A 12-month note for $1,200 carries a finance charge of $108 (9% add-on interest) and $109 monthly payments. How much is refunded if the note is paid off with the ninth payment?

   $________, found by

For Problems 9 through 14, complete the table.

	Duration of Loan (months)	*Sum of the Digits*	*Assume Loan Is Paid Off with This Payment*	*Refund Fraction*
9.	6	______	4th	________
10.	36	______	12th	________
11.	48	______	30th	________
12.	30	______	6th	________
13.	42	______	24th	________
14.	60	______	10th	________

15. The Chevy ½-ton truck was purchased for $1,170 down and the remainder financed with a 24-month loan at 9% add-on interest. The finance charge was $540. Monthly payments were $147.50. The buyer decided to pay off the loan at the end of one year (with the 12th payment). Under the Rule of 78, determine the amount of the final payment.

$____________, found by

Stock No. T-157
'79 CHEVY ½ TON
Pickup
6 cylinder, stick shift
List price $4889
Will Dennis Price
$4170

16. John and Mary Piersall purchased $2,200 worth of furniture by making a $400 down payment and signing a note for the remaining $1,800. The note called for 15 monthly payments of $138 each (a finance charge of $270). If the Piersalls choose to pay off the note with their sixth payment and the Rule of 78 applies, find what that sixth payment will be.

$____________, found by

17. The purchase of a new automobile was financed for three years at 8% add-on interest. The amount financed was $3,000. If the loan is paid off with the 20th payment and the Rule of 78 applies, find the:

A. Finance charge.
$________, found by

B. Monthly payment.
$________, found by

C. Annual percentage rate.
________%, found by

D. Unearned finance charge.
$__________, found by

E. Amount of the final payment.
$____________, found by

18. A motorcycle was purchased for $750. The down payment was $50, and the remaining $700 was financed at 7% add-on interest for 1.5 years. The owner of the cycle decided to sell it and pay off the loan with the sixth payment. Find the:

A. Finance charge.
$________, found by

B. Monthly payment.
$________, found by

C. Annual percentage rate.
________%, found by

D. Unearned finance charge.
$__________, found by

E. Amount of the final payment.
$____________, found by

19. A used motor home was purchased for $1,200. After a $150 down payment, the remainder is to be paid for in 15 monthly payments of $78 each. Using the Rule of 78, what final payoff is necessary to pay off the motor home with the 12th payment?

$_______, found by

20. What amount is necessary to pay off a $3,200, three-year note, at 8% add-on interest, with the 18th payment? Assume the Rule of 78 applies.

$____________, found by

REVIEW ASSIGNMENT FOR CHAPTER 6
CONSUMER CREDIT—INSTALLMENT CREDIT

Name ______________________ Date Due ____________ Grade _____

1. A used Chevrolet two-door is advertised for $679. A local bank will loan Jim Harrison $600 for six months with a finance charge of $45.

   A. What down payment is required?

   $________, found by

   B. What is the monthly payment?

   $________, found by

2. Tom and Mary Marker plan to purchase a swimming pool for their small children. They can pay $432.55 cash or make a down payment of $82.55 and pay the balance in 15 monthly installments, with a finance charge of $39.40. If they decide on the loan, what is their monthly payment?

   $________, found by

MAZDA
Sale Price From
$3499
only
$95.62
per month*
with $95 down
Payment includes sales tax, title, freight & dealer prep.
*for 48 months

3. Find the annual percentage rate for the $3,499 Mazda. ________%, found by

4. A sofa is advertised for $319 cash or with nothing down and $28.71 a month for 12 months. Determine the:

   A. Finance charge.

   $________, found by

   B. Annual percentage rate.

   ________%, found by

5. The May Company advertised a Broyhill chair for $159. Laura Miller made a down payment of $15 and financed the remainder through her credit union. If the finance charges are $8.40 and she makes six monthly payments,

   A. What is the amount of each payment?

   $________, found by

   B. What is the annual percentage rate?

   ________%, found by

6. A new small station wagon was purchased for $4,791.44, including tax. A down payment of $836.72 was made, leaving $3,954.72 to be financed. To the unpaid balance of $3,954.72 a finance charge of $823.20 was added for three years's financing.

   A. What is the monthly payment?

   $________, found by

   B. What is the annual percentage rate?

   ________%, found by

7. A combination garden tractor/lawnmower is on sale for $1,250. A down payment of $250 is made, and the remainder is financed at 8% add-on interest for one year. Find the:

A. Finance charge. $________, found by

B. Amount of monthly payment. $________, found by

C. Annual percentage rate. ________%, found by

Suppose that the owner of the tractor decides to pay off the original loan with the fourth payment and the Rule of 78 applies.

D. What is the unearned finance charge? $________, found by

E. What is the total amount of the final payment? $__________, found by

8. Edna Harrison purchased the '71 Olds Vista Cruiser. The dealer allowed her $395 on her old car as a trade-in. She financed the remainder with a finance company which charged an add-on interest rate of 12% for two years. Find the:

'71 OLDS Vista Cruiser . . . .$1295 Wagon, full power, factory air, 3 seats.

A. Finance charge. $__________, found by

B. Monthly payment. $________, found by

C. Annual percentage rate. ________%, found by

If Harrison decides to pay off the installment contract with her 17th payment and the Rule of 78 applies,

D. What is the unearned finance charge? $________, found by

E. What is the total amount of the final payment? $__________, found by

9. A home improvement loan of $2,800 for 15 months carries a finance charge of $245. Assume the Rule of 78 applies. If the loan were paid off with the 13th payment, what amount would be refunded to the homeowner?

$_______, found by

10. The Impala Sport Coupe is paid off with the third payment. The Rule of 78 applies. What is the final payment?

$____________, found by

IMPALA SPORT COUPE
$4820
$99 down, 48 months, $129 per month

11. Joan O'Brien is buying a new Ford and must finance $2,200. By comparing finance charges and annual percentage rates, which of the following credit plans should she choose, and why?

A. The dealer's plan requires 24 monthly payments of $103.57 each.
B. The local bank charges 6.5% add-on interest for two years.

Choose credit plan ____

TO THE STUDENT: There is a SELF-REVIEW TEST for this chapter in Appendix A, *with answers* in Appendix C.

7

Home Mortgage Loans

SECTION 7-1: FINANCING THE PURCHASE OF A HOME

Objective: To compute the monthly amortization payment on a home mortgage loan and to allocate that payment to principal and interest.

DETERMINING THE MONTHLY PAYMENT

The purchase of a home is usually the largest investment most families make. Generally, a down payment is required to purchase a new or older home, and the remaining amount is financed by a loan, usually referred to as a **mortgage loan** or a **real estate loan.** A large percentage of home mortgages is obtained either from savings and loan associations or commercial banks.

A real estate loan is usually repaid by the homeowner in equal monthly payments. The monthly payment is a fixed amount, part of which (1) reduces the principal, and (2) pays the interest on the unpaid balance. The total amount of the principal and interest to be paid each month can be determined from a monthly **amortization table.** (See Table 7-1.)

LOVELY HIDEAWAY — For your summer enjoyment. Furnished and ready to move in. Price is low only $27,500.00. Approx. Acre Lot. Off Hwy #276 West

Table 7-1 gives the monthly payment needed to pay off a $1,000 loan. The interest rates given range from 7½% to 13%, and the time from 5 to 35 years.

The monthly payment on loans other than $1,000 is determined by multiplying the payment for a $1,000 loan by the number of thousands in the desired loan.

$$\text{Monthly mortgage payment} = \frac{\text{Amount of mortgage}}{\$1{,}000} \times \text{Payment for a \$1,000 loan found in Table 7-1}$$

TABLE 7-1. Equal Monthly Amortization Payments of $1,000 Loan

	No. of Years of Loan						
Rate	*5*	*10*	*15*	*20*	*25*	*30*	*35*
7½%	$20.04	$11.88	$ 9.28	$ 8.06	$ 7.39	$ 7.00	$ 6.75
7¾	20.16	12.01	9.42	8.21	7.56	7.17	6.93
8	20.28	12.14	9.56	8.37	7.72	7.34	7.11
8¼	20.40	12.27	9.71	8.53	7.89	7.52	7.29
8½	20.52	12.40	9.85	8.68	8.06	7.69	7.47
8¾	20.64	12.54	10.00	8.84	8.23	7.87	7.66
9	20.76	12.67	10.15	9.00	8.40	8.05	7.84
9¼	20.88	12.81	10.30	9.16	8.57	8.23	8.03
9½	21.01	12.94	10.45	9.33	8.74	8.41	8.22
9¾	21.13	13.08	10.60	9.49	8.92	8.60	8.41
10	21.25	13.22	10.75	9.66	9.09	8.78	8.60
10¼	21.38	13.36	10.90	9.82	9.27	8.97	8.79
10½	21.50	13.50	11.06	9.99	9.45	9.15	8.99
10¾	21.62	13.64	11.21	10.16	9.63	9.34	9.18
11	21.75	13.78	11.37	10.33	9.81	9.53	9.37
11¼	21.87	13.92	11.53	10.50	9.99	9.72	9.57
11½	22.00	14.06	11.69	10.67	10.17	9.91	9.77
11¾	22.12	14.21	11.85	10.84	10.35	10.10	9.96
12	22.25	14.35	12.01	11.02	10.54	10.29	10.16
12¼	22.38	14.50	12.17	11.19	10.72	10.48	10.36
12½	22.50	14.64	12.33	11.37	10.91	10.68	10.56
12¾	22.63	14.79	12.49	11.54	11.10	10.87	10.76
13	22.76	14.94	12.66	11.72	11.28	11.07	10.96

Problem What is the monthly payment on a $20,000 mortgage loan at 9% for ten years?

Solution Refer to Table 7-1. Read down the left-hand column headed "Rate" to 9%. Then move to the right to the column headed by 10 years and read the payment on a $1,000 loan. It is $12.67. To find the monthly mortgage payment on the $20,000 loan:

$$\text{Monthly mortgage payment} = \frac{\text{Amount of mortgage}}{\$1{,}000} \times \text{Payment for a \$1,000 loan found in Table 7-1}$$

$$= \frac{\$20{,}000}{\$1{,}000} \times \$12.67$$

$$= 20 \times \$12.67$$

$$= \$253.40$$

It should be emphasized that the $253.40 monthly payment is *for principal and interest only*. The bank or savings and loan association might add an amount for insurance and for real estate taxes. This will be discussed in Section 7-2.

1 SELF-REVIEW

A reminder: Cover the answers in the margin.

A. (1) $8.41
(2) Monthly mortgage payment:
$= \frac{\$20{,}000}{\$1{,}000} \times \$8.41$
$= 20 \times \$8.41$
$= \$168.20$

B. $218.60 (rounded), found by
$\frac{\$19{,}500}{\$1{,}000} \times \$11.21$
$= \$218.595$

A. Suppose the $20,000 mortgage in the preceding problem had been at 9½% for 30 years. From Table 7-1:

(1) The monthly payment on a $1,000 loan at 9½% for 30 years is $_______.

(2) The monthly payment on $20,000 at 9½% for 30 years is:

Monthly mortgage payment $= \frac{\$20{,}000}{\$1{,}000} \times$ $_______

= 20 × $_______

= $_______

B. A bank determined that the maximum amount it would loan on an older home was $19,500 at 10¾% for 15 years. What is the monthly payment for principal and interest? $_______

PAYMENT FOR INTEREST, PRINCIPAL, AND NEW BALANCE

Each month the bank must compute how much of the payment is to be allocated for interest, how much to be allocated for principal, and the new balance. The procedure is:

Step 1. Calculate the interest for the month using the current principal, at the stated loan rate, for a time of one month. Use the simple interest formula:

Where: $I = P \times r \times t$ ← I is the interest; P is the principal; r is the rate of interest; t is the time

Step 2. Determine the amount used to reduce the principal. It is the difference between the interest and the monthly payment.

> **Reduction of principal = Payment − Interest**

Step 3. Determine the new principal (or new balance). This is the principal minus the amount calculated for reduction of principal.

> **New principal = Principal − Reduction of principal**

Problem A $30,000 mortgage loan at 9% for 20 years has a monthly payment of $270. For the first two months, compute the interest, reduction of principal, and new principal.

Solution Step 1. Interest for the first month is $225.00, found by:

$$\begin{aligned} I &= P \times r \times t \\ &= \$30{,}000 \times 9\% \times \frac{1}{12} \\ &= \$30{,}000 \times 0.09 \times \frac{1}{12} \\ &= \$225 \end{aligned}$$

> **The time is one month, thus $\frac{1}{12}$ of a year.**

Step 2. Amount used to reduce the principal is $45, found by:

$$\begin{aligned} \text{Reduction of principal} &= \text{Payment} - \text{Interest} \\ &= \$270 - \$225 \\ &= \$45 \end{aligned}$$

Step 3. The new principal is $29,955.00, found by:

$$\begin{aligned} \text{New principal} &= \text{Principal} - \text{Reduction of principal} \\ &= \$30{,}000 - \$45 \\ &= \$29{,}955 \end{aligned}$$

For the second payment the process is repeated. However, the new principal becomes the principal for the second month.

Step 1. Interest for the second month is $224.66, found by:

$$\begin{aligned} I &= P \times r \times t \\ &= \$29{,}955 \times 0.09 \times \frac{1}{12} \\ &= \$224.6625 \\ &= \$224.66 \text{ (rounded)} \end{aligned}$$

Step 2. Amount used to reduce principal is $45.34, found by:

$$\begin{aligned} \text{Reduction of principal} &= \text{Payment} - \text{Interest} \\ &= \$270.00 - \$224.66 \\ &= \$45.34 \end{aligned}$$

Step 3. The new principal is $29,909.66, found by:

$$\begin{aligned} \text{New principal} &= \text{Principal} - \text{Reduction of principal} \\ &= \$29{,}955.00 - \$45.34 \\ &= \$29{,}909.66 \end{aligned}$$

Summary for the first two payments on $30,000 loan at 9% for 30 years:

Payment No.	*Principal*	*Payment*	*Payment on Interest*	*Reduction of Principal*	*New Principal*
1	$30,000.00	$270.00	$225.00	$45.00	$29,955.00
2	29,955.00	270.00	224.66	45.34	29,909.66

2 SELF-REVIEW

Continue with the above problem for payment No. 3.
For payment No. 3:

A. Interest = $P \times r \times t$

= \$____________ X _____% X $\frac{1}{12}$

= $29,909.66 X 0.09 X $\frac{1}{12}$

= \$________

B. Reduction of principal = Payment – Interest

= \$________ – \$________

= \$________

C. New principal = Principal – Reduction of principal

= \$____________ – \$________

= \$____________

D.

Payment No.	*Principal*	*Payment*	*Payment on Interest*	*Reduction of Principal*	*New Principal*
1 . . .	$30,000.00	$270.00	$225.00	$45.00	$29,955.00
2 . . .	29,955.00	270.00	224.66	45.34	29,909.66
3 . . .	29,909.66	270.00	______	______	______

A. Interest:
= $29,909.66 X 9% X $\frac{1}{12}$
= $224.32

B. Reduction of principal:
= $270.00 – $224.32
= $45.68

C. New principal:
= $29,909.66 – $45.68
= $29,863.98

D.

Payment No.	*Payment on Interest*
3	$224.32

Reduction Principal	*New Principal*
$45.68	$29,863.98

Exhibit 7-1 shows a computer printout of a complete repayment schedule for a $10,000 home loan at 8% for ten years.

EXHIBIT 7-1

Repayment Schedule, $10,000 Home Loan at 8%, for Ten Years

	INTEREST RATE	MONTHLY PAYMENT TO PRINCIPAL AND INTEREST	FACE AMOUNT
	8.00	121.33	10,000.00

PAYMENT NUMBER	PAYMENT TO INTEREST	PAYMENT TO PRINCIPAL	BALANCE DUE
1	66.67	54.66	9,945.3
2	66.30	55.03	9,890.31
3	65.94	55.39	9,834.92
4	65.57	55.76	9,779.16
5	65.19	56.14	9,723.02
6	64.82	56.51	9,666.51
7	64.44	56.89	9,609.62
8	64.06	57.27	9,552.35
9	63.68	57.65	9,494.70
10	63.30	58.03	9,436.67
11	62.91	58.42	9,378.25
12	62.52	58.81	9,319.44
YEAR TOTAL	775.40*	680.56*	
13	62.13	59.20	9,260.24
14	61.74	59.59	9,200.65
15	61.34	59.99	9,140.66
16	60.94	60.39	9,080.27
17	60.54	60.79	9,019.48
18	60.13	61.20	8,958.28
19	59.72	61.61	8,896.67
20	59.31	62.02	8,834.65
21	58.90	62.43	8,772.22
22	58.48	62.85	8,709.37
23	58.06	63.27	8,646.10
24	57.64	63.69	8,582.41
YEAR TOTAL	718.93*	737.03*	
25	57.22	64.11	8,518.30
26	56.79	64.54	8,453.76
27	56.36	64.97	8,388.79
28	55.93	65.40	8,323.39
29	55.49	65.84	8,257.55
30	55.05	66.28	8,191.27
31	54.61	66.72	8,124.55
32	54.16	67.17	8,057.38
33	53.72	67.61	7,989.77
34	53.27	68.06	7,921.71
35	52.81	68.52	7,853.19
36	52.36	68.97	7,784.22
YEAR TOTAL	657.77*	798.19*	
37	51.90	69.43	7,714.79
38	51.43	69.90	7,644.89
39	50.97	70.36	7,574.53
40	50.50	70.83	7,503.70
41	50.03	71.30	7,432.40
42	49.55	71.78	7,360.62
43	49.07	72.26	7,288.36
44	48.59	72.74	7,215.62
45	48.10	73.23	7,142.39
46	47.62	73.71	7,068.68
47	47.12	74.21	6,994.47
48	46.63	74.70	6,919.77
YEAR TOTAL	591.51*	864.45*	
49	46.13	75.20	6,844.57
50	45.63	75.70	6,768.87
51	45.13	76.20	6,692.67
52	44.62	76.71	6,615.96
53	44.11	77.22	6,538.74
54	43.59	77.74	6,461.00
55	43.07	78.26	6,382.74
56	42.55	78.78	6,303.96
57	42.03	79.30	6,224.66
58	41.50	79.83	6,144.83
59	40.97	80.36	6,064.47
60	40.43	80.90	5,983.57
YEAR TOTAL	519.76*	936.20*	

	INTEREST RATE	MONTHLY PAYMENT TO PRINCIPAL AND INTEREST	FACE AMOUNT
	8.00	121.33	10,000.00

PAYMENT NUMBER	PAYMENT TO INTEREST	PAYMENT TO PRINCIPAL	BALANCE DUE
61	39.89	81.44	5,902.13
62	39.35	81.98	5,820.15
63	38.80	82.53	5,737.62
64	38.25	83.08	5,654.54
65	37.70	83.63	5,570.91
66	37.14	84.19	5,486.72
67	36.58	84.75	5,401.97
68	36.01	85.32	5,316.65
69	35.44	85.89	5,230.76
70	34.87	86.46	5,144.30
71	34.30	87.03	5,057.27
72	33.72	87.61	4,969.66
YEAR TOTAL	442.05*	1,013.91*	
73	33.13	88.20	4,881.46
74	32.54	88.79	4,792.67
75	31.95	89.38	4,703.29
76	31.36	89.97	4,613.32
77	30.76	90.57	4,522.75
78	30.15	91.18	4,431.57
79	29.54	91.79	4,339.78
80	28.93	92.40	4,247.38
81	28.32	93.01	4,154.37
82	27.70	93.63	4,060.74
83	27.07	94.26	3,966.48
84	26.44	94.89	3,871.59
YEAR TOTAL	357.89*	1,098.07*	
85	25.81	95.52	3,776.07
86	25.17	96.16	3,679.91
87	24.53	96.80	3,583.11
88	23.89	97.44	3,485.67
89	23.24	98.09	3,387.58
90	22.58	98.75	3,288.83
91	21.93	99.40	3,189.43
92	21.26	100.07	3,089.36
93	20.60	100.73	2,988.63
94	19.92	101.41	2,887.22
95	19.25	102.08	2,785.14
96	18.57	102.76	2,682.38
YEAR TOTAL	266.75*	1,189.21*	
97	17.88	103.45	2,578.93
98	17.19	104.14	2,474.79
99	16.50	104.83	2,369.96
100	15.80	105.53	2,264.43
101	15.10	106.23	2,158.20
102	14.39	106.94	2,051.26
103	13.68	107.65	1,943.61
104	12.96	108.37	1,835.24
105	12.24	109.09	1,726.15
106	11.51	109.82	1,616.33
107	10.78	110.55	1,505.78
108	10.04	111.29	1,394.49
YEAR TOTAL	168.07*	1,287.89*	
109	9.30	112.03	1,282.46
110	8.55	112.78	1,169.68
111	7.80	113.53	1,056.15
112	7.04	114.29	941.86
113	6.28	115.05	826.81
114	5.51	115.82	710.99
115	4.74	116.59	594.40
116	3.96	117.37	477.03
117	3.18	118.15	358.88
118	2.39	118.94	239.94
119	1.60	119.73	120.21
120	.80	120.21	.00
YEAR TOTAL	61.15*	1,394.49*	
FINAL TOTAL	4,559.28	10,000.00	

ASSIGNMENT 7-1
FINANCING THE PURCHASE OF A HOME

Name ______________________ Date Due ______________ Grade ______

Answers to selected problems are given in Appendix B.

Supply the missing data in Problems 1 through 6.

	Amount of Mortgage	*Years*	*Rate*	*Payment per $1,000*	*Monthly Mortgage Payment*
Ex.	$ 35,000	30	9¾%	$ 8.60	$301.00
1.	20,000	10	10½	13.50	________
2.	40,000	10	9½	12.94	________
3.	67,500	25	10¼	________	________
4.	54,750	20	11½	________	________
5.	112,610	30	10	________	________
6.	97,400	35	12	________	________

7. The Andersons purchased a $50,000 home. They made a 20% down payment. The remainder was financed at the First National Bank at 9¼% for 35 years.

   A. What is the down payment?
   $________, found by

   B. How much is the mortgage loan?
   $________, found by

   C. What is the monthly payment per $1,000?
   $________, found by

   D. What is the monthly payment?
   $______, found by

8. The Allens had $5,900 and assumed the $36,100 loan for the pictured house at 8.75% for 25 years.

   A. What is the monthly payment per $1,000?
   $______, found by

   B. What is their monthly payment?
   $________, found by

A SUNKEN CONVERSATION PIT enhances the brick fireplace in the great room of this nearly new 3 bedroom, 2 bath frame/masonry home. Split bedroom plan, cathedral ceilings, large 2-car garage. **ONLY $5,900 TO ASSUME LOAN AT 8.75%. $42,000. HL 073.**

Supply the missing data for Problems 9 through 14.

	Amount of Mortgage	*Yrs.*	*Rate*	*Monthly Mortgage Payment*	*First Payment*		*Balance after First Payment*	*Second Payment*		*Balance after Second Payment*
					Interest	*Principal*		*Interest*	*Principal*	
Ex.	$25,000	20	9%	$225.00	$187.50	$37.50	$24,962.50	$187.22	$37.78	$24,924.72
9.	18,000	15	10	193.50	150.00	43.50	________	________	________	________
10.	15,000	20	9¾	142.35	121.88	________	________	________	________	________
11.	30,000	30	10½	274.50	________	________	________	________	________	________
12.	40,000	25	11½	________	________	________	________	________	________	________
13.	50,000	35	10¼	________	________	________	________	________	________	________
14.	60,000	30	12	________	________	________	________	________	________	________

15. Alice and Barry Rossi purchased a $35,000 home. After a 20% down payment, they secured a mortgage at 9% for 30 years.

A. What is their monthly payment?

$__________, found by

B. How much of their first payment goes for interest?

$__________, found by

C. How much out of their first payment goes to reduce the principal?

$__________, found by

D. What is the new principal after the first payment?

$______________, found by

E. What is the new principal after the second payment?

$______________, found by

16. On a $50,000 mortgage at 12% for 30 years, how much of the first payment goes to reduce the principal?

$_________, found by

17. Determine the new principal after the first payment on the home on Archer Road if a 10% down payment is made and the remainder is financed at 10% for 35 years.

$______________, found by

JUST THREE MILES OUT of city on Archer Road. Two-acre lot zoned for business. Great location for nursery, beauty shop or any small home-based business. Three bedroom block home in excellent condition. $45,000. HL 028.

18. Determine the new principal after the second payment on the Brent Valley home if a 10% down payment is made and the remainder is financed at 11% for 25 years. $______________, found by

BRENT VALLEY
$110,000
4 bedroom 2 story in a custom building area. 2½ baths, large corner lot. Although it doesn't matter today, there is $4,000 worth of landscaping on huge corner lot and two fireplaces.

19. This is a portion of an amortization schedule from the Kissell Company. The original loan was made in 1950 for $14,700 at 6% for 30 years. The monthly payment is $88.14. Calculate the missing figures labeled A-F.

Monthly Payment No.	*Interest*	*Principal*	*Principal Balance*
33	$70.97	$17.17	$14,176.14
34	70.88	17.26	A. ________
35	70.79	B. ________	C. ________
36	D. ________	E. ________	F. ________

20. Refer to Problem 19. Nearly 30 years have elapsed. Calculate the missing figures labeled A-F for the last few payments. (The last payment is adjusted to leave a principal balance of zero.)

Monthly Payment No.	*Interest*	*Principal*	*Principal Balance*
355	$2.57	$85.57	$428.14
356	2.14	86.00	342.14
357	1.71	86.43	A. ________
358	1.28	B. ________	C. ________
359	D. ________	E. ________	F. ________
360	G. ________	H. ________	.00

SECTION 7-2: MORE ON FINANCING THE PURCHASE OF A HOME

Objective: To calculate the monthly escrow payment, the total monthly payment, and closing costs.
To analyze the effect of the interest rate, the term of the mortgage, and the monthly payment on the total interest paid.

ESCROW ACCOUNTS

The monthly home mortgage payments discussed previously included only interest and princpal. Most lending institutions require, for their own protection, that one-twelfth of the annual cost of insurance and one-twelfth of the annual real estate taxes be added to each monthly payment. If these charges are added, the amount is set aside in a special account called an **escrow account.** When it is time to pay the insurance and taxes, the bank takes the money out of the escrow account and makes the payment.

Problem

Banco Savings and Loan is preparing to loan Lewis Crowner $25,000 at 9½% for 20 years. The annual taxes are $774, and the yearly insurance premium for fire, theft, and other possible losses is $342. Determine the total monthly amount Crowner will pay.

Solution

Using a calculator with memory:
ESCROW ACCOUNT

Enter	Press	Display
1	÷	1
12	= ×	0.08333333
774	= m+	64.499974
1	÷	1
12	= ×	0.0833333
342	=	28.499988
	+ RM	64.499974
	=	92.99962

The payment on the mortgage is $233.25, found by:

$$\text{Monthly mortgage payment} = \frac{\text{Amount of mortgage}}{\$1{,}000} \times \text{Payment for a \$1,000 loan found in Table 7-1}$$

$$= \frac{\$25{,}000}{\$1{,}000} \times \$9.33$$

$$= \$233.25$$

Escrow account:

Taxes	=	1/12 of $774	=	$64.50
Insurance	=	1/12 of $342	=	$28.50
		Total escrow	=	$93.00

Total monthly payment = $233.25 + $93.00 = $326.25

1 SELF-REVIEW

A home mortgage loan was granted for $48,000 at 10% for 25 years. The annual property taxes are $1,260. The annual insurance premium is $295.80. The bank requires that 1/12 of the annual taxes and 1/12 of the insurance premium be paid along with the regular monthly payment.

A. What is the monthly amount for principal and interest? $________

B. What is the monthly amount to be put in escrow each month for taxes? $________

C. What is the monthly amount to be put in escrow each month for insurance? $________

D. What is the total monthly payment? $________

E. How much is in the escrow account in four months? $________

Answers:

A. $436.32, found by $\frac{\$48{,}000}{\$1{,}000} \times \$9.09$

B. $105.00, found by $\frac{\$1{,}260}{12}$

C. $24.65, found by $\frac{\$295.80}{12}$

D. $565.97, found by $436.23 + $105 + $24.65

E. $518.60, found by ($105 + $24.65) × 4

THE IMPORTANCE OF THE INTEREST RATE

Exhibit 7-2 shows the total interest on a $20,000 loan for 20 years at various rates, from 8% to 11%. A $20,000 loan at 8½% for 20 years would cost the homeowner $21,664 in interest. The same principal at 9% for the 20 years would carry an interest charge of $23,200. The seemingly minute difference of ½% in the interest rate could save the homeowner $1,536 in interest!

The *total interest* on a home loan is determined by multiplying the monthly payment by the total number of payments and then subtracting the amount of the loan.

EXHIBIT 7-2

TOTAL INTEREST FOR 20 YEARS ON A $20,000 LOAN

Rate	*Total Interest*
8%	$20,176
8½	21,664
9	23,200
9½	24,784
10	26,368
11	29,536

Total interest = (Monthly payment X Number of payments) – Amount of loan

Problem What is the total interest on a $30,000 loan at 10% for 30 years?

Solution Determine the monthly payment.

Monthly payment = $30,000 / $1,000 X $8.78 ← From Table 7-1

= $263.40

Then:

Total interest = (Monthly payment X Number of payments) – Amount of loan
= ($263.40 X 12 X 30) – $30,000.00
= $94,824.00 – $30,000.00
= $64,824.00

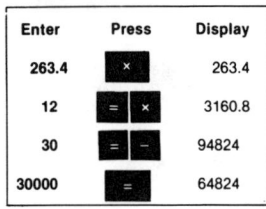

Using a calculator:
TOTAL INTEREST

Enter	Press	Display
263.4	×	263.4
12	= ×	3160.8
30	= –	94824
30000	=	64824

2 SELF-REVIEW

Suppose the home buyer in the preceding problem had been able to secure the $30,000, 30-year loan at 9½%. (A) What is the total interest? (B) How much would be saved by having the 9½% loan instead of the 10% loan?

A. Determine the monthly payment.

Monthly payment = $30,000 / $1,000 X $________

= $252.30

Total interest = (Monthly payment X Number of payments) – Amount of loan
= ($__________ X 12 X ______) – $__________
= $________________ – $________________
= $________________

B. The savings is found by:

Savings = Total interest at 10% – Total interest at 9½%
= $________________ – $________________
= $________________

A. Monthly payment:
$30,000 / $1,000 X $8.41

Total interest:
= ($252.30 X 12 X 30) – $30,000
= $90,828.00 – $30,000.00
= $60,828.00

B. Savings:
= $64,824.00 – $60,828.00
= $3,996.00

THE IMPORTANCE OF THE LENGTH OF TIME OF THE LOAN

While the rate of interest has a significant effect on the total amount of interest the home buyer pays during the duration of the loan, the duration, or **length of time**, of the loan is also important. The longer the time needed for paying off the mortgage loan, the greater the total amount of interest paid.

Exhibit 7-3 shows the total amount paid in interest on a $35,000 mortgage loan at 8%, 9%, and 10% for various periods, ranging from 5 to 35 years.

EXHIBIT 7-3

TOTAL INTEREST ON A $35,000 LOAN

Duration of Loan (years)	*Interest Rate (percent) and Total Amount of Interest* 8%	9%	10%
5 . . .	$ 7,588	$ 8,596	$ 9,625
10 . . .	15,988	18,214	20,524
15 . . .	25,228	28,945	32,725
20 . . .	35,308	40,600	46,144
25 . . .	46,060	53,200	60,445
30 . . .	57,484	66,430	75,628
35 . . .	69,517	80,248	91,420

Note that for the $35,000 mortgage loan at 10% for 5 years, the total interest charge is $9,625. The same loan for 10 years carries total interest charges of $20,524; and for 20 years the total interest is $46,144.

3 SELF-REVIEW

Clare and Norman Delang are considering the purchase of a home advertised for $42,000. They will need a $33,000 mortgage. A bank will grant them the loan at 9¾% for either 20 or 25 years. How much interest will they save if they take the 20-year loan instead of the 25-year loan?

20-year loan:

Monthly payment:

$= \frac{\$33{,}000}{\$1{,}000} \times \$9.49$

= $313.17

Total interest:

= $33,000

= $75,160.80 – $33,000

= $42,160.80

25-year loan:

Monthly payment:

$= \frac{\$33{,}000}{\$1{,}000} \times \$8.92$

= $294.36

Total interest:

= ($294.36 × 12 × 25) – $33,000

= $88,308 – $33,000

= $55,308.00

Savings:

= $55,308.00 – $42,160.80

Total interest on 20-year loan is found by:

$$\text{Monthly payment} = \frac{\$33{,}000}{\$1{,}000} \times \$\_\_\_\_\_\_$$

= $______

Then:

Total interest = ($313.17 × 12 × 20) – $______

= $______ – $33,000

= $42,160.80

Total interest on 25-year loan is found by:

$$\text{Monthly payment} = \frac{\$33{,}000}{\$1{,}000} \times \$\_\_\_\_\_\_$$

= $______

Total interest = ($294.36 × 12 × ____) – $33,000

= $88,308 – $33,000

= $______

Savings is found by:

Savings = $______ – $______

= $13,147.20

THE IMPORTANCE OF THE MONTHLY PAYMENT

In order to reduce the total interest charge it may appear that the most logical decision would be to pay off the loan in five or fewer years. If it were decided to pay off a $20,000 loan at 8% in 5 years, the monthly payment for principal and interest would be $405.60. Other monthly payments are:

Duration in Years	*Monthly Payment*
5	$405.60
10	242.80
15	191.20
20	167.40
25	154.40

For prospective homeowners earning about $10,000 a year, a monthly payment of $405.60 would no doubt be too burdensome. After adding required amounts for taxes and insurance, the monthly payment for home ownership would represent about half of their income. As a result of many studies, the federal government recommends that for a family earning about $10,000 a year, not more than 24% of the total budget should be spent on housing. In this case the maximum would be about $2,400 a year, or $200 a month. Thus it appears that a loan duration of 15 years—or possibly 20 years—would be advisable.

CLOSING COSTS OR SETTLEMENT COSTS

Closing or settlement is the formal process by which ownership of real estate or real property passes from seller to buyer. It is the last step in the home buying process. It is the time when **title** to the property is transferred from the seller to the buyer.

Under provisions of the Real Estate Settlement Procedures Act (a federal statute), when a consumer files an application for a loan, the lender must provide a good-faith estimate of the settlement or closing costs the borrower is likely to incur. Such closing costs might include:

1. Fees or premiums for title insurance, title examination, and an abstract of title.
2. Fees for preparation of deeds, settlement statements or other documents.
3. Amounts required to be placed into an escrow or trustee account for future payments of taxes, assessments, and insurance.
4. Fees for notarizing deeds and other documents.
5. Appraisal fees.
6. Credit reports.

ATTORNEY AT LAW

Announces his availability to perform Real Estate Closings for the Basic Fee of:
1% of the first $10,000 purchase price, plus ½% of the balance.

Basic Fee Includes:
Consultation on contract, preparation of closing documents, title examination, issuance of title insurance policy and attendance at the closing.

Other legal services also available at reasonable fees.

Call for an appointment or more information.

For illustration: First Federal Savings and Loan of Fort Myers, Florida, gave the following as the estimated closing costs on a $23,000 home mortgage loan:

Loan origination fee: 2% of mortgage loan	$460.00
Credit report	25.00
Application fee	25.00
Interest on loan from date of closing to 1st of month—maximum	162.91
Abstract of title	50.00
Attorney fee	10.00
Documentation stamp	46.00
Intangible tax on mortgage	34.50
Total	$813.41

4 SELF-REVIEW

Marcia Voss is going to have a closing on a small apartment house she is buying. Her mortgage is $24,000. The various costs are indicated on the statement below. Complete the statement.

A.	Loan origination fee: (2% of the mortgage + $400)	$______
B.	Credit report	40
C.	Mortgage insurance (0.65% of the mortgage)	______
D.	Legal fees (0.5% of the mortgage)	______
E.	Loan application fee	60
F.	Recording costs	7
G.	Appraisal	55
	Total	$______

A.	$ 880
B.	40
C.	156
D.	120
E.	60
F.	7
G.	55
Total	$1,318

ASSIGNMENT 7-2
MORE ON FINANCING THE PURCHASE OF A HOME

Name ______________________ **Date Due** ______________ **Grade** ______

Answers to selected problems are given in Appendix B.

For Problems 1 through 6, refer to Table 7-1 and supply the missing data.

	Amount of Mortgage	*Yrs.*	*Rate*	*Monthly Mortgage Payment*	*Annual Fire Insurance Premium*	*Annual Taxes*	*Escrow*		*Total Monthly Payment*
							Insurance	*Taxes*	
Ex.	$28,500	25	10¼%	$264.20	$101.00	$ 769.50	$8.42	$64.13	$336.75
1.	35,000	30	9¾	________	164.00	840.00	________	________	________
2.	40,000	35	11½	________	193.00	1,240.00	________	________	________
3.	50,000	30	10	________	238.00	1,400.00	________	________	________
4.	75,000	25	9½	________	306.00	2,062.50	________	________	________
5.	20,000	15	10½	________	87.00	560.00	________	________	________
6.	18,000	20	10¾	________	84.00	522.00	________	________	________

7. A home mortgage loan was granted for $42,500 at 9½% for 35 years. The annual property taxes are $1,317.50. The annual insurance premium is $207.60. The bank requires that 1/12 of the annual taxes and 1/12 of the insurance premium be paid into escrow, along with the regular monthly payment.

A. What is the monthly payment for principal and interest only?

$________, found by

B. What amount is put into escrow for taxes each month?

$________, found by

C. What amount is put into escrow for insurance each month?

$________, found by

D. What is the total monthly payment for principal, interest, and escrow?

$________, found by

E. How much is deposited in the escrow account in six months?

$________, found by

8. Peter and Helen Parkos purchased this home for \$36,900. After a 15% down payment, they financed the remainder at 12% for 30 years. Their annual taxes are \$1,180.80; their annual insurance premium is \$137.00.

EXCITING ARCHITECT-DESIGNED CONTEMPORARY—Cathedral ceilings and a dramatic stone planter enhance this new 3 bedroom modern home with many luxury conveniences! Discover how easy home ownership can be. Several models to choose from. \$36,900 FHA/VA. HL 072.

A. What is the monthly payment for principal and interest?

\$__________, found by

B. What is the amount put into escrow for taxes and insurance each month?

\$__________, found by

C. What is their total monthly payment?

\$__________, found by

9. Assume you need a \$40,000 mortgage. You plan to take 35 years to pay it off. Find the total interest paid over those 35 years at the following rates:

A. 10½%

\$__________, found by

B. 9½%

\$__________, found by

C. 8½%

\$__________, found by

D. 7½%

\$__________, found by

10. Wanda and James Cookson plan to purchase this Atlanta home. After a 5% down payment, they will obtain a loan for 30 years. Find the total interest paid in those 30 years at the following rates:

NEW HOME — N. HENRY CO.

\$41,650

100% VA, 95% CON.

3 BR ranch w/foyer, great rm., formal DR, kit., sep. breakfast rm., 2 full BA plus walk-in wet bar, carpet, wallpaper, ceramic tile, range, dishwasher, C/A, and flagstone fpl. are included. This home has over 1800 sq. ft. plus 2 car garage. We pay closing cost & points. All homes have economical gas for heating, hot water, cooking & clothes drying.

A. 9%

\$______________, found by

B. 10%

\$______________, found by

C. 11%

\$______________, found by

11. How much can be saved by financing \$60,000 for 25 years at 8% rather than 10%?

\$__________, found by

12. How much can be saved by financing \$80,000 for 35 years at 9% rather than 12%?

\$________________, found by

13. Assume you need a \$40,000 mortgage. City National Bank will loan you the money at 10% interest. Find the total interest paid if you finance the loan for:

A. 5 years.

\$__________, found by

B. 15 years.

\$__________, found by

C. 25 years.

\$__________, found by

D. 35 years.

\$___________, found by

14. Angel and Maria Delgado purchase this Brooklyn home for a 10% down payment and an 11% mortgage loan on the remainder. Find the total interest paid if they finance the loan for:

> E. 30's nr Linden – 1 fam det. garage, gas heat, 4 brs, 220 wiring, fin bsmt, 3 bths, \$42,500. Mr. Qualls, 773-3425

A. 10 years.

\$________________, found by

B. 20 years.

\$________________, found by

C. 30 years.

\$________________, found by

15. How much can be saved by financing \$55,000 at 10½% for 15 years rather than 30 years?

\$__________, found by

What might prevent you from taking out a 15-year loan? ______________________________

____

16. How much can be saved by financing \$75,000 at 11½% for 10 years rather than 35 years?

\$________________, found by

What might prevent you from taking out a 10-year loan? ______________________________

____

17. A $14,700 mortgage loan had the following closing costs: survey, $30.00; title insurance, $90.00; loan origination fee, 1% of loan; recording fee, $6.35; credit report, $5.00; appraisal, $30.00; and VA funding fee, ½% of loan. What is the total for the closing costs?

$__________, found by

18. People's Savings Association lists these closing costs for a $20,000 loan at 9% for 25 years:

Title guarantee/title insurance/preliminary letter . . .	$35.00
Recording and transfer fees	$15.00
Processing fees	1½% of loan
Escrow closing fee/title	$75.00
Title examination for lender	$30.00

What are the total closing costs?

$__________, found by

19. Mr. and Mrs. Frank Jankowski have their offer of $65,000 accepted for this Florida home. After a 20% down payment, they finance the remainder at 10¼% for 25 years.

GORGEOUS SPANISH-STYLE HOME on extra-large treed lot in quality Northwest area. Appraised at $72,500, asking a mere $68,900. Call 376-8580. Financing can be arranged. HL 897.

A. What is their down payment?

$__________, found by

B. What is their monthly payment for principal and interest?

$__________, found by

C. The total amount of interest paid over the 25 years is:

$__________, found by

D. Annual real estate taxes are $2,175, and the annual insurance premium is $416. What amount is required to be deposited to escrow every month?

$__________, found by

E. What is their total monthly payment?

$__________, found by

F. The Jankowskis paid closing costs of 2% of the amount of the mortgage plus $249.50. What would the total closing costs be?

$__________, found by

REVIEW ASSIGNMENT FOR CHAPTER 7
HOME MORTGAGES

Name ______________________________ Date Due ______________ Grade _____

1. Find the payment on a $35,000 mortgage loan at 10% for 20 years.

   $__________, found by

2. Find the payment on a $20,000 mortgage loan at 11% for 15 years.

   $__________, found by

3. Construct an amortization table (repayment schedule) for the first six months of a $35,000 mortgage loan at 10% for 30 years.

Month	*Interest*	*Reduction in Principal*	*New Principal*
1	________	________	____________
2	________	________	____________
3	________	________	____________
4	________	________	____________
5	________	________	____________
6	________	________	____________

4. Complete the amortization schedule for payments 68 and 69 for this Federal Housing Administration (FHA) loan of $16,200 at 5¼% for 30 years. Note that the principal and interest monthly payment is $89.59.

FEDERAL HOUSING ADMINISTRATION
AMORTIZATION SCHEDULE
Monthly Payment to Principal and Interest, $89. 59

______________ (SERIAL OR PROJECT NO.)

PAYMENT NO.	PAYMENT TO INTEREST (5 1/4 PERCENT)	PAYMENT TO PRINCIPAL	BALANCE DUE	PAYMENT NO.
61	6527	2432	1489482	61
62	6516	2443	1487039	62
63	6506	2453	1484586	63
64	6495	2464	1482122	64
65	6484	2475	1479647	65
66	6473	2486	1477161	66
67	6463	2496	1474665	67
68	6452	a	b	
69	c	d	e	
70	6430	2529	1467111	70

A. ____________

B. ____________

C. ____________ D. ____________ E. ____________

5. For the same loan as in Problem 4, about 15 years later, complete payments 249, 250, and 251.

A. ______________

B. ______________

C. ______________

D. ______________

E. ______________ F. ______________

FEDERAL HOUSING ADMINISTRATION

AMORTIZATION SCHEDULE ______________ (SERIAL OR PROJECT NO.)

Monthly Payment to Principal and Interest, $ 89. 59

PAYMENT DATE M	DAY	YR.	NO.	PAYMENT TO INTEREST 5 1/4 PERCENT	PAYMENT TO PRINCIPAL	BALANCE DUE	NO.	PAYMENT DATE M	DAY	YR.
			241	36 23	53 36	8 228 14	241			
			242	36 00	53 59	8 174 55	242			
			243	35 76	53 83	8 120 72	243			
			244	35 53	54 06	8 066 66	244			
			245	35 29	54 30	8 012 36	245			
			246	35 05	54 54	7 957 82	246			
			247	34 82	54 77	7 903 05	247			
			248	34 58	55 01	7 848 ∪4	248			
			249	34 34	55 25	a	249			
			250	34 09	b	c	250			
			251	d	e	f	251			
			252	33 61	55 98	7 625 57	252			

6. The Ison family was able to make a 20% down payment on this $75,000 Florida home and was, therefore, able to obtain a 9¾% mortgage loan for 25 years. Property taxes are estimated to be $2,400 annually. The annual home insurance premium will be $420. Closing costs will be 2% of the amount of the loan. Find the:

IN THE HEART OF MICANOPY—Lovely old Victorian home. Four bedrooms, 4 fireplaces, 2 baths. Zoned business or residence. Acre-plus lot with fruit trees. $75,000. HL 932.

A. Down payment.

$__________, found by

B. Amount of the mortgage loan.

$__________, found by

C. Closing costs.

$__________, found by

D. Monthly payment for principal and interest.

$__________, found by

E. Monthly payment for taxes and insurance (escrow).

$__________, found by

F. Total monthly payment.

$__________, found by

G. Total interest paid over the 25 years.

$__________, found by

H. Amount saved if they had obtained a 9% loan.

$__________, found by

I. Amount saved if they had gone for 20 years rather than 25 years with the 9¾% loan.

$__________, found by

TO THE STUDENT: There is a SELF-REVIEW TEST for this chapter in Appendix A, *with answers* in Appendix C.

8

Insurance

SECTION 8-1: HOME INSURANCE

Objective: To calculate the amounts of home insurance coverage, to compute the part of a partial loss the insurance company pays, and to determine the annual premium on a typical homeowners' insurance policy.

INTRODUCTION

Daily newspaper headlines are evidence that fire, theft, and property damage are common occurrences in the United States and abroad. The financial loss resulting from one of these catastrophes is often very substantial. Most individuals are unable to set aside, say, \$60,000 to cover a possible loss of their home by fire, or \$200,000 to settle a lawsuit resulting from an accident in the home. Instead, they join a risk-sharing group called an **insurance company.** A legal contract, called the **policy**, is signed by the company and the **policyholder.** The policyholder periodically pays a sum of money called the **premium.** Should a financial loss occur resulting from tornado damage, a fire, or theft, the policyholder is paid a specified amount as stipulated in the policy.

Many mortgage lenders, such as savings and loan associations, require that the home buyer take out an insurance policy as a condition for obtaining a mortgage. The present-day policy includes, in addition to fire insurance, **extended coverage provisions** by which coverage is extended to losses caused by lightning, hail, windstorms, explosion, vandalism, and burglary. Also included are liability insurance and provision of additional living expenses in case the family has to move into an apartment or motel while a damaged home is being repaired or rebuilt.

COINSURANCE

Insurance agents urge homeowners to carry full insurance on their homes to cover the total replacement cost should the home be completely destroyed by fire or other causes. Most insurance companies, however, allow homeowners to insure for less than 100% of the home's replacement value. The practice varies by company. Equitable General, for example, will not insure a home for less than 90% of its replacement value, Nationwide Insurance for not less than 80%. These clauses in the insurance policy are called **coinsurance clauses.** State Farm Insurance has an 80% coinsurance clause, but it will insure for a smaller percent (such as 60% or 70%).

Replacement Cost Feature

Make sure the insurance on your home equals at least 80% of its replacement cost. That way...

...for small losses — you'll get protection to full replacement cost on covered losses of less than \$1,000 and less than 5% of the insurance on your house.

...for larger losses — claim settlement will not be based on depreciated values...but on "current replacement costs" up to your policy limits!·

If homeowners insure their home for at least the percent stated in the coinsurance clause (such as 80%), the company will pay the full amount of *any* loss *up to the face amount of the policy.* For illustration, suppose an insurance company has an 80% coinsurance clause. If the owner of a house with a replacement value of \$40,000 insures it for at least \$32,000 (80% of \$40,000), the company would pay for any loss up to \$32,000.

If the face of the policy is *less* than the amount computed according to the coinsurance clause, most insurance companies will only pay a part of the loss. The part of a partial loss paid by the company is equal to the percent of replacement value carried, divided by percent of replacement value specified in the coinsurance clause of the policy.

$$\text{Part of partial loss paid} = \frac{\text{Percent of replacement value carried}}{\text{Percent of replacement value specified in coinsurance clause}}$$

Problem It is estimated that if Tom and Sue Sloan's home were completely destroyed, it would cost \$56,000 to replace it. Their insurance company has an 80% coinsurance clause, but it will allow the Sloans to insure their home for 70% of its replacement value.

A. What is the face value of the policy?
B. What part of a partial loss will the company pay?
C. How much will the company pay on a loss of \$16,000?
D. If the Sloans had insured the home for 80% of the replacement value, how much of the \$16,000 loss would the insurance company pay?

Solution A. Face value = 70% × \$56,000
= 0.70 × \$56,000
= \$39,200

B. $$\text{Part of partial loss} = \frac{\text{Percent of replacement value carried}}{\text{Percent of replacement value specified in coinsurance clause}}$$

$$= \frac{70\%}{80\%}$$

$$= \frac{7}{8} \quad \text{or} \quad 0.875$$

C. Payment on \$16,000 loss:

$$\text{Payment} = \frac{7}{8} \times \$16{,}000$$

$$= \$14{,}000$$

D. If the home is insured for 80% of the replacement value, the company will pay all of the \$16,000 loss.

Note that if the home is completely destroyed the insurance company will pay the face value of the policy, or \$39,200.

1 SELF-REVIEW

A reminder: Cover the answers in the margin.

The company insuring the Cooper's \$80,000 home has a 90% coinsurance clause in its policies; however, the company will allow homeowners to insure for less than 90% of the replacement value. The Coopers insured for 60% of the replacement value.

A. Face value:
= 60% × \$80,000
= 0.60 × \$80,000
= \$48,000

A. Find the face value of the policy.

Face value = ____% × \$________
= 0.____ × \$________
= \$________

B. Part of partial loss:

$= \frac{60\%}{90\%} = \frac{2}{3}$

B. What part of the partial loss will the company pay?

$$\text{Part of partial loss} = \frac{\text{Percent of replacement value carried}}{\text{Percent of replacement value specified in coinsurance clause}}$$

$$= \frac{\_\_\_\%}{\_\_\_\%}$$

$$= \_\_\_\_$$

C. Payment:

$= \frac{2}{3} \times \$21{,}000$

$= \$14{,}000$

C. How much will the company pay on a $21,000 loss?

$$\text{Payment} = \frac{2}{3} \times \$\_\_\_\_\_\_\_\_$$

$$= \$\_\_\_\_\_\_\_\_$$

D. $21,000

D. If the home is insured for 90% of the replacement value, the company will pay $________ on the $21,000 loss.

E. Face value of policy, or $48,000.

E. The Coopers insured for 60% of replacement value, so the company will pay $________ if the home is completely destroyed.

Most companies have several types of policies, depending on the number of perils the property is insured against. One company (Allstate) calls its types of policies the standard and the deluxe forms. Other companies designate them as named peril and all risk.

Exhibit 8-1 is the prospectus for a $40,000 Deluxe policy from Allstate in a recent year. Note that an annual premium of $143 buys $40,000 of protection on the home, plus $4,000 on the garage and other buildings on the property. In addition, should the contents of the house (such as hi-fi, furniture, television set, and cameras) be destroyed by fire or be stolen, the insurance company would pay up to $20,000. And should a major fire occur, the homeowner would receive up to $8,000 to pay for living expenses at a motel, hotel, or elsewhere while the home is being repaired. The amount of the policy, $40,000 in this case, is the face of the policy.

Another aspect of many homeowners' policies is that the amount of coverage purchased on the dwelling becomes the basis for determining the amounts of coverage which are assigned to the private structures (garages, etc.), the personal property (furniture, clothes, etc.), and the additional living expenses. Some of these percents of the face value allowed for various other coverages are shown in Table 8-1.

TABLE 8-1
Percent of Dwelling Coverage Allowed for Other Coverages

	Percent of Face Value Allowed
Private structures	10%
Personal property	50
Additional living expense	20

EXHIBIT 8-1

To find the best plan for your home, open these pages one by one.

Here's Allstate's low cost for the plan you choose!

☐ Standard ☒ Deluxe (FORM III)

Protection against loss to dwelling or family property is available with or without deductible (with certain state exceptions). Mandatory deductibles apply to some or all property perils in some states.

Coverage is: ☐ Without Deductible
☒ With $50 Deductible ☐ With $100 Deductible
☐ With $50 Windstorm-Hail Deductible*
☐ With $100 Windstorm-Hail Deductible*

*Mandatory states only

Protection up to	Covering:	Premium
$ 40,000	Dwelling	
	Multi-family Dwelling	$
$ 4,000	Private Structures (Garages, etc.)	
$ 20,000	Family Property On Premises ☒ Including Theft ☐ Excluding Theft — available only in N.Y. Metro. and suburbs	
$ 8,000	Additional Living Expense	
$ 50,000	Family Liability	$
$ 500	Medical Payments Per Person	
$ 250	Damage to Property of Others	
$ —	"All Risks" Coverage-jewelry, furs, watches	$
$ —	Earthquake	$
$		$
	Basic Annual Premium	$
	Total Annual Premium	$ 143.00 / YEAR

"Deluxe" Policy Best Protection

Fire
1. Fire
2. Hail
3. Lightning
4. Smoke
5. Windstorm
6. Explosion
7. Vandalism — Riot
8. Aircraft — Vehicles
9. Up to $50 for Glass Breakage (dwelling)

Family Liability (for occurrences such as those illustrated)
10. Guest Slips on Skate, Falls Down Stairs
11. Burning Trash Sets Neighbor's Roof on Fire
12. Your Son Breaks Neighbor's Window

Theft
13. Theft on Premises
14. Damage by Thieves
15. Theft off Premises
16. Hold-up, Pickpockets, Burglary
17. Credit Cards

"Deluxe" Homeowners Insurance also includes these added hazards and more.

Added "Fire"
18. Falling Objects
19. Bursting of Home Heating System (Steam or Hot Water)
20. Electrical Damage to Electrical Appliances, Wiring, etc. (except tubes, transistors and similar items)
21. Weight of Ice or Snow
22. Glass Breakage Over $50
23. Water Damage from Plumbing or Heating systems
24. Collapse of Building
25. Freezing of Plumbing or Heating Systems
26. Wall Damaged by Rain
27. Counter Top Scorched by Hot Iron
28. Hole Broken in Wall While Moving Furniture

You get all the protection shown, plus protection against loss to your dwelling from practically any other loss (except for a few common exclusions such as loss from termites, wear and tear, deterioration, smog, settling, cracking, earthquake*, flood†, water, backed up through sewers or drains, war, radiation, etc.)

*Earthquake coverage may be added to your policy at an additional cost.
†While flood insurance is not available under your Allstate Homeowners policy, it can be obtained through the National Flood Insurers Association. Ask your Allstate Agent for the details.

And you get:
- Replacement Cost Feature
- Additional Living Expense Feature

Optional:
- **"All Risks" Coverage for jewelry, furs, watches — to $4,000!**

Problem Using the percent indicated in Table 8-1, how much insurance would Tim O'Malley, who is insuring his home for $40,000, have on (A) the private structure; (B) personal property; (C) additional living expenses?

Solution A. Insurance on private structure is $4,000, found by:

10% of $40,000 = $4,000

B. Insurance on personal property is $20,000 found by:

50% of $40,000 = $20,000

C. Insurance on additional living expenses is $8,000, found by:

20% of $40,000 = $8,000

2 SELF-REVIEW

A. Amount of insurance:
= 80% × $60,000
= 0.80 × $60,000
= $48,000

B. Private structures:
= 10% × $48,000
= $4,800

C. Personal property:
= 50% × $48,000
= $24,000

D. Living expense:
= 20% × $48,000
= $9,600

Suppose that Judy Wilson is buying a new home for $60,000. She is going to insure the home for 80% of its replacement value (cost, in this case). She will be assigned coverage as indicated in Table 8-1. The amount of insurance is found by:

A. Amount of insurance = ____% × $_________
= 0.80 × $_________
= $_________

The amount of coverage assigned to private structures, personal property, and additional living expense is found by:

B. Private structures: ____% × $48,000 = $________

C. Personal property: ____% × $_________ = $_________

D. Additional living expenses: ____% × $_________ = $________

POLICY EXCLUSIONS

Excluded from most policies are losses due to termites, floods, earthquakes, landslides, tidal waves, sewer backups or overflows, wear and tear, smog, war, and nuclear radiation (see Exhibit 8-1). Also, many homeowners' policies have a stated maximum amount of coverage on certain items. Exhibit 8-2 shows a portion of a homeowners' policy dealing with "Special Limits of Liability" on the part of the insurance company (State Farm Insurance).

EXHIBIT 8-2

SPECIAL LIMITS OF LIABILITY

a. This Company shall be liable for loss to trees, shrubs, plants and lawns (EXCEPT THOSE GROWN FOR BUSINESS PURPOSES) only when the loss is caused by fire, lightning, explosion, riot, civil commotion, vandalism, malicious mischief, theft, aircraft or vehicles not owned or operated by an occupant of the premises. THIS COMPANY'S LIABILITY FOR LOSS IN ANY ONE OCCURRENCE UNDER THIS PROVISION SHALL NOT EXCEED IN THE AGGREGATE FOR ALL SUCH PROPERTY 5% OF THE LIMIT OF LIABILITY OF COVERAGE A, NOR MORE THAN $250 ON ANY ONE TREE, SHRUB OR PLANT, INCLUDING EXPENSE INCURRED FOR REMOVING DEBRIS THEREOF.

b. UNDER COVERAGE B, THIS COMPANY SHALL NOT BE LIABLE FOR LOSS IN ANY ONE OCCURRENCE WITH RESPECT TO THE FOLLOWING PROPERTY FOR MORE THAN:
(1) $100 IN THE AGGREGATE ON MONEY, BULLION, NUMISMATIC PROPERTY AND BANK NOTES;
(2) $500 IN THE AGGREGATE ON SECURITIES, ACCOUNTS, BILLS, DEEDS, EVIDENCES OF DEBT, LETTERS OF CREDIT, NOTES OTHER THAN BANK NOTES, PASSPORTS, RAILROAD AND OTHER TICKETS OR STAMPS, INCLUDING PHILATELIC PROPERTY;
(3) $1,000 ON MANUSCRIPTS;
(4) $500 IN THE AGGREGATE FOR LOSS BY THEFT OF JEWELRY, WATCHES, NECKLACES, BRACELETS, GEMS, PRECIOUS AND SEMI-PRECIOUS STONES, GOLD, PLATINUM AND FURS INCLUDING ANY ARTICLE CONTAINING FUR WHICH REPRESENTS ITS PRINCIPAL VALUE;
(5) $500 IN THE AGGREGATE ON WATERCRAFT, INCLUDING THEIR TRAILERS (WHETHER LICENSED OR NOT), FURNISHINGS, EQUIPMENT AND OUTBOARD MOTORS;
(6) $500 ON TRAILERS, NOT OTHERWISE PROVIDED FOR, WHETHER LICENSED OR NOT; OR
(7) $500 IN THE AGGREGATE ON FIREARMS AND RELATED EQUIPMENT

3 SELF-REVIEW

A. $100
B. $500
C. $500

From Exhibit 8-2:

A. The company is not liable for a loss of more than $_______ in money, bullion, coins, or bank notes.

B. The maximum amount on watercraft is $______.

C. The maximum amount on firearms is $______.

FACTORS DETERMINING THE PREMIUM

The three main factors that affect the premiums for a homeowners' policy are:

1. The **amount of insurance**, which is the dollar value that the property is being insured for.
2. The **type of construction**, which is generally masonry or masonry veneer construction or wood construction, referred to as simply frame construction.
3. The **protection class**, which refers to the location of the property.

A house located in a low fire hazard area with excellent fire protection will have a lower premium than a similar house located miles from the nearest fire department. Most cities, towns, villages, counties, and townships in the United States have been assigned a rate classification. The rate classification, usually a number from 1 to 10, is determined generally by the quality of the fire protection available.

Classes 1-6: Metropolitan area with good fire department.

Classes 7-8: Rural area with fire hydrants.

Class 9: Rural area without fire hydrants, but with a good fire department within six miles.

Class 10: Rural area without fire hydrants and the fire department more than six miles away.

Table 8-2 gives the annual premiums for selected amounts of insurance with a $100 **deductible clause.** The $100 deductible clause means that the homeowner must pay the first $100 of any loss, and the insurance company will pay the remainder.

TABLE 8-2
Annual Premiums for a Typical Homeowner's Policy, $100 Deductible, by Protection Class and Type of Construction

Insurance Amount	MASONRY OR MASONRY VENEER *Protection Class*				FRAME *Protection Class*			
	1-6	*7-8*	*9*	*10*	*1-6*	*7-8*	*9*	*10*
$ 15,000	$109	$115	$ 136	$ 144	$115	$ 123	$ 144	$ 154
20,000	114	120	142	151	120	129	151	161
25,000	119	126	149	158	126	135	158	169
30,000	130	137	162	172	137	147	172	184
35,000	141	149	177	188	149	160	188	201
40,000	152	161	191	203	161	173	203	217
45,000	163	173	206	219	173	186	219	234
50,000	179	189	226	240	189	204	240	257
60,000	223	236	282	300	236	254	300	322
70,000	266	282	338	360	282	304	360	386
80,000	309	328	394	420	328	354	420	450
90,000	353	375	450	480	375	404	480	515
100,000	396	421	506	539	421	454	539	579
150,000	614	652	786	839	652	705	839	901
200,000	913	970	1,171	1,250	970	1,049	1,250	1,343

Problem Using Table 8-2, determine the annual premium on a dwelling to be insured for $50,000. The home is located in Protection Class 9 and is of frame construction.

Solution The annual premium is found by reading down the insurance amount column to $50,000. Then read across to the column for frame construction and Class 9. The annual premium is $240.

4 SELF-REVIEW

A. $189

A. If the $50,000 home in the above problem were located in Protection Class 5, then the premium would be $______.

B. $137

B. The annual premium on a $30,000 home of masonry veneer construction in Protection Class 7 is $______.

HOMEOWNERS' POLICY–RELATED INSURANCE

Renter's Insurance. Most insurance companies have a special policy for those who rent an apartment or house. The provisions of the policy are similar to a homeowners' policy in that the renter receives financial protection against the loss of the contents and personal belongings by such perils as fire, lightning, explosion, smoke, vandalism, wind, hail, and theft. The renter does *not* carry insurance on the dwelling itself; the owner insures the dwelling.

Condominium Unit Owner Insurance. The person who owns a unit in a condominium buys a special insurance policy designed specifically for condominium owners. It insures contents and personal property and any special additions or alterations made to the unit that are not covered by the insurance on the building itself. The building is usually insured by the condominium association, which is made up of the individual unit owners.

Mobile Home Owner Insurance. The mobile home policy provides basically the same coverage as in a conventional homeowners' policy. However, the premiums are substantially higher because of the difference in construction and the fact that mobile homes are very susceptible to wind damage.

Flood Insurance. Flood insurance was not generally available until 1969, when the federal government and private insurance companies introduced a joint program to provide flood insurance at rates subsidized by the government. Certain standards must be met, depending on local community measures.

Earthquake Insurance. Earthquake insurance is usually provided as an addition to the regular homeowners' insurance policy.

And, you may add Earthquake coverage to your policy at a slight additional cost.

Allstate's Condominium Owners Insurance was designed with those needs in mind.
Protects the furniture in your residential condominium unit, your clothing and most other personal belongings against loss from fire, theft, vandalism and many other hazards.

ASSIGNMENT 8-1
HOME INSURANCE

Name ______________________________ Date Due ____________ Grade _____

Answers to selected problems are given in Appendix B.

For problems 1 through 6, complete the table.

	Replacement Value of Home	% of Replacement Value Carried	Amount of Insurance	10% Private Structures	50% Personal Property	20% Additional Living Expenses	Coinsuranace Clause	Part of Partial Loss Paid by Company
Ex.	$ 75,000	80%	$60,000	$6,000	$30,000	$12,000	90%	$\frac{80}{90} = \frac{8}{9}$
1.	30,000	80	24,000	______	______	______	80	______
2.	45,000	70	31,500	______	______	______	90	______
3.	18,500	80	______	______	______	______	90	______
4.	39,500	60	______	______	______	______	80	______
5.	112,750	80	______	______	______	______	90	______
6.	97,790	100	______	______	______	______	80	______

For Problems 7 through 10, refer to Table 8-1 and Exhibit 8-2.

7. Norma and Leo Brickman have purchased a house for $46,900. They want to insure their home for 80% of its replacement cost. The insurance company has a 90% coinsurance clause.

A. What amount of insurance must they buy?

$__________, found by

B. How much is their insurance on private structures?

$__________, found by

C. How much is their insurance for personal property?

$__________, found by

D. How much is their insurance for additional living expenses?

$__________, found by

E. What is their maximum coverage for money, bullion, coins, or bank notes?

$__________, found by

F. How much would the company pay on a loss of $18,900?

$__________, found by

8. Newlyweds Marie and John Weidner purchased a new house for $29,800. They decided to insure it for 80% of its cost. The company has an 80% coinsurance clause.

A. What amount of insurance did they buy?

$__________, found by

B. How much is their insurance on private structures?

$__________, found by

C. How much is their insurance for personal property?

$__________, found by

D. How much is their insurance for additional living expenses?

$__________, found by

E. What is the maximum amount of insurance on their boat and outboard motor not otherwise provided for?

$__________, found by

F. How much would the company pay on a wind damage loss of $1,200?

$__________, found by

9. The Takamuras recently purchased a home for $112,500. They chose to insure their home for the full replacement cost ($112,500).

A. What is their insurance on private structures?

$________, found by

B. What is their insurance for personal property?

$________, found by

C. What is their insurance for additional living expenses?

$________, found by

D. What is the maximum amount on manuscripts?

$________, found by

10. Helen and James Duggan purchased their retirement home in Florida for $42,500. They decided to insure it for its full replacement cost ($42,500).

A. What is their insurance on private structures?

$________, found by

B. What is their insurance for personal property?

$________, found by

C. What is their insurance for additional living expenses?

$________, found by

D. What is the maximum amount on securities, accounts, bills, deeds, and so on?

$______, found by

For Problems 11 through 20, refer to Table 8-2 and supply the missing data.

	Amount of Insurance	*Type of Construction*	*Location of the Property Protection Class*	*Annual Premium, $100 Deductible*
Ex.	$ 60,000	Masonry veneer	8	$236
11.	25,000	Frame	4	________
12.	35,000	Frame	9	________
13.	15,000	Masonry veneer	7	________
14.	40,000	Frame	5	________
15.	90,000	Masonry	10	________
16.	150,000	Masonry	9	________

17. The Sofos insured their brick (masonry) home for $40,000. Their home is located in Protection Class 2. What is their annual premium on a typical homeowners' policy?

$________, found by

18. The Steins insured their new home for $25,000. Their home is frame and located in Protection Class 7. What is the annual premium on a typical homeowners' policy?

$________, found by

19. A frame home located in a rural area without fire hydrants and the fire department more than six miles away (Class 10) is insured for $20,000. What is the annual premium on a typical homeowners' policy?

$________, found by

20. A brick home located in a rural area without fire hydrants, but with a good fire department within six miles (Class 9), is insured for $100,000. What is the annual premium on a typical homeowners' policy?

$________, found by

SECTION 8-2: LIFE INSURANCE

Objective: To determine the annual, semiannual, quarterly, and monthly premiums for various types of life insurance policies.

> The exact origin of modern life insurance has apparently been lost in antiquity, but as early as 1583 there is reference to a "William Gybbons, citizen and salter of London," who bought a year's protection for £32 and died within the year. His heirs collected £400.
>
> The first life insurance company in America was founded in 1759 in Philadelphia, known as "A corporation for the Relief of Poor and Distressed Presbyterian Ministers and of the Poor and Distressed Widows and Children of Presbyterian Ministers." It is still operating under the title of the "Presbyterian Ministers' Fund."

Americans purchase over $367 billion worth of life insurance every year. Some form of life insurance is carried by 86% of adult males and 74% of adult females. The average amount of coverage per family is $36,900. The most common reason for buying life insurance is to provide financial protection for the surviving family should the income producer die.

Insurance on the life of a single person, spouse, or children can be purchased either directly from a life insurance company, such as the Travelers Insurance Company or Mutual of Omaha, or through one of their insurance agents. It can also be obtained by members of a particular group, usually called **group insurance.**

Group insurance is issued on the lives of a specified group of persons, such as all the employees of a company, a group of teachers, or members of a particular profession or occupation. Usually, no medical examination is required. If the insurance is offered as an employee fringe benefit, the employer may pay some of the cost, with the employee paying the remainder, or the employer may pay the entire cost of the insurance.

If insurance is purchased directly from a company, the individual may be required to have a medical examination, and the policy is issued only upon approval of the company. The premiums are generally paid annually, semiannually, quarterly, or monthly.

TYPES OF LIFE INSURANCE

There are about 1,750 life insurance companies in the United States offering a wide variety of policies in order to satisfy different insurance needs. The majority of insurance plans, however, are modifications or combinations of four basic types of insurance: (1) term insurance, (2) straight life insurance (also known as whole life or ordinary life), (3) limited-payment life insurance, and (4) endowment insurance.

TERM INSURANCE

Term insurance provides insurance protection for a specified term or period of time. The term might be 5, 10, 15, 20, or 30 years or to a specific age, such as age 65. At the end of the term, say 15 years, the protection ends. Generally the policy can be renewed for another specified term, upon proof of insurability and *at a higher premium.* If the term policy is renewed for ten years, the protection would end at the end of ten years. Some term insurance policies can be converted to one of the other types of policies (straight life, limited-pay life, or endowment) at the end of the term.

Term insurance is the *least expensive* form of life insurance. Unlike some of the other types of life insurance, term insurance usually has *no cash value,* meaning that the premiums are used to provide life insurance only. Thus, no money is refunded at the end of the term.

STRAIGHT LIFE INSURANCE

Straight life insurance provides financial protection from the time the policy is taken out until the death of the insured. *The premium remains the same from year to year for as long as the insured lives.* A straight life policy combines life insurance with a modest savings plan; thus the policy builds up some *cash value* over the years. If the insured dies, the company will pay the designated beneficiary(s) either the amount stated in the policy, usually called the *face value,* or the cash value, if it is higher than the face value.

LIMITED-PAYMENT LIFE

Limited-payment life insurance also gives the insured lifetime protection. However, the premiums are paid for a limited time period or a specified number of years. A 20-payment life policy is fully paid for in 20 years, and the insured has life insurance protection for as long as he or she lives. Another type of limited-payment life policy is paid up when the insured reaches the age stated in the policy, such as age 65.

In general, the premiums for a limited-payment life policy are higher than the premiums for a straight life policy or a term policy.

ENDOWMENT INSURANCE

Endowment insurance is a combination of life insurance and an accelerated savings plan. It is usually purchased for a specified period of time, such as 20 years, or until a specified age, such as age 65. Many families with young children purchase endowment insurance in order to force them to save money for their children's college education. Others might purchase endowment insurance in order to save money for retirement and at the same time have life insurance protection.

1 SELF-REVIEW

The four basic types of life insurance discussed are: (1) term, (2) straight life, (3) limited-payment life, and (4) endowment. In the space in front of each statement indicate which of the four basic types the statement applies to.

A. 1
B. 3
C. 1
D. 2
E. 2
F. 4
G. 4

____ A. Is the least expensive of the four.

____ B. The premiums are paid for a stipulated number of years, after which the policy is paid up for life.

____ C. Usually does *not* build up any cash values.

____ D. Is the least expensive of the three forms of permanent insurance (straight life, limited-payment, endowment).

____ E. The premiums are usually paid for as long as the insured lives.

____ F. The premiums are the highest of the four types.

____ G. Is a combination of life insurance and accelerated savings. It results in the highest cash value.

LIFE INSURANCE PREMIUMS

The initial calculation of life insurance premiums is performed by persons called *actuaries,* employed by the various insurance companies. Numerous factors are considered by the actuaries in determining premiums, including the life expectancy of the person applying for the insurance. Other factors include the general health of the applicant and occupation.

Each life insurance company has a set of rather extensive rate tables. A simplified form of a typical rate table is shown in Table 8-3.

As an illustration, the premium for a \$1,000, ten-year term insurance policy for a female, 25 years old, is \$3.63. A male age 20 would pay the same premium.

For a policy with a face value greater than \$1,000, the premium given in Table 8-3 would be multiplied by the number of thousands of dollars of insurance being purchased.

$$\text{Annual premium} = \frac{\text{Face value of policy}}{\$1{,}000} \times \begin{array}{c}\text{Premium per } \$1{,}000 \\ \text{(from Table 8-3)}\end{array}$$

TABLE 8-3
Annual Premiums per $1,000 of Life Insurance

Age		Term Insurance			Limited-Payment Life		Endowment	
Male	Female	To Age 65	10-Year	Straight Life	Paid Up at 65	20-Payment Life	At Age 65	20-Year
18	23	$ 5.92	$ 3.63	$12.91	$14.14	$24.27	$ 16.51	$45.15
19	24	6.04	3.63	13.25	14.56	24.70	17.03	45.19
20	25	6.17	3.63	13.61	15.00	25.16	17.57	45.22
21	26	6.31	3.63	13.99	15.46	25.62	18.15	45.27
22	27	6.46	3.64	14.38	15.95	26.10	18.75	45.31
23	28	6.62	3.64	14.79	16.46	26.59	19.39	45.36
24	29	6.78	3.66	15.22	17.00	27.11	20.07	45.42
25	30	6.96	3.69	15.67	17.58	27.63	20.79	45.49
30	35	8.02	4.05	18.30	21.06	30.60	24.98	46.04
35	40	9.62	4.89	21.74	25.89	34.22	30.98	47.11
40	45	11.82	6.58	26.25	32.63	38.69	39.69	49.13
45	50	14.63	9.76	32.15	43.07	44.20	52.27	52.27
50	55	18.40	15.77	39.92	59.46	51.40	72.35	56.82
55	60	19.27	19.27	49.95	89.24	60.15	112.68	63.00

Source: Rates courtesy of State Farm Life Insurance Company.

Problems Determine the annual premium for the life insurance as indicated.

A. Male, age 18, or female age 23
Policy: Straight life
Face value: $8,000
Premium per $1,000: $12.91
(from Table 8-3)

B. Female, age 26, or male age 21
Policy: Ten-year term
Face value: $15,000
Premium per $1,000: $3.63
(from Table 8-3)

Solutions

A. $\text{Annual premium} = \frac{\$8{,}000}{\$1{,}000} \times \$12.91$

$= 8 \times \$12.91$

$= \$103.28$

B. $\text{Annual premium} = \frac{\$15{,}000}{\$1{,}000} \times \$3.63$

$= 15 \times \$3.63$

$= \$54.45$

2 SELF-REVIEW

Janet DePrisco is considering the purchase of life insurance. She is 30 years old and in good health. Refer to Table 8-3.

A. If she buys an $8,000, ten-year term insurance policy, the annual premium is $________, found by multiplying 8 times $_______.

B. If she buys a $12,000, limited-payment life insurance policy paid up at age 65, the annual premium is $__________, found by ____ X $_________.

C. If she buys a 20-year endowment policy with a face value of $20,000, the annual premium is $__________, found by ____ X $_________.

A. $29.52, found by 8 × $3.69

B. $210.96, found by 12 × $17.58

C. $909.80, found by 20 × $45.49

SEMIANNUAL, QUARTERLY, AND MONTHLY PREMIUMS

Paying one rather large annual premium may put undue stress on the budgets of some policyholders. Most insurance companies, therefore, have premium payment plans whereby the policyholder can pay twice a year, quarterly, or on a monthly basis. Because of the additional clerical work involved, a small charge is made. Table 8-4 shows the method one company uses in determining the premiums for these time periods.

TABLE 8-4
Method of Determining Semiannual, Quarterly, and Monthly Insurance Premiums

Premium	*Percent of Annual Premium*
Semiannual	50.5%
Quarterly	25.5
Monthly	8.5

Source: Courtesy of State Farm Insurance.

Problem Determine the (A) annual, (B) semiannual, (C) quarterly, and (D) monthly premiums for a 20-payment life policy with a face value of $8,000 taken out by a 22-year-old man.

Solution A. Annual premium is $208.80, found by:

$$\text{Annual premium} = \frac{\$8{,}000}{\$1{,}000} \times \$26.10 \leftarrow \text{From Table 8-3}$$
$$= 8 \times \$26.10$$
$$= \$208.80$$

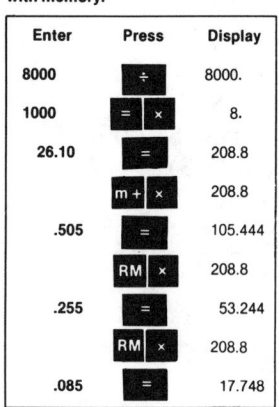

Using a calculator with memory:

Enter	Press	Display
8000	÷	8000.
1000	= ×	8.
26.10	=	208.8
	m+ ×	208.8
.505	=	105.444
	RM ×	208.8
.255	=	53.244
	RM ×	208.8
.085	=	17.748

B. Semiannual premium is $105.44, found by:

$$\text{Semiannual premium} = 50.5\% \text{ of annual premium}$$
$$= 0.505 \times \$208.80$$
$$= \$105.44$$

C. Quarterly premium is $53.24, found by:

$$\text{Quarterly premium} = 25.5\% \text{ of annual premium}$$
$$= 0.255 \times \$208.80$$
$$= \$53.24$$

D. Monthly premium is $17.75, found by:

$$\text{Monthly premium} = 8.5\% \text{ of annual premium}$$
$$= 0.085 \times \$208.80$$
$$= \$17.75$$

3 SELF-REVIEW

The annual premium on a straight-life policy with a face of $24,000 for a male aged 40 is $630 (found by 24 × $26.25). Using the State Farm Insurance system in Table 8-4:

A. The semiannual premium is found by taking 50.5% of the annual premium. Thus the semiannual premium is found by ________ × ________ = $________.

B. The quarterly premium is ________% of the annual premium. Thus the quarterly premium is found by ________ × ________ = $________.

C. The monthly premium is ________% of the annual premium. The monthly premium is found by ________ × ________ = $________.

A. 0.505 × $630 = $318.15

B. 25.5%
0.255 × $630 = $160.65

C. 8.5%
0.085 × $630 = $53.55

ASSIGNMENT 8-2
LIFE INSURANCE

Name ______________________ **Date Due** ______________ **Grade** _____

Answers to selected problems are given in Appendix B.

For Problems 1 through 6, refer to Table 8-3 and supply the missing data.

	Sex	*Age*	*Type of Life Insurance*	*Face Value of Policy*	*Premium per $1,000*	*Annual Premium*
Ex.	F	28	20-payment life	$15,000	$26.59	$398.85
1.	M	18	Endowment at age 65	20,000	16.51	________
2.	M	50	10-year term	10,000	15.77	________
3.	F	60	Term to age 65	25,000	________	________
4.	F	24	20-year endowment	45,000	________	________
5.	M	35	Limited pay–Paid up at 65	12,500	________	________
6.	F	40	Straight life	7,500	________	________

7. Michael Tupelo is considering the purchase of life insurance. He is 24 years of age and in good health. He would like to purchase $10,000 in life insurance.

   A. What is the annual premium if he buys ten-year term?

   $________, found by

   B. What is the annual premium if he buys straight life?

   $________, found by

   C. What is the annual premium if he buys 20-year endowment?

   $________, found by

8. Faye Bartlett desires to purchase $15,000 worth of life insurance. She is 45 years of age and in good health. What is her annual premium, if she purchases:

   A. Term to age 65?

   $________, found by

   B. Limited pay–paid up at 65?

   $________, found by

   C. Endowment at age 65?

   $________, found by

9. Anthony Graber, 21 years of age and in good health, buys a $20,000 limited pay–20 payment life insurance policy. He lives to age 43.

   A. What was his annual premium?

   $________, found by

   B. What was the total amount of annual premiums he paid?

   $________, found by

   C. What did his beneficiaries receive?

   $________, found by

10. A 30-year-old female took out a ten-year term policy for $20,000. She died at age 41.

    A. What was her annual premium?

    $________, found by

    B. What was the total amount of annual premiums paid?

    $________, found by

    C. What did her beneficiary receive?

    $________, found by

For Problems 11 through 16, supply the missing data, using Tables 8-3 and 8-4.

	Sex	Age	*Type of Life Insurance*	*Face Value of Policy*	*Annual Premium*	*Semiannual Premium*	*Quarterly Premium*	*Monthly Premium*
Ex.	M	40	10-year term	$30,000	$197.40	$99.69	$50.34	$16.78
11.	F	23	20-payment life	9,000	218.43	______	______	______
12.	F	55	10-year term	5,000	78.85	______	______	______
13.	M	23	Limited pay–paid up at 65	20,000	______	______	______	______
14.	M	30	20-yr. endowment	40,000	______	______	______	______
15.	F	50	Term to age 65	4,000	______	______	______	______
16.	M	55	Straight life	11,000	______	______	______	______

17. Donald Mix, 24 years of age and in good health, decides to buy a $10,000, 20-year endowment plan. What is his quarterly premium?

    $__________, found by

18. Jean Sobel, 45 years of age and in good health, decides to buy a $15,000 term to age 65 policy. What is her semiannual premium?

    $_________, found by

19. Tommy O'Brien, age 18, can afford $22 per month for life insurance. He needs to buy a policy worth at least $20,000. Which of the different types of life insurance policies can he afford to buy?

    ____

    ____

    ____

    ____

20. Lynn Cramer, age 40, has budgeted $50 per quarter for life insurance. She would like to buy a policy worth at least $10,000. Which of the different types of life insurance policies can she afford to buy?

    ____

    ____

21. A 30-year-old female takes out a $15,000 straight life policy. How much more does she pay per year if she pays the premium quarterly rather than annually?

    $_______, found by

22. A 50-year-old male takes out a $7,500 endowment to age 65 life insurance policy. How much more does he pay per year if he pays the premium monthly rather than semiannually?

    $_______, found by

SECTION 8-3: AUTOMOBILE INSURANCE

Objective: To determine the semiannual premium for automobile insurance.

Man Injured Sunday When Sister's Auto Struck From Behind

The man referred to in the newspaper clipping suffered severe bodily injury, and the automobile was demolished. Hospital and medical bills, the replacement cost of the automobile, and subsequent settlement of a lawsuit brought by the man against the other driver amounted to $120,000. Very few motorists have sufficient cash to pay such an amount. Even the theft of a $3,000 auto would be a major loss for most people!

BASIC COVERAGES

Instead of facing such a large financial loss, most automobile, truck, van, and recreational vehicle owners carry insurance against such risks as bodily injury, property damage, and collision.

The four basic categories of automobile insurance are: (1) automobile liability, (2) medical payments, (3) collision, and (4) comprehensive.

Automobile liability insurance provides protection to the policyholder against claims for bodily injury and property damage as a result of an accident. The combined coverage is often listed as 100/300/50. The 100/300 refers to the bodily injury coverage and means that the insurance company will pay up to $100,000 for the bodily injury of one person, or if more than one is involved in an accident, a maximum of $300,000 for all those in the accident. The 50 refers to a property damage limit of $50,000.

Medical payments coverage pays for medical expenses resulting from injuries suffered by the insured and passengers while riding in the insured's car. Payments are made up to the policy's limit.

Almost every state has a minimum liability coverage requirement, but you must remember that it is a bare minimum, the very **least** amount anyone can carry. In the majority of states, this amount is: $10,000 for each injured person; $20,000 total bodily injury payments for each accident; and $5,000 for total property damage payments.

Collision coverage pays for damages to the insured vehicle caused by collision with another motor vehicle or another object (such as a tree), or by upsetting (rolling over in a ditch). Repair costs, less the deductible (if any), are paid up to the cash value of the vehicle at the time of the accident. Most collision insurance is sold with a deductible clause. A $100 deductible policy means that the insured pays the first $100 on any repair bill; the insurance company pays the remainder.

Comprehensive coverage pays for damage to the insured car from numerous perils, such as fire, theft, flood, windstorm, hail, rain, vandalism, explosion, and earthquake, plus just about any cause other than collision or upset. Comprehensive coverage may also carry a deductible clause.

1 SELF-REVIEW

A. Liability insurance provides protection to the policy holder against claims for __________ injury and __________________ damage.

B. Collision insurance pays for damages to the insured auto caused by ________ __________________________.

C. Comprehensive insurance pays for damages to the insured auto for other than ________________ or upset.

D. Medical coverage pays for the medical expenses of the insured and/or passengers if the injuries result from an ______________________________________ ____.

A. bodily; property

B. a collision

C. collision

D. accident while riding in the insured's car

OPTIONAL COVERAGES

In addition to the four basic categories of liability, medical payments, collision, and comprehensive, numerous other types of coverage are available on an optional basis. Some *optional* coverages are:

1. **Uninsured motorist insurance** pays for injuries caused by a motorist with no insurance.
2. **Loss-of-earnings insurance** reimburses the insured for a percent of earnings lost because of automobile accident injuries.
3. **Disability insurance** provides the insured a weekly amount for a specified time, if the insured is disabled because of an automobile accident.
4. **Automobile death insurance** pays the designated person(s) a specified amount for the accidental death of the insured resulting from an automobile accident.

AUTOMOBILE INSURANCE PREMIUMS

The following discussion of automobile insurance premiums is limited to the four basic coverages of liability, medical, collision, and comprehensive insurance. No attempt has been made to discuss the premiums for the various optional coverages.

Insurance company actuaries have collected detailed information regarding millions of accidents, including the sex, age, and marital status of the driver, and whether the automobile was used mainly for pleasure or business.

It was discovered, for example, that for every 100 accidents involving adult drivers using the automobile mainly for pleasure, there were 200 accidents involving married males under 21 years. And, for every 100 accidents there were 390 accidents involving *unmarried* males under 21 years.

RATING FACTORS

It seems logical that for every $1.00 in premiums paid by adults, married males under 21 years should pay $2.00, and unmarried males under 21 years should pay $3.90. The actuaries have used this concept to develop a set of **rating factors** (see Table 8-5).

TABLE 8-5
Driver Classification–Rating Factors

	Multiples of Base Premium	
	Adult	*Senior–Over Age 65*
Adult and senior operators		
Pleasure	1.00	0.95
Average weekly mileage to and from work:		
Over 30 not over 100	1.05	1.00
Over 100	1.15	1.10
Business use (salesperson, etc.)	1.35	1.30
Farm automobile	0.80	0.70

	Multiples of Base Premium		
	Under 21 Years	*21 or 22 Years*	*23 or 24 Years*
*Married youthful male operators**			
Pleasure	2.00	1.55	1.30
To and from work or business use	2.20	1.80	1.45
Farm automobile	1.50	1.15	0.95

TABLE 8-5 *(continued)*

	Multiples of Base Premium				
	Under 21 Years		*21-24 Years*		*25-29 Years*
	Occasional Operator	*Principal Operator*	*Occasional Operator*	*Principal Operator*	*Principal Operator*
Unmarried youthful operators					
Females					
Pleasure	1.55	1.80	1.30	1.60	Classify
To and from work or business use	1.70	1.95	1.50	1.85	as adult
Farm automobile	1.15	1.35	0.95	1.20	
Males					
Pleasure	2.30	3.90	1.70	2.90	1.65
To and from work or business use	2.50	4.10	1.95	3.10	1.90
Farm automobile	1.70	2.95	1.30	2.15	1.30

*All married youthful female operators are classified as adults.
Source: Insurance rates courtesy of State Farm Mutual Automobile Insurance Company.

The rating factor for an individual driver depends on the age and sex of the person, as well as the way the vehicle being insured is used. For illustration, see the table below.

Description of Operator	*Rating Factor*
Adult—male or female driving for pleasure	1.00
Senior—male or female business use	1.30
Married male, age 20, farm use	1.50
Unmarried female, age 16, to and from work, occasional operator	1.70
Unmarried female, age 16, to and from work, principal operator	1.95
Unmarried male, age 19, business use, principal operator	4.10

2 SELF-REVIEW

Determine the rating factor for the operators described.

A. Adult female, to and from work, over 100 miles .... ______

B. Married male, age 22, business use, occasional operator .... ______

C. Unmarried female, age 23, business use, principal operator ...... ______

D. Unmarried male, age 20, pleasure use, principal operator .... ______

E. Married female, age 21, pleasure use .... ______

A. 1.15
B. 1.80
C. 1.85
D. 3.90
E. 1.00

Note that most insurance companies will *lower* the rating factor for certain individuals if they have had driver training, or if they are good students (B average or better). Also, the rating factor may be *increased* if the driver has an accident or traffic violations.

BASE PREMIUMS

The appropriate **rating factor** is multiplied by a **base premium** to determine the **total premium.** Thus:

Total premium = Rating factor × Base premium

Table 8-6 contains the semiannual base premiums for liability insurance, property damage, and bodily injury. Also included are the base premiums for medical coverage and for both forms of physical damage coverage—comprehensive and collision.

Observe that the physical damage premiums are classified by *age group* and *insurance rating group.* The age group column is related to the age of an automobile—the older the automobile, the *higher* the age group number. The insurance rating group classifies automobiles from 1 to 12. Generally, the higher priced the automobile, the higher the insurance rating group. See Table 8-7 for a partial listing. For illustration:

1. An American Motors 1980 Gremlin is in Age Group 1, Insurance Rating Group 7.
2. A 1977 Volkswagen Rabbit is in Age Group 4, Insurance Rating Group 8.
3. A 1980 Cadillac DeVille is in Age Group 1, Insurance Rating Group 12.

Obviously Table 8-7 is only a partial list of automobiles. An insurance agent would have a list for all vehicles.

TABLE 8-6
Typical State Farm Mutual Automobile Insurance Company Private Passenger Semiannual Base Premiums

	BODILY INJURY AND PROPERTY DAMAGE LIABILITY						MEDICAL PAYMENTS COVERAGE (Broad Form)			
Property Damage Limits	*Bodily Injury Limits (in thousands)*									
	15/30	*25/50*	*25/100*	*50/100*	*100/200*	*100/300*	*$1,000*	*$2,000*	*$3,000*	*$5,000*
10,000	$40.20	$43.20	$45.00	$47.00	$51.00	$51.80	$2.20	$3.20	$3.60	$4.00
25,000	42.00	45.00	46.60	48.80	52.80	53.60				
50,000	43.20	46.20	48.00	50.20	54.00	54.80				

PHYSICAL DAMAGE COVERAGES

Coverage	*Age Group*	*Insurance Rating Group* 1-5	6	7	8	9	10	11	12
Full comprehensive	1	$ 8.00	$ 8.80	$11.00	$14.00	$18.40	$23.80	$29.00	$32.00
	2-3	6.80	7.40	9.40	12.00	15.60	20.20	24.60	27.00
	4-5	6.00	6.60	8.20	10.60	13.80	17.80	21.80	24.00
	6	4.80	5.20	6.60	8.40	11.00	14.20	17.40	19.20
Comprehensive, $50 deductible	1	6.00	6.60	8.20	10.60	13.80	17.80	21.80	24.00
	2-3	5.20	5.60	7.00	9.00	11.80	15.20	18.60	20.40
	4-5	4.60	5.00	6.20	8.00	10.40	13.40	16.40	18.00
	6	3.60	4.00	5.00	6.40	8.20	10.60	13.00	14.40
Collision, $50 deductible	1	36.60	43.00	47.40	56.00	64.60	73.20	81.80	85.80
	2-3	31.20	36.60	40.20	47.60	55.00	62.20	69.60	73.00
	4-5	27.40	32.20	35.60	42.00	48.40	55.00	61.40	64.40
	6	23.80	28.00	30.80	36.40	42.00	47.60	53.20	55.80
Collision, $100 deductible	1	29.20	34.40	37.80	44.80	53.40	62.00	70.60	74.20
	2-3	24.80	29.20	32.20	38.00	45.40	52.80	60.00	63.00
	4-5	22.00	25.80	28.40	33.60	40.00	46.60	53.00	55.60
	6	19.00	22.40	24.60	29.20	34.80	40.40	45.80	48.00

TABLE 8-7. Automobile Age Groups and Insurance Rating Groups for Selected Automobiles

Make	*Model*	*Year*	*Age Group*	*Insurance Rating Group*
American Motors	Gremlin	1980	1	7
	Pacer	1979	2	8
Buick	Apollo	1978	3	8
	Riviera	1979	2	9
Chevrolet	Camaro-Z	1975	6	7
	Estate Wagon	1977	4	11
Ford	Mustang	1980	1	8
	LTD	1976	5	9
	Falcon	1969	6	6
Cadillac	DeVille	1980	1	12
Chrysler	New Yorker	1978	3	12
Datsun	RZ 801	1972	6	5
Volkswagen	Rabbit	1977	4	8

Problem Determine the *semiannual base premium* for a 1980 Ford Mustang if the liability coverage is $10,000 property damage and 50/100 bodily injury, medical payment for $1,000, physical damage coverage of $50 deductible comprehensive and $100 deductible collision.

Solution The 1980 Ford Mustang is in Age Group 1, Insurance Rating Group 8 (from Table 8-7). Using Table 8-6, the premiums are:

Property damage $10,000, 50/100 bodily injury . .	$ 47.00
Medical coverage for $1,000	2.20
Comprehensive, $50 deductible	10.60 ←
Collision, $100 deductible	44.80 ←
Semiannual base premium	$104.60

Vehicle in Age Group 1, Insurance Rating Group 8

Suppose that the driver of the 1980 Ford Mustang had a rating factor of 1.95. The total semiannual premium is found by:

Total semiannual premium = Rating factor × Base premium
= 1.95 × $104.60 = $203.97

3 SELF-REVIEW

Jose Garcia is 24 years old, unmarried, and drives to work each day. He owns a 1980 AMC Gremlin. His insurance coverage is to include $25,000 property damage and 25/100 bodily injury, $3,000 medical coverage, $50 deductible comprehensive, and $100 deductible collision. The total semiannual premium is determined by calculating the semiannual base premiums and rating factor, as follows:

A. Property damage $25,000, 25/100 bodily injury: . . . $_________

B. Medical coverage for $3,000: . . . . $_________

C. Age group of the 1980 Gremlin: ____

Insurance rating group: _____

D. Comprehensive, $50 deductible: . . . . $_________

E. Collision, $100 deductible: . . . . $_________

F. Total semiannual base premium: . . . . $_________

G. Rating factor: _____

H. Total semiannual premium = Rating factor × Base premium
= ______ × $_________ = $__________

A. $46.60
B. $3.60
C. 1; 7
D. $8.20
E. $37.80
F. $96.20
G. 3.10
H. Semiannual premium:
= 3.10 × $96.20
= $298.22

So **it really pays to shop around** for car insurance. Get several quotations; compare the costs, coverages and service; and choose the one that can give you the most for your money.

NO-FAULT AUTO INSURANCE

Many states have some form of **no-fault automobile insurance.** No-fault insurance is based on the premise that the accident victim's actual injury losses should be covered by his or her own insurance company, *regardless of who was at fault.* Thus, it is reasoned that there is no need for a costly lawsuit to determine who was to blame for an accident.

Michigan was one of the first states to pass a no-fault automobile insurance law. Following are some of the highlights of the Michigan no-fault law.

EXHIBIT 8-3

Here's Your Guide to the Michigan No-Fault Law.

It's intended to provide you with a general understanding of the law and tell you how the new law may affect you.

What No-Fault Means To You

In most cases your injury losses covered by the new law will be paid by your own insurance company no matter who causes the accident.

In addition, the law requires everyone who owns a car, truck, bus or trailer to have insurance. If you don't, you can be fined $500, jailed for one year and lose your driver's license and license plates. To get your Michigan license plates, you must prove you have insurance.

Vehicles Covered By The Michigan No-Fault Law.

Any motor vehicle required to be registered in Michigan is covered by the law. "Motor Vehicle" means a vehicle with more than two wheels, operated or designed for operation on a public highway by power other than muscular.

Vehicles Not Covered by the Michigan No-Fault Law.

Motor Vehicles not covered are those not required to be licensed under the laws of Michigan and two-wheeled motorcycles (including sidecars).

Required Coverage.

Bodily Injury Liability—with limits of at least $20,000 per person and $40,000 per accident. We encourage anyone with minimum limits to increase them.

Property Damage Liability—with limits of at least $10,000 per accident. *Your* policy will now provide a limit of $100,000 per accident. The $100,000 limit is the only one we offer. However, the $100,000 protection will cost you no more than what you previously paid for $10,000 limits.

Personal Protection Insurance—a new No-Fault coverage which is described below.

Property Protection Insurance—another new coverage—also described below.

Personal Protection Insurance

This "No-Fault" protection provides payment, for you and members of your family living with you, for injuries received in a covered auto accident anywhere in the U.S. or Canada. We pay you the following benefits regardless of who was at fault.

- *Medical Expenses*—Pays all reasonable expenses for medical treatment, hospital services and rehabilitation services that result from injuries received in a covered auto accident. There is no limit to the dollar amount or to the length of time expenses may be incurred.
- *Work Loss*—Pays 85% of wages or salary lost. If you can show proof of a lower tax advantage, a greater percentage of your wage loss will be paid. Also pays up to $20 a day when someone must be hired to perform duties the injured person would normally do for himself or his dependents if he were not injured.

  These two combined work loss benefits extend up to a period of three years after the accident, and are subject to a maximum of $1,000 per 30 day period.
- *Survivors' Loss*—Pays an eligible insured person's dependent survivors for services and support that would have been provided by the deceased person. Pays up to $1,000 a month . . . for up to three years after the accident occurred.
- *Funeral Expenses*—Pays a maximum benefit of $1,000.

Personal Protection benefits are not payable when an injury is intentionally caused.

ASSIGNMENT 8-3
AUTOMOBILE INSURANCE

Name ______________________ Date Due ______________ Grade ______

Answers to selected problems are given in Appendix B.

For Problems 1 through 6, use Table 8-5.

	Sex	*Age*	*Marital Status*	*Automobile Use*	*Principal/Occasional Operator if Applicable*	*Rating Factor*
Ex.	M	23	Married	To and from work	Not applicable	1.45
1.	F	20	Unmarried	Pleasure	Occasional	______
2.	F	27	Unmarried	Business use	Not applicable	______
3.	M	53	Unmarried	125 miles weekly to and from work	Not applicable	______
4.	M	22	Unmarried	Farm automobile	Principal	______
5.	F	23	Married	Pleasure	Not applicable	______
6.	M	27	Unmarried	Pleasure	Principal	______

For Problems 7 through 12, complete the table.

	Automobile	*Age Group*	*Ins. Rating Group*	*Property Damage*	*Bodily Injury*	*Premium*	*Medical Payment*	*Premium*	*Comprehensive*	*Premium*	*Collision*	*Premium*	*Semiannual Base Premium*
Ex.	77 Chev. Estate Wagon	4	11	$25,000	25/50	$45.00	$3,000	$3.60	Full	$21.80	$50 ded.	$61.40	$131.80
7.	79 Buick Riviera			50,000	100/300		5,000		Full		$50 ded.		
8.	80 AMC Gremlin			10,000	15/30		1,000		$50 ded.		$100 ded.		
9.	72 Datsun			25,000	50/100		2,000		None		None		
10.	69 Ford Falcon			10,000	25/100		1,000		None		None		
11.	80 Ford Mustang			50,000	100/200		5,000		$50 ded.		$100 ded.		
12.	78 Chrysler New Yorker			25,000	50/100		3,000		Full		$50 ded.		

For Problems 13 through 16, use Table 8-5.

13. Janet Nichols, female, age 19, is unmarried and drives her own car (principal operator) to and from work. What is her rating factor?

____

14. Kent Sloan, male, age 21, is unmarried and drives the family car (occasional operator) for pleasure. What is his rating factor?

____

15. Terri Graves, female, age 22, is married and drives the family car (occasional operator) for pleasure. What is her rating factor?

____

16. Don Soldwich, male, age 25, is married and drives the family car to and from work (principal operator) a weekly total distance of 80 miles? What is his rating factor?

____

17. Determine the semiannual base premium for a 1979 Buick Riviera if the liability coverage is $50,000 property damage and $100,000/ $200,000 bodily injury, medical payment for $3,000, physical damage coverage of full comprehensive and $50 deductible collision.

$__________, found by

18. Determine the semiannual base premium for a 1977 VW Rabbit if the liability coverage is $25,000 property damage and $25,000/ $100,000 bodily injury, medical payment for $2,000, physical damage coverage of $50 deductible comprehensive, and $50 deductible collision.

$__________, found by

19. An unmarried male operator, William Vickers, age 20, is the occasional operator, driving for pleasure, of a 1978 Buick Apollo. His insurance coverage is to include $50,000 property damage and $100,000/ $300,000 bodily injury, $1,000 medical payment coverage, $50 deductible comprehensive, and $100 deductible collision.

A. What is his rating factor? ________

B. What are the age and insurance rating groups of the 78 Buick Apollo? ________ ________

Find the semiannual base premiums for:

C. Bodily injury and property damage: $__________

D. Medical payments coverage: $__________

E. $50 deductible comprehensive: $__________

F. $100 deductible collision: $__________

G. What is the semiannual base premium? $__________

H. What is the total semiannual premium? $__________

20. Alice Robie is under 21 years of age, unmarried, and is the principal operator of her 1976 Ford LTD, which she uses for business. Her insurance coverage is to include $50,000 property damage and $50,000/$100,000 bodily injury, $5,000 medical payments coverage, $50 deductible comprehensive, and $100 deductible collision. What is her total semiannual premium?

$__________, found by

REVIEW ASSIGNMENT FOR CHAPTER 8
INSURANCE

Name ______________________ Date Due ______________ Grade _____

1. When the Hazeltines retired to Florida, they purchased this \$67,500 home. They insured the home for 70% of its replacement value. The company has an 80% coinsurance clause.

ANTIQUED BRICK—Home has 2,607 sq. ft., 3 bedrooms, 3 baths. Living room/vaulted ceiling, brick fireplace, large game room adjoining full bath. Could be a nice mother-in-law suite. Close to campus. \$67,500. HL 046.

   A. What amount of insurance did they buy?

   \$__________, found by

   B. How much is their insurance on private structures?

   \$__________, found by

   C. How much is their insurance for personal property?

   \$__________, found by

   D. How much is their insurance for additional living expenses?

   \$__________, found by

   E. How much would the company pay on a damage claim of \$2,400?

   \$__________

2. The Johnsons insured their home for \$70,000. Their home is brick (masonry or masonry veneer) and located in Protection Class 4. What is the annual premium?

   \$__________, found by

3. The Clarks insured their masonry veneer home, which has a replacement value of \$50,000, for 80% of its replacement value. The Clarks live in a rural area without fire hydrants, but with a good fire department within six miles. What is their annual insurance premium?

   \$__________, found by

4. Tom Miller, male, age 45, took out an endowment at age 65 life insurance policy for \$20,000.

   A. What is his annual premium?

   \$____________, found by

   B. Why would his annual premium on a \$20,000 20-year endowment policy be the same?

   ____

5. What is the *monthly* premium on a \$40,000 10-year term policy written on a female, 29 years of age?

   \$__________, found by

6. What is the *quarterly* premium on a \$30,000 straight life policy written on a male, 35 years of age?

   \$__________, found by

7. Lutheran Brotherhood (an insurance company) uses 50.8% for semiannual payment of premiums, 25.7% for quarterly payment, and 8.7% for monthly payments. At these rates, how much can be saved per year by paying the premiums on a $20,000 term to age 65 policy for a 50-year-old female annually rather than monthly?

   $________, found by

8. Beth Spencer, married, female, age 22, drives her 1975 Chevrolet Camaro-Z to and from work over 100 miles per week. What is her rating factor?

   ____

9. Find Beth Spencer's semiannual base premium on her 1975 Chevrolet Camaro-Z if she desires $50,000 property damage, 50/100 bodily injury, $2,000 medical payments coverage, $50 deductible comprehensive, and $100 deductible collision.

   $________, found by

10. Find the semiannual premium for automobile insurance for James Lindren, age 66, who drives his 1966 Rambler for pleasure. He only has $10,000 property damage and 15/30 bodily injury coverage.

   $________, found by

11. Find the semiannual premium for car insurance for a 23-year-old unmarried female who drives her car (principal operator) for pleasure. Her car is a 1979 AMC Pacer, and her coverage is $25,000 property damage, $50,000/$100,000 bodily injury, $2,000 medical payments coverage, full comprehensive, and $50 deductible collision.

   $________, found by

12. Bill Roberts, 19-year-old male, unmarried, drives his 1977 VW Rabbit to and from work. He is the principal operator. He has $50,000 property damage, 100/200 bodily injury, $5,000 medical payments coverage, $50 deductible comprehensive, and $100 deductible collision. What is his semiannual premium?

   $________, found by

TO THE STUDENT: There is a SELF-REVIEW TEST for this chapter in Appendix A, *with answers* in Appendix C.

9

Income and Deductions

SECTION 9-1: INCOME

Objective: To compute gross pay using hourly wages, salary, commission, or incentive pay plans.

Ford Motor Co. Chairman Henry Ford II was paid $992,420 in 1977 while his counterpart at General Motors Corp., Thomas A. Murphy, made $975,000 in salary, bonuses, and stocks, according to proxy statements released Friday by the two auto giants.

Using charge accounts, paying insurance premiums, and buying automobiles and houses all require that the purchaser have some form of income. Being employed by a firm represents one possible source of income. An employee may earn money under a variety of plans, including **hourly wages, salary, commission,** or **incentive plans.** Total earnings are classified as **gross pay.** Various amounts are usually subtracted from gross pay, with the most common being for social security contributions; federal, state, and local income taxes; medical insurance; and union dues. These amounts are referred to as **deductions.** When deductions are subtracted from gross pay, the resulting amount is called **net pay,** or **take-home pay.**

GROSS PAY: HOURLY WAGES

For hourly employees who work a *standard* workweek (generally 40 hours), the usual way of computing *gross pay* is to multiply the number of hours worked times the hourly wage rate.

$$\text{Gross pay} = \text{Hours worked} \times \text{Rate per hour}$$

Problem Fraizer Reems was hired for the cashier's job advertized. Determine his gross pay for a week in which he worked (A) 40 hours; (B) 35 hours.

CASHIER — Count, prove cash, must have good head for figures and heavy lifting ability. Congenial office. $4/hr. plus benefits. Call LIBRA EMPLOYMENT SERVICES, 335 N. Superior, 243-5236.

Solution A. Gross pay for 40 hours is $160, found by:

$$\begin{aligned}\text{Gross pay} &= \text{Hours worked} \times \text{Rate per hour}\\ &= 40 \times \$4.00\\ &= \$160.00\end{aligned}$$

B. Gross pay for 35 hours is $140, found by:

$$\begin{aligned}\text{Gross pay} &= \text{Hours worked} \times \text{Rate per hour}\\ &= 35 \times \$4.00\\ &= \$140.00\end{aligned}$$

An employee who works more than the standard work day or week is normally paid **overtime pay.** Overtime work is usually rewarded with an excess (premium) amount based on the employee's hourly rate. Quite often it is stated as *time-and-a-half* pay, but it might be *double-time* or even *triple-time* pay for all hours worked over 40 hours a week. In some cases it is paid on all hours worked over eight hours a day.

Problem Suppose Reems, who earns $4 per hour, with time and a half for overtime hours past 40 a week, works 50 hours during the week of October 6. What is his gross pay for the week?

Solution Gross pay may be determined two ways:

Using a calculator with memory (wage-earner view):

Enter	Press	Display
40	×	40
4	= m+	160
10	×	10
1.5	×	15
4	= +	60
	RM	160
	=	220

A. Wage earner's view:

Regular workweek:	
40 X $4	$160
Plus overtime earnings:	
10 X 1.5 X $4	60
Gross pay	$220

B. Management view:

Earnings at regular rate:	
50 X $4	$200
Overtime excess pay:	
10 X 0.5 X $4	20
Gross pay	$220

The management view specifically identifies the *extra* or *overtime excess pay* that is being paid by the company to have an employee work *overtime.*

1 SELF-REVIEW

A reminder: Cover the answers in the margin.

An electronics manufacturer pays $5.80 an hour, with time and a half for all hours over 40 hours a week. If an employee worked 48 hours one week, find the:

A. 40 × $5.80 = $232.00
plus
Overtime earnings, found by
8 × 1.5 × $5.80 = $69.60
Gross pay = $301.60

A. Gross pay using the *wage earner's view.*

Earnings for the regular workweek: ______ (Hours) X $______ (Hourly rate) = $______

Plus
Overtime earnings: ______ (Overtime hours) X ______ (Overtime factor) X $______ (Hourly earnings) = $______

Gross weekly pay = $______

B. 48 × $5.80 = $278.40
plus
8 × 0.5 × $5.80 = $23.20
Gross pay = $301.60

B. Gross pay using the *management view.*

Earnings at the regular rate: ______ (Total hours worked) X $______ (Regular rate) = $______

Plus
Overtime excess earnings: ______ (Excess hours) X ______ (Overtime excess factor) X $______ (Hourly earnings) = $______

Gross weekly pay = $______

GROSS PAY: SALARY

Managers, middle managers, and professional personnel are usually paid a fixed annual amount called a **salary.** The pay period may be monthly (12 times a year), semimonthly (24 times a year), biweekly (26 times a year), or weekly (52 times a year).

Problem

Rose Newland applied for the position of chief accountant advertised. If she is hired at $15,000 a year, find how much she would receive as gross pay each paycheck if she is paid: (A) monthly; (B) semimonthly; (C) biweekly; (D) weekly.

★
CHIEF ACCOUNTANT
ASSISTANT to comptroller for construction company. Fully bi-lingual. Salary commensurate to experience up to $15,000. CPA will interview Send resume to Herald News Adv 2160A

Solution

A. Monthly gross pay is $1,250, found by:

$$\text{Monthly pay} = \frac{\text{Annual pay}}{12} = \frac{\$15{,}000}{12} = \$1{,}250$$

B. Semimonthly gross pay is $625, found by:

$$\text{Semimonthly pay} = \frac{\text{Annual pay}}{24} = \frac{\$15{,}000}{24} = \$625$$

C. $$\text{Biweekly pay} = \frac{\text{Annual pay}}{26} = \frac{\$15{,}000}{26} = \$576.92$$

D. $$\text{Weekly pay} = \frac{\text{Annual pay}}{52} = \frac{\$15{,}000}{52} = \$288.46$$

ENGINEER: project........ $18-26,000
CHECKER: dimensions.... $12-21,000
LIAISON: service............. $21-18,000
SUPERVISOR: shift......... $13-16,000
INSPECTOR: machine...... $13-15,000
COORDINATOR: time...... $10-14,000
all salaried fee paid
SNELLING & SNELLING
WORLD's LARGEST

2 SELF-REVIEW

Carlos Ortega was hired for the sales manager position advertised. Determine his gross pay if he is:

WORLDWIDE SALES
Assist Senior Sales Manager for International Equipment firm, $11,000. Call Paul Collins at 940-1141, David Wood Personnel, 2020 NE 163rd St NMB

A. Paid monthly.

$$\text{Monthly pay} = \frac{\text{Annual pay}}{\quad} = \frac{\$11{,}000}{\quad} = \$\_\_\_\_\_\_$$

B. Paid semimonthly.

$$\text{Semimonthly pay} = \frac{\text{Annual pay}}{\quad} = \frac{\$11{,}000}{\quad} = \$\_\_\_\_\_\_$$

C. Paid biweekly.

$$\text{Biweekly pay} = \frac{\text{Annual pay}}{\quad} = \frac{\$11{,}000}{\quad} = \$\_\_\_\_\_\_$$

D. Paid weekly.

$$\text{Weekly pay} = \frac{\text{Annual pay}}{\quad} = \frac{\$11{,}000}{\quad} = \$\_\_\_\_\_\_$$

A. Monthly pay:

$$= \frac{\text{Annual pay}}{12} = \frac{\$11{,}000}{12} = \$916.67$$

B. Semimonthly pay:

$$= \frac{\text{Annual pay}}{24} = \frac{\$11{,}000}{24} = \$458.33$$

C. Biweekly pay:

$$= \frac{\text{Annual pay}}{26} = \frac{\$11{,}000}{26} = \$423.08$$

D. Weekly pay:

$$= \frac{\text{Annual pay}}{52} = \frac{\$11{,}000}{52} = \$211.54$$

GROSS PAY: COMMISSION

Employees involved in a selling capacity are quite often paid a commission. The **commission** may be a fixed amount for each item sold, or it may be a percent of the dollar value of the item sold.

Straight Commission. When a salesperson is paid *only* a commission, he or she is working on what is called straight commission. This commission is found by two methods.

Method 1: Commission paid is based on quantity sold.

Commission = Rate of commission X Quantity sold

Problem Jim Morrison works on straight commission. He receives 65 cents commission on each book he sells. He sold 40 books during the day. What is his commission?

Solution

Commission = Rate of commission X Quantity sold
= \$0.65 X 40
= \$26.00

Method 2: Commission paid is based on the value of goods sold.

Commission = Rate of commission X Value of sales

Problem Helen Watson works on straight commission as a real estate salesperson. The commission rate is 2½%. She sold property for \$40,200. What is her commission?

Solution

Commission = Rate of commission X Value of sales
= 2½% X \$40,200
= \$1,005

3 SELF-REVIEW

A. (1) 32 × \$0.55 = \$17.60
(2) 11 × \$1.15 = \$12.65
(3) 64 × \$0.85 = \$54.40
(4) Total comm. = \$84.65

A. Bob Carr sells cards, stationery, and books for Ace Door-to-Door Sales. He receives 55 cents for each box of cards, \$1.15 for each "memo pad," and 85 cents for each child's coloring book. Complete the following:

(1) Commission for 32 boxes of cards is: 32 X \$______ = \$________

(2) Commission for 11 memo pads is: ____ X \$______ = \$________

(3) Commission for 64 coloring books is: ____ X \$______ = \$________

(4) Total commission is: \$________

B. (1) Commission:
= 40% × \$95.00
= \$38.00

(2) Commission:
= 40% × \$128.50
= \$51.40

B. Laura Weissenberger sells cosmetics for Avon, Inc. She receives a straight commission of 40% on most items. What is her commission for a week in which she sells:

(1) \$95 worth of merchandise

Commission = ____% X \$________
= \$________

(2) \$128.50 worth of merchandise

Commission = ____% X \$________
= \$________

Salary Plus Commission. Some salespersons are paid a salary or an hourly rate called a *guarantee* or *base, plus* a commission on the value of goods sold.

Problem Lester Archila sells clothing for Hughes & Hatcher. He is guaranteed \$3.50 per hour plus 6% commission. What is his gross pay for a week in which he worked 50 hours and sold \$1,450 worth of clothing?

Solution

Gross pay = Hourly wages + Commission
= (50 × \$3.50) + (6% × \$1,450)
= \$175 + \$87
= \$262

Minimum Salary or Commission. Some companies pay their salespersons a minimum salary, often called a *draw,* or a straight commission, *whichever is greater.*

Problems A salesperson at Wards is guaranteed a minimum of \$135 a week, or a 6% commission on all sales, whichever is greater. Determine Lillie Laver's gross pay for a week in which she had sales of (A) \$2,100; (B) \$4,260.

Solutions

A. Week with sales of \$2,100.

Commission = 6% of \$2,100
= \$126

She would be paid \$135 because it is greater than the commission of \$126.

B. Week with sales of \$4,260.

Commission = 6% of \$4,260
= \$255.60

She would be paid \$255.60 commission because it is greater than the draw of \$135.

4 SELF-REVIEW

A. A salesperson for Steins is paid \$2.60 per hour, plus 3% commission. What is the gross pay for a week in which 39 hours were worked and sales were \$465?

Gross pay = Hourly wages + Commission
= (____ × \$_______) + (____% × \$_________)
= \$_________ + \$________
= \$_________

A. (39 × \$2.60) + (3% × \$465)
= \$101.40 + \$13.95
= \$115.35

B. Suppose the salesperson for Steins is paid a 6% commission on all sales or \$100 per week, whichever is greater. Determine the gross pay for a week with sales of (1) \$1,300; (2) \$3,800.

(1) Sales of \$1,300

Commission = ____% × \$_________
= \$_________

Salesperson would be paid \$________ because

____

(2) Sales of \$3,800

Commission = ____% × \$_________
= \$_________

Salesperson would be paid \$________ because

____

B. (1) Commission:
= 6% × \$1,300
= \$78.00

Paid: \$100, because \$100 is greater than \$78

(2) Commission:
= 6% × \$3,800
= \$228

Paid: \$228, because \$228 greater than \$100

INCENTIVE PAY

Many payroll plans are designed to provide incentive pay for employees to work harder, sell more, or produce more. Commission on sales is an incentive plan. One plan based on the productivity of the individual is called the Gantt Task and Bonus Plan. Under this plan a designated output per time period is agreed upon between labor and management. This output is referred to as the *task* and is usually established by time and motion studies. If a person performs at *less than task,* only hourly wages are paid. However, if an employee performs *at or more than task,* then a *bonus* is paid.

If task is equaled or exceeded, wages are found by multiplying the incentive factor times hourly rate times hours worked times the ratio of production to task:

$$\text{Wages} = \text{Incentive factor} \times \text{Hourly rate} \times \text{Hours} \times \frac{\text{Production}}{\text{Task}}$$

Problem John Anspach has a daily task during an eight-hour period of assembling 96 calculators. If he assembles 96 or more calculators, he qualifies for the bonus, which has an incentive factor of 120%. What are his wages for an eight-hour day in which he assembles 112 calculators? He earns $4.25 an hour.

Solution

$$\begin{aligned}\text{Wages} &= \text{Incentive factor} \times \text{Hourly rate} \times \text{Hours} \times \frac{\text{Production}}{\text{Task}}\\ &= 120\% \times \$4.25 \times 8 \times \frac{112}{96}\\ &= \$47.60\end{aligned}$$

Note for comparison that his daily pay for less than 96 calculators is $34.

5 SELF-REVIEW

Refer to the previous problem. Suppose that Anspach assembled 124 calculators in an eight-hour period. What would he earn?

$$\begin{aligned}\text{Wages} &= \text{Incentive factor} \times \text{Hourly rate} \times \text{Hours} \times \frac{\text{Production}}{\text{Task}}\\ &= \_\_\_\_ \times \$\_\_\_\_ \times \_\_\_ \times \frac{\_\_\_}{96}\\ &= \$\_\_\_\_\end{aligned}$$

$$\begin{aligned}&= 1.20 \times \$4.25 \times 8 \times \frac{124}{96}\\ &= \$52.70\end{aligned}$$

ASSIGNMENT 9-1
INCOME

Name ______________________________ Date Due ______________ Grade _____

Answers to selected problems are given in Appendix B.

For Problems 1 through 6, compute gross pay if time and a half is paid for over 40 hours per week.

	Hourly Wage Rate	Hours Worked	*Wage Earner's View* Regular Workweek	*Wage Earner's View* Overtime	*Management View* Earnings at Regular Rate	*Management View* Overtime Excess	Gross Pay
Ex.	$4.70	45	$188.00	$35.25	$211.50	$11.75	$223.25
1.	3.25	39	________	________	________	________	________
2.	2.90	40	________	________	________	________	________
3.	4.50	45	________	________	________	________	________
4.	5.10	43	________	________	________	________	________
5.	3.75	51	________	________	________	________	________
6.	5.37	49	________	________	________	________	________

7. Michelle Trabert worked for the J. C. Penney Company over Christmas vacation. Calculate her gross pay.

   $________, found by

SOCIAL SECURITY NUMBER	RATE OF PAY	REG HOURS	OVER TIME HRS	OTHER HOURS	REG EARNINGS	OVERTIME EARNINGS	OTHER EARNINGS DESCRIPTION	OTHER EARNINGS AMOUNT	GROSS EARNINGS
999 54 0927	3.4000	170							

8. David Turner works for the Pilliod Cabinet Company. He earns $4.04 per hour. What is his gross pay for a week in which he worked 40 hours?

   $__________, found by

9. Carmel Pigliotti earns \$3.30 per hour working for Lasalles. She earns time and a half for overtime (over eight hours per day). Find:

A. Regular earnings. \$________, found by

B. Overtime earnings. \$________, found by

C. Gross pay. \$________, found by

EMP. NO.	HOURS		EARNINGS										GROSS PAY
	REG.	O.T.	REG.	O.T.	COMMISSION	PM'S	SICK PAY	HOLIDAY	VACATION	MISC.	MEALS GRATUITIES		
35691	19.25	6.50	(A)	(B)									(C)

10. Joan Lowe is a teller for the Huntington Bank. She earns \$3.75 per hour, with time and a half for over 40 hours per week. She is paid biweekly. Find her biweekly:

A. Earnings at the regular rate.

\$__________, found by

B. Overtime excess pay.

\$__________, found by

C. Gross pay.

\$__________, found by

REGULAR HOURS	80.0	O.T. 1 HOURS	2.5

EARNINGS		DEDUC
REGULAR O.T.	rate (A) excess (B)	
TOTAL EARNINGS	\$(C)	TOTAL DEDU

JEAN LOWE

PERIOD ENDING	10 31	ACCOUNT NO.	4170237

For Problems 11 through 16, find the weekly, biweekly, semimonthly, monthly, and annual salaries.

	Position	*Weekly*	*Biweekly*	*Semimonthly*	*Monthly*	*Annual*
Ex.	Clerk	\$156	\$312	\$338	\$676	\$ 8,112
11.	GM chairman	______	______	______	______	975,000
12.	Ford Motor Co. chairman	______	______	______	______	992,420
13.	Manager, Forum Cafeteria	______	______	______	900	______
14.	Hess Oil Co. salaried manager	______	______	725	______	______
15.	Idaho Edison Co. office manager	______	450	______	______	______
16.	Texas school-teacher	312	______	______	______	______

17. Calculate the biweekly and semimonthly salary for this marketing position advertised in the *London Sunday Times* (p.a. means per annum).

We require two experienced and keen personnel to join our export team marketing high quality lighting and transmission poles throughout North Africa and the Middle East. General Sales Marketing or Technical Design Knowledge and Qualification or French speaking should be offered as prequalification. Although our Export Drive is directed from Madrid Spanish is not necessary. Attractive Working conditions and a salary of £10,000 p.a. tax free are offered

A. Biweekly, £__________, found by

B. Semimonthly, £__________, found by

18. Assume you answer the *New York Times* ad for a watchman. You are to be paid semimonthly. What is your gross pay?

WATCHMAN m/f
36 hrs. 6 nights, \$106/wk 11pm-5am.
See Supt 305 W 45 St 10am-4pm M-F

\$__________, found by

For Problems 19 through 24, complete the table.

	Position	Pay Plan	Hours Worked	Sales	Hourly Wages		Commission	Gross Pay
Ex.	Thom McCann shoe sales	$2.65/hr. + 3% commission	36	$ 970.00	$95.40	+	$29.10	$124.50
19.	Discount Promo, Inc.	$0.50 per book of tickets	—	87 books			________	________
20.	Direct hosiery mill sales	6% straight commission	—	$ 732.00			________	________
21.	K-G Men's Store	$3.75/hr. + 3½% commission	70	2,410.00	________	+	________	________
22.	dba Violets	$3.10/hr. + 5% commission	40	1,072.00	________	+	________	________
23.	Wards	$3.375/hr. or 6% comm., whichever is greater	40	2,435.00	________	or	________	________
24.	Chemical industrial sales	$5.20/hr. or 5.5% comm., whichever is greater	152	13,979.80	________	or	________	________

25. Pete Sahadi took this sales job advertised in the *Los Angeles Times.* He was guaranteed $3.20/hr. plus 4% commission. Find his gross pay for a week in which he worked 50 hours and had $120 in sales.

    $__________, found by

> SALES Ind. Prods. Telephone
> **$300/WEEK & UP**
> GUARANTEE & COMM.
> Young aggressive company now hiring management trainees—no exp. nec.—full training—age no barrier. 3 shifts avail. AM, afternoon, PM. Canoga Park loc. Xlnt. work cond. Mr. Long for info.
> 213/347-4882

26. Markheims pays salesclerks $2.95 an hour or 6½% commission, whichever is greater. Determine the gross pay for a clerk who worked 40 hours one week and had $1,300 in sales.

    $__________, found by

27. A labor-management contract for a local manufacturer specifies the Gantt Task and Bonus Plan for certain production jobs. On one job task is set at 240 units per eight-hour shift. The bonus is 130%. An employee earning $4.80 an hour will have what gross pay if the following number of units is produced?

    A. 200. $________, found by B. 240. $________, found by C. 288. $________, found by

28. Assume the Gantt Task and Bonus Plan applies. Task is 200 subassemblies; the bonus is 140%; the hourly rate is $4.20. Find the gross pay for an eight-hour day in which the following number of subassemblies is produced.

    A. 200. $________, found by B. 240. $________, found by C. 288. $________, found by

SECTION 9-2: DEDUCTIONS

Objective: To calculate social security (FICA) and federal income tax deductions, and net pay.

Taxes, in the form of federal income tax and social security tax, make up the main deductions from gross pay. Some other common deductions are for:

State income tax	Dental insurance	Unemployment insurance
City income tax	Union dues	Disability insurance
Retirement	Charity	Stocks and bonds
Medical insurance	Uniforms	Savings bonds
Hospitalization	Credit union	

Deductions are subtracted from gross pay to arrive at net pay. Thus:

Net pay = Gross pay − Deductions

Problem Linda Chase, a clerk-typist, earned \$4.50 per hour and worked a 40-hour week. Determine her net pay if she had five deductions from her gross pay.

Solution Deductions:

Federal income tax	\$25.00
Social security tax	11.03
City income tax	2.70
State income tax	1.50
Credit union	15.00
Total deductions	\$55.23

Then: Net pay = Gross pay − Deductions
= (40 × \$4.50) − \$55.23
= \$180 − \$55.23
= \$124.77

1 SELF-REVIEW

Boyd Cayne was hired as an installer at a wage of \$5.80 per hour. His first week he worked 36 hours and had the following deductions: federal income tax, \$24.70; social security tax, \$12.80; union dues, \$9.00; and medical insurance, \$17.50. Determine his net pay.

INSTALLERS
NO LAYOFFS NO STRIKES
Start with a clean slate, due to expansion we need people with no experience, many jobs available in installation sales and service dept. Call Tues.-Wed. Mr. Sawyers
up to
\$6.63 Per Hr.
475-4602

Total deductions are found by:

Federal tax	\$________
Social security	________
Union dues	________
Medical insurance	________
Total deductions . .	\$________

Then:

Net pay = Gross pay − Deductions
= (36 × \$________) − \$________
= \$________ − \$________
= \$________

Federal tax	\$24.70
Social security	12.80
Union dues	9.00
Medical insurance . . .	17.50
Total	\$64.00

Net pay:
= (36 × \$5.80) − \$64.00
= \$208.80 − \$64.00
= \$144.80

FEDERAL INSURANCE CONTRIBUTIONS ACT (FICA) OR SOCIAL SECURITY

Social security, technically known as the **Federal Insurance Contributions Act** (abbreviated FICA), began as a modest retirement plan in 1937. It has expanded into a giant pension and insurance network that currently collects FICA or social security taxes from over 100 million workers in the United States. Nearly one out of every seven persons in the United States receives a monthly social security check.

Table 9-1 gives the maximum yearly wage subject to social security tax, the maximum tax, and the rate of taxation for an employer and employee as well as for self-employed persons.

The social security tax deduction is found by multiplying the tax rate times gross pay (up to the maximum yearly wage subject to tax).

Social security tax = Tax rate X Gross pay ← Up to maximum yearly wage subject to tax

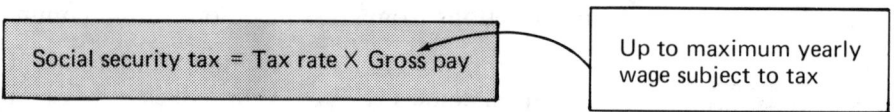

Problem Frank DeWitt has gross earnings the week of January 15, 1979, of $372.50. How much will be deducted from his gross pay for social security?

Solution

Social security tax = Tax rate X Gross pay
= 6.13% X $372.50
= 0.0613 X $372.50
= $22.83 (rounded to nearest cent)

Note that both the employee and the employer pay the tax. In the above problem DeWitt would have $22.83 deducted from his pay, and his employer would contribute another $22.83.

2 SELF-REVIEW

Refer to the previous problem. Suppose that DeWitt earned $19,370 in 1979.

A. $1,187.38
Tax rate X Gross pay
= 6.13% X $19,370
= 0.0613 X $19,370
= $1,187.381
= $1,187.38

A. His social security tax for the year is $__________, found by:

Social security tax = Tax rate X ________ pay
= ______% X $__________
= 0.______ X $__________
= $1,187.381
= $__________ (rounded to nearest cent)

B. $1,187.38

B. His employer would also contribute $__________ in social security taxes for DeWitt.

C. $22,900

C. Table 9-1 shows the maximum wage subject to tax in 1979 is $__________.

D. $1,403.77

D. Suppose DeWitt earned $24,000 in 1979. His social security tax for the year would be $__________, found by either looking in Table 9-1 or taking 6.13% of $22,900.

In Table 9-1 the maximums apply to a single employer. A person who works for more than one employer may pay more than the maximum for the year. In that case a refund can be applied for in the person's federal income tax return. The employers are not entitled to refunds.

For illustration: In 1979, Peter March earned $14,500 working on his regular job for Acme Corporation and $9,300 working part time and weekends for Bender Tool Company. The social security tax withheld by each company is:

TABLE 9-1
Social Security Taxes for Selected Periods

Year	Maximum Yearly Wage Subject to Tax	Tax Rate	Maximum Tax	Self-Employed Tax Rate	Self-Employed Maximum Tax
1975	$14,100	5.85%	$ 824.85	7.90%	$1,113.90
1976	15,300	5.85	895.05	7.90	1,208.70
1977	16,500	5.85	965.25	7.90	1,303.50
1978	17,700	6.05	1,070.85	8.10	1,433.70
1979	22,900	6.13	1,403.77	8.10	1,854.90
1980	25,900	6.13	1,587.67	8.10	2,097.90
1981	29,700	6.65	1,975.05	9.30	2,762.10
1982	31,800	6.70	2,130.60	9.35	2,973.30
1983	33,900*	6.70	2,271.30*	9.35	3,169.65*
1984	36,000*	6.70	2,412.00*	9.35	3,366.00*
1985	38,100*	7.05	2,686.05*	9.90	3,771.90*
1986	40,200*	7.15	2,874.30*	10.00	4,020.00*
1987	42,600*	7.15	3,045.90*	10.00	4,260.00*

*Denotes estimates.
Source: Department of the Treasury, Internal Revenue Service.

Acme Corporation withheld:	$ 888.85,	found by 6.13% of $14,500
Bender Tool withheld:	570.09,	found by 6.13% of $9,300
Total withheld:	$1,458.94	
Maximum tax:	-1,403.71	(from Table 9-1 or 6.13% of $22,900)
Overpayment:	$ 55.17	

March is entitled to a refund of $55.17. He would claim $55.17 as a tax credit on his 1979 federal income tax return.

3 SELF-REVIEW

In 1978 Sam Doebler earned $15,800 working for R&R Chemical Company and $3,400 working part time for Party Time Carryouts. The social security tax withheld by each employer is:

A. R&R Chemical Company withheld: $________, found by 6.05% of $________

B. Party Time Carryouts withheld: ________, found by 6.05% of $________

C. Total withheld: $________

D. Maximum tax: ________ (from Table 9-1, or ________% of $17,700)

E. Overpayment: $________

F. How can he get a refund of his overpayment? ________________________________

Answers:

A. 6.05% × $15,800 = $955.90

B. 6.05% × $3,400 = $205.70

C. $1,161.60

D. $1,070.85 or 6.05% × $17,700

E. $90.75

F. Claim $90.75 as a tax credit on his 1978 federal income tax return.

FEDERAL INCOME TAX (FIT)

The graduated income tax is one of the main sources of federal monies. The process of determining the amount of tax to be withheld from an employee's paycheck begins with the employee filing a withholding certificate, referred to as Form W-4, with the employer (see Exhibit 9-1). It identifies the employee's name, address, social security number, marital status, and number of allowances.

In the following discussion, for all practical purposes allowances, exemptions, and number of dependents are the same. The federal government has a number of qualifications that must be met for an individual to qualify as a dependent. For example, the dependent must receive over half of his or her support from the employee and receive less than $750 income (unless under 19 or a full-time student). For further information see Internal Revenue Service, *Employer's Tax Guide,* Circular E, Pub. 15.

EXHIBIT 9-1
Employee's Withholding Allowance Certificate

Form **W-4**
(Rev. May 1977)
Department of the Treasury
Internal Revenue Service

Employee's Withholding Allowance Certificate
(Use for Wages Paid After May 31, 1977)
This certificate is for income tax withholding purposes only. It will remain in effect until you change it. If you claim exemption from withholding, you will have to file a new certificate on or before April 30 of next year.

Type or print your full name	Your social security number
Home address (number and street or rural route)	Marital Status: ☐ Single ☐ Married ☐ Married, but withhold at higher Single rate
City or town, State, and ZIP code	Note: *If married, but legally separated, or spouse is a nonresident alien, check the single block.*

1 Total number of allowances you are claiming . . . .
2 Additional amount, if any, you want deducted from each pay (if your employer agrees) . . . . $
3 I claim exemption from withholding (see instructions). Enter "Exempt" . . . .

Under the penalties of perjury, I certify that the number of withholding exemptions and allowances claimed on this certificate does not exceed the number to which I am entitled. If claiming exemption from withholding, I certify that I incurred no liability for Federal income tax for last year and that I anticipate that I will incur no liability for Federal income tax for this year.

Signature ▶ .... Date ▶ ...., 19......

Source: Department of the Teasury, Internal Revenue Service, Publication 15 (supplement), May 1977.

There are basically two methods of determining FIT withholding—the **percentage method** and the **wage-bracket table method.**

PERCENTAGE METHOD OF CALCULATING FEDERAL INCOME TAX

If the employer chooses the **percentage method** of calculating the federal income tax to be withheld from the employee's paychecks, Tables 9-2 and 9-3 are used. The process is as follows:

Step 1. Determine the number of withholding allowances the employee claims on Form W-4.
Step 2. Consult Table 9-2 to determine the amount that *each* allowance is worth, depending upon the payroll period.
Step 3. Multiply the amount each allowance is worth (from Step 2) by the number of allowances.
Step 4. The product from Step 3 is subtracted from gross pay to arrive at adjusted (taxable) gross pay.
Step 5. Consult tax tables (Table 9-3), taking into account payroll period and marital status—married or single.
Step 6. Compute FIT as indicated in tax tables.

Problem

Use the percentage method to compute the federal income tax to be withheld from Mary Bell. She is married, claims three allowances, and earns $228 a week.

TABLE 9-2
Amount of One Withholding Exemption
Using the Percentage Method

Payroll period	One withholding allowance
Weekly	$19.23
Biweekly	38.46
Semimonthly	41.66
Monthly	83.33
Quarterly	250.00
Semiannually	500.00
Annually	1,000.00
Daily or miscellaneous (each day of the payroll period)	2.74

Solution

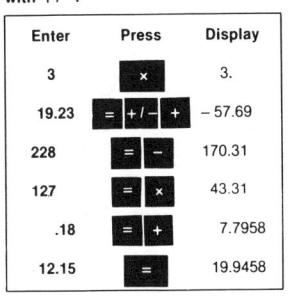

Using a calculator with +/−:

Enter	Press	Display
3	×	3.
19.23	= +/− +	− 57.69
228	= −	170.31
127	= ×	43.31
.18	= +	7.7958
12.15	=	19.9458

Step 1. She claims three allowances (herself, her husband, her son).

Step 2. Refer to Table 9-2. Since she is paid weekly, each allowance is worth $19.23.

Step 3. Multiply: $19.23 X 3 = $57.69.

Step 4. Compute adjusted gross income: $228 − $57.69 = $170.31.

Step 5. Find the appropriate place in Table 9-3: weekly payroll, married person with wages over $127 but not over $210 (wages = adjusted gross income).

Step 6. Compute the tax withheld:

FIT = $12.15 plus 18% of excess over $127
= $12.15 + [0.18 X ($170.31 − $127.00)]
= $12.15 + (0.18 X $43.31)
= $12.15 + $7.7958
= $12.15 + $7.80
= $19.95

4 SELF-REVIEW

Cassius Spiros is paid a semimonthly salary of $620. He is single and claims two allowances. Use the percentage method to compute the federal income tax withheld.

Step 1. He claims ____ allowances (himself and his mother).

Step 2. Refer to Table 9-2. Each allowance is worth $________.

Step 3. Multiply ____ X $41.66 = $________.

Step 4. Compute adjusted gross: $_________ − $83.32 = $_________.

Step 5. Find the appropriate place in Table 9-3. It is semimonthly, single person.

Step 6. Compute the FIT.

FIT = $________ + [______ X ($_________ − $_________)]
= $________ + $________
= $________

1. 2 allowances
2. $41.66
3. 2 × $41.66 = $83.32
4. $620 − $83.32 = $536.68
6. FIT:
   = $67.77 + [0.26 × ($536.68 − $425.00)]
   = $67.77 + $29.04
   = $96.81

TABLE 9-3
Tables for Percentage Method of Withholding

WEEKLY Payroll Period

(a) SINGLE person—including head of household:

If the amount of wages is:		The amount of income tax to be withheld shall be:	
Not over $27		0	
Over—	But not over—		of excess over—
$27	—$63	15%	—$27
$63	—$131	$5.40 plus 18%	—$63
$131	—$196	$17.64 plus 21%	—$131
$196	—$273	$31.29 plus 26%	—$196
$273	—$331	$51.31 plus 30%	—$273
$331	—$433	$68.71 plus 34%	—$331
$433		$103.39 plus 39%	—$433

(b) MARRIED person—

If the amount of wages is:		The amount of income tax to be withheld shall be:	
Not over $46		0	
Over—	But not over—		of excess over—
$46	—$127	15%	—$46
$127	—$210	$12.15 plus 18%	—$127
$210	—$288	$27.09 plus 21%	—$210
$288	—$369	$43.47 plus 24%	—$288
$369	—$454	$62.91 plus 28%	—$369
$454	—$556	$86.71 plus 32%	—$454
$556		$119.35 plus 37%	—$556

SEMIMONTHLY Payroll Period

(a) SINGLE person—including head of household:

If the amount of wages is:		The amount of income tax to be withheld shall be:	
Not over $59		0	
Over—	But not over—		of excess over—
$59	—$138	15%	—$59
$138	—$283	$11.85 plus 18%	—$138
$283	—$425	$37.95 plus 21%	—$283
$425	—$592	$67.77 plus 26%	—$425
$592	—$717	$111.19 plus 30%	—$592
$717	—$938	$148.69 plus 34%	—$717
$938		$223.83 plus 39%	—$938

(b) MARRIED person—

If the amount of wages is:		The amount of income tax to be withheld shall be:	
Not over $100		0	
Over—	But not over—		of excess over—
$100	—$275	15%	—$100
$275	—$454	$26.25 plus 18%	—$275
$454	—$625	$58.47 plus 21%	—$454
$625	—$800	$94.38 plus 24%	—$625
$800	—$983	$136.38 plus 28%	—$800
$983	—$1,204	$187.62 plus 32%	—$983
$1,204		$258.34 plus 37%	—$1,204

WAGE-BRACKET TABLE METHOD OF CALCULATING FEDERAL INCOME TAX

If the employer chooses the **wage-bracket table method** of calculating the federal income tax to be withheld from an employee's paychecks, Table 9-4 is used. The process is:

Step 1. Determine the number of withholding allowances the employee claims on Form W-4.
Step 2. Consult Table 9-4, taking into account the marital status and payroll period.
Step 3. Determine the federal income tax.
- *a.* Read down left column locating *gross* pay in the correct brackets.
- *b.* Read across to the number of allowances claimed.
- *c.* Read the tax.

Problem Use the wage-bracket table method to determine the federal income tax for Zeno Kmonk, who earns $212 a week, is single, and claims one allowance (himself).

Solution Step 1. He claims one allowance.
Step 2. Consult Table 9-4, and the section labeled "single person, weekly payroll period."
Step 3. Determine the federal income tax.
- *a.* Read down to the brackets $210-$220.
- *b.* Read across to one allowance column.
- *c.* The tax is $31.20.

TABLE 9-4
Tax Tables for Wage-Bracket Method of Withholding

SINGLE Persons—WEEKLY Payroll Period

And the wages are—		And the number of withholding allowances claimed is—										
At least	But less than	0	1	2	3	4	5	6	7	8	9	10 or more
		The amount of income tax to be withheld shall be—										
$110	$115	$14.30	$10.80	$7.30	$4.10	$1.20	$0	$0	$0	$0	$0	$0
115	120	15.20	11.70	8.20	4.90	2.00	0	0	0	0	0	0
120	125	16.10	12.60	9.10	5.70	2.70	0	0	0	0	0	0
125	130	17.00	13.50	10.00	6.60	3.50	.60	0	0	0	0	0
130	135	17.90	14.40	10.90	7.50	4.20	1.40	0	0	0	0	0
135	140	19.00	15.30	11.80	8.40	5.00	2.10	0	0	0	0	0
140	145	20.00	16.20	12.70	9.30	5.80	2.90	0	0	0	0	0
145	150	21.10	17.10	13.60	10.20	6.70	3.60	.70	0	0	0	0
150	160	22.60	18.60	15.00	11.50	8.10	4.70	1.80	0	0	0	0
160	170	24.70	20.70	16.80	13.30	9.90	6.40	3.30	.50	0	0	0
170	180	26.80	22.80	18.80	15.10	11.70	8.20	4.80	2.00	0	0	0
180	190	28.90	24.90	20.90	16.90	13.50	10.00	6.50	3.50	.60	0	0
190	200	31.00	27.00	23.00	18.90	15.30	11.80	8.30	5.00	2.10	0	0
200	210	33.60	29.10	25.10	21.00	17.10	13.60	10.10	6.70	3.60	.70	0
210	220	36.20	31.20	27.20	23.10	19.10	15.40	11.90	8.50	5.10	2.20	0
220	230	38.80	33.80	29.30	25.20	21.20	17.20	13.70	10.30	6.80	3.70	.80
230	240	41.40	36.40	31.40	27.30	23.30	19.20	15.50	12.10	8.60	5.20	2.30
240	250	44.00	39.00	34.00	29.40	25.40	21.30	17.30	13.90	10.40	6.90	3.80
250	260	46.60	41.60	36.60	31.60	27.50	23.40	19.40	15.70	12.20	8.70	5.30
260	270	49.20	44.20	39.20	34.20	29.60	25.50	21.50	17.50	14.00	10.50	7.10
270	280	51.80	46.80	41.80	36.80	31.80	27.60	23.60	19.60	15.80	12.30	8.90
280	290	54.80	49.40	44.40	39.40	34.40	29.70	25.70	21.70	17.60	14.10	10.70
290	300	57.80	52.10	47.00	42.00	37.00	32.00	27.80	23.80	19.70	15.90	12.50
300	310	60.80	55.10	49.60	44.60	39.60	34.60	29.90	25.90	21.80	17.80	14.30
310	320	63.80	58.10	52.30	47.20	42.20	37.20	32.20	28.00	23.90	19.90	16.10

MARRIED Persons—WEEKLY Payroll Period

And the wages are—		And the number of withholding allowances claimed is—										
At least	But less than	0	1	2	3	4	5	6	7	8	9	10 or more
		The amount of income tax to be withheld shall be—										
$150	$160	$17.20	$13.70	$10.60	$7.70	$4.80	$1.90	$0	$0	$0	$0	$0
160	170	19.00	15.50	12.10	9.20	6.30	3.40	.50	0	0	0	0
170	180	20.80	17.30	13.80	10.70	7.80	4.90	2.00	0	0	0	0
180	190	22.60	19.10	15.60	12.20	9.30	6.40	3.50	.60	0	0	0
190	200	24.40	20.90	17.40	14.00	10.80	7.90	5.00	2.10	0	0	0
200	210	26.20	22.70	19.20	15.80	12.30	9.40	6.50	3.60	.80	0	0
210	220	28.10	24.50	21.00	17.60	14.10	10.90	8.00	5.10	2.30	0	0
220	230	30.20	26.30	22.80	19.40	15.90	12.50	9.50	6.60	3.80	.90	0
230	240	32.30	28.30	24.60	21.20	17.70	14.30	11.00	8.10	5.30	2.40	0
240	250	34.40	30.40	26.40	23.00	19.50	16.10	12.60	9.60	6.80	3.90	1.00
250	260	36.50	32.50	28.50	24.80	21.30	17.90	14.40	11.10	8.30	5.40	2.50
260	270	38.60	34.60	30.60	26.60	23.10	19.70	16.20	12.70	9.80	6.90	4.00
270	280	40.70	36.70	32.70	28.60	24.90	21.50	18.00	14.50	11.30	8.40	5.50
280	290	42.80	38.80	34.80	30.70	26.70	23.30	19.80	16.30	12.90	9.90	7.00
290	300	45.10	40.90	36.90	32.80	28.80	25.10	21.60	18.10	14.70	11.40	8.50
300	310	47.50	43.00	39.00	34.90	30.90	26.90	23.40	19.90	16.50	13.00	10.00
310	320	49.90	45.30	41.10	37.00	33.00	28.90	25.20	21.70	18.30	14.80	11.50
320	330	52.30	47.70	43.20	39.10	35.10	31.00	27.00	23.50	20.10	16.60	13.20
330	340	54.70	50.10	45.50	41.20	37.20	33.10	29.10	25.30	21.90	18.40	15.00
340	350	57.10	52.50	47.90	43.30	39.30	35.20	31.20	27.20	23.70	20.20	16.80
350	360	59.50	54.90	50.30	45.70	41.40	37.30	33.30	29.30	25.50	22.00	18.60
360	370	61.90	57.30	52.70	48.10	43.50	39.40	35.40	31.40	27.30	23.80	20.40
370	380	64.60	59.70	55.10	50.50	45.90	41.50	37.50	33.50	29.40	25.60	22.20
380	390	67.40	62.10	57.50	52.90	48.30	43.70	39.60	35.60	31.50	27.50	24.00
390	400	70.20	64.80	59.90	55.30	50.70	46.10	41.70	37.70	33.60	29.60	25.80

5 SELF-REVIEW

Use the wage-bracket table method to determine the federal income tax for Lourdes Topez. She is married, earns $220 a week, and claims two allowances (herself, her husband).

1. 2 allowances

2. married

Step 1. She claims ____ allowances.

Step 2. Consult Tax Table 9-4, ______________ persons, weekly payroll.

(Continued on page 168.)

TABLE 9-4 *(continued)*

SINGLE Persons—SEMIMONTHLY Payroll Period

And the wages are—		And the number of withholding allowances claimed is—										
At least	But less than	0	1	2	3	4	5	6	7	8	9	10 or more
		The amount of income tax to be withheld shall be—										
$290	$300	$40.90	$32.60	$25.10	$17.60	$10.40	$4.10	$0	$0	$0	$0	$0
300	320	43.60	35.30	27.80	20.30	12.80	6.40	.10	0	0	0	0
320	340	47.80	39.10	31.40	23.90	16.40	9.40	3.10	0	0	0	0
340	360	52.00	43.30	35.00	27.50	20.00	12.50	6.10	0	0	0	0
360	380	56.20	47.50	38.70	31.10	23.60	16.10	9.10	2.90	0	0	0
380	400	60.40	51.70	42.90	34.70	27.20	19.70	12.20	5.90	0	0	0
400	420	64.60	55.90	47.10	38.40	30.80	23.30	15.80	8.90	2.60	0	0
420	440	69.10	60.10	51.30	42.60	34.40	26.90	19.40	11.90	5.60	0	0
440	460	74.30	64.30	55.50	46.80	38.00	30.50	23.00	15.50	8.60	2.40	0
460	480	79.50	68.60	59.70	51.00	42.20	34.10	26.60	19.10	11.60	5.40	0
480	500	84.70	73.80	63.90	55.20	46.40	37.70	30.20	22.70	15.20	8.40	2.10
500	520	89.90	79.00	68.20	59.40	50.60	41.90	33.80	26.30	18.80	11.40	5.10
520	540	95.10	84.20	73.40	63.60	54.80	46.10	37.40	29.90	22.40	14.90	8.10
540	560	100.30	89.40	78.60	67.80	59.00	50.30	41.50	33.50	26.00	18.50	11.10
560	580	105.50	94.60	83.80	73.00	63.20	54.50	45.70	37.10	29.60	22.10	14.60
580	600	110.70	99.80	89.00	78.20	67.40	58.70	49.90	41.20	33.20	25.70	18.20
600	620	116.60	105.00	94.20	83.40	72.50	62.90	54.10	45.40	36.80	29.30	21.80
620	640	122.60	110.20	99.40	88.60	77.70	67.10	58.30	49.60	40.80	32.90	25.40
640	660	128.60	116.10	104.60	93.80	82.90	72.10	62.50	53.80	45.00	36.50	29.00
660	680	134.60	122.10	109.80	99.00	88.10	77.30	66.70	58.00	49.20	40.50	32.60
680	700	140.60	128.10	115.60	104.20	93.30	82.50	71.70	62.20	53.40	44.70	36.20
700	720	146.60	134.10	121.60	109.40	98.50	87.70	76.90	66.40	57.60	48.90	40.10
720	740	153.10	140.10	127.60	115.10	103.70	92.90	82.10	71.20	61.80	53.10	44.30
740	760	159.90	146.10	133.60	121.10	108.90	98.10	87.30	76.40	66.00	57.30	48.50
760	780	166.70	152.60	139.60	127.10	114.60	103.30	92.50	81.60	70.80	61.50	52.70

MARRIED Persons—SEMIMONTHLY Payroll Period

And the wages are—		And the number of withholding allowances claimed is—										
At least	But less than	0	1	2	3	4	5	6	7	8	9	10 or more
		The amount of income tax to be withheld shall be—										
$480	$500	$66.00	$57.50	$50.00	$42.50	$35.00	$27.50	$21.00	$14.80	$8.50	$2.30	$0
500	520	70.20	61.50	53.60	46.10	38.60	31.10	24.00	17.80	11.50	5.30	0
520	540	74.40	65.70	57.20	49.70	42.20	34.70	27.20	20.80	14.50	8.30	2.00
540	560	78.60	69.90	61.10	53.30	45.80	38.30	30.80	23.80	17.50	11.30	5.00
560	580	82.80	74.10	65.30	56.90	49.40	41.90	34.40	26.90	20.50	14.30	8.00
580	600	87.00	78.30	69.50	60.80	53.00	45.50	38.00	30.50	23.50	17.30	11.00
600	620	91.20	82.50	73.70	65.00	56.60	49.10	41.60	34.10	26.60	20.30	14.00
620	640	95.60	86.70	77.90	69.20	60.40	52.70	45.20	37.70	30.20	23.30	17.00
640	660	100.40	90.90	82.10	73.40	64.60	56.30	48.80	41.30	33.80	26.30	20.00
660	680	105.20	95.20	86.30	77.60	68.80	60.10	52.40	44.90	37.40	29.90	23.00
680	700	110.00	100.00	90.50	81.80	73.00	64.30	56.00	48.50	41.00	33.50	26.00
700	720	114.80	104.80	94.80	86.00	77.20	68.50	59.70	52.10	44.60	37.10	29.60
720	740	119.60	109.60	99.60	90.20	81.40	72.70	63.90	55.70	48.20	40.70	33.20
740	760	124.40	114.40	104.40	94.40	85.60	76.90	68.10	59.40	51.80	44.30	36.80
760	780	129.20	119.20	109.20	99.20	89.80	81.10	72.30	63.60	55.40	47.90	40.40
780	800	134.00	124.00	114.00	104.00	94.00	85.30	76.50	67.80	59.00	51.50	44.00
800	820	139.20	128.80	118.80	108.80	98.80	89.50	80.70	72.00	63.20	55.10	47.60
820	840	144.80	133.60	123.60	113.60	103.60	93.70	84.90	76.20	67.40	58.70	51.20
840	860	150.40	138.70	128.40	118.40	108.40	98.40	89.10	80.40	71.60	62.90	54.80
860	880	156.00	144.30	133.20	123.20	113.20	103.20	93.30	84.60	75.80	67.10	58.40
880	900	161.60	149.90	138.20	128.00	118.00	108.00	98.00	88.80	80.00	71.30	62.50
900	920	167.20	155.50	143.80	132.80	122.80	112.80	102.80	93.00	84.20	75.50	66.70
920	940	172.80	161.10	149.40	137.80	127.60	117.60	107.60	97.60	88.40	79.70	70.90
940	960	178.40	166.70	155.00	143.40	132.40	122.40	112.40	102.40	92.60	83.90	75.10
960	980	184.00	172.30	160.60	149.00	137.30	127.20	117.20	107.20	97.20	88.10	79.30

(Continued from page 167.)

Step 3. Determine the federal income tax.

a. Read down the brackets to $______ to $______.

b. Read across to _____ allowance column.

c. The tax is $_________.

3. *a.* $220 to $230
   b. 2 allowances
   c. tax is $22.80

ASSIGNMENT 9-2
DEDUCTIONS

Name ______________________ Date Due ______________ Grade _____

Answers to selected problems are given in Appendix B.

For Problems 1 through 6, find the net pay.

	Gross Pay	*Deductions from Gross* FIT	FICA	State	City	Blue Cross	Life Ins.	Disabl. Ins.	Un. Dues	Cr. Union	Bonds	Dona-tions	Misc.	Net Pay
Ex.	$ 76.85	$ 1.90	$ 4.65	$ .38	$ 1.15	$ 0.00	$ 0.00	$0.00	$ 4.00	$ 5.00	$ 0.00	$ 0.00	$ 0.00	$59.77
1.	425.32	93.57	26.07	8.51	0.00	5.00	0.00	8.51	20.00	10.00	1.00	10.00	0.00	________
2.	378.91	83.36	23.23	7.58	0.00	5.00	0.00	7.58	15.00	5.00	1.50	10.00	0.00	________
3.	146.25	23.40	8.97	0.00	3.66	0.00	0.00	1.46	5.75	0.00	0.50	2.00	0.00	________
4.	125.97	17.00	7.72	0.00	3.15	0.00	0.00	1.26	4.50	0.00	0.50	1.50	0.00	________
5.	1,245.50	149.00	76.35	37.37	18.68	10.00	12.50	0.00	0.00	100.00	25.00	50.00	12.00	________
6.	1,961.75	234.69	120.26	58.85	29.43	5.00	12.50	0.00	0.00	150.00	25.00	40.00	20.00	________

7. Nancy Drummond accepted the garment sorter job Van Dyne Crotty advertised. Her first week she worked 38 hours and had the following deductions: Federal income tax (FIT), \$10.80; social security tax (FICA), \$6.99; hospitalization, \$3; and credit union, \$5. Find her:

> Industrial Laundry
> **GARMENT SORTER**
> Be responsible for final preparations of garments plus office cleaning. $3 per hr. Immediate employment. Interviews Mon. only from noon-5. Van Dyne Crotty, 3835 Haverhill, Toledo.

A. Gross pay.
$__________, found by

B. Total deductions.
$________, found by

C. Net weekly pay.
$________, found by

8. An apprentice carpenter earns \$6 an hour and works 40 hours a week. Deductions are: FICA, \$14.71; FIT, \$26.40; state income tax, \$4.80; city income tax, \$3.60; and union dues, \$12. What is the apprentice carpenter's net pay?

$__________, found by

9. Mark Heppinstall is hired for the dental receptionist job advertised at \$600/month. He is paid semimonthly, with the following deductions: FICA, \$18.39; FIT, \$43.60; health insurance, \$12.50; uniforms, \$5; and savings bonds, \$10. Find his:

> DENTAL receptionist: $600 salary. Type 45 wpm. Call 243-2222, IMPERIAL, 705 Spitzer Building.

A. Semimonthly gross pay.
$__________, found by

B. Total semimonthly deductions.
$________, found by

C. Semimonthly net pay.
$__________, found by

10. An elementary schoolteacher took a job at an annual salary of $14,690. The school pays biweekly. Deductions are: FIT, $61.40; state income tax, $11.30; city income tax, $16.95; retirement, $42.38; charity, $7.50; and credit union, $5. What is the teacher's biweekly net pay?

$__________, found by

For Problems 11 through 16, complete the table.

	Year	Wage	Status	*Deducted from Pay for Social Security*	*Contributed by Employer for Social Security*
Ex.	1979	$ 475.00	Employee	$29.12	$29.12
11.	1980	215.00	Employee	________	________
12.	1978	178.00	Employee	________	________
13.	1981	615.20	Self-employed	________	
14.	1977	578.50	Self-employed	________	
15.	1982	33,500.00	Employee	________	________
16.	1983	35,000.00	Self-employed	________	

17. Tom Smith earned $450 a week for the first 15 weeks of 1980 while working at Able Manufacturing Company. The last 37 weeks of 1980 he earned $600 per week as a foreman with Baker Construction Company.

A. How much FICA did Able Mfg. Co. withhold for the first 15 weeks?

$__________, found by

B. How much FICA did Baker Construction Co. withhold for the last 37 weeks?

$__________, found by

C. Was there any FICA overpayment?

____

D. If so, how much was the overpayment?

$__________, found by

E. How would Smith get a refund? ____________________

____

18. Beatrice Armagio is a self-employed interior design consultant. She earns $30,350 during 1981. How much does she pay to social security?

$__________, found by

For Problems 19 through 24, complete the table.

	Pay Period	*Gross Pay*	*Method Used to Calculate FIT*	*Marital Status*	*No. of Allowances*	*FIT Withheld*
Ex.	Weekly	$ 215.00	Wage bracket	Married	3	$17.60
Ex.	Semimonthly	450.00	Percentage	Single	2	55.52
19.	Semimonthly	780.00	Wage bracket	Married	4	________
20.	Weekly	315.00	Wage bracket	Single	0	________
21.	Weekly	375.00	Percentage	Married	3	________
22.	Semimonthly	1,415.00	Percentage	Married	5	________
23.	Weekly	148.50	Percentage	Single	1	________
24.	Semimonthly	778.00	Wage bracket	Single	2	________

25. A sales clerk at Lazarus is paid $3.10 per hour plus 3% commission on all sales. Lazarus pays weekly. During one week, 43 hours were worked. Sales totaled $4,670. The year is 1980; the sales clerk is married and claims four exemptions. Deductions are: FICA, FIT (wage-bracket method); state income tax of 2.5%; city income tax of 1.5%; and credit union, $10. Find the:

A. Gross weekly pay $________

B. FICA deduction ________

C. FIT deduction ________

D. State income tax deduction ________

E. City income tax deduction ________

F. Credit union ________

G. Total deductions ________

H. Net weekly pay ________

26. Suppose you take the job advertised at $14,000 per year. You are paid semimonthly. You are single and claim one exemption (yourself). Your deductions are: FICA (1981); FIT (percentage method); city income tax of 4.5%; hospitalization, $17.50; credit union, $25; and charitable contributions, $20. Find the:

PHARMACEUTICALS ....$14K Free
M.I.T. Employment Systems Agency
15300 Ventura, Sh. Oaks 213/990-3200

A. Semimonthly gross pay (nearest cent) $________

B. FICA deduction ________

C. FIT deduction ________

D. City income tax deduction ________

E. Other deductions ________

F. Total deductions ________

G. Net pay ________

REVIEW ASSIGNMENT FOR CHAPTER 9
INCOME AND DEDUCTIONS

Name ______________________________ Date Due ____________ Grade _____

1. Sue Clark is an employee of the Nordson Corporation. She is paid \$5.44 per hour with time and a half for all hours over 40 per week. Find her gross pay for a week in which she worked 40 hours.

   \$__________, found by

2. Toby Cardone takes a job as a security guard at \$3.75 an hour, with time and a half for all hours over 40 per week. Find his gross pay for a week in which 48 hours were worked.

   \$__________, found by

SECURITY
WACKENHUT
\$2.70—\$4.00 Per Hour
Become a member of the world's largest international full service security company. Immediate security openings in prime locations throughout metro area and other cities in Ga., Ala. & Tenn. Licensed personnel preferred; will train. Free uniforms and equipment, paid vacation, holiday pay. Call 955-0974 between 8:30 a.m.—5 p.m. for appointment and interview. E.O.E.

3. Calculate the weekly and monthly income for the "top dog" in the:

	Weekly Salary	*Monthly Salary*
A. Tobacco industry:	\$________	\$________
B. Pharmaceutical industry:	________	________
C. Transportation equipment industry:	________	________
D. Electrical machinery and instruments industry:	________	________
E. Chemicals and petroleum industry:	________	________

Q I know that in some industries the top executives receive outrageously high salaries. Which bosses are getting the biggest bucks?

A Last year's average total compensations for the top dog in the firm were: tobacco, \$448,500; pharmaceuticals, \$392,000; transportation equipment, \$391,000; electrical machinery and instruments, \$377,700; and chemicals and petroleum, \$353,600.

4. Assume that you are now being paid a biweekly salary of \$680. Your company is converting to a semimonthly pay plan. What will be your semimonthly gross pay?

   \$__________, found by

5. Helen Mathews answered the ad for telephone sales personnel. She was guaranteed \$250 per month plus 4 cents for every call made; and an additional 4 cents for every call which ultimately led to a sale. Find her salary for a month in which she made 4,230 calls, 987 of which led to ultimate sales?

   \$_________, found by

TELEPHONE SALES
\$250 Per Month Salary +
Opportunity to work for reputible company. Part-time hours. Permanent positions available in our telephone sales department. Sales No experience necessary. If you need extra income and pleasant telephone voice. Call 1—9 for appointment. Smyrna, 432-9308, Jonesboro, 471-1858, Stone Mountain, 299-3084.

6. Bob Sanchez is a salesman for Winkelmans. He earns \$3.15 an hour or 5% commission, whichever is greater. Find his gross pay for a week in which he worked 46 hours and had \$3,431.80 in sales.

   \$__________, found by

7. R&R Manufacturing uses the Gantt Task and Bonus Plan. They pay $4.10 an hour, with a bonus of 125% for meeting or exceeding task of 270 pieces for an eight-hour day. Find the gross pay for an eight-hour day for these three employees:

A. Sherry Anspach: 295 pieces

$________, found by

B. Bill Klass: 265 pieces

$________, found by

C. Tom Rinehart: 310 pieces

$________, found by

8. A management-union contract includes the Gantt Task and Bonus Plan for certain jobs. The task for buffing a short pinion gear is 120 gears a day. The bonus is 120%. The hourly rate is $4.50. If an employee buffed 150 short pinion gears during an eight-hour day, what would the gross pay equal?

$_______, found by

9. What amount would be withheld for social security from John Bartowski's salary of $24,800 earned in 1981?

$____________, found by

10. During 1982 Jane Martinez earns $27,800 at Ace Construction and $13,650 at Collins Construction. What amount is withheld for social security at each job, what is the total withheld, and what is the FICA overpayment?

A. At Ace, $____________, found by

B. At Collins, $_________, found by

C. Total, $____________, found by

D. Overpayment, $_________, found by

11. A traveling salesperson is guaranteed a semimonthly salary of $420 plus a commission of 3% on all sales. Find the:

A. Total gross earnings for a semimonthly pay period when sales totaled $13,300.00.

$_______, found by

B. Federal income tax withheld by the wage-bracket method if the salesperson is married and claims three withholding allowances.

$_________, found by

12. You are single and claim no withholding allowances. How much is withheld for FIT (wage-bracket method) for a week in which you had a gross of $195?

$________, found by

13. Darrell Williams has an annual salary of $22,560. He is paid semimonthly. Find the FIT withheld (percentage method) if he is single and claims one withholding exemption.

$_________, found by

14. Pat Friedman earns $8.50 per hour with time and a half for overtime over 40 hours per week. Find the FIT withheld (percentage method) for a week in which 46 hours were worked if Pat is married and claims five exemptions.

$________, found by

15. Mary Murphy earns $750 semimonthly as a keypunch supervisor. The year is 1980. She is married and claims four withholding allowances. Per pay period:

A. What FICA is withheld?

$________, found by

B. What FIT (wage-bracket method) is withheld?

$________, found by

C. What city income tax at 2.5% of gross pay is withheld?

$________, found by

D. If union dues, charitable contributions, and so on total $47.50, what is Mary's net pay?

$________, found by

16. Georgia McKnight, an assembler, earns $6.50 an hour with time and a half being paid for any work over eight hours a day. During the week of August 4, 1982, she works six, ten, ten, six, and ten hours.

A. What is her gross pay?

$________, found by

B. McKnight is single and claims three exemptions. Using the percentage method, what is the amount of FIT withheld?

$________, found by

C. What amount is withheld for Social Security (FICA)?

$________, found by

D. Also deducted from her check is a state income tax of 3.75%. What is this amount?

$________, found by

E. A city income tax of 1.0% must also be deducted. What is this amount?

$_______, found by

F. What is Georgia's net pay?

$________, found by

TO THE STUDENT: There is a SELF-REVIEW TEST for this chapter in Appendix A, *with answers* in Appendix C.

10

Taxes

SECTION 10-1: SALES TAXES

Objective: To compute the sales tax and the total purchase price of an item.

TAXES PEOPLE PAY — IN U.S. AND OTHER MAJOR NATIONS

■ ■	Direct Taxes (on incomes, corporate profits, estates, gifts)	Indirect Taxes (sales and property taxes, excises)	Social Security Taxes	Total Tax Burden
Denmark	21.2¢	19.0¢	3.8¢	44.0¢
Netherlands	14.4¢	12.8¢	15.0¢	42.2¢
Sweden	19.6¢	14.7¢	7.5¢	41.8¢
Norway	12.2¢	18.6¢	10.7¢	41.5¢
Austria	9.6¢	17.5¢	9.7¢	36.8¢
Britain	14.6¢	16.1¢	5.0¢	35.7¢
Italy	5.8¢	13.4¢	11.7¢	30.9¢
UNITED STATES	12.2¢	9.9¢	5.7¢	27.8¢
Switzerland	9.8¢	8.5¢	5.7¢	24.0¢

A state **sales tax**, often referred to as a **use tax**, is imposed on the retail sale of a large number of tangible items, including refrigerators, glue, fishing rods, and the rental of a floor sander. Certain items are usually exempt. These vary from state to state. However, edible groceries, take-out orders of food, and alcohol and cigarettes (taxed separately) are exempt from the sales tax in most states.

The tax rate is expressed as a percent and varies from state to state. The rates for the states having sales taxes are shown in Table 10-1.

TABLE 10-1
Sales Tax Rate, by State

State	*Percent Rate*	*State*	*Percent Rate*	*State*	*Percent Rate*
Alabama	4	Louisiana	3	Ohio	4
Arizona	4	Maine	5	Oklahoma	2
Arkansas	3	Maryland	5	Pennsylvania	6
California	4.75	Massachusetts	5	Rhode Island	6
Colorado	3	Michigan	4	South Carolina	4
Connecticut	7	Minnesota	4	South Dakota	5
D.C.	5	Mississippi	5	Tennessee	4.5
Florida	4	Missouri	3.125	Texas	4
Georgia	3	Nebraska	3	Utah	4
Hawaii	4	Nevada	3	Vermont	3
Idaho	3	New Jersey	5	Virginia	3
Illinois	4	New Mexico	3.75	Washington	4.6
Indiana	4	New York	4	West Virginia	3
Iowa	3	North Carolina	3	Wisconsin	4
Kansas	3	North Dakota	3	Wyoming	3
Kentucky	5				

Note: Local and county taxes, if any, are additional.

STRAIGHT SALES TAX

The tax rates shown in Table 10-1 are referred to as **straight sales taxes.** The sales tax on an item is computed by multiplying the tax rate times the selling price.

Sales tax = Sales tax rate X Selling price

The total purchase price of an item is equal to the selling price plus the sales tax. Thus:

> **Total purchase price = Selling price + Sales tax**

Problem A Sears store in Texas advertised a smoke alarm at a selling price of \$14.95. What is the sales tax? What is the total purchase price?

Solution

Sales tax = Sales tax rate × Selling price
= 4% × \$14.95
= 0.04 × \$14.95
= 0.598
= 0.60 (rounded)

Total purchase price = Selling price + Sales tax
= \$14.95 + \$0.60
= \$15.55

> Note that \$15.55 is 104% of \$14.95

1 SELF-REVIEW

A reminder: Cover the answers in the margin.

In the Montgomery Ward store advertisement shown, if the gloves are purchased in a store located in the state of Washington, what is the sales tax? What is the total purchase price?

> **sale 8.99**
> **women's suede gloves**
> **Special purchase.** Warm acrylic pile (on cotton back) lining. 5 colors.

A. 4.6%

A. The sales tax rate is ______% from Table 10-1.

B. Sales tax:
= 4.6% × \$8.99
= 0.046 × \$8.99
= \$0.41

B. Sales tax = Sales tax rate × Selling price
= ______% × \$______
= ________ × \$______
= \$______

C. Total purchase price:
= \$8.99 + \$0.41
= \$9.40

C. Total purchase price = Selling price + Sales tax
= \$______ + \$______
= \$______

> Note: \$9.40 is 104.6% of \$8.99

Many states permit counties and/or municipalities to add on an additional sales tax to the state sales tax. This added tax rate for selected cities is given in Table 10-2.

TABLE 10-2
Sales Tax Rates for Selected Cities*

City	*Percent Rate*	*City*	*Percent Rate*	*City*	*Percent Rate*
Amarillo, Tex.	1	Ithaca, N.Y.†	3	Richmond, Va.	1
Anaheim, Calif.† . . .	1.25	Jefferson City, Mo. . .	1	Roanoke, Va.	1
Austin, Tex.	1	Lincoln, Neb.	1	Sacramento, Calif.†	1.25
Baton Rouge, La. . . .	3	Los Angeles, Calif.† . .	1.25	St. Louis, Mo.	1
Berkeley, Calif.†	1.75	Lynchburg, Va.	1	San Antonio, Tex.	1
Birmingham, Ala. . . .	1	Mobile, Ala.	2	San Diego, Calif.†	1.25
Boulder, Colo.	2	Montgomery, Ala. . . .	2	San Francisco, Calif.†. . .	1.75
Chicago, Ill.†	2	New Orleans, La. . . .	3	Seattle, Wash.†	0.925
Dallas, Tex.	1	New York, N.Y.	4	Shreveport, La.	2
Denver, Colo.	3	Nome, Alaska	3	Spokane, Wash.†	0.925
Duluth, Minn.	1	Norfolk, Va.	1	Springfield, Ill.†	2
El Paso, Tex.	1	Oakland, Calif.†	1.75	Topeka, Kan.	0.5
Fort Worth, Tex. . . .	1	Oklahoma City, Okla..	2	Troy, N.Y.†	3.5
Fresno, Calif.†	1.25	Omaha, Neb.	1	Tucson, Ariz.	2
Glendale, Calif.†	1.25	Pasadena, Calif.†	1.25	Tulsa, Okla.	2
Houston, Tex.	1	Phoenix, Ariz.	1	Washington, D.C.	5
Huntsville, Ala.	2	Rapid City, S.D.	1.5	Yonkers, N.Y.†	4

*Excludes state and county sales taxes unless otherwise indicated.
†Combined city and county rate.
Source: Tax Foundation, Incorporated.

Using Tables 10-1 and 10-2, the combined state and city sales tax rate for items purchased in Oakland, California, is 4.75% + 1.75%, or 6.50%.

2 SELF-REVIEW

A. Using Tables 10-1 and 10-2, determine the combined state and city sales tax rates for the following locations.

	City	+	*State*	=	*Total Tax Rate*
(1) Amarillo, Tex.:	1%	+	4%	=	______%
(2) Berkeley, Calif.:	1.75%	+	______%	=	______%
(3) Seattle, Wash.:	______%	+	______%	=	______%
(4) Nome, Alaska:	______%	+	______%	=	______%

A.

	City	*State*	*Total*
(1)	1%	4%	5%
(2)	1.75%	4.75%	6.5%
(3)	0.925%	4.6%	5.525%
(4)	3%	0%	3%

B. A shopper in Yonkers, New York, purchased a new calculator for $15.45. Determine the following:

(1) The combined state and city sales tax rate is ___% + ___% = ___%.

(2) Sales tax = Sales tax rate × Selling price
= ___% × $______
= ______ × $______ = $______

(3) Total purchase price = Selling price + Sales tax
= $______ + $______ = $______

Note: $16.69 is 108% of $15.45

B. (1) 4% + 4% = 8%

(2) Sales tax:
= 8% × $15.45
= 0.08 × $15.45
= $1.24

(3) Total purchase price:
= $15.45 + $1.24
= $16.69

SOLVING FOR THE SELLING PRICE

Occasionally a consumer or businessperson knows the total purchase price of an item and the sales tax rate and desires to compute the *selling price.*

Problem

At the end of a day a store clerk counted \$2,412.80 in the cash register. The \$2,412.80 is the total purchase price of all items sold during the day. If the sales tax rate is 5%, what is the selling price of the items sold?

Solution

$$\begin{aligned} \text{Total purchase price} &= \text{Selling price} + \text{Sales tax} \\ \$2{,}412.80 &= (\text{SP}) + (5\% \text{ of selling price}) \\ 2{,}412.80 &= (100\% \times \text{SP}) + (5\% \text{ of selling price}) \\ 2{,}412.80 &= 105\% \times \text{SP} \end{aligned}$$

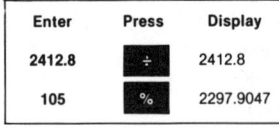

Using a calculator with %:

Enter	Press	Display
2412.8	÷	2412.8
105	%	2297.9047

Solving for the selling price:

$$\text{Selling price} = \frac{\$2{,}412.80}{105\%} = \$2{,}297.90$$

3 SELF-REVIEW

A used Rolls Royce was purchased in Baton Rouge, Lousiana. The total purchase price, including state and city sales tax, is \$29,680. The combined city and state sales tax is 6%. What is the selling price of the Rolls?

Total purchase price = Selling price + Sales tax

\$________ = (SP) + (6% of selling price)

\$________ = (100% X SP) + (6% of selling price)

\$________ = _____% X SP

Selling price = \$________ / _____%

= \$________

Answers (margin): \$29,680; \$29,680; \$29,680 = 106%; $\frac{\$29{,}680}{106\%}$ = \$28,000

If the amount of the sales tax and the tax rate is given, the selling price can be determined by dividing the sales tax by the sales tax rate.

$$\text{Selling price} = \frac{\text{Sales tax}}{\text{Sales tax rate}}$$

For example, if the sales tax on a refrigerator is \$15.50 and the sales tax rate is 5%, the selling price is \$310, found by \$15.50 ÷ 0.05.

ASSIGNMENT 10-1
SALES TAXES

Name ______________________ Date Due ____________ Grade ______

Answers to selected problems are given in Appendix B.

For Problems 1 through 6, use Table 10-1 to find the state sales tax rate; then find the state sales tax and total purchase price.

	Item	*Selling Price*	*State*	*State Sales Tax Rate*	*State Sales Tax*	*Total Purchase Price*
Ex.	Razor	$24.95	Kentucky	5%	$1.25	$26.20
1.	AM/FM radio	39.49	Alabama	______	______	______
2.	Calculator	18.99	Rhode Island	______	______	______
3.	Shampoo	1.79	Alaska	______	______	______
4.	Film	3.29	Wyoming	______	______	______
5.	Shirt	14.97	Missouri	______	______	______
6.	Shoes	42.90	California	______	______	______

7. Talia Stein purchased a plaid shirt for $9.88 and a pair of pants for $8.88. Find the state sales tax and total purchase price if purchased in the following states (use Table 10-1):

	State	*Tax*	*Total Purchase Price*
A.	Ohio	$______	$______
B.	Virginia	______	______
C.	New Jersey	______	______
D.	Connecticut	______	______

8. Paul and Shirley Kendrick decide to carpet their 9' x 12' patio with thick, green-grass carpet. They need 12 square yards. Find the state sales tax and total purchase price if the carpet is purchased in the following states (use Table 10-1):

	State	*Tax*	*Total Purchase Price*
A.	Arizona	$______	$______
B.	Maryland	______	______
C.	North Dakota	______	______
D.	Oklahoma	______	______

9. Find the purchase price of a food processor bought in South Dakota if $1.25 is paid in state sales tax.

   $__________, found by

10. Find the total purchase price of a truck tire bought in the state of Washington if $8.76 is paid in state sales tax.

   $__________, found by

For Problems 11 through 16, use Tables 10-1 and 10-2 and supply the missing data.

	Selling Price	*City*	*City Sales Tax Rate*	*State*	*State Sales Tax Rate*	*Total Tax Rate*	*Sales Tax*	*Total Purchase Price*
Ex.	$ 9.87	Ithaca	3%	New York	4%	7%	$0.69	$10.56
11.	2.25	Austin		Texas				
12.	14.98	Chicago		Illinois				
13.	173.50	Tulsa		Oklahoma				
14.	493.75	Oakland		California				
15.	78.99	Nome		Alaska				
16.	5,489.30	Topeka		Kansas				

17. Charles Sanders purchased six tumblers and eight wine glasses. Find the total sales tax and total purchase price if purchased in the following cities:

Tumbler, Reg. 1.70	Now 1.19
Cooler, Reg. 2.30	Now 1.59
Rocks/Juice, Reg. 1.70	Now 1.19
Goblet, Reg. 2.30	Now 1.59
Wine, Reg. 2.30	Now 1.59

City	*Total Sales Tax*	*Total Purchase Price*
A. Tucson, Ariz.	$	$
B. Lynchburg, Va.		
C. Seattle, Wash.		
D. Houston, Tex.		

18. Polly Baker purchased two bath towels, two hand towels, and a washcloth. Find the total sales tax and total purchase price, if purchased in the following cities:

"Fresh Daisy" Bath Towels

2/$5

Hand Towel. 1.79

Wash Cloth . . . . . . 99¢

LINENS

City	*Total Sales Tax*	*Total Purchase Price*
A. Berkeley, Calif.	$	$
B. Yonkers, N.Y.		
C. Shreveport, La.		
D. Jefferson City, Mo.		

19. Mr. and Mrs. Peter Hernandez are planning to move from New York City to Dallas, Texas. How much can they save if they wait to buy a new car costing $12,800 until after they move to Dallas?

   $__________, found by

20. Bob Moore received $8.58 in change from a $250 check when he purchased a Bearcat #210 Scanner radio in Spokane, Washington. What amount did he pay in sales tax on the radio?

   $__________, found by

SECTION 10-2: PROPERTY TAXES

Objective: To compute the assessed value, the property tax, and the tax rate.

A tax on property, including land and buildings, is one of the oldest taxes on record. In II Kings 23:35, written in 610 B.C., reference is made to Johoiakim who "gave the silver and the gold to Pharaoh; but he taxed the land to give the money according to the commandment of Pharaoh." The monies collected go toward maintaining roads, parks, hospitals, schools, law enforcement, fire protection, and so on. The county tax assessor is the person responsible for determining the amount of tax to be levied on each piece of property in the county.

ASSESSED VALUE

The tax assessor must first determine the **market value** of each piece of property in the county. It can be defined as the worth of the property (land and buildings) if the property were to be sold today.

The assessor then calculates **assessed value** by multiplying the rate of assessment times the market value. Thus:

Seeks 1-Mill Cut, Cites Expected Surplus

Assessed value = Rate of assessment X Market value

The rate of assessment usually ranges from 15% to 50%. For illustration: The rate of assessment in Ohio is set at 35% by the state legislature. In Freemont County, Idaho, the County Board of Equalization uses a rate of assessment of 18%.

Problem Determine the assessed value of eight acres of nonirrigated agricultural land (no buildings) in Freemont County, Idaho. The market value is $1,020, and the rate of assessment is 18%.

Solution

Assessed value = Rate of assessment X Market value
= 18% X $1,020
= 0.18 X $1,020
= $183.60

1 SELF-REVIEW

Time magazine reported that the rate of assessment in Michigan is 50%, while in Ohio it is 35%. Determine the assessed value of a home with a market value of $60,000 if it were located in a community with an assessment rate of:

A. 50%

Assessed value = Rate of assessment X Market value
= ______% X $60,000
= 0.______ X $60,000
= $__________

B. 35%

Assessed value = Rate of assessment X Market value
= ______% X $__________
= 0.______ X $__________
= $__________

A. Assessed value:
= 50% X $60,000
= 0.50 X $60,000
= $30,000

B. Assessed value:
= 35% X $60,000
= 0.35 X $60,000
= $21,000

TAX RATE

Although all property owners in the county contribute toward maintaining the sheriff's department, the county home, and other county agencies, the **tax rates** in various cities, townships, school districts, and other political subdivisions within the county are usually different.

Table 10-3 gives the property tax rates for the various political subdivisions in Fulton County.

TABLE 10-3
Rates of Taxation in Fulton County

In pursuance of the law, I, Grace Nolan, Treasurer of Fulton County, do hereby give notice that the number of mills levied on each dollar of property listed for taxation with said County is as follows:

				Township			Schools		Corporations		
1978 Taxing Subdivision	*County (mills)*	*County Hospital Bond (mills)*	*Fulton County Training Center (mills)*	*Health (mills)*	*General (mills)*	*Road (mills)*	*General (mills)*	*Bonds and Interest (mills)*	*General (mills)*	*Bonds and Interest (mills)*	*Total Rate (mills)*
1. Amboy-Evergreen	2.00	.90	1.00	.20	2.10	1.40	32.60	2.30			42.50
2. Metamora Vil. Evergreen	2.00	.90	1.00	.20	2.10		32.60	2.30	13.30	.50	54.90
3. Chesterfield-Evergreen	2.00	.90	1.00	.20	1.40	1.90	32.60	2.30			42.30
4. Clinton-Pettisville	2.00	.90	1.00	.20	.80	3.00	32.70	.60			41.20
5. Clinton-Wauseon	2.00	.90	1.00	.20	.80	3.00	30.50	3.70			42.10
6. Wauseon Village	2.00	.90	1.00	.20	.80		30.50	3.70	2.20	.50	41.80
7. Dover-Pettisville	2.00	.90	1.00	.20	1.00	1.50	32.70	.60			39.90
8. Dover-Wauseon	2.00	.90	1.00	.20	1.00	1.50	30.50	3.70			40.80
9. Franklin-Archbold	2.00	.90	1.00	.20	2.50	2.00	25.80	.80			35.20
10. Franklin-Fayette	2.00	.90	1.00	.20	2.50	2.00	31.10	.60			40.30

The tax rates in Table 10-3 are given in **mills.** A mill is defined as $\frac{1}{1000}$ of a dollar, or 0.001 of a dollar. A tax rate of 44.53 mills means that a property owner must pay 44.53 mills for each \$1 of assessed value of the property. Since a tax rate in mills is difficult to work with, the mills are converted to dollars by multiplying the mills by \$0.001. For illustration:

$$44.53 \text{ mills} = 44.53 \times \$0.001 = \$0.04453 \text{ per } \$1.00 \text{ of assessed value}$$

A tax rate may be expressed as:

A tax in dollars per \$1 of assessed value.
A tax in dollars per \$10 of assessed value.
A tax in dollars per \$100 of assessed value.
A tax in dollars per \$1,000 of assessed value.

For illustration, a tax rate of 44.53 mills equals:

A tax of \$0.04453 per \$1 of assessed value.
A tax of \$0.4453 per \$10 of assessed value.
A tax of \$4.453 per \$100 of assessed value.
A tax of \$44.53 per \$1,000 of assessed value.

Note that a tax rate of 44.53 mills per \$1 of assessed value is the same as a tax rate of \$44.53 per \$1,000 of assessed value.

2 SELF-REVIEW

Table 10-3 indicates that a taxpayer in the Amboy-Evergreen tax district pays a general tax rate of 32.60 mills for school taxes. Complete the following:

A. \$0.03260

B. \$0.3260

C. \$3.26

D. \$32.60

A. 32.60 mills = 32.60 × \$0.001 = \$0________ per \$1 of assessed value. Thus:

32.60 mills = \$0.03260 per \$1 of assessed value

B. = \$___________ per \$10 of assessed value

C. = \$_________ per \$100 of assessed value

D. = \$_________ per \$1,000 of assessed value

DETERMINING THE PROPERTY TAX

The dollar amount of property tax that a property owner pays is found by multiplying the tax rate by the assessed value of the property. Thus:

Property tax = Tax rate × Assessed value

Problem A property with an assessed value of \$23,500 is taxed at a rate of 83.95 mills. Determine the property tax.

Solution Step 1. Change the tax rate to dollars per \$1,000 of assessed value.

83.95 mills = \$83.95 per \$1,000 of assessed value

Step 2. Property tax = Tax rate × Assessed value

$$= \$83.95 \times \frac{\$23{,}500}{\$1{,}000}$$

$$= \$83.95 \times 23.5 \leftarrow \text{23,500 = 23.5 thousand}$$

$$= \$1{,}972.825$$

$$= \$1{,}972.83$$

3 SELF-REVIEW

John and Freda Wertz purchased the home as advertised for the asking price of \$42,500. The property is located in Bloom Township, Elmwood School District, with the tax rate indicated. If the rate of assessment is 50%, determine the following:

LIKE NEW \$42,500
T-3935 Very attractive 2 story on 60x100 lot, has new Aluminum Siding and storms, 1½ car garage, full basement, 3 large bedrooms, formal dining room, new kitchen and bath plus new carpet throughout. Don't miss this one! Call Ron Gatton, 472-0536 or John O'Leary, 729-5859.
GROGAN - ERA
REALTY, INC. 729-3787

A. Step 1. Assessed value = Rate of assessment × Market value

= _____% × \$___________ = \$___________

A. Assessed value:
= 50% × \$42,500
= \$21,250

B. Step 2. County tax is:

Property tax = Tax rate × Assessed value

= 3.80 mills × \$_________

$$= \$3.80 \times \frac{\$\_\_\_\_\_}{\$1{,}000}$$

= \$80.75

Bloom Township, Elmwood Schools TAX SCHEDULE (in mills)	
County	3.80
Township	2.40
Schools	38.70
Vocational school	1.80
Total	46.70

B. Property tax:
= 3.80 mills × \$21,250

$$= \$3.80 \times \frac{\$21{,}250}{\$1{,}000}$$

= \$80.75

C. Township tax is: Property tax = Tax rate × Assessed value

= ________ mills × \$___________

$$= \$\_\_\_\_\_ \times \frac{\$\_\_\_\_\_}{\$} = \$\_\_\_\_\_$$

C. Township tax:
= 2.40 mills × \$21,250

$$= \$2.40 \times \frac{\$21{,}250}{\$1{,}000}$$

= \$51.00

D. Schools tax:

$= 38.70 \text{ mills} \times \$21{,}250$

$= \$38.70 \times \frac{\$21{,}250}{\$1{,}000}$

$= \$822.38$

D. Schools tax is:

Property tax = ________ mills × $__________

= $________ × $\frac{\$\_\_\_\_\_\_}{\$}$ = $__________

E. Vocational school tax:

$= 1.80 \text{ mills} \times \$21{,}250$

$= \$1.80 \times \frac{\$21{,}250}{\$1{,}000}$

$= \$38.25$

E. Vocational school tax is:

Property tax = ________ mills × $__________

= $________ × $\frac{\$\_\_\_\_\_\_}{\$}$ = $__________

F. Total tax:

= Tax rate × Assessed value

$= 46.70 \text{ mills} \times \$21{,}250$

$= \$46.70 \times \frac{\$21{,}250}{\$1{,}000}$

$= \$992.38$

F. Total tax is:

Property tax = __________ × ______________

= ________ mills × $__________

= $________ × $\frac{\$\_\_\_\_\_\_}{\$}$ = $__________

COMPUTING THE TAX RATE

Governing boards, such as county commissioners, township trustees, city councils, and school boards must determine the **tax rate** needed to raise a certain amount of money. The tax rate is computed by:

$$\text{Tax rate} = \frac{\text{Total amount of taxes needed}}{\text{Total assessed value}}$$

Problem The county commissioners determined that they needed an additional $900,000 in taxes to balance the budget. The total assessed value in the county is $100 million. Determine the tax rate necessary to raise the needed funds.

Solution

$$\text{Tax rate} = \frac{\text{Total amount of taxes needed}}{\text{Total assessed value}}$$

$$= \frac{\$900{,}000}{\$100{,}000{,}000}$$

$$= 0.009 = 9 \text{ mills}$$

4 SELF-REVIEW

The county assessor revealed that the assessed valuation of all property in Bloomfield Township, Tonto Local School District, is $200 million. The amount of taxes needed to maintain the schools and provide other services such as law enforcement is $10 million. What is the tax rate?

Tax rate = $\frac{\$\_\_\_\_\_\_\_\_}{\$}$

= 0.________ = ______ mills

$\text{Tax rate} = \frac{\$10 \text{ million}}{\$200 \text{ million}}$

$= 0.050$

$= 50 \text{ mills}$

ASSIGNMENT 10-2
PROPERTY TAXES

Name ______________________ Date Due ______________ Grade _____

Answers to selected problems are given in Appendix B.

For Problems 1 through 6, find the assessed value and the property tax.

	Market Value	*Rate of Assessment*	*Assessed Value*	*Tax Rate in Mills*	*Property Tax*
Ex.	$ 45,000	38%	$17,100	42.50	$726.75
1.	115,000	50	________	54.90	________
2.	34,800	35	________	35.20	________
3.	68,750	22	________	79.80	________
4.	51,900	25	________	116.40	________
5.	84,750	70	________	64.52	________
6.	21,600	17	________	88.70	________

7. The James Scott family purchased a home with a market value of $64,900 in the Franklin-Fayette tax subdivision (Table 10-3). The rate of assessment for Fulton County is 35%. Find the:

   A. Assessed value, $__________
   B. County tax, $__________
   C. County hospital bond tax, $__________
   D. Fulton County Training Center tax, $__________
   E. Township–health tax, $__________
   F. Township–general tax, $__________
   G. Township–road tax, $__________
   H. Schools–general tax, $__________
   I. Schools–bonds and interest tax, $__________
   J. Total tax, $__________

8. A $30,000 home in Metamora Vil. Evergreen (Table 10-3; rate of assessment is 35%) would incur what amount in taxes for:

   A. Township–general? $__________
   B. Schools–general? $__________
   C. Corporation–general? $__________
   D. Total tax? $__________

For Problems 9 through 14, use the table on the next page.

9. Find the total levy tax on a home with a market value of $74,900 located in Benton Township, if the rate of assessment is 40%.

   $__________, found by

10. Find the annual tax a resident of Carroll Township, living in a $40,000 home, pays to support Penta County School, if the rate of assessment is 45%.

    $__________, found by

11. What does a family living in a $92,400 home in Rocky Ridge pay annually to support the corporation? The rate of assessment is 35%.

    $__________, found by

12. The rate of assessment in Bay Township is 50%. What does a family living in a $35,000 home pay annually to support Vanguard School?

    $__________, found by

Line No.	Names of Townships, Corporations, and School Districts	Total County (mills)	School Purposes: General (mills)	Vote (mills)	Debt (mills)	Penta County (mills)	Ehove (mills)	Van-guard (mills)	Total Schools (mills)	Total Town-ship (mills)	Total Corpo-ration (mills)	Dec. Levy (mills)	June Levy (mills)	Total Levy (mills)
1.	Allen Township . .	4.40	4.80	34.75	2.35	1.50			43.40	4.80		26.30	26.30	52.60
2.	Clay Center Corporation	4.40	4.80	34.75	2.35	1.50			43.40	1.20	2.00	25.50	25.50	51.00
3.	Lake School in Allen	4.40	4.70	27.00	.70	1.50			33.90	4.80		21.55	21.55	43.10
4.	Benton Town-ship	4.40	4.00	23.50	3.00	1.50			32.00	4.20		20.30	20.30	40.60
5.	Rocky Ridge Corporation	4.40	4.00	23.50	3.00	1.50			32.00	2.00	8.00	23.20	23.20	46.40
6.	Ben. Car. Salem School in Bay . . .	4.40	4.00	23.50	3.00	1.50			32.00	5.30		20.85	20.85	41.70
7.	Bay Township . . .	4.40	3.80	31.20	1.30			1.70	38.00	5.30		23.85	23.85	47.70
8.	Carroll Town-ship	4.40	4.00	23.50	3.00	1.50			32.00	3.40		19.90	19.90	39.80
9.	Sand Beach Cons. District	4.40	4.00	23.50	3.00	1.50			32.00	3.40		19.90	19.90	39.80
10.	Woodmore School in Clay	4.40	4.00	23.20	.60	1.50			29.30	3.20		18.45	18.45	36.90

13. The market value of all taxable property in Allen Township is $432,750,000. The rate of assessment is 42%. What total levy taxes is collected annually in Allen Township?

    $________________, found by

14. Clay Center Corporation collects $6,298,500 in total levy taxes annually. The rate of assessment is 38%. What is the market value of all property in Clay Center Corporation?

    $__________________, found by

15. If you live in a $42,500 home and the rate of assessment is 35%, what will the 6.1 mill school levy cost you annually?

    $__________, found by

> **FACT**
> The school levy on which you will be asked to vote on November 8 is for 6.1 mills, the amount recommended by the Citizens Committee For Effective Government.

16. Bedford Township, Michigan, voters recently passed a 6.78 mill operating levy. If the rate of assessment is 50%, an owner of a home having a market value of $67,900 will pay what amount annually for this levy?

    $___________, found by

17. This portion of a tax statement for a house trailer shows an assessed valuation of $1,828, a tax rate of 45.10 mills, and a total tax of $82.44. Verify the total tax and find the market value, if the rate of assessment is 20%.

Valuation	*Rate*	*Total Tax*
1,828	45.10	$82.44

    A. $__________ tax, found by

    B. $__________ market value, found by

18. You are a member of a small library board that needs an additional $17,600 annually. The market value of all taxable property in your district is $5 million. The rate of assessment is 44%. What additional operating millage is needed (nearest hundredth mill)?

    ______ mills, found by

19. What millage would a municipality need to balance an operating budget of $492,000 if the market value of the taxable property is $150 million and the rate of assessment is 40% (nearest hundredth mill)?

    __________ mills, found by

SECTION 10-3: OTHER TAXES

Objective: To calculate other taxes, such as gasoline tax, federal excise tax, and cigarette tax.

There are a multitude of federal, state, and local taxes collected to support various projects and governmental units. To mention a few, there is the **highway use tax**, which includes a state and federal gasoline tax, a **tax on tires**, and a **truck use tax**. There is a state **tax on cigarettes**, an **alcoholic beverage tax**, a **meals tax**, a **tax on admission** to sporting events, and so on.

HIGHWAY USE TAX

The term "highway use tax" stems from the idea that the people who *use* the highways and streets should pay a share of the construction and maintenance cost. The tax started in 1919, when the state of Oregon levied the first tax on gasoline. Use charges include taxes on fuels; vehicle registration fees; taxes on tires, lubricants, parts, and accessories; and taxes on vehicles when purchased.

STATE AND FEDERAL GASOLINE TAXES

The federal government taxes each gallon of gasoline at the rate of 4 cents per gallon. In addition, each state taxes each gallon at rates that vary from 5 to 11 cents per gallon.

Table 10-4 lists the combined state and federal tax rate on a gallon of gasoline in each state.

TABLE 10-4
State and Federal Gasoline Tax Table

Alabama	$0.11	Illinois	$0.135	Montana	$0.12	Rhode Island	$0.14
Alaska	0.12	Indiana	0.12	Nebraska	0.135	South Carolina	0.13
Arizona	0.12	Iowa	0.125	Nevada	0.10	South Dakota	0.12
Arkansas	0.125	Kansas	0.12	New Hampshire	0.14	Tennessee	0.11
California	0.11	Kentucky	0.13	New Jersey	0.12	Texas	0.09
Colorado	0.11	Louisiana	0.12	New Mexico	0.11	Utah	0.13
Connecticut	0.15	Maine	0.13	New York	0.12	Vermont	0.13
Delaware	0.13	Maryland	0.13	North Carolina	0.13	Virginia	0.13
Dist. of Columbia	0.14	Massachusetts	0.125	North Dakota	0.12	Washington	0.15
Florida	0.12	Michigan	0.13	Ohio	0.11	West Virginia	0.145
Georgia	0.115	Minnesota	0.13	Oklahoma	0.1058	Wisconsin	0.11
Hawaii	0.125	Mississippi	0.13	Oregon	0.11	Wyoming	0.12
Idaho	0.135	Missouri	0.11	Pennsylvania	0.13		

The tax is paid at the time of purchasing gasoline at a gas station. The tax is added directly to the retail price.

The amount of gasoline tax paid is equal to the tax per gallon times the number of gallons.

Gasoline tax = Tax per gallon × Number of gallons

Problem Use Table 10-4 to compute the gasoline tax on 22.8 gallons of gasoline purchased in (A) Alabama, (B) Hawaii, and (C) Washington.

Solution Gasoline tax = Tax per gallon × Number of gallons

A. Alabama

Tax = $0.11 × 22.8
= $2.508
= $2.51 rounded

B. Hawaii

Tax = $0.125 × 22.8
= $2.85

C. Washington

Tax = $0.15 × 22.8
= $3.42

1 SELF-REVIEW

Alva and Albert Schelman traveled across the United States and purchased the amounts of gasoline in the states indicated. Determine the gasoline tax in each state and the total taxes paid. Use Table 10-4 to find the tax rates.

	Rate	*Tax*
A.	$0.13	$ 2.42
B.	0.12	2.44
C.	0.12	2.33
D.	0.125	1.98
E.	0.135	2.94
F.	0.11	2.34
G.	0.13	2.65
H.	0.10	1.99
I.	0.11	2.18
	Total	$21.27

State	*Rate*		*Gallons*		*Tax*
A. Maine	$________	X	18.6	=	$________
B. New York	________	X	20.3	=	________
C. Indiana	________	X	19.4	=	________
D. Iowa	________	X	15.8	=	________
E. Nebraska	________	X	21.8	=	________
F. Colorado	________	X	21.3	=	________
G. Utah	________	X	20.4	=	________
H. Nevada	________	X	19.9	=	________
I. California	________	X	19.8	=	________
			Total	=	$________

FEDERAL TAX ON TIRES, TUBES, AND TREAD RUBBER

Another aspect of the highway use tax is the federal tax on tires, tubes, and the tread rubber used in retreading tires. The tax is often called a **federal excise tax.** The tax on tires and tubes is computed at the rate of 10 cents per pound of rubber used in the manufacture of the item. The actual computation of the tax is done by the manufacturer of the tire.

Note in Exhibit 10-1, from an advertisement for tires, that the federal excise tax (FET) is indicated in a separate column. Also note that the tax does not depend on the selling price of the tire. For example, both the blackwall and whitewall A78-13 tires contain 17.2 pounds of rubber. The tax is $0.10 X 17.2 lbs. = $1.72.

EXHIBIT 10-1

Size	Blackwall	Whitewall	F.E.T.
A78-13	**$19.00**	**$21.00**	$1.72
B78-13	**21.00**	**23.00**	1.82
C78-14	**22.00**	**24.00**	2.01
D78-14	**23.00**	**25.00**	2.09
E78-14	**24.00**	**26.00**	2.23
F78-14	**26.00**	**29.00**	2.37
G78-14	**27.00**	**30.00**	2.53
H78-14	**30.00**	**32.00**	2.73
G78-15	**29.00**	**31.00**	2.59
H78-15	**31.00**	**33.00**	2.79
L78-15	**33.00**	**35.00**	3.09

All prices plus tax and old tire.

2 SELF-REVIEW

Amy Sahadi bought two new H78-14 whitewall tires for her car. Use Exhibit 10-1 to complete the following:

A. Selling price of the two tires is:

\$________ X 2 = \$________

B. The federal excise tax is:

\$________ X 2 = \$________

C. If she purchased the tires in St. Louis, Missouri, she would have to pay a city and state sales tax of 4.125% of the selling price.

Sales tax = 4.125% X \$64.00

= ______ X \$________

= \$________

D. The total cost of the tires is:

\$________ + \$________ + \$________ = \$72.10

A. \$32.00 X 2 = \$64.00

B. \$2.73 X 2 = \$5.46

C. Sales tax:
= 4.125% X \$64.00
= 0.04125 X \$64.00
= \$2.64

D. Total cost:
\$64 + \$5.46 + \$2.64 = \$72.10

CIGARETTE TAX

State taxes on cigarettes and other tobacco products provide the states with over \$3 billion in revenue. Table 10-5 lists the state tax on a pack of cigarettes in each state.

TABLE 10-5
State Tax on a Pack of Cigarettes

Alabama	\$0.12	Illinois	\$0.12	Montana	\$0.12	Rhode Island	\$0.18
Alaska	0.08	Indiana	0.105	Nebraska	0.13	South Carolina	0.07
Arizona	0.13	Iowa	0.13	Nevada	0.10	South Dakota	0.12
Arkansas	0.1775	Kansas	0.11	New Hampshire	0.12	Tennessee	0.13
California	0.10	Kentucky	0.03	New Jersey	0.19	Texas	0.185
Colorado	0.10	Louisiana	0.11	New Mexico	0.12	Utah	0.08
Connecticut	0.21	Maine	0.16	New York	0.15	Vermont	0.12
Delaware	0.14	Maryland	0.10	North Carolina	0.02	Virginia	0.025
District of Columbia	0.13	Massachusetts	0.21	North Dakota	0.11	Washington	0.16
Florida	0.21	Michigan	0.11	Ohio	0.15	West Virginia	0.17
Georgia	0.12	Minnesota	0.18	Oklahoma	0.13	Wisconsin	0.16
Hawaii*		Mississippi	0.11	Oregon	0.09	Wyoming	0.08
Idaho	0.091	Missouri	0.09	Pennsylvania	0.18		

*40% of wholesale price.

The tax, which is paid at the time of purchasing the cigarettes, is added directly to the retail price. The amount of cigarette tax paid is equal to the tax per pack times the number of packs:

Cigarette tax = Tax per pack X Number of packs

Problem Use Table 10-5 to compute the state cigarette tax on two cartons (20 packs) of cigarettes if purchased in (A) Arkansas, (B) Massachusetts, and (C) Virginia.

Solution Cigarette tax = Tax per pack X Number of packs

A. Arkansas

Tax = \$0.1775 X 20
= \$3.55

B. Massachusetts

Tax = \$0.21 X 20
= \$4.20

C. Virginia

Tax = \$0.025 X 20
= \$0.50

3 SELF-REVIEW

Daniel Swigart, a highly skilled computer installer for a large company, travels throughout the country. He purchased cigarettes as indicated at various airports. Determine the total cigarette taxes he paid.

	City, State	Tax per Pack		Packs		Tax
A.	San Diego, Calif.	$0.____	X	1	=	$____
B.	Amarillo, Tex.	____	X	3	=	____
C.	Mobile, Ala.	____	X	2	=	____
D.	Chicago, Ill.	____	X	6	=	____
E.	Topeka, Kan.	____	X	1	=	____
F.	Yonkers, N.Y.	____	X	5	=	____
				Total	=	$____

	Tax per Pack	Tax
A.	$0.10	$0.10
B.	0.185	0.56
C.	0.12	0.24
D.	0.12	0.72
E.	0.11	0.11
F.	0.15	0.75
	Total =	$2.48

ASSIGNMENT 10-3
OTHER TAXES

Name ______________________ Date Due ______________ Grade _____

Answers to selected problems are given in Appendix B.

For Problems 1 to 6, use Table 10-4 to find the gasoline tax per gallon and the gasoline tax.

	State	*Gasoline Tax per Gallon*	*No. of Gallons*	*Gasoline Tax*
Ex.	New Mexico	$0.11	18.4	$2.02
1.	Wyoming	________	19.2	________
2.	Arkansas	________	23.4	________
3.	Maryland	________	8.6	________
4.	Ohio	________	13.0	________
5.	Idaho	________	24.8	________
6.	Texas	________	21.7	________

7. During Spring break, Ted Rose and some of his friends drove from Ohio to Florida. They purchased 18.6 gallons of gasoline in Ohio; 14.3 gallons in Kentucky; 17.8 gallons in Georgia; and 20.4 gallons in Florida. Using Table 10-4, determine the total gasoline tax they paid.

   $________, found by

8. The federal gasoline tax (4 cents per gallon) is what percent of the state tax in:

   A. Texas, ________%, found by

   B. Oklahoma, ________%, found by

   C. Nebraska, ________%, found by

   D. Washington, ________%, found by

For Problems 9 through 14, use Exhibit 10-1 to find the price per tire, federal excise tax per tire, selling price, federal excise tax, and the total cost of the tires.

	Size/Wall	*No. of Tires Purchased*	*Price per Tire*	*FET per Tire*	*Total Selling Price*	*Total FET*	*Total Cost*
Ex.	B78-13/white	4	$23.00	$1.82	$92.00	$7.28	$99.28
9.	L78-15/black	2	________	________	________	________	________
10.	A78-13/black	1	________	________	________	________	________
11.	G78-14/white	4	________	________	________	________	________
12.	H78-15/white	2	________	________	________	________	________
13.	C78-14/black	5	________	________	________	________	________
14.	L78-15/white	4	________	________	________	________	________

15. When Ted Rose drove to Florida he had to buy four new G78-15 whitewalls. Sales tax in Lexington, Kentucky, where the tires were purchased, is 5% of the selling price. What was the total cost of the tires?

$__________, found by

16. Two E78-14 blackwall tires are purchased in St. Louis, Missouri.

A. What is the total cost of the tires?

$__________, found by

B. Why won't 4.125% of $52.46 give the sales tax?

____

For Problems 17 through 22, use Table 10-5 to find the state tax per pack and total cigarette tax.

	State	No. of Packs	Tax per Pack	Cigarette Tax
Ex.	North Dakota	20	$0.11	$2.20
17.	Alabama	10	________	________
18.	Virginia	40	________	________
19.	New York	2	________	________
20.	Idaho	10	________	________
21.	Texas	20	________	________
22.	California	10	________	________

23. Refer to Table 10-5. The wholesale price of cigarettes in Hawaii is $5.20 a carton (ten packs). What is the state tax on a pack of cigarettes?

$__________, found by

24. Notice that the state tax on cigarettes is lowest in North Carolina. The state tax on gasoline is lowest in Texas. What is a possible explanation?

____

____

25. When Bill and Tammy Sofo drove from Chicago to New York City, they made the following purchases:

Gasoline: Illinois . . . . 20.2 gallons
Ohio . . . . 18.6 gallons
Pennsylvania . . . 21.6 gallons
New York . . . . . 15.4 gallons

Tires: Two F78-14 whitewalls purchased in Pennsylvania.

Cigarettes: Two packs in Illinois; one pack in Ohio; one pack in New York.

A. What gasoline tax did the Sofos pay on this trip?

$__________, found by

B. What FET on tires did they pay?

$__________, found by

C. What state sales tax on the tires did they pay? Pennsylvania charges 6% of the selling price.

$__________, found by

D. What cigarette tax did they pay?

$__________, found by

26. Find at least five other taxes being levied in your area and report on them: what is taxed, how much, and so on.

REVIEW ASSIGNMENT FOR CHAPTER 10
TAXES

Name ______________________ Date Due ____________ Grade _____

Use the appropriate tables in Chapter 10 for these problems.

1. What is the total purchase price of a pair of Haggar slacks if the selling price is $18 and they are purchased in Amarillo, Texas?

   $________, found by

2. What change do you receive from a $20 bill if you purchase these Footnotes in:

   A. Richmond, Virginia

   $________, found by

   B. Pasadena, California

   $________, found by

Footnotes by Fanfare
Reg. 17.00 **13.99**
Entire stock of these leather upper summer sandals, 5 to 10 medium.
WOMEN'S SHOES

3. How much can be saved in state sales tax by buying a $10,000 auto in Little Rock, Arkansas, rather than in New Haven, Connecticut?

   $________, found by

4. A living room suite is purchased in St. Louis, Missouri. The sales tax is $20.58. What is the total purchase price of the living room suite?

   $________, found by

5. Five cents in change is received from $125 when a Kent rocker is purchased in Washington, D.C. What is the total selling price of the rocker?

   $________, found by

6. Bev Petri lives in Topeka, Kansas. She has $5.56 in her purse. She would like to buy the Royal Deb jeans. How much more money does she need?

   $________, found by

Royal Deb® Girls' Jeans
Reg. 7.99 **5.99**
Western 13¾ oz. denim straight legs. Navy, 7-14.
GIRLS

7. The total purchase price for a $9.90 item when purchased in Cleveland, Ohio, is $10.44. The state sales tax in Ohio is 4%. What sales tax did Cleveland add on?

   $________, found by

8. A king-size, three-piece mattress set is purchased in Duluth, Minnesota. The customer gave the salesperson a check for $500 and received $28.55 in change. What sales tax was paid on the purchase?

   $________, found by

For Problems 9 through 12, use the table below.

		County				*Township*			*Vocational School*		*Local School*		*Corporation*		
Line	*Taxing District (School District)*	*Gen.*	*County Home*	*Spec. Levy*	*Health*	*Gen.*	*Road*	*Spec. Levy*	*Gen.*	*Bond*	*Gen.*	*Bond*	*Gen.*	*Bond*	*Total Rate*
1.	Bellevue Corp. . .	2.60	1.10	1.70					2.05	0.15	37.20	1.50	3.10	0.90	50.30
2.	Burgoon Corp. . .	2.60	1.10	1.70	0.20	0.20			1.50	0.20	24.40	1.20	4.80		37.90
3.	Clyde Corp.	2.60	1.10	1.70	0.20	0.40			1.50	0.20	28.40	1.00	2.80	0.90	40.20
4.	Freemont Corp . .	2.60	1.10	1.70	0.20				1.50	0.20	27.20	2.00	3.20		39.70
5.	Gibsonburg Corp.	2.60	1.10	1.70	0.20	0.50		1.80	1.50	0.20	21.80	.90	2.60		34.90
6.	Green Springs Corp.	2.60	1.10	1.70	0.20				1.50	0.20	28.40	1.00	6.80	1.70	45.20
7.	Helena Corp. (Jackson)	2.60	1.10	1.70	0.20	0.20			1.50	0.20	21.80	.90	10.00		40.20
8.	Helena Corp. (Washington) . . .	2.60	1.10	1.70	0.20	0.30		1.00	1.50	0.20	21.80	.90	10.00		41.30

9. Assuming a 37% rate of assessment, what are the annual property taxes on a $94,500 home located in Bellevue Corporation?

$__________, found by

10. Green Springs Corporation uses a 45% rate of assessment. Mr. And Mrs. Viceroy live in a home having a market value of $58,900. What do the Viceroys pay annually in taxes to the Local School–General fund?

$__________, found by

11. Gibsonburg Corporation assesses at a 25% rate. How much less would the Viceroys (Problem 10) pay annually for Local School–General if they lived in Gibsonburg Corporation?

$__________, found by

12. The Sanders live in Helena Corporation (Washington) in a home with a market value of $42,750. The rate of assessment is 35%. If $\frac{1}{12}$ of their annual property taxes are paid into an escrow account monthly, what amount do the Sanders pay into escrow every month for their property taxes?

$__________, found by

13. Susan Gross is a member of the board of education of United Consolidated School District. The district needs an additional $350,000 annually to meet operating expenses. The market value of property in their school district is $98 million. The rate of assessment is 40%. What operating levy millage do they need to meet their operating expenses (nearest tenth mill)?

__________, found by

14. A *Time* article entitled "Those Wild, Wild Property Taxes" said:

> The growing chorus of protests highlights the numerous inequities in the system. In communities that have no sales or income levies, property owners are grossly overtaxed. Boston has no other local taxes, and homeowners pay the highest tax rate in the country–$252.90 per $1,000 of assessed valuation. Though Boston assesses property at one-third of its true market value . . .

A. The property tax in Boston is how many mills?

__________, found by

B. The assessed value of a home with a market value of $90,000 is:

$__________, found by

C. The property tax on a home with a market value of $90,000 is:

$__________, found by

15. A 350-mile trip was taken in a car requiring 16.9 gallons of gasoline. What state gasoline tax was paid if the entire trip took place in the state of:

A. Hawaii

$________, found by

B. West Virginia

$________, found by

16. Why is there no difference in the federal excise tax paid on four C78-14 whitewalls and four C78-14 blackwalls?

____

17. How much more would you pay in state taxes for a carton of cigarettes in New Jersey compared to a carton of cigarettes purchased in Kentucky?

$________, found by

TO THE STUDENT: There is a SELF-REVIEW TEST for this chapter in Appendix A, *with answers* in Appendix C.

11

Banking Services

SECTION 11-1: CHECKING ACCOUNTS

Objective: To write checks, record checks and deposits, and reconcile bank statements.

Most business firms and individuals have checking accounts. Paying bills with checks is generally more convenient, and much safer, than paying cash. A bank provides checking account customers with checkbooks and deposit slips either at no cost or at a very small fee. The amount of the check, the date, and other information are included on each check written by a business firm or individual. A record of the payment is kept on a **check stub**, or in a **check register**.

FREE CHECKING FOR SAVINGS

Here's a special Ohio Citizens savings feature. When you maintain a $400 balance in your Regular Passbook or Golden Passbook savings account, you're assured of a free Ohio Citizens checking account.

WRITING AND RECORDING CHECKS

A **check** is a written order to the bank to pay a specified amount of money to a business or individual, called the **payee**, named on the check. The check reproduced in Exhibit 11-1 is for $821.06 and is payable to Throm Plumbing Supply (the payee).

EXHIBIT 11-1

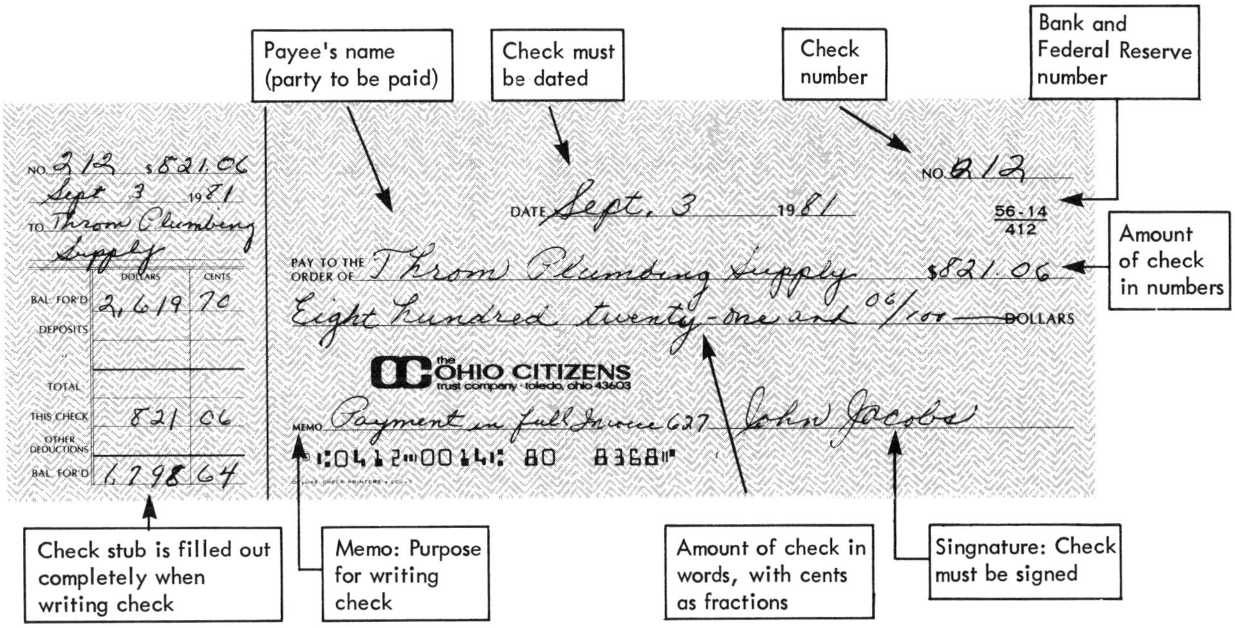

1 SELF-REVIEW

A reminder: Cover the answers in the margin.

Using your name, today's date, and check No. 453, make the following check out to Hartman Electronics for $167.16. The check is payment for a new calculator, No. 2416. Also fill out the check stub. The balance to be brought forward is $714.59.

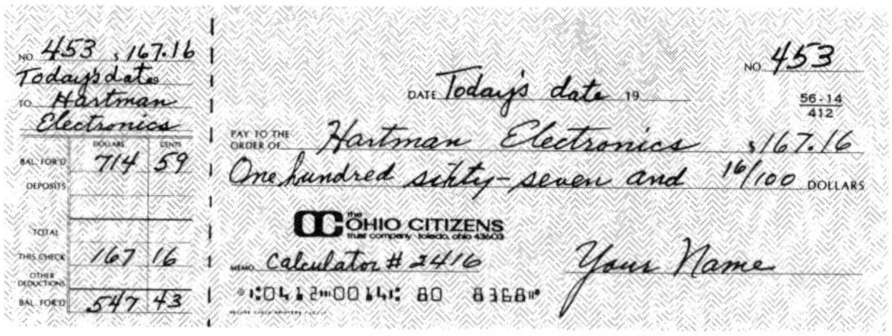

MAKING A DEPOSIT

John Jacobs deposited $200 in his account. The check stub would appear as shown.

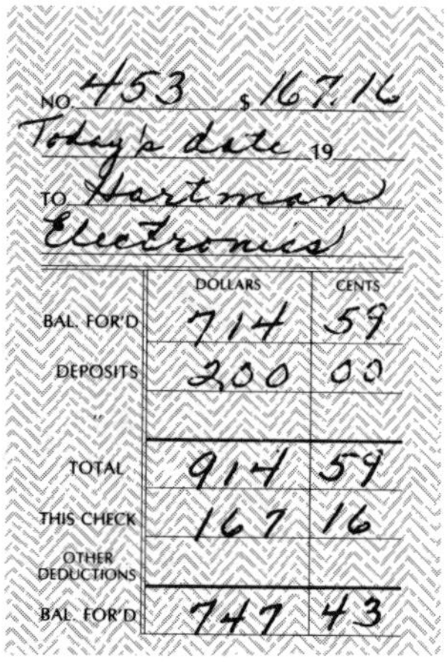

RECONCILING THE BANK STATEMENT

When a check is written, the bank is directed to pay the amount of the check to a business or individual. The check is then **canceled** by the bank, meaning that payment has been made. The canceled checks are returned each month to the checking account customer, along with a monthly bank statement.

The canceled checks are compared with those shown on the bank statement and the customer's check stubs. The balance on the bank statement and the checkbook balance are usually not the same, because the customer may have made deposits or written checks since the bank statement was issued. Also, the customer may not know the exact amount of the **service charge**, if any, assessed by the bank each month. A bank may charge a small fee for each check cashed and a monthly fee for handling the transactions.

The customer should verify that the checking account records agree with the bank's record. This is called **reconciling the bank statement.** The following steps are necessary to reconcile the customer's checkbook with the bank statement.

Step 1. The checkbook balance must be adjusted or revised:

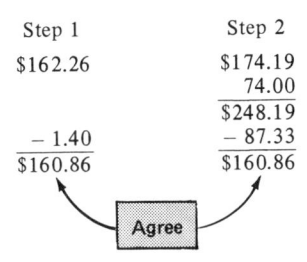

Revised checkbook balance = Checkbook balance − Service charge

Step 2. The bank statement must be adjusted or revised:

Revised bank statement = Ending balance + Deposits not on the statement − Checks outstanding

(Checks outstanding: Checks written but not as yet cashed by the bank)

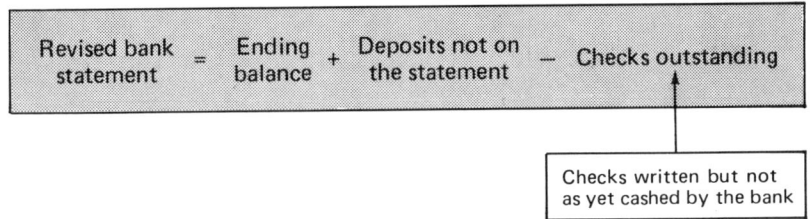

The revised checkbook balance and the revised bank statement should be equal. If they are not, either the bank or the customer has made an error.

Problem Evelyn Kime has just received her bank statement. It shows a new balance of $465.19 and a service charge of $1.65. It does not show a deposit of $294 or checks for $15.95 and $137.50. Her checkbook balance is $607.39. Reconcile her bank statement.

Solution Step 1. Adjust checkbook balance:

Checkbook balance	=	$607.39
Service charge	=	− 1.65
Revised balance	=	$605.74

Step 2. Adjust bank statement balance:

Statement balance	=	$465.19
Deposits not credited	=	294.00
		$759.19
Checks outstanding ($15.95 + $137.50)	=	− 153.45
Revised bank statement	=	$605.74

Must agree

2 SELF-REVIEW

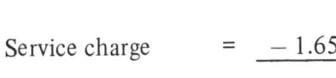

Wayne Hebler has just received his bank statement. It shows a balance of $174.19 and a service charge of 10 cents per check. During the statement period he wrote 14 checks. It does not show a deposit of $74 or checks for $63.19 and $24.14. His checkbook balance is $162.26. Reconcile his bank statement.

Step 1.

Checkbook balance = $__________

Service charge = − __________

Revised balance = $__________

Step 2.

Statement balance = $__________

Deposits not shown = + __________

$__________

Checks outstanding ($63.19 + $24.14) = − __________

Revised bank statement = $__________

Step 1	Step 2
$162.26	$174.19
	74.00
	$248.19
− 1.40	− 87.33
$160.86	$160.86

Agree

ASSIGNMENT 11-1
CHECKING ACCOUNTS

Name ______________________ Date Due ______________ Grade ______

Answers to selected problems are given in Appendix B.

1. Using today's date, make check No. 198 out to DeKarte Wholesale Hardware Supply Company for $473.79. The check is to pay invoice No. 12357. You sign as treasurer of the Village Hardware Co.

2. Using today's date and check No. 867, make out the following check and check stub to William Vickers for $221.75. The check is a payroll check for the preceding week. The balance forwarded was $2,863.38. You sign the check as treasurer of Henry's Landscape Company.

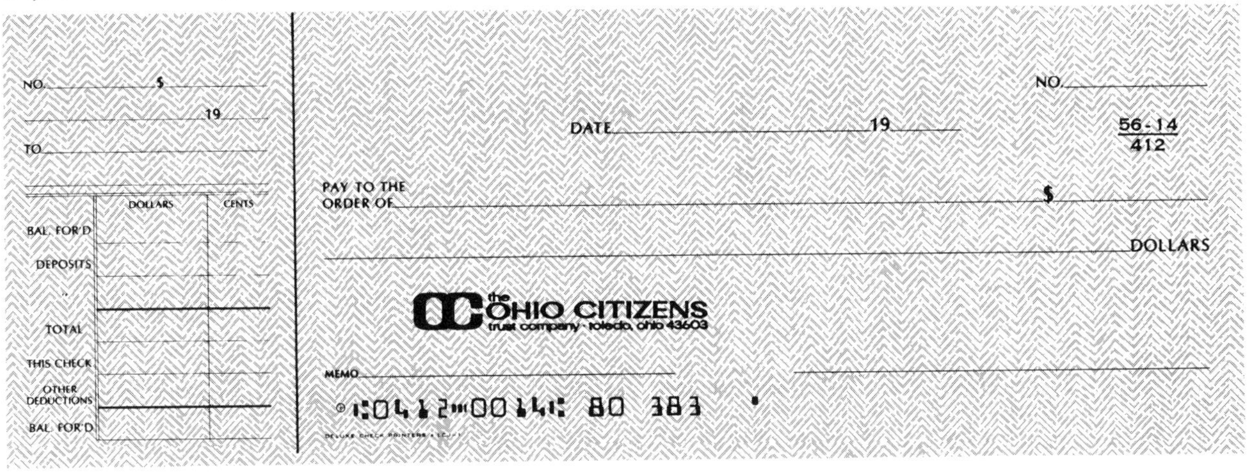

3. Porky's Restaurant has just received its bank statement. It shows a balance of $217.89 and a service charge of $5.35. The bank statement does not show a deposit of $190.70 or three outstanding checks for $117.90, $84.75, and $17.63. The restaurant's checkbook balance is $193.66. Reconcile the bank statement.

Checkbook balance	$ ______	Statement balance	$ ______
Service charge	______	Deposits not shown	______
Revised balance	$ ______	Checks outstanding	______
		Revised bank statement	$ ______

4. Complete this check stub. The balance brought forward is \$143.50. Deposits of \$451.70 and \$513.60 have been made. This check, No. 1,093, is for \$317.80. The check is to Manufacturers Supply House. Use today's date.

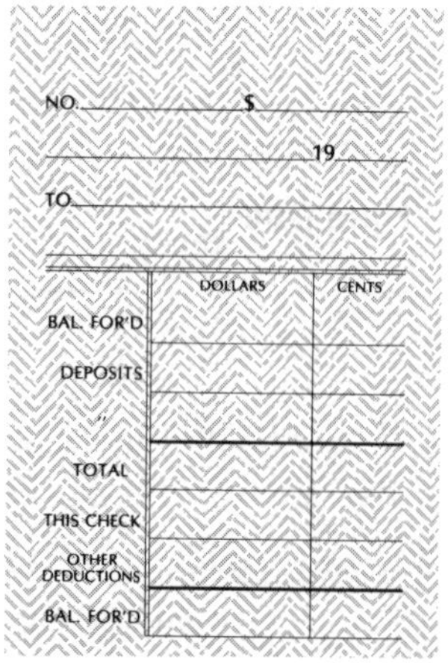

5. Complete this check stub. The balance brought forward is \$713.98. Deposits of \$350 have been made. This check No. 789 is for \$171.89. The check is to City Edison Company. Use today's date.

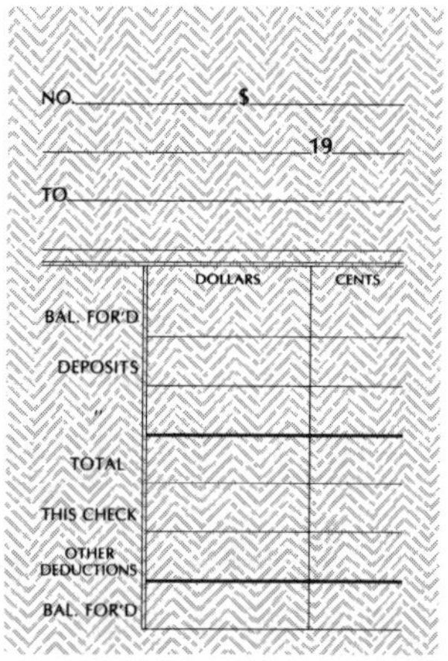

6. Dee's Clothes has just received its monthly bank statement. It shows a balance of \$431.64 and a service charge of \$1.35. The bank statement does not include two deposits of \$150 and \$210 or two outstanding checks for \$384.60 and \$196.74. Dee's Clothes' checkbook balance is \$211.65. Reconcile its bank statement.

Checkbook balance	\$__________	Statement balance	\$__________
Service charge	__________	Deposits not shown	__________
Revised balance	\$__________	Checks outstanding	__________
		Revised bank statement	\$__________

7. Federal Trust's "Tronichex" checking account carries service charges of 10 cents per check written and a 50-cent monthly statement charge. Reconcile a Tronichex statement showing a balance of \$316.70, with eight checks having been written. One deposit of \$200 is not shown, and there are two checks outstanding, for \$107.60 and \$74.98. The checkbook balance is \$335.42.

Checkbook balance	\$__________	Statement balance	\$__________
Service charge	__________	Deposits not shown	__________
Revised balance	\$__________	Checks outstanding	__________
		Revised bank statement	\$__________

8. Federal Trust's business checking account computes service charges as indicated. Reconcile a business checking account showing a balance of \$2,178.43; 43 checks paid; and 12 checks deposited. There were 24 deposits of currency and coin (no charge). Three deposits of \$416.70, \$715.00, and \$319.20 are not shown. There are five outstanding checks of \$116.80, \$91.73, \$415.50, \$19.20, and \$217.50. The checkbook balance is \$2,773.34.

BUSINESS CHECKING ACCOUNT

\$1.00 monthly statement fee
.08 per check paid
.025 per check deposited
.40 deposits of currency and coin per \$1,000.

Checkbook balance	\$__________	Statement balance	\$__________
Service charge	__________	Deposits not shown	__________
Revised balance	\$__________	Checks outstanding	__________
		Revised bank statement	\$__________

SECTION 11-2: SIMPLE INTEREST

Objective: To calculate simple interest and maturity value.

Loans involving simple interest are made by commercial banks and finance companies. For example, a homeowner can borrow $1,000 at 6% interest from Dial Finance for three months and repay $1,000 plus $15 in interest, for a total of $1,015.

DETERMINING INTEREST

The **interest**, designated by I, is the amount of money paid for the use of money.

The **principal**, designated by P, is the total amount of money borrowed.

The **interest rate**, designated by r, is the percent per year charged for the use of the principal.

The **time**, designated by t, is the length of the loan, usually given in days, months, or years. For purposes of calculation, however, time must be expressed in years or part of a year.

The interest is determined by finding the product of the principal, rate, and time. Expressed as a formula:

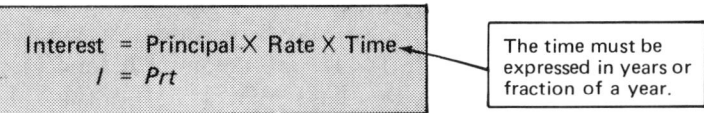

> Interest = Principal × Rate × Time
> $I = Prt$

The time must be expressed in years or fraction of a year.

The *maturity value* of a loan is found by adding the principal and interest.

> Maturity value = Principal + Interest

Problem

In the Dial Finance Company advertisement, what is the interest if $1,000 is borrowed for three months at 6%? What is the maturity value of the loan?

Solution

Interest = Principal × Rate × Time

or $I = Prt$

$= \$1{,}000 \times 6\% \times \frac{3}{12}$ ← 3 months = $\frac{3}{12}$ of a year

$= \$1{,}000 \times 0.06 \times \frac{1}{4}$

$= \$15.00$

Maturity value = Principal + Interest

= $1,000 + $15.00

= $1,015.00

Using a calculator:

Enter	Press	Display
1000	×	1000
.06	×	60
3	÷	180
12	=	15

1 SELF-REVIEW

Find the interest and maturity value for the following loans.

A. A $12,000 loan at 12% for two years.

Interest = Prt

= $______ × _____% × ____

= $______

A. I = $12,000 × 12% × 2
= $2,880.00

MV = $12,000 + $2,880
= $14,880

Maturity value = Principal + Interest
= $__________ + $__________
= $__________

B. $I = \$5{,}000 \times 9.5\% \times \frac{8}{12}$
$= \$316.67$

B. A $5,000 loan for eight months at 9.5% interest.

$I = Prt$
= $__________ × ________% × ______
= $__________

MV = Principal + Interest
= $5,000 + $316.67
= $5,316.67

In words, Maturity value = ______________ + ______________
= $__________ + $__________
= $__________

30-DAY-MONTH TIME AND EXACT TIME

Time in the preceding problems was a full number of either years or months. In calculating the interest on a loan for periods of time *less than* one year, the days may be counted by two methods:

1. **The 30-day-month time method.** A year is considered as having exactly 360 days; that is, 12 months of 30 days each.
2. **The exact time method.** The actual number of days in a month are counted.

Problem

The date of origin of a loan is April 1, and the maturity date, or due date, is June 1. Determine the number of days from April 1 to June 1 using (A) 30-day-month time, and (B) exact time.

Solution

A. Using 30-day-month time there are 60 days, found by:

April 1 to May 1	30 days
May 1 to June 1	30 days
Total	60 days

B. Using exact time there are 61 days, found by:

April 1 to April 30	29 days
Month of May	31 days
May 31 to June 1	1 day
Total	61 days

> *"Let us all be happy and live within our means, even if we have to borrow the money to do it."*
> Artemus Ward

Technical Note. The day a loan is made is not included in the computation of the number of days. Using a simple example, if a loan is made September 8 and is due September 12, the duration of the loan (time) is four days—even though the days are September 8, 9, 10, 11, and 12.

As another example, how many days are there from July 15 to October 20? (This means that the loan was made July 15 and is due October 20.)

30-Day-Month Time Method:

July 15 to October 15	90 days
October 15 to October 20 . . .	5 days
Total	95 days

Exact Time Method:

July 15 to July 31	16 days
Month of August	31 days
Month of September	30 days
20 days in October	20 days
Total	97 days

or

October 20	10th month	20th day
July 15	– 7th month	– 15th day
Total	3 months +	5 days = 95 days

2 SELF-REVIEW

A.

	30 days
	30 days
Nov. 21	11 days
Total	71 days

B.

	20 days
	31 days
21 days	21 days
Total	72 days

If a loan is made on September 10 and is due on November 21, how many days are there using the:

A. 30-day-month time method

Sept. 10 to Oct. 10 . . . . _____ days

Oct. 10 to Nov. 10 . . . . _____ days

Nov. 10 to _____ . . . . . _____ days

Total . . . . _____ days

B. Exact time method

Sept. 10 to Sept. 30 . . . _____ days

Month of October . . . . . _____ days

_____ days in Nov. . . . _____ days

Total . . . . _____ days

EXACT TIME USING A TABLE

As an aid to calculating exact time, Table 11-1 can be used. Notice that the first day of the year, January 1, has been assigned the number 1, January 2, the number 2, and so on. To use the table:

1. Locate the number of the day of the year for the *date of origin.*
2. Locate the number of the day of the year for the *due date.*
3. Subtract the number corresponding to the date of origin from the number corresponding to the due date.

TABLE 11-1. Exact Number of Days between Two Dates

Day of Month	*Jan.*	*Feb.*	*Mar.*	*Apr.*	*May*	*June*	*July*	*Aug.*	*Sept.*	*Oct.*	*Nov.*	*Dec.*
1	1	32	60	91	121	152	182	213	244	274	305	335
2	2	33	61	92	122	153	183	214	245	275	306	336
3	3	34	62	93	123	154	184	215	246	276	307	337
4	4	35	63	94	124	155	185	216	247	277	308	338
5	5	36	64	95	125	156	186	217	248	278	309	339
6	6	37	65	96	126	157	187	218	249	279	310	340
7	7	38	66	97	127	158	188	219	250	280	311	341
8	8	39	67	98	128	159	189	220	251	281	312	342
9	9	40	68	99	129	160	190	221	252	282	313	343
10	10	41	69	100	130	161	191	222	253	283	314	344
11	11	42	70	101	131	162	192	223	254	284	315	345
12	12	43	71	102	132	163	193	224	255	285	316	346
13	13	44	72	103	133	164	194	225	256	286	317	347
14	14	45	73	104	134	165	195	226	257	287	318	348
15	15	46	74	105	135	166	196	227	258	288	319	349
16	16	47	75	106	136	167	197	228	259	289	320	350
17	17	48	76	107	137	168	198	229	260	290	321	351
18	18	49	77	108	138	169	199	230	261	291	322	352
19	19	50	78	109	139	170	200	231	262	292	323	353
20	20	51	79	110	140	171	201	232	263	293	324	354
21	21	52	80	111	141	172	202	233	264	294	325	355
22	22	53	81	112	142	173	203	234	265	295	326	356
23	23	54	82	113	143	174	204	235	266	296	327	357
24	24	55	83	114	144	175	205	236	267	297	328	358
25	25	56	84	115	145	176	206	237	268	298	329	359
26	26	57	85	116	146	177	207	238	269	299	330	360
27	27	58	86	117	147	178	208	239	270	300	331	361
28	28	59	87	118	148	179	209	240	271	301	332	362
29	29	*	88	119	149	180	210	241	272	302	333	363
30	30		89	120	150	181	211	242	273	303	334	364
31	31		90		151		212	243		304		365

*Add one day for February 29 for leap year. (Leap years are 1980, 1984, and so on.)

Problem The due date of a loan is October 20 and the date of origin is July 15. How many days are there between the two dates, using exact time?

Solution There are 97 days between the two dates, found by:

	Day of Year	
Due date, October 20	293	
Date of origin, July 15	– 196 ←	Subtract
Exact time	97	

3 SELF-REVIEW

Determine the number of days for the following loans using the *exact time* method.

A. Origin of loan May 7; due date June 29.

	Day of Year
Due date, June 29	180
Date of origin, May ___ . .	______
Exact time	______

B. Origin of loan August 20; maturity date December 20.

	Day of Year
Due date, Dec. 20	______
Date of origin, Aug. 20 . .	______
Exact time	______

C. Suppose the days for the above loan are counted using 30-day-month time. How many days are there?

May 7 to ______ 7 is . . . 30 days

June 7 to June 29 is . . . . _____ days

Total . . . . _____ days

D. Suppose the days for the above loan are counted using 30-day-month time. How many days are there?

August 20 to Sept. 20 . . . _____ days

Sept. 20 to ______ 20 . . _____ days

Oct. 20 to ______ 20 . . . _____ days

Nov. 20 to ______ ___ . . _____ days

Total . . . . _____ days

A.

	Day of Year
May 7	127
Exact time . . .	53

B.

	Day of Year
Dec. 20	354
Aug. 20	232
Exact time . . .	122

C. June; 30 days
22 days
Total = 52 days

D.

Sept. 20	30 days
Oct. 20	30 days
Nov. 20	30 days
Dec. 20	30 days
Total	120 days

DUE DATE OF A LOAN WHEN TIME IS IN MONTHS AND IN DAYS The term of a loan may be in months. If it is, then the due date will be the same day of the month, the stated number of months later.

Illustrations:

1. The due date of a three-month loan dated February 5 is May 5.
2. The due date of a five-month loan dated June 24 is November 24.
3. The due date of a six-month loan dated September 28 is March 28.

A. Sept. 7

B. July 18

C. Nov. 30

4 SELF-REVIEW

Find the due date:

A. Date of origin is May 7; term is four months.

Due date is ________

B. Date of origin is Nov. 18; term is eight months.

Due date is ________

C. Date of origin is Aug. 31; term is three months.

Due date is ________

Note: Since November has only 30 days, the due date cannot be November 31. It is the last day of the month.

The term of a loan may be in days. If it is, then the due date is the exact number of days past the date of origin.

The due date of a 30-day loan dated January 1 is January 31, exactly 30 days later.

Another illustration: The due date of a 60-day loan dated March 5 is May 4. Referring to Table 11-1:

March 5 is day No.	64
Time of loan	+ 60
	124

The 124th day of the year is May 4.

A. Time = +65
Total = 217
August 5

B. Jan. 19

C. Time = 90
Total = 146
May 26

5 SELF-REVIEW

Find the due date:

A. Date of origin is June 1; time is 65 days.

June 1 is day No.	152
Time of loan . . +	____
Total	____

The 217th day of the year is August ____.

B. Date of origin is Aug. 22; time is 150 days.

Aug. 22 is day No.	234
Time of loan . . .	+ 150
Total	384

Since this goes into the next year, 365 is subtracted from 384, giving 19. The 19th day of the year is Jan. _____.

C. Date of origin is Feb. 25; time is 90 days. Nonleap year.

Feb. 25 is day No.	56
Time of loan . . .	+ ____
Total	____

The 146th day of the year is May _____.
If a leap year, the due date is May 25.

COMPUTING THE AMOUNT OF INTEREST ON A LOAN

Recall that time, t, in the interest formula $I = Prt$ is found either by using 30-day-month time or exact time. In addition, the amount of interest due on a loan depends on whether the year is considered to be 360 days or 365 days. The interest, using the assumption that the year has 360 days, is called **ordinary interest.** If the year is considered as having 365 days, it is called **exact interest.**

Thus there are four possible combinations used in computing the amount of interest to be charged. In summary:

Ordinary Interest (year considered as having 360 days)

Method 1: Ordinary interest, 30-day-month time. Year has 360 days, each month 30 days.

Method 2: Ordinary interest, exact time. Year has 360 days, exact number of days in each month used.

Exact Interest (year considered as having 365 days)

Method 3: Exact interest, 30-day-month time. Year has 365 days, each month 30 days.

Method 4: Exact interest, exact time. Year has 365 days, exact number of days in each month used.

Shown schematically:

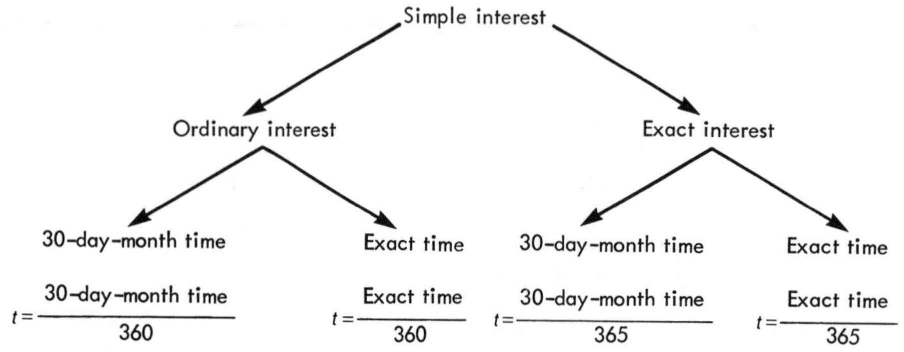

Problem The amount of interest charged under the four methods is illustrated using the following problem. A $9,000, 10% loan has been negotiated by the owner of a small retail women's apparel shop to purchase a special group of winter coats. The date of origin is September 14, and the due date is November 14. Determine the number of days from the date of origin to the due date by (A) 30-day-month time and (B) exact time.

Solution A. Using 30-day-month time there are 60 days, found by:

Sept. 14 to Oct. 14	30 days
Oct. 14 to Nov. 14	30 days
Total	60 days

B. Using exact time there are 61 days, found by:

	Day of Year
Due date, Nov. 14	318
Date of origin, Sept. 14 . .	− 257
Exact time	61 days

Method 1: *Ordinary interest, 30-day-month time.* The time, t, is computed by:

$$t = \frac{\text{30-day-month time}}{360}$$

Computing the interest on the $9,000 loan:

$$\begin{aligned} \text{Interest} &= \text{Principal} \times \text{Rate} \times \text{Time} \\ I &= Prt \\ &= \$9{,}000 \times 10\% \times \frac{60}{360} \\ &= \$150 \end{aligned}$$

Method 2: *Ordinary interest, exact time.* The time, t, is computed by:

$$t = \frac{\text{Exact days}}{360}$$

Computing the interest on the loan:

$$\begin{aligned} I &= Prt \\ &= \$9{,}000 \times 10\% \times \frac{61}{360} \\ &= \$152.50 \end{aligned}$$

Method 2 results in a higher interest charge. It is often referred to as the *Banker's Rule* because many banks use it to calculate the interest on personal, commercial, and industrial loans.

Technical Note. The U.S. District Court for the District of Oregon [*American Timber and Trading Co.* v. *First National Bank of Oregon,* Civil No. 72-1066 (9th Cir., Jan. 22, 1975)] found that the Oregon National Bank had violated the state's usury law when the bank calculated interest by the exact time over 360-day method when the interest rate was at the state's maximum rate. Also, the U.S. Supreme Court refused to review the district court's decision, thus leaving it in effect. First National Bank of Oregon charged some borrowers 10% and some corporate borrowers 12% interest; both interest rates are the maximum limits allowed by state law. When the bank calculated its interest on the loans in question using 365 over 360 method, the effective interest rates were 10.139% and 12.167%, respectively.

Method 3: *Exact interest, 30-day-month time.* The time, t, is computed by:

$$t = \frac{\text{30-day-month time}}{365}$$

Computing the interest on the $9,000 loan:

$$I = Prt$$
$$= \$9{,}000 \times 10\% \times \frac{60}{365}$$
$$= \$147.95 \text{ (rounded to nearest cent)}$$

Method 4: *Exact interest, exact time.* Time, t, is computed by:

$$t = \frac{\text{Exact days}}{365}$$

Computing the interest on the $9,000 loan:

$$I = Prt$$
$$= \$9{,}000 \times 10\% \times \frac{61}{365}$$
$$= \$150.41 \text{ (rounded to nearest cent)}$$

6 SELF-REVIEW

Village Sports Shop borrows $12,000 at 11.5% to pay for spring and summer merchandise. The loan is made on May 10 and is due in three months.

A. August 10, found by May 10 + 3 months

A. The due date is ______________, found by

Determine the number of days from the date of origin to the due date by:

B. 90 days

C. 92 days

B. 30-day-month time.

_____ days, found by three months of 30 days each.

C. Exact time.

Due date, Aug. 10, day:	222
Origin date, May 10, day:	– 130

Exact time: _____ days

D. $I = \$12{,}000 \times 11.5\% \times \frac{90}{360}$

$= \$12{,}000 \times 0.115 \times \frac{90}{360}$

$= \$345.00$

$MV = \$12{,}345$

D. Suppose the $12,000 loan is at 11.5% ordinary interest at 30-day-month time. Then:

$$I = Prt$$
$$= \$12{,}000 \times 11.5\% \times \frac{\_\_\_}{360}$$
$$= \$12{,}000 \times 0.115 \times \frac{90}{360}$$
$$= \$\_\_\_\_\_\_\_\_$$

$$\text{Maturity value} = P + I$$
$$= \$12{,}000 + \$345$$
$$= \$\_\_\_\_\_\_\_\_$$

E. $I = \$12{,}000 \times 11.5\% \times \frac{92}{360}$

$= \$12{,}000 \times 0.115 \times \frac{92}{360}$

$= \$352.67$

$MV = \$12{,}352.67$

E. Suppose the $12,000 loan is at 11.5% ordinary interest at exact time. Then:

$I = Prt$

$= \$\_\_\_\_\_\_\_\_ \times \_\_\_\_\_\_\_\_ \% \times \_\_\_\_$

$= \$\_\_\_\_\_\_\_\_ \times 0.115 \times \frac{92}{360}$

$= \$\_\_\_\_\_\_\_\_$

Maturity value $= P + I$

$= \$12{,}000 + \$352.67$

$= \$\_\_\_\_\_\_\_\_\_\_$

F. $I = \$12{,}000 \times 11.5\% \times \frac{92}{365}$

$= \$12{,}000 \times 0.115 \times \frac{92}{365}$

$= \$347.84$

$MV = \$12{,}347.84$

F. Suppose the $12,000 loan is at 11.5% exact interest at exact time. Then:

$I = Prt$

$= \$12{,}000 \times 11.5\% \times \_\_\_\_$

$= \$\_\_\_\_\_\_\_\_$

Maturity value $= P + I$

$= \$12{,}000 + \$347.84$

$= \$\_\_\_\_\_\_\_\_\_\_$

ASSIGNMENT 11-2
SIMPLE INTEREST

Name ______________________ **Date Due** ____________ **Grade** _____

Answers to selected problems are given in Appendix B.

For Problems 1 through 6, find the due date, interest, and maturity value.

	Principal	*Interest Rate*	*Date of Origin*	*Term of Loan*	*Due Date*	*Type of Interest and Time*	*Interest*	*Maturity Value*
Ex.	$ 4,200	7½%	Mar. 5	3 months	June 5	Ordinary interest/ exact time	$80.50	$4,280.50
1.	1,500	8	Feb. 20	6 months	________	Ordinary interest/ 30-day-month	________	________
2.	3,250	9	Apr. 3	90 days	________	Exact interest/ 30-day month	________	________
3.	965	6½	July 15	4 months	________	Exact interest/ exact time	________	________
4.	12,430	8½	Oct. 5	1 month	________	Ordinary interest/ exact time	________	________
5.	565	10¼	Nov. 10	60 days	________	Ordinary interest/ 30-day month	________	________
6.	1,725	11¼	Aug. 21	180 days	________	Exact interest/ exact time	________	________

7. Find the (A) interest and (B) maturity value for a $7,640 loan at 11% for three years.

   A. Interest, $____________, found by B. Maturity value, $____________, found by

8. Find the interest and maturity value for a $560 loan at 13½% for 6 months.

   A. Interest, $____________, found by B. Maturity value, $____________, found by

9. The date of origin of a loan is June 17. The loan is due in four months.

   A. What is the due date? ____________ found by

   B. What is the number of days from the date of origin to the due date using exact time? ____________, found by

   C. What is the number of days from the date of origin to the due date using 30-day-month time? ____________, found by

10. The date of origin of a loan is April 7. The loan is due in 120 days.

    A. What is the due date? ____________ found by

    B. What is the number of days from the date of origin to the due date, using exact time? ____________, found by

    C. What is the number of days from the date of origin to the due date using 30-day-month time? ____________, found by

11. A manufacturer of plastic products charges 18% ordinary interest at exact time on overdue accounts. An account of $800 was due on March 15 but not paid until June 5.

    A. What was the interest (late charge)? $__________, found by

    B. What was the full amount due on June 5? $__________, found by

12. The Swancreek Trust Company charges exact interest, while the Merchant's Bank charges ordinary interest. Sam Whitaker plans to borrow $3,000 for 120 days at 8%.

A. Which bank offers him the better deal? ______________

B. Explain: ____

____

13. In order to meet its June 5 payroll, a firm borrows $9,000 on that date at 8½% exact interest using exact time. The maturity date for the loan is August 2. What is the maturity value of the loan?

$____________, found by

14. The owner of the Hat Boutique Shop borrowed $1,525 to pay for incoming merchandise. The loan was made on October 1 for 90 days at 10% ordinary interest at exact time. What is the maturity value?

$____________, found by

15. Sally Fuller, in order to pay her federal income tax, borrowed $850 at 9¼% ordinary interest using 30-day-month time. She borrowed the money on April 9 for 120 days. What amount must she repay?

$__________, found by

16. Tom Urbaniak borrowed $500 on December 17 to complete his holiday shopping. He borrowed the money at 8¾% exact interest, exact time, for 90 days. What is the maturity value?

$__________, found by

17. Twin Timbers Bowling Lanes, Inc., borrowed $47,500 to complete its remodeling. The money was borrowed at 12¾% exact interest, exact time, on May 20 for six months. What is the maturity value?

$______________, found by

18. Assume you borrowed $1,000 on July 1 at 11% ordinary interest at exact time. If the loan was not paid until July 1 of the following year (a nonleap year) what interest rate did you really pay?

__________%, found by

19. Two loan agreements for $14,750 were signed on January 31 (a nonleap year). Both were at 12½% ordinary interest at 30-day-month time. One agreement was for 270 days, the other for nine months. What is the difference in the interest charges?

$_________, found by

20. In order to pay the tuition for summer school, a student borrowed $650 for three months at 9% ordinary interest at exact time. The loan was signed on June 1. Find the:

A. Due date.

__________, found by

B. Number of days at interest.

__________, found by

C. Amount of interest.

$_________, found by

D. Maturity value.

$_________, found by

SECTION 11-3: DETERMINING PRINCIPAL, RATE, AND TIME

Objective: To determine the principal, rate, or time.

In Section 11-2, the amount of interest was determined, given the principal, rate, and time. Suppose, however, that the amount of interest is known, but the principal, rate of interest, or time is unknown. In the following illustration the **principal** is not known.

DETERMINING THE PRINCIPAL

The interest, I, rate, r, and time, t, are given; the principal, P, is the unknown. If the simple interest formula $I = Prt$ is solved for P:

$$\text{Principal} = \frac{\text{Interest}}{\text{Rate} \times \text{Time}} \quad \text{or} \quad P = \frac{I}{r \times t}$$

Problems

A. A small firm invested surplus cash in an account paying 6% interest. In a quarter of a year the money earned $90 in interest. How much surplus cash did the firm have initially?

B. Find the principal that results in $3 interest when invested at 8% for 30 days (ordinary interest at 30-day-month time).

Solutions

A.
$$P = \frac{I}{r \times t} = \frac{\$90.00}{0.06 \times \frac{1}{4}} = \frac{\$90.00}{0.015} = \$6{,}000$$

Using a calculator with memory:

Enter	Press	Display
.06	×	0.06
1	÷	0.06
4	= m+	0.015
90	÷ RM	0.015
	=	6000

or

Using a calculator:

Enter	Press	Display
90	÷	90
.06	÷	1500
1	×	1500
4	=	6000

B.
$$P = \frac{I}{r \times t} = \frac{\$3.00}{\frac{8}{100} \times \frac{30}{360}} = \frac{\$3}{\frac{2}{300}} = \$450$$

Technical Note: If any of the numbers are rounded before the final answer is determined, some degree of error will be introduced. In this example, if $^{2}/_{300}$ is changed to the decimal 0.0067, the calculations are:

$$P = \frac{\$3}{\frac{2}{300}} = \frac{\$3}{0.0067} = \$447.76$$

This answer is significantly different from the other answer of $450. To avoid this type of rounding error, *do not* round off any numbers until the last step in the problem.

A. $P = \dfrac{\$9.75}{9\% \times \dfrac{72}{360}}$

$= \dfrac{\$9.75}{0.018}$

$= \$541.67$

B. $P = \dfrac{\$33.83}{9\% \times \dfrac{85}{360}}$

$= \dfrac{\$33.83}{0.02125}$

$= \$1,592.00$

1 SELF-REVIEW

Woodville Auto Parts invested surplus funds in an account paying 9% ordinary interest. Determine the principal if:

A. The interest is \$9.75 and the time is 72 days.

$P = \dfrac{I}{r \times t}$

$= \dfrac{\$\_\_\_\_\_\_}{\_\_\% \times \dfrac{\_\_\_}{360}}$

$= \dfrac{\$\_\_\_\_\_\_}{0.\_\_\_}$

$= \$\_\_\_\_\_\_$

B. The interest is \$33.83 and the time is 85 days.

$P = \dfrac{I}{r \times t}$

$= \dfrac{\$\_\_\_\_\_\_}{9\% \times \dfrac{\_\_\_}{360}}$

$= \dfrac{\$\_\_\_\_\_\_}{0.\_\_\_}$

$= \$\_\_\_\_\_\_$

DETERMINING THE RATE OF INTEREST

Suppose that the interest, I, principal, P, and time, t, are known, but the rate, r, is not known. If the simple-interest formula, $I = Prt$, is solved for r:

$$\text{Rate} = \frac{\text{Interest}}{\text{Principal} \times \text{Time}}, \quad \text{or} \quad r = \frac{I}{P \times t}$$

Problems

A. What is the rate of interest if \$500 is invested for six months and it yields \$22.50 in interest?

B. The Employees' Credit Union posted \$56.44 interest for a 90-day period on an account containing \$3,225. What is the ordinary interest rate at 30-day-month time?

Solutions

A. $r = \dfrac{I}{P \times t}$

$= \dfrac{\$22.50}{\$500 \times \dfrac{6}{12}}$

$= \dfrac{\$22.50}{\$250}$

$= 0.09$

$= 9\%$

Using a calculator with memory:

Enter	Press	Display
500	×	500
6	÷	3000
12	= m+	250
22.5	÷ RM	250
	=	0.09

or

Using a calculator:

Enter	Press	Display
22.5	÷	22.5
500	÷	0.045
6	×	0.0075
12	=	0.09

B. $r = \dfrac{I}{P \times t}$

$= \dfrac{\$56.44}{\$3,225 \times \dfrac{90}{360}}$

$= 0.07, \quad \text{or} \quad 7\%$

2 SELF-REVIEW

A. Helen Jones borrowed \$125 from CBA Finance Company for 20 days and paid \$0.90 in interest. Determine the ordinary interest rate.

$$r = \frac{I}{P \times t}$$

$= \dfrac{\$\_\_\_\_\_\_}{\$125 \times \_\_\_}$

$= \dfrac{\$\_\_\_\_\_\_}{\$\_\_\_\_\_\_}$

$= \_\_\_\_\_\_\%$

B. If James Seger maintains a minimum balance of \$200 in his checking account, he will not have to pay the \$1.50 monthly service charge. He is, in effect, investing \$200 to earn \$1.50 a month. What is his rate of return?

$$r = \frac{I}{P \times t}$$

$= \dfrac{\$\_\_\_\_\_\_}{\$200 \times \frac{1}{12}}$

$= \dfrac{\$\_\_\_\_\_\_}{\$16.\_\_\_\_\_\_}$

$= 0.09$

$= \_\_\_\%$

A. $r = \dfrac{\$0.90}{\$125 \times \frac{20}{360}}$

$= \dfrac{\$0.90}{\$6.9444444}$

$= 12.96\%$

B. $r = \dfrac{\$1.50}{\$200 \times \frac{1}{12}}$

$= \dfrac{\$1.50}{\$16.666666}$

$= 0.09$

$= 9\%$

DETERMINING THE TIME

If the time, t, is to be determined, the principal, P, interest, I, and rate, r, must be known. If the simple-interest formula $I = Prt$ is solved for t:

$$\text{Time} = \frac{\text{Interest}}{\text{Principal} \times \text{Rate}}, \quad \text{or} \quad t = \frac{I}{P \times r}$$

Problems

A. A bank has a minimum charge of \$4 interest on all loans. \$300 is borrowed at 8% ordinary interest at 30-day-month time. How many days does the \$4 interest charge represent?

B. Alpha Simmons paid \$42.16 in interest charges for paying her federal income taxes after April 15. She owed \$1,500 in taxes. If the federal government charges 9% exact interest at exact time, how many days late was her payment?

Solutions

A. $t = \dfrac{I}{P \times r}$

$t = \dfrac{\$4.00}{\$300 \times \frac{8}{100}}$

$= \dfrac{\$4.00}{24}$

$= \dfrac{1}{6}$ of a year or $\dfrac{1}{6}(360)$

$= 60$ days

360 because it is ordinary interest

B. $t = \dfrac{I}{P \times r}$

$= \dfrac{\$42.16}{\$1{,}500 \times 9\%}$

$= \dfrac{\$42.16}{\$135}$

$= 0.31229$ of a year $= 0.31229 \times 365$

$= 113.988$ days

$= 114$ days (rounded)

365 because it is exact interest

3 SELF-REVIEW

A. Interest of $72 was received on a $1,200 loan at 8% ordinary interest. What was the length of the loan in days?

$t = \frac{I}{P \times r}$

$= \frac{\$\_\_\_\_}{\$\_\_\_\_ \times \_\_\_\%}$

$= \frac{\$72}{\$96}$

= ________ of a year

= ________ days, found by

B. Interest of $415 was received on a $9,000 loan at 12% exact interest at exact time. What was the length of the loan in days?

$t = \frac{I}{P \times r}$

$= \frac{\$\_\_\_\_}{\$\_\_\_\_ \times \_\_\_\%}$

$= \frac{\$\_\_\_\_}{\$}$

= 0.________ of a year

= ________ days, found by

A. $t = \frac{\$72}{\$1{,}200 \times 8\%}$

$= \frac{\$72}{\$96}$

= 0.75

= 270 days, found by 0.75 × 360

B. $t = \frac{\$415}{\$9{,}000 \times 12\%}$

$= \frac{\$415}{\$1{,}080}$

= 0.3842592

= 140 days, found by 0.3842592 × 365

ASSIGNMENT 11-3
DETERMINING PRINCIPAL, RATE, AND TIME

Name ____________________ Date Due ____________ Grade _____

Answers to selected problems are given in Appendix B.

For Problems 1 through 6, find the principal, rate of interest (nearest tenth percent), and time (in days).

	Interest	*Type of Interest*	*Principal*	*Rate of Interest*	*Time (in days)*
Ex.	$ 19.49	Ordinary	$ 985.00	9½%	75
1.	37.50	Ordinary	________	8¾	120
2.	516.75	Exact	________	7½	90
3.	8.50	Exact	234.90	________	10
4.	212.35	Ordinary	4,175.00	________	200
5.	10.00	Ordinary	54.96	18	________
6.	1,416.70	Exact	10,000.00	12¼	________

7. The Comer Sporting Goods Company invested money at 8½% ordinary interest. It earned $70 in 30 days. How much money was invested?

   $____________, found by

8. As Perry Comis leaves home for college, he would like to establish a savings account paying him $50 every 28 days. What principal would he require if he can invest it at 9% exact interest?

   $____________, found by

9. A bank pays interest quarterly. At the end of the first quarter, $12.28 was paid on an account containing $893. What is the rate of interest (nearest tenth percent)?

   ______%, found by

10. Metropolitan Edison charged a late fee of $5.94 on an electric bill for $118.80 which was ten days late. What exact interest rate is being charged (nearest tenth of a percent)?

   ________%, found by

11. Sandburg Interior Decorators deposited $8,500 at 6½% ordinary interest and earned $138.13. How many days was the $8,500 deposited?

   ______, found by

12. Janet Brown borrowed $550 at 8% exact interest in order to pay her tuition. On the due date she paid the bank $561. What was the term of the loan (nearest day)?

   ____________, found by

13. Joseph Ward maintains a minimum balance of $200 in his checking account. As a result, he does not pay the $1.38 monthly service charge. By maintaining the minimum balance he, in effect, is investing the money. What is the rate of return?

________%, found by

14. What principal is necessary to establish a trust fund paying $100 per month in interest if it can be invested at 13% ordinary interest using 30-day-month time?

$______________, found by

15. A $1,000 loan agreement signed on March 10 states that $1,053 is to be paid back. The rate is 8½% ordinary interest. When must the loan be paid back?

__________________, found by

16. Huntington Bank offers a home improvement loan of $3,500 for 24 months (two years). A total of $4,060 is paid back. What rate of interest is being charged?

______%, found by

17. A friend agreed to loan Sam Wilkins $200 for one month on the condition that he pay back $210. What is the ordinary interest rate?

_______%, found by

18. How long will it take $273 to double at 10½% exact interest (to nearest day)?

________________, found by

19. The Alice Bainey Howell Scholarship pays a needy student $300 every three months from interest earned. What amount of money is necessary to sustain this scholarship if the money is deposited at 9¼% ordinary interest?

$________________, found by

20. An auto loan payment for $197.41 is due Continental Trust Company on June 19. After June 28, $200.41 is to be paid. If the payment is made June 30, what rate (exact interest) is being charged?

_________%, found by

SECTION 11-4: COMPOUND INTEREST

Objective: To compute compound interest and amount in the account.

Millions of Americans have savings accounts at commercial banks or savings and loan associations. The money accumulated is used for various purposes, including paying for a college education, purchasing a new automobile, and retirement income. In order to encourage depositors to save and leave their money in the accounts, financial institutions offer interest rates ranging from 4% to about 8%.

COMPUTING COMPOUND INTEREST

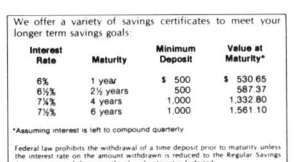

Banks calculate interest annually, semiannually, quarterly, or daily, with quarterly and daily interest being the most common forms. One of the unique features of a savings account is that the amount of interest paid on the original deposit is added to it. Then, based on this total, the interest for the next period is determined. Thus, *interest is earned on interest.* Adding interest to an initial principal, thus forming a new and larger principal in the next time period, is the procedure for computing **compound interest.**

In a sense, *compound interest is just simple interest calculated many times on a sum that grows larger and larger every time the interest is added.*

We offer a variety of savings certificates to meet your longer term savings goals:

Interest Rate	Maturity	Minimum Deposit	Value at Maturity*
6%	1 year	$ 500	$ 530.65
6½%	2½ years	500	587.37
7¼%	4 years	1,000	1,332.80
7½%	6 years	1,000	1,561.10

*Assuming interest is left to compound quarterly

Federal law prohibits the withdrawal of a time deposit prior to maturity unless the interest rate on the amount withdrawn is reduced to the Regular Savings Account rate, and three months of such interest is forfeited

Problem Compute the compound interest on $100 deposited in a bank that compounds interest only once a year. The initial deposit of $100 is left on deposit for four years at an annual rate of interest of 6%.

Solution

Original principal	$100.00
Interest for the 1st year ($100 × 6% × 1)	6.00
Principal at end of 1st year	106.00
Interest for the 2nd year ($106 × 6% × 1)	6.36
Principal at end of 2nd year	112.36
Interest for the 3rd year ($112.36 × 6% × 1)	6.74
Principal at end of 3rd year	119.10
Interest for the 4th year ($119.10 × 6% × 1)	7.15
Principal at end of 4th year	$126.25

Compound interest is the difference between the amount in the account, after computing and adding the interest a specified number of times, and the original principal.

Compound interest = Amount in account − Original principal

Problem In the preceding problem the amount in the account at the end of the fourth year is $126.25. The original principal is $100. What is the compound interest?

Solution

Compound interest = Amount in account − Original principal
= $126.25 − $100
= $26.25

1 SELF-REVIEW

A. $500.00
B. ($500 × .06 × 1) 30.00
C. 530.00
D. ($530 × .06 × 1) 31.80
E. 561.80
F. ($561.80 × .06 × 1) 33.71
$595.51

Find the compound interest on $500 for 3 years at 6% compounded annually.

A. Original principal . . . . $________

B. Interest for the 1st year ($________ × ________ × 1) 30.00

C. Principal at end of 1st year . . . . ________

D. Interest for the 2nd year ($530 × ________ × ____) 31.80

E. Principal at end of 2nd year . . . . ________

F. Interest for the 3rd year ($561.80 × ________ × ____) . . . . ________

Principal at end of 3rd year $595.51

G. $95.51, found by $595.51 – $500.00

G. The compound interest for the 3-year period is $________, found by $________ – $________.

CONVERSION PERIODS

Savings deposited and compounded *semiannually* means that interest is calculated every six months. If the annual rate of interest on the savings account is 4%, interest is calculated every six months at 2% (½ of the 4% annual rate). Thus, there are *two conversion periods each year.*

An investment at 5% compounded quarterly means that interest would be calculated four times a year at 1.25% per conversion period (¼ of the 5% annual rate).

The interest rate per conversion period is found by dividing the given annual rate by the number of conversion periods per year.

$$\text{Rate per conversion period} = \frac{\text{Given annual rate}}{\text{Number of conversion periods per year}}$$

Annual	=	1
Semiannual	=	2
Quarterly	=	4
Monthly	=	12

Consider the following illustration:

Stated Annual Rate of Interest	*Compounded*	*Conversion Periods per Year*	*Interest Rate per Period*
8%	Annually	1	8% ← $\frac{8\%}{1}$
8	Semiannually	2	4% ← $\frac{8\%}{2}$
8	Quarterly	4	2% ← $\frac{8\%}{4}$
8	Monthly	12	8/12%
4	Quarterly	4	1%
4	Monthly	12	4/12%
5	Quarterly	4	5/4% or 1¼%

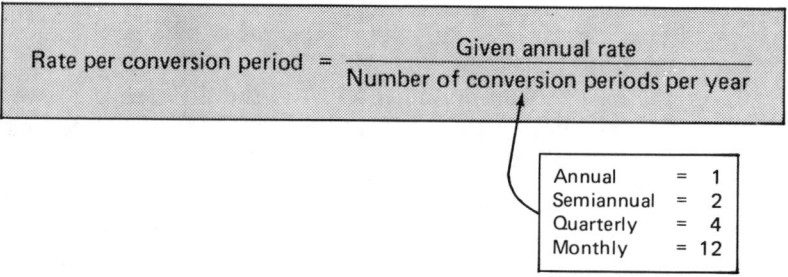

2 SELF-REVIEW

Complete the following:

	Stated Annual Rate of Interest	*Compounded*	*Conversion Periods per Year*	*Interest Rate per Period*
A.	6%	Quarterly	4	$\frac{6\%}{4}$ = ______%
B.	4½%	Semiannually	_____	$\frac{\_\_\%}{2}$ = ______%
C.	6%	Monthly	_____	___% = ______%
D.	5%	Annually	_____	___% = ______%

	Conversion Periods	*Interest Rate*
A.	4	1.5%
B.	2	$\frac{4½\%}{2}$ = 2.25%
C.	12	$\frac{6\%}{12}$ = 0.5%
D.	1	$\frac{5\%}{1}$ = 5%

Problem To illustrate the use of the rate per conversion period, suppose that $1,000 is deposited in a savings account paying 4% compounded quarterly. What is the amount in the account at the end of one year? The rate per conversion period is

$$\frac{4\%}{4} = 1\%.$$

Solution

Original principal	$1,000.00
Interest for 1st period ($1,000 X 1%)	10.00
Principal for 2d period	1,010.00
Interest for 2d period ($1,010 X 1%)	10.10
Principal for 3d period	1,020.10
Interest for 3d period ($1,020.10 X 1%)	10.20
Principal for 4th period	$1,030.30
Interest for 4th period ($1,030.30 X 1%)	10.30
Amount at end of one year	$1,040.60

3 SELF-REVIEW

Suppose that the person who deposited the original $1,000 in the problem above decided not to withdraw the $1,040.60. Determine the value of the account at the end of the second year.

Principal for the 5th period	$1,040.60
Interest for 5th period ($1,040.60 X 1%)	10.41
Principal for the 6th period	$1,051.01

A. Interest for 6th period (____________ X _____%) .... $____________

B. Principal for 7th period .... $____________

C. Interest for 7th period (____________ X _____%) .... $____________

D. Principal for 8th period .... $____________

E. Interest for 8th period (____________ X _____%) .... $____________

F. Amount at end of two years .... $____________

	$1,051.01
A ($1,051.01 X 1%)	10.51
B.	1,061.52
C. ($1,061.52 X 1%)	10.62
D.	$1,072.14
E. ($1,072.14 X 1%)	10.72
F.	$1,082.86

TABLE 11-2
Amount of $1 at Compound Interest

N	1.000%	1.125%	1.250%	1.375%	1.500%	1.625%	1.750%	1.875%	2.000%	N
1	1.01000	1.01125	1.01250	1.01375	1.01500	1.01625	1.01750	1.01875	1.02000	1
2	1.02010	1.02263	1.02516	1.02769	1.03023	1.03276	1.03531	1.03785	1.04040	2
3	1.03030	1.03413	1.03797	1.04182	1.04568	1.04955	1.05342	1.05731	1.06121	3
4	1.04060	1.04577	1.05095	1.05614	1.06136	1.06660	1.07186	1.07714	1.08243	4
5	1.05101	1.05753	1.06408	1.07067	1.07728	1.08393	1.09062	1.09733	1.10408	5
6	1.06152	1.06943	1.07738	1.08539	1.09344	1.10155	1.10970	1.11791	1.12616	6
7	1.07214	1.08146	1.09085	1.10031	1.10984	1.11945	1.12912	1.13887	1.14869	7
8	1.08286	1.09362	1.10449	1.11544	1.12649	1.13764	1.14888	1.16022	1.17166	8
9	1.09369	1.10593	1.11829	1.13078	1.14339	1.15613	1.16899	1.18198	1.19509	9
10	1.10462	1.11837	1.13227	1.14633	1.16054	1.17491	1.18944	1.20414	1.21899	10
11	1.11567	1.13095	1.14642	1.16209	1.17795	1.19400	1.21026	1.22672	1.24337	11
12	1.12683	1.14367	1.16075	1.17807	1.19562	1.21341	1.23144	1.24972	1.26824	12
13	1.13809	1.15654	1.17526	1.19427	1.21355	1.23313	1.25299	1.27315	1.29361	13
14	1.14947	1.16955	1.18995	1.21069	1.23176	1.25316	1.27492	1.29702	1.31948	14
15	1.16097	1.18271	1.20483	1.22733	1.25023	1.27353	1.29723	1.32134	1.34587	15
16	1.17258	1.19601	1.21989	1.24421	1.26899	1.29422	1.31993	1.34611	1.37279	16
17	1.18430	1.20947	1.23514	1.26132	1.28802	1.31525	1.34303	1.37135	1.40024	17
18	1.19615	1.22308	1.25058	1.27866	1.30734	1.33663	1.36653	1.39707	1.42825	18
19	1.20811	1.23684	1.26621	1.29624	1.32695	1.35835	1.39045	1.42326	1.45681	19
20	1.22019	1.25075	1.28204	1.31407	1.34685	1.38042	1.41478	1.44995	1.48595	20
21	1.23239	1.26482	1.29806	1.33213	1.36706	1.40285	1.43954	1.47713	1.51567	21
22	1.24472	1.27905	1.31429	1.35045	1.38756	1.42565	1.46473	1.50483	1.54598	22
23	1.25716	1.29344	1.33072	1.36902	1.40838	1.44881	1.49036	1.53305	1.57690	23
24	1.26973	1.30799	1.34735	1.38784	1.42950	1.47236	1.51644	1.56179	1.60844	24

COMPOUND INTEREST USING TABLES

Computing compound interest using the procedures from the foregoing examples can be very tedious, especially if there are a large number of conversion periods involved. Compound-interest tables are available which greatly reduce the mathematics involved. Table 11-2 gives the amount of $1 at various conversion period rates.

In order to use the compound-interest table, it is necessary to know:

1. The interest rate per period:

$$\text{Rate per conversion period} = \frac{\text{Given annual rate}}{\text{Number of conversion periods per year}}$$

2. The total number of conversion periods:

$$\text{Total number of conversion periods} = \text{Conversion periods per year} \times \text{Number of years}$$

4 SELF-REVIEW

Complete the following table.

	Stated Annual Rate	Conversion Periods per Year	Rate per Conversion Period	Time at Interest (years)	Total No. of Conversion Periods
A.	8% compounded annually	1	8%	2	2
B.	8% compounded semiannually	2	4%	2	4
C.	8% compounded quarterly	4	2%	2	8
D.	8% compounded monthly	12	8/12% or 2/3%	2	24
E.	6% compounded annually	____	________%	3	3
F.	6% compounded quarterly	4	________%	5	20

	Conv. Periods per Year	Rate	Total Conv. Periods
E.	1	6%	3
F.	4	1.5%	20

G. 5% compounded semiannually	____	________%	3	____
H. 4% compounded monthly	____	$\frac{4}{12}$% or $\frac{1}{3}$%	4	____
I. 4% compounded quarterly	____	________%	8	____
J. 5% compounded quarterly	____	________%	10	____

G.	2	2.5%	6
H.	12	–	48
I.	4	1%	32
J.	4	1.25%	40

After the number of conversion periods and the interest rate per period have been determined, the compound-interest table is used to give the amount of \$1 at the previously determined rate and number of conversion periods.

Problem Suppose that \$1,000 is deposited in a bank that pays 4% interest compounded quarterly. The money is left on deposit for two years. What is the amount in the account at the end of two years?

Solution Step 1. The rate per conversion period is 1%, found by $\frac{4\%}{4} = 1\%$.

Step 2. The total number of conversion periods is eight, found by:
4 per year × 2 years = 8

Step 3. Consult the compound-interest table, Table 11-2.

a. Locate the 1% column.

b. Read down the column until the value opposite 8 conversion periods is located.

c. The number is \$1.08286.

d. Since the number \$1.08286 is the amount of \$1 compounded quarterly for two years at 1% per period, it must be multiplied by the number of dollars in the account (1,000). Thus:

Amount in account = \$1.08286 × 1,000 = \$1,082.86

It follows then that the compound interest is \$82.86, found by:

Compound interest = Amount in account – Original principal
= \$1,082.86 – \$1,000 = \$82.86

5 SELF-REVIEW

Suppose that \$8,000 is deposited in a certificate of deposit account that pays 7½% compounded quarterly, and the money must be left in the account five years. What is the amount in the account at the end of five years? What is the compound interest?

A. The rate per conversion period is $\frac{\_\_\_\_\%}{4}$ = ________%

B. The number of conversion periods is ____ × ____ = 20.

C. Table 11-2 indicates that the amount of \$1 at 1.875% per conversion period for 20 periods is \$____________.

D. The amount in the account = \$____________ × __________
= \$____________

E. The compound interest = Amount in account – Original principal
= \$____________ – \$____________
= \$____________

A. $\frac{7\frac{1}{2}\%}{4}$ = 1.875%

B. 4 × 5 = 20

C. \$1.44995

D. \$1.44995 × 8,000
= \$11,599.60

E. Compound interest:
= \$11,599.60 – \$8,000.00
= \$3,599.60

DAILY COMPOUNDING

EARN FROM DAY-IN TO DAY-OUT
$500 MINIMUM 90-DAY NOTICE

Most banks and savings and loan associations offer savings plans involving **daily compounding.** Daily compounding means that interest is computed each day and added to the account so that the interest can earn interest. The actual computations are not made each day; instead high-speed computers, or tables such as Table 11-3, are used.

Table 11-3 shows the amount of $1 at 5½% interest, compounded daily, using a 365-day year.

TABLE 11-3
Amount of $1 at 5½% Interest, Compounded Daily, 365-Day Basis

N		N		N		N		N	
1	1.0001506	21	1.0031691	41	1.0061967	61	1.0092334	81	1.0122793
2	1.0003013	22	1.0033203	42	1.0063483	62	1.0093855	82	1.0124318
3	1.0004521	23	1.0034715	43	1.0064999	63	1.0095376	83	1.0125844
4	1.0006028	24	1.0036227	44	1.0066516	64	1.0096897	84	1.0127370
5	1.0007536	25	1.0037739	45	1.0068033	65	1.0098418	85	1.0128896
6	1.0009044	26	1.0039251	46	1.0069550	66	1.0099940	86	1.0130422
7	1.0010552	27	1.0040764	47	1.0071067	67	1.0101462	87	1.0131948
8	1.0012061	28	1.0042277	48	1.0072585	68	1.0102984	88	1.0133475
9	1.0013569	29	1.0043790	49	1.0074103	69	1.0104507	89	1.0135002
10	1.0015078	30	1.0045304	50	1.0075621	70	1.0106029	90	1.0136529
11	1.0016587	31	1.0046818	51	1.0077139	71	1.0107552	91	1.0138057
12	1.0018097	32	1.0048331	52	1.0078658	72	1.0109075	92	1.0139584
13	1.0019606	33	1.0049846	53	1.0080176	73	1.0110598	93	1.0141112
14	1.0021116	34	1.0051360	54	1.0081695	74	1.0112122	94	1.0142640
15	1.0022626	35	1.0052875	55	1.0083214	75	1.0113646	95	1.0144169
16	1.0024136	36	1.0054389	56	1.0084734	76	1.0115170		
17	1.0025647	37	1.0055904	57	1.0086253	77	1.0116694		
18	1.0027158	38	1.0057420	58	1.0087773	78	1.0118218		
19	1.0028668	39	1.0058935	59	1.0089293	79	1.0119743		
20	1.0030180	40	1.0060451	60	1.0090814	80	1.0121268		

Problem Suppose that $4,000 is deposited in an account paying 5½% interest, compounded daily, 365-day basis. What is the amount in the account after 92 days? What is the compound interest?

Solution Table 11-3 indicates that the amount of $1 at 5½% compounded daily for 92 days is $1.0139584. Thus:

Amount in the account = $1.0139584 × 4,000
= $4,055.83

Compound interest = $4,055.83 – $4,000
= $55.83

6 SELF-REVIEW

What would $2,490 earn in interest if the money is invested at 5½% compounded daily, 365-day basis, for 60 days?

A. From Table 11-3, $1 in 60 days would be worth $________.

B. The amount in the account = $________ × ______
= $________

C. The compound interest = $________ – $________
= $______

A. $1.0090814

B. In account:
= $1.0090814 × 2,490
= $2,512.61

C. Compound interest:
= $2,512.61 – $2,490.00
= $22.61

Tables are also available to facilitate the computations for *whole* years. Table 11-4 is for daily compounding at 5½% for a selected number of years.

TABLE 11-4
5½% Compounded Daily–365-Day Year

Years	*Amount of $1*
1	1.056536237
2	1.116268820
3	1.179378458
4	1.246056078
5	1.316503400
10	1.733181201
15	2.281738943
20	3.003917076
30	5.206332605

Problem A certificate of deposit pays 5½% interest compounded daily, 365-day basis. A minimum deposit of $1,000 is left on deposit for four years. What is the amount in the account at the end of four years? What is the interest?

Solution

Amount in account = $1.246056078 × 1,000
= $1,246.06

Compound interest = $1,246.06 – $1,000.00
= $246.06

7 SELF-REVIEW

A deposit of $2,000 earned 5½% interest compounded daily, 365-day year, for five years.

A. What is the amount in the account at the end of five years?

$______________, found by

A. $2,633.01, found by $1.3165034 × 2,000

B. What is the interest?

$___________, found by

B. $633.01, found by $2,633.01 – $2,000.00

ASSIGNMENT 11-4
COMPOUND INTEREST

Name ______________________ Date Due ______________ Grade _____

Answers to selected problems are given in Appendix B.

For Problems 1 through 6, find the rate of interest per period, number of periods, amount of $1 (from Table 11-2), amount in account, and compound interest.

	Principal	*Compounded*	*Rate*	*Yrs.*	*Rate per Period*	*No. of Periods*	*Amount of $1*	*Amount in Account*	*Compound Interest*
Ex.	$ 5,400	Quarterly	6½%	3	1.625%	12	$1.21341	$6,552.41	$1,152.41
1.	2,500	Quarterly	7½%	2½	______	___	______	______	______
2.	1,900	Quarterly	5½%	5	______	___	______	______	______
3.	21,650	Semiannually	3¾%	7	______	___	______	______	______
4.	13,790	Semiannually	4%	10	______	___	______	______	______
5.	485	Annually	2%	15	______	___	______	______	______
6.	916	Monthly	15%	2	______	___	______	______	______

7. First Federal Savings and Loan pays 7½% compounded quarterly on certificates of deposit left on deposit a minimum of four years and exceeding $1,000 on deposit. What would $3,000 be worth at the end of five years at 7½% compounded quarterly?

   $____________, found by

8. What will $15,000 earn in interest in two years at 12% compounded monthly?

   $____________, found by

9. An investment of $4,000 earned 4½% compounded quarterly for three years, and then, 5½% compounded quarterly for an additional four years. What was the amount in the account at the end of seven years?

   $____________, found by

10. A trust fund was established for Jean Mauch at age nine by her grandparents. The initial deposit was $4,000 compounded semiannually at 4%. How much did she receive at age 21?

    $____________, found by

11. The amount of $255 was deposited in a bank account paying 5½% compounded daily. The bank uses a 365-day year. If the money was left on deposit for 14 days, how much interest would be earned?

    $________, found by

12. Referring to Problem 11, suppose that the $255 was left on deposit for three years.

    A. How much was the account worth at the end of the third year?

       $__________, found by

    B. How much interest did the account earn?

       $__________, found by

13. The Anheim Trust Company and the Tinsdale Savings and Loan use a 365-day year in computing interest on their savings accounts. Both banks have savings accounts which pay interest at an annual rate of 5½%. Anheim Trust uses daily compounding and Tinsdale uses quarterly compounding. Sam Hutsong has $1,000 to deposit for 90 days (one quarter).

A. How much interest will Anheim Trust pay?

$__________, found by

B. How much interest will Tinsdale Savings pay?

$__________, found by

14. The Defiance Savings and Loan Association has a savings account which pays 5½% compounded daily on a 365-day-a-year basis. Jack Soo deposited $2,500. The account was withdrawn at the end of the 80th day.

A. What was the value of the account when the money was withdrawn?

$______________, found by

B. How much interest was earned?

$__________, found by

15. $20,000 was deposited with the Pueblo First National Bank in a five-year savings certificate paying 8% compounded quarterly.

A. Assuming no additions or withdrawals, what was the value of the account at the end of the fifth year?

$_______________, found by

B. What was the total amount of interest accumulated?

$_____________, found by

16. $500 was deposited in a passbook savings account paying 5½% compounded daily based on a 365-day year. No additions or withdrawals were made for a period of two years.

A. What was the value of the account at the end of the second year?

$___________, found by

B. At the end of the second year, $1,700 was added to the account. Three years later the account was worth $____________, found by

17. A trust fund was established for a newborn baby with an initial deposit of $9,000. For the first six years, the trust earned interest at 5½% compounded quarterly. Then, for the next 15 years, 75 days, the trust earned interest at 5½% compounded daily (365-day year). What is the trust fund worth at age 21 years, 75 days?

$_______________, found by

18. A deposit of $3,000 earned 3.75% compounded semiannually for ten years, and then the bank increased the interest rate to 4½% compounded quarterly for five years, and then, finally, the bank increased the interest rate to 5½% compounded daily (365-day year) for ten years. What was the amount in the account at the end of the 25 years?

$_____________, found by

REVIEW ASSIGNMENT FOR CHAPTER 11
BANKING SERVICES

Name ______________________________ Date Due ______________ Grade _____

1. Using today's date and check No. 71, make the following check and stub out to General Cleaning Company for $52.73. The check pays for cleaning services provided. The balance forwarded was $217.80, and one deposit of $175.00 has been made. You sign the check for the Mall Jewelry Store.

NO. ________ $ ________
________ 19 ____
TO ________

	DOLLARS	CENTS
BAL. FOR'D		
DEPOSITS		
TOTAL		
THIS CHECK		
OTHER DEDUCTIONS		
BAL. FOR'D		

NO. ________
DATE ________ 19 ____
56-14
412
PAY TO THE ORDER OF ________ $ ________
________ DOLLARS
the OHIO CITIZENS trust company · toledo, ohio 43603
MEMO ________ ________

2. Main Distributors has just received its bank statement. It shows a balance of $1,714.35 and a service charge of $8.35. The bank statement does not show two deposits of $491.70 and $325.50 or four outstanding checks for $205.70, $161.73, $321.75, and $79.80. Main Distributors's checkbook balance is $1,770.92. Reconcile its bank statement.

Checkbook balance	$________	Statement balance	$________
Service charge	________	Deposits not shown	________
Revised balance	$________	Checks outstanding	________
		Revised bank statement	$________

3. On March 10, Sam Wilson borrowed $6,000 at 10% ordinary interest at 30-day-month time. The loan was for 120 days.

   A. What is the due date? __________, found by

   B. What is the interest? $__________, found by

   C. What is the maturity value? $__________, found by

4. The Fidelity Trust Company offers all unsecured loans on an exact interest basis. The American Bank offers similar loans on an ordinary interest basis. If Jim Jefferson wants to borrow $9,000 for 90 days at 9%:

   A. What interest would Fidelity Trust Company charge? $__________, found by

   B. What interest would American Bank charge? $__________, found by

   C. Where should he borrow the money? __________ Why? ____________________

   ____

5. On May 15 a small manufacturing firm borrowed $10,200 to meet outstanding bills and the payroll. It was a 120-day note at 11½% ordinary interest at exact time. At the end of the 120 days the firm was able to repay $4,200 (including the interest). The bank accepted the payment and wrote a new 90-day loan for the remaining principal at the same 11½% ordinary interest at exact time.

   A. When was the original note due?

   __________, found by

   B. How much interest was paid on the original loan?

   $__________, found by

   C. When was the second loan due?

   __________, found by

   D. How much interest was paid on the second loan?

   $__________, found by

6. Find the exact interest, exact time on a four-month, $4,250 loan dated October 20 at 10½%.

   $__________, found by

7. The Ace Hardware Company invested surplus cash at 7½% ordinary interest at 30-day-month time for 60 days. The money earned $10 interest. How much surplus cash was invested?

   $__________, found by

8. What principal is required to earn $75 every 30 days at 8% exact interest?

   $______________, found by

9. An overdue invoice for $900 is assessed an interest charge of $12 for being paid 60 days late. Assuming ordinary interest, what is the interest rate (nearest percent)?

   ____%, found by

10. If the water bill is paid by the tenth of the month, the net amount is $112.40. If the bill is paid after the tenth, the gross amount is $123.64. A bill was paid two days late and, therefore, the gross amount was paid. What exact interest rate (nearest tenth percent) is being charged?

    ________%, found by

11. Wilson Swap Shop deposited $6,000 at 8% interest and earned $120. If the money is invested at ordinary interest, determine the number of days of interest (nearest day).

    ____________, found by

12. When will a $1,000 loan at 9% exact interest, exact time be due if the interest is $35 and the date of origin is June 7?

    ____________, found by

13. Find the amount in the account and the compound interest on $1,500 at 7% compounded quarterly for three years.

    A. Amount in account, $____________, found by

    B. Compound interest, $__________, found by

14. Find the amount in the account and the compound interest on $12,000 at 18% compounded monthly for two years.

    A. Amount, $__________, found by

    B. Compound interest, $_________, found by

15. The amount of $10,000 is deposited for ten years in an account paying 4% compounded semiannually. The next five years the account paid 6% compounded quarterly. What is the account worth after the 15 years?

    $______________, found by

16. What will $400,000 earn in 54 months at 8% compounded quarterly?

    $___________, found by

17. What would $551.20 deposited for 65 days at 5½% interest compounded daily (365-day year) be worth?

    $__________, found by

18. On June 15, 1980, $1,000 is deposited in a savings account paying 5½% interest compounded daily (365-day year).

    A. How much will the account be worth on June 15, 1990?

       $____________, found by

    B. How much will the account be worth on June 15, 2000?

       $____________, found by

19. What is $5,000 worth at 5½% interest in five years at:

A. Simple interest, $__________, found by

B. Compounded quarterly, $______________, found by

C. Compounded daily (365-day year), $______________, found by

20. What is the interest on $7,500 at 5½% for five years if the:

A. Interest is simple interest? $______________, found by

B. Interest is compounded quarterly? $______________, found by

C. Interest is compounded daily (365-day year)? $______________, found by

21. Grace Jones received the total amount deposited in a trust fund on the day she became 21 years of age. The trust fund was established by her parents on her seventh birthday with an initial deposit of $11,000. For the first four years the account earned 4% interest compounded semiannually. The next five years the account earned 5% interest compounded quarterly. The last five years the account earned 5½% interest compounded daily (365-day year). How much did Jones receive on her 21st birthday?

$_______________, found by

22. On January 1, 1978, Sam Walker deposited $2,100 in a savings account paying 4½% compounded quarterly. On January 1, 1980, his bank changed to daily compounding (365-day year) and raised the interest rate to 5½%. How much will be in his account on March 15, 1982? (Use 30-day-month time.)

$_______________, found by

TO THE STUDENT: There is a SELF-REVIEW TEST for this chapter in Appendix A, *with answers* in Appendix C.

12

Promissory Notes, Discounting, and Partial Payment

SECTION 12-1: PROMISSORY NOTES AND DISCOUNTING

Objective: To compute the discount and proceeds of a noninterest-bearing note.

PROMISSORY NOTES

Derek Richards needed $75 to pay for repairs on his car. He borrowed it from Tony Angelo and gave him this informal note: "Tony, I owe you $75. Signed Derek." This same I.O.U. concept is used in business, where the note is called a **promissory note.**

Problem

Bill Spinner manufactures graphite fishing rods in a small building adjacent to his home. He sells them wholesale for $25 apiece to sporting goods stores, bait and tackle shops, and other retail outlets. Since most of the orders total less than $1,000, he is usually paid cash upon delivery.

Spinner loaded 40 rods in his van for delivery to Karen's Marina. Unfortunately, the owner had just sold her business, and the new owner refused to accept delivery. Spinner then offered the rods to John Walton, owner of Walton's Bait and Tackle Shop, for $20, $5 off the regular price. Walton wanted the rods but had just paid a large remodeling bill and did not have $800 cash (computed by $20 × 40 = $800).

PROMISSORY NOTE
NATIONAL DIRECT STUDENT LOAN PROGRAM

Based on a long-time friendship, Walton offered to purchase the fishing rods if Spinner would accept a promissory note for the $800 payable in 60 days. What should the promissory note contain?

PROMISSORY NOTE

$800.00 March 15 1981

Sixty days after date, for value received, I

promise to pay to the order of Bill Spinner

Eight hundred and 00/100 DOLLARS

with interest at the rate of 0 per centum per annum, payable — annually,

at Drand County, Arkansas

No. 9340 John Walton [SEAL]

[SEAL]

Due May 14, 1981 [SEAL]

Legal News, Toledo, Ohio

Solution

The promissory note signed by Walton meets the criteria as set forth by the Uniform Commercial Code.

> Refer back to Table 11-1:
>
> March 15 is day No. 74
> Time of loan is + 60
> 134
>
> The 134th day of the year is May 14.

1. It is in writing and signed by the **maker** of the promissory note, John Walton.
2. It contains an unconditional promise to pay a certain sum of money at a fixed or determinable future time. Walton promised to pay Spinner $800, called the **face** of the note. The **date of origin** is March 15. The **term** of the note is 60 days. May 14 is the **due date** of the note, often called the **maturity date.**
3. It is payable to a specified party, called the **payee.** Spinner is the payee.

Another very important characteristic of Walton's promissory note is that it is **negotiable** (although it does not specifically state this in the note). Negotiable means that the note can be transferred from one owner to another. (Spinner will take advantage of this aspect.)

DISCOUNTING A NONINTEREST-BEARING NOTE

In the above problem, Walton pays no interest on the note. Based on Spinner's experience with several other noninterest-bearing notes he has accepted in the past, he knows that he can keep it until the maturity date, May 14, and then collect $800 from Walton. The $800 is called the **maturity value** of the note. *In a noninterest-bearing note, the maturity value equals the face value of the note.*

Another possibility Spinner has is to take the note to his bank and have the note *discounted.*

> *Technical Note.* It is assumed that the bank is one of the few in the United States still discounting notes. In recent years many banks have discontinued this practice and instead are requiring that a line of credit (see Section 12-2) be established. Discounting is a common practice in other domestic and international financial transactions, however.

Spinner held Walton's note until April 24, when he needed cash to meet his small payroll and to purchase more graphite blanks to manufacture his fishing rods. Spinner therefore decided to discount the note at his bank. This means that he will receive cash from the bank for his promissory note. However, since the bank will not be able to collect the $800 from Walton until May 14, Spinner will receive less than the $800 from the bank. The bank will discount the note. The process of determining the discount is equivalent to calculating interest on the maturity value of the note and is generally referred to as discounting the note.

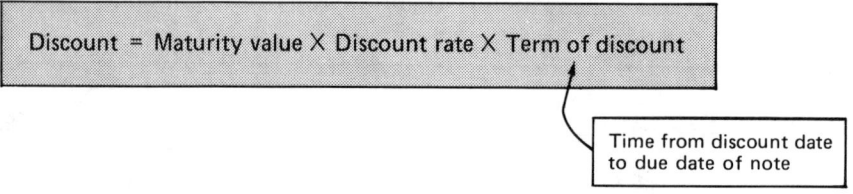

> Discount = Maturity value × Discount rate × Term of discount
>
> (Term of discount: Time from discount date to due date of note)

Notes are generally discounted using *exact time* and *ordinary interest* (360 days).

The amount that Spinner receives is known as the **proceeds** of the note. It is found by subtracting the discount from the maturity value.

> Proceeds = Maturity value − Discount

Problem If Walton's note is discounted on April 24, at a discount rate of 12%, what proceeds will Spinner receive?

Solution Spinner will be charged 12% interest on \$800 for 20 days (April 24 to May 14 is 20 days). The 20-day time period, known as the **term of discount**, is the number of days from the discount date to the due date of the note.

Using a calculator:

Enter	Press	Display
800	×	800
.12	×	96
20	÷	1920
360	=	5.3333333

The discount is found by:

$$\text{Discount} = \text{Maturity value} \times \text{Discount rate} \times \text{Term of discount}$$

$$= \$800 \times 12\% \times \frac{20}{360}$$

(20 ← Exact time; 360 ← Ordinary interest)

$$= \$5.33$$

The proceeds are found by:

$$\text{Proceeds} = \text{Maturity value} - \text{Discount}$$
$$= \$800 - \$5.33$$
$$= \$794.67$$

Thus Spinner will receive \$794.67 from the bank on April 24. The bank will collect \$800 from Walton on May 14.

1 SELF-REVIEW

A reminder: Cover the answers in the margin.

Spinner delivered an order of graphite fishing rods totaling \$1,000 to Kramer's Bait and Tackle Shop on August 26. Kramer did not have the \$1,000 but offered to sign a noninterest-bearing promissory note due September 26. Spinner accepted.

\$1,000

If Spinner keeps the note until September 26, he will receive \$________ from Kramer. On September 5, however, he needs cash and takes the note to his bank to have it discounted. The bank has raised the discount rate to 13%. Find the amount of the discount and proceeds.

A. Discount:
= Maturity value
× Discount rate
× Term of discount

$= \$1{,}000 \times 13\% \times \frac{21}{360}$

$= \$7.58$

A. Discount = ________ × ________ × ________

= \$______ × ____% × $\frac{}{360}$ ← Ordinary interest

= \$______

B. Proceeds:
= Maturity value
− Discount

= \$1,000 − \$7.58
= \$992.42

B. Proceeds = ________ ________

= \$______ − \$______

= \$______

ASSIGNMENT 12-1
PROMISSORY NOTES AND DISCOUNTING

Name ______________________ Date Due ____________ Grade _____

Answers to selected problems are given in Appendix B.

For Problems 1 through 6, find the maturity value, due date, term of discount, discount, and proceeds for these noninterest-bearing notes. (Notes are ordinary interest at exact time.)

	Face	*Maturity Value*	*Date of Origin*	*Term*	*Due Date*	*Discount Date*	*Term of Discount (days)*	*Discount Rate*	*Discount*	*Proceeds*
Ex.	$ 1,200	$1,200	Sept. 20	3 months	Dec. 20	Nov. 10	40	7%	$9.33	$1,190.67
1.	5,000	________	June 5	90 days	________	June 20	_____	8	__________	____________
2.	750	________	Aug. 20	120 days	________	Oct. 25	_____	11	__________	____________
3.	43,600	________	Mar. 20	2 months	________	Mar. 20	_____	9½	__________	____________
4.	4,100	________	May 2	1 month	________	May 2	_____	10¾	__________	____________
5.	1,000	________	Nov. 20	60 days	________	Dec. 15	_____	8¼	__________	____________
6.	200	________	Dec. 2	1 month	________	Dec. 2	_____	7½	__________	____________

7. John Barker gave Arrin James a $1,200 noninterest-bearing note dated September 3 and due in three months. James discounted the note on October 10 at 10½%

   A. What is the discount term? ____________, found by

   B. What is the discount? $__________, found by

   C. What are the proceeds? $____________, found by

8. Herman Houser needed cash. He took a $550 noninterest-bearing note dated July 5 and due in 30 days to his bank on July 10 for discounting. If the discount rate is 9%:

   A. What is the discount term? ____________, found by

   B. What is the discount? $________, found by

   C. What are the proceeds? $___________, found by

9. On August 26 Asa Tang, maker of fine chairs, delivered a truckload of ladderback chairs valued at $400 to Grandma's Antique Shop. Jean Gibbons, the owner of the shop, did not have the $400 on hand and offered Tang this note, which he accepted.

PROMISSORY NOTE

$ 400.00 August 26 1980

One Month *after date, for value received,* I

promise to pay to the order of Asa Tang

Four hundred 00/100 *DOLLARS*

with interest at the rate of 0 *per centum per annum, payable* — *annually,*

at Hopewell County, Arkansas

No. 3291 (Mrs.) Jean Gibbons [SEAL]

[SEAL]

Due September 26, 1980 [SEAL]

Legal News, Toledo, Ohio

A. Who is the maker of the note?

____

B. What is the note called?

____

C. What is the maturity date of the note?

____

D. What is the maturity value of the note?

$________

E. If Tang kept the note for one month, how much would he collect from Gibbons?

$________

F. On September 5 Tang needed cash and took the note to his bank and asked for payment. How much would Tang receive if the bank had raised its discount rate to 9%?

$__________, found by

10. A 90-day noninterest-bearing note with a face of $12,000 was sold on the date of origin to a finance company. If the discount rate was 7%, what were the proceeds?

$__________, found by

11. On September 3 the ABC Finance Company discounted a $900 noninterest-bearing note dated August 12 and due in four months. The finance company discounts this type of note at 12%. What are the proceeds of the note?

$__________, found by

SECTION 12-2: DISCOUNTING AN INTEREST-BEARING NOTE AND ESTABLISHING A LINE OF CREDIT

Objective: To compute the interest, maturity value, discount and proceeds of an interest-bearing note.

Promissory notes are usually **interest-bearing notes.** The **maturity value** of the note on the **due date** is calculated by adding the interest to the **face** of the note.

Maturity value = Face + Interest

Problem Bill Spinner sold $2,000 worth of graphite fishing rods to Mall Sporting Goods, a new shop in the Northside Mall, on June 15. He was anxious to add this new account and agreed to accept an interest-bearing note for the $2,000 for four months at 10% ordinary interest at exact time. What is the maturity value of the note at the end of the four months, that is, October 15?

Solution There are 122 days from June 15 to October 15. Calculating the interest on the $2,000 note at 10%:

Refer to Table 11-1:

	Day of Year
Due date, Oct. 15	288
Date of origin, June 15	− 166
Exact time	122

Interest = Principal × Rate × Time

$I = Prt$

$= \$2{,}000 \times 10\% \times \frac{122}{360}$

$= \$67.78$

Determining the maturity value:

Maturity value = Face + Interest

= $2,000 + $67.78

= $2,067.78

Amount to be received October 15.

1 SELF-REVIEW

Hsu and Ten Wong manufacture lacquered bowls and other art objects. They sold $3,000 worth of merchandise to a retail shop on April 10 and accepted a promissory note due July 10 at 10% interest. What is the maturity value of the note?

Interest = *Prt*

= $_________ × ______% × ______

= $_________

$I = Prt$

$= \$3{,}000 \times 10\% \times \frac{91}{360}$

$= \$75.83$

Maturity value = Face + Interest

= $_________ + $_________

= $_________

$MV = \$3{,}000 + \$75.83$

$= \$3{,}075.83$

Problem Bill Spinner presented the $2,000 promissory note he received from Mall Sporting Goods to a finance company for discounting, instead of holding it for the full four months. How much would he receive from the Hudson Finance Company if he had the promissory note from Mall Sporting Goods discounted on July 15? Hudson's current discount rate is 11%.

Solution July 15 to October 15 is 92 days.

Calculating the discount on the maturity value of $2,067.78 (computed in previous problem):

Discount = Maturity value × Rate × Term of discount

$$= \$2{,}067.78 \times 11\% \times \frac{92}{360}$$

$$= \$58.13$$

Determining the proceeds received on July 15:

Proceeds = Maturity value − Discount
= $2,067.78 − $58.13
= $2,009.65

2 SELF-REVIEW

Hsu and Ten Wong (see Self-Review 1) need cash and decide to have the promissory note for $3,000 discounted at their bank on April 20. The bank's current discount rate is 10½%. How much would they receive on April 20?

Discount = Maturity value × Rate × Term of discount
= $________ × ______% × ——
= $________

Discount:
$= \$3{,}075.83 \times 10\tfrac{1}{2}\% \times \frac{81}{360}$
= $72.67

Proceeds = Maturity value − ________
= $________ − $________
= $________

Proceeds:
= Maturity value − Discount
= $3,075.83 − $72.67
= $3,003.16

LINE OF CREDIT

As an alternative to discounting the notes from his customers, Bill Spinner could have established with his bank a **line of credit**, which he could use to secure needed cash. Initially, the bank would investigate Spinner's business, check his credit, and so on. Then it would extend to him a line of credit, meaning that, for example, he would be allowed to borrow on a short-term basis up to $10,000, provided he had the proper collateral.

The promissory note of $2,000 from Mall Sporting Goods would be sufficient collateral for Spinner to borrow $2,000. If the bank charged him 10% per annum, he would pay back $2,067.78 at the end of four months (that is, on October 15). The calculations are:

Interest = Prt

$$= \$2{,}000 \times 10\% \times \frac{122}{360}$$

$$= \$67.78$$

Maturity value = Face + Interest
= $2,000 + $67.78
= $2,067.78

This is the same amount he would collect from Mall Sporting Goods on October 15.

Banks' Line Of Credit Gives Go-Ahead To CPB Expansion Plans

WASHINGTON (AP) — The Corporation for Public Broadcasting announced Tuesday an agreement with a consortium of banks to establish a $32.5 million line of credit to finance the corporation's nationwide satellite transmission system.

The satellite system will permit the nation's public TV stations to have several channels to receive and send programs instead of the one now devoted to the Public Broadcasting Service network.

Bank of America will act as agent for a group of lenders. The line of credit will be reduced over a 10-year period, beginning in fiscal year 1979.

Interest charges will be based on Bank of America's prime rate, plus fractional increments over the last years of the credit.

ASSIGNMENT 12-2
DISCOUNTING AN INTEREST-BEARING NOTE AND ESTABLISHING A LINE OF CREDIT

Name ______________________ **Date Due** ______________ **Grade** _____

Answers to selected problems are given in Appendix B.

For Problems 1 through 6, find the due date, interest term, interest, maturity value, discount term, discount, and proceeds for these interest-bearing notes.

	Date of Origin	*Term*	*Due Date*	*Interest Term*	*Interest Rate*	*Face*	*Interest*	*Maturity Value*	*Discount Date*	*Discount Rate*	*Discount Term (days)*	*Discount*	*Proceeds*
Ex.	Mar. 3	3 mo.	June 3	92	8½%	$ 4,800	$104.27	$4,904.27	Apr. 20	10¼%	44	$61.44	$4,842.83
1.	Sept. 7	60 days			7%	2,500			Sept. 30	9½%			
2.	Jan. 10	30 days			12%	5,000			Jan. 30	13%			
3.	Jul. 20	2 mo.			6½%	1,500			Jul. 20	8¾%			
4.	May 1	4 mo.			14%	12,615			May 1	15%			
5.	Aug. 3	6 mo.			7½%	4,625			Dec. 20	11%			
6.	Oct. 10	3 mo.			7¼%	14,825			Oct. 31	11½%			

7. The American Bank discounted a $900, 60-day, 8% note dated April 10 on May 15 at 9%. Find the:

   A. Due date ______________

   B. Interest term ______________

   C. Interest ______________ found by

   D. Maturity value ______________ found by

   E. Discount term ______________

   F. Discount ______________ found by

   G. Proceeds ______________ found by

8. The County Trust discounted a $1,415.20, two-month, 7½% note dated August 1 on September 1 at 9¼%. Find the:

   A. Due date ______________

   B. Interest term ______________

   C. Interest ______________ found by

   D. Maturity value ______________ found by

   E. Discount term ______________

   F. Discount ______________ found by

   G. Proceeds ______________ found by

9. On January 16 of a nonleap year, Mrs. John Stillwell sold to her bank a $3,000 note dated January 1, bearing interest at 9% for four months. If the rate of discount was 10½%, what were the proceeds?

$______________, found by

10. On July 14, William Brothers Hardware sold $1,314.85 worth of items to Standard Homebuilders Company, Inc. In lieu of cash payment they accepted an 8% interest-bearing note due in 90 days. On September 10 the note was discounted at National Bank at a discount rate of 10%. What amount did William Brothers Hardware receive?

$______________, found by

11. If William Brothers Hardware (Problem 10) had established a line of credit with National Bank, it could have used the Standard Homebuilders Company note as collateral to borrow $1,314.85.

A. Assuming the company could borrow $1,314.85 at 8% on July 14 for 90 days, what would it pay back?

$______________, found by

B. How does that compare to the maturity value of the note in Problem 10?

____

____

SECTION 12-3: PARTIAL PAYMENT

Objective: To determine how partial payments are allocated and the amount due at maturity using the United States Rule and the Merchants' Rule.

From an Adrian, Michigan, farmer:

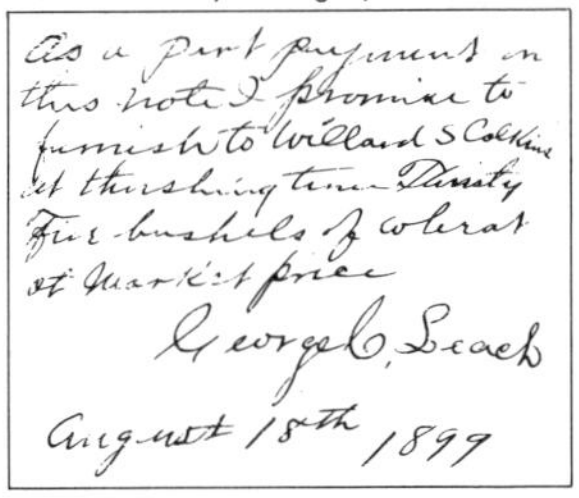
As a part payment on
this note I promise to
furnish to Willard S Colkins
at threshing time Ninety
Five bushels of wheat
at market price
George C. Leach
August 18th 1899

The signer of an interest-bearing note may want to pay off part of the debt *prior* to the maturity date. This payment is referred to as a **partial payment.**

Usually the reason for making one or more partial payments on a note before its maturity date is to reduce the total interest charge. Most notes contain a clause stating that the borrower will not pay a penalty for reducing the debt, or paying it in full, prior to the maturity date.

There is another situation where a partial payment is made. If the borrower is unable to meet the payment when due, a partial payment may be made and an extension of time requested.

In order to avoid any disagreement regarding how partial payments are to be applied and how the interest is to be reduced, one of two methods is commonly used. The two methods—The **United States Rule** and the **Merchants' Rule**—are used to *determine the balance of the loan after a partial payment is made.*

THE UNITED STATES RULE

The U.S. Supreme Court in a ruling (*Story* vs. *Livingston*, 1839) made a decision as to how partial payments are to be applied. The rule has since been incorporated into the statutes of many states. It is known as the **United States Rule.**

The United States Rule is relatively simple to apply:

1. The partial payment is used first to *pay the interest* on the principal to the date of the partial payment.
2. Any money left over after the interest is paid goes toward reducing the principal.
3. Should the partial payment not fully pay the interest to date, it is held by the holder of the note until the total of all the partial payments equals or exceeds the interest to date. Then the interest to date is paid.

Problem A note for $3,000 was signed on February 1 in a nonleap year. It was due in four months. The interest rate was 10%. The borrower made a partial payment of $1,000 on March 3 and another payment of $500 on May 2. How were the partial payments allocated? What is the amount due at maturity?

Solution The following figure and computations show how the partial payments were allocated.

Shown schematically:

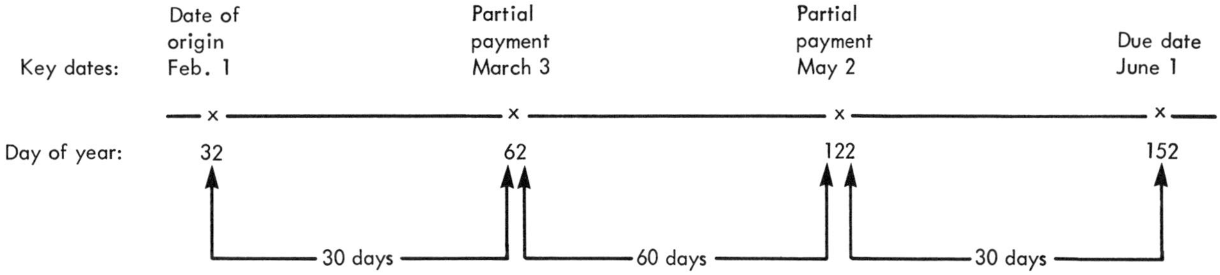

To compute the amount due on the maturity date using the United States Rule:

$3{,}000 \times 10\% \times \frac{30}{360}$

$2{,}025 \times 10\% \times \frac{60}{360}$

$1{,}558.75 \times 10\% \times \frac{30}{360}$

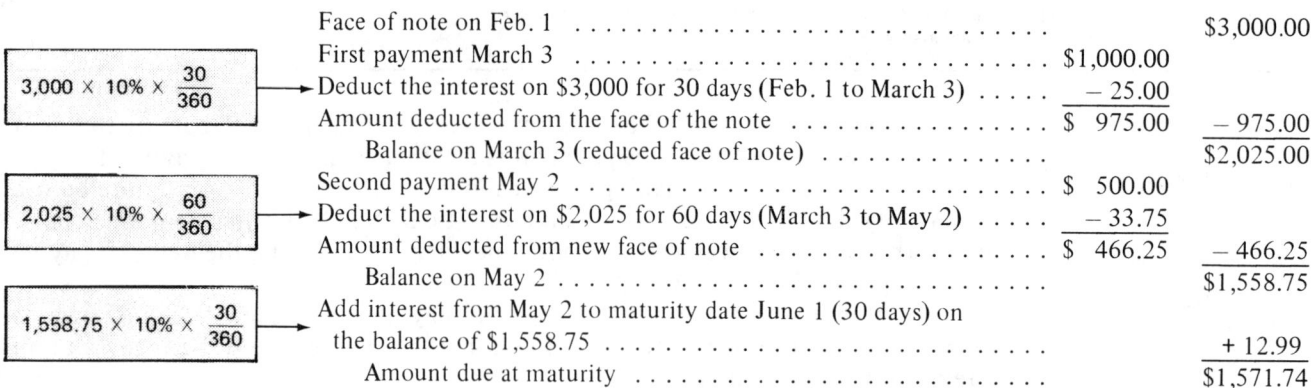

Face of note on Feb. 1		$3,000.00
First payment March 3	$1,000.00	
Deduct the interest on $3,000 for 30 days (Feb. 1 to March 3)	– 25.00	
Amount deducted from the face of the note	$ 975.00	– 975.00
Balance on March 3 (reduced face of note)		$2,025.00
Second payment May 2	$ 500.00	
Deduct the interest on $2,025 for 60 days (March 3 to May 2)	– 33.75	
Amount deducted from new face of note	$ 466.25	– 466.25
Balance on May 2		$1,558.75
Add interest from May 2 to maturity date June 1 (30 days) on the balance of $1,558.75		+ 12.99
Amount due at maturity		$1,571.74

1 SELF-REVIEW

On July 5, $8,000 was borrowed by signing a 12% promissory note due in 150 days. Two partial payments were made, the first on September 3 for $2,000 and the second on October 23 for $3,000.

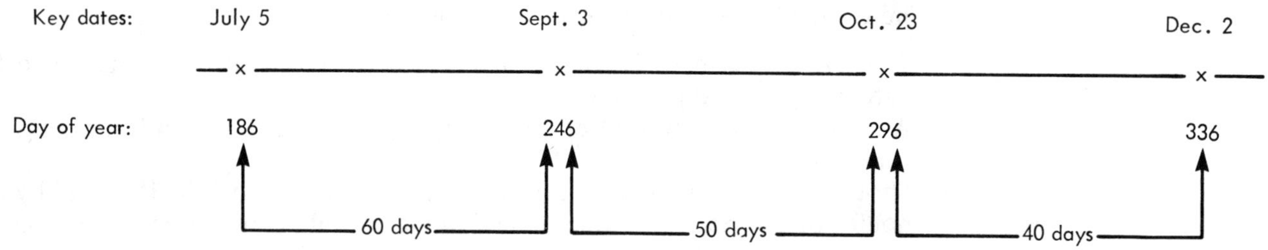

What is the amount due on the maturity date using the United States Rule?

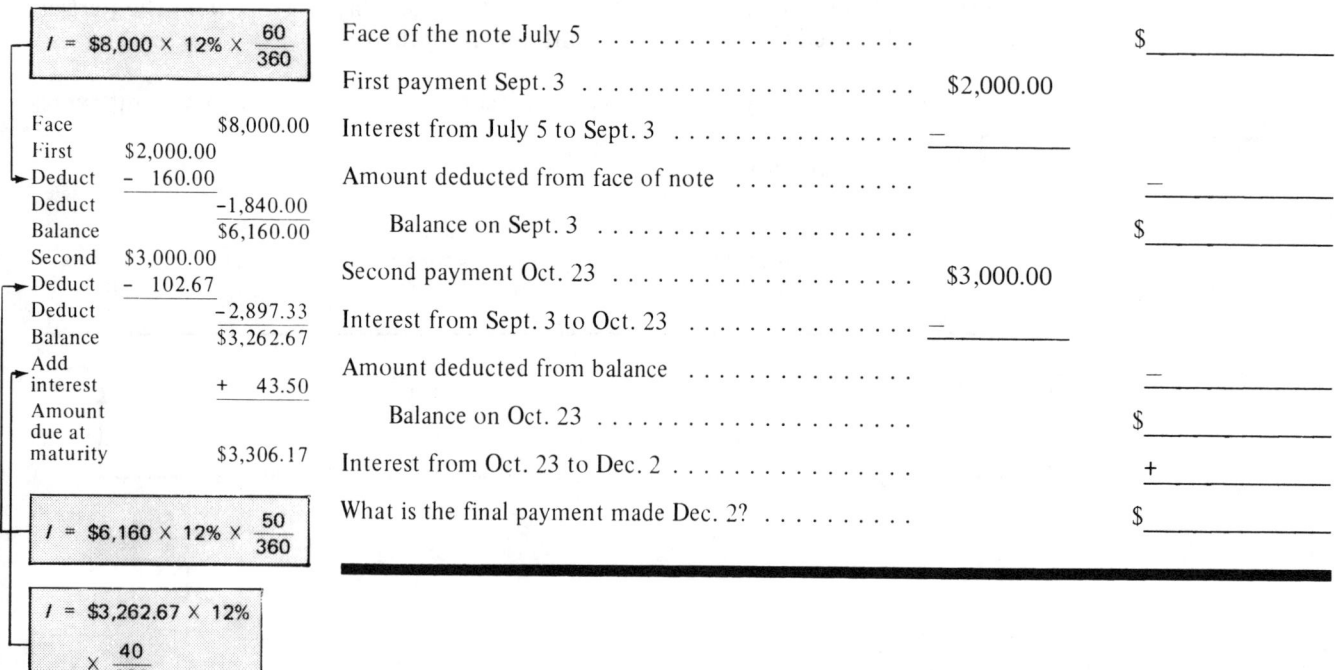

Face of the note July 5		$
First payment Sept. 3	$2,000.00	
Interest from July 5 to Sept. 3	–	
Amount deducted from face of note		–
Balance on Sept. 3		$
Second payment Oct. 23	$3,000.00	
Interest from Sept. 3 to Oct. 23	–	
Amount deducted from balance		–
Balance on Oct. 23		$
Interest from Oct. 23 to Dec. 2		+
What is the final payment made Dec. 2?		$

$I = \$8{,}000 \times 12\% \times \frac{60}{360}$

Face		$8,000.00
First	$2,000.00	
Deduct	- 160.00	
Deduct		-1,840.00
Balance		$6,160.00
Second	$3,000.00	
Deduct	- 102.67	
Deduct		- 2,897.33
Balance		$3,262.67
Add interest		+ 43.50
Amount due at maturity		$3,306.17

$I = \$6{,}160 \times 12\% \times \frac{50}{360}$

$I = \$3{,}262.67 \times 12\% \times \frac{40}{360}$

THE MERCHANTS' RULE

The second method used to determine the balance of a loan after a partial payment is made is known as the **Merchants' Rule.** A step-by-step procedure for applying the Merchants' Rule is:

Step 1. Determine the maturity value of the note. It is the principal plus interest for the full term of the note.
Step 2. Determine the interest on each partial payment from the date of the payment to the *due date of the loan.*
Step 3. Sum the partial payments and the interest on the payments.
Step 4. Subtract the total (Step 3) from the maturity value of the note (Step 1). This is the balance due—that is, the amount due at maturity.

Problem To illustrate the computations required under the Merchants' Rule, see the preceding problem involving a loan of $3,000 on February 1 for four months and partial payments of $1,000 and $500 on March 3 and May 2, respectively. The final payment is due June 1 (which is four months from February 1).

Shown schematically:

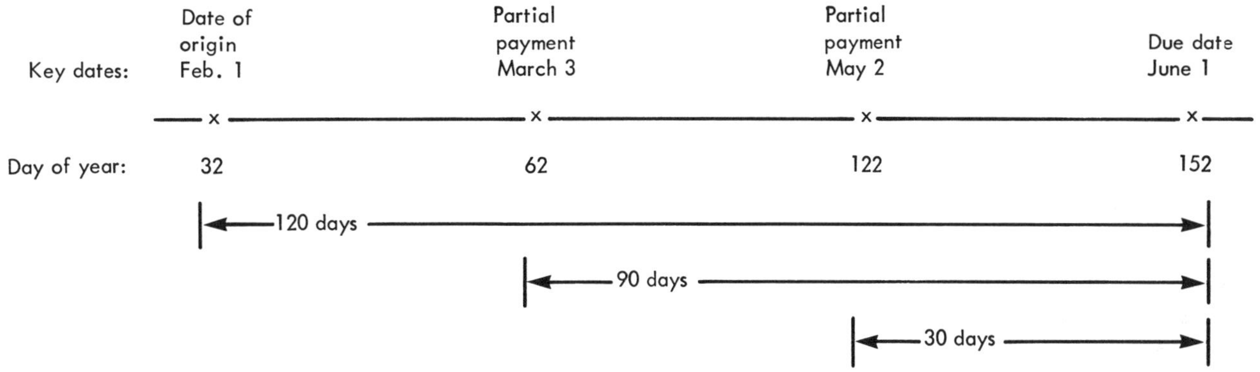

Solution

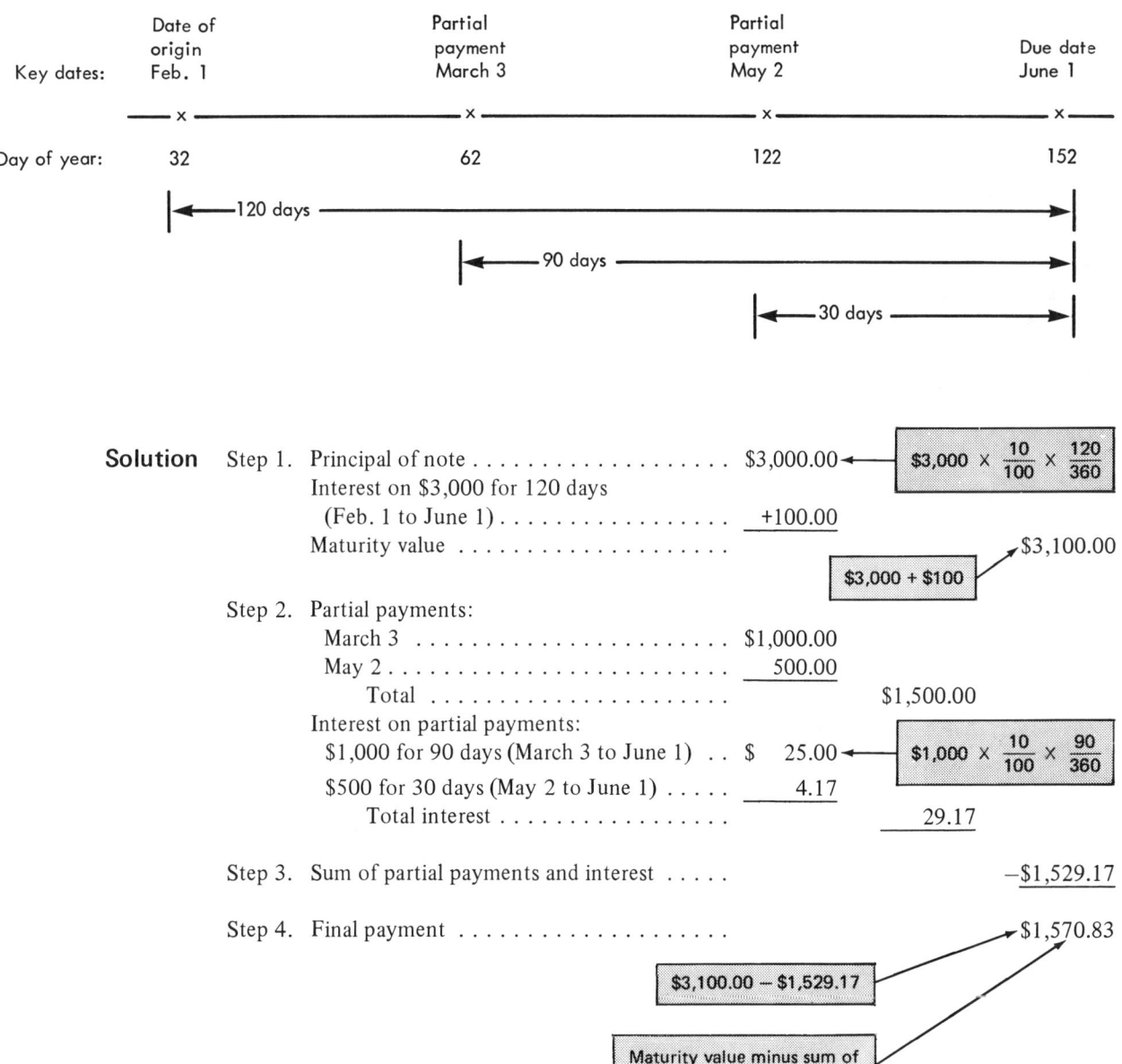

Step 1.	Principal of note	$3,000.00	
	Interest on $3,000 for 120 days (Feb. 1 to June 1)	+100.00	
	Maturity value		$3,100.00
Step 2.	Partial payments:		
	March 3	$1,000.00	
	May 2	500.00	
	Total		$1,500.00
	Interest on partial payments:		
	$1,000 for 90 days (March 3 to June 1) . .	$ 25.00	
	$500 for 30 days (May 2 to June 1)	4.17	
	Total interest		29.17
Step 3.	Sum of partial payments and interest		−$1,529.17
Step 4.	Final payment		$1,570.83

$3,000 \times \frac{10}{100} \times \frac{120}{360}$ (→ $3,000.00 / interest)

$3,000 + $100 (→ $3,100.00)

$1,000 \times \frac{10}{100} \times \frac{90}{360}$ (→ $25.00)

$3,100.00 − $1,529.17 (→ $1,570.83)

Maturity value minus sum of partial payments and interest (→ $1,570.83)

Note that as a result of the two partial payments the borrower received interest credit of $29.17 (which, of course, the borrower never had to pay). Thus, the interest payment of $60 was reduced by $29.17. In essence, only $30.83 interest charge was paid, found bv $60 – $29.17.

The Merchants' Rule favors the borrower. The same problem ($3,000 loan for four months at 10%) resulted in a final payment at maturity of $1,571.74 using the United States Rule, but only $1,570.83 under the Merchants' Rule.

2 SELF-REVIEW

In Self-Review 1, the problem stated that $8,000 was borrowed on July 5, and a 12% promissory note was signed, due in 150 days. Two partial payments were made—the first on September 3 for $2,000 and the second on October 23 for $3,000. What is the amount due at maturity using the Merchants' Rule?

Face of note	$________		
Interest on note for 150 days . . .	________		
Maturity value of note			$________
Partial payments			
Sept. 3	$________		
Oct. 23	________		
Total		$________	
Interest on partial payments			
Sept. 3	$________		
Oct. 23	________		
Total		$________	
Sum of partial payments and interest			–$________
Final payment			$________

$I = \$8{,}000 \times 12\% \times \frac{150}{360}$

Face	$8,000		
Interest . . .	400		
Maturity value			$8,400
Payment . . .	$2,000		
Payment . . .	3,000		
Total . . .		$5,000	
Interest . . .	$ 60		
Interest . . .	40		
Total . . .		$ 100	
Sum of payments and interest . .			5,100
Final payment . .			$3,300

$I = \$2{,}000 \times 12\% \times \frac{90}{360}$

$I = \$3{,}000 \times 12\% \times \frac{40}{360}$

The final payment on the $8,000 loan at 10% for 4 months using the United States Rule (Self-Review 1) is $__________. For comparison, had the bank used the Merchants' Rule in applying the partial payments, the final payment would be only $__________.

U.S. Rule = $3,306.17
Merchants' Rule = $3,300.00

ASSIGNMENT 12-3
PARTIAL PAYMENT

Name ______________________ **Date Due** ______________ **Grade** _____

Answers to selected problems are given in Appendix B.

1. An individual signed a note for $3,000 dated February 4 (nonleap year) bearing ordinary interest at 9% and due in 120 days. Payments were made on March 6 for $1,000 and on April 25 for $1,500. Using the United States Rule:

A.	Face of note Feb. 4		$__________
	First payment March 6	$1,000.00	
B.	Interest from Feb. 4 to March 6	– __________	
C.	Amount deducted from face of note		– __________
D.	Balance on March 6		$__________
	Second payment	$1,500.00	
E.	Interest from March 6 to April 25	– __________	
F.	Amount deducted from balance		– __________
G.	Balance on April 25		$__________
H.	Interest from April 25 to June 4		+ __________
I.	What is the final payment made June 4?		$__________

2. A six-month note for $3,550 dated April 15 and bearing interest at 9% had partial payments of $1,250 on May 12, $25 on July 1, and $975 on August 1. What was the amount due at maturity using the United States Rule?

   $______________, found by

3. On August 7, $1,000 was borrowed from the United Trust Company. A note was signed bearing interest at 8% due in 3 months. A partial payment was made of $300 on September 8, and a second partial payment of $400 on October 8. Using the Merchants' Rule:

A. Face of note . . . . $________

B. Interest on note for 92 days . . . . ________

C. Maturity value of note . . . . $__________

D. Partial payments

Sept. 8 . . . . $________

Oct. 8 . . . . ________

Total . . . . $________

E. Interest on partial payments

Sept. 8 . . . . $________

Oct. 8 . . . . ________

Total . . . . $________

F. Sum of partial payments and interest . . . . . . – $__________

G. Final payment . . . . $__________

4. A clothing merchant signed a 90-day note on July 1 for $1,350 at 10% interest. A condition of the note was that a $500 partial payment be made on August 15 and a $700 partial payment be made on September 15. What is the amount due at maturity using the Merchants' Rule?

$__________, found by

5. A six-month note for $6,500 dated May 7 bears interest at 10%. Partial payments were made on June 10 for $1,200, on June 30 for $25, and on September 15 for $3,475. Use the United States Rule to determine the amount due on the maturity date.

$______________, found by

6. Solve Problem 5 using the Merchants' Rule.

$______________, found by

REVIEW ASSIGNMENT FOR CHAPTER 12
PROMISSORY NOTES, DISCOUNTING, AND PARTIAL PAYMENT

Name ______________________________ Date Due ____________ Grade _____

1. On October 12, the owner of the Fireplace and Barbeque Shop took a noninterest-bearing note to the bank, where it was discounted at 12%. The note for $1,200 was dated July 15 and due in four months. Determine the:

A. Due date.

__________, found by

B. Maturity value.

$________, found by

C. Discount term.

__________, found by

D. Bank discount.

$________, found by

E. Proceeds.

$____________, found by

2. The owner of a small plastics firm needed cash to meet the weekly payroll. A $2,500, 60-day note dated May 15 and bearing interest at 8% was taken to a finance company on June 21. The note was discounted at 11½%. Determine the:

A. Due date.

__________, found by

B. Interest.

$________, found by

C. Maturity value.

$__________, found by

D. Discount term.

__________, found by

E. Bank discount.

$________, found by

F. Proceeds.

$__________, found by

3. A $6,500, 9% interest-bearing note due in four months and dated March 10 was accepted by a small manufacturer. Determine the net proceeds if the note was discounted at a bank at 9% on the date of origin.

$____________, found by

4. Palloti Pizza used its line of credit to borrow \$5,000 at 8¾% for three months on June 15. What did Palloti Pizza pay back in three months?

\$______________, found by

5. The owner of a building supply company accepted a four-month note for \$5,250 dated August 12 and bearing 9% interest. Two partial payments were made, the first on September 11 for \$2,000 and the second on November 10 for \$3,000. Using the United States Rule, determine the amount due on the maturity date.

\$____________, found by

6. Solve Problem 5 using the Merchants' Rule.

$\$$__________, found by

7. A wholesale appliance dealer accepted a $14,550 note from a retail store. It was dated June 4, bearing 9% interest, and the duration was three months. Partial payments of $6,000 and $5,500 were made on July 10 and August 10, respectively. Using the Merchants' Rule, determine the amount due at the maturity date.

$\$$____________, found by

8. Solve Problem 7 using the United States Rule.

$______________, found by

TO THE STUDENT: There is a SELF-REVIEW TEST for this chapter in Appendix A, *with answers* in Appendix C.

13

Opening a Business

SECTION 13-1: ASSETS, LIABILITIES, AND OWNER EQUITY

Objective: To determine the assets, liabilities, and owner equity of a business.

A large number of new businesses begin operation in the United States every day. These include gasoline stations, machine shops, banks, furniture manufacturers, TV repair shops, and gift shops.

ASSETS

Cash is one of the primary concerns in opening any business. It must be available to pay such expenses as rent and the utility bills. **Supplies** are needed. For example, to open a plant to manufacture plastic toys, items such as plastic sheets and paint are essential. Equipment to form dolls, soldiers, and the plastic wheels of a truck is required. The total value of these items (cash, supplies, and equipment) is referred to as **assets.** Thus, an **asset** is something of value owned by a firm.

In the United States:

2,024,000	Corporations
1,073,000	Partnerships
10,882,000	Proprietorships
13,979,000	Total

Assets = Cash + Supplies + Equipment + Other items owned

Might be land and buildings

LIABILITIES

Money borrowed to start a business or money owed for supplies, equipment, or other items is referred to as **liabilities.** Thus, a **liability** is a claim against the assets of the firm by creditors.

OWNER EQUITY

Owner equity is sometimes called just **equity**. Other names sometimes used are **capital, net worth,** or **proprietorship.** It is the claim against the assets by the owner(s) of the business. It is found by subtracting the liabilities from the assets.

Owner equity = Assets − Liabilities

According to the Department of Commerce:

28.1 out of every 10,000 businesses failed last year.

It follows thus, that:

Assets = Liabilities + Owner equity

This relationship is called the **accounting equation.**

Problem Amy and Tom Hanna made plastic toys as a hobby. So unique were some of their toys that friends encouraged them to open their own manufacturing business. As a first step, they transferred $15,000 from their savings account to a business checking account in order to account for business expenditures separately.

Transaction A: They purchased plastic sheets and paint for $3,500 **on account,** meaning that they charged them and will be billed at a later date. Unpaid amounts are called *accounts payable.*

Transaction B: They bought used precision equipment for $6,000, paying cash.

What are the assets, liabilities, and owner equity after those two transactions?

Solution Assets = Cash + Supplies + Equipment + Other items owned

$ 9,000	Cash balance ← $15,000 – $6,000 paid for equipment
3,500	Supplies on hand
6,000	Equipment for production
$18,500	Total (total value of all assets owned by the Hanna Toy Manufacturing Company)

Liabilities

$3,500	Supplies not paid for
$3,500	Total (total owned by the Hanna Toy Manufacturing Company to creditors)

Owner equity = Assets – Liabilities
= $18,500 – $3,500
= $15,000 (the amount owned outright by the Hannas)

To verify:
Assets = Liabilities + Owner equity
$18,500 = $3,500 + $15,000

1 SELF-REVIEW

A reminder: Cover the answers in the margin.

Sam Columbo started Columbo's TV Repair Shop by using $8,000 of his savings and borrowing $2,000 from his bank. He purchased repair equipment for $2,500, paying $1,000 in cash and promising to pay the balance due in 90 days. He paid cash for supplies (tubes, transistors, etc.) amounting to $3,200. What were the assets, liabilities, and owner equity *after* these transactions?

A. Assets:
$________ Cash, found by ________________
$________ Supplies
$________ Equipment
$________ Total

B. Liabilities:
$________ Bank loan
$________ Equipment, balance due
$________ Total

C. Owner equity = Assets – Liabilities
= $________ – $________
= $________

D. To verify, the accounting equation is:

Assets = Liabilities + Owner equity
$________ = $________ + $________

Answers in margin:

A. $5,800 found by: $10,000 – 1,000 – 3,200 = $5,800
3,200
2,500
11,500

B. $2,000
1,500
3,500

C. $11,500 – $3,500 = $8,000

D. $11,500 = $3,500 + $8,000

ASSIGNMENT 13-1
ASSETS, LIABILITIES, AND OWNER EQUITY

Name ______________________________ **Date Due** ______________ **Grade** _____

Answers to selected problems are given in Appendix B.

1. Betty and Jim McDougal plan to open the McDougal Upholstery Shop using $12,000 of their savings. Prior to the opening, they purchased supplies such as foam cushioning, staples, tacks, and Dacron filling for $3,000, paying $1,800 cash and promising to pay the balance due in 60 days. Sewing machines, automatic staplers, and other professional equipment amounting to $4,300 were purchased on account.

   After these purchases, the assets, liabilities, and owner equity are:

Assets:

$________ Cash, found by

________ Supplies

________ Equipment

$________ Total

Liabilities:

$________ (explain) ______________________

Owner equity:

Owner equity = __________ – __________

$________ = $________ – $________

To verify, the accounting equation is:

In words: __________ = __________ + __________

$________ = $________ + $________

With respect to the McDougal Upholstery Shop, describe:

Assets ____

____.

Liabilities ____

____.

Owner equity ____

____.

2. Jay and Jerry Walinski opened an automobile service garage using $20,000 of their savings. They purchased supplies such as fan belts, spark plugs, gaskets, oil, grease, and so on for $5,000, paying $2,000 cash and promising to pay the remaining in 30 days. Hydraulic lifts, jacks, tools, and other automotive repair equipment amounting to $9,000 was purchased with cash.

Find the assets, liabilities, and owner equity after these transactions:

Assets:		*Liabilities:*
$________ Cash, found by ____________		$________ Supplies and equipment not paid for
________ Supplies		
________ Equipment		*Owner Equity:*
$________ Total		$________ = $________ – $________

3. George and Kiriaki Pappas have opened the Krio Ice Cream Parlor. They started with only $5,000 of their savings. They obtained a bank loan of $12,000 with which to buy supplies, fixtures, and equipment. They used $4,000 cash to buy their needed supplies. They made a $10,000 down payment on fixtures and equipment worth $25,000. The remaining amount is to be paid off in six months. Find:

Assets = $________, found by

Liabilities = $________, found by

Owner equity = $________, found by

The accounting equation is: $________ = $________ + $________

4. Sara and Bernice Rosenberg opened The Sisters Dress Shoppe with $10,000 of their own money and a $15,000 small-business loan. They made a down payment of $12,500 on $25,000 worth of fixtures. The balance was placed on account. They paid $10,000 cash for merchandise and supplies. Find:

Assets = $________, found by

Liabilities = $________, found by

Owner equity = $________, found by

The accounting equation is: $________ = $________ + $________

SECTION 13-2: THE BALANCE SHEET

Objective: To complete a balance sheet for a small business.

Most firms must prepare a number of financial statements periodically. These will allow management to evaluate the financial condition of the firm and aid in planning the future. One such statement is the **balance sheet.** A balance sheet is simply a list of the assets, liabilities, and owner equity as of a certain date—usually the end of the month, or the end of the quarter, or the end of the year.

ANDERS WATCH AND CLOCK SHOP
Balance Sheet January 31,

Assets	*Amount*
Cash	$7,300
Supplies	700
Equipment (less depreciation)	2,950
Total	$10,950
Liabilities	
Accounts payable	$600
Owner Equity	
Paula Anders, capital	10,350
Total liabilities and owner equity	$10,950

The balance sheet is aptly named because the **total assets** must equal the **liabilities** plus **owner equity**. As noted in Section 13-1, this relationship is referred to as the **accounting equation** and is stated as:

Assets = Liabilities + Owner equity

Where:

An **asset** is something of value owned by a firm.

A **liability** is a claim against the assets of the firm by creditors.

Owner equity is a claim against the assets of the business by its owner(s).

Problem

When Amy and Tom Hanna decided to start a toy manufacturing plant (see Section 13-1), they transferred $15,000 from their savings account. Prior to opening their business on October 1, they purchased supplies totaling $3,500 on account and bought several used precision machines for $6,000.

During October they manufactured and sold toys amounting to $5,200, paid $2,500 to their creditors, and depreciated their equipment $50. Examine the effect of each of these transactions on the accounting equation and the balance sheet as of October 31.

Solution

Prior to opening their toy manufacturing plant, the Hannas' financial position (continued from Section 13-1) was:

	Assets			=	*Liabilities*	+	*Owner equity*
	Cash	+ Supplies	+ Equipment	=	Accounts payable	+	Hanna, capital
Balance:	$9,000	+ $3,500	+ $6,000	=	$3,500	+	$15,000

Transaction C: The Hannas sold toys for cash amounting to $5,200 during their first month of operation. The result was to increase their cash by $5,200 and, on the other side of the equation, the owner equity by $5,200. Note that after the transaction, the accounting equation is in balance.

	Assets			=	*Liabilities*	+	*Owner Equity*
	Cash	+ Supplies	+ Equipment	=	Accounts payable	+	Hanna, capital
Balance:	$ 9,000	+ $3,500	+ $6,000	=	$3,500	+	$15,000
Transaction C:	+ 5,200						+ 5,200
Balance:	$14,200	+ $3,500	+ $6,000	=	$3,500	+	$20,200

Transaction D: The Hannas paid $2,500 to the creditors who had advanced them supplies on account. This reduced their cash by $2,500 and, on the other side of the equation, reduced owner equity (their capital) by-$2,500. Again, note that after the transaction the accounting equation is in balance.

	Assets			=	*Liabilities*	+	*Owner Equity*
	Cash	+ Supplies +	Equipment	=	Accounts payable	+	Hanna, capital
Balance:	$14,200 +	$3,500 +	$6,000	=	$3,500	+	$20,200
Transaction D:	– 2,500						– 2,500
Balance:	$11,700 +	$3,500 +	$6,000	=	$3,500	+	$17,700

Transaction E: Precision equipment wears out gradually due to use. In accounting, this decline in the "usefulness" of an asset is called **depreciation.** It is considered a business expense the same as rent expense or heating expense. Instead of deducting the estimated depreciation from equipment, the usual procedure is to record it under a separate heading called accumulated depreciation. Suppose that the Hannas estimated the depreciation on their equipment for the first month to be $50. The effect on the accounting equation follows:

	Assets				=	*Liabilities*	+	*Owner Equity*
	Cash	+ Supplies +	Equipment	– Accumulated depreciation	=	Accounts payable	+	Hanna, capital
Balance:	$11,700 +	$3,500 +	$6,000		=	$3,500	+	$17,700
Transaction E:				– + 50				– 50
Balance:	$11,700 +	$3,500 +	$6,000	– $50	=	$3,500	+	$17,650

Technical Note: The accumulated depreciation of $50 is shown as a positive number. However, note in the accounting equation that it is subtracted because the equipment has declined in value.

A balance sheet which reflects these transactions is shown in the exhibit. Note that the balance sheet amounts are the same as found in the accounting equation for the last transaction for October.

Hanna Toy Manufacturing Company Balance Sheet October 31, 1980		
Assets		
Cash		$11,700 00
Supplies		3,500 00
Equipment	$6,000 00	
Less accumulated depreciation	50 00	5,950 00
Total assets		$21,150 00
Liabilities		
Accounts payable		$3,500 00
Owner Equity		
Hanna, capital		17,650 00
Total liabilities and owner equity		$21,150 00

These two totals MUST BE EQUAL

1 SELF-REVIEW

Suppose that due to an oversight, the following expenses, paid in cash, were omitted from the October 31 balance sheet for the Hanna Toy Manufacturing Company. Rent expense, $200; electricity, $160; heat expense, $100; telephone, $40; miscellaneous expense, $30.

Show how these cash transactions would alter the accounting equation.

	Assets								=	*Liabilities*	+	*Owner Equity*
	Cash	+	Supplies	+	Equipment	–	Accumulated depreciation		=	Accounts payable	+	Hanna, capital
Balance:	$11,700	+	$3,500	+	$6,000	–	$50		=	$3,500	+	$17,650
Transaction:	– ______		______		______		______			______		– ______
Balance:	$ ______	+	$3,500	+	$6,000	–	$50		=	$3,500	+	$ ______

$11,700	$17,650
– 530	– 530
$11,170	$17,120

Revise the Hannas' balance sheet.

HANNA TOY MANUFACTURING COMPANY
Balance Sheet
As of October 31

Assets

Answer				
$11,170		Cash		$ ______
$ 3,500		Supplies		______
	$6,000	Equipment	$ ______	
$ 5,950	$ 50	Less accumulated depreciation	$ ______	______
$20,620		Total assets		$ ______

Liabilities

Answer		
$ 3,500	Accounts payable	$ ______

Owner Equity

Answer		
$17,120	Hanna, capital	$ ______
$20,620	Total liabilities and owner equity	$ ______

These two totals must be equal

ASSIGNMENT 13-2
THE BALANCE SHEET

Name ______________________ Date Due ______________ Grade _____

Answers to selected problems are given in Appendix B.

1. Betty and Jim McDougal opened the McDougal Upholstery Shop using $12,000 of their savings. Prior to the opening, they purchased supplies, such as foam cushioning, staples, tacks, and Dacron filling for $3,000. They paid $1,800 cash and promised to pay the balance due in 60 days. Sewing machines, staplers, and other professional equipment amounting to $4,300 were purchased on account.
   Show the upholstery shop's financial position before opening for business.

	Assets					=	*Liabilities*	+	*Owner Equity*
	Cash	+	Supplies	+	Equipment	=	Accounts payable	+	McDougal, capital
Balance:	$ ______	+	$ ______	+	$ ______	=	$ ______	+	$ ______

Transaction A: They reupholstered sofas, chairs, and other furniture during April, for which they received $3,600 cash. Show the effect of this transaction:

	Assets					=	*Liabilities*	+	*Owner Equity*
	Cash	+	Supplies	+	Equipment	=	Accounts payable	+	McDougal, capital
Balance:	$ ______	+	$ ______	+	$ ______	=	$ ______	+	$ ______
Transaction:	+ ______							+	$ ______
Balance:	$ ______	+	$ ______	+	$ ______	=	$ ______	+	$ ______

Other transactions: The McDougals paid $900 to the creditors who had advanced them the supplies and $400 to the distributor who sold them the equipment. They depreciated the equipment $80 and paid their rent and other expenses, amounting to $350. Show how these transactions alter the accounting equation.

	Assets							=	*Liabilities*	+	*Owner Equity*
	Cash	+	Supplies	+	Equipment	–	Accumulated depreciation	=	Accounts payable	+	McDougal, capital
Balance:	$ ______	+	$ ______	+	$ ______			=	$ ______	+	$ ______
Transaction:	– ______						______		– ______		– ______
Balance:	$ ______	+	$ ______	+	$ ______	–	$ ______	=	$ ______	+	$ ______

Design a balance sheet in the space provided.

McDOUGAL UPHOLSTERY SHOP
Balance Sheet
as of April 30

2. Jay and Jerry Walinski opened an automobile service garage using $20,000 of their savings. They purchased supplies such as fan belts, spark plugs, gaskets, oil, grease, and so on for $5,000. They paid $2,000 cash and promised to pay the balance due in 30 days. Hydraulic lifts, jacks, tools, and other automotive repair equipment amounting to $9,000 was purchased with cash.

Prior to opening their automotive service garage the Walinski's financial position was:

	Assets					=	*Liabilities*	+	*Owner Equity*
	Cash	+	Supplies	+	Equipment	=	Accounts payable	+	Walinski, capital
Balance:	$______	+	$______	+	$______	=	$______	+	$______

Transaction A: They paid the $3,000 balance due on their supplies out of cash during the month of October. Show the effect of this transaction.

	Assets					=	*Liabilities*	+	*Owner Equity*
	Cash	+	Supplies	+	Equipment	=	Accounts payable	+	Walinski, capital
Balance:	$______	+	$______	+	$______	=	$______	+	$______
Transaction:	–______						–______		
Balance:	$______	+	$______	+	$______	=	$______	+	$______

Other transactions: The Walinskis repaired numerous autos and trucks, receiving $4,400 in cash. They used $750 worth of supplies. They depreciated their equipment $90 and paid other expenses amounting to $520. Show how these transactions would change the respective values in the accounting equation.

	Assets				=	Liabilities	+	Owner Equity
	Cash	+ Supplies	+ Equipment	− Accumulated depreciation	=	Accounts payable	+	Walinski, capital
Balance:	$______	+ $______	+ $______		=	$______	+	$______
Transaction:	+______	−______		+______				______
Balance:	$______	+ $______	+ $______	− $______	=	$______	+	$______

Make a balance sheet in the space provided using the new figures.

WALINSKI AUTOMOTIVE SERVICE GARAGE
Balance Sheet
As of October 30

SECTION 13-3: INCOME STATMENTS

Objective: To prepare an income statement for a small business.

An **income statement**, also called a **profit and loss statement**, is a report of the revenues earned and the expenses incurred by a firm for a specified period of time—such as a month, a quarter, or a year.

Problem When the Hannas started their toy manufacturing company, sales for the first three months of operation totaled $35,000, but toys valued at $1,000 were returned for various reasons. Returns and allowances for lost goods, unpaid debts, and trade-ins are subtracted from sales to arrive at **net sales.**

Net sales = Sales − Returns and allowances

= $35,000 − $1,000
= $34,000

The cost of the goods sold is subtracted from net sales to give **gross profit.** The cost of the goods sold (raw plastic, paint, etc.) used in manufacturing the toys amounted to $10,000.

Gross profit = Net sales − Cost of goods sold

= $34,000 − $10,000
= $24,000

Gross profit minus operating expenses gives **net income.**

Net income = Gross profit − Operating expenses

To be subtracted from the Hannas' three-month gross profit of $24,000 are such operating expenses as the wages of a number of part-time employees, $2,800; utilities, $920; rent, $600; advertising, $300; shipping, $200; office supplies, $180; depreciation, $150; insurance, $120; and miscellaneous expenses of $100. Total operating expenses amounted to $5,370.

Net income = Gross profit − Operating expenses
= $24,000 − $5,370
= $18,630

Make an income statement for the Hanna Toy Manufacturing Company.

Solution The toy company's **income statement** shows one of the more common ways of listing the operating expenses, namely, from the largest amount to the smallest.

HANNA TOY MANUFACTURING COMPANY
Income Statement
For Quarter Ended December 31

Income:		
Sales	$35,000	
Less: Sales returns and allowances	– 1,000	
Net sales		$34,000
Cost of goods sold		10,000
Gross profit on sales		$24,000
Operating expenses:		
Salaries and wages	$ 2,800	
Utilities	920	
Rent	600	
Advertising	300	
Shipping	200	
Office supplies	180	
Depreciation	150	
Insurance	120	
Miscellaneous expenses	100	
Total operating expenses		5,370
Net Income		$18,630

1 SELF-REVIEW

Betty and Jim McDougal opened an upholstery shop April 1. During the three months ending June 30, they had income from upholstering sofas, chairs, and other furniture totaling $22,500. A set of pillows priced at $50 was returned by a dissatisfied customer.

The foam rubber, tacks, and other goods used in their business cost $2,100. Operating expenses included rent, $160; depreciation, $240; utilities, $180; delivery charges, $210; insurance, $80; wages of a part-time employee, $360; advertising, $70; office supplies, $30; miscellaneous expenses, $40.

Make an income statement for the McDougals for the three months ending June 30, using this form.

MCDOUGAL UPHOLSTERY SHOP

____

____

Income:		
Revenues from upholstery	$______	
Less ________	–______	
Net revenue		$______
Cost of goods sold		______
Gross profit		$______
Operating Expenses:		
Wages	$360	
____________	______	
____________	______	
____________	______	
____________	______	
____________	______	
____________	______	
____________	______	
____________	______	
Total operating expenses		______
Net income		$______

Income Statement
For Quarter Ended June 30

$22,500
Returns; –$50

$22,450
$2,100
$20,350

Depreciation	$240	
Delivery charges	210	
Utilities	180	
Rent	160	
Insurance	80	
Advertising	70	
Misc.	40	
Office supplies	30	
Total		$ 1,370
Net income		$18,980

ASSIGNMENT 13-3
INCOME STATEMENTS

Name ______________________ Date Due ____________ Grade _____

Answers to selected problems are given in Appendix B.

For Problems 1 through 4, find the total operating expenses for each quarter (horizontal) and totals by activity (vertical). Cross-check the sums of the totals.

	Quarter	*Salaries and Wages*	*Utilities*	*Rent*	*Advertising*	*Shipping*	*Office Supplies*	*Depreciation*	*Miscellaneous*	*Total Operating Expenses*
Ex.	First	$14,620	$1,515	$1,050	$630	$450	$540	$240	$1,070	$20,115
1.	Second	13,960	1,200	1,050	450	360	420	240	915	________
2.	Third	8,725	720	1,050	540	270	390	240	845	________
3.	Fourth	14,315	1,625	1,050	900	480	600	240	975	________
4.	Totals	$51,620	$______	$______	$______	$______	$______	$______	$______	$______

5. Jay and Jerry Walinski opened an automobile service garage on October 1. During the three months ending December 31, they had income from automotive repair work totaling $17,650. Several credit allowances amounted to $185.

   They used supplies costing $1,700. Operating expenses included rent, $900; depreciation, $270; utilities, $240; insurance, $90; wages, $300; and miscellaneous expenses, $30. Make an income statement for the Walinskis for the three months ending December 31.

WALINSKI AUTOMOTIVE SERVICE GARAGE
Income Statement
For Quarter Ended December 31

Income:		
Revenue from service	$________	
Less ________________	________	
Net revenue		$________
Cost of supplies		________
Gross profit		$________
Operating expenses:		
Rent	$900	
________________	________	
________________	________	
________________	________	
________________	________	
________________	________	
Total operating expenses		$________
Net income		$________

6. Sara and Bernice Rosenberg opened The Sisters Dress Shoppe. During their first quarter of business (July 1 to September 30) they had sales of $13,790. Returns amounted to $78. The cost of goods sold totaled $5,650. Operating expenses were: salaries and wages, $1,200; rent, $1,200; depreciation, $75; utilities, $120; insurance, $120; advertising, $1,200; supplies, $150; and miscellaneous expenses, $60. Make an income statement for the Sisters Dress Shoppe for the three months ending September 30.

SECTION 13-4: VERTICAL AND HORIZONTAL ANALYSIS

Objective: To analyze financial statements using vertical and horizontal analysis.

VERTICAL ANALYSIS

Percents can be used to portray the relationship of the various parts of a balance sheet to the total. This is usually referred to as **vertical analysis.** For example, ple, to express cash as a percent of total assets, the procedure is:

$$\text{Cash as a percent of total assets} = \frac{\text{Cash}}{\text{Total assets}}$$

The usual practice is to round each percent to the nearest tenth of a percent. The percents total 100%. (Rounding may cause a slight deviation from 100%.)

Problem

Express each asset on the Hanna Toy Manufacturing Company balance sheet as of October 31 (see Section 13-2) as a percent of the total.

Solution

Assets	*Amount*	*Percent of Total*	*Found by*
Cash	$11,700	55.3	$11,700 ÷ $21,150
Supplies	3,500	16.5	3,500 ÷ 21,150
Equipment (less depreciation)	5,950	28.1	5,950 ÷ 21,150
Total	$21,150	99.9	

An analysis of these percents reveals that the Hannas are in a very "liquid" financial position–meaning that a large percent (55.3%) of their assets are in cash.

1 SELF-REVIEW

Express the liabilities and owner equity from the Hanna balance sheet as percents of the total.

	Amount	*Percent of Total*	*Found by*
Liabilities	$ 3,500	________	________________
Owner equity	17,650	________	________________
Total	$________	________	

16.5%; $3,500 ÷ $21,150

83.5%; $17,650 ÷ $21,150

$21,150; 100.0%

HORIZONTAL ANALYSIS

Another use of percents as applied to balance sheets is called **horizontal analysis.** The purpose is to show the percent increase or decrease in corresponding balance sheet items, or income statement items, when two time periods are involved. If the analysis involves two months, such as October and November, the amount in the earlier month (October) automatically becomes the base when determining the percent change. In general:

$$\text{Percent change} = \frac{\text{Amount of change}}{\text{Original (base) amount}}$$

Problem Determine the percent change in each asset in the Hanna Toy Manufacturing Company balance sheet from October to November. (The following figures for November are hypothetical and are given only to illustrate the calculation of percents used in horizontal analysis.)

Solution

Assets	*November*	*October*	*Increase or Decrease*		*Found by*
			Amount	*Percent*	
Cash	$14,220	$11,700	$ 2,520	21.5%	$ 2,520 ÷ $11,700
Supplies	1,950	3,500	– 1,550	– 44.3%	– 1,550 ÷ 3,500
Equipment, less depreciation	15,270	5,950	9,320	156.6%	9,320 ÷ 5,950
Totals	$31,440	$21,150	$10,290	47.7%	$10,290 ÷ $21,150

Using a calculator:

Enter	Press	Display
14220	−	14220
11700	÷	2520
11700	=	0.2153846

This horizontal analysis reflects a 21.5% increase in cash, a drastic drop (44.3%) in the supplies needed to conduct the toy manufacturing business, and a substantial percent increase (156.6%) in equipment.

2 SELF-REVIEW

Make a horizontal analysis of the major items on the Hanna Toy Manufacturing Company income statement (see Section 13-3). Compute the percent change from the fourth quarter last year (December 31) to the first quarter of this year (ending March 31).

	Quarter Ending		*Increase or Decrease*		
	Mar. 31	*Dec. 31*	*Amount*	*Percent*	*Found by*
Net sales	$51,000	$34,000	$17,000	50.0%	$17,000 ÷ $34,000
Cost of goods sold	19,000	10,000	______	______	______
Gross profit on sales	32,000	______	______	______	______
Total operating expenses	4,960	5,370	______	______	______
Net income	27,040	______	______	______	______

$9,000; 90.0%;
$9,000 ÷ $10,000

$24,000; $8,000; 33.3%
$8,000 ÷ $24,000

–$410; –7.6%;
–$410 ÷ $5,370

$18,630; $8,410; 45.1%;
$8,410 ÷ $18,630

ASSIGNMENT 13-4
VERTICAL AND HORIZONTAL ANALYSIS

Name ______________________ Date Due ______________ Grade _____

Answers to selected problems are given in Appendix B.

For Problems 1 through 6, make a horizontal analysis of the percent change from last year to this year (last year is the base) for each of these items in an income statement.

		This Year	*Last Year*	*Percent Change*
Ex.	Sales	$300,000	$200,000	+ 50.0%
1.	Returns and allowances	10,000	20,000	_______
2.	Net sales	___________	180,000	_______
3.	Cost of goods sold	100,000	80,000	_______
4.	Gross profit on sales	___________	100,000	_______
5.	Operating expenses	60,000	40,000	_______
6.	Net income	___________	60,000	_______

Problems 7 and 8 are based on the following data from the balance sheet of the Continental Clothing Company.

Assets	*Last Year (000 omitted)*	*This Year (000 omitted)*
Cash	$12,000	$15,000
Supplies	520	480
Equipment	1,420	2,160
Inventory	415	380
Total	$14,355	$18,020
Liabilities		
Accounts payable	$ 2,100	$ 1,800
Notes payable	1,500	2,500
Current liabilities	800	600
Total	$ 4,400	$ 4,900
Owner Equity		
Capital	$ 9,955	$13,120

7. Vertical analysis (round to nearest tenth of a percent).

A. Express cash as a percent of total assets for last year. ________%, found by

B. Express cash as a percent of total assets for this year. ________%, found by

C. Express supplies as a percent of total assets for this year. ________%, found by

D. Express equipment as a percent of total assets for this year. ________%, found by

E. Express inventory as a percent of total assets for this year. ________%, found by

F. Do the percents for B + C + D + E = 100%? ________

Why or why not? ________________________________

G. Express total liabilities as a percent of assets for last year. ________%, found by

H. Express owner equity, capital as a percent of cash for last year. ________%, found by

I. Express current liabilities as a percent of cash for last year. ________%, found by

8. Horizontal analysis (round to the nearest tenth of a percent).

A. Find the percent change in cash from last year to this year. ________%, found by

B. Find the percent change in supplies from last year to this year. ________%, found by

C. Find the percent change in equipment from last year to this year. ________%, found by

D. Find the percent change in inventory from last year to this year. ________%, found by

E. Find the percent change in total assets from last year to this year. ________%, found by

F. Do the percents for A + B + C + D equal the percent for E? ______

Why or why not? ________________________________

G. Find the percent change in total liabilities from last year to this year. ________%, found by

H. Find the percent change in owner equity, capital from last year to this year. ________%, found by

I. Find the percent change in what percent cash is of total assets from last year (Problem 7A) to this year (Problem 7B). ________%, found by

SECTION 13-5: RATIO ANALYSIS

Objective: To compute current ratio, the acid-test ratio, and the return on owner investment.

The relationship of one number to another number is called a **ratio.** The key term in computing a ratio is the word **to.** The number which precedes this word is the numerator; the number following it is the denominator. For example, suppose that there are nine men and two women in a class. The ratio of men *to* women is 9 to 2, or 4.5 to 1, found by 9 ÷ 2. The usual way of citing this ratio is 4.5:1. In ratio analysis of balance sheets and other financial statements, ratios are usually given to the nearest tenth, such as 2.6:1 or 146.8:1.

If a company needed a short-term business loan, one of the financial ratios which would be of interest to a lender is the **current ratio**, also referred to as **the working capital ratio**, or the **bankers' ratio**. It is the *ratio of current assets to current liabilities.*

$$\text{Current ratio} = \frac{\text{Current assets}}{\text{Current liabilities}}$$

Another important business ratio is the **acid-test ratio**, also called the **quick ratio.**

$$\text{Acid-test ratio} = \frac{\text{Current assets} - \text{Inventory}}{\text{Current liabilities}}$$

This shows the ability of the business to pay all current liabilities (debts) almost immediately.

Another important ratio is **return on owner investment.**

$$\text{Return on owner investment} = \frac{\text{Net income}}{\text{Owner equity}}$$

This shows how much the company (owners or stockholders) earned on each dollar invested. It is generally represented as a percent.

Problems Use the data on the next page to compute the current ratio, the acid-test ratio, and the return on owner investment for the Standard Oil Company of California.

Solutions *Current ratio:*

$$\text{Current ratio} = \frac{\text{Current assets}}{\text{Current liabilities}}$$

$$= \frac{\$5{,}199{,}154{,}000}{\$3{,}652{,}720{,}000}$$

$$= 1.4233, \text{ expressed as } 1.4{:}1$$

The ratio means that for every $1.00 in current liabilities, the company has $1.40 in current assets.

Standard Oil Company of California

Chevron

Assets

CURRENT ASSETS:	
Cash	**$ 280,408,000**
Marketable securities, at cost which approximates market value	**642,711,000**
Accounts and notes receivable, less reserve	**3,177,113,000**
Inventories:	
Crude oil and products	**917,655,000**
Other merchandise	**82,580,000**
Materials and supplies	**98,687,000**
Total Current Assets	**5,199,154,000**

Liabilities

CURRENT LIABILITIES:	
Accounts payable	**$ 3,043,706,000**
Notes payable to banks	**54,393,000**
Current installments of long-term debt	**68,062,000**
Federal and other taxes on income	**292,810,000**
Other taxes payable	**193,749,000**
Total Current Liabilities	**3,652,720,000**

Acid-test ratio:

$$\text{Acid-test ratio} = \frac{\text{Current assets} - \text{Inventory}}{\text{Current liabilities}}$$

$$= \frac{\$5{,}199{,}154{,}000 - \$1{,}098{,}922{,}000}{\$3{,}652{,}720{,}000}$$

$ 917,655,000
82,580,000
98,687,000
$1,098,922,000

$$= \frac{\$4{,}100{,}232{,}000}{\$3{,}652{,}720{,}000}$$

$$= 1.122, \text{ expressed as } 1.1{:}1$$

The ratio means that for every $1.00 in current liabilities, the company has $1.10 in liquid assets.

Return on owner investment:

The net income for Standard Oil of California (from another financial statement) is \$154,400,000, and owner equity is \$1,546,434,000, found by (assets – liabilities).

$$\text{Return on owner investment} = \frac{\text{Net income}}{\text{Owner equity}}$$

$$= \frac{\$154{,}400{,}000}{\$1{,}546{,}434{,}000}$$

\$5,199,154,000
–3,652,720,000
\$1,546,434,000

$$= 0.0998$$

$$= 9.98\%$$

The ratio means that for each \$100 invested, a stockholder is receiving \$9.98.

1 SELF-REVIEW

Selected balance sheet items and other data from the annual report of the International Business Machines Corporation and Subsidiary Companies are given in the table.

Current assets

Current ratio:

$= \frac{\$7{,}010}{\$3{,}210}$

= 2.18

Expressed as 2.2:1

A. Current ratio = ____ / Current liabilities

= \$____ / \$

= ____

Expressed as ____:1

Current Assets	*(in millions)*
Cash	\$ 176
Marketable securities	3,629
Notes and accounts receivable	2,083
Inventories	688
Prepaid expenses	434
Total current assets	\$7,010
Current liabilities	\$3,210
Net income	\$1,838
Stockholders' equity	\$10,110

Source: International Business Machines Corporation.

Current assets – Inventory

Acid-test ratio:

$= \frac{\$7{,}010 - \$688}{\$3{,}210}$

$= \frac{\$6{,}322}{\$3{,}210}$

= 1.97

Expressed as 2.0:1

B. Acid-test ratio = ____ – ____ / Current liabilities

= \$____ – \$____ / \$

= \$____ / \$

= ____

Expressed as ____:1

Net income

ROI:

$= \frac{\$1{,}838}{\$10{,}110}$

= 0.1818

= 18.18%

C. Return on owner investment = ____ / Owner equity

= \$____ / \$

= ____

= ____%

ASSIGNMENT 13-5
RATIO ANALYSIS

Name ______________________ Date Due ______________ Grade ______

Answers to selected problems are given in Appendix B.

For Problems 1 through 6, find the ratio (nearest tenth), show how it is found, and interpret it.

	Ratio	*Found by*	*Interpretation*
Ex. 5 men to 2 women	2.5:1	5 ÷ 2	There are 2.5 men to every 1 woman
Ex. 2 women to 5 men	0.4:1	2 ÷ 5	There are 0.4 women to every 1 man
1. 255 production workers to every 10 supervisors	________	________________	________________________
2. $280,000 in sales to every $20,000 spent on advertising	________	________________	________________________
3. 200 hits to every 500 at bats	________	________________	________________________
4. 215 yards gained on 18 carries	________	________________	________________________
5. 82 salespersons to 5 secretaries	________	________________	________________________
6. 7,212 applications received by a medical school; only 600 openings. Ratio of applicants to openings.	________	________________	________________________

For Problems 7 through 12, use these selected items from the Farmer Chemical Corporation balance sheet.

Assets	*This Year*	*Last Year*
Current Assets:		
Cash	$ 33,879	$ 28,400
Marketable securities, at cost which approximates market	1,149	3,177
Receivables, net of reserves	239,950	194,946
Inventories, at cost	245,433	149,251
Prepaid expenses	9,212	5,333
Total current assets	$529,623	$381,107
Liabilities		
Current Liabilities:		
Notes payable and current maturities of long-term debt	$ 42,739	$ 35,852
Accounts payable and accrued liabilities	225,409	142,541
Domestic and foreign income, franchise and other taxes	42,622	22,848
Total current liabilities	$310,770	$201,241

7. Find the current ratio for the Farmer Chemical Corporation for this year.

   Current ratio = $\frac{\$\_\_\_\_\_\_}{\$\_\_\_\_\_\_}$ = ______

8. Interpret the current ratio for the Farmer Chemical Corporation for this year.

   ____

9. Find the current ratio for the Farmer Chemical Corporation for last year.

   Current ratio = $\frac{\$\_\_\_\_\_\_}{\$\_\_\_\_\_\_}$ = ______

10. Find the acid-test ratio for the Farmer Chemical Corporation for this year.

    Acid-test ratio = $\frac{\$\_\_\_\_\_\_ - \$\_\_\_\_\_\_}{\$\_\_\_\_\_\_}$ = $\frac{\$\_\_\_\_\_\_}{\$\_\_\_\_\_\_}$ = ______ = ______

11. Interpret the acid-test ratio for the Farmer Chemical Corporation for this year.

    ____

12. Find the acid-test ratio for the Farmer Chemical Corporation for last year.

    Acid-test ratio = $\frac{\$\_\_\_\_\_\_ - \$\_\_\_\_\_\_}{\$\_\_\_\_\_\_}$ = $\frac{\$\_\_\_\_\_\_}{\$\_\_\_\_\_\_}$ = ______ = ______

13. Find the return on owner investment for the Farmer Chemical Corporation for last year. Assume the net income was $20,145 and owner equity was $179,866.

    Return on owner investment = $\frac{\$\_\_\_\_\_\_}{\$\_\_\_\_\_\_}$ = ______ = ______%

14. Find the return on owner investment for the Farmer Chemical Corporation for this year. Assume the net income is $26,043 and owner equity is $218,853.

    Return on owner investment = $\frac{\$\_\_\_\_\_\_}{\$\_\_\_\_\_\_}$ = ______ = ______%

REVIEW ASSIGNMENT FOR CHAPTER 13
OPENING A BUSINESS

Name ______________________________ Date Due ______________ Grade _____

1. George and Kiriaki Pappas opened the Krio Ice Cream Parlor with $5,000 of their own money. They obtained a bank loan of $12,000. They purchased $4,000 in supplies for cash. They used $10,000 cash as a down payment on fixtures and equipment worth $25,000. The balance due of $15,000 they put on account. Prior to opening the Krio Ice Cream Parlor, the Pappases' financial position was:

Assets						=	*Liabilities*			+	*Owner Equity*
Cash	+	Supplies	+	Equipment		=	Accounts payable	+	Loan payable	+	Pappas, capital
$______	+	$______	+	$______		=	$______	+	$______	+	$______

Transaction A: They paid $2,500 out of cash on their $12,000 bank loan. Show the effect of this transaction.

	Assets					=	*Liabilities*			+	*Owner Equity*
	Cash	+	Supplies	+	Equipment	=	Accounts payable	+	Loan payable	+	Pappas, capital
Balance:	$______	+	$______	+	$______	=	$______	+	$______	+	$______
Transaction:	– ______							–	$______		
Balance:	$______	+	$______	+	$______	=	$______	+	$______	+	$______

Other transactions: During July, their first month of operation, the Pappases earned \$9,715 in ice cream sales. They used \$2,870 in supplies. They depreciated their equipment and fixtures \$120 and paid other expenses amounting to \$1,370. Design a balance sheet in the space provided.

KRIO ICE CREAM PARLOR
Balance Sheet
As of July 31

2. During the three months ending September 30, the Krio Ice Cream Parlor (Problem 1) had income from sales of ice cream totaling \$25,450. There were no credit allowances.

The Pappases used \$8,640 in supplies. Operating expenses included rent, \$1,200; depreciation, \$360; utilities, \$300; insurance, \$75; wages, \$1,500; and miscellaneous expenses, \$725. Construct an income statement for the Krio Ice Cream Parlor for the three months ending September 30.

KRIO ICE CREAM PARLOR
Income Statement
For Quarter Ended September 30

For Problems 3 through 7, use the financial statement from Western Electronics Inc. Dollars are in millions.

Assets	*This Year*	*Last Year*
Current Assets:		
Cash	$ 37.3	$ 34.6
Short-term securities and time deposits, at cost which approximates market	282.9	281.7
Receivables	731.1	734.2
Inventories	631.8	630.2
Total	$1,683.1	$1,680.7
Liabilities and Owner Equity		
Current Liabilities:		
Accounts payable and accruals	$ 517.6	$ 515.8
Income taxes	34.3	33.7
Current portion of long-term debt	25.3	27.8
Total	$ 577.2	$ 577.3

3. Vertical analysis (round to the nearest tenth of a percent).

   A. Express inventories as a percent of total assets for this year. ________%, found by

   B. Express inventories as a percent of total assets for last year. ________%, found by

   C. Interpret and compare your answers to 3A and 3B. ____

   ____

   D. Express income taxes as a percent of total current liabilities for this year. ______%, found by

   E. Express income taxes as a percent of total current liabilities for last year. ______%, found by

   F. Interpret and compare your answers to D and E. ____

   ____

   G. Express total current assets as a percent of total current liabilities for this year. _________%, found by

   H. Express total current assets as a percent of total current liabilities for last year. _________%, found by

4. Horizontal analysis (round to the nearest tenth of a percent).

   A. Find the percent change in cash from last year to this year. _______%, found by

   B. Find the percent change in receivables from last year to this year. ________%, found by

   C. Find the percent change in total current assets from last year to this year. ______%, found by

   D. Find the percent change in total current liabilities from last year to this year. _________%, found by

   E. Interpret and compare your answers to 4C and 4D. ____

   ____

5. A. Find the current ratio for this year.

Current ratio = $\dfrac{\$\_\_\_\_\_\_\_\_\_\_\_\_}{\$}$ = ________________

B. Find the current ratio for last year.

Current ratio = $\dfrac{\$\_\_\_\_\_\_\_\_\_\_\_\_}{\$}$ = ________________

C. Interpret and compare your answers to 5A and 5B.

____

____

6. A. Find the acid-test ratio for this year.

Acid-test ratio = $\dfrac{\$\_\_\_\_\_\_\_\_\_\_\_\_\_\_\_\_\_\_\_\_}{\$}$ = ________________

B. Find the acid-test ratio for last year.

Acid-test ratio = $\dfrac{\$\_\_\_\_\_\_\_\_\_\_\_\_\_\_\_\_\_\_\_\_}{\$}$ = ________________

C. Interpret and compare your answers to 6A and 6B.

____

7. A. Assume a net income this year of $119.4 million. Find the owner equity and the return on owner investment for this year.

Owner equity = $____________ − $__________ = $____________

Return on owner investment = $\dfrac{\$\_\_\_\_\_\_\_\_\_\_\_\_}{\$}$ = __________ = _____%

B. Assume a net income last year of $99.5 million. Find the owner equity and the return on owner investment for last year.

Owner equity = $____________ − $__________ = $____________

Return on owner investment = $\dfrac{\$\_\_\_\_\_\_\_\_\_\_\_\_}{\$}$ = __________ = _____%

C. Interpret and compare your answers to 7A and 7B.

____

____

TO THE STUDENT: There is a SELF-REVIEW for this chapter in Appendix A, *with answers* in Appendix C.

14

Business Expenses

SECTION 14-1: PAYROLL REGISTER

Objective: To construct a payroll register.

In Amy and Tom Hannas' firm for the manufacture of plastic toys (see Chapter 13), the income statement reveals that wages and salaries account for the largest single operating expense. A **payroll register** is developed to keep an accurate record of the number of regular and overtime hours their employees work, the hourly rate of each employee, gross income, deductions, and net income.

Problem

The Hannas employ two production workers who work on an hourly basis, a sales representative who has a salary plus 7% commission on sales, and an office manager-secretary who is on a straight salary.

Ted Cox is a machine operator who earns \$6.20 an hour for 40 hours a week. Time and a half is paid for any overtime work beyond the 40 hours. He is married and claims two withholding allowances for federal income tax purposes (himself and his wife).

Sue Green is also a machine operator, she earns \$6.60 an hour, with time and a half for overtime. She is married and claims three withholding allowances (herself, her husband, and a child).

> This kind of intervention in the labor market had as its origin the Fair Labor Standards Act of 1938 which provided for a minimum wage of 25 cents per hour which has been periodically increased until \$2.65 per hour was achieved in January 1978. The current legislation requires that the minimum wage be periodically increased until \$3.50 per hour is achieved in 1981.

Atu Fong is the sales representative. In an outstanding week, he earned \$395. He is married and claims six withholding allowances (himself, his wife, and 4 children).

Jean Mix, office manager-secretary, is single. She claims one withholding allowance (herself). Her salary is \$215 a week.

Each employee pays half of the premium for medical insurance and the employer (the Hannas) pay the other half. Some of the employees have regular deductions every week for a savings plan offered by a local credit union. Federal law requires deductions for income taxes and social security (FICA).

Construct the payroll register for the week of September 8.

Solution

Income Tax Deductions. The Hannas use the *wage-bracket method* to determine how much is to be deducted every week from an employee's paycheck for federal income tax.

Cox worked 40 hours. His gross income for the week of September 8 is \$248. Refer to the section in Table 14-1 entitled "Married persons, weekly payroll period." Go down the left margin to "\$240 but less than \$250." Then move horizontally to the column headed by two exemptions. The amount to be deducted from his paycheck is \$26.40.

TABLE 14-1
Withholding Tax Tables

SINGLE Persons—WEEKLY Payroll Period

And the wages are—		And the number of withholding allowances claimed is—										
At least	But less than	0	1	2	3	4	5	6	7	8	9	10 or more
		The amount of income tax to be withheld shall be—										
$110	$115	$14.30	$10.80	$7.30	$4.10	$1.20	$0	$0	$0	$0	$0	$0
115	120	15.20	11.70	8.20	4.90	2.00	0	0	0	0	0	0
120	125	16.10	12.60	9.10	5.70	2.70	0	0	0	0	0	0
125	130	17.00	13.50	10.00	6.60	3.50	.60	0	0	0	0	0
130	135	17.90	14.40	10.90	7.50	4.20	1.40	0	0	0	0	0
135	140	19.00	15.30	11.80	8.40	5.00	2.10	0	0	0	0	0
140	145	20.00	16.20	12.70	9.30	5.80	2.90	0	0	0	0	0
145	150	21.10	17.10	13.60	10.20	6.70	3.60	.70	0	0	0	0
150	160	22.60	18.60	15.00	11.50	8.10	4.70	1.80	0	0	0	0
160	170	24.70	20.70	16.80	13.30	9.90	6.40	3.30	.50	0	0	0
170	180	26.80	22.80	18.80	15.10	11.70	8.20	4.80	2.00	0	0	0
180	190	28.90	24.90	20.90	16.90	13.50	10.00	6.50	3.50	.60	0	0
190	200	31.00	27.00	23.00	18.90	15.30	11.80	8.30	5.00	2.10	0	0
200	210	33.60	29.10	25.10	21.00	17.10	13.60	10.10	6.70	3.60	.70	0
210	220	36.20	31.20	27.20	23.10	19.10	15.40	11.90	8.50	5.10	2.20	0
220	230	38.80	33.80	29.30	25.20	21.20	17.20	13.70	10.30	6.80	3.70	.80
230	240	41.40	36.40	31.40	27.30	23.30	19.20	15.50	12.10	8.60	5.20	2.30
240	250	44.00	39.00	34.00	29.40	25.40	21.30	17.30	13.90	10.40	6.90	3.80
250	260	46.60	41.60	36.60	31.60	27.50	23.40	19.40	15.70	12.20	8.70	5.30
260	270	49.20	44.20	39.20	34.20	29.60	25.50	21.50	17.50	14.00	10.50	7.10
270	280	51.80	46.80	41.80	36.80	31.80	27.60	23.60	19.60	15.80	12.30	8.90
280	290	54.80	49.40	44.40	39.40	34.40	29.70	25.70	21.70	17.60	14.10	10.70
290	300	57.80	52.10	47.00	42.00	37.00	32.00	27.80	23.80	19.70	15.90	12.50
300	310	60.80	55.10	49.60	44.60	39.60	34.60	29.90	25.90	21.80	17.80	14.30
310	320	63.80	58.10	52.30	47.20	42.20	37.20	32.20	28.00	23.90	19.90	16.10

MARRIED Persons—WEEKLY Payroll Period

And the wages are—		And the number of withholding allowances claimed is—										
At least	But less than	0	1	2	3	4	5	6	7	8	9	10 or more
		The amount of income tax to be withheld shall be—										
$150	$160	$17.20	$13.70	$10.60	$7.70	$4.80	$1.90	$0	$0	$0	$0	$0
160	170	19.00	15.50	12.10	9.20	6.30	3.40	.50	0	0	0	0
170	180	20.80	17.30	13.80	10.70	7.80	4.90	2.00	0	0	0	0
180	190	22.60	19.10	15.60	12.20	9.30	6.40	3.50	.60	0	0	0
190	200	24.40	20.90	17.40	14.00	10.80	7.90	5.00	2.10	0	0	0
200	210	26.20	22.70	19.20	15.80	12.30	9.40	6.50	3.60	.80	0	0
210	220	28.10	24.50	21.00	17.60	14.10	10.90	8.00	5.10	2.30	0	0
220	230	30.20	26.30	22.80	19.40	15.90	12.50	9.50	6.60	3.80	.90	0
230	240	32.30	28.30	24.60	21.20	17.70	14.30	11.00	8.10	5.30	2.40	0
240	250	34.40	30.40	26.40	23.00	19.50	16.10	12.60	9.60	6.80	3.90	1.00
250	260	36.50	32.50	28.50	24.80	21.30	17.90	14.40	11.10	8.30	5.40	2.50
260	270	38.60	34.60	30.60	26.60	23.10	19.70	16.20	12.70	9.80	6.90	4.00
270	280	40.70	36.70	32.70	28.60	24.90	21.50	18.00	14.50	11.30	8.40	5.50
280	290	42.80	38.80	34.80	30.70	26.70	23.30	19.80	16.30	12.90	9.90	7.00
290	300	45.10	40.90	36.90	32.80	28.80	25.10	21.60	18.10	14.70	11.40	8.50
300	310	47.50	43.00	39.00	34.90	30.90	26.90	23.40	19.90	16.50	13.00	10.00
310	320	49.90	45.30	41.10	37.00	33.00	28.90	25.20	21.70	18.30	14.80	11.50
320	330	52.30	47.70	43.20	39.10	35.10	31.00	27.00	23.50	20.10	16.60	13.20
330	340	54.70	50.10	45.50	41.20	37.20	33.10	29.10	25.30	21.90	18.40	15.00
340	350	57.10	52.50	47.90	43.30	39.30	35.20	31.20	27.20	23.70	20.20	16.80
350	360	59.50	54.90	50.30	45.70	41.40	37.30	33.30	29.30	25.50	22.00	18.60
360	370	61.90	57.30	52.70	48.10	43.50	39.40	35.40	31.40	27.30	23.80	20.40
370	380	64.60	59.70	55.10	50.50	45.90	41.50	37.50	33.50	29.40	25.60	22.20
380	390	67.40	62.10	57.50	52.90	48.30	43.70	39.60	35.60	31.50	27.50	24.00
390	400	70.20	64.80	59.90	55.30	50.70	46.10	41.70	37.70	33.60	29.60	25.80

Green worked 45 hours. Her gross income was $313.50. Refer again to "Married persons, weekly payroll period," and read down the left margin to "$310 but less than $320." Moving across to three withholding allowances gives the deduction of $37.

Fong earned $395. He has six withholding allowances. Go down the left column in the "Married persons, weekly payroll period" section of the table to "$390 but less than $400." Under six withholding allowances, the tax is $41.70.

Mix's weekly gross income is $215. Refer to "Single persons, weekly payroll period" and one withholding allowance. The deduction is $31.20.

Social Security Deductions. The Hannas are required to deduct 6.13% from the gross income of each employee for social security, abbreviated FICA. For Cox's weekly gross of $248, the deduction is $15.20; and for Fong the deduction is $24.21.

The Hanna's payroll register for the week of September 8 is:

	Hours Worked						*Deductions*						
Employee	*Regular*	*Overtime*	*Rate*	*M/S*	*Allowances*	*Gross Pay*	*FIT*	*FICA*	*Medical Insurance*	*Credit Union*	*Total Deductions*	*Net Income*
Ted Cox	40		$6.20	M	2	$ 248.00	$ 26.40	$15.20	$ 8.50		$ 50.10	$197.90
Sue Green	40	5	6.60	M	3	313.50	37.00	19.22	8.50	$ 5.00	69.72	243.78
Atu Fong				M	6	395.00	41.70	24.21	8.50	10.00	74.41	320.59
Jean Mix				S	1	215.00	31.20	13.18	5.20		59.58	155.42
Totals						$1,171.50	$136.30	$71.81	$30.70	$15.00	$253.81	$917.69

Check: $1,171.50 = $253.81 + $917.69.

1 SELF-REVIEW

A reminder: Cover the answers in the margin.

Construct a weekly payroll register for the Lewandowski Dry Cleaning Company. Lewandowski pays time and a half for all work over 40 hours a week. Each employee contributes $4.90 a week toward hospital insurance. Of course, federal income tax and social security (6.13%) must be deducted. The employees are:

Jim Mack. Earns $5.50 an hour, married, has four withholding allowances. Worked 39 hours during the week of April 17.

Alex Hart. Earns $5.80 an hour, single, has two withholding allowances. Worked 42 hours during the week.

Dot Hunt. Earns $6.00 an hour, single, one withholding allowance. Worked 48 hours during the week.

Payroll Register for Lewandowski Dry Cleaning Company
Week of April 27

	Hrs. Worked						*Deductions*				
Emp.	*Regular*	*Overtime*	*Rate*	*M/S*	*Allowances*	*Gross Pay*	*FIT*	*FICA*	*Medical Ins.*	*Total Deductions*	*Net Pay*
Jim Mack	____	____	$____	____	____	$____	$____	$____	$____	$____	$____
Alex Hart	____	____	____	____	____	____	____	____	____	____	____
Dot Hunt	____	____	____	____	____	____	____	____	____	____	____
Totals						$____	$____	$____	$____	$____	$____

	Reg.	*OT*	*Rate*	*M/S*	*Allowances*	*Gross Pay*	*FIT*	*FICA*	*Med. Ins.*	*Total Deduct.*	*Net Pay*
Jim	39	0	$5.50	M	4	$214.50	$ 14.10	$13.15	$ 4.90	$ 32.15	$182.35
Alex	40	2	5.80	S	2	249.40	34.00	15.29	4.90	54.19	195.21
Dot	40	8	6.00	S	1	312.00	58.10	19.13	4.90	82.13	229.87
Totals						$775.90	$106.20	$47.57	$14.70	$168.47	$607.43

ASSIGNMENT 14-1
PAYROLL REGISTER

Name ______________________ **Date Due** ____________ **Grade** _____

Answers to selected problems are given in Appendix B.

For Problems 1 through 6, find the amount to be deducted from weekly gross income for federal income tax (FIT) and social security (FICA) at 6.13%.

	Employee	*Weekly Gross Income*	*Marital Status*	*No. of Withholding Allowances*	*Deductions for FIT*	*Deductions for FICA*
Ex.	Ted Koontz	$317.50	S	1	$58.10	$19.46
1.	Sam Stein	398.75	M	3	________	________
2.	Sue Ober	391.50	M	4	________	________
3.	Art Kahn	262.45	S	2	________	________
4.	Gene Conner	291.50	S	0	________	________
5.	April Freed	346.50	M	2	________	________
6.	Totals	$________			$________	$________

7. Construct a weekly payroll register for Gus and Nick's Service Station. They pay time and a half for all work over 40 hours a week. A 2½% state income tax is deducted from each employee's gross pay. Federal income tax and social security at 6.13% are the only other deductions. The employees are:

Tom Trianon: Paid weekly salary of $350, married, has four withholding allowances.
Joe Nader: Paid weekly salary of $350, married, has five withholding allowances.
Charles Trakos: Earns $4.90 an hour, single, has two withholding allowances. Worked 46 hours last week.
Bob Bailey: Earns $4.25 an hour, single, has one withholding allowance. Worked 30 hours last week.

Employee	*Regular Hours*	*Overtime Hours*	*Rate*	*Marital Status*	*Withholding Allowances*	*Gross Pay*	*State Income Tax (2½%)*	*FIT*	*FICA*	*Total Deductions*	*Net Pay*
Tom Trianon			$			$	$	$	$	$	$
Joe Nader											
Charles Trakos											
Bob Bailey											

8. Construct a payroll register for the Bernard-David Clothing Company for the week of February 7. FICA rate is 6.65%. Employees are:

Amy Bernard: Weekly salary of $307.50, single, one withholding allowance, FIT, FICA, $20.00 credit union, and $7.50 health insurance are deducted.

Michael Steinman: Weekly salary of $200.00 plus 6% commission on all sales. Sales totaled $2,350. Married with three withholding allowances. FIT, FICA, $10.50 health insurance, and 1% United Appeal are deducted.

Sue Clark: Earns $1.75 per hour plus 5½% commission on all sales. She worked 36 hours and had sales totaling $3,700. She is single with two withholding allowances. FIT and FICA are the only deductions.

Ben Moore: Earns $3.90 per hour plus time and a half for all hours over 40 per week. Worked 50 hours, married, claiming five withholding allowances. FIT, FICA, $12.50 health insurance, and $10 credit union are deducted.

PAYROLL REGISTER FOR BERNARD-DAVID CLOTHING COMPANY

9. Finish the payroll register for Specialty Tooling Company. Time and a half is paid for all Saturday work and double time for Sunday work. (SIT = state income tax, CIT = city income tax).

Emp. No.	Hourly Rate	Hours Worked M T W T F S S	Gross Pay	Marital Status	Allowances	Deductions FIT	FICA (6.65%)	SIT (2%)	CIT (1½%)	Total Deductions	Net Pay
A47	$5.35	7 8 8 6 8 4 0	$240.75	S	1	$39.00	$14.76	$4.82	$3.61	$62.19	$178.56
B16	4.97	8 8 8 8 4 4 4		M	4						
C31	4.45	9 8 8 8 8 0 0		S	2						
D93	5.25	8 8 8 8 8 4 4		S	3						
E04	4.80	7 8 8 8 8 0 0		S	0						
F23	5.40	8 8 8 8 6 4 4		M	6						
G86	6.45	9 8 8 8 9 4 4		M	5						

SECTION 14-2: ADVERTISING EXPENSES

Objective: To compute the cost of newspaper and television advertising.

Most businesses advertise in order to encourage customers to purchase their products or services. As the table shows, the total annual advertising volume in the United States is in excess of $37 billion.

Medium	*Total*
Newspapers	$11,070,000,000
Television	7,630,000,000
Direct mail	5,340,000,000
Radio	2,595,000,000
Magazines	2,165,000,000
Business papers	1,180,000,000
Outdoor	420,000,000
Farm publications	100,000,000
Miscellaneous	7,490,000,000
Total	$37,990,000,000

Source: *Advertising Volume in the United States,* Television Bureau of Advertising, Inc., January 1978.

NEWSPAPER ADVERTISING

Most newspapers offer businesses attractive rates if they contract for space a year in advance. The actual rate is based on the numoer of lines of advertising contracted. The rates for *The Blade* (Toledo, Ohio), with a daily circulation of about 175,000 and a Sunday circulation of about 200,000, are given in Table 14-2. Note that as the number of lines contracted for increases, the rate per line decreases. (For reference, a full-page ad is about 2,800 lines.)

The cost of newspaper advertising generally varies according to circulation. Small newspapers charge less than those with large circulations, such as *The New York Times.* Color is more expensive than black and white.

The actual cost of an advertisement is computed by multiplying the number of lines by the cost per line.

Cost of advertisement = No. of lines X Cost per line

Problem The First National Bank contracted with *The Blade* for 200,000 lines to be used during the year. (This is equivalent to about 70 pages a year.) On October 4 the bank plans to advertise a new checking account service available to bank customers. The advertisement consists of 1,418 lines (about one-half page). It will appear in the evening paper. What is the cost of the advertisement?

TABLE 14-2
The Blade Newspaper Advertising Rates

	Evening, per Line	*Sunday, per Line*
No contract rates	$0.88	$1.04
Annual contract rates (No. of lines)		
700	0.735	0.865
1,400	0.730	0.860
4,200	0.725	0.855
7,000	0.720	0.850
14,000	0.715	0.845
28,000	0.710	0.840
48,000	0.705	0.835
70,000	0.700	0.830
84,000	0.695	0.825
100,000	0.690	0.820
200,000	0.685	0.815

Solution Refer to Table 14-2. Go down the left column to 200,000 lines and read across to the column headed by the word "Evening." The rate is 68.5 cents a line.

Cost of advertisement = Number of lines × Cost per line
= 1,418 × $0.685
= $971.33

1 SELF-REVIEW

An automobile dealer contracted with *The Blade* for 100,000 lines annually. Plans are for two advertisements next week. One is to be in the evening paper, consisting of 945 lines (about one-third of a page) and another in the Sunday paper, consisting of 265 lines. What is the total cost of the advertisements?

	No. of Lines		*Cost per Line*		*Total*
Daily	______	×	$______	=	$______
Sunday	______	×	______	=	______
Total					$______

Daily	945 ×	$0.690 =	$652.05
Sun.	265 ×	0.820 =	217.30
Total			$869.35

TELEVISION ADVERTISING

Television advertising volume has increased from $53 million in 1949 to over $7.6 billion—an increase of over 14,000%. The breakdown of television advertising expenditures is shown in the table.

Medium	Amount
Network	$3,455,000,000
Spot	2,260,000,000
Local	1,915,000,000
Total	$7,630,000,000

The cost of *network advertising* depends in part on the time of day and the number of potential viewers. The largest concentration of viewers is between the hours of 8 P.M. and 11 P.M. (called *prime time*). Logically, the cost of advertising during prime time is higher than in the daytime hours (9 A.M. to 4 P.M.), or at news time (6 P.M. to 7 P.M.), or during late hours (11:30 P.M. to conclusion).

Another factor affecting the cost of advertising is the rating of the program. The well-known Nielsen ratings, and others, give the networks a fairly accurate indicator of the audience viewing daily or weekly programs. The cost of advertising on a high-rated network program is greater than on a low-rated program (because the advertisement is viewed by more people).

★ ★ ★
The American Broadcasting Company will charge $200.000 per commercial-minute during the World Series. Baseball will get $54.4 million for broadcasting rights

About 8 out of 10 television advertisements have a duration of 30 seconds. The cost of a 10-second advertisement is half the 30-second rate. A 60-second ad is double the 30-second rate.

COST FACTORS FOR TELEVISION ADS

Base is cost of 30-second ad
10-second ad = ½ of cost of 30-second ad
60-second ad = 2 × cost of 30-second ad

The actual cost per 30-second ad on network television varies from about $4,000 on a low-rated daytime program, or one during the late hours, to over $150,000 for a spectacular such as the World Series, the Super Bowl, or the Olympics.

Problem The Florida citrus industry plans to introduce a new drink. Its advertising campaign for the week of October 15 calls for:

1. Two 30-second ads and one 10-second ad on a popular network show. The ad price for a 30-second spot is $7,600.
2. Three 30-second ads and a 60-second ad on a popular prime-time network program. A 30-second spot costs $24,400.

What is its advertising expense for the week?

Solution

Daytime:

30-sec.:	2 ads × $7,600	= $15,200
10-sec.:	1 ad × (½ × $7,600)	= 3,800
	Total	= $19,000

10-second ad costs ½ the 30-second ad

Prime time:

30-sec.:	3 ads × $24,400	= $ 73,200
60-sec.:	1 ad × (2 × $24,400)	= 48,800
	Total	= $122,000

Total = Daytime + Prime time
= $19,000 + $122,000
= $141,000

2 SELF-REVIEW

Visa wants to have one 30-second and two 10-second advertisements on the early-evening NBC news. The cost per 30-second ad is $10,000. Also, one 30-second ad and one 60-second ad are to appear on a prime-time special Emmy Award program. The 30-second cost is $30,000. What is the total advertising budget for the week?

Evening news:

30-second:

___ ad × $_________ = $_________

10-second:

___ ad × ___ × $_________ = $_________

Total = $_________

Prime time:

30-second:

___ ad × $_________ = $_________

60-second:

___ ad × ___ × $_________ = $_________

Total = $_________

The total weekly budget is $__________.

Evening news:

1 × $10,000	= $10,000
2 × (½ × $10,000)	= 10,000
Total	= $20,000

Prime time:

1 × $30,000	= $30,000
1 × (2 × $30,000)	= 60,000
Total	= $90,000

$20,000 + $90,000 = $110,000

ASSIGNMENT 14-2
ADVERTISING EXPENSES

Name ______________________ Date Due ____________ Grade _____

Answers to selected problems are given in Appendix B.

For Problems 1 through 6, use Table 14-2 to find the cost per line and the cost of the newspaper advertisement.

	Annual Contract Rates	*Edition*	*Cost per Line*	*No. of Lines*	*Cost of Advertisement*
Ex.	14,000 lines	Evening	$0.715	1,418	$1,013.87
1.	200,000 lines	Evening	________	945	________
2.	100,000 lines	Evening	________	715	________
3.	No contract	Sunday	________	2,800	________
4.	7,000 lines	Sunday	________	1,418	________
5.	70,000 lines	Evening	________	600	________
6.	No contract	Evening	________	265	________

7. The Lion Store contracts for 200,000 lines annually with *The Blade.* Using Table 14-2, find the cost of two full-page ads (each is 2,800 lines) in the Sunday paper.

   $__________, found by

8. Best Products contracted for 84,000 lines with *The Blade.* Use Table 14-2 to determine the cost of running a one-third page (945 lines) ad in the Monday through Friday (5 days) evening editions.

   $____________, found by

9. When Rudy's Hot Dogs opened its new South Toledo store, it ran a full page (2,800 lines) ad on Sunday and a half-page (1,418 lines) ad in three evening editions of *The Blade.* The stand had not contracted for a minimum number of lines. What did Rudy's four ads cost?

   $______________, found by

10. Joseph's Food Stores contracted for 100,000 lines per year. The company routinely takes a third of a page (945 lines) every Sunday. What does the routine advertising policy cost Joseph's for 52 Sundays?

   $_______________, found by

For Problems 11 through 16, find the cost of the 10-second ads, 30-second ads, 60-second ads, and the total advertising expense.

	Cost of 30-Second Ad	*No. of Ads for 10 Sec.*	*30 Sec.*	*60 Sec.*	*Cost of Ads for 10 Sec.*	*30 Sec.*	*60 Sec.*	*Total Advertising Expense*
Ex.	$ 50,000	3	2	2	$75,000	$100,000	$200,000	$375,000
11.	5,000	4	1	0	______	______	______	______
12.	8,000	5	0	1	______	______	______	______
13.	74,700	0	3	1	______	______	______	______
14.	65,000	1	4	2	______	______	______	______
15.	137,500	2	4	4	______	______	______	______
16.	148,750	1	3	5	______	______	______	______

17. When Ford Motor Company introduced a new line of subcompact automobiles, its television advertising plans for one week called for:
    A. Four 30-second ads, two 10-second ads, and one 60-second ad on a popular network show. The ad price for a 30-second spot is $12,500.
    B. Four 60-second ads and four 10-second ads on a prime-time special. A 30-second spot costs $32,500.

    What is the advertising expense for the week? $__________, found by

18. General Mills is involved in the sponsorship of many television programs. A breakdown of its commitment for one quarter is shown below. Complete this table as in Problems 11-16 above.

    What is General Mills's TV advertising cost for the quarter?

30-Second Spot Cost	*No. of Spots 10 Sec.*	*30 Sec.*	*60 Sec.*	*Cost of Ads for 10 Sec.*	*30 Sec.*	*60 Sec.*	*Total Advertising Expense*
$ 4,000	12	24	16	______	______	______	______
11,700	8	20	12	______	______	______	______
32,500	4	20	8	______	______	______	______
90,000	4	8	4	______	______	______	______
150,000	2	4	4	______	______	______	______
Total							______

SECTION 14-3: BUSINESS INSURANCE

Objective: To compute the annual premium for a businessowners' insurance policy.

Another necessary business expense is insurance against fire, theft, wind damage, bodily injury, and other possible disasters. Most insurance underwriters offer a **businessowners' policy** similar to the homeowners' insurance policy discussed in Chapter 8. Allstate, for example, has a basic policy and a deluxe policy. Exhibit 14-1 shows the cost and briefly describes the coverage for a deluxe businessowners' policy for a real estate office in a recent year.

Burglary, Robbery and Employee Dishonesty

Note in Exhibit 14-1 that the **building** is insured for $60,000, the **business personal property** for $13,000, including $1,000 for merchandise and $12,000 for furniture, lighting fixtures, and equipment (typewriters, calculators, etc.).

Further, the policy provides for liability up to $1 million should, for example, the building collapse and an injured client sue. The insurance company also pays should a dishonest employee steal from the business. The owner will also be reimbursed up to $1,000 should a messenger be robbed while transporting money to the bank.

Items *not* covered are losses resulting from wear and tear (a rug wearing out, for example), floods, landslides, freezing of plumbing, and credit defaults.

FACTORS AFFECTING THE PREMIUM

The premium on a businessowners' insurance policy depends on:

1. Type of coverage (deluxe or basic).
2. Amount of insurance.
3. Rating territory (geographic location of business).
4. Degree of fire protection (fire protection class).
5. Type of building construction.
6. Type of business and general building use.

Rating territory and degree of fire protection. The **rating territory** is the general geographic location of a business within a state. For illustration, in Ohio, Territory 1 consists of Mahoning County; Territory 2 consists of Cuyahoga, Franklin, and Summit counties. Table 14-3 gives the annual premium per $1,000 of property value for a business located in Territory 2.

The *degree of fire protection* is indicated by a rate classification system ranging from 1 to 10. In Table 14-3 note that the heading for one of the columns is "Protected-Town Classes 1-8." This includes metropolitan areas with a good fire department and rural areas with fire hydrants.

The other column heading is "Unprotected-Town Classes 9-10." These are rural areas without fire hydrants. Some of the rural areas have good fire departments within six miles, others do not.

Type of building construction. Note in Table 14-3 that there are three types of building construction, labeled Type 1, Type 2, and Type 3 at the head of the columns. These are:

Type 1. A structure of predominantly wood construction.

Type 2. A structure constructed predominantly with wood floors, wood roof, and with either brick, hollow block, or brick veneer walls.

Type 3. A structure predominantly constructed of concrete.

Type of business and general building use. Another factor affecting the premium is the type of business and general building use. "Classifications" on the left side of the exhibit refer to the building use, such as apartment buildings, motels, or mercantile buildings (retail stores). Note that retail stores are further classified as Class A, B, or C. In Class A are stores such as hardware stores and shoe stores; in Class B are department stores and drugstores; and in Class C are clothing stores and television-radio stores.

EXHIBIT 14-1

Here's Allstate's low cost for the Businessowners Deluxe Policy

Prepared for Barlet Real Estate

Address

Territory 2

Town Class 7

Classification Office building owner occupied

Building Construction Type 2

Values and Premiums — Mandatory Coverages		
Buildings & Specified Personal Property		**Annual Premium or minimum**
Show cost to replace	Replacement Cost Value	
Buildings at described premises	$ 60,000	
Appurtenant buildings on same premises	$	
Property furnished for use of tenants	$	
TOTAL BUILDING REPLACEMENT COST VALUE	$ 60,000	
Annual Composite Rate per $1,000	$ 3.30	
Annual Premium....................		$ 198.00
Business Personal Property		
Show Actual Cash Value	Actual Cash Value	
Stock of Merchandise	$ 1,000	
Furniture, Fixtures and Equipment	$ 12,000	
Property of others in Applicant's custody	$	
Tenant's Improvements and Betterments	$	
TOTAL BUSINESS PERSONAL PROPERTY ACV	$ 13,000	
Annual Composite Rate per $1,000	$ 8.20	
Annual Premium....................		$ 106.60

Total Annual Premium........$ 304.60

Buildings & Specified Personal Property

When Buildings and Specified Personal Property are covered, the Deluxe Policy protects . . .

Your buildings, including all permanently installed fixtures and machinery, plus all exterior glass.

Also covered . . .

All garages and similar structures on the same premises.

Personal Property used for servicing the building.

Personal Property furnished for the use of tenants.

Money and other negotiable instruments used in your business, including up to $1,000 while enroute off premises.

Deductibles per occurrence

Glass	$50
Earthquake	$1,000
Loss by Theft (including Employee Dishonesty)	$250
All Other Loss	$100

Business Personal Property

When Business Personal Property is covered, the Deluxe Policy protects . . .

Personal Property used in your business, including stock, furniture, fixtures and equipment while on your premises. Also included is money and other negotiable instruments on your premises or in a bank, including up to $1,000 while enroute off premises.

Business Personal Property at other locations for up to 30 days.

The property of others in your custody while on your premises.

Your Business Personal Property and the property of others while in due course of transit within 100 miles of your premises for pickup and delivery.

Tenant's Improvements and Betterments.

Deductibles per occurrence

Loss by Theft (including Employee Dishonesty)	$250
All Other Loss	$100

Business Liability

The Deluxe Policy provides an equally new approach to insuring your business liability, affording:

A Combined Single Limit of liability of . . . One Million Dollars . . . $1,000,000 Per Occurrence Plus Premises Medical Payments of $5,000 Each Person, $25,000 Each Accident!

The Liability Limit applies to bodily injury, property damage and to personal injury. (Personal injury is broad protection for such hazards as false arrest, libel or slander, wrongful entry or eviction and invasion of the right of privacy.)

TABLE 14-3

BUSINESSOWNERS POLICY — ANNUAL COMPOSITE RATES PER $1,000 OF PROPERTY VALUE — OHIO - TERRITORY 2

OHIO TERRITORY 2 - CONSISTING OF THE FOLLOWING COUNTIES: CUYAHOGA, FRANKLIN, SUMMIT

CLASSIFICATIONS	ANNUAL MINIMUM PREMIUM	PROTECTED-TOWN CLASSES 1-8 BUILDING CONSTRUCTION			UNPROTECTED-TOWN CLASSES 9-10 BUILDING CONSTRUCTION		
		Type 1	Type 2	Type 3	Type 1	Type 2	Type 3
DELUXE POLICY — **BUILDINGS AND SPECIFIED PERSONAL PROPERTY**	$	$	$	$	$	$	$
Apartment Buildings - 4 families or less, with no Mercantile or Office occupancy. Specified Personal Property included.	125	6.40	4.80	3.60	8.60	6.40	4.70
Apartment Buildings - Over 4 families, with no Mercantile or Office occupancy. Specified Personal Property included.	150	9.20	6.90	5.20	12.40	9.20	6.80
Apartment Buildings - with Mercantile or Office occupancy. Specified Personal Property included.	150	9.60	7.30	5.60	12.80	9.60	7.20
Motel Buildings. Specified Personal Property included.	150	11.10	9.00	6.90	14.80	11.80	8.90
Mercantile Buildings, Leased to Others, with no apartment occupancy.	150	10.60	7.30	5.50	14.30	9.70	7.20
Mercantile Buildings, Owner occupied as a Retail Store, in whole or in part. Rate Business Personal Property separately using rates shown below.	50	9.20	6.30	4.70	12.40	8.40	6.10
Office Buildings, Leased to Others, with no apartment occupancy.	150	5.30	4.00	3.00	7.10	5.30	3.90
Office Buildings. Owner occupied as an office, barber or beauty shop, in whole or in part. Rate Business Personal Property separately using rates shown below.	50	4.40	3.30	2.50	5.90	4.40	3.30
BUSINESS PERSONAL PROPERTY							
Barber Shops	100	16.20	13.90	11.60	21.00	17.70	14.60
Beauty Shops	125	20.00	17.40	14.50	26.00	22.00	18.30
Retail Stores - Class A	150	17.30	13.70	11.70	22.00	17.10	14.40
Retail Stores - Class B	200	23.00	18.00	15.40	29.00	22.00	18.90
Retail Stores - Class C	250	30.00	24.00	20.00	37.00	29.00	25.00
Offices	100	10.60	8.20	6.80	13.60	10.40	8.60
BASIC POLICY — **BUILDINGS AND SPECIFIED PERSONAL PROPERTY**							
Apartment Buildings - 4 families or less, with no Mercantile or Office occupancy. Specified Personal Property included.	100	5.60	4.00	2.80	7.80	5.60	3.90
Apartment Buildings - Over 4 families, with no Mercantile or Office occupancy. Specified Personal Property included.	100	8.00	5.70	4.00	11.20	8.00	5.60
Apartment Buildings - with Mercantile or Office occupancy. Specified Personal Property included.	100	8.00	5.70	4.00	11.20	8.00	5.60
Motel Buildings. Specified Personal Property included.	100	9.20	7.10	5.00	12.90	9.90	7.00
Mercantile Buildings, Leased to Others, with no apartment occupancy.	100	9.30	6.00	4.20	13.00	8.40	5.90
Mercantile Buildings, Owner occupied as a Retail Store, in whole or in part. Rate Business Personal Property separately using rates shown below.	25	8.10	5.20	3.60	11.30	7.30	5.00
Office Buildings, Leased to Others, with no apartment occupancy.	100	4.60	3.30	2.30	6.40	4.60	3.20
Office Buildings. Owner occupied as an office, barber or beauty shop, in whole or in part. Rate Business Personal Property separately using rates shown below.	25	3.80	2.70	1.90	5.30	3.80	2.70
BUSINESS PERSONAL PROPERTY							
Barber Shops	75	13.80	11.50	9.20	18.40	15.30	12.20
Beauty Shops	100	17.30	14.40	11.50	23.00	19.20	15.30
Retail Stores - Class A	100	13.80	10.20	8.20	18.40	13.60	10.90
Retail Stores - Class B	150	17.80	13.20	10.60	24.00	17.60	14.10
Retail Stores - Class C	200	24.00	17.40	13.90	31.00	23.00	18.50
Offices	75	9.20	6.80	5.40	12.20	9.00	7.20

Rates courtesy Allstate Insurance Company. The rates are for illustration only.

Problem Verify that the annual premium for the businessowners' policy for the Barlet Real Estate office shown in Exhibit 14-1 is $304.60.

Solution For the real estate office:

1. Type of coverage: Deluxe.
2. Amount of insurance: Building, $60,000; contents ("business personal property"), $13,000.
3. Rating territory: Territory 2.
4. Degree of fire protection (fire protection class): Class 7.
5. Type of building construction: Type 2.
6. Classification of building: Office building–owner occupied.
7. Type of business: Office.

Refer to Table 14-3. Find "Deluxe Policy" in the margin. Then read down the left column under "Buildings and Specified Personal Property" to the line entitled "Office Buildings–Owner Occupied." Go across to the column headed "Type 2" construction under the heading "Protected-Town Classes 1-8." The premium is $3.30 per $1,000 of property value. Logically, the premium for $60,000 is 60 times the premium for $1,000. It is $198.00, found by 60 × $3.30.

The rate for *business personal property,* that is, the contents of the real estate office, is given under "Business Personal Property." Read down to "Offices." Then read across to the column heading "Type 2" construction under "Protected-Town Classes 1-8." The premium for $1,000 protection is $8.20 and for $13,000 it is $106.60, found by 13 × $8.20.

The total annual premium for this deluxe businessowners' policy is $304.60, found by adding the premium for buildings and specified personal property ($198.00) and the premium for business personal property ($106.60). This agrees with the amount stated in Exhibit 14-1.

Another aspect of the rate schedule which should be noted is the column titled "Annual Minimum Premium." The insurance company charges a minimum amount, regardless of the replacement value of the building or the business personal property. For a deluxe policy the minimum annual premium for a motel building, including the contents, is $150, and the minimum annual premium on the business personal property of a Class C retail store is $250.

Many businessowners' insurance policies have *coinsurance clauses* (described in detail in Section 8-1 on homeowners' insurance in Chapter 8).

1 SELF-REVIEW

Peter and Jan Allan want a *basic* businessowners' policy to protect their antique shop, which they operate from their own mercantile building. They want $90,000 protection on the buildings and specified personal property, and $150,000 on their business personal property (the antiques for sale). The building is of predominantly wood construction. The shop is located in a Protection Class 5 area. For business personal property purposes, antique shops are in Class B.

For the basic policy, the *building construction* is classified as Type ____.

Type 1

The annual premium per $1,000 of protection is $________ and for $90,000 it is $________, found by $________ × ______.

$8.10;

$729, found by $8.10 × 90

For *business personal property* (the antiques), the antique shop is in Class B.

The annual premium per $1,000 of protection is $__________, and for $150,000 it is $__________.

$17.80

$2,670

The total annual premium is $__________, found by $________ + $__________.

$3,399, found by $729 + $2,670

ASSIGNMENT 14-3
BUSINESS INSURANCE

Name ______________________ Date Due ______________ Grade _____

Answers to selected problems are given in Appendix B.

For Problems 1 through 6, find the building premium, business personal property premium, and the total annual premium. Use Table 14-3.

	Amount of Insurance		*Type of Cover-age*	*Fire Protec-tion Class*	*Building Const. Type*	*Type of Business*	*Building Premium*		*Business Personal Property Premium*		*Total Annual Premium*
	Building	*Personal Property*					*Per $1,000*	*Total*	*Per $1,000*	*Total*	
Ex.	$ 70,000	Included	Deluxe	9	1	Motel	$14.80	$1,036	0	Included	$1,036
1.	120,000	$ 50,000	Basic	10	3	Mercantile, owner occupied; Class B, retail					
2.	180,000	40,000	Basic	2	2	Office building; owner occupied					
3.	940,000	Included	Deluxe	7	1	Apartment building; over 4 families			0	Included	
4.	95,000	105,000	Deluxe	8	2	Office building; owner occupied; beauty shop					
5.	740,000	450,000	Deluxe	5	3	Mercantile building; owner occupied; Class A, retail					
6.	1,250,000	Included	Basic	1	1	Apartment building; less than 4 families			0	Included	

7. Determine the annual premium for a deluxe policy on an apartment building with mercantile or office occupancy of Type 2 construction in a Class 5 area. The building and personal property are valued at $265,000 (note that this is an instance where business personal property is included in the buildings and specified personal property).

   $______________, found by

8. An all-brick eight-family apartment located in a large metropolitan area, Class 5 fire protection district, is to be insured for $120,000. What is the annual premium for a basic businessowners' policy?

   $_______, found by

9. A drugstore (retail store, Class B) is located in a mercantile building owned by the druggist. The building is of Type 3 construction, in a Class 8 district, and is valued at $225,000. The business personal property is valued at $190,000. For the deluxe policy, find the:

   A. Annual premium on the building.

   $______________, found by

   B. Annual premium on the business personal property.

   $______________, found by

   C. Total annual premium.

   $______________, found by

10. A sporting goods store (retail store, Class C) is located in a Class 9 protection district and is in an owner-occupied mercantile building of Type 1 construction. The building is valued at $95,000, and the business personal property is valued at $75,000. For the basic policy, find the:

A. Annual premium on the building.

$______________, found by

B. Annual premium on the business personal property.

$______________, found by

C. Total annual premium.

$______________, found by

11. A barber shop is located on the ground floor of an office building. The building is located in a metropolitan area with a good fire department and is a structure predominantly constructed of concrete. The shop owner does not carry insurance on the building but does carry insurance (a basic policy) on the business personal property, which is valued at $26,000. What is the annual premium?

$___________, found by

12. A shoe store (retail store, Class A) is housed in a mercantile building (owner occupied) of predominantly wood construction located in a rural area with fire hydrants. The building is valued at $165,000, and the business personal property is valued at $152,000. What is the total annual premium for the deluxe policy?

$______________, found by

13. A motel predominantly constructed of concrete is located in Protection Class 7. What is the annual premium on a deluxe policy for $20,000?

$__________, found by (careful)

14. A builder erects two four-family apartment buildings of Type 2 construction at a cost of $190,000 each. One building is located in a Class 6 fire protection district, and the other is located in a Class 10 district. How much higher is the annual premium for the building in the Class 10 district than it is for the building in the Class 6 district on a *basic* policy?

$_______, found by

What is the difference in the annual premiums for Class 6 and Class 10 on *deluxe* policies?

$_______, found by

SECTION 14-4: OTHER BUSINESS EXPENSES

Objective: To compute the cost of workers' compensation and unemployment insurance, and freight costs.

Several business expenses have been discussed: wages and salaries of employees, premiums for businessowners' insurance, advertising expense, and matching social security contributions of employees. There are other business expenses, including **workers' compensation insurance, unemployment insurance,** and **freight costs.**

WORKERS' COMPENSATION INSURANCE

Every state has established an insurance system which provides compensation to an employee, or the employee's dependents, in the event the employee is injured on the job, incurs an illness on the job which prevents him or her from working, or is killed on the job. So all-inclusive are these laws that 84 percent of the civilian labor force has this protection. Many states include medical care, physical and vocational rehabilitation programs, and other related programs as part of their workers' compensation system.

What is unemployment insurance?

The unemployment insurance program pays benefits to insured workers who are involuntarily unemployed and looking for work. The benefits are of limited duration and are based on an individual's insured wages and not upon need. They help tide a worker over until he can find a job for which he is suited by reason of past experience and training.

Who is covered?

More than 4 out of 5 wage and salaried workers are covered by unemployment insurance. Domestic, agricultural, and State and local government workers make up the majority of the workers still not covered.

The premiums for **workers' compensation insurance** are paid to the state by the *employer, not the employee.* They are therefore considered as a business expense, the same as payroll, advertising, and other insurance.

The premiums vary by state but are based on the total payroll of a firm and the type of business engaged in. The state classifies every business according to the frequency and severity of accidents. The number and seriousness of accidents in underground coal mining are greater than in retail establishments. It is logical, therefore, that a coal mine operator would pay a higher premium than the owner of a toy store.

In most states the premium for workers' compensation insurance is computed by multiplying a *base rate by the total payroll.*

Premium for workers' compensation insurance = Base rate X Total payroll

Problem

The base rate for workers' compensation insurance for underground coal mining in Ohio is $30.26 per $100 paid to employees. The total monthly payroll for a small underground mine is $40,000. What is the monthly premium for workers' compensation insurance?

Solution

The base rate of $30.26 per $100 paid in wages can be expressed as 30.26 cents per $1, or $0.3026 per $1. Thus:

Monthly premium = Base rate X Total payroll
= $0.3026 X 40,000
= $12,104

1 SELF-REVIEW

In Ohio, the owner of a toy store pays a base rate of only $0.73 per $100 paid in wages. The payroll for the Fun Toy Store for October is $2,600. What is the monthly premium for workers' compensation insurance?

$0.0073

The base rate of $0.73 per $100 in wages is the same as $__________ per $1.

Monthly premium = Base rate X Total payroll
= $__________ X 2,600
= $__________

Monthly premium:
= $0.0073 X 2,600
= $18.98

UNEMPLOYMENT INSURANCE

The Federal Unemployment Tax Act requires that every state must have an unemployment insurance program. Qualified persons who, through no fault of their own, become unemployed are given financial aid. *The employers, not the employees, pay for this insurance.* This is another expense of doing business.

The federal government administers the unemployment insurance program. The money to administer it comes from a 0.7% federal tax on the first $6,000 every employee earns during the year. In addition, each state levies its own tax.

The state programs vary. In Ohio, for example, the amount an employer pays depends on past employment experience. An employer with good experience (very few layoffs) might pay less than 1% on the first $6,000 paid each employee during the year. A firm with a large number of seasonal layoffs might pay the maximum of 4.6%. *The amount paid by the employer goes to the state and is paid out in benefits by the state to qualified unemployed persons.*

Problem

A sewer contractor in Ohio has four employees. The firm has considerable unemployment during the year—especially during the winter months—and must pay the maximum of 4.6%. The annual wages of the four employees are shown at right.

Name	*Annual Wages*
Tom Richards	$17,600
John Stribbling	4,500
Jean Cox	19,200
Art Cable	5,950

What is the sewer contractor's annual contribution to the federal unemployment insurance program and to the state unemployment insurance program?

Solution

Employee	*Annual Wage*	*Amount Taxed*	*Federal Tax (0.7%)*	*State Tax (4.6%)*
Tom Richards	$17,600	$ 6,000	$ 42.00	$ 276.00
John Stribbling	4,500	4,500	31.50	207.00
Jean Cox	19,200	6,000	42.00	276.00
Art Cable	5,950	5,950	41.65	273.70
Totals		$22,450	$157.15	$1,032.70

0.7% × $6,000

4.6% × $4,500

As checks: 0.7% × $22,450 = $157.15 and 4.6% × $22,450 = $1,032.70

2 SELF-REVIEW

A small manufacturer of ceramic products has good experience with respect to layoffs. The firm pays a state tax of only 1.1% on the first $6,000 of each employee's annual wage. What is the total federal and state unemployment insurance tax paid on the wages of the five employees?

Employee	*Annual Wage*	*Amount Taxed*	*Federal Tax (0.7%)*	*State Tax (1.1%)*
Bob Zuiko	$12,850	$ ______	$ ______	$ ______
Sue Tarbell	21,275	______	______	______
Alan Knox	5,250	______	______	______
Alex Karem	5,695	______	______	______
Luis Lopez	22,750	______	______	______
Totals		$ ______	$ ______	$ ______

As checks: Federal ______% × $______ = $______

State ______% × $______ = $______

Emp.	*Amount Taxed*	*Federal*	*State*
Zuiko	$ 6,000	$ 42.00	$ 66.00
Tarbell	6,000	42.00	66.00
Knox	5,250	36.75	57.75
Karem	5,695	39.87	62.65
Lopez	6,000	42.00	66.00
Totals	$28,945	$202.62	$318.40

0.7% × $28,945 = $202.62
1.1% × $28,945 = $318.40

FREIGHT COSTS

The cost of shipping automobile parts, refrigerators, flowers, electronic parts, and other goods from a manufacturer to the customer is another expense of doing business. There are a number of ways goods can be shipped, including truck, rail, UPS, U.S. Postal Service, Greyhound express, and air freight.

The cost of shipping by air includes: (1) pickup of the package, (2) air freight to the destination, (3) delivery to the customer, and (4) a 5% federal tax on the total shipping charge.

Problem

A 750-pound electronic computer is to be shipped from a San Diego, California, manufacturer by Delta's 3D air freight service to a customer in Philadelphia. An air freight pickup service in San Diego, which is typical of metropolitan areas, has the rates shown in Table 14-4. The rates are for regular service (8 A.M. to 6 P.M. Monday through Friday).

Rate per 100 pounds for items weighing less than 1,000 pounds

Rate per 100 pounds for items weighing between 3,000 and 5,000 pounds

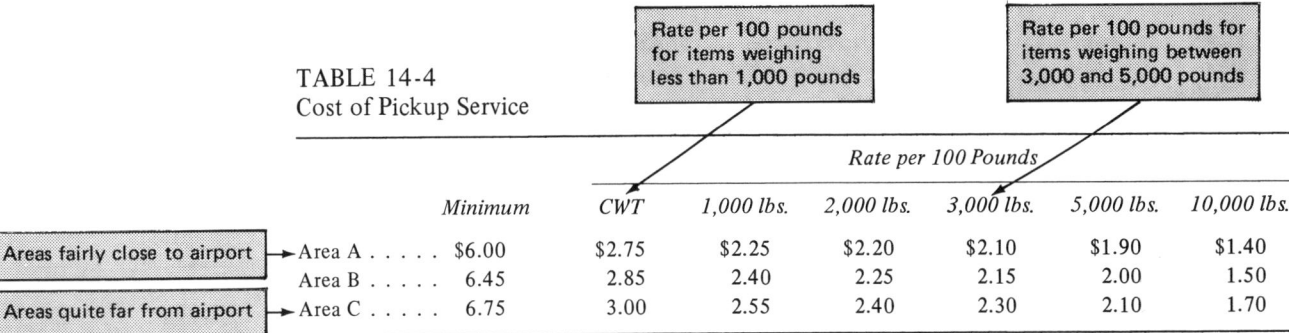

TABLE 14-4
Cost of Pickup Service

		Rate per 100 Pounds					
	Minimum	*CWT*	*1,000 lbs.*	*2,000 lbs.*	*3,000 lbs.*	*5,000 lbs.*	*10,000 lbs.*
Area A	$6.00	$2.75	$2.25	$2.20	$2.10	$1.90	$1.40
Area B	6.45	2.85	2.40	2.25	2.15	2.00	1.50
Area C	6.75	3.00	2.55	2.40	2.30	2.10	1.70

Areas fairly close to airport (Area A)

Areas quite far from airport (Area C)

A schedule of Delta 3D air freight rates is given in Table 14-5.

TABLE 14-5
Cost of Air Freight

	3D Rate per Hundred Pounds		
	100 lbs.	*1,000 lbs.*	*3,000 lbs.*
Atlanta to Dallas/Ft. Worth	$10.26	$ 9.45	$ 8.04
Boston to Miami	13.71	12.87	11.88
Chicago to Houston	12.15	10.35	9.21
Detroit to Tampa	12.21	10.20	9.21
Los Angeles to Atlanta	16.41	14.94	12.42
Los Angeles to New York	19.92	16.80	15.87
Memphis to Miami	11.70	10.14	9.36
New York to New Orleans	13.71	11.58	10.56
San Diego to Philadelphia	19.41	16.08	15.06
San Francisco to Dallas/Ft. Worth	14.46	13.47	11.28

Note: Minimum charge is $19.00.

Rate per 100 pounds for items weighing less than 1,000 pounds

Delivery rates from the Philadelphia airport to customers in that area by the Speedy Delivery Service are shown in Table 14-6. These rates also are typical for metropolitan areas.

TABLE 14-6
Cost of Delivery Service

		Rate per 100 Pounds					
	Minimum	*CWT*	*1,000 lbs.*	*2,000 lbs.*	*3,000 lbs.*	*5,000 lbs.*	*10,000 lbs.*
Area A	$6.50	$2.90	$2.50	$2.30	$2.20	$2.00	$1.50
Area B	7.00	3.05	2.70	2.40	2.35	2.10	1.60
Area C	7.50	3.25	2.90	2.60	2.50	2.20	1.80

What is the total cost of shipping the computer by air freight?

Solution

The manufacturer of the computer is located fairly close to the San Diego airport (in Area A). The customer is located in Valley Forge (quite some distance from the Philadelphia airport, in Area C).

Using a calculator with memory:

Enter	Press	Display
750	÷	750
100	= m+	7.5
	×	7.5
2.75	=	20.625
	RM ×	7.5
19.41	=	145.575
	RM ×	7.5
3.25	=	24.375
24.38	+	24.38
145.58	+	169.96
20.63	= ×	190.59
.05	= +	9.5295
190.59	=	200.1195

	Pounds	*Rate per 100 Pounds*		*No. of 100 Pounds*		*Cost*
Pickup (Table 14-4)	750	$ 2.75	×	7.5	=	$ 20.63
Air freight (Table 14-5)	750	19.41	×	7.5	=	145.58
Delivery (Table 14-6)	750	3.25	×	7.5	=	24.38
Total						$190.59
		5% federal tax × $190.59			=	9.53
				Total cost	=	$200.12

3 SELF-REVIEW

Refer to Tables 14-4, 14-5, and 14-6. Aircraft parts weighing 2,200 pounds are shipped via Delta 3D air freight from Area C near San Diego to quite near the Philadelphia airport (Area A). What is the total cost?

	Pounds	*Rate per 100 lbs.*		*No. of 100 lbs.*		*Cost*
Pickup (Table 14-4)	2,200	$______	×	______	=	$______
Air freight (Table 14-5)	______	______	×	______	=	______
Delivery (Table 14-6)	______	______	×	______	=	______
Total						$______
		5% federal tax × $______			=	$______
				Total cost	=	$______

Lbs.	*Rate*	*No.*		*Cost*
2,200	$ 2.40	22	=	$ 52.80
2,200	16.08	22	=	353.76
2,200	2.30	22	=	50.60
				$457.16
5% × $457.16			=	22.86
Total cost			=	$480.02

ASSIGNMENT 14-4
OTHER BUSINESS EXPENSES

Name ____________________ Date Due ____________ Grade ______

Answers to selected problems are given in Appendix B.

For Problems 1 through 6, find the monthly premium for workers' compensation insurance.

	Type of Business	*Monthly Payroll*	*Base Rate per $100*	*Monthly Premium*
Ex.	Building construction	$52,100	$11.42	$5,949.82
1.	Delivery service	2,450	2.05	________
2.	Janitorial service	980	2.46	________
3.	Window washing service	3,960	12.54	________
4.	Painting contractor	7,860	3.64	________
5.	Clothing store	4,650	0.73	________
6.	Underground coal mining	74,700	30.26	________

7. The base rate for a state's workers' compensation insurance for a service station attendant is $3.12 per $100 paid in wages. The payroll for City Park Service Station for March is $3,450. What is the monthly premium for workers' compensation insurance?

   $__________, found by

8. Eloise and Alice Manley operate a bakery. The base rate for unemployment compensation insurance is $2.80 per $100 paid in wages. The payroll for the bakers employed by the Manleys is $2,870. What is the monthly premium for workers' compensation insurance?

   $__________, found by

For Problems 9 through 14, the maximum annual wage taxed for both federal and state unemployment insurance is $6,000. Find the amount taxed and the federal and state unemployment insurance taxes.

	Employee	*Annual Wage*	*Amount Taxed*	*Federal Tax (0.7%)*	*State Tax (2.4%)*
Ex.	Sam Welch	$ 3,600	$3,600	$25.20	$86.40
9.	Tammy Shore	5,700	______	______	______
10.	Mary Murdock	4,800	______	______	______
11.	Bob Faust	9,240	______	______	______
12.	Dave Priest	22,860	______	______	______
13.	Lana Smith	17,450	______	______	______
14.	John Miller	5,198	______	______	______

15. Hannibul Exterminating Company has an above-average unemployment experience. Its state tax for unemployment insurance is, therefore, 3.2% on the first $6,000 of each employee's annual wage. What are the federal and state unemployment insurance taxes paid on the annual wages of these four employees?

Employee	Annual Wage	Amount Taxed	Federal Tax (0.7%)	State Tax (3.2%)
A. Tom Harris	$ 7,850	$______	$______	$______
B. Ben Wanamaker	9,142	______	______	______
C. Nick Iorio	11,400	______	______	______
D. Bev Pinciotti	8,615	______	______	______

16. Mark Sardis is a carpenter hired frequently by the Main City Building Construction Company for seasonal work. Main City's unemployment rate is high. Their state tax rate is 4.6% on the first $6,000. What state and federal taxes did Main City pay for Mark Sardis if he earned $5,900 during the year?

$__________, found by

For Problems 17 through 22, refer to Tables 14-4, 14-5, and 14-6. Find the rate per 100 pounds and total cost for pickup, air freight, and delivery. Find the 5% federal tax, and total cost.

	Shipped from	*Weight (lbs.)*	*Pickup Area*	*Cost per 100 lbs.*	*Pickup Cost*	*Air Freight Cost per 100 lbs.*	*Air Freight Cost*	*Delivery Area*	*Cost per 100 lbs.*	*Delivery Cost*	*Pickup, Air Freight, Delivery, Total*	*5% Federal Tax*	*Total Cost*
Ex.	New York to New Orleans	1,400	B	$2.40	$33.60	$11.85	$165.90	A	$2.50	$35.00	$234.50	$11.73	$246.23
17.	Boston to Miami	3,500	A					B					
18.	San Francisco to Dallas/ Fort Worth	620	C					C					
19.	Detroit to Tampa	6,200	A					B					
20.	Los Angeles to Atlanta	2,250	C					C					
21.	Memphis to Miami	987	A					A					
22.	Chicago to Houston	1,643	B					C					

23. A major television network, in order to adequately cover the NIT finals in Madison Square Garden, had to fly 1,140 pounds of extra TV equipment from Los Angeles to New York. Their studio is quite far from the airport in Los Angeles (Area C), while the Garden is in Area B in New York City. What was the total cost?

Pickup $__________

Air freight __________

Delivery __________

Total __________

5% tax __________

Total cost $__________

REVIEW ASSIGNMENT FOR CHAPTER 14
BUSINESS EXPENSES

Name ______________________ **Date Due** ______________ **Grade** _____

1. Construct a payroll register for the Fteno Finance Company. All employees are salaried, paid weekly, and have social security tax (FICA) (6.13%), federal income tax (FIT) (wage-bracket), state income tax (SIT) (2½%), and contributions of 1% withheld.

	Name	Weekly Salary	Marital Status	Allow-ances	Deductions: FICA	FIT	SIT	Contri-butions	Total Deductions	Net Pay
A.	Alice Manore	$215.00	S	1	$____	$____	$____	$____	$____	$____
B.	Thomas Axleton	241.70	M	3						
C.	Mary Bassett	298.50	M	3						
D.	Edward Young	317.50	S	2						
E.	Barbara Parsons	345.00	M	4						

2. Construct a payroll register for the Quick-Stop Food Shop. All employees are paid weekly, paid time and a half for all hours over 40 per week, and have only social security tax (FICA) (6.13%) and federal income tax (FIT) withheld.

	Name	Hourly Rate	Hours Worked	Gross Pay	Marital Status	Allow-ances	Deductions: FIT	FICA	Total Deductions	Net Pay
A.	Bill Troup	$2.90	40	$____	S	1	$____	$____	$____	$____
B.	Sue Carr	2.90	38		S	0				
C.	Mike Farley	3.50	42		M	2				
D.	Jill Urbanski	3.75	45		M	3				
E.	Greg Descamps	4.15	50		M	4				

3. Refer to Table 14-2. Kesslers Men's Wear bought a full-page ad (2,800 lines) in *The Blade's* Sunday edition to announce its annual spring sale. The shop does not contract for any space with *The Blade.* What did the full-page ad cost?

   $______________, found by

4. Refer to Table 14-2. State Savings and Loan Company contracts for 100,000 lines per year. One week it ran three half-page ads (1,418 lines each) in the evening edition and a one-third page ad (945 lines) in the Sunday edition. What did its newspaper advertising cost that week?

   $______________, found by

5. Mel North has invented a new potato peeler. He markets it by mail. Plans are to buy a ten-second spot on his wife's favorite TV soap opera. Assuming a 30-second ad costs $4,000 on the soap, what will it cost Mel?

   $__________, found by

6. Colgate-Palmolive sponsors many television programs. Their commitments for one month are:

Cost of 30-Second Ad	*No. of Ads* 10 Sec.	30 Sec.	60 Sec.
$ 5,500	10	8	4
14,700	4	8	4
82,500	4	6	2
127,450	2	4	2

   What is Colgate Palmolive's TV advertising cost for this month?

   $________________, found by

For Problems 7 through 10, refer to Table 14-3.

7. A dentist has her office in a building which she owns. A lawyer has his office in an adjacent building which he owns. Both buildings are in a Class 8 protection district and are of Type 3 construction.

   A. Determine the annual premium for the deluxe policy for the dentist, if the building is worth $200,000 and the contents $150,000.

      $__________, found by

   B. Determine the annual premium for the deluxe policy for the lawyer, if the building is worth $220,000 and the contents $35,000.

      $_______, found by

8. Samuel Walker owns a small shopping center (mercantile building). He leases the stores to various retailers. There are no apartments in his building. The replacement cost of the building is $265,000. How much is the annual premium for a basic policy if:

A. The structure is of predominantly wood construction and is located in a rural area without fire hydrants. $______________, found by

B. The structure has wood floors, wood roof, and brick walls and is located in a rural area with fire hydrants. $______________, found by

C. The structure is predominantly constructed of concrete and is located in a metropolitan area with a good fire department. $______________, found by

9. The Kampos Real Estate office is located in an office building owned by Connie Kampos. The building is constructed of wood and is in Protection Class 10. It is insured for $30,000, and the business personal property is insured for $2,000. What does Kampos pay in annual premiums for the business-owners' deluxe policy?

$____________, found by

10. The *Daily's* district circulation "shack" (office building, owner occupied) is constructed of cinder block (Type 3) and is located in Protection Class 1. What will it cost to insure (deluxe policy) the building for:

A. $10,000?

$__________, found by

B. $15,000?

$__________, found by

C. $20,000?

$__________, found by

11. A nursing home operator pays a base rate of only $0.88 per $100 paid in wages for workers' compensation insurance. The payroll for Sleepy Acres Nursing Home, Inc., for July is $4,650. What is the monthly premium for workers' compensation insurance?

$__________, found by

12. High Voltage, Inc., engaged in construction and repair of power lines, pays a base rate of $17.65 per $100 paid in wages for workers' compensation insurance. Its payroll for one month totaled $12,650. What was its monthly premium for workers' compensation insurance?

$______________, found by

13. A fast-food drive-in restaurant has had average experience with respect to layoffs. It pays a state tax of 2.3% and a federal tax of 0.7% on the first $6,000 of each employee's annual wage. What are the state, federal, and total unemployment insurance taxes paid on the wages of the four employees?

Employee	*Annual Wage*	*Amount Taxed*	*Federal Tax*	*State Tax*	*Total*
A. Amy Botkin	$7,120	$______	$______	$______	$______
B. Daryl Clay	5,240	______	______	______	______
C. Jerry Mumford	4,916	______	______	______	______
D. Susan Moore	5,862	______	______	______	______

14. Wallace Jordan works at B-N Parts Corporation. The company has experienced very few layoffs. Therefore, B-N pays only 1.7% state tax and the 0.7% federal tax on the first $6,000 of each employee's annual wage for unemployment insurance. If Jordan earned $17,450 last year:

A. How much was withheld from his pay for unemployment insurance?

$______, found by

B. How much did B-N Parts Corporation pay for Jordan's unemployment insurance?

$________, found by

15. Find the total cost of shipping a 950-pound engine prototype from Detroit to Tampa. Pickup is in Area B; Delta 3D air freight service is used (see Table 14-5); and the delivery is in Area A. There is a 5% federal tax on the total shipping charge.

$________, found by

16. Assume you had to ship a 100-pound item from your area to some other agreed-upon area. Investigate and report on the cost and time involved if shipped one of these ways.
A. Air freight
B. Greyhound
C. United Parcel Service
D. Rail
E. U.S. Postal Service

TO THE STUDENT: There is SELF-REVIEW TEST for this chapter in Appendix A, *with answers* in Appendix C.

15

Trade and Cash Discounts

SECTION 15-1: TRADE DISCOUNTS

Objective: To determine the trade discount and the net price.

TRADE DISCOUNT

Department stores, hardware stores, drugstores, and other retail stores purchase most of their merchandise either from a wholesaler (often called a distributor) or directly from the manufacturer. They are sometimes provided with rather elaborate catalogs which describe and illustrate with photographs and diagrams all the details of the items. Most catalogs include the catalog or **list price** of each item. *The list price is simply the suggested retail price the retail store is to charge the customer.*

The retailer receives a discount, called a **trade discount**, from the list price in the catalog. *It is usually stated as a percent.* Many of these catalogs have over 1,000 pages and are very expensive to print and distribute. The wholesaler or manufacturer cannot issue a new catalog every time a single price changes or an item is added or deleted. Instead, the manufacturer or wholesaler simply sends to the retailer a sheet indicating a new set of trade discounts to be applied to the list prices in the catalog. An example is given in Exhibit 15-1.

EXHIBIT 15-1
Trade Discounts Offered by a Wholesaler

CARBIDE TOOLS—CONFIDENTIAL DISTRIBUTOR
DISCOUNT SCHEDULE

Pages 2-3-4:	Hammer type, one-piece masonry drills and accessories. . .	40%
Page 4:	Hammer type, core style, masonry drills	40%
Page 5:	Vibrating type hammer drills—Ram-tip, bulk	50-20%
Page 7:	Carbide-tipped hole saws	30%

Trade discount

Additional Discounts Available

These additional discounts are available *only* on *single* orders shipped at *one* time to *one* destination from factory in Arcadia, California.

1. Invoices totaling $250, an additional 5%.
2. Invoices totaling $500, an additional 10%.
3. Invoices totaling $1,000, an additional 20%.

Inducement to retailer to purchase a greater quantity of merchandise. If retailer purchases $1,000 or more of merchandise, an additional 20% is deducted.

NET PRICE The amount remaining after the trade discount has been taken from the list price in the catalog is called the **net price.** *This is the amount the retailer pays for the merchandise.* To calculate the net price:

Step 1. Find the *amount* of the trade discount by multiplying the list price in the catalog by the rate of discount.

Amount of trade discount = Rate of discount × List price

Step 2. Subtract the amount of the discount from the list price in the catalog to arrive at the net price.

Net price = List price − Amount of trade discount

Problem Note in Exhibit 15-1 that carbide-tipped hole saws on page 7 of the catalog are offered to a retail hardware store at a 30% trade discount. The list price in the catalog is \$10 for a package of seven saws. What is the net price to the dealer?

Solution Step 1. The amount of the trade discount is calculated by:

$$\begin{aligned}\text{Amount of trade discount} &= \text{Rate of discount} \times \text{List price}\\ &= 30\% \times \$10\\ &= \$3\end{aligned}$$

Step 2. Arrive at the net price by:

$$\begin{aligned}\text{Net price} &= \text{List price} - \text{Amount of trade discount}\\ &= \$10 - \$3\\ &= \$7\end{aligned}$$

1 SELF-REVIEW

A reminder: Cover the answers in the margin.

The list price of a 19-inch color television set in a manufacturer's catalog is \$625. A discount sheet sent by the manufacturer to all dealers shows a discount rate of 40%.

A. The amount of discount is:

Discount = Rate of discount × List price

= ______% × \$________

= \$________

A. Discount = 40% × \$625
= \$250

B. The net price to the dealer is:

Net price = List price − Amount of trade discount

= \$________ − \$________

= \$________

B. Net price = \$625 − \$250
= \$375

COMPLEMENT METHOD FOR COMPUTING NET PRICE

A more direct method of determining the net price the retailer pays is by using the **complement** of the trade discount. Exhibit 15-1 shows that the carbide-tipped hole saws are discounted 30%. The hardware dealer, therefore, pays 70% of the list price in the catalog. The complement of 30% is 70%, found by 100% – 30%. The complement is multiplied by the list price to arrive at the net price.

> Net price = Complement of trade discount X List price

Problem

A manufacturer of Western-style boots shows a list price of $200 a pair for the Sagebrush boot in the catalog. The trade discount to dealers is 40%. Using the complement method, what is the net price of a pair of Sagebrush boots?

Solution

The complement of the trade discount of 40% is 60%, found by 100% – 40%. Then:

Net price = Complement of the trade discount X List price
= 60% X $200
= $120

2 SELF-REVIEW

The Rite Writer pen has a catalog list price of $4.80 a box. (As noted, this is the same as the suggested list price.) The distributor offers a 35% discount to bookstores. Find the:

A. Complement of the trade discount. ______%, found by _______ – ______

B. Net price. $________, found by _____% X $________

A. 65%, found by 100% – 35%

B. $3.12, found by 65% X $4.80

ASSIGNMENT 15-1
TRADE DISCOUNTS

Name ______________________ Date Due ______________ Grade _____

Answers to selected problems are given in Appendix B.

For Problems 1 through 5, determine the trade discount and the net price (to the nearest cent) for these items.

	Item	*List Price in Catalog*	*Discount Rate*	*Amount of Trade Discount*	*Net Price to Retailer*
Ex.	Opal ring	$200.00	40%	$80.00	$120.00
1.	LED watch	85.00	30	25.50	________
2.	Diamond brooch	395.00	60	________	________
3.	Cuff links	4.50	45	________	________
4.	Pearl necklace	214.00	50	________	________
5.	Silver locket	15.00	47	________	________

6. The list price of a washer-dryer combination is $719. The rate of discount is 40%. Find the:

   A. Amount of the trade discount.

   $__________, found by

   B. Net price of the washer-dryer to an appliance dealer.

   $__________, found by

7. Custom draperies list for $89.50 a panel. The rate of discount is 50%. Find the:

   A. Amount of the trade discount.

   $_________, found by

   B. Net price to a department store.

   $_________, found by

8. The suggested list price of a diesel earth mover is $67,800. The rate of discount is $33\frac{1}{3}$%. Find the:

   A. Amount of the discount.

   $__________, found by

   B. Net price to the dealer.

   $__________, found by

For Problems 9 through 12, determine the complement and the net price (to nearest cent).

	Item	*List Price*	*Rate of Discount*	*Complement of Trade Discount*	*Net Price*
Ex.	Early American sofa	$ 800	40%	60%	$480.00
9.	Loafer-boy chair	320	30	_____	____________
10.	Maple coffee table	695	60	_____	____________
11.	Highboy	1,295	45	_____	____________
12.	Bedroom suite	3,680	42	_____	____________

13. The Heath Company is offering a discount on several discontinued models of stereo receivers. All these closeout items are discounted 65%. Using the complement method, what is the net price of an item which has a list price in the catalog of $385?

$__________, found by

14. Dirksen Distributors shows a suggested retail list price of $425.00 in its catalog for the Easy Wheeler. It offers a 42% discount to dealers. Argon Wholesalers suggests a $410 retail price for the Easy Wheeler and offers a 37% discount. Find:

A. Dirksen's net price.

$__________, found by

B. Argon's net price.

$__________, found by

15. Bartolo Wholesale Company offers a 35% discount on all plumbing items in its catalog. Topper Discount Stores ordered the following items from the catalog.

Item	*No. Ordered*	*List Price (each)*	*Amount*
Single-control washerless kitchen faucet	42	$34.99	$__________
Rinser spray head	450	2.99	__________
Antique white lavatory faucet	80	49.95	__________
Copper tubing; ½ inch, 5-foot section	210	4.99	__________
Reducing tee, ½ X ¼ X ¼	100	0.89	__________
Stop and waste valve, ½ inch	25	3.29	__________
		Total	$__________

In addition, Bartolo offers an *additional* 10% discount on orders between $500 and $1,000 and a 15% discount on orders over $1,000. What net price did Topper Discount Stores pay for these plumbing items?

$__________, found by ______________________________

____

16. If the list price in the catalog and the net price to the retailer are known, the rate of discount can be calculated. (The solution is an application of the percent decrease formula given in Chapter 3.)

A. The list price in the catalog of a CB radio is $100. The net price to the dealer is $60. What is the rate of discount?

_____%, found by

B. The list price of a toaster is $21.95. The net price to the dealer is $13.42. What is the discount rate?

_____%, found by

SECTION 15-2: CHAIN DISCOUNTS

Objective: To compute the net price when given a chain discount.

CHAIN DISCOUNTS

When a manufacturer or wholesaler gives the retailer a discount, such as 40%, based on the catalog list price, it is called a trade discount. Additional discounts may be offered, however, on certain catalog items. For example, a manufacturer of CB radios with a new model in production might offer the retailer additional discounts in order to sell the current model in stock. If the *usual* trade discount is 40% and the *additional* discount is 20%, the discount announced to the retailer would be "40% less 20%," or just 40/20. This type of a discount is called a **chain discount**. Another term often used is **series discount**, meaning it is a series of discounts.

A chain discount of 40% less 20% less 10% means that discounts of 40%, 20%, and 10% are deducted successively from the list price in the catalog.

Problem

Khan Importers wants to celebrate its 50th year in the import business. Its usual rate of discount on a hand-made Kalimar rug from India is 40%. The new chain discount just announced is 40% less 20% less 10%. What is the net price to a department store of a Kalimar rug which has a catalog list price of $500?

Solution

Catalog list price	$500
Less first discount (0.40 X $500)	– 200
First net price	300
Less second discount (0.20 X $300)	– 60
Second net price	240
Less third discount (0.10 X $240)	– 24
Final net price to a department store	$216

1 SELF-REVIEW

Feldman, Inc. is offering a chain discount of 30/20 on plaid shirts with a catalog list price of $20. What is the final net price?

	Catalog list price	$20
A.	Less first discount (0.30 X $20)	–_______
B.	First net price	_______
C.	Less second discount (_______ X $_____)	–_______
D.	Final net price	$_______

Catalog price	=	$20.00
A. 0.30 X $20	=	– 6.00
B. First net price	=	14.00
C. 0.20 X $14	=	– 2.80
D. Final net price	=	$11.20

COMPLEMENT METHOD FOR COMPUTING NET PRICE

A more direct method of arriving at the net price is to multiply the list price in the catalog by the product of the complements of the chain discounts.

> Net price = List price X Product of complements of the chain discounts

Problem Khan Importers is offering a chain discount of 40% less 20% less 10% on a $500 Kalimar rug.

A. What is the product of the complements of the chain discounts?
B. What is the net price of the rug to a retailer?

Solution A. Complement of 40% is 60% ← 100% − 40%

Complement of 20% is 80% ← 100% − 20%

Complement of 10% is 90% ← 100% − 10%

The product of the complements = 0.60 X 0.80 X 0.90 = 0.432

B. Net price = List price X Product of complements of the chain discounts
= $500 X 0.432
= $216 ← Same net price as computed previously

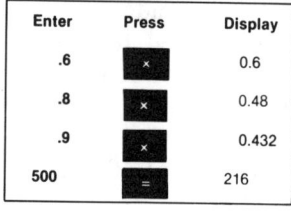

Using a calculator:

Enter	Press	Display
.6	×	0.6
.8	×	0.48
.9	×	0.432
500	=	216

2 SELF-REVIEW

Feldman, Inc. is offering a chain discount of 30/20 on plaid shirts with a catalog list price of $20. Use the complement method to determine the net price.

A. What is the complement of 30%? ______%, found by ______% − ______%
B. What is the complement of 20%? ______%, found by ______% − ______%
C. What is the product of the complements? ______
D. In words:

Net price = ______ X ______

E. Net price = $______ X ______
= $______ (must be same answer as in Self-Review 1)

A. 70%, found by 100% − 30%
B. 80%, found by 100% − 20%
C. 0.56, found by 0.70 X 0.80
D. Net price = List price X Product of complements of chain discounts
E. Net price = $20 X 0.56
= $11.20

3 SELF-REVIEW

A chain discount of 35% less 15% less 5% is being offered by a manufacturer on a discontinued group of brass hanging lamps. The catalog list price on one of the lamps is $600. Use the complement method to find:

A. The complement of 35%, ______; of 15%, ______; of 5%, ______
B. The product of the complements. ______
C. The net price of the lamp. ______, found by $______ X ______

A. 65%, 85%, 95%
B. 0.65 X 0.85 X 0.95 = 0.524875
C. $314.93, found by $600 X 0.524875

ASSIGNMENT 15-2
CHAIN DISCOUNTS

Name ______________________ **Date Due** ____________ **Grade** _____

Answers to selected problems are given in Appendix B.

For Problems 1 through 5, find the discounts and net prices.

	Item	*List Price*	*Chain Discount*	*First Discount*	*First Net Price*	*Second Discount*	*Second Net Price*	*Third Discount*	*Final Net Price*
Ex.	Sofa	$ 400.00	30/20/10	$120	$280	$56	$224	$22.40	$201.60
1.	Bed	200.00	40/30/10	______	______	______	______	______	______
2.	Hammer	10.00	20/10/10	______	______	______	______	______	______
3.	Rug	10,000.00	50/20/5	______	______	______	______	______	______
4.	Shirt	7.50	40/20	______	______	______	______	______	______
5.	Motor	200.00	50/10	______	______	______	______	______	______

6. The list price of a dining table in a manufacturer's catalog is $950. The chain discount to a dealer is 40%/20%.

List price $950.00

A. Less the first discount . . . . . . $__________, found by ________% × $________

B. First net price . . . . $__________, found by $________ − $________

C. Less the second discount . . . . $__________, found by ________% × $________

D. Final net price . . . . $__________, found by $________ − $________

7. The list price of a 52-piece set of dinnerware is $425. The chain discount to a department store is 30% less 20% less 10%.

List price $425.00

A. Less the first discount . . . . . . $__________, found by ______________________

B. First net price . . . . $__________, found by ______________________

C. Less the second discount . . . . $__________, found by ______________________

D. Second net price . . . . $__________, found by ______________________

E. Less the third discount . . . . . $__________, found by ______________________

F. Final net price . . . . $__________, found by ______________________

8. The list price of a three-horsepower Terrance lawn mower is $110. Terrance Manufacturing offers dealers a 35/20/5 chain discount. What is the net price to a dealer?

$________ found by

For Problems 9 through 12, determine the product of the complements.

	Chain Discount	*Complement of First Discount*	*Complement of Second Discount*	*Complement of Third Discount*	*Product of Complements*
Ex.	40/30/10	0.60	0.70	0.90	0.378
9.	50/20/10	________	________	________	________
10.	45/20/5	________	________	________	________
11.	40/30	________	________		________
12.	50/20	________	________		________

13. Aunt Dorothy's Distributors sells art needlework to its dealers throughout the United States and Canada. In order to move a group of slow-moving kits, a chain discount of 30% less 20% less 5% was announced. Kits and Things of Detroit placed an order amounting to $2,450.

    A. What is the complement of the first discount? ________, found by ______________

    B. What is the complement of the second discount? ________, found by ______________

    C. What is the complement of the third discount? ________, found by ______________

    D. What is the product of the complements? ________

    E. What is the net price to Kits and Things of Detroit? $__________, found by ______________

14. Mr. Muscles, a distributor of barbells and other muscle-building equipment, has a promotion on a select group of equipment. The chain discount is 55/10. A health spa placed an order which had a total list price of $4,700. Using the complement method, what is the net price to the spa?

    $__________, found by

15. Small Appliance Wholesalers offers a variety of discounts from the list price in their catalog. Jensen's Department Store ordered the following. Using the complement method, determine the net prices.

Item	*No. Ordered*		*List Price (each)*			*Discount*	*Product of Complements*	*Net Price*
Toaster	20	X	$ 21.50	=	$__________	50/10/5	________	$__________
Mixer	14	X	$ 89.95	=	$__________	40/20/10	________	$__________
Broiler	86	X	$129.60	=	$__________	50/10	________	$__________
Fan	25	X	$ 36.00	=	$__________	40%	________	$__________

In addition, an additional 5% discount is offered on orders of $1,000 to $1,500; 10% on orders between $1,500 and $3,000; and 20% on orders of $3,000 and over. What is the total net price of the Jensen order?

$__________

SECTION 15-3: CASH DISCOUNTS

Objective: To compute the cash discount and the cash price of an invoice.

CASH DISCOUNTS

When retailers order merchandise from a manufacturer or distributor, they usually are not required to pay in advance. In fact, they are not expected to pay upon receipt of the shipment. The common practice is to grant credit periods of 30 days or more from the date of the invoice to the date when payment is expected.

Despite the fact that credit is granted to retailers, manufacturers or distributors would prefer to receive payment as soon as possible. As an incentive to the retailer to pay for the merchandise *before* the end of the credit period, a **cash discount** is frequently offered. It is determined by multiplying the rate of cash discount by the *net* price.

Cash discount = Rate of cash discount × Net price

The cash discount is then subtracted from the *net price* on the invoice. The retailer pays the resulting amount, generally called the *cash price.*

Cash price = Net price − Cash discount

The three most common ways of granting a cash discount are known as **ordinary dating, end-of-month dating,** and **receipt-of-goods dating.**

ORDINARY DATING

BOSS MANUFACTURING COMPANY

DATE SHIPPED: 4/7	
TERRITORY 25	INVOICE DATE 4/7
TERMS: 2% 20, Net 40	

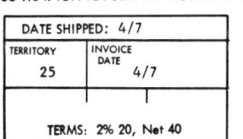

A portion of an actual invoice from the Boss Manufacturing Company of Kewanee, Illinois, with respect to leather gloves sold to Mangus Metals of Houston, Texas, is used to illustrate **ordinary dating.** Note that the **terms** are: 2% 20, net 40. This means that Mangus Metals has 20 days from the invoice date of 4/7 (April 7) to take the 2% discount off the net price of the leather gloves. That is, Mangus has until April 27 to take the 2% discount. If the discount is not taken, the full amount is due within 40 days of the invoice date. The date *exactly* 40 days after April 7 is May 17.

Problem A shipment of steel bars from a steel mill to a steel broker dated September 8 has terms of 3/10, net 30.

A. What do these terms mean?
B. If the net price of the steel bars is $4,000, what are the cash discount and the cash price to the broker?

Solution A. A 3% discount can be taken from the net amount of $4,000 for ten days, that is, until September 18. The invoice must be paid in full by October 8, exactly 30 days after September 8.

B. Cash discount = Rate of cash discount × Net price
= 3% × $4,000
= $120

Cash price = Net price − Cash discount
= $4,000 − $120
= $3,880 ← Steel broker pays $3,880

1 SELF-REVIEW

An importer of artificial flowers prints these terms on all invoices: 4/15, net 30.

A. On an invoice to Denver Flowers dated June 6, this means:

____

____

____

B. The net price of the order from Denver Flowers is $2,300. The cash discount is: $______, found by ____% X $__________

C. The cash price to Denver Flowers is $__________, found by $__________ – $______.

Answers:

A. A 4% discount can be taken from the net amount of the invoice for 15 days, that is, until June 21. The invoice must be paid in full by July 6.

B. $92; 4% × $2,300

C. $2,208; $2,300 – $92

END-OF-MONTH DATING

End-of-month dating, abbreviated EOM, is often called **proximo dating** (abbreviated prox). The word *proximo* is translated as "in the following month." Note, for illustration, the partial invoice from Bradley Knitwear, Inc., is dated 11-3 (November 3) and has terms of 8/10 EOM. This means that the retailer ordering the knitwear has until ten days after the *end* of the month of November to take advantage of the cash discount of 8%, that is, until December 10. Although not stated, it is implied that the full amount is due 20 days after the last day for taking the discount, or December 30.

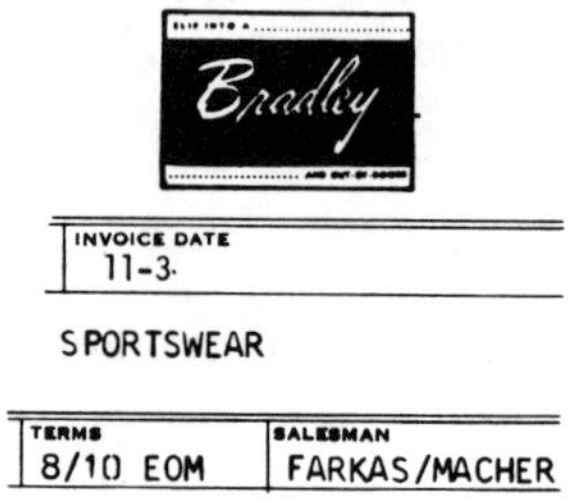

Problem

The net price on an invoice dated June 8 is $180. Terms are 2/10 EOM, net 30.

A. Interpret 2/10 EOM, net 30.
B. What is the cash discount?
C. What is the cash price?

Solution

A. Retailer receives 2% off net price of $180 if invoice is paid by July 10. Full amount due 20 days after last day for taking discount, or July 30.

B. Cash discount = Rate of cash discount X Net price
= 2% X $180 = $3.60

C. Cash price = Net price – Cash discount
= $180.00 – $3.60 = $176.40

2 SELF-REVIEW

The net amount of an invoice is $1,860. It is dated March 15 and carries terms of 3/10 prox, net 30.

A. The last date on which the cash discount may be taken is ______________.

B. The amount of the cash discount, if taken, is $__________, found by ________________________.

C. If the invoice is paid on April 5, the cash price is $__________, found by ________________________.

D. In order to avoid a late charge, the invoice must be paid by ______________.

Answers:

A. April 10

B. $55.80, found by 3% × $1,860

C. $1,804.20, found by $1,860 – $55.80

D. April 30

When EOM or proximo dating is involved, it is common business practice to grant a month's extension on invoices dated on or after the 26th of the month. In other words, the invoice is treated as though it carried a date at the beginning of the *next* month. Thus an invoice dated June 27 with terms of 3/10 EOM is considered to be dated as of July 1, and the cash discount may be taken if the invoice is paid by August 10.

3 SELF-REVIEW

An invoice for $200 is dated May 28 and carries terms of 3/10 EOM.

A. The last date on which the discount may be taken is ______________.

B. The amount of the discount is $________.

C. If the invoice is paid within the discount period, then the amount paid is $________.

D. The final date for payment without a late charge is ______________.

A. July 10

B. $6.00

C. $194

D. July 30

RECEIPT-OF-GOODS DATING

Merchandise involved in long-distance shipments can be over a month in transit. Obviously, buyers are reluctant to pay for goods which have not been received. *Receipt-of-goods dating,* abbreviated *rog,* is used in these cases. In brief, 4/10, net 30 *rog* means that a 4% discount may be taken from the net amount on the invoice within 10 days *after the goods are received.* If not paid, the net amount is due between the 11th and 30th days. If paid after the 30-day period, the invoice may be subject to a late charge, just as in ordinary dating and EOM dating.

4 SELF-REVIEW

What does 2/10, net 30 rog mean with respect to merchandise shipped from the manufacturer on May 2 but not received until June 6?

2/10, net 30 rog means that a 2% discount may be taken from the net amount of the invoice within ten days of June 6, that is, June 16. The full net amount is due on or before July 6.

INVOICES

The wholesaler or manufacturer prepares a document, called an *invoice,* which is either included with the merchandise or mailed separately to the retailer. It usually contains such information as how the merchandise is being shipped, description and unit price of the goods, cost of transportation, trade discounts, and the terms (cash discounts). (See Exhibit 15-2.)

EXHIBIT 15-2

EASTMAN KODAK COMPANY **INVOICE** Kodak

D.U.N.S. CODE 00-220-6183

343 STATE STREET

ROCHESTER, N.Y. 14650

ORD. RCVD.	SHIP DATE
01/08	01/10

ORDER NO.	ORDER DATE	ACCOUNT NO.	INVOICE DATE	INVOICE NO.	PAGE
	01/04	36R2767	JAN 13 19	001753057	1

9 S1

SHIP TO/CHARGE TO

KUHLMAN ASSOC/DESIGN

406 MADISON AVE

TOLEDO OH 43604

QUANTITY	DESCRIPTION	UNIT PRICE	AMOUNT
	SHIPPED VIA UNITED PARCEL SERVICE		
	A36R276720250130		
	PAYMENT RECEIVED		
	102.20		
2	RL 16MM 7252 PRF 1 T WN B 400EC0457 CAT. NO. 173 8145	32.40	64.80
2	RL 16MM 7247 PERF 2 S90 100ECN449 CAT. NO. 165 5109	10.48	20.96
	ALL SAME EMULSION		
2	RL 16MM 7247 PRF1 S90 WNB 100ECN455 CAT. NO. 165 4987	10.48	20.96
	TRANSPORTATION		1.20

We certify that in our production of the goods covered by this invoice we have complied with all applicable requirements of the Fair Labor Standards Act of 1938, as amended

Terms 2/10 EOM Net 30 EOM except where noted below and subject to Credit Department approval.

INVOICE TOTAL

$ 107.92

6 - 001001
000372-00 -75009-A00304-

VISUAL GRAPHICS CORPORATION
VGC Park
5701 N.W. 94th Ave.
Tamarac, Florida 33321

TELEPHONE 305-722-3000
CABLE VISUGRAPH FTL

REMIT TO:
P.O. BOX 019033
MIAMI, FL 33101

3-343525

INVOICE NUMBER	INVOICE DATE	PAGE NO.
56761	4/24/79	1

THIS IS YOUR INVOICE

IN ACCORDANCE WITH OUR STANDARD TERMS, A CHARGE OF 1½% PER MONTH WILL BE MADE ON PAST DUE BALANCES

SHIP TO
343525
KUHLMAN ASSOCIATES
406 MADISON AVE
TOLEDO
OH 43604

F.O.B. SHIPPING POINT

CUSTOMER PURCHASE ORDER NUMBER	SALESPERSON NUMBER	OUR SHIPPING NUMBER	NUMBER CARTONS	TOTAL WEIGHT	SHIPPED VIA	TERMS
BILL	SC	2-177 3	3	49	UPS	NET 30 DAYS

PRODUCT NUMBER	DESCRIPTION	QUANTITY ORDERED	QUANTITY BACK ORDERED	QUANTITY SHIPPED	UNIT PRICE	AMOUNT
ECH-31-60026-201	SOL,PCS ONE RINSE CT.	1		1	10.70	10.70
ECH-31-60027-201	SOL,PCS 1 DEV. CTN	1		1	18.30	18.30
ECH-31-60037-201	SOL,PCS ONE FIXER CTN	1		1	18.30	18.30
	SUBTOTAL					47.30
	FREIGHT AND HANDLING					1.70
	TOTAL					49.00

F.O.B. means Free on Board. F.O.B. Destination means seller pays freight. F.O.B. Shipping Point means buyer pays freight.

Late charge of $1\frac{1}{2}$%, or $0.74 per month, if payment not made by May 24.

Buyer pays $1.70 for freight and handling.

Toledo Blue Print AND PAPER COMPANY
617 ADAMS ST./TOLEDO, OHIO 43604/PH. (419) 243-7224
Supplies, For The Engineer, Architect, Artist, Draftsman
COMPLETE PHOTOGRAPHIC REPRODUCTION SERVICES

INVOICE
10084

SHIP TO:

SOLD TO
WILLIAM KUHLMAN STUDIO
406 Madison Ave.
Toledo, Ohio 43604

VIA

DATE	YOUR ORDER NO		TERMS 2/10,N/30
11-24-78			DUE AND PAYABLE 12-24-78

	QUANTITY	DESCRIPTION	UNIT	PRICE	NET AMOUNT
03881	2	Drawing Book		1.50	3.00
	2	Boxes Conte Crayons		3.75	7.50
	6	Illustration Board #172 30 x 40		2.95	17.70
	1	Portfolio			29.95
					58.15
		Less 10%			5.82
					52.33

Seller represents that with respect to the production of the articles and/or the performance of the services covered by this invoice it has fully complied with the provisions of the Fair Labor Standards Act of 1938 as amended. We hereby certify that the amounts invoiced herein do not exceed maximum levels established in accordance with excise order #11615 Dated August 15, 1971

ORIGINAL INVOICE

Cash discounts of 2% or $1.05 if paid by December 4.

These are called EXTENSIONS
2 x $1.50
2 x 3.75
6 x 2.95

Trade discount of 10%

Net amount of $52.33 subject to cash discount of $1.05. Thus, $51.28 if paid by Dec. 4; $52.33 if paid between Dec. 4 and Dec. 24. Delinquent after Dec. 24.

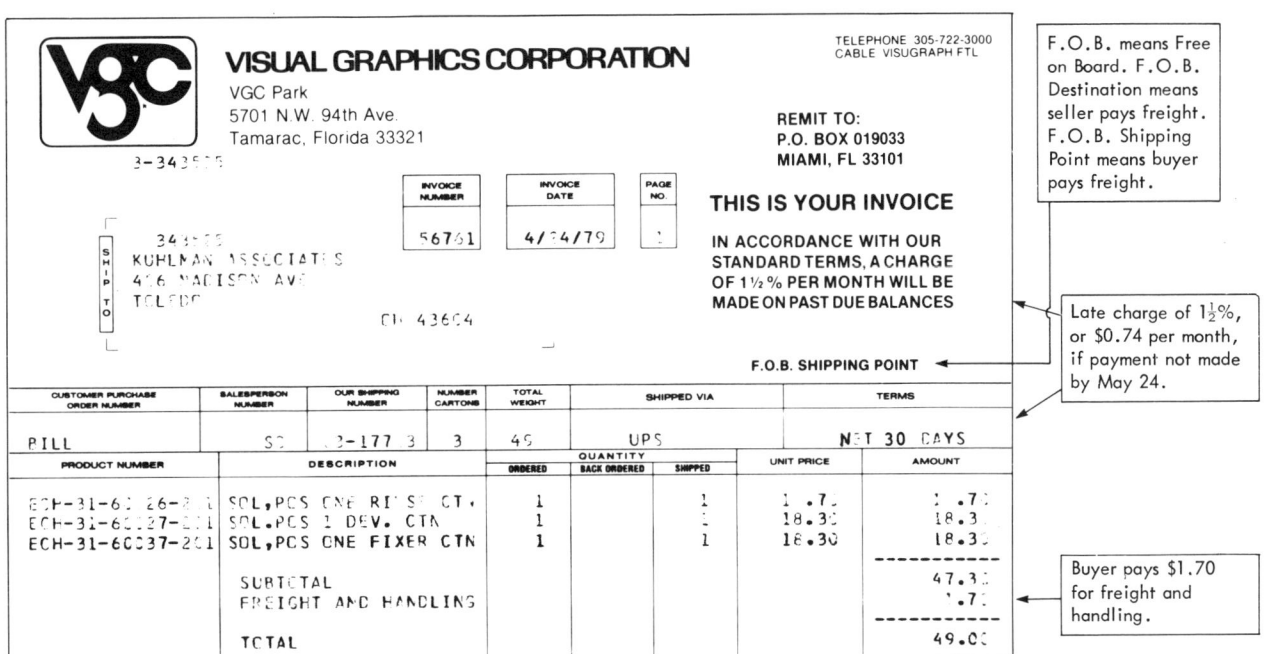

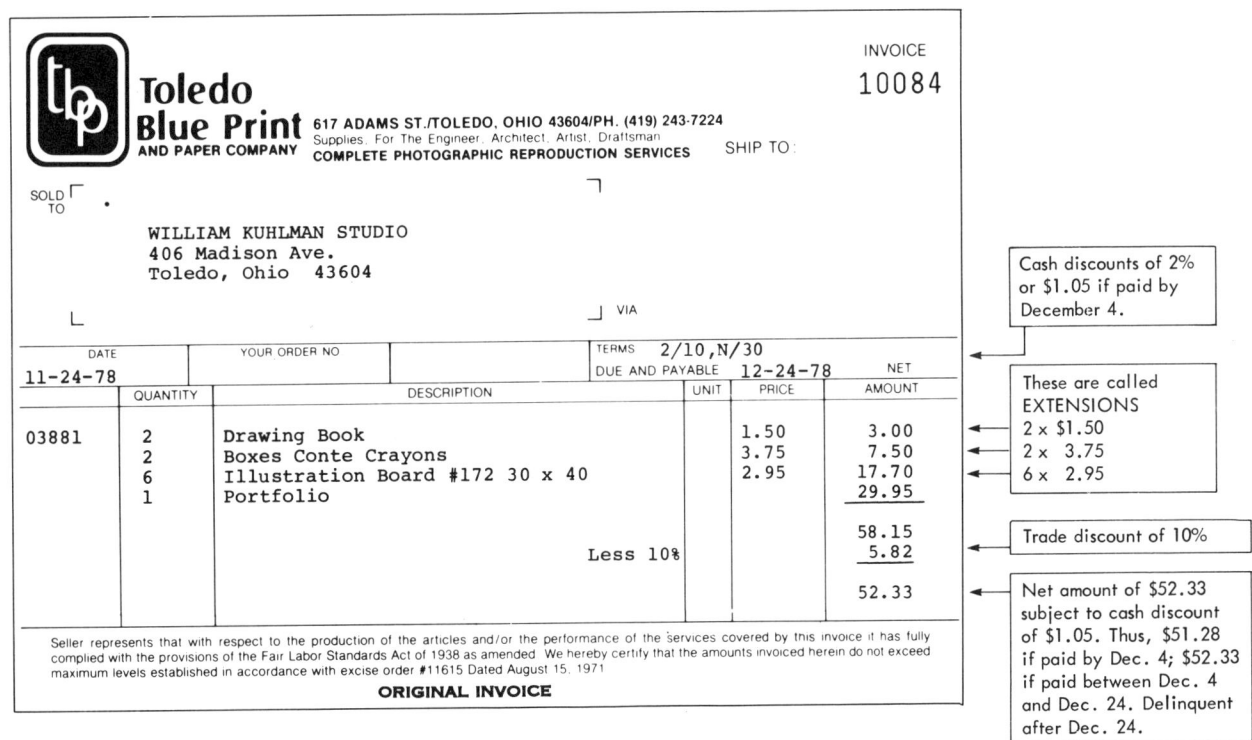

ASSIGNMENT 15-3
CASH DISCOUNTS

Name ______________________ Date Due ______________ Grade _____

Answers to selected problems are given in Appendix B.

For Problems 1 through 5, give the last date for taking the discount and determine the cash discount and the cash price.

	Invoice Date	*Net Amount of Invoice*	*Terms*	*Last Date for Taking Discount*	*Date Paid*	*Cash Discount*	*Cash Price*
Ex.	Jan. 10	$ 500	3/10, net 30	Jan. 20	Jan. 18	$15.00	$485.00 ← $500 – $15
1.	Mar. 3	1,200	2/10, net 30	______	Mar. 10	______	______
2.	Oct. 8	67,000	4/20, net 40	______	Nov. 3	None	______
3.	July 5	170	2/10, net 30	______	July 12	______	______
4.	Dec. 28	810	3/10, net 30	______	Jan. 2	______	______
5.	Apr. 4	2,000	2/10, net 30	______	May 1	______	______

6. The dating in Problems 1 through 5 is called ______________ dating.

7. Sherman Manufacturing forwards an order for transistors to a dealer in Rhode Island. The net invoice amount is $942. Terms stated on the invoice dated August 2 are 4/10, net 30.

   A. What is the last date the cash discount can be taken? ______________

   B. What is the cash discount? $__________, found by

   C. What is the cash price? $__________, found by

8. Motorcycle parts with a net price of $1,940 were sent by Round Wheel Distributors to Mark's Cycles. The invoice date was 5/2; the terms 5/10, net 40.

   A. The last date for taking the cash discount is ______________.

   B. The last date for paying the invoice without a penalty is ______________.

   C. If paid promptly, the cash price paid by Mark's Cycles is $______________, found by

For Problems 9 through 13, give the last date for taking the discount and determine the cash discount and the cash price.

	Invoice Date	*Net Amount of Invoice*	*Terms*	*Last Date for Taking Discount*	*Date Paid*	*Cash Discount*	*Cash Price*
Ex.	May 16	$ 400.00	3/10, net 30 EOM	June 10	June 5	$12	$388
9.	Nov. 8	12,000.00	5/20, net 30 rog, rec'd. Jan. 6	________	Jan. 21	________	________
10.	Apr. 21	156.80	4/10 prox	________	May 9	________	________
11.	June 9	840.00	2/10, net 40 rog, rec'd. July 14	________	Aug. 14	________	________
12.	Jan. 4	310.50	8/10, net 30	________	Jan. 14	________	________
13.	Oct. 26	1,000.00	3/10, EOM	________	Nov. 7	________	________

14. The dating in Problems 9 through 13 includes ____________ dating, ____________ dating, and ____________ dating.

15. An invoice for $767.40 has terms of 3/10, net 60 and is dated March 14.

A. The last date the discount may be taken is ____________.

B. The invoice must be paid in full by ____________ to avoid a late charge, found by

C. The cash discount, if taken is $____________, found by

D. The cash price is: $____________, found by

16. An invoice for $800 is dated May 7. Terms are 3/10 EOM. Find how much would be paid if payment is made in full on:

A. June 3. $____________, found by

B. September 20. $____________, found by

17. Merchandise invoiced August 8 carried a net price of $752.80. Terms were 4/10, net 30 rog. The goods were received September 11. Find how much would be paid if payment is made in full on:

A. November 6. $____________, found by

B. September 20. $____________, found by

REVIEW ASSIGNMENT FOR CHAPTER 15
TRADE AND CASH DISCOUNTS

Name ______________________ Date Due ______________ Grade _____

For Problems 1 through 6, determine the trade discount and the net price (nearest cent).

	Item	*List Price*	*Discount(s)*	*Amount of Discount*	*Net Price*
1.	Ladies' skirt	$ 24.98	45%	________	________
2.	Umbrella	12.79	25%	________	________
3.	Men's shoes	44.95	40%	________	________
4.	Irrigation tray	18.35	30/20	________	________
5.	Distributor cap	3.45	20/10	________	________
6.	Part No. B55	112.30	40/25/5	________	________

7. A GE lighted make-up mirror has a list price of $26.98. The trade discount is 35%.

   A. What is the amount of the trade discount (nearest cent)?

   $__________, found by

   B. What is the net price?

   $__________, found by

8. A Remington hand-held hair dryer has a list price of $19.95. The trade discount is 30%.

   A. What is the complement of the trade discount?

   _______%, found by

   B. What is the net price (nearest cent)?

   $__________, found by

9. Part No. C5AZ has a list price of $55.45. The chain discounts are 40% less 25%.

   A. What is the first discount?

   $__________, found by

   B. What is the first net price?

   $__________, found by

   C. What is the second discount (nearest cent)?

   $__________, found by

   D. What is the final net price?

   $__________, found by

10. Prestolite condenser No. SRP-1824 carries a suggested list price of \$3.12 and a dealer trade net price of \$1.87. What is the trade discount rate (nearest tenth percent)?

________%, found by

11. Zarkin Corporation's ram-tip hammer drill lists at \$74.59. Chain discounts of 50/20/10 are offered.

A. What is the net price?

\$__________, found by

B. What is the amount of trade discount?

\$__________, found by

12. A portable tape recorder is listed in the catalog for \$145. The discount sheet indicates a trade discount of 40%.

A. What is the amount of discount?

\$__________, found by

B. What is the net price?

\$__________, found by

13. Two television suppliers offer comparable sets at these prices: Hilton Company quotes \$260 less discounts of 30%, 25%, and 10%. Williams Brothers Wholesalers quotes \$270 less discounts of 40%, 10%, and 10%. Which company has the lower net price?

______________________, found by

14. The Paoli Chair Company of Paoli, Indiana, states on the cover of its catalog: "Prices in this price list are retail prices and are subject to a 50/10 discount." What is the final net price for a desk with a list price of \$329.50?

\$___________, found by

15. The product of the complements of chain discounts of 40/30 is (0.60) (0.70), or 0.42. The net price is 42% of the list price. The buyer, therefore, saves 58% (100% – 42%). This 58% is called the single equivalent discount (SED) to chain discounts of 40/30. Find the SED to chain discounts of:

A. 30/20. ________, found by

B. 40/10. ________, found by

C. 30/10/10. ________, found by

D. 25/15/5. ____________, found by

For Problems 16 through 21, give the last date for taking the discount, and determine the cash discount and the cash price.

	Invoice Date	*Net Amount of Invoice*	*Terms*	*Last Date for Taking Discount*	*Date Paid*	*Cash Discount*	*Cash Price*
16.	2/7	$ 530.00	2/10, net 30	________	2/16	________	________
17.	10/23	1,470.00	3/20, net 40	________	11/10	________	________
18.	5/7	475.00	2/10, EOM	________	6/9	________	________
19.	7/30	163.75	4/10, EOM	________	8/20	________	________
20.	1/12	964.80	3/10 prox	________	1/29	________	________
21.	9/15	2,479.70	2/10, net 30 rog, rec'd. 11/15	________	11/23	________	________

22. The net amount of an invoice is $270. The invoice is dated March 4. The terms are 2/10, net 30.

A. What is the last date the discount may be taken?

____________, found by

B. What is the cash price of the invoice if paid on or before that date?

$____________, found by

23. The net amount of an invoice is $700. The invoice is dated January 10. The terms are 3/10 EOM.

A. What is the last date the discount may be taken?

____________, found by

B. What is the cash price of the invoice if paid on or before that date?

$____________, found by

24. Reynolds Metals Company's invoice to Kroger was dated 11/14 and had a net amount of $14,135.78. What amount did Kroger pay if the invoice was paid on 11/28?

$________________, found by

SOLD TO:	
THE KROGER CO. 31008 AURORA SOLON OH 44139	
TERMS (FROM INVOICE DATE)	SHIPPING POINT
2% 15, NET 30	346 CLEV

25. Standard Printing Company received an invoice from the Millcraft Paper Company with a net amount of \$109.50. The invoice and purchase date was 6/11. The terms are: "2% if paid by 10th of month following purchase." What cash price does Standard pay on 7/8?

\$____________, found by

26. Kuhlman Associates/Design received an invoice from National Camera Company for a list amount of \$973.50. Kuhlman receives chain discounts of 30/20/5 from National. The terms of the invoice are 2/10, net 30. The invoice is dated 10/15.

A. What is the net amount of the invoice?

\$____________, found by

B. What is the cash amount of the invoice if paid on 11/9?

\$____________, found by

C. What is the cash amount of the invoice if paid on 10/24?

\$____________, found by

27. Suburban Excavation Company received an invoice from France Stone Company with a list amount of \$435. France Stone Company offers chain discounts of 35% less 25%. The terms of the invoice are 2/10 EOM. The invoice is dated 10/15.

A. What is the net amount of the invoice?

\$____________, found by

B. What is the cash amount of the invoice if paid on 11/9?

\$____________, found by

C. What is the cash amount of the invoice if paid on 10/24?

\$____________, found by

TO THE STUDENT: There is a SELF-REVIEW TEST for this chapter in Appendix A, *with answers* in Appendix C.

16

Markup and Markdown

SECTION 16-1: MARKUP

Objective: To compute the cost, markup, and selling price of an item.
To compute the cost, markup, and selling price as percents of selling price or cost.

THE BASIC RETAILING EQUATION

Std. Pkg.	Suggested Wholesaler Price Each	Suggested Dealer Price Each	Suggested Consumer Price Each
SE-1	$2.16	$2.83	$4.73
SE-2	3.77	4.82	8.06
SE-3	3.77	4.82	8.06
SE-4	4.61	5.77	9.68

The Ford Motor Company, J. C. Penney, Pizza Hut and thousands of other manufacturers and retailers expect to make a profit. J. C. Penney, for example, in order to make a profit on its Towncraft shirt, must sell it at a higher price than the shirt costs them. Some important terms are:

Cost: For a retailer, it is the amount paid to a wholesaler or manufacturer for an item. For a manufacturer, it is the cost of producing the item.

Selling price: The price the customer pays for the item.

Markup: The difference between the cost of the item and its selling price.

These three terms are included in what is commonly referred to as the **basic retailing equation**:

Cost + Markup = Selling price, or $C + M = SP$

Problem J. C. Penney purchases a man's Towncraft shirt for $4.95 and marks it up $5.00. What is the selling price?

Solution

Cost + Markup = Selling price
$4.95 + $5.00 = $9.95

1 SELF-REVIEW

A reminder: Cover the answers in the margin.

Determine the selling price for food items purchased at the 5-Star Food Chain.

Cost + Markup = Selling price

A. 16-oz. jar of Hellman's mayonnaise costs $0.76. The markup is $0.43. $______ + $______ = $______

B. 15-oz. jar of Mott's applesauce costs $0.37. The markup is $0.18. $______ + $______ = $______

C. 10-count Hefty trash can bags costs $0.98. The markup is $0.47. $______ + $______ = $______

A. $0.76 + $0.43 = $1.19

B. $0.37 + $0.18 = $0.55

C. $0.98 + $0.47 = $1.45

The basic retailing equation includes cost, markup, and selling price. If two of the dollar amounts are known, the third amount can be determined.

Problem

A. Find the *selling price:* The *cost* of a toaster is \$20; the *markup* is \$5. What is the *selling price?*

B. Find the *cost:* A retailer *marked up* a lamp \$30. Its *selling price* is \$50. What is the *cost* of the lamp?

C. Find the *markup:* A stereo receiver *cost* a hi-fi dealer \$200. The *selling price* is \$300. What is the *markup?*

Solution

A.

$$C + M = SP$$
$$\$20 + \$5 = \$25$$

B.

$$C + M = SP$$
$$C + \$30 = \$50$$
$$C = \$20$$

$$C = SP - M = \$50 - \$30 = \$20$$

C.

$$C + M = SP$$
$$\$200 + M = \$300$$
$$M = \$100$$

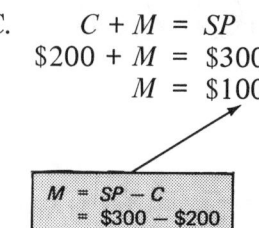

$$M = SP - C = \$300 - \$200 = \$100$$

2 SELF-REVIEW

A. The cost of a Parker pen to the bookstore is \$2.49. It is marked up \$1.20. What is the selling price?

$$C + M = SP$$

\$______ + \$______ = \$______

A. \$2.49 + \$1.20 = \$3.69

B. Sears marked up a chain saw \$30. Its selling price is \$89. What is the cost of the saw?

$$C + M = SP$$

C + \$______ = \$______

C = \$______, found by

= \$______ – \$______

= \$______

B. C + \$30 = \$89
C = \$59, found by
= \$89 – \$30
= \$59

C. A truck costs a manufacturer \$3,000 to produce. Its selling price to the dealer is \$3,750. What is the markup?

$$C + M = SP$$

\$______ + M = \$______

M = \$______, found by

= \$______ – \$______

= \$______

C. \$3,000 + M = \$3,750
M = \$750, found by
= \$3,750 – \$3,000
= \$750

In the preceding discussion the basic retailing equation was expressed in terms of *dollars.* *C, M,* and *SP,* however, can be expressed as *percents of the selling price* or as *percents of the cost.*

THE BASIC RETAILING EQUATION EXPRESSED AS PERCENTS OF THE SELLING PRICE

In retailing, generally cost, markup, and selling price are expressed as percents of the *selling price.*

To illustrate, suppose that the cost of a silk pillow to a retailer is \$20. The markup is \$5. The selling price of the pillow is, therefore, \$25. Inserting the dollar amounts in the basic equation:

$$C + M = SP$$

$$\$20 + \$5 = \$25$$

$$\frac{\$20}{\$25} + \frac{\$5}{\$25} = \frac{\$25}{\$25}$$

$$80\% + 20\% = 100\%$$

To express the cost, markup, and selling price as a percent of the selling price, divide each by SP. Thus *SP* becomes the *base.*

Cost as % of selling price (80%); Markup as % of selling price (20%); Selling price as % of selling price (100%)

To reemphasize: *Cost* is 80% of the selling price, *markup* is 20% of the selling price. Selling price is 100% of the selling price (the base).

3 SELF-REVIEW

A. The cost of a sofa to a furniture store is \$200. The markup is \$300. The selling price to the customer is, therefore, \$500. The basic retailing equation:

In words:

Cost + ________ = ____________

Inserting dollar amounts:

\$_____ + \$_____ = \$_____

Converting to percent of selling price:

$$\frac{\$\_\_\_\_}{\$500} + \frac{\$\_\_\_\_}{\$500} = \frac{\$\_\_\_\_}{\$}$$

_____% + _____% = 100%

A. Cost + Markup = Selling price

$$\$200 + \$300 = \$500$$

$$\frac{\$200}{\$500} + \frac{\$300}{\$500} = \frac{\$500}{\$500}$$

$$40\% + 60\% = 100\%$$

B. If the cost of a refrigerator is 40% of the selling price, the markup is _____% of the selling price, found by:

$$C + M = SP$$

40% + _____% = 100%

B. Markup = 60%, found by

40% + 60% = 100%

C. Suppose M is 25% of SP. Then C = _____% of SP, found by

C. C = 75% of SP, found by

75% + 25% = 100%

THE BASIC RETAILING EQUATION EXPRESSED AS PERCENTS OF THE COST

Retailers usually mark up their merchandise based on the *selling price.* Manufacturers, however, generally mark up their items based on *cost.*

To illustrate, suppose a tire costs \$40 to manufacture. It is marked up \$20 and sold to dealers for \$60. Inserting the dollar amounts in the basic equation:

$$C + M = SP$$

$$\$40 + \$20 = \$60$$

$$\frac{\$40}{\$40} + \frac{\$20}{\$40} = \frac{\$60}{\$40}$$

$$100\% + 50\% = 150\%$$

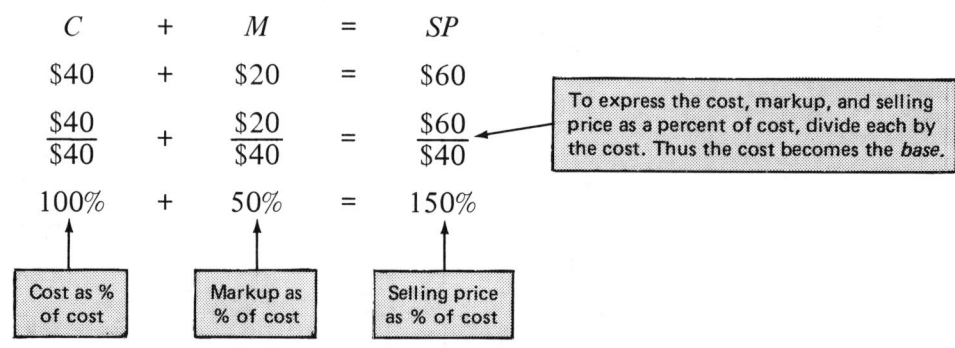

To express the cost, markup, and selling price as a percent of cost, divide each by the cost. Thus the cost becomes the ***base.***

100%: Cost as % of cost

50%: Markup as % of cost

150%: Selling price as % of cost

To reemphasize: The markup is 50% of the cost. The selling price is 150% of cost. Cost is 100% of cost (the base).

4 SELF-REVIEW

A. The cost to manufacture a concrete block is \$0.25. The markup is \$0.15. The selling price is, therefore, \$0.40. The basic equation, in words:

Cost + __________ = ______________

\$______ + \$______ = \$______

Converting to percent of cost:

$$\frac{\$\_\_\_\_}{\$0.25} + \frac{\$\_\_\_\_}{\$0.25} = \frac{\$\_\_\_\_}{\$0.25}$$

____% + ____% = ____%

A. Cost + Markup = Selling price

$$\$0.25 + \$0.15 = \$0.40$$

$$\frac{\$0.25}{\$0.25} + \frac{\$0.15}{\$0.25} = \frac{\$0.40}{\$0.25}$$

$$100\% + 60\% = 160\%$$

B. The markup on a wheelbarrel is 70% of the cost of manufacturing it. The selling price is ______% of the cost, found by

$$C + M = SP$$

$$100\% + 70\% = \_\_\_\_\_\%$$

B. 170%, found by 100% + 70% = 170%

C. Suppose the selling price is 140% of cost. The markup is ______% of cost, found by

C. 40% of the cost, found by 140% − 100% = 40%

DETERMINING THE SELLING PRICE GIVEN MARKUP BASED ON SELLING PRICE

Retailers know the cost of an item (from the invoice received from the wholesaler or manufacturer). Many retailers express the markup as a specified percent of the selling price. For illustration, a jewelry store has a policy of marking up all silverware 80%, based on selling price. This implies that the cost is 20% of the selling price.

Problem

A set of silverware costs Jarcko Jewelry $40. Markup is 80% of the selling price. What is the selling price of the silverware?

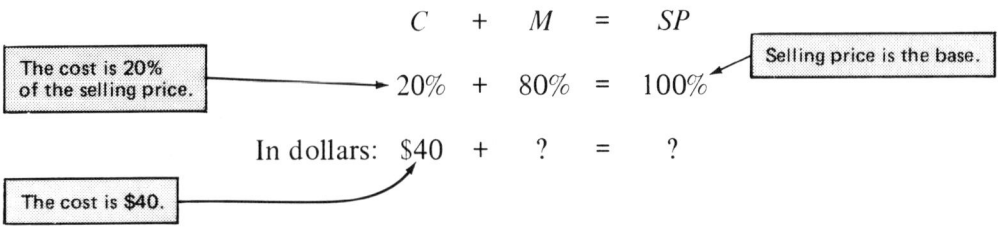

Solution

	C	+	M	=	SP
	20%	+	80%	=	100%
In dollars:	$40	+	?	=	?

The cost is 20% of the selling price. → 20%

Selling price is the base. → 100%

The cost is $40. → $40

Using a calculator:

Enter	Press	Display
40	÷	40
.20	= −	200
40	=	160

Since the cost is $40 and the cost is 20% of the selling price, it follows that $40 equals 20% of the selling price. That is, $40 = 20% of *SP*.

The question is: What is the selling price?

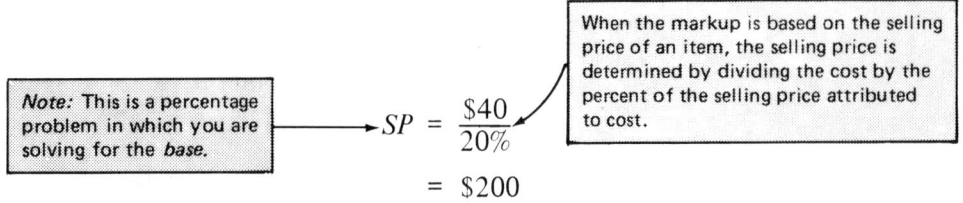

Note: This is a percentage problem in which you are solving for the *base*.

$$SP = \frac{\$40}{20\%}$$

$$= \$200$$

When the markup is based on the selling price of an item, the selling price is determined by dividing the cost by the percent of the selling price attributed to cost.

The markup is, therefore, $160, found by $200 – $40.

5 SELF-REVIEW

A. A calculator costs the Mainstreet Bookstore $35. The store's policy is to mark up most items 30% of the selling price. What is the selling price?

C	+	M	=	SP
____%	+	30%	=	100%
$35	+	?	=	?

It follows that $35 equals 70% of the selling price. Thus:

$$SP = \frac{\$\_\_\_\_}{70\%}$$

$$= \$\_\_\_\_$$

The markup is $15.

B. Apple trees cost Frank's Nursery $12. Frank's marks up nursery stock 40% based on the selling price. What is the selling price?

C	+	M	=	SP
____%	+	____%	=	____%
$12	+	?	=	?

It follows that: $____ equals ____% of the selling price. Thus:

$$SP = \frac{\$\_\_\_\_}{\%}$$

$$= \$\_\_\_\_$$

The markup is $______.

Answers:

A. 70% + 30% = 100%

$$SP = \frac{\$35}{70\%}$$

$$= \$50$$

B.

C	+	M	=	SP
60%	+	40%	=	100%
$12	+	?	=	?

It follows that $12 equals 60% of the selling price. Thus:

$$SP = \frac{\$12}{60\%}$$

$$= \$20$$

The markup is $8.

DETERMINING THE SELLING PRICE GIVEN MARKUP BASED ON THE COST

Manufacturers know the cost of producing an item. Many manufacturers express the markup as a specific percent of the cost.

For illustration: A manufacturer of fine furniture has a policy of marking up all chairs 70% based on the cost. This implies that the selling price is 170% of the cost.

Problem A Queen Anne chair costs \$120 to produce. Markup is 70% of cost. What is the selling price of the chair?

Solution Applying the basic retailing equation:

$$C + M = SP$$

In percent: $100\% + 70\% = 170\%$ ← The selling price is 170% of the cost.

$\$120 + ? = ?$

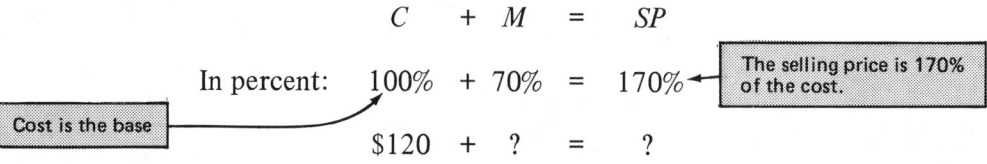

Cost is the base → 100%

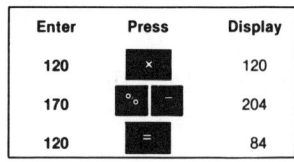

Using a calculator with %:

Enter	Press	Display
120	×	120
170	% −	204
120	=	84

Since the cost is \$120 and the selling price is 170% of the cost, it follows that the selling price equals 170% of \$120.

The question is: What is the selling price?

Note: This is a percentage problem in which you are solving for the *percentage.*

$$SP = 170\% \text{ of } \$120$$
$$= \$204$$

The markup is, therefore, \$84, found by \$204 − \$120.

6 SELF-REVIEW

A. The cost of manufacturing a pound of Hickory Farms beef stick is \$1.40. The markup is 165% of cost. What is the selling price?

$C + M = SP$

100% + 165% = ________%

\$1.40 + ? = ?

It follows that the selling price equals 265% of \$1.40. Thus:

SP = ______% × \$________

= \$________

The markup is \$2.31.

B. Mrs. Smith's preserves cost \$0.24 a jar to produce. Markup is 120% of cost. What is the selling price?

$C + M = SP$

100% + ________% = ________%

\$0.24 + ? = ?

Thus:

SP = ______% × \$________

= \$________

The markup is \$________.

A. 100% + 165% = 265%

SP = 265% × \$1.40
= \$3.71

B. $C + M = SP$
100% + 120% = 220%

SP = 220% × \$0.24
= \$0.53

The markup is \$0.29.

ASSIGNMENT 16-1
MARKUP

Name ______________________ Date Due ______________ Grade _____

Answers to selected problems are given in Appendix B.

For Problems 1 through 6, find the cost, markup, selling price, percent markup based on selling price, or the percent markup based on cost.

	Item	*Cost*	*Markup*	*Selling Price*	*% Markup Based on Selling Price*	*% Markup Based on Cost*
1.	Comic book	$ 0.40	$ 0.10	$______	20%	25%
2.	Stanley hammer	5.00	______	7.00	28.6	______
3.	Sofa	______	90.00	240.00	______	60
4.	Blouse	8.00	______	______	50	______
5.	Wheelchair	300.00	______	______	______	120
6.	Jelly donuts	______	1.39	______	______	231

7. Fleeger's Pro Hardware Store buys Cape Craft wooden paper towel holders at a cost of $6 each. The selling price is $9. What is the markup?

   $________, found by

8. A bookstore pays $0.79 for a pack of notebook paper that is sold for $1.09. What is the markup?

   $________, found by

9. Cramer Furniture Company paid $795 for a living room set. The set is marked up 60% based on the selling price.

   A. The cost is what percent of the selling price?

      ______%, found by

   B. What is the selling price?

      $______________, found by

   C. What is the markup?

      $______________, found by

10. Violet's Boutique received a shipment of sweaters costing $14.50 each. Violet's operates on 71% markup based on the selling price.

    A. The cost is what percent of the selling price?

       ______%, found by

    B. What is the selling price?

       $___________, found by

    C. What is the markup?

       $___________, found by

11. A small manufacturer of wicker chairs sells them to retailers for $24. Commodore House marks them up 40%, based on the retail selling price. What is the retail selling price?

$_____, found by

12. A Canon Model A35F camera is purchased by Kolor Photo Company at a cost of $75. The markup is 25% based on the selling price. What is the selling price?

$________, found by

13. A dealer in large marine batteries purchases them for $200. The price is marked up 70% of cost.

A. What is the markup?

$________, found by

B. What is the selling price?

$________, found by

14. Yost's Bakery calculates the cost of making an eclair to be $0.04. The markup based on cost is 775%.

A. What is the markup?

$________, found by

B. What is the selling price?

$________, found by

15. Sound, Inc., purchased a Pioneer tape cassette player from a U.S. distributor for $420. The selling price is $560.

A. What was the markup?

$________, found by

B. What was the percent markup based on cost?

________%, found by

16. Suppose that a grocer buys Florida grapefruit for $0.14½ each and sells them two for $0.45.

A. What is the markup per grapefruit?

$________, found by

B. What is the percent markup based on cost?

________%, found by

17. "Keystoning" is the term used for the common business practice of doubling the cost to arrive at the selling price. Under this situation, the markup is what percent of the selling price?

_____%, found by

18. A jewelers catalog shows:

ALL PRICES "TRIPLE KEYSTONE"
Prices subject to change without notice

In this case, what is the percent markup based on cost?

________%, found by

SECTION 16-2: MARKDOWN

Objective: To determine the markdown, the percent markdown, and the sale price.

MARKDOWN

Most retailers offer one or more items below the regular selling price practically every day. The reasons for these price reductions are varied. Some items are even offered below the wholesale price to attract shoppers! (This kind of a sale item is often called a "leader item.") The retailer also uses "sales" to clear out summer merchandise, damaged goods, discontinued items, and slow-moving goods.

This price reduction is usually referred to as a **markdown.** It is the *difference between the selling price and the sale price.*

Markdown = Selling price − Sale price

Problem Sterling Sound advertised the Fisher RS 1022 in the *Dallas Morning News* at a special sale price of $189. The selling price is $300. What is the markdown?

Solution

Markdown = Selling price − Sale price
= $300 − $189
= $111

1 SELF-REVIEW

In the *Detroit Sunday News,* Federal Stores advertised Pennzoil 10W-40 on sale for 89 cents a quart. The usual selling price is $1.09. What is the markdown?

In words: Markdown = ________________ − ________________
= $________ − $________
= $________

Selling price − Sale price
= $1.09 − $0.89
= $0.20

PERCENT MARKDOWN

The **percent markdown** on an item is computed by *dividing the markdown by the selling price.*

$$\text{Percent markdown} = \frac{\text{Markdown}}{\text{Selling price}}$$

Problem Saks Fifth Avenue has a group of women's shoes advertised on sale in the *Chicago Tribune* for $36 a pair. The usual selling price is $90 a pair. What is the percent markdown?

Solution

$$\text{Percent markdown} = \frac{\text{Markdown}}{\text{Selling price}}$$

$$= \frac{\$90 - \$36}{\$90}$$

$$= 0.60$$

$$= 60\%$$

2 SELF-REVIEW

Pennzoil 10W-40 is on sale for 89 cents a quart. The usual selling price is $1.09. The markdown is $0.20. What is the percent markdown?

In words: Percent markdown = ______________ ÷ ________________

= $\frac{\$\_\_\_\_\_\_ - \$\_\_\_\_\_\_}{\$\_\_\_\_\_\_}$

= __________ = ________%

Markdown ÷ Selling price

$= \frac{\$1.09 - \$0.89}{\$1.09}$

= 0.183 = 18.3%

SALE PRICE If the *percent markdown* and the *selling price* are known, the *sale price* can be determined. Two ways are:

Method 1: Find the markdown by multiplying the percent markdown times the selling price.

Markdown = Percent markdown X Selling price

Then find the sale price by subtracting the markdown from the selling price.

Sale Price = Selling price – Markdown

Method 2: The complement of the percent markdown is multiplied by the selling price to arrive at the sale price.

Sale price = Complement of percent markdown X Selling price

Problem The selling price of a GE refrigerator is $800. Highland Appliance advertised it in the *Toledo Blade* for 20% off. What is the sale price of the refrigerator?

Solution *Method 1:*

Find the markdown.

Markdown = Percent markdown X Selling price
= 0.20 X $800
= $160

Subtract the markdown from the selling price to arrive at the sale price.

Sale price = Selling price – Markdown
= $800 – $160
= $640

Method 2:

Find the complement of percent markdown.

Complement = 100% – 20% = 80%

Multiply the complement by the selling price to arrive at the sale price.

Sale price = Complement of percent markdown × Selling price
= 0.80 × $800
= $640 (same answer as Method 1)

3 SELF-REVIEW

Kentucky Fried Chicken has a Founder's Day Special on its bucket of chicken. The usual price is $6. The markdown is 30%. What is the sale price?

Method 1:

% markdown × Selling price
= 30% × $6
= $1.80

Selling price – Markdown
= $6.00 – $1.80
= $4.20

Method 2:

70%, found by 100% – 30%

Complement of % markdown × Selling price
= 0.70 × $6.00
= $4.20

Method 1:

In words: Markdown = %__________ × __________ price
= _____% × $_____
= $______

Then, in words: Sale price = __________ – __________
= $______ – $______
= $______

Method 2:

Complement of percent markdown is _____%, found by _____% – _____%.

In words:

Sale price = ____________________ × __________
= 0._____ × $______
= $______ (should be same answer as found by Method 1)

ASSIGNMENT 16-2
MARKDOWN

Name ______________________ Date Due ______________ Grade _____

Answers to selected problems are given in Appendix B.

For Problems 1 through 6, find the sale price, markdown, or percent markdown (nearest tenth percent).

	Item	*Selling Price*	*Markdown*	*Percent Markdown*	*Sale Price*
Ex.	ER 78-14 tire	\$42.88	\$10.72	25%	\$32.16
1.	Electronic calculator	14.95	________	________	10.95
2.	Pair of shoes	10.99	________	________	8.99
3.	Jovan Musk Oil	2.00	0.40	________	________
4.	Regal Griller	27.99	6.00	________	________
5.	Sweaters	18.00	________	20%	________
6.	Dry cleaning (trousers)	1.80	________	25%	________

7. In *The Los Angeles Times,* K-Mart advertised a Hook-a-Rug kit for \$6.00. The usual selling price is \$7.88. What is the markdown?

   \$________, found by

8. In *The New York Times,* Macy's advertised men's winter gloves for \$9.99. The usual selling price is \$15.00. What is the markdown?

   \$________, found by

9. Staff all-purpose enriched flour, 5-pound bag, is on sale for 49 cents. The usual selling price is 79 cents. What is the percent markdown (nearest tenth percent)?

   _____%, found by

10. Royal Knight pinwale corduroy shirts are on sale for \$10.99. The usual selling price is \$12.99. What is the percent markdown (nearest percent)?

    _____%, found by

11. The *Sunday Magazine Supplement* carried an advertisement for a shimmering rhinestone glimmer-point ring. The usual price is \$7. The markdown is 22%. What is the sale price?

    \$________, found by

12. Burger King has a Thanksgiving Day special on a Whopper, fries, and regular-size drink. The usual price is \$1.89. The markdown is 16%. What is the sale price?

    \$________, found by

13. The Bergen/Passak/Hudson County, New Jersey *Record* carried an ad for a Buick Regal on sale for \$5,995. The regular price is \$6,833.54.

    A. What is the markdown?

    \$______________, found by

    B. What is the percent markdown (nearest tenth percent)?

    ________%, found by

14. A Bond's ad from the Chicago *Tribune* is shown:

A. Find the (1) markdown and (2) percent markdown (nearest percent) for the $65 blazer on sale for $39.

(1) Markdown

$_____, found by

(2) % markdown

_____%, found by

B. Find the markdown and percent markdown (nearest percent) for a $90 sportcoat on sale for $49.

(1) Markdown

$_____, found by

(2) % markdown

_____%, found by

15. Find the regular price and percent markdown (nearest percent) on the Thrifty Maid catsup advertised in the *Atlanta Constitution.*

A. Regular price

________¢, found by

B. Percent markdown

_____%, found by

16. Star Draperies Manufacturing's ad in *The Los Angeles Times* appears at the right. To the nearest tenth percent, find the percent markdown for:

A. 2-tone boucle

_____%, found by

B. "Mirage" sheer

________%, found by

C. 2-ply satins

________%, found by

17. You are to mark down a group of slacks 30%. Find the sale price you would put on a pair of slacks that regularly sells for:

A. $24.99, $___________, found by

B. $12.49, $________, found by

C. $42.95, $___________, found by

D. $9.99, $________, found by

REVIEW ASSIGNMENT FOR CHAPTER 16
MARKUP AND MARKDOWN

Name ______________________ Date Due ____________ Grade _____

For Problems 1 through 10, complete the table.

	Item	*Cost*	*Markup*	*% Markup Based on Selling Price*	*% Markup Based on Cost*	*Selling Price*	*Percent Markdown*	*Markdown*	*Sale Price*
1.	Wrist-watch	$ 97.50	______	______	______	$195.00			
2.	Desk	114.70	______	______	______	184.49			
3.	Washing machine	162.50	$81.25	______	______	______	20%	______	______
4.	Television set	361.70	98.29	______	______	______	10	______	______
5.	Screwdriver set	21.88	______	______	25%	______	25	______	______
6.	Birthday cake	1.14	______	______	350	______	33⅓	______	______
7.	Shock absorber	6.60	______	67%	______	______	______	______	$17.50
8.	Dictionary	2.37	______	70	______	______	______	______	5.90
9.	Desk lamp	______	______	______	150	50.00	______	$10.00	______
10.	Pump fixture	______	______	______	90	950.00	______	50.00	______

11. Sweaters, Inc., purchased a group of sweaters at a cost of $7.20 each. The selling price is $18.00. What is the markup?

    $__________, found by

12. A jewelry store sold a group of fine watches at $149.95 each. The cost to the jewelry store was $85.69 per watch. What is the markup?

    $__________, found by

13. Ace Manufacturing produces wooden pallets at a cost of $6.70 each. They mark up each pallet $5.20. What is the selling price?

    $__________, found by

14. The Hendersons buy aluminum lawn chairs for $2.37 each and mark them up $2.62 each. What is the selling price?

    $________, found by

15. The Hat Boutique operates on a markup of 55% of the selling price. They have a line of winter hats that cost $12.64 each. What is the selling price?

    $__________, found by

16. A men's clothing store marks up most items 48%, based on the selling price. If a vest costs the store $10.40, what is the selling price?

    $__________, found by

17. Tiger Stores buy Silk-O-Lite shades at a cost of $6.26. The price of the shade was marked up 60% based on its cost. Determine:

    A. The markup.

    $________, found by

    B. The selling price.

    $__________, found by

18. Home Furniture buys a Singer four-piece pecan-tone bedroom suite at a cost of $375.27. Home marks up the suite 70% based on cost. Determine:

A. The markup.

$____________, found by

B. The selling price.

$____________, found by

19. A Kenmore sewing machine costs $99.78 and sells for $179.95. Determine:

A. The markup.

$__________, found by

B. The percent markup based on cost.

________%, found by

20. An Early One fire detector costs James Hardware $6.80. James sells the fire detector at a selling price of $14.99. Determine:

A. The markup.

$________, found by

B. The percent markup based on cost.

__________%, found by

21. Old Oaks Farms buys beefstick for $1.36 per pound. The company marks it up 60% based on the selling price.

A. The cost is what percent of the selling price?

_____%, found by

B. What is the selling price?

$________, found by

22. Bargains Galore buys an Essex automatic electric blanket at a cost of $8.73. They mark it up 50% based on the selling price.

A. What percent of the selling price is the cost?

_____%, found by

B. What is the selling price?

$__________, found by

C. What is the markup?

$________, found by

23. A Pioneer stereo 8-track recording system costs $154.94 and sells for $238.95. Determine:

A. The markup.

$__________, found by

B. The markup as a percent of the selling price.

________%, found by

24. Naturalizer ladies' boots cost $11.60 and sell for $24.99. Determine:

A. The markup.

$__________, found by

B. The percent markup based on selling price.

________%, found by

25. Stuart McGuire leather demiboots are on sale at $28.97 a pair. They regularly sell at $38.99 a pair. Determine:

A. The markdown.

$__________, found by

B. The percent markdown.

________%, found by

26. The *Sunday Supplement* carried an advertisement for Value City Furniture indicating a savings of $72.95 on a dinette set. The sale price was $197.00. What was the percent markdown?

_____%, found by

27. Hong Kong Tailors is offering 27% off on its $299 wool suit package (includes suit, sport coat, slacks, and shirt). What is the sale price?

$____________, found by

TO THE STUDENT: There is a SELF-REVIEW TEST for this chapter in Appendix A, *with answers* in Appendix C.

17

Depreciation

SECTION 17-1: STRAIGHT-LINE METHOD

Objective: To compute annual depreciation, accumulated depreciation, and book value using the straight-line method.

INTRODUCTION

It is common knowledge that a new or used automobile begins to decrease in value almost the moment it is driven out of the dealer's showroom. A new Buick costing $9,000 might be worth, if sold at the end of one year, only $7,500, and $6,000 at the end of two years. This decrease in value is called **depreciation.**

> Johnson said acceptance of simplified depreciation would be a major step for small businesses who don't have the expertise to deal with complicated depreciation tax breaks geared to big business.

Equipment such as typewriters, forklifts, drill presses, and tools also depreciate in value due to prolonged usage, obsolescence, and other reasons. So do buildings, furniture, and other similar properties. All these long-lived assets are usually referred to as **fixed assets.**

The decrease in the value of a *fixed asset* is part of the cost of doing business. The Internal Revenue Service, therefore, permits a business firm to recognize this depreciation by deducting it from profits when filling out its income tax return.

STRAIGHT-LINE METHOD

One method of determining the amount of the annual depreciation is called the **straight-line method.** In order to calculate depreciation, it is necessary to know:

1. The **useful life** of the fixed asset, that is, an estimate of how long it will last. This is usually stated in years, although in the case of a machine, it might be stated either as the number of hours of operation or the total number of units produced. Trade and government tables are available to assist in estimating the useful life.
2. The estimated resale, trade-in, scrap, or **salvage value** of the asset at the end of its useful life.
3. The **original cost** of the asset.

The **annual depreciation** is computed by subtracting the salvage value from the original cost and then dividing by the estimated useful life of the asset.

$$\text{Annual depreciation} = \frac{\text{Original cost} - \text{Salvage value}}{\text{Estimated useful life of asset}}$$

The **book value** of a fixed asset at the end of a specified period of time is found by subtracting the *accumulated depreciation* from the original cost. Accumulated depreciation is the total depreciation for all previous years and includes the present year.

$$\text{Book value} = \text{Original cost} - \text{Accumulated depreciation}$$

Problem A small portable electric welding machine cost $13,000. It has an estimated useful life of five years. At the end of the five years it is predicted that the salvage, or resale, value will be $3,000. What is the annual depreciation using the straight-line method? What is the book value for each of the five years?

Solution

$$\text{Annual depreciation} = \frac{\text{Original cost} - \text{Salvage value}}{\text{Estimated useful life of asset}}$$

$$= \frac{\$13{,}000 - \$3{,}000}{5}$$

$$= \$2{,}000$$

Book value = Original cost − Accumulated depreciation
= $13,000 − $2,000
= $11,000 (at end of first year)

The depreciation record for each of the five years is shown in the table.

End of Year	*Original Cost*	*Depre- ciation*	*Accumulated Depreciation*	*Book Value*
1	$13,000	$2,000	$ 2,000	$11,000 ← $13,000 − $2,000
2	13,000	2,000	4,000	9,000 ← $13,000 − $4,000
3	13,000	2,000	6,000	7,000
4	13,000	2,000	8,000	5,000
5	13,000	2,000	10,000	3,000

Note that the book value at the end of the fifth year is the same as the estimated salvage value.

1 SELF-REVIEW

A reminder: Cover the answers in the margin.

Using the straight-line method, determine the annual depreciation, the accumulated depreciation, and the book value for an IBM Selectric typewriter which cost $900 and has an estimated useful life of six years and a salvage value at the end of six years of $150.

Annual depreciation = $\frac{\$\_\_\_\_ - \$\_\_\_\_}{6}$

= $____

End of Year	*Original Cost*	*Depre- ciation*	*Accumulated Depreciation*	*Book Value*
1	$900	$125	$____	$____
2	900	____	____	____
3	____	____	____	____
4	____	____	____	____
5	____	____	____	____
6	____	____	____	____

Annual depreciation:

$$= \frac{\$900 - \$150}{6}$$

= $125

Year	*Orig. Cost*	*Deprec.*	*Accum. Deprec.*	*Book Value*
1	$900	$125	$125	$775
2	900	125	250	650
3	900	125	375	525
4	900	125	500	400
5	900	125	625	275
6	900	125	750	150

Recall that the estimated useful life of a machine may be stated in terms of the *number of hours of operation* or in terms of *units produced.* The depreciation after a certain *number of hours of operation* is determined by:

$$\text{Depreciation after No. of hours} = \frac{\text{No. of hours operated}}{\text{Tl. estimated hours machine will last}} \times (\text{Original cost} - \text{Salvage value})$$

Likewise, the depreciation after a certain *number of units have been produced* is found by:

$$\text{Depreciation after No. of units produced} = \frac{\text{No. of units produced}}{\text{Total estimated units machine will produce}} \times (\text{Original cost} - \text{Salvage value})$$

2 SELF-REVIEW

A. A small punch press costs $10,000. It is estimated that it will operate 50,000 hours before it is scrapped. Its salvage value at the end of the 50,000 hours is estimated to be $500. What is the depreciation after 6,500 hours of use?

Depreciation after 6,500 hours = $\frac{\_\_\_\_\text{ hours}}{\_\_\_\_\text{ hours}}$ × ($____ – $____)

= $____

What is the book value of the punch press after 6,500 hours of operation? $____,

found by $____ – $____.

A. Depreciation:

$= \frac{6{,}500}{50{,}000}$

× ($10,000 – $500)

= $1,235

$8,765, found by $10,000 – $1,235

B. A lathe costs $50,000. It is estimated that it will produce 2,000,000 units (pieces) during its lifetime. The scrap value at that time is estimated to be $10,000. An accountant needs to know the depreciation expense for income tax purposes. The production engineer reported that the lathe had produced 80,000 units since it had been purchased. What is the depreciation?

Depreciation after 80,000 units = $\frac{\_\_\_\_\text{ units}}{\_\_\_\_\text{ units}}$ × ($____ – $____)

= $____

What is the book value of the lathe after it produced 80,000 units? $____,

found by $____ – $____.

B. Depreciation:

$= \frac{80{,}000}{2{,}000{,}000}$

× ($50,000 – $10,000)

= $1,600

Book value = $48,400, found by $50,000 – $1,600

ASSIGNMENT 17-1
STRAIGHT-LINE METHOD

Name ______________________ Date Due ______________ Grade _____

Answers to selected problems appear in Appendix B.

For Problems 1 through 6, determine the annual depreciation using the straight-line method.

	Asset	*Original Cost*	*Salvage Value*	*Useful Life (years)*	*Annual Depreciation*	*Found by*
Ex.	Oil pump	\$ 15,000	\$ 2,000	5	\$2,600	(\$15,000 – \$2,000) ÷ 5
1.	Typewriter	1,200	200	10	________	________________
2.	Cement mixer	800	50	10	________	________________
3.	Computer	72,000	8,000	8	________	________________
4.	Molding machine	120,000	10,000	6	________	________________
5.	Router	6,000	800	10	________	________________
6.	Bottling machine	400,000	20,000	8	________	________________

For Problems 7 through 10, use the straight-line method.

7. Complete the depreciation record for a compact van used by Pizza Inn for delivering pizzas. The original cost is \$4,500, with an estimated useful life of three years and a trade-in value of \$600.

End of Year	*Annual Depreciation*	*Accumulated Depreciation*	*Book Value*
1	\$1,300, found by (\$4,500 – \$600) ÷ 3	\$1,300	\$3,200
2	________________	________	________
3	________________	________	________

8. Complete the depreciation record for office equipment costing \$16,500, with an estimated life of five years and a salvage value of \$500.

End of Year	*Annual Depreciation*	*Accumulated Depreciation*	*Book Value*
1	\$3,200, found by $\frac{1}{5}$ (\$16,500 – \$500)	\$3,200	\$13,300
2	________________	________	________
3	________________	________	________
4	________________	________	________
5	________________	________	________

9. Construct a depreciation record for an electric welding machine costing $9,000, having an estimated life of 6 years, and a salvage value after 6 years of $1,500.

End of Year

1

2

3

4

5

6

10. Construct a depreciation record for a commercial chain saw costing $980 with an estimated life of two years and a trade-in value of $200.

End of Year

1

2

11. Find the depreciation and book value after 4,500 hours of operation for a duplicator costing $6,500, with an estimated life of 18,000 hours and a salvage value of $500.

A. The depreciation is $__________, found by

B. The book value is $__________, found by

12. The anticipated life span of a central processing unit (CPU) of an electronic computer is estimated to be 14,448 hours. The original cost of the CPU is $122,000, with a salvage value of $19,000 after 14,448 hours. After 6,700 hours:

A. The depreciation is $__________, found by

B. The book value is $__________, found by

13. Find the depreciation and book value after 15,000 units for a machine costing $250,000, with an estimated life of 300,000 units and a salvage value of $50,000.

A. The depreciation is $__________, found by

B. The book value is $__________, found by

14. A numerically controlled (NC) drill press is estimated to last for 140,000 units. The cost was $95,000 with an estimated salvage value of $5,000 after 140,000 units of production. After 20,000 units:

A. The depreciation is $__________, found by

B. The book value is $__________, found by

SECTION 17-2: SUM-OF-THE-YEARS'-DIGITS METHOD

Objective: To compute annual depreciation, accumulated depreciation, and book value, using the sum-of-the-years'-digits method.

SUM-OF-THE-YEARS'-DIGITS METHOD

The **sum-of-the-years'-digits method** allows for more depreciation in the early years of an asset's life and less and less as it approaches the end of its useful life. To calculate the annual depreciation:

Step 1. Estimate the useful life of the item in years.

Step 2. Calculate the sum of the years' digits.

For illustration, if the useful life is estimated to be 5 years, the sum of the years' digits is: 5 + 4 + 3 + 2 + 1 = 15 or, by formula from Chapter 6:

$$\text{Sum} = \frac{N(N+1)}{2} = \frac{5(5+1)}{2} = 15$$

Step 3. Convert each digit to a fraction, with the sum of the digits as the denominator. The digits 5, 4, 3, 2 and 1 convert to the fractions $5/15$, $4/15$, $3/15$, $2/15$, and $1/15$.

Step 4. Multiply each of these fractions by (Original cost − Salvage value) to arrive at the depreciation for each year.

Problem A steel chipping machine cost \$45,000. The useful life of the machine is estimated to be six years. At the end of the sixth year, its salvage value is estimated to be \$3,000. What is the annual depreciation using the sum-of-the-years'-digits method? What is the book value for each year?

Solution Step 1. The estimated useful life is six years.

Step 2. Sum the digits.

$$6 + 5 + 4 + 3 + 2 + 1 = 21, \quad \text{or} \quad \text{Sum} = \frac{N(N+1)}{2} = \frac{6(6+1)}{2} = 21$$

Step 3. Convert each digit to a fraction. The fractions are $6/21$, $5/21$, $4/21$, $3/21$, $2/21$, and $1/21$.

Step 4. Multiply each of these fractions by (Original cost − Salvage value) to arrive at the annual depreciation for each year.

Using a calculator with memory:

Enter	Press	Display
45000	−	45000
3000	m+ ×	42000
6	÷	252000
21	= −	12000
	RM	42000
	=	−30000
	RM ×	42000
5	÷	210000
21	=	10000

and so on

Year	*Calculations*	*Depreciation*	*Accumulated Depreciation*	*Book Value*	
1	$\frac{6}{21}$ (\$45,000 − \$3,000) =	\$12,000	\$12,000	\$33,000 ←	\$45,000 − \$12,000
2	$\frac{5}{21}$ (\$45,000 − \$3,000) =	10,000	22,000	23,000 ←	\$45,000 − \$22,000
3	$\frac{4}{21}$ (\$45,000 − \$3,000) =	8,000	30,000	15,000 ←	\$45,000 − \$30,000
4	$\frac{3}{21}$ (\$45,000 − \$3,000) =	6,000	36,000	9,000	
5	$\frac{2}{21}$ (\$45,000 − \$3,000) =	4,000	40,000	5,000	
6	$\frac{1}{21}$ (\$45,000 − \$3,000) =	2,000	42,000	3,000	

Note that book value at the end of the sixth year is the same as the estimated salvage value of the steel chipping machine.

Note also that the sum-of-the-years'-digits method gives a higher amount of depreciation in the early life of the chipping machine and less and less as it approaches the end of its useful life.

1 SELF-REVIEW

A special glass furnace cost $8,000 to build. Its useful life is estimated to be only four years. Its scrap value at the end of the four years is estimated to be $200. What is the annual depreciation using the sum-of-the-years'-digits method? What is the book value for each year?

Step 1. The estimated useful life is ____ years.

Step 2. Calculate the sum of the digits two ways.

$$\_\_ + \_\_ + \_\_ + \_\_ = \_\_\_, \quad \text{or} \quad \text{Sum} = \frac{N(N+1)}{2} = \frac{(\ \ +\ \ )}{2} = \_\_\_$$

Step 3. Express each digit as a fraction: ——, ——, ——, ——.

Step 4. Multiply each fraction by (Original cost – Salvage value)

Year	*Calculations*	*Depreciation*	*Accumulated Depreciation*	*Book Value*
1	—— ($______ – $______) =	$______	$______	$______
2	—— ($______ – $______) =	______	______	______
3	—— ($______ – $______) =	______	______	______
4	—— ($______ – $______) =	______	______	______*

*Must be same as salvage value.

Step 1: 4 years

Step 2: 4 + 3 + 2 + 1 = 10,

or $\text{Sum} = \frac{4(4+1)}{2} = 10$

Step 3: $\frac{4}{10}$ $\frac{3}{10}$ $\frac{2}{10}$ $\frac{1}{10}$

Step 4:

Yr.	*Calculations*	*Deprec.*	*Accum. Deprec.*	*Book Value*
1	$\frac{4}{10}$ ($8,000 – $200) =	$3,120	$3,120	$4,880
2	$\frac{3}{10}$ ($8,000 – $200) =	$2,340	$5,460	$2,540
3	$\frac{2}{10}$ ($8,000 – $200) =	$1,560	$7,020	$ 980
4	$\frac{1}{10}$ ($8,000 – $200) =	$ 780	$7,800	$ 200

ASSIGNMENT 17-2
SUM-OF-THE-YEARS'-DIGITS METHOD

Name ______________________ Date Due ______________ Grade ______

Answers to selected problems appear in Appendix B.

For Problems 1 through 6, find the sum of the digits both ways.

	Useful Life (years)	*Summing the Digits*	*Using the formula,* Sum $= \frac{N(N+1)}{2}$
Ex.	3	3 + 2 + 1 = 6	$\frac{3(3+1)}{2} = \frac{12}{2} = 6$
1.	5	______	______
2.	8	______	______
3.	7	______	______
4.	10	______	______
5.	9	______	______
6.	15	______	______

For Problems 7 through 10, use the sum-of-the-years'-digits method.

7. Complete the depreciation record for a compact van used by Pizza Inn for delivering pizzas. The original cost is $4,500, with an estimated useful life of three years and a trade-in value of $600.

End of Year	*Annual Depreciation*	*Accumulated Depreciation*	*Book Value*
1	$1,950, found by $\frac{3}{6}$($4,500 – $600)	$1,950	$2,550
2	______	______	______
3	______	______	______

8. Complete the depreciation record for office equipment costing $16,500 with an estimated life of five years and salvage value of $500.

End of Year	*Annual Depreciation*	*Accumulated Depreciation*	*Book Value*
1	$5,333.33, found by $\frac{5}{15}$($16,500 – $500)	$5,333.33	$11,166.67
2	______	______	______
3	______	______	______
4	______	______	______
5	______	______	______

9. Construct a depreciation record for an electric welding machine costing $9,000, having an estimated useful life of six years and a salvage value after six years of $1,500.

End of Year

10. Construct a depreciation record for a commercial chain saw costing $980 with an estimated life of two years and a trade-in value of $200.

End of Year

1

2

11. Find the sum of the first 100 whole numbers (1 + 2 + ... + 100). ____________, found by

SECTION 17-3: THE DECLINING-BALANCE METHOD

Objective: To compute annual depreciation, accumulated depreciation, and book value, using the declining-balance method.

DECLINING-BALANCE METHOD

Application of the **declining-balance method**, often called the **double-declining method**, results in much higher annual depreciation for the early life of a fixed asset, but the depreciation diminishes as the asset approaches the end of its useful life. To compute the depreciation:

Step 1. Estimate the *useful life.*

Step 2. Determine the annual rate of depreciation by *dividing one by the useful life.* Thus:

$$\text{Annual rate of depreciation} = \frac{\text{One}}{\text{Useful life}}$$

For illustration: An asset with a useful life of 5 years would have an annual depreciation rate of $\frac{1}{5} = 0.20$, or 20%. An asset with a useful life of ten years would have an annual rate of depreciation of $\frac{1}{10} = 0.10 = 10\%$.

Step 3. *Double the annual rate* computed in Step 2. For illustration:

Double $\frac{1}{5}$ is $\frac{2}{5}$, or $0.40 = 40\%$. Double $\frac{1}{10}$ is $\frac{2}{10}$, or $0.20 = 20\%$.

Step 4. The depreciation for the first year is found by *multiplying the doubled rate by the original cost of the asset.*

First year depreciation = Doubled rate × Original cost

Step 5. *Subtract the accumulated depreciation from the original cost* to arrive at the declining balance. This is the same as the book value of the asset.

Step 6. Second year depreciation = Doubled rate × Declining balance

This procedure is continued to find the depreciation for the following years.

Problem The useful life of a commercial van used by a grocery store is four years. The original cost is $10,000. What is the annual depreciation for the first two years, using the declining-balance method?

Solution Step 1. The useful life is four years.

Step 2. The annual rate of depreciation = $\frac{1}{4} = 0.25$, or 25%.

Step 3. Doubling the annual rate of $\frac{1}{4}$ is $\frac{2}{4}$, or $0.50 = 50\%$.

Step 4. Compute:

First year depreciation = Doubled rate × Original cost
= 50% × $10,000
= $5,000

Step 5. Subtract the accumulated depreciation from the original cost to arrive at the declining balance.

Declining balance = Original cost − Accumulated depreciation
= $10,000 − $5,000
= $5,000

Step 6. Compute the second year depreciation.

Second year depreciation = Doubled rate × Declining balance
= 50% × $5,000
= $2,500

The third- and fourth-year depreciation is found by multiplying the doubled rate by the declining balance at the end of the year.

Using a calculator with memory and +/−:

Enter	Press	Display
.5	m+ ×	0.5
10000	= −	5000
10000	= +/− ×	5000
	RM	0.5
	= +	2500
5000	= −	7500
10000	= +/− ×	2500
	RM	0.5
	= +	1250
7500	= −	8750
10000	= +/− ×	1250
	RM	0.5
	= +	625
8750	= −	9375
10000	= +/−	625

Depreciation record for each of the four years:

Year	*Double Rate of Depreciation*		*Annual Depreciation*	*Accumulated Depreciation*	*Declining Balance (Book Value)*	
1	50% × $10,000	=	$5,000	$5,000	$5,000 ←	$10,000 − $5,000
2	50% × 5,000	=	2,500	7,500	2,500 ←	10,000 − 7,500
3	50% × 2,500	=	1,250	8,750	1,250 ←	10,000 − 8,750
4	50% × 1,250	=	625	9,375	625 ←	10,000 − 9,375

The Internal Revenue Service will not allow the declining balance to be less than the salvage value. If the computation of the declining balance results in an amount *less than* the salvage value, the annual depreciation for that year is recalculated to be: Previous year's declining balance − Salvage value. Thus, the *declining balance* at the end of that year will be equal to the salvage value.

Suppose in the above problem that the salvage value of the commercial van is $750. Then annual depreciation for the fourth year is recalculated to be $500, found by $1,250 − $750.

The fourth year of the depreciation record would read as follows:

Year	*Double Rate of Depreciation*	*Annual Depreciation*	*Accumulated Depreciation*	*Declining Balance (Book Value)*
4		$500	$9,250	$750
		↑ $1,250 − $750	↑ $8,750 + $500	↑ $10,000 − $9,250, same as salvage value

1 SELF-REVIEW

The useful life of a large earth-moving machine is estimated to be five years. The original cost is $30,000, and its salvage value is $3,000. Determine the annual depreciation, the accumulated depreciation, and the declining balance.

Step 1. The estimated life is 5 years.

Step 2. Annual rate of depreciation as a fraction is —, and as a percent ____%.

Step 3. The doubled rate is _____%.

Step 4. First-year depreciation = _____% × $_________ = $_________.

Step 5. Declining balance at end of first year =
$_________ − $_______ = $________

Step 6. Second-year depreciation = _____% × $_________ = $_________.

Complete the depreciation record.

Year	*Double Rate of Depreciation*		*Annual Depreciation*	*Accumulated Depreciation*	*Declining Balance (Book Value)*
1	40% × $30,000	=	$12,000	$12,000	$18,000
2	40% × 18,000	=	7,200	19,200	10,800
3	________	=	______	______	______
4	________	=	______	______	______
5	________	=	888*	______	______

*Only $888 can be recorded on the firm's federal income tax for depreciation. This results in a declining balance (salvage value) of $3,000 at the end of the fifth year. The $888 is found by: declining balance at end of the fourth year minus the salvage value, that is, $3,888 − $3,000 = $888.

Step 2: $\frac{1}{5}$; 20%

Step 3: 40%

Step 4:
40% × $30,000 = $12,000

Step 5:
$30,000 − $12,000 = $18,000

Step 6:
40% × $18,000 = $7,200

3. 40% × $10,800 = $4,320; 23,520; 6,480
4. 40% × $ 6,480 = $2,592; 26,112; 3,888
$ 888; 27,000; 3,000

40% × $3,888 = $1,555.20, which is not equal to $888.

ASSIGNMENT 17-3
THE DECLINING-BALANCE METHOD

Name ______________________ **Date Due** ______________ **Grade** ______

Answers to selected problems are given in Appendix B.

For Problems 1 through 6, compute the doubled rate of depreciation.

	Years of Useful Life	*Annual Rate of Depreciation*		*Doubled Rate of Depreciation*	
		As a Fraction	*As a Percent*	*As a Fraction*	*As a Percent*
Ex.	4	$\frac{1}{4}$	25%	$\frac{2}{4}$ or $\frac{1}{2}$	50%
1.	10	______	______	______	______
2.	5	______	______	______	______
3.	20	______	______	______	______
4.	8	______	______	______	______
5.	3	______	______	______	______
6.	6	______	______	______	______

For Problems 7 through 10, use the declining-balance method.

7. Complete the depreciation record for a compact van used by Pizza Inn for delivering pizzas. The original cost is $4,500, with an estimated useful life of three years and a trade-in value of $600.

End of Year	*Annual Depreciation*	*Accumulated Depreciation*	*Book Value*
1	$3,000, found by $66\frac{2}{3}\%$ × $4,500	$3,000	$1,500
2	______	______	______
3	______	______	______

8. Complete the depreciation record for office equipment costing $16,500, with an estimated life of five years and a salvage value of $500.

End of Year	*Annual Depreciation*	*Accumulated Depreciation*	*Book Value*
1	$6,600, found by 40% × $16,500	$6,600	$9,900
2	______	______	______
3	______	______	______
4	______	______	______
5	______	______	______

9. Construct a depreciation record for an electric welding machine costing $9,000, having an estimated life of six years and a salvage value after six years of $1,500.

End of Year
1
2
3
4
5
6

10. Construct a depreciation record for a commercial chain saw costing $980, with an estimated life of two years and a trade-in value of $200.

End of Year
1
2

11. Discuss what happens when using the declining-balance method of determining depreciation and the estimated useful life of the item is one year.

12. If the salvage value is $0, will the book value (declining balance) after the last year of depreciation equal the salvage value? Why or why not?

REVIEW ASSIGNMENT FOR CHAPTER 17
DEPRECIATION

Name ______________________ Date Due ______________ Grade _____

1. Use the straight-line, sum-of-the-years'-digits, and declining-balance methods to construct depreciation records for a store fixture costing $15,000, with an estimated life of four years and a salvage value of $1,000.

Straight-line method:

End of Year	*Annual Depreciation*	*Accumulated Depreciation*	*Book Value*
1	______________	$______________	$______________
2	______________	______________	______________
3	______________	______________	______________
4	______________	______________	______________

Sum-of-the-years'-digits method:

End of Year	*Annual Depreciation*	*Accumulated Depreciation*	*Book Value*
1	______________	$______________	$______________
2	______________	______________	______________
3	______________	______________	______________
4	______________	______________	______________

Declining-balance method:

End of Year	*Annual Depreciation*	*Accumulated Depreciation*	*Book Value*
1	______________	$______________	$______________
2	______________	______________	______________
3	______________	______________	______________
4	______________	______________	______________

2. A robotic delivery unit (rdu) used in a hospital is expected to last 45,000 hours. The unit costs $74,500 and has a scrap value of $2,500 after 45,000 hours of use. After 20,000 hours:

   A. The depreciation is $____________, found by

   B. The book value is $____________, found by

3. A punch press is expected to produce 300,000 units before it is traded in. The cost of a punch press is $17,500, with a trade-in value of $2,000 after 300,000 units have been produced. After 60,000 units are produced:

   A. The depreciation is $____________, found by

   B. The book value is $____________, found by

TO THE STUDENT: There is a SELF-REVIEW TEST for this chapter in Appendix A, *with answers,* in Appendix C.

18

Valuing an Inventory and Inventory Turnover

SECTION 18-1: VALUING AN INVENTORY USING THE AVERAGE-COST METHOD

Objective: To determine the value of an inventory using the average-cost method.

INTRODUCTION

A visit to J. C. Penney, Sears, or Macys' reveals a wide variety of merchandise, including clothing, cameras, jewelry, and furniture. The value of this merchandise on hand on a specified date is referred to as the **merchandise inventory.**

One way of finding out how many of each item are on hand is to actually count the items. This is usually referred to as taking a **physical inventory.** Many retail establishments close for a day or two at the end of the fiscal year, and all employees, plus others hired for this specific job, count all the sweaters, the hammers, the television sets, and so on.

Decline In Inventories Posted By U.S. Firms

Another way of determining how many of each item are on hand is to maintain a **perpetual inventory.** This means that inventory records are constantly being adjusted for **receipts** (incoming items) and **issues** (outgoing shipments or sales). The receipts are added to the inventory, the issues are subtracted. With the advent of high-speed electronic computers, maintaining perpetual inventory records has become less time-consuming. A recent development involves the use of light pens or wands, as now done extensively in discount and other retail stores.

Inventory is an asset of a firm. As such, its value must be determined to arrive at the worth of the firm. The value of the inventory is recorded on the balance sheet sent to the stockholders. It must also be known and verified for insurance and tax purposes.

AVERAGE-COST METHOD

An inventory can be valued several different ways. One is called the **average-cost method.** As the name implies, the average cost of each item (unit) must be determined.

$$\text{Average cost per unit} = \frac{\text{Total cost of all incoming units}}{\text{Total number of units received}}$$

The average cost per unit is multiplied by the number of units on hand to arrive at the total value of the items.

$$\text{Total value} = \text{Average cost per unit} \times \text{Number of units on hand}$$

Problem The following inventory record shows that Gimbles Wholesale Electronics, Inc., received 100 Model TI hand calculators on June 1 at a price of $10 each. Another shipment of 70 arrived June 15, but the unit cost had risen to $12. A third incoming shipment of 60 calculators on June 29 was priced even higher ($13). During the month 120 calculators were sold. A count on June 30 revealed 110 on hand.

Date	*Unit Cost*	*Receipts Quantity IN*	*Issues Quantity OUT*	*Balance on Hand at End of Day*	
6/1	$10	100		100	
6/4			40	60 ←	100 – 40
6/15	$12	70		130 ←	60 + 70
6/17			50	80 ←	130 – 50
6/29	$13	60		140 ←	80 + 60
6/30			30	110 ←	140 – 30

What is the total value of the 110 Model TI calculators as of June 30, using the average-cost method?

Solution The table below shows that the 100 calculators received June 1 priced at $10 each cost Gimbles $1,000, found by 100 × $10. Likewise, the incoming June 15 shipment of 70 calculators with a unit cost of $12 amounted to $840. The June 29 receipt of 60 calculators at $13 each totaled $780. The total value of the 230 calculators is $2,620, found by $1,000 + $840 + $780.

Date	*Receipts*		*Unit Cost*		*Value*
June 1	100	×	$10	=	$1,000
June 15	70	×	12	=	840
June 29	60	×	13	=	780
Totals	230				$2,620

To find the average cost per unit:

$$\text{Average cost per unit} = \frac{\text{Total cost of all incoming units}}{\text{Total number of units received}}$$

$$= \frac{\$2{,}620}{230}$$

$$= \$11.39$$

To find the total value of the 110 units on hand as of June 30:

$$\text{Total value} = \text{Average cost per unit} \times \text{Number of units on hand}$$

$$= \$11.39 \times 110$$

$$= \$1{,}252.90$$

1 SELF-REVIEW

A reminder: Cover the answers in the margin.

The garden department received a shipment of 50 Christmas cactus plants from a supplier on December 2 at a unit cost of $1.50. An incoming shipment of 80 plants on December 8 was priced at $1.55 a plant. A final shipment of 70 cactus arrived December 18 at a reduced price of $1.10. There were 40 plants on hand (not sold) on December 31.

Using the average-cost method, what is the total value of the year-end inventory of the 40 Christmas cactus plants?

To compute the average cost per unit:

Date	*Receipts*	*Unit Cost*	*Value*
December 2	50	$1.50	$______
December 8	______	______	______
December 18	______	______	______
Totals	______		$______

Margin answer:

Receipts	*Unit Cost*	*Value*
50	$1.50	$ 75
80	1.55	124
70	1.10	77
200		$276

$$\text{Average cost per unit} = \frac{\text{Total cost of all incoming units}}{\text{Total number of units received}}$$

$= \_\_\_\_\_\_$

$= \$\_\_\_\_\_\_$

Margin answer: Average cost $= \frac{\$276}{200}$ $= \$1.38$

Total value of the 40 plants on hand December 31:

Total value = Average cost per unit × Number of units on hand

= $______ × ____

= $______

Margin answer: Total value = $1.38 × 40 = $55.20

ASSIGNMENT 18-1
VALUING AN INVENTORY USING THE AVERAGE-COST METHOD

Name ______________________ **Date Due** ______________ **Grade** _____

Answers to selected problems are given in Appendix B.

For Problems 1 through 6, determine the number of units on hand July 31. Receipts are incoming shipments from suppliers; issues are sales to customers.

	Item	*July 1 Receipts*	*July 9 Issues*	*July 15 Issues*	*July 18 Receipts*	*July 22 Issues*	*July 26 Receipts*	*July 31 Balance on Hand*
Ex.	Lamp	+100	−10	−5	+12	−6	+20	111
1.	5-inch saw	30	27	2	40	30	50	______
2.	Sheet	120	60	40	200	10	0	______
3.	Bath mat	45	22	8	0	14	0	______
4.	35-mm film	200	140	20	35	18	50	______
5.	Garden hose	0	0	0	40	40	0	______
6.	Paperweight	40	0	1	45	2	0	______

7. Clearwater Wholesalers Supply Company carries this inventory card on a claw hammer:

	Date	*Unit Cost*	*Receipts*	*Issues*	*Balance*
Part No.: CO-127	9/1	$5.00	50		50
Description: claw hammer	9/15			20	30
Location:	10/1	4.00	30		60
72	10/15			40	20

A. Determine the average cost per unit.

$______________, found by

B. Determine the total value of the inventory at end of the day, October 15, using the average-cost method.

$______________, found by

8. The inventory card showed these transactions on a box of spark plugs.

Date	*Unit Cost*	*In*	*Out*	*Balance*
12/1	$5.75			130
12/6			25	105
12/14			80	25
12/19	7.00	200		225
12/24			150	75
12/31	6.50	100		175

A. Determine the average cost per unit. $________, found by

B. Determine the total value of the inventory at end of the day, December 31, using the average-cost method.

$______________, found by

9. A. Complete this plumbing supply house inventory record for a Briggs faucet set.

Date	*Unit Cost*	*Receipts*	*Shipments*	*Balance*
4/1	$35.00			75
4/3	33.00	100		________
4/10			95	________
4/12			20	________
4/15	30.00	100		________
4/30			75	________

B. Calculate the value of the inventory at end of the day, April 30, using the average-cost method.

$______________, found by

10. A. Complete this perpetual inventory card maintained by Bostwick-Braun Wholesale Hardware Supply Company for a 14-inch gas chain saw:

Date	*Unit Cost*	*Received from Manufacturer*	*Shipped to Retailers*	*Balance on Hand*
7/1	$64.75			150
7/7	67.50	75		________
7/18			110	________
7/23	69.95	90		________
7/31			80	________

B. Determine the value of the inventory at the end of the day on July 31 using the average-cost method.

$______________, found by

SECTION 18-2: VALUING AN INVENTORY USING THE FIRST-IN, FIRST-OUT (FIFO) METHOD

Objective: To determine the value of an inventory using the first-in, first-out method.

FIFO METHOD Fifo stands for **first-in, first-out** and implies that the oldest (first-in) items are sold before items acquired later. The value of the inventory is calculated accordingly.

Problem The price and number of several incoming shipments of ceramic vases received by Ceramics Wholesalers, Inc., and the number sold to retail outlets for the month of March is:

Date	*Unit Cost*	*Receipts Quantity IN*	*Issues Quantity OUT*	*Balance on Hand at End of Day*	
3/1	$ 8	100		100	
3/5			20	80 ←	100 – 20
3/14	10	50		130 ←	80 + 50
3/19			90	40 ←	130 – 90
3/27	12	70		110 ←	40 + 70
3/31			30	80 ←	110 – 30

What is the value of the inventory of vases at the end of the month, using the first-in, first-out (Fifo) method?

Solution The simplest way to calculate the value of the inventory on March 31, using the Fifo method, is to start with the ending balance and work *backward* through the incoming shipments until the current stock is accounted for.

Of the 80 ceramic vases on hand March 31, 70 came from the March 27 receipts and are valued at $12 each. The remaining 10, (80 – 70), came from the March 14 receipts and are valued at $10 each. To compute the value of the inventory:

Received March 27	70 vases × $12 each	= $840	
Received March 14	10 vases × $10 each	= 100	
Ending balance	80	$940 ←	Value using Fifo

1 SELF-REVIEW

A reminder: Cover the answers in the margin.

Compute the value of the inventory of pens as of May 31 using the first-in, first-out (Fifo) and average-cost methods.

A. Complete the table:

Date	*Unit Cost*	*Receipts of Pens*	*Issues of Pens*	*On Hand*
May 2	$5	200		200
May 8			120	______
May 16	6	100		______
May 23	7	60		______
May 31			110	______

A.

Date	*On Hand*
May 8	80
May 16 ...	180
May 23 ...	240
May 31 ...	130

B. 60; 70; May 16

B. How many of the 130 pens on hand at the end of May came from the incoming shipment dated May 23? _______. The remaining _______ (number) pens on hand May 31 were (theoretically) from the shipment dated ___________.

C.

Date	No.	Unit Cost	Value
May 23	60	$7	$420
May 16	70	6	420
Balance	130		$840

C. Compute the value of the inventory of pens using the *Fifo method:*

Date Received	*No. of Pens*	*Unit Cost*	*Value*
May 23	_______	X $_______	= $_______
___________ . . .	_______	X $_______	= _______
Ending Balance . . .	_______		$_______ ← Total value using Fifo

D. Average cost:

$$= \frac{\$2,020}{360}$$

= $5.61111

= $5.61 (rounded)

where:

	200 × $5 =	$1,000
	100 × 6 =	600
	60 × 7 =	420
Totals	360	$2,020

Total value:

= $5.61 × 130

= $729.30

D. Using the *average-cost method,* determine the total value of the pens at the end of the day, May 31:

$$\text{Average cost per unit} = \frac{\text{Total cost of all incoming units}}{\text{Total number of units received}}$$

= $\frac{\$\_\_\_\_\_\_\_\_}{\_\_\_\_\_\_\_\_}$

= $_________ = $_________ (rounded)

Total value = Average cost per unit × Number of units on hand

= $_______ × _______

= $_______ ← Total value using average-cost method

E. Using FIFO, $840; using average-cost method, $729.30—a difference of $110.70.

E. Compare the value of the inventory at the end of May 31 using the Fifo and average-cost methods.

____

____

ASSIGNMENT 18-2
VALUING AN INVENTORY USING THE FIRST-IN, FIRST-OUT (FIFO) METHOD

Name ______________________________ **Date Due** ______________ **Grade** _____

Answers to selected problems are given in Appendix B.

For Problems 1 through 6, determine the balance on hand, and, using Fifo, explain the composition (make-up) of that balance.

	Item	*Aug. 1 IN*	*Aug. 8 OUT*	*Aug. 15 OUT*	*Aug. 22 IN*	*Aug. 31 Balance on Hand*	*Composition*
Ex.	Hats	50	20	20	30	40	10 from 8/1 and 30 from 8/22
1.	Shoes	65	20	15	25	_____,	____________________
2.	Scarves	120	10	10	15	_____,	____________________
3.	Belts	115	65	50	50	_____,	____________________
4.	Shirts	50	30	20	100	_____,	____________________
5.	Trousers	20	5	5	50	_____,	____________________
6.	Sweaters	70	15	37	45	_____,	____________________

7. Clearwater Wholesalers Supply Company carries this inventory card on a claw hammer:

	Date	*Unit Cost*	*Receipts*	*Issues*	*Balance*
Part No.: CO-127	9/1	$5.00	50		50
Description: Claw hammer	9/15			20	30
	10/1	4.00	30		60
Location: 72	10/15			40	20

Use Fifo to determine the value of the claw hammer inventory.

$__________, found by

8. The inventory card showed these transactions on a box of spark plugs.

Date	*Unit Cost*	*IN*	*OUT*	*Balance*
12/1	$5.75			130
12/6			25	105
12/14			80	25
12/19	7.00	200		225
12/24			150	75
12/31	6.50	100		175

Find the value of the inventory using the first-in, first-out (Fifo) method.

$______________, found by

9. A. Complete this plumbing supply house inventory record for a Briggs faucet set:

Date	*Unit Cost*	*Receipts*	*Shipments*	*Balance*
4/1	$35.00			75
4/3	33.00	100		_______
4/10			95	_______
4/12			20	_______
4/15	30.00	100		_______
4/30			75	_______

B. Calculate the value of the inventory using Fifo.

$__________, found by

10. A. Complete the perpetual inventory card maintained by Bostwick-Braun Wholesale Hardware Supply Company for a 14-inch gas chain saw:

Date	*Unit Cost*	*Received from Manufacturer*	*Shipped to Retailers*	*Balance On Hand*
7/1	$64.75			150
7/7	67.50	75		_______
7/18			110	_______
7/23	69.95	90		_______
7/30			80	_______

B. Calculate the value of the inventory using Fifo.

$______________

SECTION 18-3: VALUING AN INVENTORY USING THE LAST-IN, FIRST-OUT (LIFO) METHOD

Objective: To determine the value of an inventory using the last-in, first-out method.

LIFO METHOD

Another method of computing the worth of an inventory is called the **Lifo** method. Lifo is the abbreviation for **last-in, first-out.** Under this method, the *records would indicate* that the *most recent* items added to the inventory are shipped out *first.*

Problem

A farm store received three large shipments of cans of oil in cases during the month. Each incoming shipment was priced slightly higher than the previous one. These incoming shipments and sales to customers for August were:

Date	*Unit Cost*	*Receipts Quantity IN*	*Issues Quantity OUT*	*Balance on Hand at End of Day*	
Aug. 1	$10	100		100	
Aug. 6			40	60 ←	100 − 40
Aug. 16	12	70		130 ←	60 + 70
Aug. 18			50	80 ←	130 − 50
Aug. 27	15	60		140 ←	80 + 60
Aug. 31			30	110 ←	140 − 30

What is the value of the inventory of 110 cases at the end of the day, August 31, using the last-in, first-out (Lifo) method?

Solution

The simplest way to calculate the value of the inventory on August 31 using the Lifo method is to start with the beginning balance and work *forward* through the incoming shipments until the current stock is accounted for.

Of the 110 cases of oil on hand August 31, 100 came from the August 1 receipts and are valued at $10 each. The remaining 10, (110 − 100), came from the August 16 receipts and are valued at $12 each. To compute the value of the inventory:

Received August 1	100 cases	×	$10 each =	$1,000	
Received August 16	10 cases	×	12 each =	120	
Ending balance	110 cases			$1,120 ←	Value using Lifo

But for a change to LIFO, Amstar's earnings would have been up 420% in a year

1 SELF-REVIEW

A. The incoming shipments of Smell Nice Perfume and the sales to customers for January are shown. Compute the balance on hand at the end of the day.

Date	*Unit Cost*	*Receipts Quantity IN*	*Issues Quantity OUT*	*Balance on Hand at End of Day*
January 2	$5	200		200
January 8			40	______
January 12	4	250		______
January 20			50	______
January 22	2	150		______
January 31			240	______

A.

Date	*Balance*
Jan. 8	160
Jan. 12	410
Jan. 20	360
Jan. 22	510
Jan. 31	270

B. The balance of Smell Nice on hand January 31 is __________.

B. 270

C. Using the *Lifo method,* what is the value of this inventory balance?

Date Received	*Quantity IN*		*Unit Cost*		*Value*
January 2	______	×	$______	=	$______
January ____	______	×	______	=	______
Totals	______				$______ ← Total value using Lifo

C.

Date	*IN*	*Cost*	*Value*
Jan. 2	200	$5.00	$1,000
Jan. 12	70	4.00	280
Totals	270		$1,280

D. Now using the first-in, first-out *(Fifo) method,* determine the value of the 270 bottles of Smell Nice on hand at the end of the day, January 31.

Date Received	*Quantity IN*		*Unit Cost*		*Value*
January 22	______	×	$______	=	$______
January ____	______	×	______	=	______
Totals	______				$______ ← Total value using Fifo

D.

Date	*IN*	*Cost*	*Value*
Jan. 22	150	$2.00	$300
Jan. 12	120	4.00	480
Totals	270		$780

E. Now using the *average-cost method,* determine the value of the 270 bottles of Smell Nice on hand at the end of the day, January 31.

$$\text{Average cost per unit} = \frac{\text{Total cost of all incoming units}}{\text{Total number of units received}}$$

$$= \frac{\$\_\_\_\_\_\_}{\_\_\_\_\_\_}$$

= $__________ = $________ (rounded)

Total value = Average cost per unit × Number of units on hand

= $________ × ________

= $__________ ← Total value using average-cost method

E. Average cost:

$$= \frac{\$2{,}300}{600}$$

= $3.83333
= $3.83 (rounded)

where:

	200 ×	$5 =	$1,000
	250 ×	4 =	1,000
	150 ×	2 =	300
Totals	600		$2,300

Total value:
= $3.83 × 270
= $1,034.10

F. Compare valuing the inventories using Lifo, Fifo, and average cost. ________

____

F. LIFO gives the largest value of $1,280; FIFO gives the smallest value of $780; Average cost is $1,034.10, the middle value.

ASSIGNMENT 18-3
VALUING AN INVENTORY USING THE LAST-IN, FIRST-OUT (LIFO) METHOD

Name ______________________________ **Date Due** ______________ **Grade** _____

Answers to selected problems are given in Appendix B.

For Problems 1 through 6, determine the balance on hand as of September 30 using Lifo. Explain the composition of that balance.

	Item	*Sept. 1 IN*	*Sept. 8 OUT*	*Sept. 15 IN*	*Sept. 22 OUT*	*Sept. 30 Balance on Hand*	*Composition*
Ex.	Ring	40	25	15	25	5	5 from Sept. 1
1.	Watch	20	10	40	20	_____	______________________
2.	Necklace	25	5	20	20	_____	______________________
3.	Bracelet	25	15	90	15	_____	______________________
4.	Choker	30	20	40	10	_____	______________________
5.	Necklace	60	20	25	35	_____	______________________
6.	Earrings	15	5	20	20	_____	______________________

7. Clearwater Wholesalers Supply Company carries this inventory card on a claw hammer:

	Date	*Unit Cost*	*Receipts*	*Issues*	*Balance*
Part No.: CO-127 Description: Claw hammer Location: 72	9/1	$5.00	50		50
	9/15			20	30
	10/1	4.00	30		60
	10/15			40	20

Use Lifo to determine the value of the claw hammer inventory at the end of the day, October 15.

$__________, found by

8. The inventory card showed these transactions on a box of spark plugs.

Date	*Unit Cost*	*IN*	*OUT*	*Balance*
12/1	$5.75			130
12/6			25	105
12/14			80	25
12/19	7.00	200		225
12/24			150	75
12/31	6.50	100		175

Find the value of the inventory using the last-in, first-out (Lifo) method.

$____________, found by

9. A. Complete this plumbing supply house inventory record for a Briggs faucet set:

Date	*Unit Cost*	*Receipts*	*Shipments*	*Balance*
4/1	$35.00			75
4/3	33.00	100		______
4/10			95	______
4/12			20	______
4/15	30.00	100		______
4/30			75	______

B. Calculate the value of the inventory using Lifo.

$__________, found by

10. A. Complete this perpetual inventory card maintained by Bostwick-Braun Wholesale Hardware Supply Company for a 14-inch gas chain saw:

Date	*Unit Cost*	*Received from Manufacturer*	*Shipped to Retailers*	*Balance On Hand*
7/1	$64.75			150
7/7	67.50	75		______
7/18			110	______
7/23	69.95	90		______
7/30			80	______

B. Use Lifo to determine the value of this inventory at the end of the day, July 30.

$____________, found by

SECTION 18-4: INVENTORY TURNOVER

Objective: To find the inventory turnover for a business.

INVENTORY TURNOVER BASED ON COST

Inventory turnover is the number of times during a specified period that the inventory of a firm has been converted into sales. McDonalds, Wendys, Kentucky Fried Chicken, and other fast-food chains must have a very high turnover to convert inventory (hamburgers, buns, chicken, and so on) to sales. A computer manufacturer or an aircraft manufacturer producing very high-cost goods has a relatively small turnover. The rate of inventory turnover is based on the **average value** of the inventory either at **cost** or at **retail.**

If the rate of turnover is calculated based on the **cost** of the goods:

$$\text{Rate of inventory turnover at cost} = \frac{\text{Cost of goods sold}}{\text{Average inventory at cost}}$$

Problem

Carlton's Tire and Battery Shop takes an inventory every quarter, that is, four times a year. Inventory is based on the cost of the goods on hand. Carlton's purchases its tires, batteries, and automotive accessories from a wholesale dealer. The wholesale cost of the goods *on hand* for the last four inventories was $14,300, $17,600, $12,900, and $16,200. The wholesale cost of all the tires, batteries, and automotive accessories *sold* during the year was $183,000.

What is the rate of inventory turnover at cost?

Solution

Compute the average value of the inventory *on hand* based on wholesale cost:

Quarter	*Cost of Inventory*
First	$14,300
Second	17,600
Third	12,900
Fourth	16,200
Total	$61,000

$$\text{Average inventory at cost} = \frac{\$61{,}000}{4} = \$15{,}250$$

Using a calculator with memory:

Enter	Press	Display
14300	+	14300
17600	+	31900
12900	+	44800
16200	+ ÷	61000
4	= m+	15250
183000	÷ RM	15250
	=	12

Then:

$$\text{Rate of inventory turnover at cost} = \frac{\text{Cost of goods sold}}{\text{Average inventory at cost}} = \frac{\$183{,}000}{\$15{,}250} = 12.0$$

Usually given to nearest tenth

Interpretation: The inventory of tires, batteries, and automotive accessories turned over 12 times during the year. That is, theoretically, Carlton's had a complete turnover of all goods every month for each of the 12 months.

1 SELF-REVIEW

The Cute Boutique Shop takes an inventory based on cost three times a year, that is, every four months. The value of the inventory (at cost) for the last three inventories was: $8,420, $7,680, and $5,620. The cost of all the goods sold during the year was $95,480. What is the rate of inventory turnover at cost for the year?

Compute the average value of the inventory on hand based on cost:

Total: $21,720

Average inventory at cost $= \frac{\$21,720}{3}$

$= \$7,240$

Date	*Cost of Inventory*
April 30	$8,420
August 31	7,680
December 31	5,620
Total	$________

Average inventory at cost = $________

= $________

Rate of inventory turnover at cost $= \frac{\$95,480}{\$7,240}$

$= 13.2$

Interpret: Cute Boutique turns over all its merchandise about 13 times a year, or approximately once a month.

Then: Rate of inventory turnover at cost $= \frac{\text{Cost of goods sold}}{\text{Average inventory at cost}}$

$= \frac{\$\_\_\_\_\_\_\_\_}{\$} = \_\_\_\_\_\_\_\_$

Interpretation: ________________________________

INVENTORY TURNOVER BASED ON RETAIL SALES

The rate of inventory turnover can be based on *retail sales* instead of on cost.

$$\text{Rate of inventory turnover at retail} = \frac{\text{Net sales}}{\text{Average inventory at retail}}$$

Problem My Lords Men's Shop takes an inventory twice a year. The retail price of each item on hand is recorded. The two inventories last year were: June 30, $82,960; December 31, $67,490. The retail value of all goods sold during the year was $315,945. What is the rate of inventory turnover at retail?

Solution

Inventory Date	*Inventory at Retail*
June 30	$ 82,960
December 31	67,490
Total	$150,450

Average inventory at retail $= \frac{\$150,450}{2}$

$= \$75,225$

Rate of inventory turnover at retail $= \frac{\text{Net sales}}{\text{Average inventory at retail}}$

$= \frac{\$315,945}{\$75,225} = 4.2$

Interpretation: The inventory of suits, ties, and so on turned over about four times a year, that is, about every three months.

2 SELF-REVIEW

Garvey's Appliance takes inventory four times a year. The retail prices on refrigerators and other appliances are totaled. For the last four inventories the totals were $42,941, $41,678, $36,218, and $39,163. Total net sales for the year were $228,000.

A. The average inventory at retail is $________, found by $________ ÷ ____

B. The rate of inventory turnover at retail is ______, found by:

$________ ÷ $________

Interpretation: ________________________________

A. $40,000; $160,000 ÷ 4

B. 5.7; $228,000 ÷ $40,000

Interpret: Garvey's turns over all of its appliances six times a year, or about once every two months.

ASSIGNMENT 18-4
INVENTORY TURNOVER

Name ______________________ Date Due ____________ Grade ______

Answers to selected problems are given in Appendix B.

For Problems 1 through 6, find the average inventory.

Period	*Value of Inventories*	*Average Inventory*
Ex. Quarterly	\$24,670; \$30,173; \$27,850; \$32,475	\$28,792, found by $\frac{\$24{,}670 + \$30{,}173 + \$27{,}850 + \$32{,}475}{4}$
1. Semiannually	\$716,470; \$821,960	____________
2. Quarterly	\$70,650; \$81,190 \$75,640; \$60,970	____________
3. Every 4 months ..	\$105,620; \$97,516; \$111,070	____________
4. Semiannually	\$4,135,610; \$3,985,720	____________
5. Bimonthly	\$4,160; \$3,980; \$4,250; \$4,070; \$3,890; \$4,050	____________
6. Monthly	\$751; \$696; \$750; \$743; \$683; \$705; \$723; \$685; \$697; \$715; \$725; \$700	____________

7. The Ribbon Alley takes an inventory based on cost every quarter (four times a year). The value of the inventory (at cost) for the last four inventories was \$5,620, \$4,972, \$5,434, and \$5,972. The cost of all the goods sold during the year was \$32,800.

   A. What is the average inventory at cost?

   \$____________, found by

   B. What is the rate of inventory turnover at cost for the year?

   _______, found by

   C. Interpret the turnover rate. ____________

   ____

8. Joe's Auto Parts, Inc., conducts a semiannual (twice a year) inventory based on cost. Joe's last two inventories were valued at \$45,570 and \$56,835. The cost of all auto parts sold during the year was \$248,780.

   A. What is the rate of inventory turnover at cost for the year?

   _______, found by

   B. Interpret the turnover rate.

   ____

   ____

9. Scott Gifts, Inc., takes inventory at retail three times a year. The last three inventories (at retail) equaled $26,870, $29,200, and $25,750. Total net sales for the year were $250,000.

A. What is the average inventory at retail?

$________________, found by

B. What is the rate of inventory turnover at retail?

________, found by

C. What does it mean?

____

10. Bernards Boutique takes inventory at retail bimonthly (six times a year). The last six inventories were $82,430, $79,860, $81,750, $83,420, $78,760, and $76,200. Total net sales for that time period were $715,800.

A. What is the rate of inventory turnover at retail?

________, found by

B. Interpretation ____

____

11. An important measure of inventory turnover is the *average number of days it takes for an item to turn over.* That is, how long does an item stay in stock before it is sold?

$$\text{Average number of days for one turnover} = \frac{\text{Days in period}}{\text{Rate of turnover}}$$

Modern Furniture Company takes an inventory at retail four times a year. The last four inventories were valued at $102,000, $99,500, $137,200, and $61,300.

A. The average inventory at retail is $______________,
found by

B. Retail sales for the year totaled $1,200,000. The rate of inventory turnover at retail is ___________,
found by

C. The average number of days for a piece of furniture to turn over (to be sold) is _________ days,
found by (365 days in a year) ÷ (rate of turnover)

12. In Problems 8 and 10, find the average number of days it takes Joe's to move an auto part and Bernards to sell a boutique item.

A. Joe's takes _________ days,
found by

B. Bernards takes _________ days,
found by

REVIEW ASSIGNMENT FOR CHAPTER 18
VALUING AN INVENTORY AND INVENTORY TURNOVER

Name ______________________ Date Due ______________ Grade _____

1. Aladdin Wholesale Jewelers handles simulated diamond rings. The inventory record for September shows the following transactions.

A. Complete the inventory record.

Date	*Unit Cost*	*In*	*Out*	*Balance*
9/3	$ 8.00			110
9/5			40	______
9/12	9.00	80		______
9/14	10.00	50		______
9/21			70	______
9/30	11.00	100		______

B. Find the value of the inventory using the average cost method.

$____________, found by

C. Find the value of the inventory using Fifo.

$____________, found by

D. Find the value of the inventory using Lifo.

$____________, found by

2. A Poor-Boy Furniture Store had the following shipments of Poor-Boy chairs from the manufacturer during October: Oct. 3, 10 chairs at $50 each; Oct. 15, 8 chairs at $45 each; Oct. 22, 16 chairs at $40 each; and Oct. 27, 10 chairs at $30 each. Sales to customers were: Oct. 4, 4 chairs; Oct. 17, 6 chairs; Oct. 19, 2 chairs; and Oct. 31, 12 chairs.

A. Organize the information into an inventory record card.

Date	*Unit Cost*	*Chairs Received (IN)*	*Chairs Sold (OUT)*	*Balance*
10/3	$________	________		________
10/4			________	________
10/15	________	________		________
10/17			________	________
10/19			________	________
10/22	________	________		________
10/27	________	________		________
10/31			________	________

B. Find the value of the inventory using the average-cost method.

$__________, found by

C. Find the value of the inventory using Fifo.

$__________, found by

D. Find the value of the inventory using Lifo.

$__________, found by

3. Korner Kitchen Kupboard, Inc., takes inventory quarterly. Net sales for the year totaled $135,650, with the cost of goods sold being $113,040.

	Inventory	
Quarter	*At Cost*	*At Retail*
1	$14,650	$17,580
2	12,500	15,000
3	16,870	20,244
4	15,120	18,144

A. What is the rate of inventory turnover at cost?

____

B. What is the rate of inventory turnover at retail?

____

TO THE STUDENT: There is a SELF-REVIEW TEST for this chapter in Appendix A, *with answers* in Appendix C.

19

The Use of Statistical Techniques in Business

SECTION 19-1: GRAPHIC PRESENTATION

Objective: To construct line charts, bar charts, two-directional bar charts, and pie charts.

INTRODUCTION

Followers of the Dallas Cowboys, the New York Yankees, the UCLA Bruins, and other professional and college teams may visualize a statistician as one who sits in the press box and records the number of yards gained, home runs, and baskets scored. Television announcers bombard the viewing audience with "statistics." We are informed that the Cowboys passed 22 times and completed 11. On the ground they rushed 235 yards, for an average of 5.2 yards per carry.

Daily newspapers and television reports reveal such statistics as 9% of Americans earn over $30,000 a year; the volume on the New York Stock Exchange totaled 22,010,000 shares, and the average price was up 21 cents; there are 30,000 members of the Midwest Old Settlers and Threshers Association; and 400,000 color television sets and 1,224,000 tons of macaroni were produced in the U.S.S.R. last year.

Most people envision statistics as being just a mass of numerical data on sports, membership in organizations, stock prices, and so on. **Statistics** has another meaning, however. It is defined as the *science of collecting, organizing, presenting, analyzing, and interpreting numerical data* for the purpose of making better decisions.

Managers of construction firms, hospitals, department stores, and the like have to make a large number of decisions. How much should we bid on a construction project? Which one of the seven applicants should we hire? How many dozen pantyhose should we purchase? The objective of this chapter is to introduce some of the basic statistical tools which might help these managers make better decisions. Three statistical techniques have been selected: graphic presentation, frequency distribution analysis, and averages.

LINE CHARTS

The old Chinese proverb, "A picture is worth a thousand words," is also endorsed by *Business Week, Fortune,* and other magazines in such areas as hospital administration, law enforcement, and engineering. One of the main purposes of a graph (also called a chart) is to attract reader attention and to present data in an easy-to-compare form.

Line charts are ideal for portraying the trend in sales, production, exports, population, and other series over a period of time.

Problem Portray the trend in urban and rural population in the United States since 1910 in the form of a line chart. The figures are given in the table below.

Year	Percent of Total Population: Urban	Percent of Total Population: Rural
1910	45.6	54.4
1920	51.2	48.8
1930	56.1	43.9
1940	56.5	43.5
1950	64.0	36.0
1960	69.9	30.1
1970	73.5	26.5
1980	75.0	25.0

Source: U.S. Bureau of the Census, *U.S. Census of Population, 1970,* vol. I, part A, and unpublished data.

Solution Most economic and business data are plotted on paper having an **arithmetic scale.** The divisions on both the x-axis (the horizontal axis) and the y-axis (the vertical axis) are equidistant. Note in Figure A that the distance between each of the lines on the x-axis represents ten years. The distance between each of the lines on the y-axis represents 10%.

In plotting data in a line chart, the years (time) are *always* placed on the x-axis. The years progress from left to right on the x-axis. The percents on the y-axis increase in magnitude from the origin of zero.

The first plot for the urban population is 1910 and 45.6%. In Figure B, you would go to 1910 on the x-axis and up to 45.6% on the y-axis and place a dot. Then you would move to 1920 on the x-axis and go up to 51.2% on the y-axis and place a dot. You would continue this process for the remaining years and connect the dots as in Figure C.

FIGURE A
Scaling the x-Axis and the y-Axis

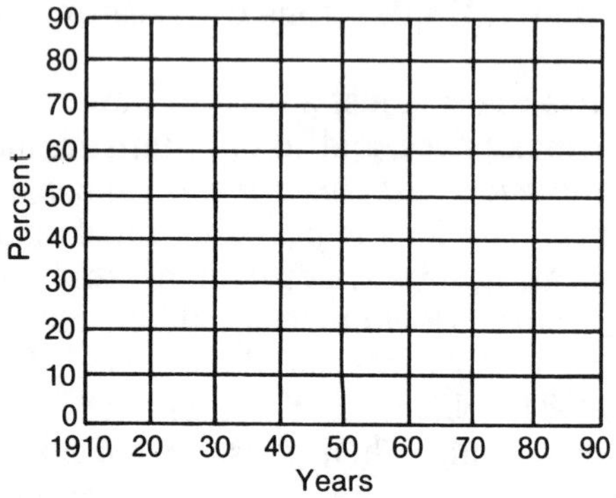

FIGURE B
Plotting the *Urban* Population

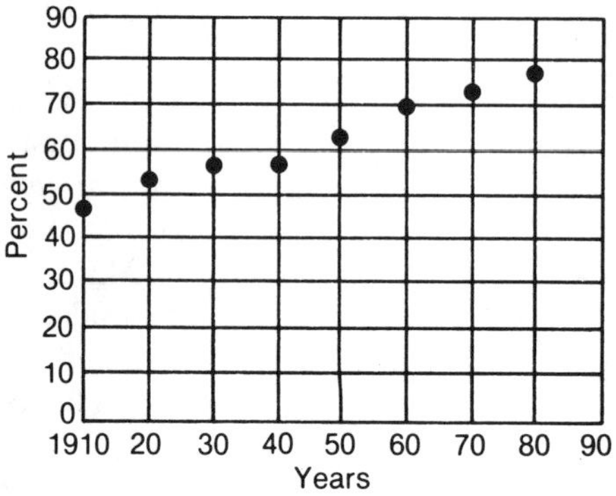

FIGURE C
Connecting the Dots to Reveal the Trend

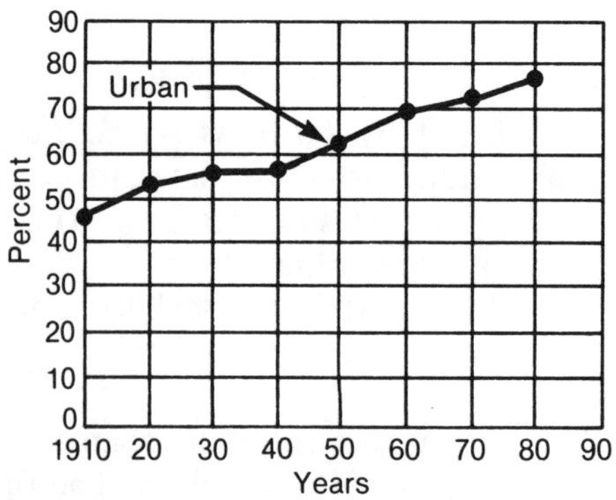

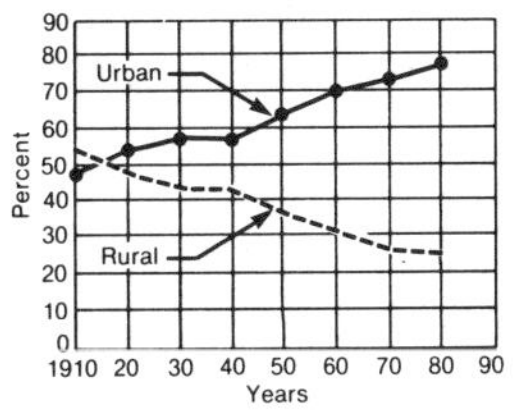

The percent of the total population living in urban areas is increasing. The percent of the total population living in rural areas is decreasing.

1 SELF-REVIEW

A reminder: Cover the answers in the margin.

A. Use Figure C and plot the rural data.

B. Briefly interpret the trend with respect to the percent of the total population living in urban and rural areas.

____

____

BAR CHARTS

Instead of depicting the data in the form of a line chart, some statisticians prefer a **bar chart.** The usual practice is to place the time (years, months, weeks, etc.) on the x-axis.

Problem Graph the sales of the company for the first six months of the year in a bar chart. The sales are:

Month	*Sales ($ millions)*	*Month*	*Sales ($ millions)*
January	$10.0	April	$17.9
February	15.1	May	26.5
March	12.6	June	37.1

Solution As shown in Figure D, the first step is to draw two vertical lines from January to $10 million. Then, as shown in Figure E, the tops of the lines are connected to form a bar. The height of the bar represents the total amount of sales for January.

This same procedure is followed for February. Note that a small space separates the sales for the two months. This makes the chart easier to read.

FIGURE D
Two Vertical Lines Drawn for January

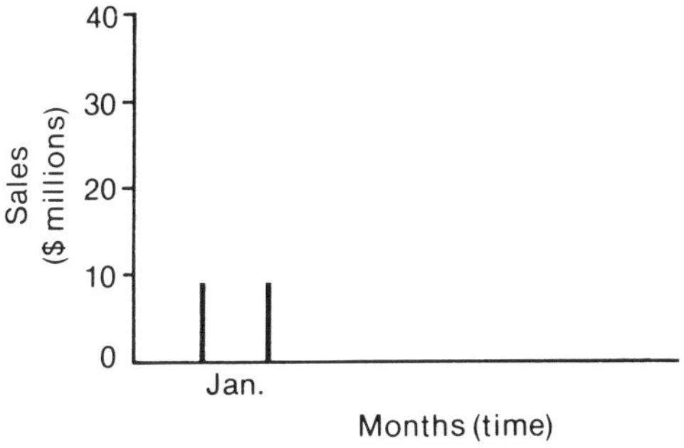

FIGURE E
Connecting the Tops of the Lines to Form a Bar

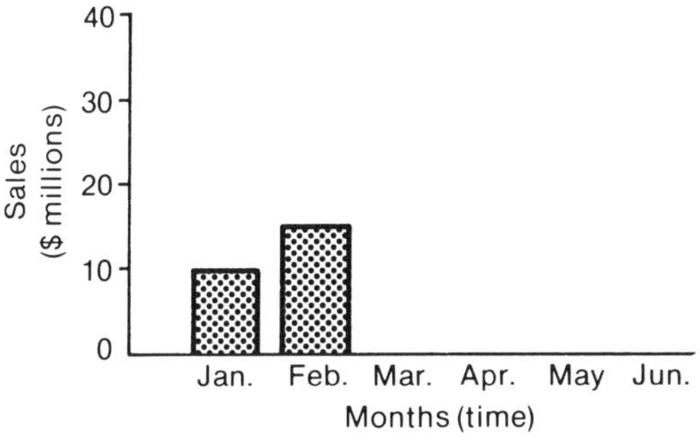

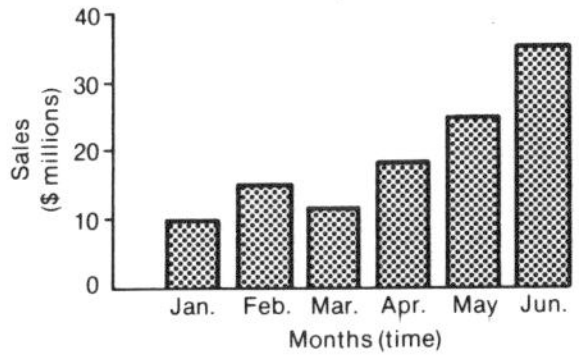

Except for March, there has been a steady increase in sales.

2 SELF-REVIEW

A. Compete Figure E by plotting the sales for March through June.

B. Interpret the trend in sales for the first six months of the year.

____

____

TWO-DIRECTIONAL BAR CHART

Another type of chart is called a **two-directional bar chart.** It is especially appropriate, for example, to describe the percent change in the sales of the divisions of a company from one year to the next.

Problem

The percent changes in the sales of the five divisions of the GAX Company from last year to this year are to be plotted in the form of a two-directional bar chart. The sales manager supplied the figures in the table below.

Division	*Sales ($ millions)* *Last Year*	*This Year*	*Percent Change*
Electronics	$100	$110	+ 10
Machine tools	10	6	− 40
Wood products	200	400	+100
Chemical	50	40	− 20
Textile	100	150	+ 50

In computing the percent change, sales last year is the *base* (denominator). The 10% increase from last year to this year for the electronics division was found by ($110 − $100) ÷ $100, and the 40% decrease in machine tools by ($6 − $10) ÷ $10 = 0.40 (decrease).

Solution

The usual procedure is to *rearrange the percent increases from the largest to the smallest.* The *percent decreases are rearranged from the smallest to the largest.*

Percent Increases		*Percent Decreases*	
+100	(Wood products)	−20	(Chemicals)
+ 50	(Textiles)	−40	(Machine tools)
+ 10	(Electronics)		

Then a line is drawn vertically in the center of the page. The percent *increases* are plotted to the right of the center line, designated as zero. The percent *decreases* are plotted to the left of zero.

The first plot is Wood products, 100% increase. As shown in Figure F, two lines are drawn from the center line (zero) to 100%, and a bar is formed. The bar for the next largest increase (Textiles) goes to +50%.

FIGURE F
A Two-Directional Bar Chart

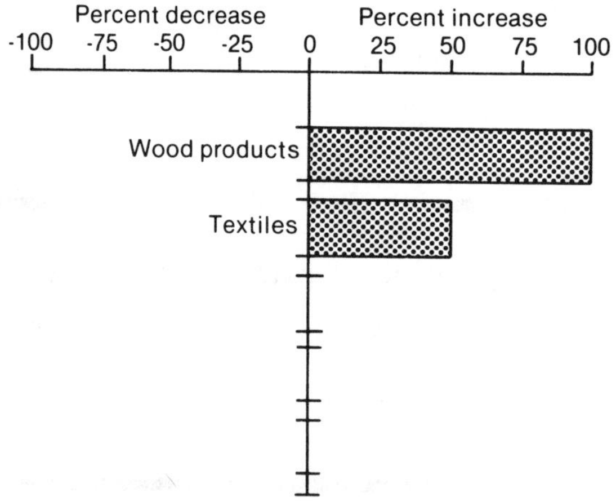

FIGURE F
A Two-Directional Bar Chart

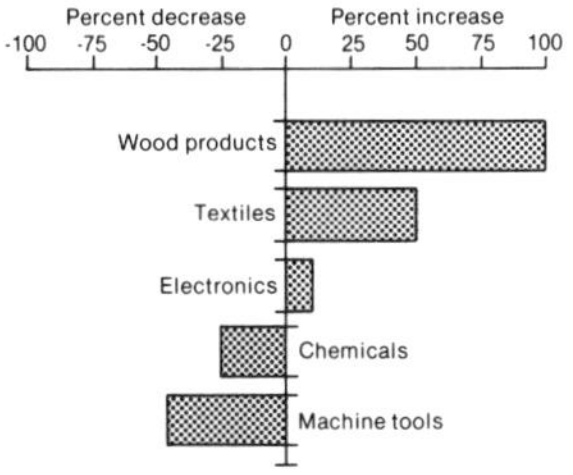

3 SELF-REVIEW

Complete Figure F. (Be careful when plotting the percent decreases. They go to the left of the center line.)

PIE CHART

A **pie chart** (sometimes called a circle chart) is a graphic presentation of ratios which allows a visual comparison of its parts. It is a popular way of describing where our tax dollar goes, the composition of sales, and so on.

Problem Show where our tax dollar goes in the form of a pie chart. The records revealed that 25 cents out of every tax dollar in a community goes for education, 50 cents for roads, 15 cents for administration, 8 cents for welfare, and 2 cents for miscellaneous.

Solution The *total area of the "pie," or circle, represents 100%,* or in this case, \$1. The division of the circle into 100 parts is shown in Figure G. The 25 cents out of every \$1 converts to 25%. To plot the 25% for education, a line is drawn from 0 to the center of the circle, and another line is drawn from the center to 25 (see Figure H). The 25% + 50% for roads gives 75%. A line is drawn from the center of the circle to 75%. Thus the area between 25% and 75% represents roads.

Adding 15% for administration to the 75% gives 90%. Again a line is drawn from the center to 90%. The piece of pie between 75% and 90% represents administration. This process is continued until all the percents are plotted (see Figure I).

FIGURE G

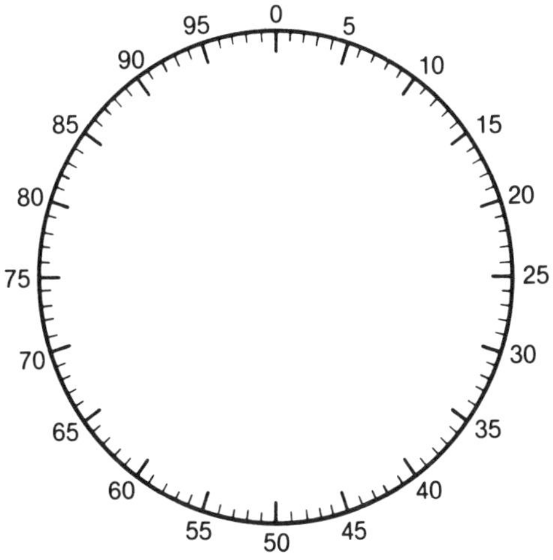

FIGURE H

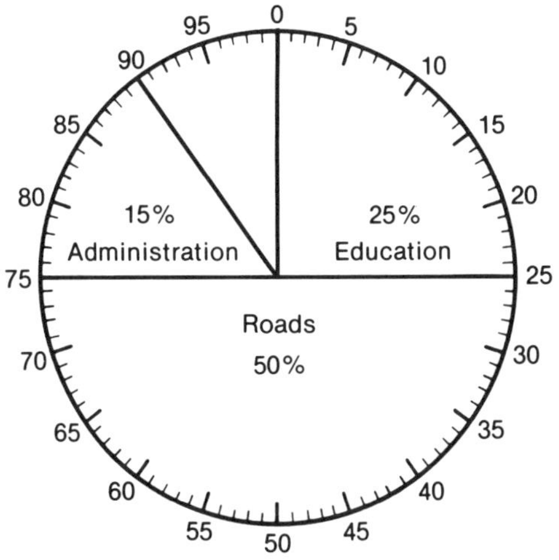

FIGURE I

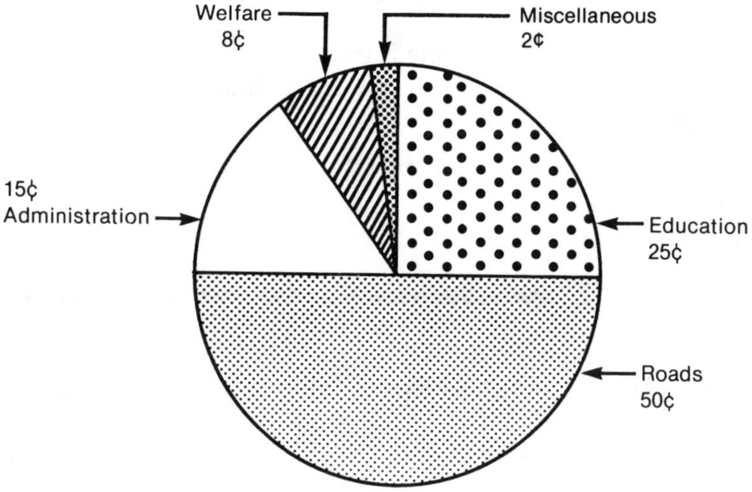

4 SELF-REVIEW

Last month a retail shop had these sales: books, $2,000; magazines, $10,000; greeting cards, $8,000.

Convert the sales of each of these items to a percent of the total. Plot the percents as a pie chart.

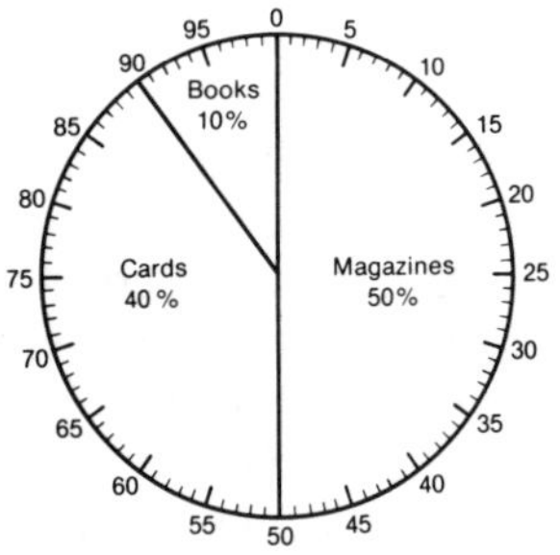

Books, 10%, found by $2,000 ÷ $20,000.
Magazines, 50%, found by $10,000 ÷ $20,000.
Cards, 40%, found by $8,000 ÷ $20,000.

Pie chart

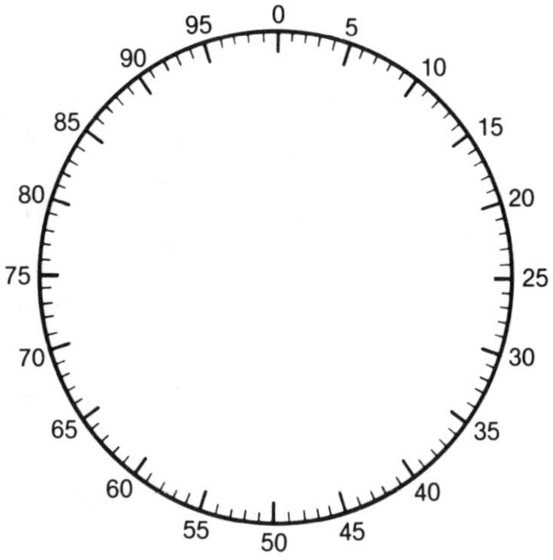

ASSIGNMENT 19-1
GRAPHIC PRESENTATION

Name ______________________ Date Due ______________ Grade _____

Answers to selected problems are given in Appendix B.

1. Plot the population of the United States and projections to 2000 in the form of a line chart.

Year	*Population (in millions)*
1950	152
1960	181
1970	205
1980	222
1990	244
2000	260

Source: U.S. Department of Commerce, *Statistical Abstract of the United States.*

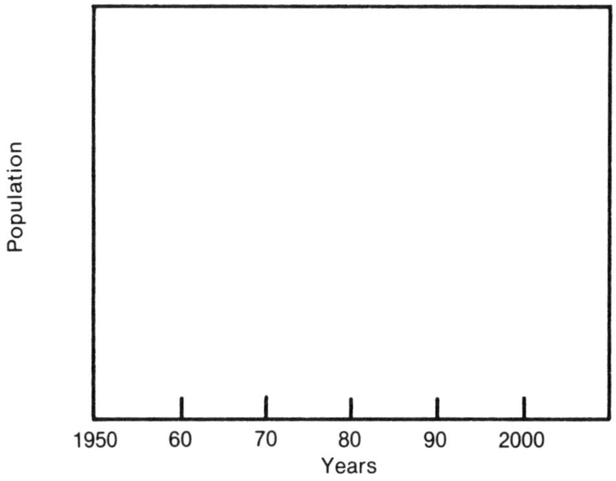

2. Plot the enrollment in all institutions of higher education and projections to 1983 in the form of a line chart. Suggestion: Use a dotted (· · ·) line for men, a dashed (----) for women, and solid line for the total.

Year	*Enrollment (thousands)* Men	*Enrollment (thousands)* Women
1966	3,577	2,351
1967	3,822	2,584
1968	4,119	2,809
1969	4,419	3,065
1970	4,637	3,284
1971	4,717	3,399
1972	4,701	3,564
1973	4,714	3,694
1983	5,292	4,478

Source: Department of Health, Education, and Welfare, *Projections of Education Statistics to 1982-83.*

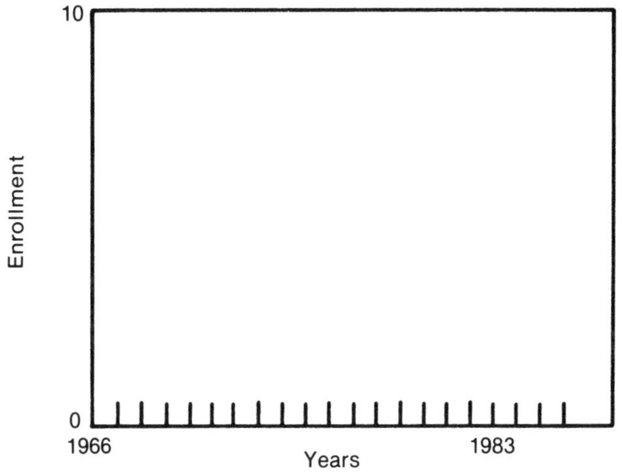

3. Portray the number of new passenger cars sold in the United States in the form of a bar chart.

Year	*No. Sold (millions)*
1960	6.6
1965	9.3
1970	8.4
1975	8.6
1980	12.0*

*Estimated
Source: U.S. Department of Commerce, *Survey of Current Business.*

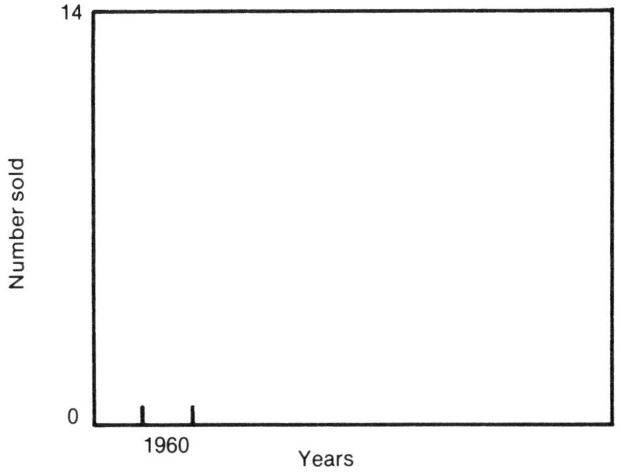

4. There are occasions where a bar chart and a line chart are combined for emphasis and eye appeal. Plot the hourly earnings in manufacturing since 1947 in the form of a *bar chart.* Then plot the hourly earnings in mining since 1947 as a *line chart* on the same graph immediately above the bars for mining.

Year	*Hourly Earnings* *Manufacturing*	*Mining*
1947	$1.22	$1.47
1951	1.56	1.93
1955	1.86	2.20
1959	2.19	2.56
1963	2.45	2.75
1967	2.82	3.19
1971	3.57	4.06
1975	4.83	5.95
1979	6.75	8.90

Source: U.S. Department of Labor, *Monthly Labor Review,* March 1979, p. 95.

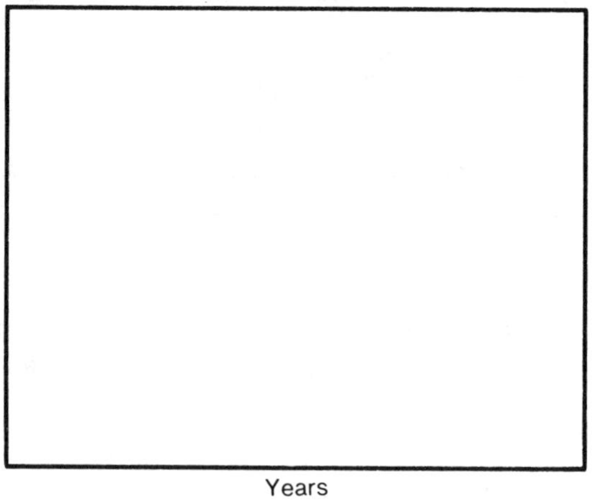

5. The sales of a department store, by department for last year and this year are:

Department	*Sales* *Last Year*	*This Year*
Shoe	$ 40,000	$ 20,000
Lingerie	1,000	2,000
Suit	100,000	110,000
Jewelry	50,000	80,000
Millinery	9,000	4,000

Convert the sales of each department for *last year* to a percent of the total for last year. Portray these percents in the form of a pie chart.

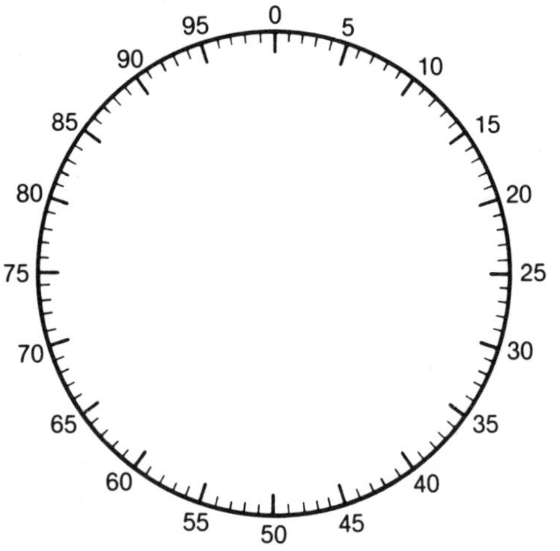

6. Refer to Problem 5. Plot the *percent change* in sales from last year to this year (last year is the base) for each of the five departments in the form of two-directional bar chart.

The percent changes are:

Shoe ______%

Lingerie ______%

Suit ______%

Jewelry ______%

Millinery ______%

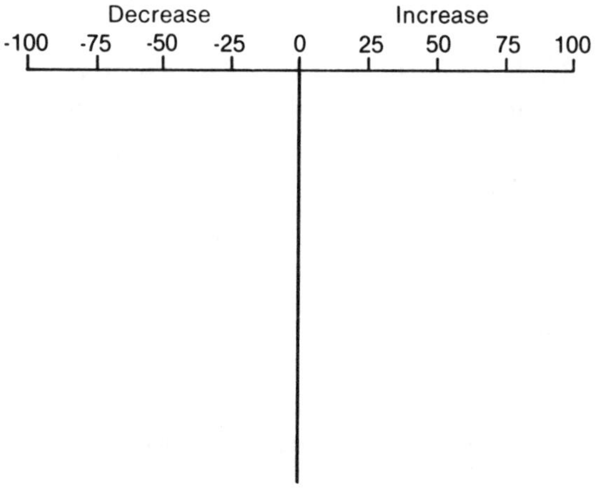

SECTION 19-2: FREQUENCY DISTRIBUTIONS

Objective: To construct a frequency distribution and to draw a histogram and frequency polygon.

FREQUENCY DISTRIBUTION

A large mass of statistical data is difficult to analyze. To organize it into a more understandable form, a **frequency distribution** may be constructed.

Problem

The personnel manager wants to analyze the weekly wages of a group of clerical employees. As a first step, the weekly wages were recorded as follows:

$152.74	$176.66	$162.48	$167.72	$181.09	$172.88	$155.00	$169.60
196.17	182.47	181.69	186.91	190.10	178.59	176.14	192.70
167.27	175.14	160.00	177.46	165.18	165.00	167.77	178.46
185.20	157.02	172.14	192.22	179.40	169.51	191.03	188.87
200.15	178.47	176.33	179.05	180.95	178.45	174.28	175.00
150.10	176.86	187.71	168.33	195.00	182.05	172.37	179.04
186.19	190.05	196.27	209.28	203.16	196.30	168.52	200.00

The data in the table (that is, the weekly wages) is usually referred to as the **raw data.** As such, it has little meaning. It reveals little about the pattern of weekly wages. The solution is to construct a frequency distribution.

Solution

One way of organizing the weekly wages into a frequency distribution is to (1) set up wage **classes,** (2) **tally** the wages into the predetermined classes, and then (3) **count** the tallies.

Note that the lowest wage is $150.10. It was arbitrarily decided to group the weekly wages into classes "$150 but under $160," "$160 but under $170," and so on. The highest wage class is "$200 but under $210," to accommodate the highest weekly wage of $209.28.

The wage in the upper-left corner of the table ($152.74) is placed into the "$150 but under $160" class by using a tally mark (/). The next wage down in the first column ($196.17) is tallied in the "$190 but under $200" class. This process is continued until all the wages are tallied.

1 SELF-REVIEW

A. The last two columns on the right in the table of weekly wages have not been tallied. Tally these wages.

B. Count the tallies in each wage class and record the number of wages in the following distribution.

Weekly Wages	*Tallies*	*No. of Wages*
$150 but under $160	///	______
160 but under 170	𝍸 ///	______
170 but under 180	𝍸 𝍸 //	______
180 but under 190	𝍸 ////	______
190 but under 200	𝍸 //	______
200 but under 210	///	______
Total		______

It should be noted that in presenting a frequency distribution in a publication, such as an annual report, the actual tallies are not shown.

A. *Completed Tallies*	B. *No. of Wages*
////	4
𝍸 𝍸 /	11
𝍸 𝍸 𝍸 ///	18
𝍸 𝍸	10
𝍸 ////	9
////	4
	56

Based on the frequency distribution, the personnel manager can now say that (1) the largest concentration of weekly wages falls in the $170 but under $180 class, (2) over half of the employees have weekly wages between $160 and $190 (actually 39 out of the 56 employees), (3) no employee has a weekly wage under $150, and (4) no employee has a weekly wage of $210 or over.

GRAPHIC PORTRAYAL OF A FREQUENCY DISTRIBUTION

It has been pointed out that a graph is an excellent statistical tool to capture the attention of the reader. Two graphs which may be drawn to bring out the important characteristics of the data in a frequency distribution are the **histogram** and the **frequency polygon.**

A **histogram** is constructed by first scaling the frequencies on the y-axis and the weekly wages on the x-axis. Note in the frequency distribution in Self-Review 1 that four employees had weekly wages between $150 and $160. To plot this, lines are drawn vertically from $150 and from $160 to 4 on the y-axis, as shown in Figure J. The tops of these two lines are then connected.

Next, lines are drawn vertically from $160 and from $170 to 11 on the y-axis. This process is continued until all the data in the frequency distribution is plotted (see Figure K). There is no space between the bars.

FIGURE J

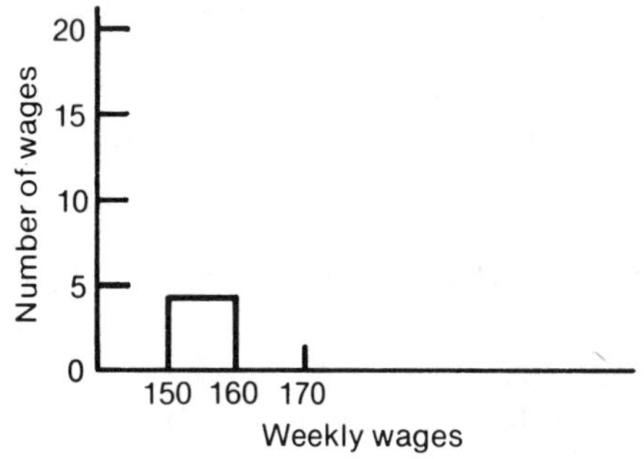

FIGURE K

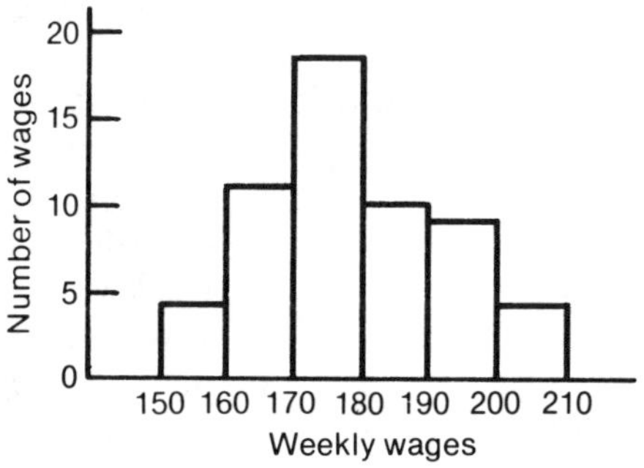

A **frequency polygon** is constructed by scaling the frequencies (number of weekly wages) on the y-axis and the weekly wages on the x-axis. Four employees had wages between $150 and $160. To plot, the **midpoint** of $155 is used to represent that class. Then you would move vertically from $155 on the x-axis to 4 on the y-axis and place a dot (see Figure L).

The next plot is $165 (midpoint of the $160 but under $170 class) and 11. The third plot is $175 and 18, and so on. The dots are connected to form the frequency polygon (see Figure M). As shown, the usual practice is to extend the lower end of the frequency polygon to the midpoint of the class prior to the first class ($145). The upper end is extended to the midpoint of the next higher class ($215).

FIGURE L

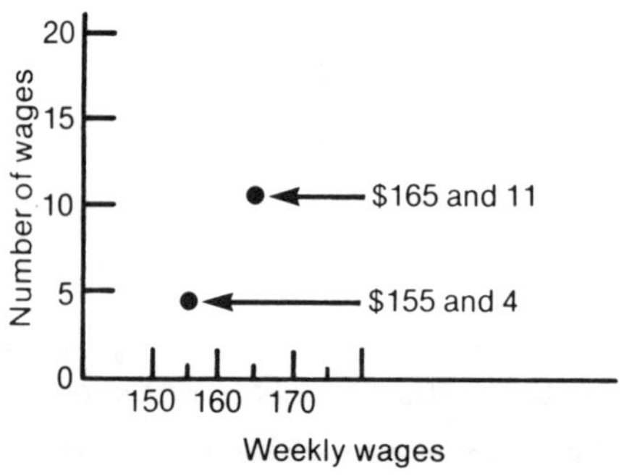

FIGURE M

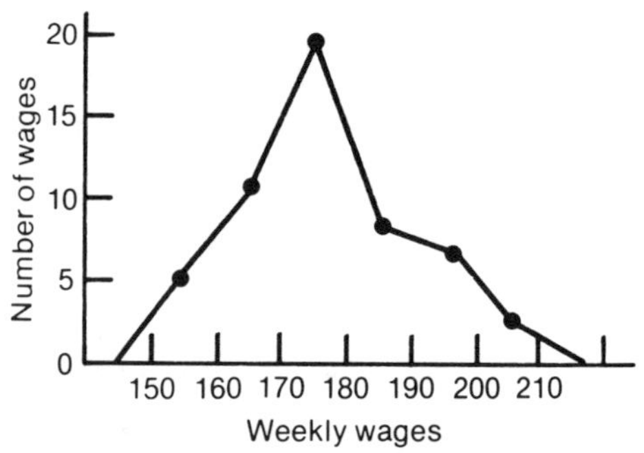

A. Histogram

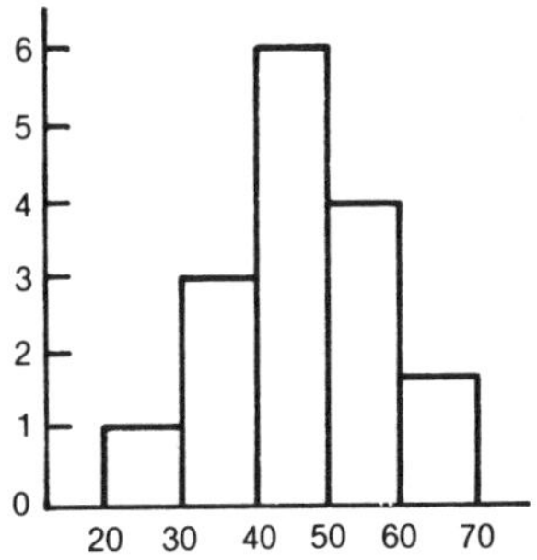

B. Frequency polygon

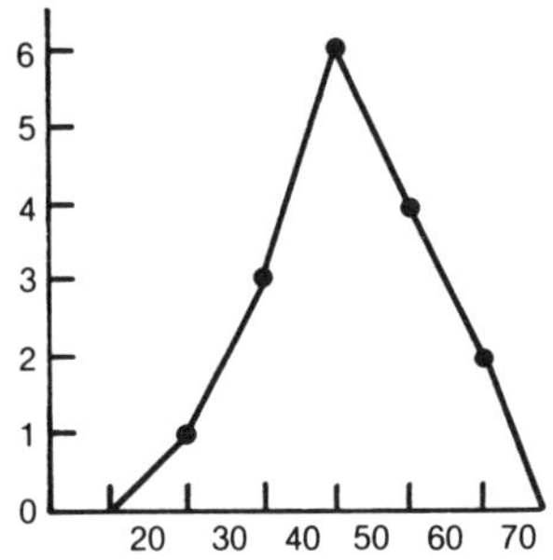

2 SELF-REVIEW

Using the following frequency distribution, plot a histogram and a frequency polygon.

Ages	*No.*
20 up to 30	1
30 up to 40	3
40 up to 50	6
50 up to 60	4
60 up to 70	2

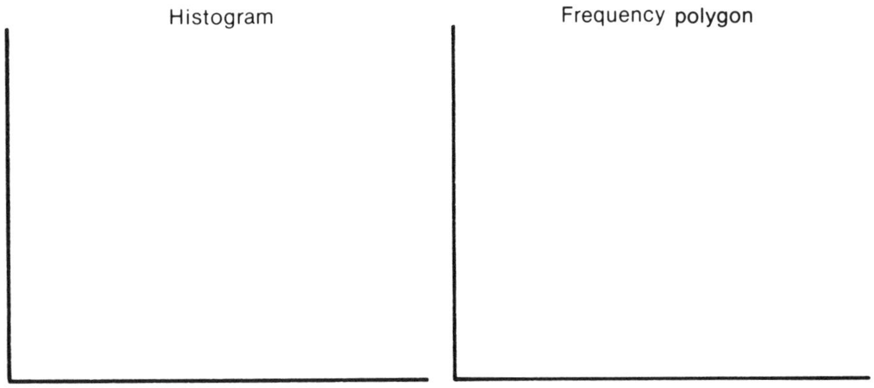

ASSIGNMENT 19-2
FREQUENCY DISTRIBUTIONS

Name ______________________ **Date Due** ______________ **Grade** _____

Problems 1 through 4 are based on the following table of per capita disposable income, by state.

Per Capita Disposable Income, by State

Region and State	*Per Capita Income*	*Region and State*	*Per Capita Income*
New England		Plains	
Connecticut	$8,914	Iowa	$ 7,873
Maine	6,333	Kansas	8,001
Massachusetts	8,063	Minnesota	7,847
New Hampshire	7,277	Missouri	7,342
Rhode Island	7,526	Nebraska	7,391
Vermont	6,541	North Dakota	7,478
Mideast		South Dakota	6,841
Delaware	8,604	Southwest	
Maryland	8,306	Arizona	7,374
New Jersey	8,818	New Mexico	6,505
New York	8,267	Oklahoma	6,951
Pennsylvania	7,733	Texas	7,697
Southeast		Rocky Mountain	
Alabama	6,247	Colorado	8,001
Arkansas	6,183	Idaho	6,813
Florida	7,505	Montana	7,051
Georgia	6,700	Utah	6,622
Kentucky	6,615	Wyoming	9,096
Louisiana	6,640	Far West	
Mississippi	5,736	California	8,850
North Carolina	6,607	Nevada	9,032
South Carolina	6,242	Oregon	7,839
Tennessee	6,489	Washington	8,450
Virginia	7,624	Alaska	10,851
West Virginia	6,456	Hawaii	8,380
Great Lakes		District of Columbia	10,022
Illinois	8,745		
Indiana	7,696		
Michigan	8,442		
Ohio	7,812		
Wisconsin	7,597		

Source: U.S. Department of Commerce, *Survey of Current Business*. April 1979, p. 20.

1. Organize the per capita incomes into a frequency distribution in the following space. Suggestion: Start the distribution with the class "$5,000 but under $6,000."

2. Draw a histogram using the distribution of per capita incomes. Insert essential numbers and label the vertical and horizontal axes.

3. Draw a frequency polygon using the distribution of per capita incomes. Insert essential numbers and label the axes.

4. Using the frequency distribution, histogram, and frequency polygon, interpret the per capita incomes by state.

SECTION 19-3: AVERAGES

Objective: To compute the arithmetic mean and the median.

Averages are probably used more extensively than any other statistical measure. An **average** is a number which represents the central value of a group of numbers. Newspapers, magazines, and other sources reveal such averages as: The federal government reported the average annual salary of a Computer Operator VI is \$16,423. The First Baptist Church in Warren, Pennsylvania, revealed that the average contribution per church member last year was \$208.81. The median age of males in the United States is 27.6 years and of females, 30.0 years.

It's a doubt shared by many young people. Last year, the median price nationally of a used house reached \$47,800 by May. By that time, new houses in Boston had reached \$72,200. Here, in San Diego, Calif., the median price of a used house was \$78,200.

There are many averages, but only two will be considered here: the **arithmetic mean** (usually shortened to just the *mean*), and **median.**

ARITHMETIC MEAN

The mean is no doubt the most widely used of all the averages. It is defined as the *sum of all the values divided by the total number of values.*

$$\text{Mean} = \frac{\text{Sum of all the values}}{\text{Number of values}}$$

From Standard Oil of California:

The Company's overall drilling expense of \$704 million represented an average of \$1,923,000 per well.

In terms of a formula:

$$\bar{X} = \frac{\Sigma X}{n}$$

Where:

$\bar{X}$ (read "X bar," or "bar X") is the designation for the arithmetic mean.

Σ is the symbol for summation. In this case, it directs you to sum all the X values.

X refers to the individual values.

n is the number of values.

Problem Company sales for the first six months of the year were: January, \$6 million; February, \$8 million; March, \$5 million; April, \$6 million; May, \$9 million; and June, \$8 million. What is the arithmetic mean monthly sales?

Solution

$$\text{Mean} = \frac{\text{Sum of all the values}}{\text{Number of values}}$$

$$\bar{X} = \frac{\Sigma X}{n}$$

$$= \frac{\$6 + \$8 + \$5 + \$6 + \$9 + \$8}{6}$$

$$= \frac{\$42}{6}$$

$$= \$7 \text{ (in millions of dollars)}$$

1 SELF-REVIEW

A salesperson had weekly sales of: $2,400, $1,910, $2,150, $2,220, and $2,270. To compute the mean:

$$\text{Mean} = \frac{\text{Sum of all the values}}{\text{Number of values}}$$

In terms of a formula:

______ = ______

= ____

= ____________

= $__________

$$\bar{X} = \frac{\Sigma x}{N}$$

$$= \frac{\$2,400 + \$1,910 + \$2,150 + \$2,220 + \$2,270}{5}$$

$$= \frac{\$10,950}{5}$$

$$= \$2,190$$

MEDIAN

The **median** is another commonly used average. It is defined as the value corresponding to the point on a scale above which are exactly half of the total frequencies and below which are the other half of the total frequencies. It is the middle point of a series of numbers.

Recall that an average is one value which is representative of all the values. There are occasions where the median is more representative than the arithmetic mean. As an illustration, suppose the annual incomes of five junior executives are $20,000, $21,000, $18,000, $23,000, and $200,000. The *arithmetic mean* income is $56,400. It does not seem to be representative of the incomes because practically all of them are in the $18,000 to $23,000 range. Only one is above $23,000.

The median annual income is simply the *midpoint of the values after they have been arranged from the smallest to the largest.*

Using a calculator:

Enter	Press	Display
20000	+	20000
21000	+	41000
18000	+	59000
23000	+	82000
200000	+ ÷	282000
5	=	56400

Problem Determine the median income of the five junior executives.

Solution The midpoint of the values after they have been arranged from the smallest to the largest is $21,000.

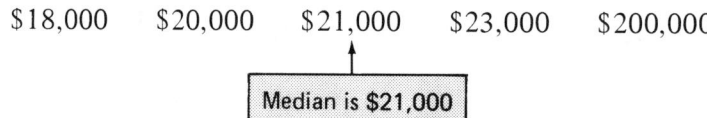

$18,000 $20,000 $21,000 $23,000 $200,000

↑

Median is $21,000

The median income of $21,000 does seem more representative of the incomes of the junior executives than the arithmetic mean of $56,400. This example illustrates one of the weaknesses of the mean, that is, *one extremely high (or low) value results in an unrepresentative average.*

Note in this example that there is an *odd* number of incomes (5). If there is an *even* number of values, the median is the value halfway between the two middle values.

Problem What is the median age of this group of six executives: Juan, 42; Sally, 59; Abe, 48; Jennifer, 62; Bob, 38; and Dean, 46.

Solution As before, the ages are arranged from the lowest to the highest. The median age is 47, which is halfway between the two center values of 46 and 48.

Ages

38 42 46 ↑ 48 59 62

Median is 47

2 SELF-REVIEW

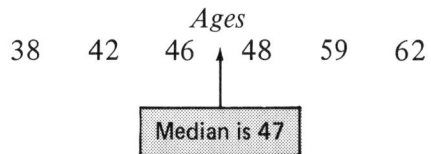

A. A group of retirees has service with the company of 32, 50, 27, 30, 30, 35, and 42 years. What is the median length of service?

______________________________ Median is ________

B. Production of stereo receivers the past eight days was: 3,271, 2,267, 3,196, 3,400, 2,281, 3,240, 3,303, and 3,270. What is the median number of receivers produced per day?

____

Median is __________, found by

A.
27 30 30 32 35 42 50

↑

Median is 32

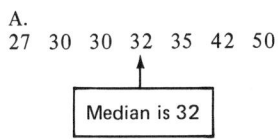

B.
2,267 2,281 3,196 3,240 3,270 3,271 3,303 3,400

Median is 3,255, found by $\frac{3,240 + 3,270}{2}$

ASSIGNMENT 19-3
AVERAGES

Name ______________________ Date Due ____________ Grade _____

Answers to selected problems are given in Appendix B.

For Problems 1 through 6, determine the arithmetic mean.

		Sum	*No. of Values*	*Arithmetic Mean*	
Ex.	Ages: 3, 6, 4, 7, 2	22	5	4.4	years
1.	Weights: 125, 132, 120, 123 pounds	______	____	______	pounds
2.	Tensile strength: 6.3, 9.7, 5.6 psi	______	____	______	psi
3.	Hourly rates: \$6.50, \$7.20, \$4.90, \$8.30, \$7.20	______	____	______	
4.	No. of children: 3, 0, 9, 4, 6, 1, 2, 7, 4, 2	______	____	______	______
5.	Daily production of sofas: 22, 31, 22	______	____	______	______
6.	Air pollution: Monday, 198; Tuesday, 198; Wednesday, 211; Thursday, 163 pph	______	____	______	pph

7. The number of insured persons in the United States who were eligible for unemployment compensation during a 12-month period are given below. Compute the arithmetic mean number and the median number.

Month	*No. Eligible (000)*
January	3,781
February	3,638
March	3,212
April	2,659
May	2,369
June	2,297
July	2,581
August	2,394
September	2,064
October	1,999
November	2,148
December	2,567

Source: U.S. Department of Labor, *Monthly Labor Review*, March 1979, p. 91

A. The arithmetic mean is

______________,

found by

$$\overline{X} = \frac{\Sigma X}{n}$$

= __________

= __________ thousand

B. The median is

____________ thousand,

found by

8. The number of new passenger automobiles sold in the United States for a 12-month period follows. Compute the arithmetic mean and the median.

Month	*No. Sold (000)*
January	687
February	777
March	1,078
April	1,043
May	1,159
June	1,137
July	930
August	958
September	828
October	1,034
November	909
December	769

Source: U.S. Department of Commerce, *Survey of Current Business,* February 1979, p. S-40.

A. The arithmetic mean is

__________, found by

$$\bar{X} = \frac{\Sigma X}{n}$$

= __________

= __________

B. The median number sold is

__________, found by

C. Explain what the median indicates in this problem.

____

____

____

____

9. The wholesale price of 93-score butter on the Chicago exchange for the week of May 14 was: Monday, \$1.2176; Tuesday, \$1.2172; Wednesday, \$1.2181; Thursday, \$1.2180; and Friday, \$1.2180.

A. The arithmetic mean weekly price is \$__________, found by

B. The median price is \$__________, found by

10. What does ΣX direct a person to do? ______________________________

11. The (arithmetic mean/median) __________ should not be used if one of the values is extremely large.

12. The (arithmetic mean/median) __________ is the midpoint of all the values after they have been arranged from low to high.

13. The (arithmetic mean/median) __________ cannot be computed for this data: \$135.00, \$138.56, over \$170.53.

14. Half of the defensive team weigh over 110.1 kilograms. Which average (arithmetic mean/median) is being used? __________

REVIEW ASSIGNMENT FOR CHAPTER 19
THE USE OF STATISTICAL TECHNIQUES IN BUSINESS

Name ______________________ Date Due ______________ Grade ______

1. Portray the average sale price for new one-family houses in the United States in the form of a line chart.

Year	*Average Price*	*Year*	*Average Price*
1971 . . .	$30,700	1976 . . .	$46,400
1972 . . .	32,700	1977 . . .	52,400
1973 . . .	35,600	1978 . . .	56,300
1974 . . .	38,900	1979* . .	59,600
1975 . . .	42,800		

*Estimated
Source: U.S. Department of Commerce, *News,* November 11, 1979 and subsequent issues.

2. Plot the imports into the United States, by quarter (in billions of dollars).

1978	First quarter	$205.8
	Second quarter	210.9
	Third quarter	220.8
	Fourth quarter	229.7
1979	First quarter	237.0

Source: U.S. Department of Commerce, *Survey of Current Business,* May 1979, p. S-1.

3. The investment portfolio of the Wells Fargo Mortgage and Equity Trust includes:

Type of Investment	*Amount Invested*
Apartments	$17,547,000
Industrial properties	14,770,000
Office buildings	6,860,000
Land leased to others . . .	4,467,000
Mobile home parks	1,114,000
Shopping centers	769,000
Total	$45,527,000

Source: Wells Fargo Mortgage and Equity Trust, *Annual Report,* 1978, p. 18.

Convert the amounts invested to percents of the total and plot them in a pie chart.

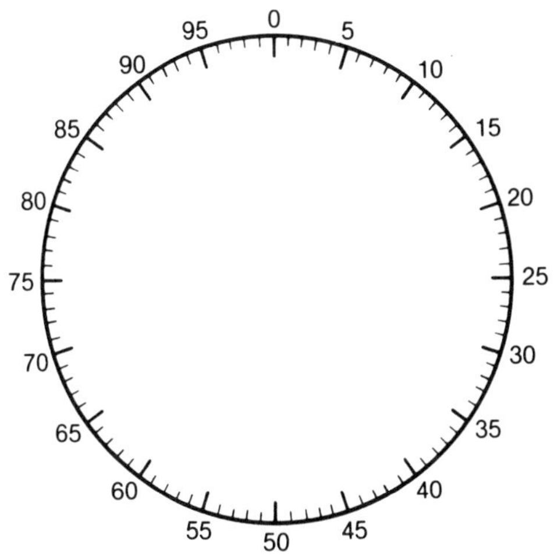

4. Selected items from the statement of consolidated earnings of Merrill Lynch & Co., Inc., are to be portrayed in the form of a two-directional bar chart.

	For the Three Months Ended	
Item	*March 30, 1979*	*March 31, 1978*
Commissions	$131,479,000	$ 90,621,000
Income taxes	101,627,000	51,913,000
Cash	65,908,000	99,817,000
Securities on deposit . .	68,949,000	151,761,000

Source: Merrill Lynch & Co., Inc., *First Quarter Report*, March 30, 1979.

Compute the percent change for each item from March 1978 to March 1979 (1978 is the base). Plot the percents in a two-directional bar chart.

5. A study by Laurette Looney of the grade point averages of a sample of 120 undergraduate students with grade point averages of 1.80 or above revealed the following grade point averages.

2.30	2.81	2.71	2.95	2.25	3.15	2.19	2.22	3.07	3.70
2.18	2.00	2.17	2.16	2.54	2.41	2.87	2.45	3.25	3.79
2.28	2.20	2.39	1.99	2.71	2.22	2.11	2.63	3.49	2.21
3.97	2.41	2.59	2.59	3.18	2.18	2.30	1.81	2.01	2.49
2.45	2.60	2.73	2.72	2.48	2.89	2.49	3.27	2.82	2.00
2.78	3.00	3.89	3.81	2.26	2.12	2.65	3.51	2.21	2.19
2.55	3.40	2.51	2.47	1.89	2.24	3.08	2.01	2.42	2.17
2.32	3.31	2.31	2.47	2.90	2.50	3.33	1.80	3.77	3.43
2.31	3.62	2.24	2.29	2.12	1.88	3.51	2.07	2.61	2.57
1.99	2.51	2.58	2.22	2.36	3.12	2.06	2.22	3.01	1.91
2.18	2.59	2.37	2.97	2.52	3.37	2.85	2.44	3.23	2.76
2.38	4.00	1.97	2.14	2.65	2.22	2.09	2.61	3.42	2.40

Source: Office of Academic Affairs Research, "Grade Inflation at the University of Toledo."

A. Organize the grade point averages into a frequency distribution. Suggestion: make the first class "1.80 but under 2.20."

B. Draw a histogram.

Grade-point averages

C. Using the first column on the left, the arithmetic mean grade point average is ________, and the median grade point average is ________.

TO THE STUDENT: There is a SELF-REVIEW TEST for this chapter in Appendix A, *with answers* in Appendix C.

20

The Metric System

Objective: To use the metric system to determine lengths, volume, weight, and temperature, and to convert between U.S. customery measures and metric.

A BRIEF HISTORY OF MEASUREMENT

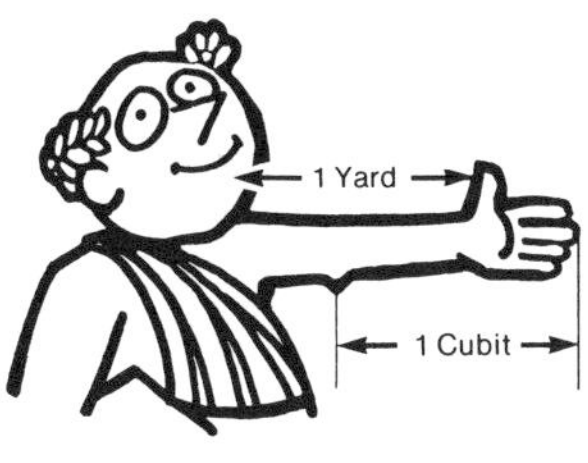

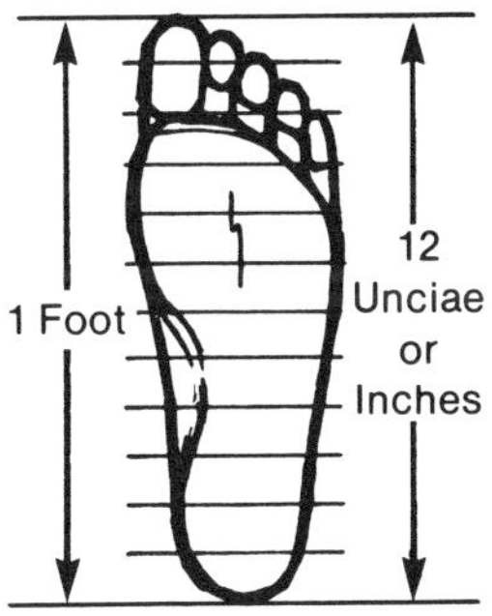

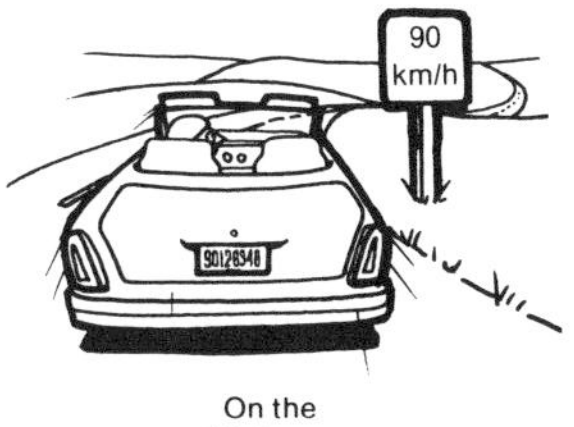

On the Highway

Early units of measurement were related to various parts of the human body. A "cubit" was the length from the elbow to the tip of the middle finger. One definition of a "yard" was the distance from a man's chin to the tip of his thumb. A man's foot was another commonly used measurement unit. The Romans subdivided a foot into 12 unciae, or inches. An inch was defined as the length of a man's thumb from the knuckle to the tip. Two steps of a soldier were considered a "pace," and 1 000 paces a mile. A pound was the weight of a pint of ale.

The English kept refining the accuracy of these measurements, which were the ones brought to America by the colonists. Included were such commonly known measurements as inches, feet, pounds, miles, quarts, pecks, and bushels. They are referred to as the **U.S. customary measurements.**

A French vicar, Gabriel Mouton, proposed a **metric** system in 1670. It was adopted by many European countries, and in 1866 the Congress of the United States recognized it, declaring it legal to use the metric system. It was not, however, made compulsory. A dual system of measurement developed in the United States. U.S. customary measures include milk sold by the quart or gallon, apples counted by the bushel, and distances given in miles. The metric system is used for camera and film sizes, such as 16 millimeter and 35 millimeter. The weight of drugs generally is expressed in milligrams, such as 325 mg Tylenol.

Most countries, encompassing about 90% of the world's population, have adopted the metric system. Great Britain, Canada, Australia, and New Zealand decided in the late 1960s to convert to this system. Finally, in 1971, the U.S. Department of Commerce recommended to Congress that the United States should change to the metric system through "a coordinated national program." The House and Senate passed the Metric Conversion Act in 1975, and the president signed it into law.

The complete conversion to the metric system will take many years to implement. Most firms are moving rapidly to convert; over 50 percent of the worldwide production of the Ford Motor Company already uses metric measurements. Many soft drink bottlers now use the metric measure (liter), and the wine industry has totally converted all bottles to metrics. Temperatures are given in degrees **Celsius** (a metric measurement). Distances are posted in kilometers, and turnpike speed limits will probably be given as 90 kilometers per hour.

METRIC DISTANCES (LENGTHS)

There are seven *base units* of measurement in the International Metric System, abbreviated SI. The base unit for length is the **meter.** A meter is slightly longer than a yard—about 39.37 inches, to be more precise. The symbol for meter is m.

If a meter is subdivided into 10 equal parts, each of these subdivisions is called a **decimeter.** The word "decimeter" is pronounced "dess-i-meter" and is expressed as a symbol as dm. A decimeter is written in decimal form as 0.1 meter. The line segment below is one decimeter in length.

Eleven decimeters extend beyond 1 meter by exactly one-tenth of a meter. It could be written 1.1 meters. Forty-seven decimeters (47 dm) is 4 meters plus seven tenths of a meter, and in decimal form it is written 4.7 meters.

The next smaller subdivision of a meter is called a **centimeter.** There are 100 centimeters to a meter. The prefix "centi" means one hundredth. One centimeter could be written in decimal form as 0.01 meter. The word is pronounced "cent-i-meter" and has the symbol cm. The line segment below is 1 centimeter in length.

35 mm Camera

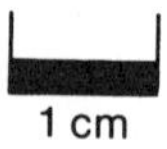

Twenty-three centimeters could be written 23 cm. Since there are 100 centimeters to a meter, 10 centimeters is one tenth of a meter and is written 0.10 meter. Two hundred sixty-one centimeters is 2.61 meters.

The next smaller subdivision of a meter is called a **millimeter.** The prefix "milli" means one thousandth. This means that a millimeter is one thousandth of a meter. There are 10 millimeters to a centimeter. The symbol for a millimeter is mm.

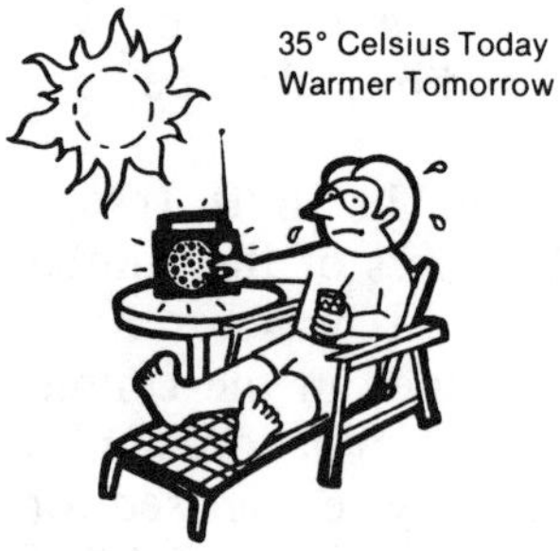

The Weather

The line segment on the left below is 1 millimeter in length. The segment on the right shows 10 mm, or 1 cm.

As an aid in remembering the subdivisions of a meter, you can think of them in the form of a metric staircase, as below.

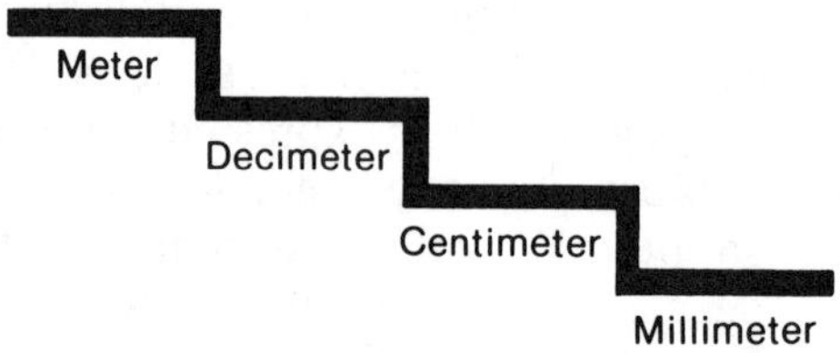

The conversion of one metric unit to another can be accomplished by moving the decimal point of the original unit to the right or left. The procedure is:

Step 1. Locate the original metric unit on one of the steps of the staircase.
Step 2. Count the number of steps to the new desired unit.
Step 3. Move the decimal point of the original unit as many places as steps, in the same left or right direction.
- *a.* When moving *down* the steps, the decimal point must be moved to the right.
- *b.* When moving *up* the steps, the decimal point must be moved to the left.

Problem A shipping crate is 2.50 meters long. Convert 2.50 meters to centimeters.

Solution Refer to the following metric staircase. Centimeters is two steps down (to the right) from meters. Thus, the decimal point must be moved two places to the *right.*

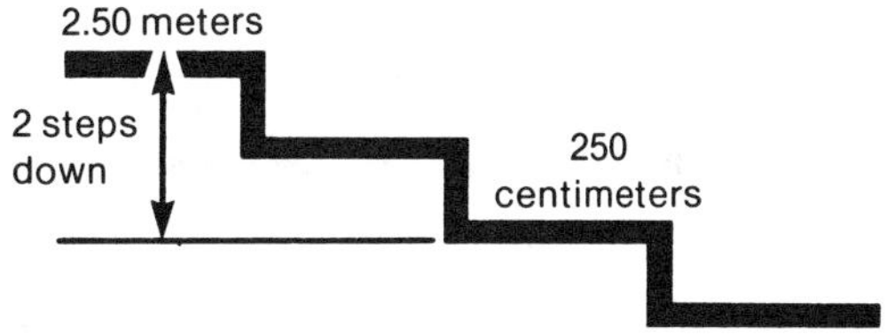

To review, the base unit for measuring distances is the meter. The **decimeter, centimeter,** and **millimeter** are units of measure **smaller** than the **meter.**

The **dekameter, hectometer,** and **kilometer** are units of length *larger* than the meter. Their position on the metric staircase is:

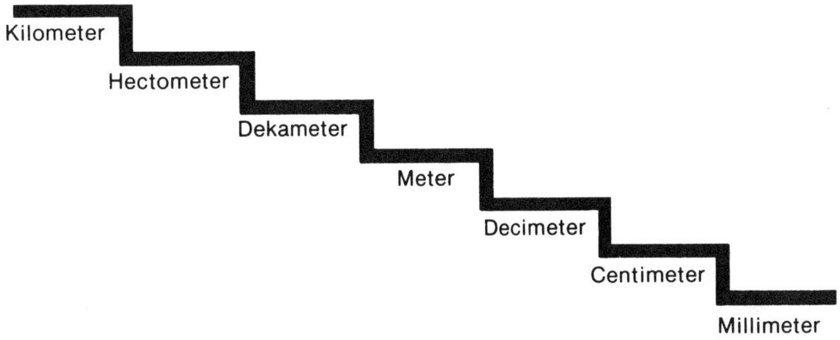

In writing numbers, the digits are separated in groups of three, starting at the decimal point. *Commas are not used.* Instead, a space is left between each group. Examples: 10 000 meters, not 10,000 meters. Note: four-digit numbers may be written either with or without the space. 7695 m or 7 695 m, not 7,695 m.

The dekameter and hectometer are seldom used in measuring long distances. Instead, the **kilometer,** pronounced "kill-o-meter" and expressed as a symbol is km, is the metric unit applied. To convert from meters to kilometers (three steps *up,* that is, left, on the metric staircase), the decimal point is moved three places to the *left.* Thus, 10 000 meters equals 10 kilometers. For reference, a kilometer is less than a mile (about ⅝ of a mile). The distance between New York and Miami is about 2 140 kilometers, and between Chicago and Seattle it is 3 320 km.

1 SELF-REVIEW

A reminder: Cover the answers in the margin.

Answer each of the following either Yes or No. If No, insert the correct answer in the space provided.

A. No. meters, kilometers, milligrams, liters

A. Metric measurements include such commonly known measurements as inches, pounds, miles, and bushels. ______ If No, ______________________________

____

B. Yes

B. A carpenter measured the height of a door in a home to be 2.1 m. Is this measurement logical? ______ If No, ______________________________

C. Yes

C. The carpenter then measured a pine board to be 21 decimeters. Converting to to meters it is 2.1 m. Is the conversion correct? ______ If No, ____________

D. Yes

D. Steel wire thick enough to hold the weight of a person is needed. The purchasing agent ordered steel wire 5.4 mm in diameter. Does this diameter appear to be about right for the job? ______ If No, ______________________________

E. No. 4 700 kilometers

E. The distance between New York and Seattle is about 4 700 meters. _______
If No, ____

VOLUME

The U.S. customary measurements for volume are units such as the pint, quart, gallon, barrel, cubic yard, peck, and bushel. This system for measuring volume is quite confusing because there is one set of measurements for liquid measures (pint, quart, etc.) and another set for dry measures (peck, bushel, etc.). The conversion from one unit to another is rather complicated. For example, how many pints are there in a gallon? How many gallons in a barrel?

The metric system is very simple. The three most commonly used *metric units* for measuring both liquid and dry measures are:

Metric Unit	*Abbreviation*	*Equal to:*	*For Measuring:*
Cubic meter	m^3	1 000 liters	Large-capacity tank cars, grain storage bins, railroad freight cars
Liter	L		Gasoline tanks in automobiles, capacity of milk containers and beer cans
Milliliter	mL	0.001 liters	Capacity of small bottles of medicine, vanilla extract

Capacity of 1 liter

One cubic decimeter

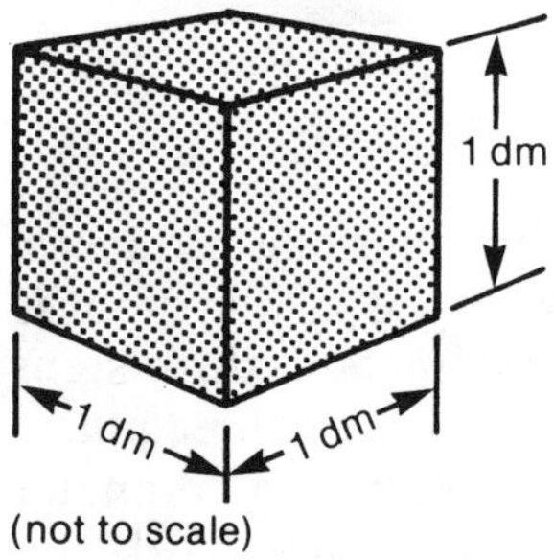

(not to scale)

A plastic container measuring 1 meter by 1 meter by 1 meter has a volume of 1 **cubic meter.** (This is the size container needed to ship a television set.) The volume of a grain bin measuring 8 meters long by 4 meters wide by 3 meters high is found by $V = lwh = 8 \times 4 \times 3 = 96$ cubic meters. A small truck bed measuring 3 m long by 2 m wide by 0.5 m high would hold 3 m^3 of topsoil. This is read as 3 cubic meters.

Because the cubic meter is a rather large unit of volume, it is not very appropriate for measuring the volume of such small items as milk cartons or soda cans, or the capacity of the gasoline tank of an automobile. These are measured in **liters.** The liter, pronounced "lee-ter" is defined as the volume of one cubic decimeter. The symbol for liter is L.

A liter is slightly larger than a quart. Probably milk will eventually be sold in 1-liter, 2-liter, and 4-liter containers.

A **milliliter** is one thousandth of a liter. One milliliter equals 1 cubic centimeter. A very small, empty container about the size of a cube of sugar measuring 1 cm x 1 cm x 1 cm has a capacity of 1 milliliter. The volume of a bottle of rubber cement or cough medicine is expressed in milliliters.

Capacity of 1 milliliter

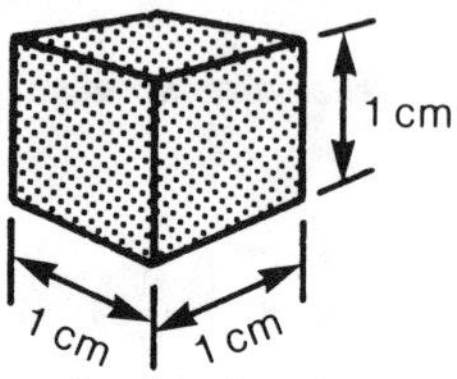

Size of cube of sugar

2 SELF-REVIEW

A. cubic meters

A. Would the capacity of a boxcar of a train be measured in milliliters, cubic meters, centimeters, or kilometers? ________________

B. milliliters

B. Would the capacity of a can of household oil be measured in liters, cubic decimeters, milliliters, or kilometers? ________________

C. liters

C. Would the capacity of a wine bottle be measured in liters, milliliters, cubic meters, or hectometers? ________________

D. 1 cm^3

D. Has a milliliter the same volume as 1 cm^3, 1 m^3, 1 dm^3, or 0.01 L?

E. quart carton

E. Is a liter a measure of volume slightly larger than a water glass, quart carton, coffee cup, or barrel? ______________________

WEIGHT AND MASS

The U.S. customary measurements used to indicate the weight of an object are units such as ounces, pounds, and tons. The metric system does not include the term "weight." Only the "mass" of an object is used. However, in everyday usage the word "weight" carries the same connotation as the metric quantity of mass. In this section, therefore, the two terms will be used interchangeably.

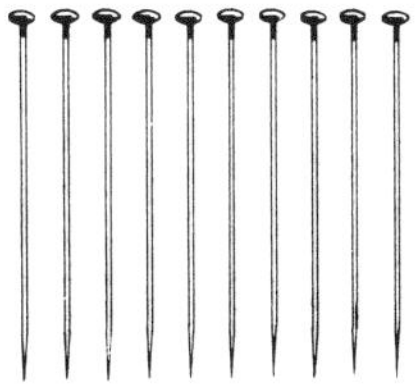

≈1 gram

As a frame of reference, ten ordinary straight pins weigh about 1 gram. A medium-sized paper clip also weighs about 1 gram. A nickel has the mass (weight) of about 5 grams. A size D flashlight battery weighs about 100 grams. A gram symbolized g, is considered to be the weight of one cubic centimeter of distilled water (about 20 drops) at 4 degrees Celsius.

The prefixes for mass units are the same as used previously for length. They include kilo, hecto, deka, deci, centi, and milli. Their relationship is shown in the metric staircase below.

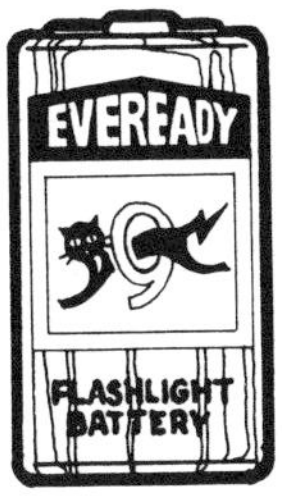

≈100 grams

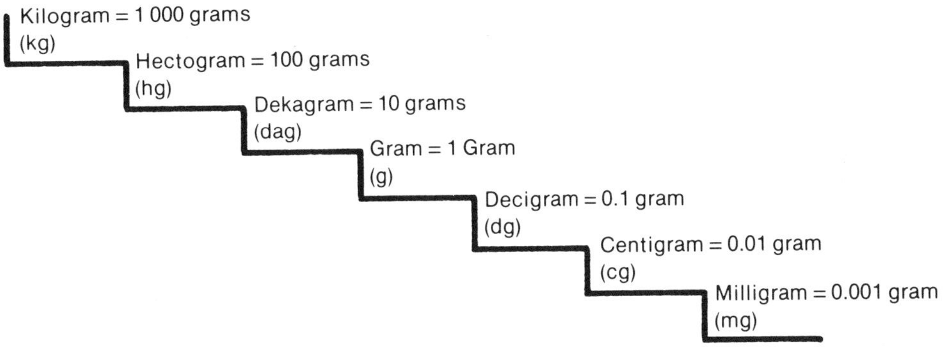

≈1 gram

The same conversion procedure as given for lengths is followed when converting grams to milligrams and kilograms. To convert the weight of a stick of butter given in grams to milligrams, note on the metric staircase that a milligram is three steps *down* (to the right) from a gram. The decimal point is moved *three* places to the right. If the stick of butter weighed 125 grams, the decimal point would be moved three places to the right, to give 125 000 milligrams.

The metric system also uses a unit known as the **metric ton**, sometimes referred to as **tonnes.** Its symbol is t. It is used to give the weight of very heavy items, such as cars, trucks, and machinery. A metric ton is equal to 1 000 kilograms. An automobile manufacturer might list the metric weight of a pickup truck as 2 162 kilograms, or 2.162 metric tons.

Four of the most commonly used metric measurements for mass (weight) are the **milligram** (mg), the **gram** (g), the **kilogram** (kg), and the **metric ton** (t). The milligram and gram are applied extensively in medicine and drugs. The kilogram is used to show the weight of such items as soap powder, butter, meat, the weight of persons, and the shipping weight of appliances. A truckload of canned goods or a railroad car loaded with coal may be given in metric tons.

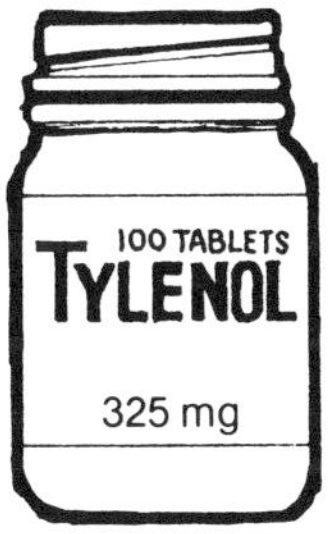

Pain reliever

3 SELF-REVIEW

A. 0.325 g

A. The weight of the 325-milligram bottle of Tylenol converted to grams is __________ g.

B. State which of the four commonly used metric measures would be applied to measure the weight of the following items:

B. (1) kilogram
(2) kilogram
(3) milligram
(4) metric ton

(1) A television set. ____________

(2) A professional football player. ____________

(3) An aspirin tablet. ____________

(4) A truck loaded with steel bars. ____________

TEMPERATURE

A weather forecaster might well say, "The high temperature for this beautiful spring day was 22 degrees Celsius." The degree Celsius (°C) is the unit used in the metric system to measure temperature. It was named after its originator, Anders Celsius of Sweden, who developed it in the mid-1700s. Several important temperatures on the degree Celsius scale are shown in the illustration of a Celsius thermometer. It depicts the differences between the familiar Fahrenheit (°F) thermometer (on the left) and the Celsius (°C) thermometer (on the right).

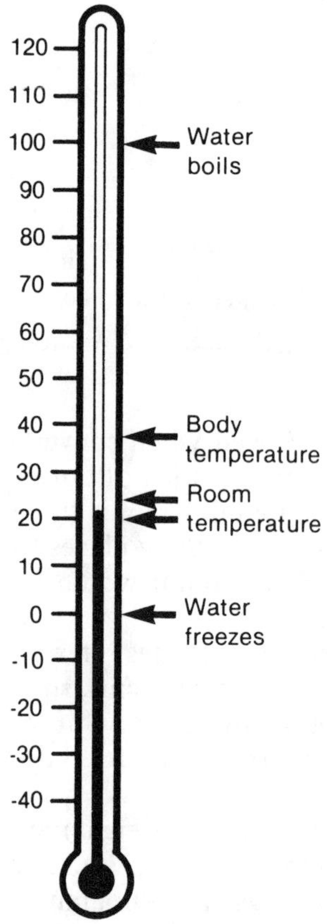

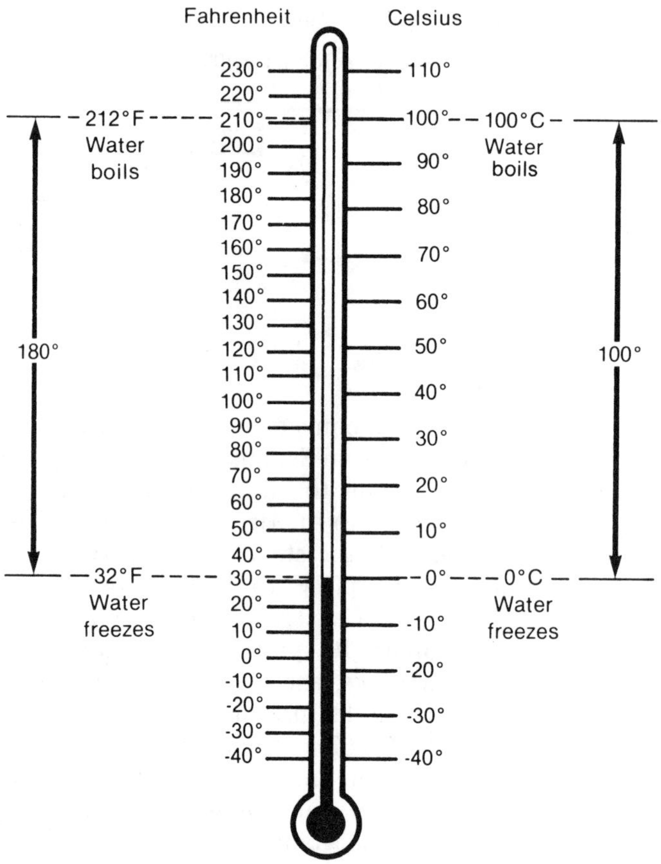

CONVERSIONS: METRIC TO U.S. CUSTOMARY AND U.S. CUSTOMARY TO METRIC

The time period for changing to metric units and away from U.S. customary units will undoubtedly last several years. Hence it will be necessary to convert units of measurement from one system to the other. The conversion can be either approximate or exact, depending on the accuracy of the conversion factor. For example, to convert from liters to quarts, an approximate conversion factor of 1.06 may be used. The exact factor is 1.056 688. A table of *approximate* conversion factors follows.

A few comparative temperatures:

°F	°C	Condition
500	260	Hot kitchen oven
350	177	Moderate kitchen oven
225	107	Low kitchen oven
212	100	Water boils
118	48	Highest temperature on record in Phoenix, Ariz.
72	22	Pleasant day; comfortable room temperature
45	7	Rather chilly
32	0	Water freezes; cold outdoors
0	−18	Bitter cold outdoors
−44	−42	Extremely cold. Lowest recorded in Bismark, N.D.

METRIC CONVERSION CARD

Approximate Conversions to Metric Measures

Symbol	When You Know	Multiply by	To Find	Symbol
		LENGTH		
in	inches	2.5	centimeters	cm
ft	feet	30	centimeters	cm
yd	yards	0.9	meters	m
mi	miles	1.6	kilometers	km
		AREA		
in^2	square inches	6.5	square centimeters	cm^2
ft^2	square feet	0.09	square meters	m^2
yd^2	square yards	0.8	square meters	m^2
mi^2	square miles	2.6	square kilometers	km^2
	acres	0.4	hectares	ha
		MASS (weight)		
oz	ounces	28	grams	g
lb	pounds	0.45	kilograms	kg
	short tons (2000 lb)	0.9	metric ton	t
		VOLUME		
tsp	teaspoons	5	milliliters	mL
Tbsp	tablespoons	15	milliliters	mL
in^3	cubic inches	16	milliliters	mL
fl oz	fluid ounces	30	milliliters	mL
c	cups	0.24	liters	L
pt	pints	0.47	liters	L
qt	quarts	0.95	liters	L
gal	gallons	3.8	liters	L
ft^3	cubic feet	0.03	cubic meters	m^3
yd^3	cubic yards	0.76	cubic meters	m^3
		TEMPERATURE (exact)		
°F	degrees Fahrenheit	5/9 (after subtracting 32)	degrees Celsius	°C

Approximate Conversions from Metric Measures

Symbol	When You Know	Multiply by	To Find	Symbol
		LENGTH		
mm	millimeters	0.04	inches	in
cm	centimeters	0.4	inches	in
m	meters	3.3	feet	ft
m	meters	1.1	yards	yd
km	kilometers	0.6	miles	mi
		AREA		
cm^2	square centimeters	0.16	square inches	in^2
m^2	square meters	1.2	square yards	yd^2
km^2	square kilometers	0.4	square miles	mi^2
ha	hectares (10 000 m^2)	2.5	acres	
		MASS (weight)		
g	grams	0.035	ounces	oz
kg	kilograms	2.2	pounds	lb
t	metric ton (1000 kg)	1.1	short tons	
		VOLUME		
mL	milliliters	0.03	fluid ounces	fl oz
mL	milliliters	0.06	cubic inches	in^3
L	liters	2.1	pints	pt
L	liters	1.06	quarts	qt
L	liters	0.26	gallons	gal
m^3	cubic meters	35	cubic feet	ft^3
m^3	cubic meters	1.3	cubic yards	yd^3
		TEMPERATURE (exact)		
°C	degrees Celsius	9/5 (then add 32)	degrees Fahrenheit	F

Source: U.S. Department of Commerce, National Bureau of Standards Special Publication 365 (Washington, D.C., May 1976).

Problems A. Convert 115 kilograms to pounds. B. Convert 3 miles to kilometers.

Solutions

	Known		*Multiply by*		
A.	115 kilograms	×	2.2	=	253 lbs.
B.	3 miles	×	1.6	=	4.8 kilometers

4 SELF-REVIEW

A. An apprentice carpenter wants to convert 7 m to feet. It is ________ feet, found by

B. The highway department wants to post the equivalent of 25 miles in kilometers. It is _______ km, found by

C. The *Pillsbury Family Cook Book* includes a recipe for pecan kisses which calls for an oven temperature of 275° F. Converted to °C, the oven setting would be _______ °C, found by

A. 24.1 feet, found by 7×3.3

B. 40 km, found by 25×1.6

C. 135°C, found by $\frac{5}{9}(275 - 32)$

D. 3.9 gal., found by 15×0.26

D. The volume of bottles shipped from Europe is given in liters. The importer wants to stamp the U.S. customary equivalent in gallons on each bottle. The bottles are marked 15 liters. Converted, it is _______ gallons, found by

ASSIGNMENT 20-1
THE METRIC SYSTEM

Name ______________________ Date Due ____________ Grade _____

For Problems 1 through 6, convert between U.S. customary and metric measurements.

	Known	*Convert to:*	*Answer*		*Found by:*
Ex.	68 degrees Fahrenheit	Degrees Celsius	20° C		$\frac{5}{9}(68 - 32)$
1.	26 millimeters	Inches	________	in.	________________
2.	7 meters	Feet	________	ft.	________________
3.	8 inches	Centimeters	________	cm	________________
4.	7 pounds	Kilograms	________	_____	________________
5.	6 cups	Liters	________	_____	________________
6.	30 degrees Celsius	Fahrenheit	________	_____	________________

For Problems 7 through 12, fill in the blanks.

7. The basic metric unit for distances (lengths) is the ____________.

8. In the correct order, the subdivisions smaller than a meter are ______________, ______________, and ______________.

9. A rug measures 2.9 m by 1.6 m. Converted to decimeters, it is ______ dm by ______ dm., found by

10. 2.1 kilometers is the same as ________ meters.

11. Note on the following drawing that the numbers are in centimeters.

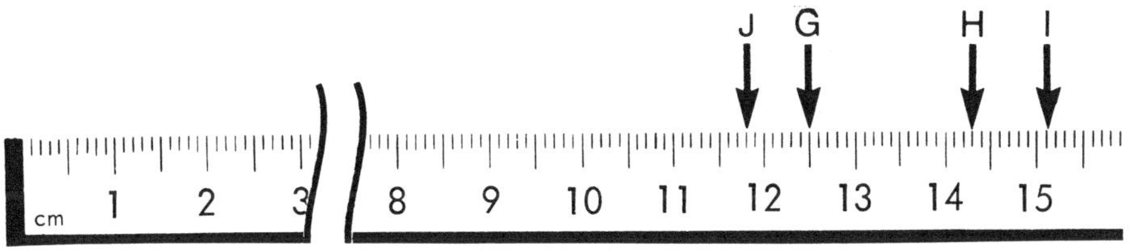

Point H is read ______ mm = ________ cm = ________ dm = _________ m.

Point I is read 0.151 meters = ________ decimeters = _________ centimeters, equals ________ millimeters.

12. A swimming pool is 8 meters long, 4 meters wide, and 2 meters deep.

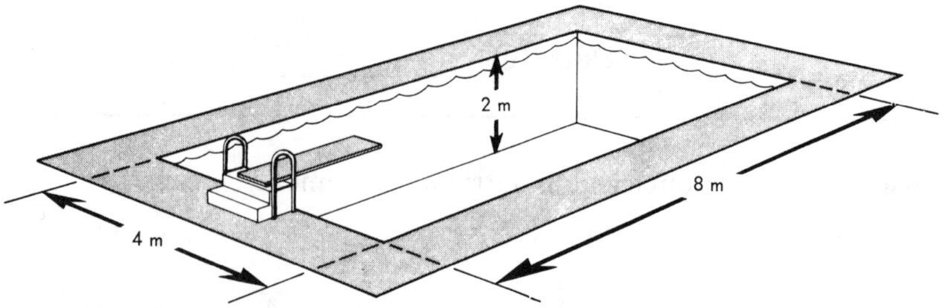

The contractor who designed the pool will need _____ cubic meters of water to fill it, found by

For Problems 13 through 18, circle the *larger* amount or *higher* temperature in each pair of figures.

13. 10 mg or 5 g

14. 2.7 t or 1 500 kg

15. 120 mm or 2 km

16. 20°C or 60°F

17. 350°F or 250°C

18. 2 L or 2 quarts

For Problems 19 through 25: Multiple choice. Insert the *letter* in front of the correct answer in the space provided.

19. ____ A meter is about how many yards: (a) 0.0001 (b) 0.01 (c) 1.1 (d) 11.5 (e) 1 000

20. ____ Converted, a mile is about how many kilometers? (a) 1.6 (b) 16 (c) 1 000 (d) 10 000

21. ____ A temperature change of 9°F is equivalent to a change of how many degrees on the Celsius scale? (a) 1 000 (b) 5 (c) 9 (d) 1.6 (e) 0.95

22. ____ 22 decimeters converted to millimeters is (a) 220 mm (b) 22 mm (c) 2.2 mm (d) 0.22 mm (e) 2 200 mm

23. ____ The distance between New York and Dallas is about: (a) 2 586 t (b) 2 586 m (c) 2 586 km (d) 2 586 dm (e) 2 586 cm

24. ____ The metric base unit of length is the (a) kilogram (b) meter (c) degree Celsius (d) cubic meter (e) tonne

25. ____ The length of a football field, excluding the end zones, is about: (a) 91 meters (b) 110 meters (c) 31 kilometers (d) 180 millimeters (d) 52 tonnes

TO THE STUDENT: There is a SELF-REVIEW TEST for this chapter in Appendix A, *with answers* in Appendix C.

appendix A

Self-Review Tests for All Chapters

SELF-REVIEW TEST
Chapter 1: A Brief Review of Basic Computations

Do all the problems. Then check your answers against those given in Appendix C. Score each problem 10 points.

1. $54\frac{3}{8} + \frac{1}{4} =$ ________

2. $14.3 \times 0.71 =$ ____________

3. $17\frac{1}{4} - \frac{3}{8} =$ ________

4. $16{,}827 \div 213 =$ ____________

5. If a loan is paid off by making 24 monthly payments of $112.91 each, how much is paid back?

   $______________, found by

6. *The New York Times* reports that gold is selling for $899.05 per ounce. To the nearest hundredth ounce, how many ounces could be purchased for $427,503.66?

   ______________ ounces, found by

7. Complete A to E.

PLEASE BE SURE TO **DEDUCT** ANY PER CHECK CHARGES OR SERVICE CHARGES THAT MAY APPLY TO YOUR ACCOUNT

CHECK NO.	DATE	CHECKS ISSUED TO OR DESCRIPTION OF DEPOSIT	(−) AMOUNT OF CHECK	✓ T	(−) CHECK FEE (IF ANY)	(+) AMOUNT OF DEPOSIT	BALANCE
							146 91
—	10/11	DEPOSIT				50 00	(A) ______
176	10/12	The Gas Company	34 73				(B) ______
177	10/12	The Phone Company	17 81				(C) ______
—	10/18	DEPOSIT				50 00	(D) ______
178	10/23	World-Wide Travel	75 00				(E) ______
179	10/23	CASH	25 00				94 37

8. The net changes in the price of a share of seven stocks listed on the New York Stock Exchange during a week were:

Stock	*Change*	*Stock*	*Change*
IBM	$+2\frac{3}{4}$	Bassett	$+2\frac{3}{4}$
Xerox	$+1$	NCR	$-\frac{1}{2}$
O-I	$-6\frac{1}{4}$	RCA	$+\frac{3}{8}$
Standard Oil, Ind.	$-2\frac{3}{8}$	U.S. Steel	$-\frac{1}{2}$

The total net change is: _______, found by

9. The produce manager at Winn-Dixie earns $6 an hour for all "regular" hours worked and $9 an hour for all overtime hours worked. For the week of February 2, she worked:

Day	*Regular Hours*	*Overtime Hours*
Monday	8	2
Tuesday	8	4¼
Wednesday	8	0
Thursday	8	1
Friday	8	½
Saturday	4	0

The total amount earned during the week of February 2 is:

$____________, found by

10. How much will be saved over the regular price if six pairs of toddler thermal underwear are purchased at the sale price?

$__________, found by

Sale! Toddler
Thermal Underwear
Reg. 3.00
Now 2/$5
Toddler bottom in solid white or pink/blue print. Sizes 2-4. INFANTS.

SELF-REVIEW TEST
Chapter 2: Percents

Do all the problems. Then check your answers against those given in Appendix C. Score each problem 10 points.

1. Convert 22.3% to its decimal equivalent. __________

2. Convert 0.7613 to its percent equivalent. __________%

3. Convert $\frac{19}{25}$ to its percent equivalent. __________%

4. Convert $\frac{5}{7}$ to its:

   A. Decimal equivalent (nearest ten-thousandth). __________

   B. Percent equivalent (nearest whole percent). __________

5. Convert $17\frac{4}{9}\%$ to:

   A. Its decimal equivalent (nearest thousandth). __________

   B. Its fraction equivalent. __________

6. Convert the given percents to their decimal equivalents and to their fraction equivalents.

   A. 30%

   Decimal ______ Fraction __________

   B. 50%

   Decimal ______ Fraction __________

   C. 70%

   Decimal ______ Fraction __________

7. *Esquire* reported on a resolution submitted to the House of Representatives which states that 92% of the traffic on the Colorado River through the Grand Canyon National Park is commercial. Convert this percent to its:

   A. Decimal equivalent. ______

   B. Fraction equivalent (reduced to lowest terms). ______

8. The Andersons had a clearance sale with everything marked "$\frac{1}{3}$ Off." Express this fraction as a:

   A. Decimal (nearest thousandth). __________

   B. Percent (nearest hundredth). __________%

9. Rod Carew had a batting average of 0.381. Express this as a:

   A. Percent. __________%

   B. Fraction. __________

10. What is the difference between $5\frac{1}{2}\%$ and $\frac{1}{20}$?

    ____

SELF-REVIEW TEST
Chapter 3: Percentages

Do all the problems. Then check your answers against those given in Appendix C. Score each problem 10 points.

1. If 6.13% of your gross pay is withheld for social security purposes and your gross pay is $215.75, what amount is withheld for social security purposes (nearest cent)?

   $__________, found by

2. Montgomery Ward is offering a savings of $6.39 on its 36-month OEE Riverside automobile battery. The regular price is $25.49. What is the percent discount (nearest percent)?

   ______%, found by

3. A Firestone Deluxe Champion 4-ply polyester cord, size 875-15 whitewall tire is on sale for $29.82, including the federal excise tax of 5%. What was the price of the tire without the federal excise tax (nearest cent)?

   $__________, found by

4. During the census years 1960 and 1970, the population of Alaska increased from 226,000 to 300,000. What was the percent increase (nearest percent)?

   ______%, found by

5. Lady Pepperell no-iron sheets are regularly priced at $6 each. For its January white sale, the Lion Store has them at two for $6.88. Based on the regular price, what would be the percent savings on two sheets (nearest percent)?

   ______%, found by

6. The *London Sunday Times* reporting on the Seaspeed Hovercraft commented on the results of extra space. Compare the percent increase in passenger capacity to the percent increase in car capacity.

   > The extra space has been achieved by inserting a £55ft. section into the middle of the traditional craft, increasing the capacity from 250 passengers to 400, and from 30 cars to 60.

   A. Passenger ______________%, found by

   B. Car ______________%, found by

   Comparison ______________________________

7. The *Chicago Tribune's* Jon Van writes on "the fat of the land." To the nearest tenth percent, what percent of the total overweight pounds is accounted for:

   > Federal figures show that Americans are a cumulative 2.3 billion pounds overweight, with men accounting for 800 million pounds of extra fat and women supplying 1.5 billion pounds, writes Hannon in the August issue of the American Journal of Public Health.

   A. By men? _______%, found by

   B. By women? _______%, found by

8. What is the percent reduction in the price of this $1,495 organ offered by Goodman Music Centers, as advertised in the *Dallas Morning News* (nearest percent)?

_______%, found by

WOULD YOU LIKE TO BUY A
$1,495.00 ORGAN*
FOR ONLY
$399
*WITH A $50 MUSIC COURSE GUARANTEED TO HELP YOU PLAY

9. *Time* reports: "On 215 occasions since the end of World War II the U.S. has seriously threatened to unleash some of its military might—from a single warship to a nuclear strike force—in order to gain diplomatic leverage. Ground combat units were involved in 20% of the incidents." On how many occasions were ground combat units involved?

_______ occasions, found by

10. Several years ago Rupert Murdoch of Australia purchased Carter Bordon's 23.8% interest in the New York Magazine Company for $3.55 million *(Newsweek).* At that rate, what would total ownership have cost him (nearest tenth of a million)?

$_______ million, found by

SELF-REVIEW TEST
Chapter 4: Consumer Spending

Do all the problems. Then check your answers against those given in Appendix C. Score each problem 10 points.

1. Find the unit price for the name and address labels advertised at the right.

   $__________ per label, found by

2. IGA supermarkets were selling General Mills Lucky Charms in the sizes and prices shown. Based on unit price, which was the best buy?

   A. 20-ounce: $1.87
   $__________ per ______, found by

   B. 14-ounce: $1.35
   $__________ per ______, found by

   C. 9-ounce: $0.95
   $__________ per ______, found by

   Best buy: ____________________

3. Five-Star supermarkets were selling Frank's Red Hot Sauce in the sizes and prices shown. Based on unit price, which was the better buy?

   A. 2½-ounce: $0.29
   $__________ per ______, found by

   B. 4½-ounce: $0.45
   $__________ per ______, found by

   Best buy: ____________________

4. In one year Teresa Appel drove her automobile 11,000 miles. Her annual auto insurance premium was $215. She calculated the depreciation cost to be $550 a year. License fees cost her $32. Her car gets 22 miles per gallon, and gasoline was 84.9 cents per gallon that year. Maintenance cost her $210 that year. The next year, Teresa drove her car 8,800 miles. Her fixed costs stayed the same. Gasoline that year cost 87.9 cents per gallon, and her maintenance costs were $187.

   A. What was her cost per mile the year she drove 11,000 miles? $__________, found by

   B. What was her cost per mile the year she drove 8,800 miles? $__________, found by

5. The Bob Watkins family rented a full-sized station wagon to move their son and his clothing, hi-fi set, and so on to college. The rental rate was $27.95 per day, plus 19 cents per mile, plus the cost of gasoline. The trip took the Watkins three days and covered 220 miles. The gasoline cost $18.12.

   A. What did renting the station wagon cost the Watkins?
   $__________, found by

   B. What was the cost per mile?
   $__________, found by

   C. What was the cost per day?
   $__________, found by

6. The Amtrak coach rate between Denver and Philadelphia is

$____________.

The distance between Denver and Philadelphia is 1,770 miles. What is the cost per mile?

$____________, found by

BETWEEN AND	NEW YORK via	NEW YORK Coach	NEW YORK Roomette	PHILADELPHIA via	PHILADELPHIA Coach	PHILADELPHIA Roomette
		$	$		$	$
Atlanta	—	67.50	111.40	—	59.00	98.65
Boston	—	19.50	s27.50	—	28.00	s40.00
Buffalo	—	33.00	s49.50	N	42.50	s65.25
Chicago	—	58.00	107.00	—	49.50	93.50
Cincinnati	W	57.50	p103.50	W	49.00	p90.75
Cleveland	—	42.50	74.00	N	52.00	p89.75
Dallas/Ft. Worth	OK	117.50	201.50	OK	112.50	192.50
Denver	C	130.00	218.50	C	121.50	205.00
Detroit	—	51.00	95.50	N	60.50	—
Fresno	CG	197.00	t325.00	CG	188.50	t311.50

7. The one-way fare on the Queen Elizabeth II from New York City to Southampton varies with the type of accommodations desired. The Queen Mary or Queen Elizabeth suite fare is $13,080 in the high season. An inside room, bed and upper, shower and toilet, costs $895 in the high season. It is approximately 3,900 miles between New York City and Southampton.

A. What is the cost per mile in the Queen Mary suite?

$____________, found by

B. What is the cost per mile in the inside room, bed and upper, shower and toilet?

$____________, found by

8. Pat and Jerry Northside are considering the purchase of a $48,000 home. Their biweekly (26 times a year) net pay is $1,150. They do not want to spend more than 35% of their net annual pay for housing. They have estimated their housing expenses to be: 11% mortgage payment, $457.12; annual insurance premium, $219.00; semiannual real estate taxes, $600.00; utilities, $1,475.00 annually; and maintenance, $800.00 annually. Should the Northsides buy the $48,000 home?

__________________ Why or why not? __________________

____

9. Pat and Jerry Northside and their two children have an annual net income of $29,900. Using the expense categories and percents in Table 4-3 (in Chapter 4), determine their monthly budget allocation for food, housing, and so on.

Food ____________

Housing ____________

____________ ____________

____________ ____________

____________ ____________

____________ ____________

____________ ____________

10. The Northside family of four (Problems 8 and 9) maintained a record of their expenditures for September and October. Analyze their budget with reference to Table 4-3.

Item	*Monthly Budget (Problem 9)*	*Actual for Sept.*	*Difference*	*Actual for Oct.*	*Difference*	*Two Months Combined*
Food	________	$670	________	$680	________	________
Housing	________	765	________	765	________	________
Transportation	________	240	________	245	________	________
Clothing	________	300	________	310	________	________
Medical	________	120	________	125	________	________
Gifts	________	190	________	212	________	________
Other	________	147	________	154	________	________
Totals			________		________	________

Are they spending over or under their budget? ________________________

Any suggestions? ____

____

SELF-REVIEW TEST
Chapter 5: Consumer Credit—Charge Accounts

Do all the problems. Then check your answers against those given in Appendix C. Score each problem 20 points.

For Problems 1 through 4, the finance charge is calculated using a monthly periodic rate of 2% of the first $200 and 1.5% on the portion over $200. The transactions are:

April 1	Previous balance	$235.00
April 6	Purchase	32.00
April 21	Payment	50.00
April 26	Purchase	20.00

If the "Highest New Balance" is:	The Minimum Monthly Payment will be:	If the "Highest New Balance" is:	The Minimum Monthly Payment will be:
$ .01 to $ 5.00	Balance	$240.01 to $280.00	$12.00
5.01 to 100.00	$ 5.00	280.01 to 320.00	13.00
100.01 to 120.00	6.00	320.01 to 360.00	14.00
120.01 to 140.00	7.00	360.01 to 400.00	15.00
140.01 to 160.00	8.00	400.01 to 440.00	16.00
160.01 to 180.00	9.00	440.01 to 470.00	17.00
180.01 to 200.00	10.00	470.01 to 500.00	18.00
200.01 to 240.00	11.00	Over $500.00,	1/28 of Highest Account Balance rounded to the next higher whole dollar amount.

1. Using the previous-balance method, as of May 1 find the:

   A. Previous balance

   $__________, found by

   B. Finance charge

   $__________, found by

   C. New balance

   $__________, found by

   D. Minimum payment

   $__________, found by

2. Using the adjusted-balance method, as of May 1 find the:

   A. Adjusted balance

   $__________, found by

   B. Finance charge

   $__________, found by

   C. New balance

   $__________, found by

   D. Minimum payment

   $__________, found by

3. Using the average daily balance—no new purchases included method, as of May 1 find the:

A. Average daily balance

$______________, found by

B. Finance charge

$______________, found by

C. New balance

$______________, found by

D. Minimum payment

$______________, found by

4. Using the average daily balance—new purchases included method, as of May 1 find the:

A. Average daily balance

$______________, found by

B. Finance charge

$______________, found by

C. New balance

$______________, found by

D. Minimum payment

$______________, found by

5. For the following Master Charge statement find the:

A. New balance for purchases, $______________, found by

B. New balance for cash advances, $______________, found by

C. New balance for totals, $______________, found by

	Previous Balance	Payments	Credits	New Debits Purchases/Advances	FINANCE CHARGES	New Balance
Purchases	153.81	15.00	8.79	77.71	2.79	(A)
Cash Advances	100.00	10.00			1.13	(B)
Totals	253.81	25.00	8.79	77.71	3.92	(C)

SELF-REVIEW TEST
Chapter 6: Consumer Credit—Installment Credit

Do all the problems. Then check your answers against those in Appendix C. Score each problem 10 points.

1. A community college student purchased a Volkswagen Rabbit priced at $4,900 with $900 as a down payment. The remainder was financed at 9% add-on interest for two years. What is the finance charge?

   $______________, found by

2. What monthly payment is required to pay off a $3,000 home improvement loan for five years at 8% add-on interest?

   $______________, found by

3. A '74 Torino wagon is for sale at $1,297. With a $46 down payment, 36-month financing is available at 10.8% add-on interest What will be the amount of the monthly payment?

   $______________, found by

4. A high school student purchased a Garelli Moped for $402.50. After a down payment of $102.50, the remainder was financed at $27 per month for 12 months. What is the annual percentage rate? (Use Table 6-1.)

   ______________%, found by

5. A used Ford is on sale at Walt Pierce's Buick-Opel used car lot for $3,779.23, including tax, title, and registration. After a down payment of $1,566, the remainder is financed at 9% add-on interest for 18 months. What is the annual percentage rate? (Use Table 6-1.)

   ______________%, found by

6. What does it cost (finance charge) to borrow $1,000 for six months at 10% add-on interest?

   $______________, found by

7. City Loan will finance a $400 home insulation loan for four years at 6% add-on interest. What is each monthly payment?

$______________, found by

8. An 18-month loan of $750 is paid off with the 12th payment, and the Rule of 78 applies. The monthly payment is $45.73. How much is saved in unearned finance charge?

$______________, found by

9. The Monza Towne Coupe is paid off with the 48th payment, and the Rule of 78 applies. What final payment is required?

$______________, found by

MONZA TOWNE COUPE Sale Price **$3651**

$300 down **$75.44 per month**

Based on annual percentage rate 12.50 for 60 months

15 OTHERS TO CHOOSE FROM

10. You are shopping around for the financing of a new car. You need to finance $5,000. By comparing the finance charges and the annual percentage rates, where should you get the financing, and why? (Use Table 6-1.)

A. Trust National Bank: 48 payments at $140.63 each.
B. Company credit union: Four years at 6.5% add-on interest.
C. Statewide Insurance Company: Four years at an annual percentage rate of 11.00%.

____

SELF-REVIEW TEST
Chapter 7: Home Mortgage Loans

Do all the problems. Then check your answers against those in Appendix C. Score each problem 10 points. Where necessary in these problems, use Table 7-1 to find the monthly payment.

1. Eugene and Maryann McGill made an $18,300 down payment on this Toronto home and financed the remainder at 10¼% for 35 years. What is their monthly payment for principal and interest?

> **→ North ←**
> EXECUTIVES TAKE NOTE
> **Perfect traffic pattern for entertaining. Great for family living. Fabulous 2 storey, 4 bedroom home, main floor library, family room, fireplace, raised hearth, Colonial large kitchen, customized wallpaper, draperies, professionally finished lower level. $168,300. Sandi Kert, 417-7101.**

$____________, found by

2. How much of the McGill's (Problem 1) first monthly payment goes for interest?

$____________, found by

3. Irene Sandaver offers $10,500 for this home located in an urban area in the Midwest. Her offer is accepted. After a $500 down payment, she financed the remaining $10,000 at 10½% for 20 years. Find her monthly payment for principal and interest.

> BY OWNER, 618 Colburn St., 2 bedroom house, very nice, for quick sale asking $11,500 only. 893-3210.

$____________, found by

4. After Sandaver (Problem 3) made her first monthly payment, what was the remaining balance?

$____________, found by

5. Assume the balance on a $30,000 mortgage at 8% for 25 years reaches $12,000 after the 200th payment. What is the balance after the 201st payment?

$____________, found by

6. Charles Stein purchases this Queens, New York, home with a $1,500 down payment and finances the remainder at 10% for 30 years. The annual taxes are $550. The annual insurance premium is $186. What is the total monthly payment (including principal, interest, taxes, and insurance)?

> **BELLEROSE—$39,990**
> Taxes $550. Cash $1500. Big Plot. ALVIN BRUCE ROPER 212/343-1100

$____________, found by

7. This Hacienda Heights home, advertised in the *Los Angeles Times*, is purchased with a $13,000 down payment. The remainder is financed for 35 years. How much in total interest can be saved by obtaining a 9½% mortgage rather than a 9¾% mortgage?

> DREAM HOUSE—by owner, 2800 sq. ft. 2 sty., 4 br., 2 3/4 ba., frplc. lrg. decor. bonus rm. 3-car garage, air, lrg. yrd. exquisitely decor, fam. rm., walk to school & shpg. close to Puente Hills Mall, $129,000. 213/330-8451

$______________, found by

8. In Problem 1, how much could the McGills have saved in total interest if they had financed their home for 20 years rather than 35 years?

$______________, found by

Why might they not have financed it for 20 years? ______________________________

____

9. Joy and Tom Jordon decide to purchase this Beverly Road home in Atlanta. They are able to obtain a 30-year mortgage at 9¼%. How much in total interest would they save if they made a 20% down payment rather than a 10% down payment?

> **46 Beverly Rd.—$92,500!**
> Open 1-5. Exceptional! 1st ad! "rock-solid" gracious lge airy rms! 3-lge BR, 3-Ba + 4th BR & Ba in finished bsmt! lge lot, pool 9944, 256-2301.

$__________________, found by

Why might they not make a 20% down payment? ______________________________

____

10. This paragraph is from Loise Cook, Associated Press, writing on "Home Buyer Should Be Aware of Closing Costs." Closing costs on a $35,000 house would run from what to what, according to the article?

> **According to Consumer's Union, closing costs can vary, depending on where you live, from just under 1 per cent to nearly 7 per cent of the price of the house. The closing costs on a $50,000 house, therefore, could run anywhere from about $500 to $3,500.**

____

What might be included in the closing costs? ______________________________

____

SELF-REVIEW TEST
Chapter 8: Insurance

Do all the problems. Then check your answers against those in Appendix C. Score each problem 10 points.

1. Assume you are living in a home that cost $100,000. You decide to take out a homeowners' policy and insure it for 80% of cost. The company has a 90% coinsurance clause. (Use Table 8-1.)

   A. How much is your home insured for?

   $____________, found by

   B. What is your insurance for private structures?

   $____________, found by

   C. What is your insurance for personal property?

   $____________, found by

   D. What is your insurance for additional living expenses?

   $____________, found by

   E. What will the company pay on a loss of $27,000?

   $____________, found by

2. Assume now that you decide to insure the house for the full $100,000. Your home is frame and located in Protection Class 9. What is your annual premium for a typical homeowners' policy? (Use Table 8-2.)

   $______, found by

3. What would your annual homeowners' insurance premium be if your $100,000 frame home were located in a metropolitan area with a good fire department? (Use Table 8-2.)

   $______, found by

4. What is the quarterly premium for a 25-year-old female taking out a $15,000 straight life policy? (Use Tables 8-3 and 8-4.)

   $________, found by

5. George Hammer, age 50, signed for a $20,000 ten-year term policy. He passed away at age 56. (Use Table 8-3.)

   A. How much did he pay in premiums?

      $______________, found by

   B. How much do his beneficiaries receive?

      $______________

6. How much can be saved annually if Betty Franklin, age 45, pays her premiums on her $100,000 20-year endowment policy annually rather than monthly? (Use Tables 8-3 and 8-4.)

   $__________, found by

7. Briefly state the reason for an unmarried female under 21 years, who is an occasional operator and drives for pleasure, having a rating factor of 1.55, while an unmarried male, 21-24 years, who is the principal operator and drives to and from work has a rating factor of 3.10.

   ____

   ____

   ____

   ____

For Problems 8 through 10, use Tables 8-5, 8-6, and 8-7.

8. Bob Morgan, age 38, uses his 1979 Buick Riviera for business. His insurance coverage includes $50,000 property damage, 100/300 bodily injury, $3,000 medical payments coverage, full comprehensive, and $50 deductible collision. What is his semiannual premium?

   $______________, found by

9. Teresa North, a 22-year-old unmarried co-ed, drives her 1972 Datsun for pleasure. She is the principal operator. She has $25,000 property damage, 25/100 bodily injury, $50 deductible comprehensive, and $100 deductible collision. What is her semiannual premium?

   $______________, found by

10. Sam Kristos, a 17-year-old unmarried male, drives his family's 1969 Ford Falcon occasionally and only for pleasure. Their insurance includes $10,000 property damage and 25/50 bodily injury. What is his semiannual premium?

   $______________, found by

SELF-REVIEW TEST
Chapter 9: Income and Deductions

Do all the problems. Then check your answers against those in Appendix C. Score each problem 10 points.

1. The front-desk clerk at a suburban Holiday Inn earns \$3.40 an hour, with time and a half for all hours over 46 hours per week. If this individual worked 49 hours last week, the gross pay is:

   \$______________, found by

2. Assume you land a job after graduation paying \$11,500 per year. What would your biweekly gross be?

   \$______________, found by

3. Harry's King Size Clothes pays one salesclerk \$2.95 an hour plus 1.75% commission on all sales. Find the salesclerk's gross pay for a period in which 80 hours were worked and \$8,470 worth of goods were sold.

   \$______________, found by

4. AB Tool and Die, Inc., uses the Gantt Task and Bonus Plan. One employee earns \$3.90 an hour for an eight-hour day. Task is set at 75 units, with a bonus of 140%. Find the gross pay for an eight-hour day when production is 100 units.

   \$______________, found by

5. A local junior executive earned a salary of \$875 biweekly for 1979. What would be the total FICA contribution for the full year of 1979?

   \$______________, found by

6. A clerk at Belaire Cleaners earns \$3.10 per hour, with time and a half for anything over 40 hours per week. If the clerk is single and claims one exemption, what FIT (wage-bracket method) will be withheld in a week in which 38 hours were worked? (Use Table 9-4.)

   \$______________, found by

7. A nurse is paid a semimonthly salary of \$700. Calculate FIT (percentage method) if the nurse is married and claims three exemptions. (Use Tables 9-2 and 9-3.)

   \$______________, found by

8. Jim Ray is married, claims two exemptions, and sells for a local retailer. He earns \$3.70 an hour or 6% commission on all sales, whichever is greater. In a weekly period when 36 hours were worked, sales totaled \$3,853.33. FIT (wage-bracket method); FICA (1980); SIT (2%); CIT (1.5%); and \$5 credit union are deductions. What is the net pay for the week?

$______________, found by

9. An employee of the Andersons is paid \$5.10 an hour with time and a half for all hours over eight a day. Calculate the net pay for a week during which 10 hours were worked on Monday, 7 on Tuesday, 12 on Wednesday, and 14 on Thursday. FICA (1979) and FIT (percentage method) were the only deductions. The employee is single and claims one exemption.

$______________, found by

10. The staffing coordinator at a private facility for retarded children is paid an annual salary of \$11,272. The coordinator is paid semimonthly, is married, and claims three withholding allowances. Determine net pay for one pay period in 1980. Deductions, in addition to FICA and FIT (percentage method), are 1.5% state income tax; 2.0% city income tax; and \$5.00 a pay period for charitable contributions.

$______________, found by

SELF-REVIEW TEST
Chapter 10: Taxes

Do all the problems. Then check your answers against those in Appendix C. Score each problem 10 points.

1. Use Tables 10-1 and 10-2, and find the total purchase price of a clock with a selling price of $49.99 if purchased in:

   A. Boulder, Colorado

   $__________, found by

   B. Denver, Colorado

   $__________, found by

   C. Jefferson City, Missouri

   $__________, found by

   D. Rapid City, South Dakota

   $__________, found by

2. Use Tables 10-1 and 10-2. The following items were bought in Los Angeles, California. Find the total purchase price.

   A. Toothbrush—$1.49

   $__________, found by

   B. Lamp—$37.50

   $__________, found by

   C. Sofa—$499.60

   $_____________, found by

   D. Tool set—$1,246.65

   $_____________, found by

3. Use Table 10-1. If the sales tax on a rug bought in New Jersey is $2.65, what is the total purchase price of the rug, including tax?

   $__________, found by

4. Use Tables 10-1 and 10-2. An orchid corsage was purchased in Spokane, Washington. Change amounting to $2.05 was received from a $10 bill. What was the selling price of the corsage?

   $__________, found by

5. What is the property tax on a home with a market value of $87,500 if the rate of assessment is 50% and the tax rate is 54.60 mills?

   $_____________, found by

6. Use Table 10-5. A person in Boston, Massachusetts, smokes two packs of cigarettes a day. What would the savings per year (365 days) in cigarette taxes alone be if the individual quit smoking?

$______________, found by

7. What millage is necessary to raise $850,000 annually if the market value is $95 million and the rate of assessment is 30% (nearest tenth mill)?

________________, found by

8. Use Table 10-4, and find the gasoline tax on 112.5 gallons if purchased in:

A. Montana.

$__________, found by

B. District of Columbia.

$__________, found by

C. West Virginia.

$__________, found by

D. Tennessee.

$__________, found by

9. Use Exhibit 10-1 and Tables 10-1 and 10-2. Four L78-15 whitewall tires are purchased in Tulsa, Oklahoma. The sales tax is calculated on the selling price only. What is the total cost of the tires?

$______________, found by

10. Use Table 10-3. For a home in Fulton County, Dover-Wauseon, having an assessed value of $32,360, find the property tax for:

A. County.

$__________, found by

B. Township–Road.

$__________, found by

C. Schools–General.

$______________, found by

D. Total rate.

$______________, found by

SELF-REVIEW TEST
Chapter 11: Banking Services

Do all the problems. Then check your answers against those in Appendix C. Score each problem 8⅓ points.

1. Using today's date and check No. 217, make out the following check and stub to Packer's Meat Supply for \$1,216.93. The check pays for invoice No. 718215. The balance forwarded was \$1,413.60, and two deposits of \$675 and \$518 had been made. Sign the check yourself for Village Meat Market.

2. Delray Cleaners has just received its bank statement. It shows a balance of \$623.50 and a service charge of \$2. The bank statement does not show a deposit of \$200 or two outstanding checks for \$61.50 and \$163.79. The checkbook balance is \$600.21. Reconcile the bank statement.

Checkbook balance	\$__________	Statement balance	\$__________
Service charge	__________	Deposits not shown	__________
Revised balance	\$__________	Checks outstanding	__________
		Revised bank statement	\$__________

3. A \$4,000, three-month note is signed on November 9. The annual rate of interest is 8%. Find:

   A. Ordinary interest at exact time.

   \$__________, found by

   B. Exact interest at 30-day-month time.

   \$__________, found by

4. A \$4,000, 90-day note is signed on November 9. The annual rate of interest is 8%. Find:

   A. Exact interest at 30-day-month time.

   \$__________, found by

   B. Ordinary interest at exact time.

   \$__________, found by

5. A Western States Power Company bill calls for a net payment of $17.36 if paid by April 30. After that date the gross amount of $18.23 must be paid. Mike Pappas paid his bill on May 3. At exact interest, to the nearest tenth percent, what rate did he pay?

_____________%, found by

6. What principal, to the nearest cent, must be deposited to earn $200 every 29 days at 7% exact interest?

$_________________, found by

7. How many days will it take $1,000 to earn $100 at 8% ordinary interest?

_______ days, found by

8. First Federal Savings and Loan Association pays 6½% compounded quarterly on an amount of $1,000 or more left on deposit for 12 months or longer. What would $5,000 earn in five years at 6½% compounded quarterly?

$______________, found by

9. A special certificate was issued paying 13.5% compounded monthly. The minimum deposit is $10,000 for six months. What would $20,000 be worth after six months at 13.5% compounded monthly?

$_________________, found by

10. Peoples Savings and Loan Association pays 5½% compounded daily (365-day year) on its passbook savings account. What would $565 earn in 72 days?

$________, found by

11. On the 11th birthday of their child, the Nellers deposited $1,100 in a savings account paying 4% compounded semiannually. On their child's 16th birthday the bank converted to 5½% compounded daily (365-day year). What was their $1,100 deposit worth on their child's 21st birthday?

$______________, found by

12. On July 1, 1975, $15,000 was deposited in an account paying 7½% compounded quarterly. On July 1, 1979, the bank converted to 5½% compounded daily (365-day year). How much will the $15,000 have earned by August 10, 1989? (Use exact time.)

$_________________, found by

SELF-REVIEW TEST
Chapter 12. Promissory Notes, Discounting, and Partial Payment

Do all the problems. Then check your answers against those in Appendix C. Score each problem 20 points.

1. The Corner Appliance Store accepted a 90-days-same-as-cash note of $965 from a customer on March 25. This is the same as a noninterest-bearing note. Finding itself in need of cash, the Corner Appliance Store had the note discounted at 13½% on April 15. What are the proceeds?

   $_____________, found by

2. The Canton Cannon Company accepted a $1,800, 8% interest-bearing note dated May 10. The note was due and payable in four months. On August 11 the company took the note to a bank, where it was discounted at 10%. What are the proceeds?

   $_____________, found by

3. Third World Construction Company used its line of credit with the Citizens Trust Company to borrow $8,400 on May 1 at 7¾% for six months. What did the Third World Construction Company pay the Citizens Trust Company on the due date?

   $_____________, found by

4. An eight-month note for \$1,500 dated June 1 bears interest at 11%. A partial payment of \$750 is made on July 30. Using the United States Rule, what is the amount due on the due date?

$______________, found by

5. A \$7,400, 120-day note, dated August 17, bears interest at 10½%. A partial payment of \$4,000 was made on October 1. Using the Merchants' Rule, what is the amount due on the due date?

$______________, found by

SELF-REVIEW TEST
Chapter 13: Opening a Business

Do all the problems. Then check your answers against those in Appendix C. Score each problem 14 points.

1. Develop a balance sheet as of October 31 for Al's Radio/TV Repair Shop. It was started by Al Herbert on October 20.
   A. He funded it by depositing $8,000 in a business checking account.
   B. Equipment was purchased for $4,750 cash.
   C. He bought $3,600 worth of supplies with $2,000 cash and put the remainder on account.
   D. From October 20 to October 31, Al's Radio/TV took in $600 in cash for repair services performed.

2. Continuation of Problem 1. During the quarter ending December 31, Al's Radio/TV Repair Shop had income from repair services totaling $2,100. He had $120 in credit and allowances. He used $915 in supplies. Operating expenses included $345 in rent, $90 for utilities and insurance, $120 for depreciation, and $205 for miscellaneous expenses. Make an income statement for Al's Radio/TV Repair Shop for the quarter ending December 31.

Questions 3 through 7 are based on the following data from the balance sheet of the Wejipum Discount Chain and Belt Company:

Assets	*This Year*	*Last Year*
Cash	$15,000	$20,000
Marketable securities	5,000	3,000
Accounts receivable	3,000	1,000
Inventory	27,000	14,000
Total	$50,000	$38,000
Current liabilities	$20,000	$16,000

3. Vertical analysis (round the the nearest tenth percent).

A. Express cash as a percent of total assets for this year. ________%, found by

B. Express marketable securities as a percent of total assets for this year. ________%, found by

C. Express accounts receivable as a percent of total assets for this year. ________%, found by

D. Express inventory as a percent of total assets for this year. ________%, found by

4. Horizontal analysis (round to the nearest tenth percent).

A. Find the percent change in cash from last year to this year. ________%, found by

B. Find the percent change in accounts receivable from last year to this year. ________%, found by

C. Find the percent change in total assets from last year to this year. ________%, found by

D. Find the percent change in current liabilities from last year to this year. ________%, found by

5. A. Find the current ratio for this year.

Current ratio = $\frac{\$\_\_\_\_\_\_\_\_}{\$\_\_\_\_\_\_\_\_}$ = ________

B. Find the current ratio for last year.

Current ratio = $\frac{\$\_\_\_\_\_\_\_\_}{\$\_\_\_\_\_\_\_\_}$ = ________

C. Interpret and compare your answers to A and B. ________________________________

____

6. A. Find the acid-test ratio for this year.

Acid-test ratio = $\frac{\$\_\_\_\_\_\_\_\_}{\$\_\_\_\_\_\_\_\_}$ = ________

B. Find the acid-test ratio for last year.

Acid-test ratio = $\frac{\$\_\_\_\_\_\_\_\_}{\$\_\_\_\_\_\_\_\_}$ = ________

C. Interpret and compare your answers to A and B. ________________________________

____

7. A. Assume a net income of $6,540 for this year. Find the owner equity and the return on owner investment for this year.

Owner equity = $____________ – $____________ = $____________

Return on owner investment = $\frac{\$\_\_\_\_\_\_\_\_}{\$\_\_\_\_\_\_\_\_}$ = ________ = ________%

B. Assume a net income of $5,500 for last year. Find the owner equity and the return on owner investment for last year.

Owner equity = $____________ – $____________ = $____________

Return on owner investment = $\frac{\$\_\_\_\_\_\_\_\_}{\$\_\_\_\_\_\_\_\_}$ = ________ = ________%

C. Interpret and compare your answers to A and B. ________________________________

____

SELF-REVIEW TEST
Chapter 14: Business Expenses

Do all the problems. Then check your answers against those in Appendix C. Score each problem 12½ points.

1. Construct a weekly payroll register for the Mall Boutique. It pays hourly rates plus commission. The year is 1980. Use wage-bracket method for FIT.

	Hourly Rate	*Hours Worked*	*Rate of Commission*	*Total Sales*	*Gross Pay*	*Marital Status*	*Allowances*	*Deductions* *FIT*	*FICA*	*SIT (3½%)*	*Total Deductions*	*Net Pay*
A.	$2.25	30	6%	$ 750.00	$_____	S	1	$_____	$_____	$_____	$_____	$_____
B.	2.30	26	6.5%	2,350.00	_____	S	0	_____	_____	_____	_____	_____
C.	2.75	40	7%	1,145.00	_____	M	2	_____	_____	_____	_____	_____
D.	3.10	40	7.5%	3,480.00	_____	M	4	_____	_____	_____	_____	_____
E.	5.75	40	–	–	_____	M	3	_____	_____	_____	_____	_____

2. Refer to Table 14-2. Dairy-Whip, Inc., contracted for 48,000 lines annually with *The Blade.* One week the firm ran a 200-line ad in the Monday, Wednesday, and Friday evening editions and a half page (1,418 lines) in the Sunday paper. What is the total cost of the advertisements for Dairy-Whip that week?

   $____________, found by

3. Revlon introduced a new lip gloss by running two 30-second and three 10-second spots on a prime time sitcom. The cost per 30-second advertisement is $17,500. Revlon also ran four 30-second and two 60-second spots on the prime-time portion of the Academy Award presentations. The 30-second cost is $92,500. What is the total cost for TV advertising that week?

   $____________, found by

For Problems 4 and 5, refer to Table 14-3.

4. A sporting goods store (retail store, Class 6) in an owner-occupied mercantile building is located on the shore of a lake 12 miles from the nearest fire department, with no fire hydrants in the area. The building is of Type 1 construction and is valued at $87,500. The contents are valued at $125,000.

   A. What is the annual premium for the basic policy?

   $____________, found by

   B. What is the annual premium for the deluxe policy?

   $____________, found by

5. Pat and Dallas Paulos bought an old wooden shack to use as an antique shop (retail store, Class B). The building is located in a rural area without fire hydrants. The Paulos wish to insure the building for $4,000 and the contents for $240,000. What is the annual premium for the deluxe policy?

$______________, found by

6. Howard's Nursery and Landscape Service, Inc., pays a base rate of $1.07 per $100 paid in wages for workers' compensation insurance. Find the firm's monthly premium for workers' compensation insurance for these summer months:

Month	*Monthly Payroll*	*Premium for Workers' Compensation*
A. June	$4,940	$______________
B. July	6,275	______________
C. August	6,140	______________

7. Howard's Nursery and Landscape Service, Inc., pays a state tax of 3.8% and a federal tax of 0.7% on the first $6,000 of each employee's annual wages. Find the state, federal, and total unemployment insurance tax paid on the wages of these three employees:

Employee	*Annual Wage*	*Amount Taxed*	*Federal Tax*	*State Tax*	*Total*
A. Alan Woodland	$8,640	$________	$________	$________	$________
B. Sue Trump	5,430	________	________	________	________
C. Pete Norris	4,260	________	________	________	________

8. Find the total cost of shipping a 175-pound tin of Bay lobsters from San Francisco to Dallas/Ft. Worth by Delta 3D air freight. Pickup is in Area A and delivery is in Area C.

$__________, found by

SELF-REVIEW TEST
Chapter 15: Trade and Cash Discounts

Do all the problems. Then check your answers against those in Appendix C. Score each problem 10 points.

1. A set of deluxe chrome wheelcovers is listed in a catalog for $125. The trade discount is 30%.

   A. What is the amount of discount?

   $__________, found by

   B. What is the net price?

   $__________, found by

2. A power lawn mower is listed in a catalog at a price of $239.95. The discount sheet indicates a discount rate of 40%. What is the net price of the lawn mower?

   $__________, found by

3. A welder's supply lists a pair of heavy-duty welder's gloves at $19 per pair. The discount sheet indicates discounts of 30%/10%/10%.

   A. What is the amount of discount?

   $__________, found by

   B. What is the net price?

   $__________, found by

4. An invoice is dated May 31 and carries terms of 2/10, net 30. The net amount of the invoice is $1,470. If the invoice is paid on June 8:

   A. What is the amount of cash discount?

   $__________, found by

   B. What is the cash price of the invoice?

   $__________, found by

5. The same item is available at the same list price from three distributors. Distributor A offers chain discounts of 20/20/20. Distributor B offers chain discounts of 25/20/15. Distributor C offers chain discounts of 35% less 20%. If price is the only consideration, from which distributor should the item be purchased?

   Why? ______________________________

   ____

6. Daisy Boutique receives an invoice from Bobbie Brooks, Ltd., with terms of 4/10, net 30. The net amount of the invoice is $2,450. What amount is necessary to pay an invoice dated March 25, if the invoice is paid on April 5?

$____________, found by

7. An invoice is dated June 3 and carries terms of 5/10 EOM. The net amount of the invoice is $750. If the invoice is paid on July 7:

A. What is the amount of cash discount?

$____________, found by

B. What is the cash price of the invoice?

$____________, found by

8. Aetna Shirt Corporation offers terms of 2/10 prox. What amount is necessary to pay an invoice dated February 27 with a net amount of $980, if the invoice is paid on March 9?

$____________, found by

9. A local department store received a shipment of toys from Hong Kong on August 15. The invoice for $490, dated May 16, carried terms 5/10 rog.

A. When is the last date to take advantage of the cash discount?

____________, found by

B. What is the cash price of the invoice if paid on or before that date?

$____________, found by

10. An invoice dated November 3 has a list amount of $2,235. Chain discounts of 20/10 apply, as well as terms of 2/10, net 30. What is the cash price of the invoice if paid on November 10?

$____________, found by

SELF-REVIEW TEST
Chapter 16: Markup and Markdown

Do all the problems. Then check your answers against those in Appendix C. Score each problem 10 points.

1. New Age Appliance buys an RCA 25-inch Colortrak television set at a cost of $265. New Age puts a selling price of $568 on the set.

   A. What is the markup?

   $__________, found by

   B. What is the percent markup based on selling price (nearest tenth percent)?

   _______%, found by

2. Open-Pit Furnace Construction builds an open-pit furnace at a cost of $12,473. The company sells the furnace for $25,980.

   A. What is the markup?

   $__________, found by

   B. What is the percent markup based on cost (nearest tenth percent)?

   _______%, found by

3. Hudson's buys Wells Fargo smoke alarms at a cost of $19.96. It marks up each smoke alarm $9.93.

   A. What is the selling price?

   $_______, found by

   B. What is the percent markup based on selling price (nearest percent)?

   _____%, found by

4. Hasting Furniture Company manufactures a sofa at a cost of $96.37. It marks it up $48.63.

   A. What is the selling price?

   $__________, found by

   B. What is the percent markup based on cost (nearest percent)?

   _____%, found by

5. A shimmering rhinestone ring cost Kay Jewelers $7.80 It sells the ring at a markup which is 80% of the selling price. What is the selling price?

$__________, found by

6. Sautters Food Stores buys lemon drops from the Franklin Candy Company at $6.24 per dozen bags. Each bag is marked to sell for 69 cents. What is the percent markup based on cost (nearest tenth percent)?

________%, found by

7. Haas Electronics manufactures CB units at a cost of $35. The markup on each unit is 120% of cost. What is the selling price?

$__________, found by

8. Hook-A-Rug kits are marked to sell at $7.88. That represents a 40% markup based on the selling price. What was the cost of the kit (nearest cent)?

$__________, found by

9. The *Cleveland Press* carried an ad listing 20% off on all full-length and short dresses. What is the sale price on a dress marked to sell regularly at $49.98 (nearest cent)?

$__________, found by

10. A Wendy's coupon entitled you to buy a hamburger, fries, and regular size drink (normally $1.99) for $1.59. What was the percent markdown (nearest percent)?

________%, found by

SELF-REVIEW TEST
Chapter 17: Depreciation

Do all the problems. Then check your answers against those in Appendix C. Score each part 20 points.

1. Use the straight-line, sum-of-the-years'-digits, and declining-balance methods to construct depreciation records for a tractor/trailer costing $85,000, with an estimated life of five years and a trade-in value of $10,000.

   A. Straight-line method:

   B. Sum-of-the-years'-digits method:

   C. Declining-balance method:

2. A commercial seed-blowing machine is expected to last 8,400 hours. The machine cost $125,000 and has a trade-in value of $15,000 after 8,400 hours of use. After 2,940 hours:

A. The depreciation is $____________, found by

B. The book value is $____________, found by

3. A plating machine is expected to produce 700,000 units during its lifetime. The cost is $47,500, with a scrap value of $2,500 after 700,000 units. After 168,000 units:

A. The depreciation is $____________, found by

B. The book value is $____________, found by

SELF-REVIEW TEST
Chapter 18: Valuing an Inventory and Inventory Turnover

Do all the problems. Then check your answers against those in Appendix C. Score each problem 12½ points.

1. Theoretically, when the first items that come in are the last items that you sell, which method of valuing the inventory are you using?

   A. Average cost B. Fifo C. Lifo

2. An annual inventory turnover rate of seven means you sell your average inventory how many times during the year?

   A. 52 B. 7 C. 1.7 D. 42

For Problems 3 through 6, use the following inventory record from Able Distributors:

Date	*Unit Cost*	*IN*	*OUT*	*Balance*
9/1	$7.40			40
9/8			30	______
9/9	8.00	50		______
9/15			35	______
9/22			20	______
9/30	8.50	50		______

3. Complete the inventory record.

4. Find the value of the inventory using the average-cost method. $____________, found by

5. Find the value of the inventory using Fifo. $____________, found by

6. Find the value of the inventory using Lifo. $____________, found by

For Problems 7 and 8, use these records from the Keystoning Klothes Kompany:

BIMONTHLY INVENTORY

Period	*Cost*	*Retail*
1	$81,700	$163,400
2	74,700	149,400
3	78,200	156,400
4	82,600	165,200
5	80,000	160,000
6	79,800	159,600

Annual sales at retail: $800,000
Annual sales at cost: $400,000

7. What is the rate of inventory turnover at cost? ______

8. What is the rate of inventory turnover at retail? ______

SELF-REVIEW TEST
Chapter 19: The Use of Statistical Techniques in Business

Do all the problems. Then check your answers against those in Appendix C. Score each problem 20 points.

1. The production of luggage in a small plant during the day is:

Hour	*No.*	*Hour*	*No.*
First	27	Fifth	28
Second	39	Sixth	35
Third	48	Seventh	51
Fourth	31	Eighth	36

Plot the production data in the form of a line graph.

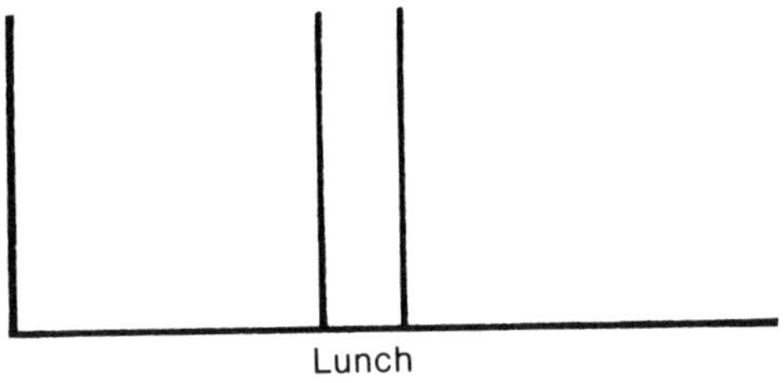

2. The sales of a department store by day of the week are:

Day	*Sales*	*Day*	*Sales*
Monday	$18,120	Thursday	$ 57,834
Tuesday	23,569	Friday	83,456
Wednesday	47,892	Saturday	103,925

Plot the sales in a bar chart.

3. The production of a lumber mill this year (millions of board feet) is:

Plywood	12
Rough lumber	2
Finished lumber	6

Plot the data in the form of a pie chart.

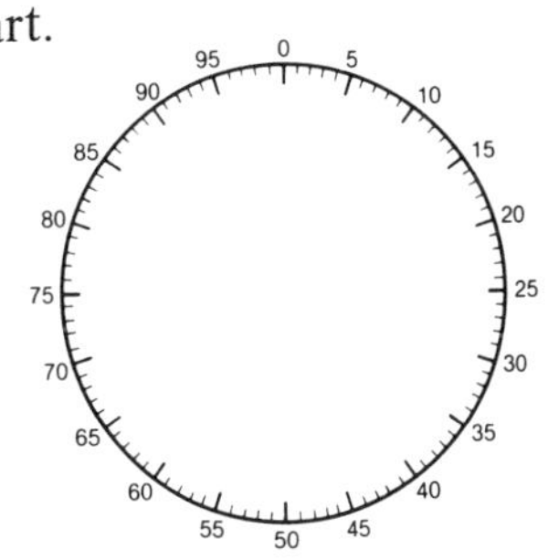

4. The exports of three groups for 1979 and 1980 (millions of dollars) are:

	1979	*1980*
Electronic parts	$ 80	$140
Machine tools	30	10
Oil	200	300

Show the percent change in the exports of each of the three groups from 1979 to 1980 in the form of a two-directional bar chart.

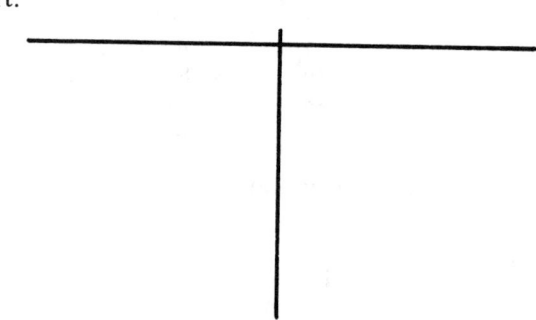

5. The hourly wages of the production workers in a small plant are:

$6.20	$5.00	$6.50	$7.90
8.40	7.20	8.20	7.10
9.55	7.80	7.65	6.40

A. Organize the wages into a frequency distribution, starting with $5 but under $6.

B. Draw a histogram and a frequency polygon.

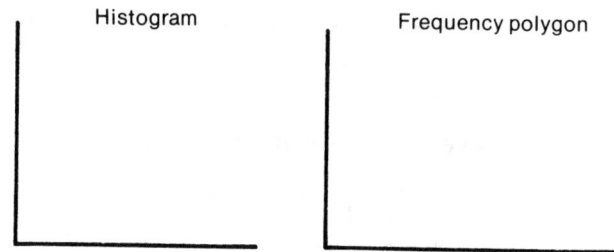

Histogram

Frequency polygon

C. The arithmetic mean hourly wage is $________, found by

D. The median hourly wage is $________, found by

SELF-REVIEW TEST
Chapter 20: The Metric System

Do all the problems. Then check your answers against those in Appendix C. Score each problem 4 points.

Insert the letter T if the statement is *true*. Insert F if it is *false*.

____ 1. Early units of measurement introduced by the Romans and English were based primarily on parts of the body such as the foot and arm.

____ 2. The development of the metric system of weights and measurements has been credited to the French.

____ 3. Words such as "mile," "bushel," and "ounce" are measurements that are part of the metric system.

____ 4. Congress passed a national metric conversion act in 1975.

____ 5. It is logical that a player for the Los Angeles Lakers basketball team is 4 meters tall.

____ 6. The capacity of a large storage bin for corn would be measured in cubic meters.

____ 7. It is logical that a giant box of Duz soap powder would weigh 3 kg.

____ 8. It is logical that a Mounds candy bar weighs 45 g.

____ 9. Under the new metric system, ground coffee will probably be packaged for the consumer in half mg, 1 mg, and 2 mg sizes.

____ 10. Sue Shapely, a college student, probably weighs 2 t.

____ 11. A liter is slightly larger than a quart.

____ 12. A yard is slightly larger than a meter.

____ 13. Converted, a mile is about 1.6 kilometers.

____ 14. A temperature change of 5° C is equivalent to a change of 9 degrees on the Fahrenheit scale.

____ 15. The distance between cities is usually measured in hectometers.

____ 16. A comfortable room temperature is about 21° C.

____ 17. A Celsius thermometer was plunged in a pan of boiling water. The scale showed 100° C.

____ 18. A body temperature of 40° C would indicate that the person has a very high fever.

____ 19. An empty container about the size of a cube of sugar will have a capacity of about 1 milliliter.

____ 20. A paper clip weighs about 1 gram.

____ 21. Two quarts is the equivalent of about 1.9 liters.

____ 22. To convert °C to °F, use the conversion formula $°C = \frac{5}{9}(°F - 32)$.

____ 23. The volume of a large shipping container measuring 4 meters by 3 meters by 2 meters is 24 cubic meters, written 24 m^3.

____ 24. It is impossible to convert from a U.S. customary measure to a metric measure.

____ 25. 10 mg is larger than 10 g.

appendix B

Answers to Selected Assignment Problems

CHAPTER 1

Assignment 1-1
Computations with Whole Numbers and Decimals

1. \$1,235.94
3. 1,229.42
5. \$5,228.17
7. \$800.48
9. 21,476
11. 200.7669, found by multiplying and marking off 4 decimal places
13. 1.7, found by dividing and rounding 1.738 to the nearest tenth
15. 0.5, found by $40\overline{)18.00}$ giving .45 (160; 200; 200)
17. \$32,470, found by the "7" in the units place being 5 or more
19. 475.57, found by multiplying and rounding 475.566 to the nearest hundredth
21. \$352.80, found by \$662.46 + \$87.19 – \$429.68 – \$58.17 + \$10.00 + \$81.00
23. \$1,673.69, found by \$1,000.00 + \$426.88 – \$86.03 – \$129.16 + \$375.00 + \$87.00
25. A. \$0.50, found by \$2.39 – \$1.89
    B. \$0.30, found by \$1.19 – \$0.89
27. \$4.74, found by \$10.00 – (\$1.29 + \$1.49 + \$1.19 + \$0.99 + \$0.30)
29. A. £3.05, found by £6.50 – £3.45
    B. £8.05, found by £20 – £11.95
31. 20.1 pounds, found by \$15.86 ÷ \$0.79 = 20.076 and rounding

Assignment 1-2
Computations with Fractions

1. $1\frac{11}{16}$, $1\frac{11}{16}$
3. $\frac{3}{30}$, $\frac{1}{10}$
5. $\frac{14}{8}$, $\frac{7}{4}$
7. –1, found by

   $(+\frac{1}{8} + \frac{3}{8} + \frac{1}{8} + \frac{3}{8} + \frac{1}{2}) +$

   $(-\frac{1}{8} - \frac{1}{4} - \frac{3}{4} - \frac{1}{4} - \frac{1}{8} - \frac{1}{4} - \frac{1}{8} - \frac{5}{8}) = \frac{12}{8} - \frac{20}{8} = -\frac{8}{8}$
9. A. \$3.50, found by ½ × \$7.00
   B. \$3.00, found by ½ × \$6.00
   C. \$2.50, found by ½ × \$5.00
   D. \$2.00, found by ½ × \$4.00
11. $\frac{1}{4}$, found by $\frac{88¢ - 66¢}{88¢} = \frac{22¢}{88¢}$
13. 5 oz., found by (3¾ ÷ 6) × 8
15. $\frac{8}{31}$, found by $\frac{40}{155}$ tons per acre
17. A. \$24,897.81, found by 7,243 × \$3.43¾
    B. \$24,553.77, found by 7,243 × \$3.39
    C. \$24,227.84, found by 7,243 × \$3.34½
    D. \$23,268.14, found by 7,243 × \$3.21¼

CHAPTER 2

Assignment 2-1
Converting a Percent to a Fraction or a Decimal

1. $\frac{16}{100}$, $\frac{4}{25}$, 0.16
3. $\frac{66\frac{2}{3}}{100}$ or $\frac{200}{300}$, $\frac{2}{3}$, 0.66⅔ or $0.66\overline{6}$
5. $\frac{1\frac{3}{4}}{100}$ or $\frac{7}{400}$, $\frac{7}{400}$, 0.0175

7. $\frac{1}{5}$, found by $\frac{20}{100}$ reduced and 0.20

9. $\frac{13}{20}$, found by $\frac{65}{100}$ reduced and 0.65

11. $\frac{1}{20}$, found by $\frac{5}{100}$ reduced and 0.05

13. A. $\frac{1}{100}$ and .01

    B. $\frac{2}{100}$ or $\frac{1}{50}$, found by $\frac{2}{100}$ reduced, and .02

15. $\frac{3}{10}$ and 0.30

17. The chances are 20 out of 100 (1 out of 5) of thundershowers on Saturday.
19. 8 out of 100 or 8¢ on a dollar (100 cents) is charged for sales tax. Ten dollars would be charged $0.80.
21. 6 out of 100 or 6¢ on every dollar (100 cents) is earned in interest. $100 would earn $6.
23. 25 out of 100 or $25 out of every $100 of net income is spent for shelter. $250 out of $1,000.
25. 30 out of 100 or $3.00 off a $10.00 item. $0.30 off a $1.00 item; $30 off a $100 item.

Assignment 2-2
Converting Decimals and Fractions to Percents

1. 6%
3. 239%
5. 92.5%, found by (37 ÷ 40) = 0.925
7. 412.5%, found by 4⅛ = 33/8 and (33 ÷ 8) = 4.125
9. 90%, found by 9 out of 10 = 9/10 = 0.9
11. A. 25%
    B. 50%
13. 9.5%, 10.5%
15. A. 0.235%, found by ($2.35 ÷ $1,000) = 0.00235
    B. 0.005%, found by ($0.05 ÷ $1,000) = 0.00005
    C. 0.080%, found by ($0.80 ÷ $1,000) = 0.00080
    D. 0.080%, found by ($0.80 ÷ $1,000) = 0.00080
    E. 0.400%, found by ($4.00 ÷ $1,000) = 0.00400
    F. 0.400%, found by ($4.00 ÷ $1,000) = 0.00400
    G. 0.330%, found by ($3.30 ÷ $1,000) = 0.00330
    H. 3.050%, found by ($30.50 ÷ $1,000) = 0.03050
    I. 0.150%, found by ($1.50 ÷ $1,000) = 0.00150
    J. 3.930%, found by ($39.30 ÷ $1,000) = 0.03930
17. A. 45.65%, found by 84 pounds ÷ 184 pounds = 0.45652
    B. 45.60%, found by 306 marks ÷ 671 marks = 0.45604
    C. 45.59%, found by 759 francs ÷ 1,665 francs = 0.45586
    D. 45.57%, found by 141,150 lira ÷ 309,734 lira = 0.45571
19. A. 0.25
    B. 0.0025, found by 0.25% = 0.0025

CHAPTER 3

Assignment 3-1
Percentage, Rate, and Base

1. 341.1, found by 461 × 0.74 = 341.14
3. 33.3%, found by 237 ÷ 711 = 0.3333
5. 50.7, found by 7.1 ÷ 0.14 = 50.71
7. $33.25, found by $95 × 0.35
9. 3.1%, found by 132.6 ÷ 4,216.72 = 0.0314
11. 987.2, found by 617 ÷ 0.625
13. $12,732.80, found by ($15,791.00 × 0.80) + $100
15. 2.66%, found by $1,252.94 ÷ $47,110.00 = 0.02660
17. 236.4 trillion cubic feet, found by 26 ÷ 0.11 = 236.36
19. $208.42, found by ($170 × 0.226) + $170
21. 1.3%, found by 0.08% ÷ 6.05% = 0.0132

Assignment 3-2
Rate of Increase or Decrease

1. 37.5% increase, found by $3.00 ÷ $8.00, where $3 = $11 – $8
3. 10% decrease, found by $0.25 ÷ $2.50, where $0.25 = $2.50 – $2.25
5. 26.7% increase, found by $4.00 ÷ $14.99 = 0.2668, where $4.00 = $18.99 – $14.99
7. A. $0.30, found by $0.89 – $0.59
   B. 50.8%, found by $0.30 ÷ $0.59 = 0.50847
9. A. 15 mph, found by 70 – 55
   B. 21%, found by 15 ÷ 70 = 0.214
11. 21.5%, found by $1.61 ÷ $7.49 = 0.2150, where $1.61 = $7.49 – $5.88
13. 69.9%, found by $1.02 ÷ $1.46 = 0.6986, where $1.02 = $2.48 – $1.46
15. 26.5%, found by $0.50 ÷ $1.89 = 0.2646, where $0.50 = $1.89 – $1.39
17. A. 3.4%, found by 572 ÷ 16,588 = 0.03448, where 572 = 17,160 – 16,588
    B. Much less, specifically 21.5% less, found by 24.9% – 3.4%
19. 30%, found by $12.50 ÷ $41.50 = 0.301, where $12.50 = $41.50 – $29.00

CHAPTER 4

Assignment 4-1
Unit Pricing—Comparison Shopping

1. $0.045625/ounce, found by $2.19 ÷ 48
3. 2.36¢ per bag, found by 59¢ ÷ 25
5. $0.2225/roll, found by $0.89 ÷ 4

7. $0.0298/ounce, found by
$0.32 ÷ 10.75 = $0.029767441
9. A. $0.0725, found by $0.29 ÷ 4
B. $0.063, found by $0.63 ÷ 10
C. $0.057, found by $1.03 ÷ 18
Best buy: C, the 18-pack for $1.03
11. A. $0.0399, found by $1.13 ÷ 28.3
B. $0.0576, found by $2.59 ÷ 45
Best buy: A, the 28.3 gram bottle for $1.13
13. A. $2.597 per pound, found by $7.79 ÷ 3
B. $2.495 per pound, found by $4.99 ÷ 2
C. $2.69 per pound, found by $2.69 ÷ 1
Best buy: B, 2-pound tin for $4.99
15. A. $0.0019 per gram, found by $0.65 ÷ 340
B. $0.0017 per gram, found by $0.89 ÷ 510
C. $0.00388 per gram, found by $0.99 ÷ 255
D. $0.0053 per gram, found by $0.75 ÷ 142
Best buy: B, 510 grams for $0.89
17. A. $0.00145, found by $0.32 ÷ 220
B. $0.00163 per gram, found by $0.22 ÷ 135
Best buy: A, 220 grams for $0.32
19. A. $0.545, found by $1.09 ÷ 2
B. 0.566\overline{6}$, found by 1 lb. 8 oz. = 1.5 lbs., $0.85 ÷ 1.5
C. $0.6068239, found by (397 g) (0.0022) = 0.8734 lbs., $0.53 ÷ 0.8734
Best buy: A, 2 lbs. for $1.09

Assignment 4-2
Cost of Transportation

1. $2,760, found by $925 + $1,835;
$0.23, found by $2,760 ÷ 12,000
3. $3,148.80, found by $1,022.90 + $2,125.90;
$0.32, found by $3,148.80 ÷ 9,840
5. $3,215.25, found by $2,416.58 + $798.67;
$0.15, found by $3,215.25 ÷ 21,435
7. A. $623.18, found by $435.68 (gasoline) + $37.50 + $115.00 + $35.00, where $435.68 = (11,400 ÷ 23) $0.879
B. $1,523.50, found by $975 (depreciation) + $516 + $32.50, where $975 = ($4,750 – $2,800) ÷ 2
C. $2,146.68, found by $623.18 + $1,523.50
D. $0.188, found by $2,146.68 ÷ 11,400
9. A. $108.45, found by $23.95 + ($0.27 X 210) + $27.80
B. $0.516, found by $108.45 ÷ 210
11. A. $3.95, found by $1.25 + $0.80 + $0.70 + $0.60 + $0.60
B. $7.90, found by 2 X $3.95
C. $1.16, found by $7.90 ÷ 6.8 or $3.95 ÷ 3.4
13. A. $0.09, found by $96.00 ÷ 1,040
B. $0.08, found by $111.50 ÷ 1,470
C. $0.07, found by $75.00 ÷ 1,085
D. Amtrak service from Cincinnati and Buffalo is via Chicago

Assignment 4-3
Cost of Owning or Renting a Home

1. $8,812.72, found by (12 X $359.81) + $2,200 + $111 + $344 + $1,840; $734.39, found by $8,812.72 ÷ 12
3. $7,270, found by (12 X $450) + $110 + $1,760; $605.83, found by $7,270 ÷ 12
5. $9,892.48, found by (12 X $438.79) + $2,000 + $287 + $430 + $1,910; $824.37, found by $9,892.48 ÷ 12
7. A. $8,168.60, found by $4,704.60 + $1,183 + $196 + $365 + $1,720
B. $680.72, found by $8,168.60 ÷ 12
9. A. $5,557, found by (12 X $425) + $142 + $315
B. $463.08, found by $5,557 ÷ 12
11. They should *not* buy; annual allowable housing expense is $6,846 = 35% X (24 X $815), while annual estimated housing expense is $8,490.60 = (12 X $428.55) + $128 + (2 X $900) + $1,120 + $300

Assignment 4-4
Budgeting

1. $4,860, found by 27% X $18,000; $5,760, found by 32% X $18,000; $1,800, found by 10% X $18,000; $2,160, found by 12% X $18,000; $900, found by 5% X $18,000; $1,440, found by 8% X $18,000; $1,080, found by 6% X $18,000
3. $4,524, found by 29% X $15,600; $4,524, found by 29% X $15,600; $1,716, found by 11% X $15,600; $1,716, found by 11% X $15,600; $1,092, found by 7% X $15,600; $1,092, found by 7% X $15,600; $936, found by 6% X $15,600
5. $7,506, found by 27% X $27,800; $8,896, found by 32% X $27,800; $2,780, found by 10% X $27,800; $3,336, found by 12% X $27,800; $1,390, found by 5% X $27,800; $2,224, found by 8% X $27,800; $1,668, found by 6% X $27,800
7. Food, $315, found by
35% X $10,800 = $3,780 ÷ 12
Housing, $207, found by
23% X $10,800 = $2,484 ÷ 12
Transportation, $81, found by
9% X $10,800 = $972 ÷ 12
Clothing, $108, found by
12% X $10,800 = $1,296 ÷ 12
Medical, $90, found by
10% X $10,800 = $1,080 ÷ 12
Gifts, $54, found by
6% X $10,800 = $648 ÷ 12
Other, $45, found by
5% X $10,800 = $540 ÷ 12

9.

Item	Monthly Budget	Actual for October	Difference	Actual for November	Difference	Two Months Combined
Food	$315	$350	+$35	$345	+$30	+ $65
Housing	207	200	– 7	200	– 7	– 14
Transportation	81	105	+ 24	112	+ 31	+ 55
Clothing	108	97	– 11	103	– 5	– 16
Medical	90	95	+ 5	95	+ 5	+ 10
Gifts	54	45	– 9	63	+ 9	0
Other	45	45	0	47	+ 2	+ 2
Totals			+$37		+$65	+$102

They are spending considerably over their income. They must cut back, especially in the areas of food and transportation, or they will be in financial trouble.

CHAPTER 5

Assignment 5-1
The Previous-Balance and the Adjusted-Balance Methods of Determining the Finance Charge

1. $6.30, found by 1½% X $420
3. $8.30, found by (1½% X $500) + (1% X $80)
5. $9.43, found by (1½% X $500) + (1% X $192.63)
7. A. $15, $190 is between $151 and $200
   B. $74.54, found by 10% X $745.36
9. $60.69, found by $32.50 – $20.00 + $0.19 + $48
11. Adjusted-balance method; because 1.5% X $12.50 equals $0.19, the finance charge
13. A. $6.90, found by 1.5% X $460
    B. $454.40, found by $460 – $50 + $6.90 + $37.50
15. A. Finance charge: $6.15, found by 1.5% X $410
    B. New balance: $453.65, found by $460 – $50 + $6.15 + $37.50
17. A. $26.40 payment
    B. $100, found by $126.40 – $26.40
    C. $1.50, found by 1.5% X $100
    D. $50.91, found by $8.59 + $3.66 + $26.13 + $8.36 + $4.17
    E. $152.41, found by $126.40 – $26.40 + $1.50 + $50.91

Assignment 5-2
Average Daily Balance Method—No New Monthly Purchases Included

1. $190, found by [(10 X $270) + (10 X $200) + (10 X $100)] ÷ 30
3. $2.85, found by 1.5% X $190
5. A. $131.33, found by [(20 X $147) + (10 X $100)] ÷ 30
   B. $1.97, found by 1.5% X $131.33
   C. $139.87, found by $147 – $47 + $1.97 + $37.90

7. A. $7.50, found by 1.5% X $500
   B. $3.00, found by 1.5% X $200
   C. $5.90, found by 1.5% X $393.55

Assignment 5-3
Average Daily Balance Method—New Monthly Purchases Included

1. $354.64, found by [(15 X $415.50) + (6 X $265.50) + (9 X $312.62)] ÷ 30
3. $5.32, found by 1.5% X $354.64
5. A. $365.09, found by [(8 X $373.50) + (4 X $398.47) + (13 X $348.47) + (6 X $367.63)] ÷ 31
   B. $5.48, found by 1.5% X $365.09
   C. $44.13, found by $24.97 + $19.16
   D. -0- no credits
   E. $50.00 given on statement
   F. $373.11, found by $373.50 + $44.13 + $5.48 – $50.00

CHAPTER 6

Assignment 6-1
Installment Credit

1. $40.00, found by $480.00 ÷ 12
3. $156.96, found by $144.00 + $12.96
   $13.08, found by $156.96 ÷ 12
5. $1,500, found by $2,000 – $500
   $1,695, found by $1,500 + $195
   $70.63, found by $1,695 ÷ 24
7. $17.80, found by [($275 – $35) + $27] ÷ 15
9. $134.66, found by [($5,695 – $895) + $1,663.63] ÷ 48
11. $55.00, found by ($300 + $30) ÷ 6
13. A. $72.50, found by $1,740.00 ÷ 24
    B. $96.66, found by $2,319.87 ÷ 24

C. \$51.66, found by \$1,859.76 ÷ 36
D. \$68.88, found by \$2,479.88 ÷ 36
E. \$41.25, found by \$1,980.00 ÷ 48
F. \$55.00, found by \$2,640.00 ÷ 48

15. \$67.13, found by (\$900.00 + \$106.88) ÷ 15 = \$67.13

Assignment 6-2
Annual Percentage Rate (APR) on Installment Accounts

1. 21.25% (Table 6-1)
3. \$12.00, found by (\$360.00 ÷ \$3,000.00) X \$100; 14.75% (table)
5. A. \$19.50, found by (\$390.00 ÷ \$2,000) X \$100
   B. 12.00% (table)
7. A. 25.50% (table), with finance charge per \$100 = \$44, found by (\$330 ÷ \$750) X \$100
   B. Greater than 25.75%; off the table with FC per 100 = \$63.20, found by (\$632 ÷ \$1,000) X \$100
9. A. \$3,761.90, found by \$3,847.00 – \$85.10
   B. \$5,106.00, found by 60 X \$85.10
   C. \$1,344.10, found by \$5,106.00 – \$3,761.90
   D. \$35.73, found by (\$1,344.10 ÷ \$3,761.90) X \$100
   E. 12.75% (table)
11. A. Much greater than 25.75%; off the table with FC per \$100 = \$20, found by (\$60 ÷ \$300) X \$100
    B. The friend selling the car is charging a very high rate of interest (over 25.75% APR).

Assignment 6-3
Installment Accounts—Add-On Interest

1. \$245.00, found by \$3,500 X 0.07 X 1
3. \$94.99, found by \$745 X 0.085 X 1.5
5. \$1,212.11, found by \$5,876.92 X 0.0825 X 2.5
7. \$280, found by \$1,750 X 0.08 X 2
9. A. \$6,000, found by \$6,495 – \$495
   B. \$1,080, found by \$6,000 X 0.06 X 3
   C. \$7,080, found by \$6,000 + \$1,080
   D. \$196.67, found by \$7,080.00 ÷ 36
   E. 11.00% (table), where FC per \$100 = \$18, found by (\$1,080 ÷ \$6,000) X \$100
11. A. \$68.75, found by [\$2,500 + (\$2,500 X 0.08 X 4)] ÷ 48
    B. 14.25% (table) where FC per \$100 = \$32, found by (\$800 ÷ \$2,500) X \$100
13. A. \$3,112.70, found by \$3,662 – (0.15 X \$3,662)
    B. \$1,120.57, found by \$3,112.70 X 0.09 X 4
    C. \$4,233.27, found by \$3,112.70 + \$1,120.57
    D. \$88.19, found by \$4,233.27 ÷ 48
    E. 16.00% (table), where FC per \$100 = \$36, found by (\$1,120.57 ÷ \$3,112.70) X \$100

Assignment 6-4
Refund of Finance Charge—The Rule of 78

1. A. 42/78, found by 12 + 11 + 10 + 9
3. A. 75/78, found by 12 + 11 + 10 + 9 + 8 + 7 + 6 + 5 + 4 + 3
   B. 3/78, found by 2 + 1
5. A. 68/78, found by 12 + 11 + 10 + 9 + 8 + 7 + 6 + 5
   B. 10/78, found by 4 + 3 + 2 + 1
7. \$64.62, found by (21/78) \$240 where 21 = (6 X 7) ÷ 2
9. 21, found by (6 X 7) ÷ 2; 3/21, found by (2 X 3) ÷ 2
11. 1,176, found by (48 X 49) ÷ 2; 171/1,176, found by (18 X 19) ÷ 2
13. 903, found by (42 X 43) ÷ 2; 171/903, found by (18 X 19) ÷ 2
15. \$1,777.10, found by (13 X \$147.50) – \$140.40 where \$140.40 = (78/300) X \$540
17. A. \$720, found by \$3,000 X 0.08 X 3
    B. \$103.33, found by (\$3,000 + \$720) ÷ 36
    C. 14.50% (table), where FC per \$100 = (\$720 ÷ \$3,000) X \$100 = \$24
    D. \$147.03, found by (136/666) X \$720
    E. \$1,609.58, found by (17 X \$103.33) – \$147.03
19. \$306, found by (4 X \$78) – \$6 where \$6 = [(6/120) X \$120] and \$120 = (15 X \$78) – \$1,050

CHAPTER 7

Assignment 7-1
Financing the Purchase of a Home

1. \$270, found by (\$20,000/\$1,000) X \$13.50
3. \$625.73, found by (\$67,500/\$1,000) X \$9.27 (table)
5. \$988.72, found by (\$112,610/\$1,000) X \$8.78 (table)
7. A. \$10,000, found by 0.20 X \$50,000
   B. \$40,000, found by \$50,000 – \$10,000
   C. \$8.03 (table)
   D. \$321.20, found by (\$40,000/\$1,000) X \$8.03
9. \$17,956.50, found by \$18,000.00 – \$43.50; I = \$149.64, found by \$17,956.50 X 0.10 X 1/12; P = \$43.86, found by \$193.50 – \$149.64; \$17,912.64, found by \$17,956.50 – \$43.86
11. I_1 = \$262.50, found by \$30,000 X 0.105 X 1/12; P_1 = \$12.00, found by \$274.50 – \$262.50; bal. \$29,988, found by \$30,000 – \$12; I_2 = \$262.40, found by \$29,988 X 0.105 X 1/12; P_2 = \$12.10, found by \$274.50 – \$262.40; bal. \$29,975.90, found by \$29,988.00 – \$12.10
13. Monthly payment = \$439.50, found by (\$50,000/\$1,000) X \$8.79 (table)

I_1 = $427.08, found by $50,000 × 0.1025 × 1/12;
P_1 = $12.42, found by $439.50 – $427.08;
bal. $49,987.58, found by $50,000.00 – $12.42;
I_2 = $426.98, found by $49,987.58 × 0.1025 × 1/12;
P_2 = $12.52, found by $439.50 – $426.98;
bal. $49,975.06, found by $49,987.58 – $12.52

15. A. $225.40, found by ($28,000/$1,000) × $8.05 (table), where $35,000 – (0.20 × $35,000) = $28,000
 B. $210.00, found by $28,000 × 0.09 × 1/12
 C. $15.40, found by $225.40 – $210.00
 D. $27,984.60, found by $28,000.00 – $15.40
 E. $27,969.08, found by $27,984.60 – [$225.40 – ($27,984.60 × 0.09 × 1/12)]
17. $40,489.20, found by $40,500 – [$348.30 – ($40,500 × 0.10 × 1/12)], where $40,500 = $45,000 – (0.10 × $45,000) and $348.30 = ($40,500/$1,000) × $8.60 (table)
19. A. $14,158.88, found by $14,176.14 – $17.26
 B. $17.35, found by $88.14 – $70.79
 C. $14,141.53, found by $14,158.88 – $17.35
 D. $70.71, found by $14,141.53 × 0.06 × 1/12
 E. $17.43, found by $88.14 – $70.71
 F. $14,124.10, found by $14,141.53 – $17.43

Assignment 7-2
More on Financing the Purchase of a Home

1. $301.00, found by ($35,000/$1,000) × $8.60 (table); $13.67, found by $164/12; $70 found by $840/12; $384.67, found by $301.00 + $13.67 + $70.00
3. $439.00, found by ($50,000/$1,000) × $8.78; $19.83, found by 238/12; $116.67, found by 1,400/12; $575.50, found by $439.00 + $19.83 + $116.67
5. $221.20, found by ($20,000/$1,000) × $11.06; $7.25, found by 87/12; $46.67, found by 560/12; $275.12, found by $221.60 + $7.25 + $46.67
7. A. $349.35, found by ($42,500/$1,000) × $8.22 (table)
 B. $109.79, found by $1,317.50 ÷ 12
 C. $17.30, found by $207.60 ÷ 12
 D. $476.44, found by $349.35 + $109.79 + $17.30
 E. $762.54, found by 6 × ($109.79 + $17.30)
9. A. $111,032, found by (420 × $359.60) – $40,000, where $359.60 = ($40,000/$1,000) × $8.99 (table), and 420 = 35 × 12
 B. $98,096, found by (420 × $328.80) – $40,000, where $328.80 = ($40,000/$1,000) × $8.22 (table)
 C. $85,496, found by (420 × $298.80) – $40,000, where $298.80 = ($40,000/$1,000) × $7.47 (table)
 D. $73,400, found by (420 × $270) – $40,000, where $270. = ($40,000/$1,000) × $6.75 (table)
11. $24,660, found by $103,620 – $78,960, where $78,960 = (300 × $463.20) – $60,000 and $103,620 = (300 × $545.40) – $60,000
13. A. $11,000, found by (60 × $850) – $40,000
 B. $37,400, found by (180 × $430) – $40,000
 C. $69,080, found by (300 × $363.60) – $40,000
 D. $104,480, found by (420 × $344.00) – $40,000
15. $71,676, found by [(360 × $503.25) – $55,000] – [(180 × $608.30) – $55,000]
 You might not be able to afford monthly payments of $608.30, while you could afford monthly payments of $503.25.
17. $381.85, found by $30.00 + $90.00 + $147.00 + $6.35 + $5.00 + $30.00 + $73.50, where $147.00 = 0.01 × $14,700 and $73.50 = 0.005 × $14,700
19. A. $13,000, found by 0.20 × $65,000
 B. $482.04, found by ($52,000/$1,000) × $9.27 (table), where $52,000 = $65,000 – $13,000
 C. $92,612, found by (300 × $482.04) – $52,000
 D. $215.92, found by ($2,175/12) + ($416/12)
 E. $697.96, found by $482.04 + $215.92
 F. $1,289.50, found by (0.02 × $52,000) + $249.50

CHAPTER 8

Assignment 8-1
Home Insurance

1. $2,400, found by 0.10 × $24,000; $12,000, found by 0.50 × $24,000; $4,800, found by 0.20 × $24,000; 100%, found by 80% ÷ 80%
3. $14,800, found by 0.80 × $18,500; $1,480, found by 0.10 × $14,800; $7,400, found by 0.50 × $14,800; $2,960, found by 0.20 × $14,800; 8/9, found by 80% ÷ 90%
5. $90,200, found by 0.80 × $112,750; $9,020, found by 0.10 × $90,200; $45,100, found by 0.50 × $90,200; $18,040, found by 0.20 × $90,200; 8/9, found by 80% ÷ 90%
7. A. $37,520, found by 0.80 × $46,900
 B. $3,752, found by 0.10 × $37,520
 C. $18,760, found by 0.50 × $37,520
 D. $7,504, found by 0.20 × $37,520
 E. $100 from Exhibit 8-2
 F. $16,800, found by 8/9 × $18,900
9. A. $11,250, found by 0.10 × $112,500
 B. $56,250, found by 0.50 × $112,500
 C. $22,500, found by 0.20 × $112,500
 D. $1,000 from Exhibit 8-2
11. $126 (table)
13. $115 (table), Protection Class 7-8
15. $480 (table)

17. $152 (table)
19. $161 (table), Protection Class 10

Assignment 8-2
Life Insurance

1. $330.20, found by ($20,000/$1,000) X $16.51
3. $19.27 (table); $481.75, found by ($25,000/$1,000) X $19.27
5. $25.89 (table); $323.63, found by ($12,500/$1,000) X $25.89
7. A. $36.60, found by ($10,000/$1,000) X $3.66 (table)
   B. $152.20, found by ($10,000/$1,000) X $15.22 (table)
   C. $454.20, found by ($10,000/$1,000) X $45.42 (table)
9. A. $512.40, found by ($20,000/$1,000) X $25.62 (table)
   B. $10,248, found by 20 X $512.40
   C. $20,000 or cash value of policy, whichever is higher
11. $110.31, found by 0.505 X $218.43;
    $55.70, found by 0.255 X $218.43;
    $18.57, found by 0.085 X $218.43
13. $329.20, found by ($20,000/$1,000) X $16.46 (table);
    $166.25, found by 0.505 X $329.20;
    $83.95, found by 0.255 X $329.20;
    $27.98, found by 0.085 X $329.20
15. $58.52, found by ($4,000/$1,000) X $14.63 (table);
    $29.55, found by 0.505 X $58.52;
    $14.92, found by 0.255 X $58.52;
    $4.97, found by 0.085 X $58.52
17. $115.82, found by 0.255 X [($10,000/$1,000) X $45.42] (table)
19. Term to age 65, 10-year term, and straight life, found by: $22.00 per month X 12 = $264 per year. The maximum amount per $1,000 that he can afford is $13.20, found by $264 ÷ 20. Thus, checking Table 8-3 for 18-year-old male, there are three policies listed under $13.20 per $1,000.
21. $4.70, found by [4 X 0.255 X ($15,000/$1,000) X $15.67] – [($15,000/$1,000) X $15.67]

Assignment 8-3
Automobile Insurance

1. 1.55 (table)
3. 1.15 (table)
5. 1.00 (table)
7. 2; 9; $54.80; $4.00; $15.60; $55.00; and $129.40, found by $54.80 + $4.00 + $15.60 + $55.00
9. 6; 5; $48.80; $3.20; 0; 0; $52.00, found by $48.80 + $3.20
11. 1; 8; $54.00; $4.00; $10.60; $44.80; $113.40, found by $54.00 + $4.00 + $10.60 + $44.80
13. 1.95 (table)
15. 1.00 (table)
17. $128.20, found by $54.00 + $3.60 + $15.60 + $55.00 using 2-9 age and insurance rating group
19. A. 2.30 (table)
    B. 3-8 (table)
    C. $54.80 (table)
    D. $2.20 (table)
    E. $9.00 (table)
    F. $38.00 (table)
    G. $104.00, found by $54.80 + $2.20 + $9.00 + $38.00
    H. $239.20, found by 2.30 X $104.00

CHAPTER 9

Assignment 9-1
Income

1. $126.75, found by 39 X $3.25; no overtime
3. $180.00, found by 40 X $4.50;
   $33.75, found by 5 X 1.5 X $4.50;
   $202.50, found by 45 X $4.50;
   $11.25, found by 5 X 0.5 X $4.50;
   $213.75, found by $180 + $33.75 or $202.50 + $11.25
5. $150.00, found by 40 X $3.75;
   $61.88, found by 11 X 1.5 X $3.75;
   $191.25, found by 51 X $3.75;
   $20.63, found by 11 X 0.5 X $3.75;
   $211.88, found by $150.00 + $61.88 or $191.25 + $20.63
7. $57.80, found by 17.0 X $3.40
9. A. $63.53, found by 19.25 X $3.30
   B. $32.18, found by 6.50 X 1.50 X $3.30
   C. $95.71, found by $63.53 + $32.18
11. $18,750, found by $975,000 ÷ 52;
    $37,500, found by $975,000 ÷ 26;
    $40,625, found by $975,000 ÷ 24;
    $81,250, found by $975,000 ÷ 12
13. $207.69, found by ($900 X 12) ÷ 52;
    $415.38, found by ($900 X 12) ÷ 26;
    $450, found by ($900 X 12) ÷ 24;
    $10,800, found by $900 X 12
15. $225, found by ($450 X 26) ÷ 52;
    $487.50, found by ($450 X 26) ÷ 24;
    $975, found by ($450 X 26) ÷ 12;
    $11,700, found by $450 X 26
17. £384.62 biweekly, found by £10,000 ÷ 26;
    £416.67 semimonthly, found by £10,000 ÷ 24
19. $43.50 commission and gross pay, found by $0.50 X 87

21. $262.50, found by 70 X $3.75;
$84.35, found by 0.035 X $2,410;
$346.85, found by $262.50 + $84.35
23. $146.10, found by 0.06 X $2,435 = $146.10 or
40 X $3.375 = $135.00
25. $164.80, found by (50 X $3.20) + (0.04 X $120)
27. A. $38.40, found by 8 X $4.80
B. $49.92, found by 1.30 X $4.80 X 8 X 240/240
C. $59.90, found by 1.30 X $4.80 X 8 X 288/240

Assignment 9-2
Deductions

1. $242.66, found by $425.32 – ($93.57 + $26.07 + $8.51 + $5.00 + $8.51 + $20.00 + $10.00 + $1.00 + $10.00)
3. $100.51, found by $146.25 – ($23.40 + $8.97 + $3.66 + $1.46 + $5.75 + $0.50 + $2.00)
5. $754.60, found by $1,245.50 – ($149.00 + $76.35 + $37.37 + $18.68 + $10.00 + $12.50 + $100.00 + $25.00 + $50.00 + $12.00)
7. A. $114.00, found by 38 X $3.00
B. $25.79, found by $10.80 + $6.99 + $3 + $5
C. $88.21, found by $114.00 – $25.79
9. A. $300, found by ($600 X 12) ÷ 24
B. $89.49, found by $18.39 + $43.60 + $12.50 + $5.00 + $10.00
C. $210.51, found by $300.00 – $89.49
11. $13.18 both, found by 0.0613 X $215.00
13. $57.21, found by 0.0930 X $615.20
15. $2,130.60 both, found by maximum for 1982, since $33,500 is greater than $31,800
17. A. $413.78, found by 0.0613 X 15 X $450
B. $1,360.86, found by 0.0613 X 37 X $600
C. Yes
D. $186.97, found by ($413.78 + $1,360.86) – $1,587.67
E. Claim a FICA overpayment tax credit when filing 1980 IRS return
19. $94.00 (table)
21. $50.50, found by $375.00 – (3 X $19.23) = $317.31 and $43.47 + 0.24 ($317.31 – $288.00)
23. $17.33, found by $148.50 – (1 X $19.23) = $129.27 and $5.40 + 0.18 ($129.27 – $63.00)
25. A. $273.40, found by (43 X $3.10) + (0.03 X $4,670.00)
B. $16.76, found by 0.0613 X $273.40
C. $24.90 (table)
D. $6.84, found by 0.025 X $273.40
E. $4.10, found by 0.015 X $273.40
F. $10.00
G. $62.60, found by $16.76 + $24.90 + $6.84 + $4.10 + $10.00
H. $210.80, found by $273.40 – $62.60

CHAPTER 10

Assignment 10-1
Sales taxes

1. 4%; $1.58, found by 0.04 X $39.49 = $1.5796; $41.07, found by $39.49 + $1.58
3. 0%; $0; $1.79
5. 3.125%; $0.47, found by 0.03125 X $14.97 = $0.4678; $15.44, found by $14.97 + $0.47
7. A. $0.75, found by 0.04 X $18.76 = 0.7504, and $19.51, found by $18.76 + $0.75
B. $0.56, found by 0.03 X $18.76 = 0.5628, and $19.32, found by $18.76 + $0.56
C. $0.94, found by 0.05 X $18.76 = 0.938, and $19.70, found by $18.76 + $0.94
D. $1.31, found by 0.07 X $18.76 = 1.3132, and $20.07, found by $18.76 + $1.31
9. $25.00, found by $1.25 ÷ 0.05
11. 1%; 4%; 5%; $0.11, found by 0.05 X $2.25; $2.36, found by $2.25 + $0.11
13. 2%; 2%; 4%; $6.94, found by 0.04 X $173.50; $180.44, found by $173.50 + $6.94
15. 3%; 0%; 3%; $2.37, found by 0.03 X $78.99; $81.36, found by $78.99 + $2.37
17. A. $1.19, found by 0.06 X $19.86, and $21.05, found by $19.86 + $1.19, where $19.86 = (6 X $1.19) + (8 X $1.59)
B. $0.79, found by 0.04 X $19.86, and $20.65, found by $19.86 + $0.79
C. $1.10, found by 0.05525 X $19.86, and $20.96, found by $19.86 + $1.10
D. $0.99, found by 0.05 X $19.86, and $20.85, found by $19.86 + $0.99
19. $384, found by $1,024 – $640, where $1,024 = 0.08 X $12,800, and $640 = 0.05 X $12,800

Assignment 10-2
Property Taxes

1. $57,500, found by 0.50 X $115,000, and $3,156.75, found by $54.90 X $57,500/$1,000
3. $15,125, found by 0.22 X $68,750, and $1,206.98, found by $79.80 X $15,125/$1,000
5. $59,325, found by 0.70 X $84,750, and $3,827.65, found by $64.52 X $59,325/$1,000
7. A. $22,715, found by 0.35 X $64,900
B. $45.43, found by $2.00 X $22,715/$1,000
C. $20.44, found by $0.90 X $22,715/$1,000
D. $22.72, found by $1.00 X $22,715/$1,000
E. $4.54, found by $0.20 X $22,715/$1,000
F. $56.79, found by $2.50 X $22,715/$1,000
G. $45.43, found by $2.00 X $22,715/$1,000

H. $706.44, found by $31.10 × $22,715/$1,000
I. $13.63, found by $0.60 × $22,715/$1,000
J. $915.41, found by $40.30 × $22,715/$1,000 or (with rounding error), $45.43 + $20.44 + $22.72 + $4.54 + $56.79 + $45.43 + $706.44 + $13.63

9. $1,216.38, found by $40.60 × $29,960/$1,000, where $29,960 = 0.40 × $74,900
11. $258.72, found by $8.00 × $32,340/$1,000, where $32,340 = 0.35 × $92,400
13. $9,560,313, found by $52.60 × $181,755,000/$1,000, where $181,755,000 = 0.42 × $432,750,000
15. $90.74, found by $6.10 × $14,875/$1,000, where $14,875 = 0.35 × $42,500
17. A. $82.44, found by $45.10 × $1,828/$1,000
    B. $9,140, found by $1,828 ÷ 0.20
19. 8.20 mills, found by $492,000 ÷ (0.40 × $150,000,000) = 0.0082

Assignment 10-3
Other Taxes

1. $0.12; $2.30, found by $0.12 × 19.2 = $2.304
3. $0.13; $1.12, found by $0.13 × 8.6 = $1.118
5. $0.135; $3.35, found by $0.135 × 24.8 = $3.348
7. $8.40, found by ($0.11 × 18.6) + ($0.13 × 14.3) + ($0.115 × 17.8) + ($0.12 × 20.4)
9. $33; $3.09; $66, found by 2 × $33; $6.18, found by 2 × $3.09; $72.18, found by $66.00 + $6.18
11. $30; $2.53; $120, found by 4 × $30; $10.12, found by 4 × $2.53; $130.12, found by $120.00 + $10.12
13. $22; $2.01; $110, found by 5 × $22; $10.05, found by 5 × $2.01; $120.05, found by $110.00 + $10.05
15. $140.56, found by $134.36 + (0.05 × $124.00) where $134.36 = 4($31.00 + $2.59) and $124 = 4 × $31
17. $0.12; $1.20, found by $0.12 × 10
19. $0.15; $0.30, found by $0.15 × 2
21. $0.185; $3.70, found by $0.185 × 20
23. $0.208, found by (0.40 × $5.20) ÷ 10
25. A. $9.43, found by ($0.135 × 20.2) + ($0.11 × 18.6) + ($0.13 × 21.6) + ($0.12 × 15.4)
    B. $4.74, found by 2 × $2.37
    C. $3.48, found by 0.06 × (2 × $29.00)
    D. $0.54, found by ($0.12 × 2) + ($0.15 × 1) + ($0.15 × 1)

CHAPTER 11

Assignment 11-1
Checking Accounts

1.

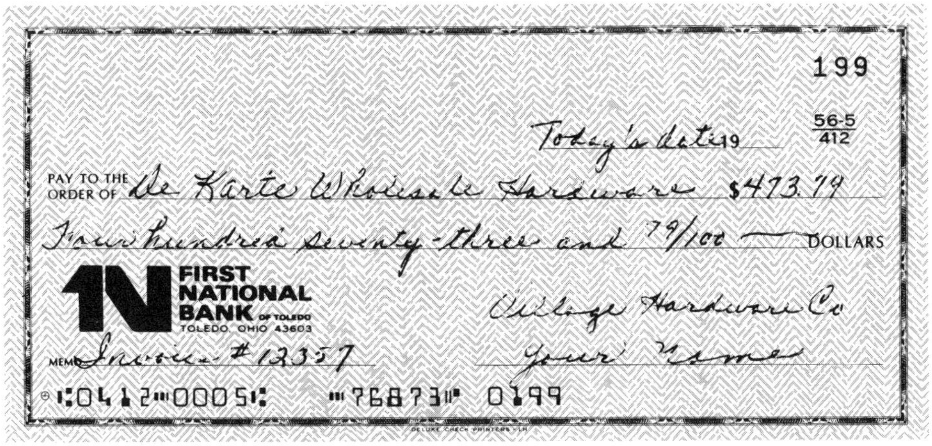

3.

Checkbook balance		$193.66
Service charge	–	5.35
Revised balance		$188.31

Statement balance		$217.89
Deposits not shown	+	190.70
		$408.59
Checks outstanding ($117.90 + $84.75 + $17.63)	–	220.28
Revised bank statement		$188.31

5. 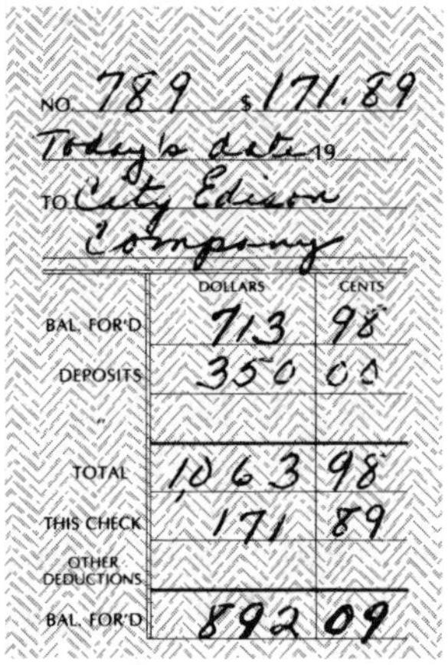

NO. 789 $171.89
Today's date 19
TO City Edison Company

	DOLLARS	CENTS
BAL. FOR'D	713	98
DEPOSITS	350	00
TOTAL	1,063	98
THIS CHECK	171	89
OTHER DEDUCTIONS		
BAL. FOR'D	892	09

7.

Checkbook balance	$335.42
Service charge (8 × 10¢ + 50¢)	− 1.30
Revised balance	$334.12

Statement balance	$316.70
Deposits not shown	+ 200.00
	$516.70
Checks outstanding ($107.60 + $74.98)	− 182.58
Revised bank statement	$334.12

Assignment 11-2
Simple Interest

1. Due August 20;
   I = $60, found by $1,500 × 0.08 × 180/360;
   MV = $1,560, found by $1,500 + $60
3. Due November 15;
   I = $21.14, found by $965 × 0.065 × 123/365;
   MV = $986.14, found by $965.00 + $21.14
5. Due January 9;
   I = $9.49, found by $565 × 0.1025 × 59/360;
   MV = $574.49, found by $565.00 + $9.49
7. I = $2,521.20, found by $7,640 × 0.11 × 3;
   MV = $10,161.20, found by $7,640.00 + $2,521.20
9. A. October 17, found by 6th month + 4 months = 10th month
   B. 122 days, found by 290 − 168
   C. 120 days, found by 4 × 30
11. A. $32.80, found by $800 × 0.18 × 82/360, where 82 = 156 − 74
    B. $832.80, found by $800.00 + $32.80
13. $9,121.56, found by $9,000.00 + $121.56, where $121.56 = $9,000 × 0.085 × 58/365, where 58 = 214 − 156
15. $875.77, found by $850.00 + $25.77, where $25.77 = $850 × 0.0925 × 118/360, where the due date is August 7; (219 = 99 + 120)
17. $50,553.01, found by $47,500 + $3,053.01, where $3,053.01 = $47,500 × 0.1275 × 184/365, where the due date is November 20; (184 = 324 − 140)
19. $15.36, found by $1,382.81 − $1,367.45, where $1,382.81 = $14,750 × 0.125 × 270/360; (9-month due date: October 31)
    $1,367.45 = $14,750 × 0.125 × 267/360; (270-day due date: October 28), found by 31 + 270 = 301

Assignment 11-3
Determining Principal, Rate, and Time

1. $1,285.71, found by $37.50 ÷ (0.0875 × 120/360)
3. 132.1%, found by $8.50 ÷ ($234.90 × 10/365) = 1.3207525
5. 364 days, found by $10.00 ÷ ($54.96 × 0.18) = 1.0108361 × 360
7. $9,882.35, found by $70 ÷ (0.085 × 30/360)
9. 5.5%, found by $12.28 ÷ ($893 × ¼) = 0.0550052
11. 90, found by $138.13 ÷ ($8,500 × 0.065) = 0.25000904 × 360 = 90.003257
13. 8.28%, found by $1.38 ÷ ($200 × 1/12) = 0.0828
15. Oct. 20, found by $53 ÷ ($1,000 × 0.085) = 0.6235294 × 360 = 224.47058; and March 10 the 69th day + 224 days = 293rd day of the year
17. 60%, found by $10 ÷ ($200 × 1/12) = 0.6
19. $12,972.97, found by $300 ÷ (0.0925 × 3/12)

Assignment 11-4
Compound Interest

1. 1.875%, found by 7½% ÷ 4; 10, found by 2½ × 4; $1.20414 (Table 11-2); $3,010.35, found by $1.20414 × 2,500; $510.35, found by $3,010.35 − $2,500.00
3. 1.875%, found by 3¾% ÷ 2; 14, found by 7 × 2; $1.29702 (Table 11-2); $28,080.48, found by $1.29702 × 21,650; $6,430.48, found by $28,080.43 − $21,650
5. 2.000%, found by 2% ÷ 1; 15, found by 15 × 1; $1.34587 (Table 11-2); $652.75, found by $1.34587 × 485; $167.75, found by $652.75 − $485.00
7. $4,349.85, found by $1.44995 × 3,000, where rate per period = 1.875% and number of periods = 20
9. $5,691.86, found by $1.14367 × 4,000 = $4,574.68, where rate per period = 1.125% and number of periods = 12; and $1.24421 × 4,574.68 = $5,691.8626, where rate per period = 1.375% and number of periods = 16
11. $0.54, found by $255.54 − $255.00 where $255.54 = $1.0021116 × 255
13. A. $13.65, found by $1,013.65 − $1,000.00, where $1,013.65 = $1.0136529 × 1,000
    B. $13.75, found by $1,013.75 − $1,000.00, where $1,013.75 = $1.01375 × 1,000, where rate per period = 1.375% and number of periods = 1

15. A. \$29,719.00, found by \$1.48595 × 20,000, where rate per period = 2.000% and number of periods = 20
    B. \$9,719.00, found by \$29,719.00 – \$20,000.00
17. \$28,824.09, found by
    For first 6 years: 5.5% ÷ 4 = 1.375% for 24 periods.
    Then, 9,000 × \$1.38784 = \$12,490.56
    For next 15 years:
    12,490.56 × \$2.281738943 = \$28,500.20
    For next 75 days:
    28,500.20 × \$1.0113646 = \$28,824.09

CHAPTER 12

Assignment 12-1
Promissory Notes and Discounting

1. \$5,000; Sept. 3; 75 days; \$83.33, found by \$5,000 × 0.08 × 75/360; \$4,916.67, found by \$5,000 – \$83.33
3. \$43,600; May 20; 61 days; \$701.84, found by \$43,600 × 0.095 × 61/360; \$42,898.16, found by \$43,600 – \$701.84
5. \$1,000; Jan. 19; 35 days; \$8.02, found by \$1,000 × 0.0825 × 35/360; \$991.98, found by \$1,000 – \$8.02
7. A. 54 days, found by October 10 to December 3
   B. \$18.90, found by \$1,200 × 0.105 × 54/360
   C. \$1,181.10, found by \$1,200 – \$18.90
9. A. (Mrs.) Jean Gibbons
   B. Promissory note
   C. September 26
   D. \$400
   E. \$400
   F. \$397.90, found by \$400 – \$2.10, where \$2.10 = \$400 × 0.09 × 21/360
11. \$870, found by \$900 – \$30, where \$30 = \$900 × 0.12 × 100/360

Assignment 12-2
Discounting an Interest-Bearing Note and Establishing a Line of Credit

1. Nov. 6; 60 days; \$29.17, found by \$2,500 × 0.07 × 60/360; \$2,529.17, found by \$2,500 + \$29.17; 37 days; \$24.69, found by \$2,529.17 × 0.095 × 37/360; \$2,504.48, found by \$2,529.17 – \$24.69
3. Sept. 20; 62 days; \$16.79, found by \$1,500 × 0.065 × 62/360; \$1,516.79, found by \$1,500 + \$16.79; 62 days; \$22.86, found by \$1,516.79 × 0.0875 × 62/360; \$1,493.93, found by \$1,516.79 – \$22.86
5. Feb. 3; 184 days; \$177.29, found by \$4,625 × 0.075 × 184/360; \$4,802.29, found by \$4,625 + \$177.29; 45 days; \$66.03, found by \$4,802.29 × 0.11 × 45/360; \$4,736.26, found by \$4,802.29 – \$66.03
7. A. June 9
   B. 60 days
   C. \$12, found by \$900 × 0.08 × 60/360
   D. \$912, found by \$900 + \$12
   E. 25 days
   F. \$5.70, found by \$912 × 0.09 × 25/360
   G. \$906.30, found by \$912.00 – \$5.70
9. \$2,995.37, found by \$3,090 – \$94.63 where \$3,090 = \$3,000 + (\$3,000 × 0.09 × 120/360) and \$94.63 = \$3,090 × 0.105 × 105/360
11. A. \$1,341.15, found by \$1,314.85 + (\$1,314.85 × 0.08 × 90/360).
    B. It is the same as the maturity value in Problem 10.

Assignment 12-3
Partial Payment

1. A. \$3,000
   B. \$22.50, found by \$3,000 × 0.09 × 30/360
   C. \$977.50, found by \$1,000 – \$22.50
   D. \$2,022.50, found by \$3,000 – \$977.50
   E. \$25.28, found by \$2,022.50 × 0.09 × 50/360
   F. \$1,474.72, found by \$1,500 – \$25.28
   G. \$547.78, found by \$2,022.50 – \$1,474.72
   H. \$5.48, found by \$547.78 × 0.09 × 40/360
   I. \$553.26, found by \$547.78 + \$5.48
3. A. \$1,000
   B. \$20.44, found by \$1,000 × 0.08 × 92/360
   C. \$1,020.44, found by \$1,000 + \$20.44
   D. \$300 + \$400 = \$700
   E. \$4.00, found by \$300 × 0.08 × 60/360
      <u>2.67</u>, found by \$400 × 0.08 × 30/360
      \$6.67
   F. \$706.67, found by \$700 + \$6.67
   G. \$313.77, found by \$1,020.44 – \$706.67

5. $2,035.37, found by

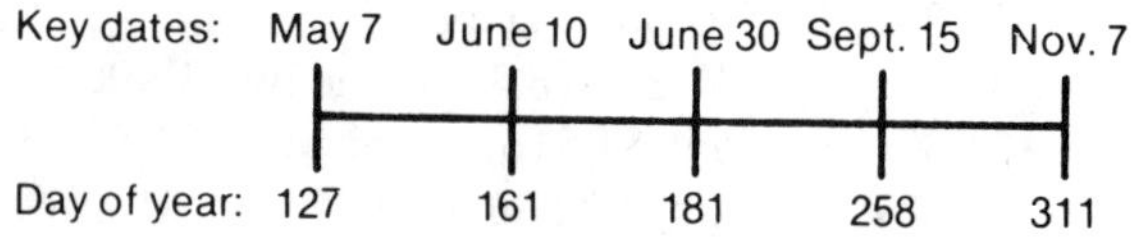

Face		$6,500.00
First payment	$1,200.00	
Deduct interest on $6,500.00 for 34 days (May 7 to June 10)	– 61.39	
Amount deducted from face		– 1,138.61
Balance on June 10		$5,361.39
Second payment	$ 25.00	
Deduct interest on $5,361.39 for 20 days (June 10 to June 30) . . .	– 29.79*	
Third payment	3,475.00	
Add second payment	+ 25.00	
	$3,500.00	
Deduct interest on $5,361.39 for 97 days (June 10 to Sept. 15) . . .	– 144.46	
Amount deducted from new face		– 3,355.54
Balance on Sept. 15		$2,005.85
Add interest on $2,005.84 for 53 days (Sept. 15 to Nov. 7) . . .		+ 29.53
Amount due on due date		$2,035.38

***Since the interest is greater than the payment, this payment is added to the next payment.**

CHAPTER 13

Assignment 13-1
Assets, Liabilities, and Owner Equity

1. *Assets:*

   $10,200 Cash, found by $12,000 – $1,800
   3,000 Supplies
   4,300 Equipment
   $17,500 Total

   Liabilities:

   $5,500 (explain) Accounts Payable: $1,200 (supplies) + $4,300 (equipment)

   Owner Equity:

   Owner equity = Assets – Liabilities
   $12,000 = $17,500 – $5,500

   The accounting equation is: Assets = Liabilities + Owner equity
   $17,500 = $5,500 + $12,000

   Assets: Cash, supplies, and equipment which the McDougals own.
   Liabilities: Money which the McDougals owe for supplies and equipment.
   Owner equity: The $12,000 the McDougals invested initially.

3. Assets = $32,000, found by $3,000 (cash) + $4,000 (supplies) + $25,000 (equipment), where $3,000 (cash) = $5,000 + $12,000 – $4,000 – $10,000
   Liabilities = $27,000, found by $12,000 (bank loan) + $15,000 (equipment on account)
   Owner equity = $5,000, found by $32,000 – $27,000 or original investment
   Accounting equation: $32,000 = $27,000 + $5,000

Assignment 13-2
The Balance Sheet

1.

	Assets					=	Liabilities	+	Owner Equity
	Cash	+	Supplies	+	Equipment	=	Accounts payable	+	McDougal, capital
Balance:	$10,200	+	$3,000	+	$4,300	=	$5,500	+	$12,000
Transaction:	+ 3,600								+ 3,600
Balance:	$13,800	+	$3,000	+	$4,300	=	$5,500	+	$15,600

	Assets							=	Liabilities	+	Owner Equity
	Cash	+	Supplies	+	Equipment	–	Accumulated depreciation	=	Accounts payable	+	McDougal, capital
Balance:	$13,800	+	$3,000	+	$4,300			=	$5,500	+	$15,600
Transaction:	– 1,650					–	+ 80		– 1,300		– 430
Balance:	$12,150	+	$3,000	+	$4,300	–	$80	=	$4,200	+	$15,170

McDOUGAL UPHOLSTERY SHOP
Balance Sheet
As of April 30

Assets		
Cash		$12,150
Supplies		3,000
Equipment	$4,300	
Less accumulated depreciation	– 80	4,220
Total assets		$19,370
Liabilities		
Accounts payable		$ 4,200
Owner Equity		
McDougal, capital		15,170
Total liabilities and owner equity		$19,370

Assignment 13-3
Income Statements

1. $18,595, found by $13,960 + $1,200 + $1,050 + $450 + $360 + $420 + $240 + $915
3. $20,185, found by $14,315 + $1,625 + $1,050 + $900 + $480 + $600 + $240 + $975

5. WALINSKI AUTOMOTIVE SERVICE GARAGE
Income Statement
For Quarter Ended December 31

Income:		
Revenue from service	$17,650	
Less: credit allowances . . .	– 185	
Net revenue		$17,465
Cost of supplies		1,700
Gross profit		$15,765
Operating Expenses		
Rent	$ 900	
Wages	300	
Depreciation	270	
Utilities	240	
Insurance	90	
Miscellaneous expenses . . .	30	
Total operating expenses. .		$ 1,830
Net income		$13,935

Assignment 13-4
Vertical and Horizontal Analysis

1. 50.0% decrease, found by ($10,000 – $20,000) ÷ $20,000
3. 25.0% increase, found by ($100,000 – $80,000) ÷ $80,000
5. 50.0% increase, found by ($60,000 – $40,000) ÷ $40,000
7. A. 83.6%, found by $12,000 ÷ $14,355 = 0.8359
   B. 83.2%, found by $15,000 ÷ $18,020 = 0.8324
   C. 2.7%, found by $480 ÷ $18,020 = 0.0266
   D. 12.0%, found by $2,160 ÷ $18,020 = 0.1199
   E. 2.1%, found by $380 ÷ $18,020 = 0.0211
   F. Yes; cash, supplies, equipment, and inventory make up all of the total assets and there is no rounding error.
   G. 30.7%, found by $4,400 ÷ $14,355 = 0.3065
   H. 83.0%, found by $9,955 ÷ $12,000 = 0.8296
   I. 6.7%, found by $800 ÷ $12,000 = 0.0667

Assignment 13-5
Ratio Analysis

1. 25.5:1; 255 ÷ 10; there are 25.5 production workers to every 1 supervisor
3. 0.4:1; 200 ÷ 500; there are 0.4 hits for every 1 at bat (0.400)
5. 16.4:1; 82 ÷ 5; there are 16.4 salespersons to every 1 secretary
7. 1.7:1; found by $529,623 ÷ $310,770
9. 1.9:1, found by $381,107 ÷ $201,241
11. An acid-test ratio of 0.9:1 means that for every 90 cents of liquid assets (quickly convertible to cash—does not include inventory) there is $1 in current liabilities. A healthy fiscal position would call for an acid-test ratio of 1.0:1.
13. 11.2%, found by $20,145 ÷ $179,866

CHAPTER 14

Assignment 14-1
Payroll Register

1. $55.30 FIT (table); $24.44 FICA, found by 6.13% X $398.75
3. $39.20 FIT (table); $16.09 FICA, found by 6.13% X $262.45
5. $47.90 FIT (table); $21.24 FICA, found by 6.13% X $346.50

7.

Employee	*Reg. Hrs.*	*OT Hrs.*	*Rate*	*M/S*	*Allow ances*	*Gross Pay*	*SIT (2½%)*	*FIT*	*FICA*	*Total Deductions*	*Net Pay*
Trianon	0	0	0	M	4	$350.00	$8.75	$41.40	$21.46	$71.61	$278.39
Nader	0	0	0	M	5	350.00	8.75	37.30	21.46	67.51	282.49
Trakos	40	6	$4.90	S	2	240.10	6.00	34.00	14.72	54.72	185.38
Bailey	30	0	4.25	S	1	127.50	3.19	13.50	7.82	24.51	102.99

Assignment 14-2
Advertising Expenses

1. $0.685 (table); $647.33, found by 945 X $0.685
3. $1.04 (table); $2,912.00, found by 2,800 X $1.04
5. $0.700 (table); $420.00, found by 600 X $0.700
7. $4,564.00, found by (2 X 2,800) X $0.815
9. $6,655.52, found by (2,800 X $1.04) + (3 X 1,418 X $0.88)
11. $10,000, found by 4 X $2,500; $5,000; $0; $15,000, found by $10,000 + $5,000
13. $0; $224,100, found by 3 X $74,700; $149,400; $373,500, found by $224,100 + $149,400
15. $137,500, found by 2 X $68,750; $550,000, found by 4 X $137,500; $1,100,000, found by 4 X $275,000; $1,787,500, found by $137,500 + $550,000 + $1,100,000
17. $412,500, found by [(4 X $12,500) + (2 X $6,250) + ($25,000)] + [(4 X $65,000) + (4 X $16,250)]

Assignment 14-3
Business Insurance

1. $5.00; $600, found by $5.00 X 120; $14.10; $705, found by $14.10 X 50; $1,305, found by $600 + $705
3. $9.20; $8,648, found by $9.20 X 940; 0; included; $8,648
5. $4.70; $3,478, found by $4.70 X 740; $11.70; $5,265, found by $11.70 X 450; $8,743, found by $3,478 + $5,265
7. $1,934.50, found by $7.30 X 265
9. A. $1,057.50, found by $4.70 X 225
   B. $2,926.00, found by $15.40 X 190
   C. $3,983.50, found by $1,057.50 + $2,926.00
11. $239.20, found by $9.20 X 26 where building is "Protected-Town Classes 1-8" and Type 3 construction
13. $150, found by annual minimum premium since $6.90 X 20 = $138. Building construction is Type 3.

Assignment 14-4
Other Business Expenses

1. $50.23, found by 0.0205 X $2,450 = $50.225
3. $496.58, found by 0.1254 X $3,960
5. $33.95, found by 0.0073 X $4,650 = $33.945
7. $107.64, found by 0.0312 X $3,450
9. $5,700; $39.90, found by 0.007 X $5,700; $136.80, found by 0.024 X $5,700
11. $6,000; $42.00, found by 0.007 X $6,000; $144.00, found by 0.024 X $6,000
13. $6,000; $42.00, found by 0.007 X $6,000; $144.00, found by 0.024 X $6,000

15. A. $6,000; $42, found by 0.007 X $6,000; $192, found by 0.032 X $6,000
B. $6,000; $42, found by 0.007 X $6,000; $192, found by 0.032 X $6,000
C. $6,000; $42, found by 0.007 X $6,000; $192, found by 0.032 X $6,000
D. $6,000; $42, found by 0.007 X $6,000; $192, found by 0.032 X $6,000

For Problems 17, 19, and 21, the answers for the left side of the problem are given above the answers for the right side.

	Shipped from	*Weight (lbs.)*	*Pickup Area*	*Cost per 100 lbs.*	*Pickup Cost*	*Found by*	*Air Freight Cost per 100 lbs.*	*Air Freight Cost*	*Found by*	*Delivery Area*	*Cost per 100 lbs.*
17.	Boston to Miami	3,500	A	$2.10	$ 73.50	$2.10 X 35	$11.88	$415.80	$11.88 X 35	B	$2.35
19.	Detroit to Tampa	6,200	A	1.90	117.80	$1.90 X 62	9.21	571.02	$9.21 X 62	B	2.10
21.	Memphis to Miami	987	A	2.75	27.14	$2.75 X 9.87	11.70	115.48	$11.70 X 9.87	A	2.90

	Delivery Cost	*Found by*	*Pickup, Air Freight, Delivery Total*	*Found by*	*5% Federal Tax*	*Found by*	*Total Cost*	*Found by*
17.	$ 82.25	$2.35 X 35	$571.55	$73.50 + $415.80 + $82.25	$28.58	0.05 X $571.55	$600.13	$571.55 + $28.58
19.	130.20	$2.10 X 62	819.02	$117.80 + $571.02 + $130.20	40.95	0.05 X $819.02	$859.97	$819.02 + $40.95
21.	28.62	$2.90 X 9.87	171.24	$27.14 + $115.48 + $28.62	8.56	0.05 X $117.24	$179.80	$171.24 + $8.56

23. $263.94, found by

$2.55 X 11.40	=	$ 29.07
$16.80 X 11.40	=	191.52
$2.70 X 11.40	=	30.78
		$251.37
5% X $251.37	=	12.57
		$263.94

CHAPTER 15

Assignment 15-1 Trade Discounts

1. $25.50, found by 0.30 X $85; $59.50, found by $85.00 – $25.50
3. $2.03, found by 0.45 X $4.50 = $2.025; $2.47, found by $4.50 – $2.03
5. $7.05, found by 0.47 X $15; $7.95, found by $15.00 – $7.05
7. A. $44.75, found by 0.50 X $89.50
   B. $44.75, found by $89.50 – $44.75
9. 70%, found by 100% – 30%; $224.00, found by 0.70 X $320.00
11. 55%, found by 100% – 45%; $712.25, found by 0.55 X $1,295.00
13. $134.75, found by 0.35 X $385.00, where 0.35 = 1.00 – 0.65
15. Net price = $4,436.70, found by 0.65 X 0.85 X $8,030.23, where $8,030.23 = (42 X $34.99) + (450 X $2.99) + (80 X $49.95) + (210 X $4.99) + (100 X $0.89) + (25 X $3.29)

Assignment 15-2 Chain Discounts

1. $80.00; $120.00; $36.00; $84.00; $8.40; $75.60
3. $5,000.00; $5,000.00; $1,000.00; $4,000.00; $200.00; $3,800.00
5. $100.00; $100.00; $10.00; $90.00
7. A. $127.50, found by 0.30 X $425.00
   B. $297.50, found by $425.00 – $127.50
   C. $59.50, found by 0.20 X $297.50
   D. $238.00, found by $297.50 – $59.50
   E. $23.80, found by 0.10 X $238.00
   F. $214.20, found by $238.00 – $23.80
9. 0.50; 0.80; 0.90; 0.36
11. 0.60; 0.70; 0.42
13. A. 0.70, found by 1.00 – 0.30
    B. 0.80, found by 1.00 – 0.20
    C. 0.95, found by 1.00 – 0.05
    D. 0.532, found by 0.70 X 0.80 X 0.95
    E. $1,303.40, found by 0.532 X $2,450.00
15. Toaster: $430.00, found by 20 X $21.50; 0.4275;

$183.83, found by 0.4275 X $430.00 = $183.825
Mixer: $1,259.30, found by 14 X $89.95; 0.432;
$544.02, found by 0.432 X $1,259.30 = $544.0176
Broiler: $11,145.60, found by 86 X $129.60; 0.45;
$5,015.52, found by 0.45 X $11,145.60
Fan: $900.00, found by 25 X $36; 0.60;
$540, found by 0.60 X $900
$5,026.70, found by 0.80 X $6,283.37, where 80% is complement of 20%

Assignment 15-3
Cash Discounts

1. March 13; $24, found by 0.02 X $1,200; $1,176, found by $1,200 – $24
3. July 15; $3.40, found by 0.02 X $170; $166.60, found by $170.00 – $3.40
5. April 14; none, paid after April 14; $2,000
7. A. August 12
   B. $37.68, found by 0.04 X $942.00
   C. $904.32, found by $942.00 – $37.68
9. January 26; $600, found by 0.05 X $12,000; $11,400, found by $12,000 – $600
11. July 24; none, paid after July 24; $840
13. December 10; $30, found by 0.03 X $1,000; $970, found by $1,000 – $30
15. A. March 24
    B. May 13, found by March 14 (73) plus 60 days (133)
    C. $23.02, found by 0.03 X $767.40 = $23.022
    D. $744.38, found by $767.40 – $23.02
17. A. $752.80, paid after Sept. 21, therefore no cash discount
    B. $722.69, found by $752.80 – $30.11 where $30.11 = 0.04 X $752.80

CHAPTER 16

Assignment 16-1
Markup

1. *SP* = $0.50, found by $0.40 + $0.10
3. *C* = $150, found by $240 – $90; % markup based on *SP* = 37.5%, found by $90 ÷ $240 = 0.375
5. *M* = $360, found by 120% X $300; *SP* = $660, found by $300 + $360; % markup based on *SP* = 54.5%, found by $360 ÷ $660
7. $3, found by $9 – $6
9. A. 40%, found by

$$\begin{aligned} C + M &= SP \\ ? + 60\% &= 100\% \\ \$795 + ? &= ? \end{aligned}$$

   B. $1,987.50, found by $795 ÷ 40%
   C. $1,192.50, found by $1,987.50 – $795.00
11. $40, found by $24 ÷ 60% where

$$\begin{aligned} C + M &= SP \\ 60\% + 40\% &= 100\% \\ \$24 + ? &= ? \end{aligned}$$

13. A. $140, found by 70% X $200 where

$$\begin{aligned} C + M &= SP \\ 100\% + 70\% &= 170\% \\ \$200 + ? &= ? \end{aligned}$$

    B. $340, found by $200 + $140
15. A. $140, found by $560 – $420
    B. 33⅓%, found by $140 ÷ $420
17. 50%, found by

$$\begin{aligned} C + M &= SP \\ 50\% + 50\% &= 100\% \end{aligned}$$

Assignment 16-2
Markdown

1. $4.00 markdown, found by $14.95 – $10.95; 26.8% markdown, found by $4.00 ÷ $14.95
3. 20.0% markdown, found by $0.40 ÷ $2.00; $1.60 sale price, found by $2.00 – $0.40
5. $3.60 markdown, found by 20% X $18.00; $14.40 sale price, found by $18.00 – $3.60
7. $1.88 markdown, found by $7.88 – $6.00
9. 38.0% markdown, found by 30¢ ÷ 79¢, where 79¢ – 49¢ = 30¢
11. $5.46 sale price, found by $7.00 – $1.54, where 22% X $7.00 = $1.54
13. A. $838.54, found by $6,833.54 – $5,995.00
    B. 12.3% markdown, found by $838.54 ÷ $6,833.54
15. 78¢ regular price, found by 59¢ + 19¢; 24% markdown, found by 19¢ ÷ 78¢
17. A. $17.49 sale price, found by 70% X $24.99 where 100% – 30% = 70%
    B. $8.74 sale price, found by 70% X $12.49
    C. $30.07 sale price, found by 70% X $42.95
    D. $6.99 sale price, found by 70% X $9.99

CHAPTER 17

Assignment 17-1
Straight-Line Method

1. \$100, found by (\$1,200 – \$200) ÷ 10
3. \$8,000, found by (\$72,000 – \$8,000) ÷ 8
5. \$520, found by (\$6,000 – \$800) ÷ 10

7.

Yr.	*Annual Depreciation*	*Accumulated Depreciation*	*Book Value*
1	\$1,300, found by (\$4,500 – \$600) ÷ 3	\$1,300	\$3,200, found by \$4,500 – \$1,300
2	\$1,300, found by (\$4,500 – \$600) ÷ 3	\$2,600, found by \$1,300 + \$1,300	\$1,900, found by \$4,500 – \$2,600
3	\$1,300, found by (\$4,500 – \$600) ÷ 3	\$3,900, found by \$2,600 + \$1,300	\$600, found by \$4,500 – \$3,900

9.

Yr.	*Annual Depreciation*	*Accumulated Depreciation*	*Book Value*
1	\$1,250, found by (\$9,000 – \$1,500) ÷ 6	\$1,250	\$7,750, found by \$9,000 – \$1,250
2	\$1,250, found by (\$9,000 – \$1,500) ÷ 6	\$2,500, found by \$1,250 + \$1,250	\$6,500, found by \$9,000 – \$2,500
3	\$1,250, found by (\$9,000 – \$1,500) ÷ 6	\$3,750, found by \$2,500 + \$1,250	\$5,250, found by \$9,000 – \$3,750
4	\$1,250, found by (\$9,000 – \$1,500) ÷ 6	\$5,000, found by \$3,750 + \$1,250	\$4,000, found by \$9,000 – \$5,000
5	\$1,250, found by (\$9,000 – \$1,500) ÷ 6	\$6,250, found by \$5,000 + \$1,250	\$2,750, found by \$9,000 – \$6,250
6	\$1,250, found by (\$9,000 – \$1,500) ÷ 6	\$7,500, found by \$6,250 + \$1,250	\$1,500, found by \$9,000 – \$7,500

11. A. \$1,500, found by (4,500/18,000) (\$6,500 – \$500)
    B. \$5,000, found by \$6,500 – \$1,500
13. A. \$10,000, found by (15,000/300,000) (\$250,000 – \$50,000)
    B. \$240,000, found by \$250,000 – \$10,000

Assignment 17-2
Sum-of-the-Years'-Digits Method

1. 15, found by 5 + 4 + 3 + 2 + 1, or $\frac{5(5+1)}{2} = \frac{30}{2}$
3. 28, found by 7 + 6 + 5 + 4 + 3 + 2 + 1, or $\frac{7(7+1)}{2} = \frac{56}{2}$
5. 45, found by 9 + 8 + 7 + 6 + 5 + 4 + 3 + 2 + 1, or $\frac{9(9+1)}{2} = \frac{90}{2}$

7.

Yr.	*Annual Depreciation*	*Accumulated Depreciation*	*Book Value*
1	\$1,950, found by (3/6) (\$4,500 – \$600)	\$1,950	\$2,550
2	\$1,300, found by (2/6) (\$4,500 – \$600)	\$3,250	\$1,250
3	\$650, found by (1/6) (\$4,500 – \$600)	\$3,900	\$ 600

9.

Yr.	*Annual Depreciation*	*Accumulated Depreciation*	*Book Value*
1	\$2,142.86, found by (6/21) (\$9,000 – \$1,500)	\$2,142.86	\$6,857.14
2	\$1,785.71, found by (5/21) (\$9,000 – \$1,500)	\$3,928.57	\$5,071.43
3	\$1,428.57, found by (4/21) (\$9,000 – \$1,500)	\$5,357.14	\$3,642.86
4	\$1,071.43, found by (3/21) (\$9,000 – \$1,500)	\$6,428.57	\$2,571.43
5	\$714.29, found by (2/21) (\$9,000) – \$1,500)	\$7,142.86	\$1,857.14
6	\$357.14, found by (1/21) (\$9,000 – \$1,500)	\$7,500.00	\$1,500.00

11. 5,050 found by $\frac{100(100+1)}{2}$

Assignment 17-3
The Declining-Balance Method

1. 1/10, 10%, 2/10 or 1/5, 20%
3. 1/20, 5%, 2/20 or 1/10, 10%
5. 1/3, 33⅓%, 2/3, 66⅔%

7.

Yr.	Annual Depreciation	Accumulated Depreciation	Book Value (Declining Balance)
1	$3,000, found by 66⅔% of $4,500	$3,000	$1,500
2	$900 adjusted; actual is $1,000, found by 66⅔% of $1,500	$3,900	$ 600
3	0	$3,900	$ 600

9.

Yr.	Annual Depreciation	Accumulated Depreciation	Book Value (Declining Balance)
1	$3,000, found by 33⅓% of $9,000	$3,000	$6,000
2	$2,000, found by 33⅓% of $6,000	$5,000	$4,000
3	$1,333.33, found by 33⅓% of $4,000	$6,333.33	$2,666.67
4	$888.89, found by 33⅓% of $2,666.67	$7,222.22	$1,777.78
5	$277.78 adjusted; actual is $592.59, found by 33⅓% of $1,777.78	$7,500.00	$1,500.00
6	0	$7,500.00	$1,500.00

11. The doubled rate is 200%, which is impossible. The annual depreciation is, therefore, equal to the original cost less salvage value.

CHAPTER 18

Assignment 18-1
Valuing an Inventory Using the Average-Cost Method

1. 61, found by 30 – 27 – 2 + 40 – 30 + 50
3. 1, found by 45 – 22 – 8 + 0 – 14 + 0
5. 0, found by 0 – 0 – 0 + 40 – 40 + 0
7. A. $4,625, found by [(50 × $5.00) + (30 × $4.00)] ÷ 80
   B. $92.50, found by $4.625 × 20
9. A. Balance:
   4/3: 175, found by 75 + 100
   4/10: 80, found by 175 – 95
   4/12: 60, found by 80 – 20
   4/15: 160, found by 60 + 100
   4/30: 85, found by 160 – 75
   B. Value: $2,758.64, found by {[(75 × $35) + (100 × $33) + (100 × $30)] ÷ 275} × 85

Assignment 18-2
Valuing an Inventory Using the First-In, First-Out (Fifo) Method

1. 55, found by 65 – 20 – 15 + 25;
   25 from 8/22 and 30 from 8/1
3. 50, found by 115 – 65 – 50 + 50;
   50 from 8/22
5. 60, found by 20 – 5 – 5 + 50;
   50 from 8/22 and 10 from 8/1
7. $80, found by 20 × $4
9. A. Balance: see Assignment 18-1, No. 9A
   B. $2,550, found by 85 × $30, where 85 comes from the 100 received 4/15

Assignment 18-3
Valuing an Inventory Using the Last-In, First-Out (Lifo) Method

1. 30, found by 20 – 10 + 40 – 20;
   20 from 9/1 and 10 from 9/15
3. 85, found by 25 – 15 + 90 – 15;
   25 from 9/1 and 60 from 9/15
5. 30, found by 60 – 20 + 25 – 35;
   30 from 9/1
7. $100, found by 20 × $5.00
9. A. Balance: see Assignment 18-1, No. 9A
   B. $2,955, found by (75 × $35) + (10 × $33)

Assignment 18-4
Inventory Turnover

1. $769,215, found by ($716,470 + $821,960) ÷ 2
3. $104,735.33, found by ($105,620 + $97,516 + $111,070) ÷ 3

5. $4,066.67, found by ($4,160 + $3,980 + $4,250 + $4,070 + $3,890 + $4,050) ÷ 6
7. A. $5,499.50, found by ($5,620 + $4,972 + $5,434 + $5,972) ÷ 4
   B. 6.0, found by ($32,800 ÷ $5,499.50) = 5.9641785
   C. The Ribbon Alley turns its inventory over six times per year. The shop sells its average inventory value six times a year. It sells one complete inventory every two months.
9. A. $27,273.33, found by ($26,870 + $29,200 + $25,750) ÷ 3
   B. 9.2, found by ($250,000 ÷ $27,273.33) = 9.166464
   C. Scott Gifts, Inc., sells its average inventory a little over nine times per year.
11. A. $100,000, found by ($102,000 + $99,500 + $137,200 + $61,300) ÷ 4
   B. 12, found by $1,200,000 ÷ $100,000
   C. 30.4, found by 365 ÷ 12

CHAPTER 19

Assignment 19-1
Graphic Presentation

1.

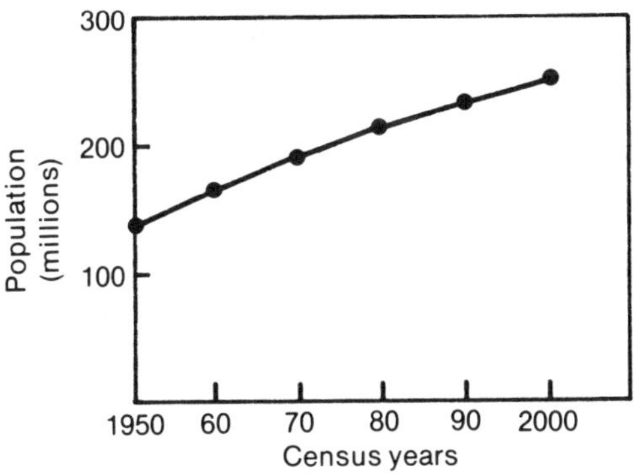

3.

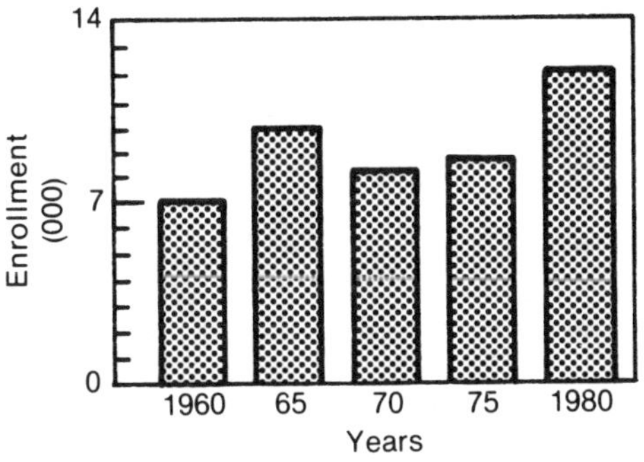

5. May be plotted in any order.

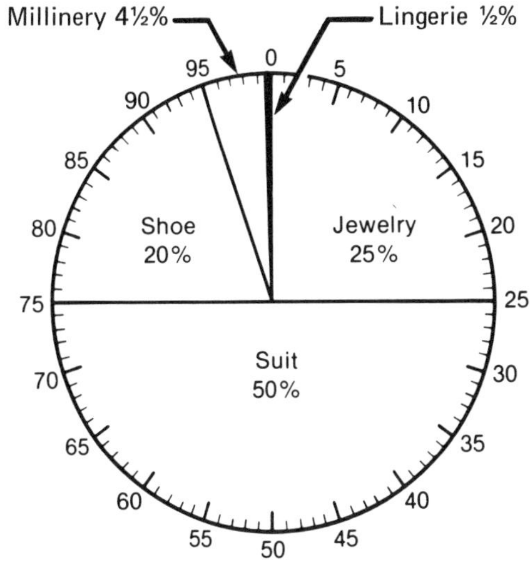

Assignment 19-2 (No answers)

Assignment 19-3
Averages

1. 500, 4, 125 pounds, found by 500 ÷ 4
3. $34.10, 5, $6.82, found by $34.10 ÷ 5
5. 75, 3, 25 sofas, found by 75 ÷ 3
7. A. $\overline{X}$ = 2,642.4 thousand, found by 31,709 ÷ 12
   B. Median = 2,480.5 thousand, found by (2,567 + 2,394) ÷ 2
9. A. $1.21778, found by $6.0889 ÷ 5
   B. Median = $1.2180
11. Arithmetic mean
13. Arithmetic mean

CHAPTER 20

(No answers)

appendix C

Answers to Chapter Self-Review Tests

Chapter 1: A Brief Review of Basic Computations

1. $54\frac{5}{8}$, found by $54\frac{3}{8} + \frac{2}{8}$
2. 10.153, found by multiplying and marking three decimal places
3. $16\frac{7}{8}$, found by $16\frac{10}{8} - \frac{3}{8}$
4. 79, found by

$$\begin{array}{r} 79 \\ 213\overline{)16827} \\ \underline{1491} \\ 1917 \\ \underline{1917} \end{array}$$

5. \$2,709.84, found by 24 X \$112.91
6. 475.51 ounces, found by \$427,503.66 ÷ \$899.05
7. A. \$196.91, found by \$146.91 + \$50.00
   B. \$162.18, found by \$196.91 – \$34.73
   C. \$144.37, found by \$162.18 – \$17.81
   D. \$194.37, found by \$144.37 + \$50.00
   E. \$119.37, found by \$194.37 – \$75.00 and check \$119.37 – \$25.00 = \$94.37
8. $-2\frac{3}{4}$, found by $(+2\frac{3}{4} + 1 + 2\frac{3}{4} + \frac{3}{8}) + (-6\frac{1}{4} - 2\frac{3}{8} - \frac{1}{2} - \frac{1}{2}) = \frac{55}{8} - \frac{77}{8} = -\frac{22}{8}$
9. \$333.75, found by 44 regular hours X \$6 + (\$9 X $7\frac{3}{4}$)
10. \$3, found by (6 X \$3) – [6 X (\$5 ÷ 2)]

Chapter 2: Percents

1. 0.223
2. 76.13%
3. 76%, found by $\frac{19}{25} = 0.76$
4. A. 0.7143, found by 5 ÷ 7 = 0.71429
   B. 71%
5. A. 0.174, found by $17\frac{4}{9}\% = 17.44\% = 0.1744$
   B. $\frac{157}{900}$, found by $17\frac{4}{9} \times \frac{1}{100}$
6. A. 30% = 0.3 = $\frac{3}{10}$
   B. 50% = 0.5 = $\frac{1}{2}$
   C. 70% = 0.7 = $\frac{7}{10}$
7. A. 0.92
   B. $\frac{23}{25}$, found by $\frac{92}{100}$ reduced
8. A. 0.333, found by 1 ÷ 3 = 0.3333
   B. 33.33%
9. A. 38.1%
   B. $\frac{381}{1000}$
10. 0.005, found by 0.055 – 0.05, where $5\frac{1}{2}\% = 5.5\% = 0.055$ and $\frac{1}{20} = 0.05$

Chapter 3: Percentages

1. \$13.23, found by \$215.75 X 0.0613 = \$13.225
2. 25%, found by \$6.39 ÷ \$25.49 = 0.251
3. \$28.40, found by \$29.82 ÷ 1.05, where 105% = 100% + 5%
4. 33%, found by 74,000 ÷ 226,000 = 0.327, where 74,000 = 300,000 – 226,000
5. 43%, found by \$5.12 ÷ \$12, where \$5.12 = \$12.00 – \$6.88
6. A. 60% increase in passenger capacity, found by 150 ÷ 250, where 150 = 400 – 250
   B. 100% increase in car capacity, found by 30 ÷ 30 where 30 = 60 – 30. Larger percent increase in car capacity, specifically 40% larger.
7. A. 34.8%, found by 800,000,000 ÷ 2,300,000,000 = 0.3478
   B. 65.2%, found by 1,500,000,000 ÷ 2,300,000,000 = 0.6522
8. 73%, found by \$1,096.00 ÷ \$1,495.00 = 0.733, where \$1,096 = \$1,495 – \$399
9. 43, found by 215 X 0.20
10. \$14.9 million, found by \$3.55 ÷ 0.238 = \$14.92

Chapter 4: Consumer Spending

1. $0.001 per label, found by $1.00 ÷ 1,000
2. A. $0.0935 per ounce, found by $1.87 ÷ 20
   B. $0.0964 per ounce, found by $1.35 ÷ 14
   C. $0.1056 per ounce, found by $0.95 ÷ 9
   Best buy: A, 20 ounces for $1.87
3. A. $0.116 per ounce, found by $0.29 ÷ 2½
   B. $0.10 per ounce, found by $0.45 ÷ 4½
   Best buy: B, 4½ ounces for $0.45
4. A. $0.13, found by {$215 + $550 + $32 + [(11,000 ÷ 22) X $0.849] + $210} ÷ 11,000
   B. $0.15, found by {$215 + $550 + $32 + [(8,800 ÷ 22) X $0.879] + $187} ÷ 8,800
5. A. $143.77, found by (3 X $27.95) + ($0.19 X 220) + $18.12
   B. $0.6535, found by $143.77 ÷ 220
   C. $47.92, found by $143.77 ÷ 3
6. $121.50. Cost per mile = $0.069, found by $121.50 ÷ 1,770
7. A. $3.35, found by $13,080 ÷ 3,900
   B. $0.23, found by $895 ÷ 3,900
8. They should buy; annual allowable housing expense is $10,465 = 35% X (26 X $1,150), while annual estimated housing expense is $9,179.44 = (12 X $457.12) + $219 + (2 X $600) + $1,475 + $800
9.

Food	$672.75,	found by (27% X $29,900) ÷ 12
Housing	797.33,	found by (32% X $29,900) ÷ 12
Transportation	249.17,	found by (10% X $29,900) ÷ 12
Clothing	299.00,	found by (12% X $29,900) ÷ 12
Medical	124.58,	found by (5% X $29,900) ÷ 12
Gifts	199.33,	found by (8% X $29,900) ÷ 12
Other	149.50,	found by (6% X $29,900) ÷ 12

10.

Item	*Monthly Budget*	*Actual for September*	*Difference*	*Actual for October*	*Difference*	*Two Months Combined*
Food	$672.75	$670	–$ 2.75	$680	+$ 7.25	+$ 4.50
Housing	797.33	765	– 32.33	765	– 32.33	– 64.66
Transportation	249.17	240	– 9.17	245	– 4.17	– 13.34
Clothing	299.00	300	+ 1.00	310	+ 11.00	+ 12.00
Medical	124.58	120	– 4.58	125	+ 0.42	– 4.16
Gifts	199.33	190	– 9.33	212	+ 12.67	+ 3.34
Other	149.50	147	– 2.50	154	+ 4.50	+ 2.00
Totals			–$59.66		–$ 0.66	–$60.32

They are spending under their budget. Considerably under in September; just barely under in October. The excess could go into some type of savings or investment plan.

Chapter 5: Consumer Credit–Charge Accounts

1. A. $235.00
   B. $4.53, found by (0.02 X $200) + (0.015 X $35)
   C. $241.53, found by $235.00 – $50.00 + $52.00 + $4.53
   D. $12.00 (table)
2. A. $185.00, found by $235 – $50
   B. $3.70, found by 0.02 X $185
   C. $240.70, found by $235.00 – $50.00 + $52.00 + $3.70
   D. $12.00 (table)
3. A. $218.33, found by [(20 X $235) + (10 X $185)] ÷ 30
   B. $4.27, found by (0.02 X $200) + (0.015 X $18.33)
   C. $241.27, found by $235.00 – $50.00 + $52.00 + $4.27
   D. $12.00 (table)
4. A. $248.33, found by [(5 X $235) + (15 X $267) + (5 X $217) + (5 X $237)] ÷ 30
   B. $4.72, found by (0.02 X $200) + (0.015 X $48.33)
   C. $241.72, found by $235.00 – $50.00 + $52.00 + $4.72
   D. $12.00 (table)
5. A. $210.52, found by $153.81 – $15 – $8.79 + $77.71 + $2.79
   B. $91.13, found by $100 – $10 + $1.13
   C. $301.65, found by $253.81 – $25 – $8.79 + $77.71 + $3.92 or $210.52 + $91.13

Chapter 6: Consumer Credit—Installment Credit

1. $720, found by ($4,900 – $900) X 0.09 X 2
2. $70, found by [$3,000 + ($3,000 X 0.08 X 5)] ÷ 60
3. $46.01, found by [($1,297 – $46) + ($1,297 – $46) X 0.108 X 3)] ÷ 36
4. 14.50% (Table 6-1), where FC per $100 = ($24/$300) X $100 = $8 and $24 = (12 X $27) – $300
5. 16.50% (Table 6-1), where FC per $100 = ($298.79/$2,213.23) X $100 = $13.50 and $298.79 = ($3,779.23 – $1,560) X 0.09 X 1.5
6. $50, found by $1,000 X 0.10 X 0.5
7. $10.33, found by [$400 + ($400 X 0.06 X 4)] ÷ 48
8. $8.98, found by (21/171) X $73.14, where 21 = (6 X 7) ÷ 2 and $8.98 = (18 X $45.73) – $750
9. $930.62, found by (13 X $75.44) – (78/1,830) X $1,175.40, where $1,175.40 = (60 X $75.44) – $3,351 and 78 = (12 X 13) ÷ 2
10. A. $1,750.24 FC, 15.50% APR, found by (48 X $140.63) – $5,000 and Table 6-1
    B. $1,300 FC, 11.75% APR, found by $5,000 X 0.065 X 4 and Table 6-1
    C. 11.00% APR
    Therefore borrow from Statewide Insurance Company; lower APR and, since all three are for four years, lower finance charge and monthly payments.

Chapter 7: Home Mortgage Loans

1. $1,318.50, found by ($150,000/$1,000) X $8.79 (Table 7-1), where $150,000 = $168,300 – $18,300
2. $1,281.25, found by $150,000 X 0.1025 X 1/12
3. $99.90, found by ($10,000/$1,000) X $9.99 (Table 7-1)
4. $9,987.60, found by $10,000 – [$99.90 – ($10,000 X 0.105 X 1/12)]
5. $11,848.40, found by $12,000 – [$231.60 – ($12,000 X 0.08 X 1/12)], where $231.60 = ($30,000/$1,000) X $7.72 (table)
6. $399.27, found by $337.94 + $550/12 + $186/12, where $337.94 = ($38,490/$1,000) X $8.78 (table) and $38,490 = $39,990 – $1,500
7. $9,256.80, found by $293,735.20 – $284,478.40, where $293,735.20 = (420 X $975.56) – $116,000 and $284,478.40 = (420 X $953.52) – $116,000 and $975.56 = ($116,000/$1,000) X $8.41 (table) and $953.52 = ($116,000/$1,000) X $8.22 (table)
8. $200,250, found by $403,770 $203,520, where $403,770 = (420 X $1,318.50) – $150,000 and $203,520 = (240 X $1,473) – $150,000 and $1,318.50 = ($150,000/$1,000) X $8.79 (table) and $1,473 = ($150,000/$1,000) X $9.82 (table)
   The McGills might not have been able to afford a monthly payment of $1,473. However, if they could afford $1,318.50 monthly it would seem another $154.50 per month could be spared to ultimately save over $200,000!
9. $18,156.80, found by $163,404.00 – $145,247.20, where $163,404.00 = (360 X $685.15) – $83,250 and $145,247.20 = (360 X $609.02) – $75,000 and $685.15 = ($83,250/$1,000) X $8.23 (table) and $609.02 = ($74,000/$1,000) X $8.23 (table)
   Perhaps they did not have $18,500, which is 20% of $92,500.
10. $350 to $2,450, found by 0.01 X $35,000 and 0.07 X $35,000.
    Fees or premiums for title insurance, title examination and an abstract of title, preparation fees, escrow, assessments, notary fees, appraisals, credit reports, etc.

Chapter 8: Insurance

1. A. $80,000, found by 0.80 X $100,000
   B. $8,000, found by 0.10 X $80,000
   C. $40,000, found by 0.50 X $80,000
   D. $16,000, found by 0.20 X $80,000
   E. $24,000, found by (8/9) X $27,000
2. $539 (Table 8-2)
3. $421 (Table 8-2, using Protection Class 1-6)
4. $52.06, found by 0.255 X ($15,000/$1,000) X $13.61 (Tables 8-3 and 8-4)
5. A. $1,892.40, found by 6 X ($20,000/$1,000) X $15.77 (Table 8-3)
   B. $20,000 (term, therefore no cash value)
6. $98.26, found by [12 X 0.085 X ($100,000/$1,000) X $49.13 (table) – ($100,000/$1,000) X $49.13]
7. Unmarried males, 21-24 years, who are principal operators and drive to and from work have *twice as many accidents* as unmarried females, under 21 years, who are occasional operators and drive for pleasure.
8. $174.15, found by 1.35 (Table 8-5) X ($54.80 + $3.60 + $15.60 + $55.00)
9. $110.72, found by 1.60 (Table 8-5) X ($46.60 + $3.60 + $19.00)
10. $99.36, found by 2.30 (Table 8-5) X ($43.20)

Chapter 9: Income and Deductions

1. $171.70, found by (46 X $3.40) + (3 X 1.5 X $3.40) or (49 X $3.40) + (3 X 0.5 X $3.40)
2. $442.31, found by $11,500 ÷ 26

3. $384.23, found by (80 × $2.95) + (0.0175 × $8,470.00)
4. $58.24, found by 1.40 × $3.90 × 8 × 100/75
5. $1,394.58, found by 0.0613 × (26 × $875.00)
6. $11.70, found by 38 × $3.10 = $117.80 and Table 9-4
7. $83.88, found by $700.00 – (3 × $41.66) = $575.02 and $58.47 + 0.21 × ($575.02 – $454.00)
8. $179.34, found by gross pay = $231.20 because (0.06 × $3,853.33) is greater than 36 × $3.70; deductions = $51.86, found by $24.60 (FIT) + $14.17 (FICA) + $4.62 (SIT) + $3.47 (CIT) + $5.00; and $231.20 – $51.86
9. $194.28, found by gross pay = $249.90, found by (31 × $5.10) + (12 × 1.5 × $5.10) or (43 × $5.10) + (12 × 0.5 × $5.10); deductions = $55.62, found by $40.30 (FIT) + $15.32 (FICA) where FIT = $40.30, found by $230.67 = $249.90 – $19.23 and $31.29 + 0.26 ($230.67 – $196.00) and FICA = 0.0613 × $249.90; and $249.90 – $55.62
10. $380.65, found by gross pay = $469.67, found by $11,272.00 ÷ 24; and deductions = $89.02, found by $38.79 (FIT) + $28.79 (FICA) + $7.05 (SIT) + $9.39 (CIT) + $5.00 (charity), where FIT = $38.79, found by $469.67 – (3 × $41.66) = $344.69 and $26.25 + 0.18 ($344.69 – $275.00); FICA = $28.79, found by 0.0613 × $469.67; SIT = $7.05, found by 0.015 × $469.67; CIT = $9.39, found by 0.02 × $469.67 and $469.67 – $89.02

Chapter 10: Taxes

1. A. $52.49, found by (0.05 × $49.99) + $49.99 or 1.05 × $49.99
   B. $52.99, found by (0.06 × $49.99) + $49.99 or 1.06 × $49.99
   C. $52.05, found by 1.04125 × $49.99
   D. $53.24, found by 1.065 × $49.99
2. A. $1.58, found by 1.06 × $1.49
   B. $39.75, found by 1.06 × $37.50
   C. $529.58, found by 1.06 × $499.60
   D. $1,321.45, found by 1.06 × $1,246.65
3. $55.65, found by ($2.65 ÷ 0.05) + $2.65
4. $7.53, found by $7.95 ÷ 1.05525
5. $2,388.75, found by $54.60 × $43,750/$1,000, where $43,750 = 0.50 × $87,500
6. $153.30, found by 365 × 2 × $0.21
7. 29.8 mills, found by $850,000 ÷ (0.30 × $95,000,000)
8. A. $13.50, found by $0.12 × 112.5
   B. $15.75, found by $0.14 × 112.5
   C. $16.31, found by $0.145 × 112.5
   D. $12.38, found by $0.11 × 112.5
9. $157.96, found by (4 × $35.00) + (4 × $3.09) + (0.04 × 4 × $35.00)
10. A. $64.72, found by $2.00 × $32,360/$1,000
    B. $48.54, found by $1.50 × $32,360/$1,000
    C. $986.98, found by $30.50 × $32,360/$1,000
    D. $1,320.29, found by $40.80 × $32,360/$1,000

Chapter 11: Banking Services

1.

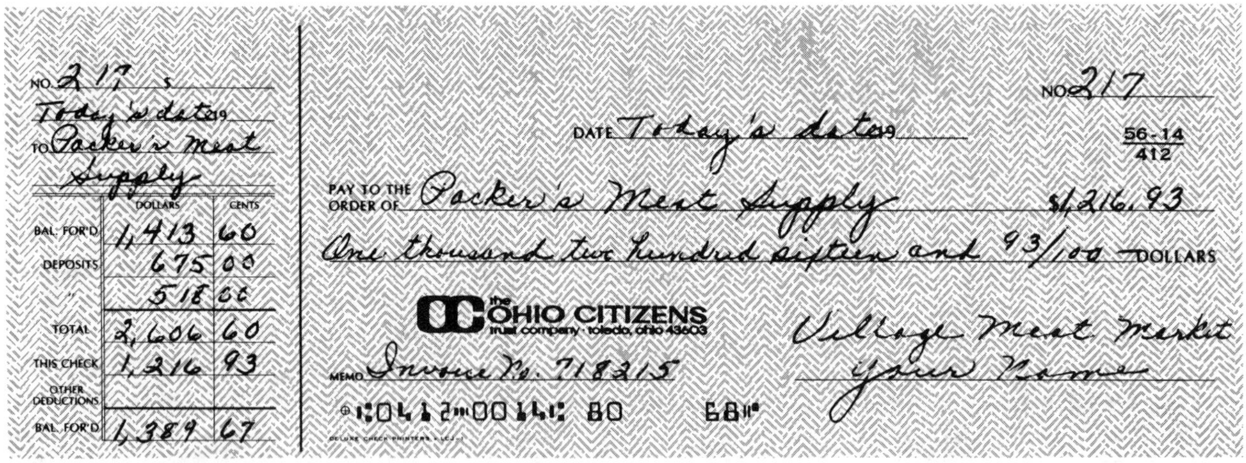
NO. 217
Today's date 19
TO Packer's Meat Supply
	DOLLARS	CENTS
BAL. FOR'D	1,413	60
DEPOSITS	675	00
	518	00
TOTAL	2,606	60
THIS CHECK	1,216	93
OTHER DEDUCTIONS		
BAL. FOR'D	1,389	67

NO. 217
DATE Today's date 19
56-14/412
PAY TO THE ORDER OF Packer's Meat Supply $1,216.93
One thousand two hundred sixteen and 93/100 DOLLARS
the OHIO CITIZENS trust company · toledo, ohio 43603
Village Meat Market
Your Name
MEMO Invoice No. 718215

2.

Checkbook balance		$600.21
Service charge	–	2.00
Revised balance		$598.21

Statement balance		$623.50
Deposits not shown	+	200.00
		$823.50
Checks outstanding ($61.50 + $163.79)	–	225.29
Revised bank statement		$598.21

3. A. \$81.78, found by \$4,000 × 0.08 × 92/360, where the due date is Feb. 9 and (365 – 313) + 40 = 92
   B. \$78.90, found by \$4,000 × 0.08 × 90/365, where 90 = 3 × 30
4. A. \$77.15, found by \$4,000 × 0.08 × 88/365, where the due date is (313 + 90) – 365 = 38 (Feb. 7)
   B. \$80.00, found by \$4,000 × 0.08 × 90/360
5. 609.7%, found by \$0.87 ÷ (\$17.36 × 3/365) = 6.097325, where \$0.87 = \$18.23 – \$17.36
6. \$35,960.59, found by \$200 ÷ (0.07 × 29/365)
7. 450 days, found by \$100 ÷ (\$1,000 × 0.08) = 1.25; then 1.25 × 360
8. \$1,902.10, found by \$6,902.10 – \$5,000.00, where \$6,902.10 = \$1.38042 × 5,000 and the rate per period is 1.625% and the number of periods is 20.
9. \$21,388.60, found by \$1.06943 × 20,000, where the rate per period is 1.125% and the number of periods is 6
10. \$6.16, found by (\$1.0109075 × 565) – \$565
11. \$1,765.29, found by \$1.21899 × 1,100 = \$1,340.89, where the rate per period is 2.000% and the number of periods is 10 (5 years); then \$1.316503400 × 1,340.89 (5 years)
12. \$20,207.34, found by \$35,207.34 – \$15,000.00, where \$1.34611 × 15,000 = \$20,191.65, with the rate per period equal to 1.875% and the number of periods equal to 16; then \$1.733181201 × 20,191.65 = \$34,995.79 (10 years to July 1, 1989); and then \$1.0060451 × 34,995.79 = \$35,207.34 (40 days exact time to August 10, 1989).

Chapter 12: Promissory Notes, Discounting, and Partial Payment

1. \$940.03, found by \$965 – (\$965 × 0.135 × 69/360)
2. \$1,833.79, found by \$1,849.20 – \$15.41, where \$1,849.20 = \$1,800 + (\$1,800 × 0.08 × 123/360) and \$15.41 = \$1,849.20 × 0.10 × 30/360
3. \$8,732.73, found by \$8,400 + (\$8,400 × 0.0775 × 184/360)
4. \$821.20, found by

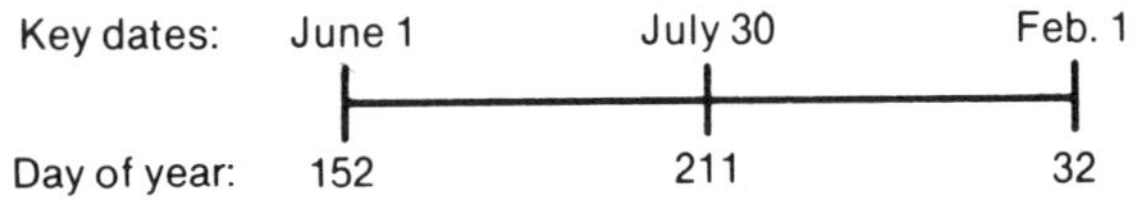

Face		\$1,500.00
First payment	\$750.00	
Deduct interest on \$1,500.00 for 59 days (June 1 to July 30)	– 27.04	
Amount deducted from face		– 722.96
Balance on July 30		\$ 777.04
Add interest on \$777.04 for 186 days (July 30 to Feb. 1)		+ 44.16
Amount due on due date		\$ 821.20

5. \$3,571.50, found by \$7,659 – \$4,087.50, where \$7,659 = \$7,400 + (\$7,400 × 0.105 × 120/360) and \$4,087.50 = \$4,000 + (\$4,000 × 0.105 × 75/360)

Chapter 13: Opening a Business

1.

AL'S RADIO/TV REPAIR SHOP
Balance Sheet
As of October 31

Assets		
Cash	\$1,850	
Supplies	3,600	
Equipment	4,750	
Total assets		\$10,200
Liabilities		
Accounts payable	\$1,600	
Owner Equity		
Al Herbert, capital	8,600	
Total liabilities and owner equity		\$10,200

2.

AL'S RADIO/TV REPAIR SHOP
Income Statement
For Quarter Ended December 31

Income:		
Income from repair services	\$2,100	
Less: Credit allowances	– 120	
Net income		\$1,980
Cost of supplies		– 915
Gross profit		\$1,065
Operating expenses:		
Rent	\$ 345	
Depreciation	120	
Utilities and insurance	90	
Miscellaneous expenses	205	
Total operating expenses		– 760
Net income		\$ 305

3. A. 30.0%, found by \$15,000 ÷ \$50,000 = 0.3000
   B. 10.0%, found by \$5,000 ÷ \$50,000 = 0.1000
   C. 6.0%, found by \$3,000 ÷ \$50,000 = 0.0600
   D. 54.0%, found by \$27,000 ÷ \$50,000 = 0.5400
4. A. 25.0% decrease, found by (\$15,000 – \$20,000) ÷ \$20,000 = 0.2500
   B. 200.0% increase, found by (\$3,000 – \$1,000) ÷ \$1,000 = 2.0000
   C. 31.6% increase, found by (\$50,000 – \$38,000) ÷ \$38,000 = 0.3158
   D. 25.0% increase, found by (\$20,000 – \$16,000) ÷ \$16,000 = 0.2500

5. A. 2.50:1, found by $50,000 ÷ $20,000 = 2.500
   B. 2.38:1, found by $38,000 ÷ $16,000 = 2.375
   C. This year there is $2.50 in current assets for every $1.00 of current liabilities. Last year there was $2.38 for every $1.00. Wejipum is in slightly better financial shape this year.
6. A. 1.15:1, found by ($50,000 – $27,000) ÷ $20,000 = 1.15
   B. 1.5:1, found by ($38,000 – $14,000) ÷ $16,000 = 1.50
   C. This year there is $1.15 in quickly convertible liquid assets for every $1.00 of current liabilities. Last year there was $1.50 for every $1.00. Wejipum had a slightly better acid-test ratio last year.
7. A. $30,000, found by $50,000 – $20,000; 21.8%, found by $6,540 ÷ $30,000 = 0.218
   B. $22,000, found by $38,000 – $16,000; 25%, found by $5,500 ÷ $22,000 = 0.25
   C. The return on owner investment, although quite high this year, is less than last year.

Chapter 14: Business Expenses

1. Gross pay:
   A. $112.50, found by (30 X $2.25) + (6% X $750);
   B. $212.55, found by (26 X $2.30) + (6.5% X $2,350);
   C. $190.15, found by (40 X $2.75) + (7% X $1,145);
   D. $385.00, found by (40 X $3.10) + (7.5% X $3,480);
   E. $230.00, found by (40 X $5.75)

	FIT	*FICA, found by (6.13% X gross)*	*SIT, found by (3½% X gross)*	*Total Deductions*	*Net Pay*
A.	$10.80	$ 6.90	$ 3.94	$21.64	$ 90.86
B.	36.20	13.03	7.44	56.67	155.88
C.	17.40	11.66	6.66	35.72	154.43
D.	48.30	23.60	13.48	85.38	299.62
E.	21.20	14.10	8.05	43.35	186.65

2. $1,607.03, found by (3 X 200 X $0.705) + (1,418 X $0.835)
3. $801,250, found by [(2 X $17,500) + (3 X $8,750)] + [(4 X $92,500) + (2 X $185,000)]
4. A. $4,863.75, found by (87.5 X $11.30) + (125 X $31.00)
   B. $5,710.00, found by (87.5 X $12.40) + (125 X $37.00)
5. $7,010.00, found by $50.00 + (240 X $29.00), where $50.00 minimum is greater than 4 X $12.40 = $49.60
6. A. $52.86, found by $1.07 X 49.40
   B. $67.14, found by $1.07 X 62.75
   C. $65.70, found by $1.07 X 61.40
7. A. $6,000, $42, found by 0.007 X $6,000; $228.00, found by 0.038 X $6,000; $270, found by $42 + $228
   B. $5,430; $38.01, found by 0.007 X $5,430; $206.34, found by 0.038 X $5,430; $244.35, found by $38.01 + $206.34
   C. $4,260; $29.82, found by 0.007 X $4,260; $161.88, found by 0.038 X $4,260; $191.70, found by $29.82 + $161.88
8. $40.75, found by $6.00 (minimum) + ($14.46 X 1.75) + $7.50 (minimum) = $38.81. Then $38.81 + (0.05 X $38.81)

Chapter 15: Trade and Cash Discounts

1. A. $37.50, found by 0.30 X $125
   B. $87.50, found by $125.00 – $37.50
2. $143.97, found by $239.95 – (0.40 X $239.95) or 0.60 X $239.95
3. A. $8.23, found by (0.30 X $19) + (0.10 X $13.30) + (0.10 X $11.97)
   B. $10.77, found by $19.00 – $8.23
4. A. $29.40, found by 0.02 X $1,470.00
   B. $1,440.60, found by $1,470.00 – $29.40
5. Distributor B, because the net is 51% of this list, compared to 51.2% (A) and 52% (C); or because the single equivalent discount for B is 49%, compared to 48.8% (A) and 48% (C).
6. $2,450.00; April 5 is 11 days after March 25, therefore no cash discount
7. A. $37.50, found by 0.05 X $750.00
   B. $712.50, found by $750.00 – $37.50
8. $960.40, found by $980.00 – (0.02 X $980.00) or 0.98 X $980.00
9. A. August 25, found by August 15 plus ten days
   B. $465.50, found by $490.00 – (0.05 X $490.00) or 0.95 X $490.00
10. $1,577.02, found by 0.80 X 0.90 X $2,235.00 = $1,609.20 (net) and 0.98 X $1,609.20 = $1,577.016

Chapter 16: Markup and Markdown

1. A. $303 markup, found by $568.00 – $265.00
   B. 53.3% markup on selling price, found by $303.00 ÷ $568.00
2. A. $13,507 markup, found by $25,780 – $12,473
   B. 108.3% markup on cost, found by $13,507 ÷ $12,473
3. A. $29.89 selling price, found by $19.96 + $9.93
   B. 33% markup on selling price, found by $9.93 ÷ $29.89
4. A. $145.00 selling price, found by $96.37 + $48.63
   B. 50% markup on cost, found by $48.63 ÷ $96.37

5. $39.00 selling price, found by $7.80 ÷ 20%, where 100% – 80% = 20%
6. 32.7% markup on cost, found by 17¢ ÷ 52¢, where $6.24 ÷ 12 = 52¢ and 69¢ – 52¢ = 17¢
7. $77.00 selling price, found by $35.00 + $42.00, where 120% X $35.00 = $42.00
8. $4.73 cost, found by 60% X $7.88, where 100% – 40% = 60%
9. $39.98 sale price, found by 80% X $49.98, where 100% – 20% = 80%
10. 20% markdown, found by $0.40 ÷ $1.99, where $1.99 – $1.59 = $0.40

Chapter 17: Depreciation

1. A. Straight-line method:

Yr.	Annual Depreciation	Accumulated Depreciation	Book Value
1	$15,000, found by ($85,000 – $10,000) ÷ 5	$15,000	$70,000
2	$15,000, found by ($85,000 – $10,000) ÷ 5	30,000	55,000
3	$15,000, found by ($85,000 – $10,000) ÷ 5	45,000	40,000
4	$15,000, found by ($85,000 – $10,000) ÷ 5	60,000	25,000
5	$15,000, found by ($85,000 – $10,000) ÷ 5	75,000	10,000

B. Sum-of-the-years'-digits method:

Yr.	Annual Depreciation	Accumulated Depreciation	Book Value
1	$25,000, found by (5/15) ($85,000 – $10,000)	$25,000	$60,000
2	$20,000, found by (4/15) ($85,000 – $10,000)	45,000	40,000
3	$15,000, found by (3/15) ($85,000 – $10,000)	60,000	25,000
4	$10,000, found by (2/15) ($85,000 – $10,000)	70,000	15,000
5	$5,000, found by (1/15) ($85,000 – $10,000)	75,000	10,000

C. Declining-balance method:

Yr.	Annual Depreciation	Accumulated Depreciation	Book Value (declining balance)
1	$34,000, found by 40% of $85,000	$34,000	$51,000
2	$20,400, found by 40% of $51,000	54,400	30,600
3	$12,240, found by 40% of $30,600	66,640	18,360
4	$7,344, found by 40% of $18,360	73,984	11,016
5	$1,016 adjusted, found by $11,016 – $10,000; actual is $4,406.40, found by 40% of $11,016	75,000	10,000

2. A. $38,500, found by (2,940/8,400) ($125,000 – $15,000)
   B. $86,500, found by $125,000 – $38,500
3. A. $10,800, found by (168,000/700,000) ($47,500 – $2,500)
   B. $36,700, found by $47,500 – $10,800

Chapter 18: Valuing an Inventory and Inventory Turnover

1. C.–Lifo; last-in, first-out is equivalent to first-in, last-out
2. B.–7; definition of turnover rate
3. 9/8; 10
   9/9; 60
   9/15; 25
   9/22; 5
   9/30, 55
4. $440.39, found by {[(40 X $7.40) + (50 X $8.00) + (50 X $8.50)] ÷ 140} X 55
5. $465.00, found by (50 X $8.50) + (5 X $8.00)
6. $416.00, found by (40 X $7.40) + (15 X $8.00)
7. 5.0, found by $400,000 ÷ [($81,700 + 74,700 + 78,200 + 82,600 + 80,000 + 79,800) ÷ 6] = 5.0314465
8. 5.0, found by $800,000 ÷ [($163,400 + 149,400 + 156,400 + 165,200 + 160,000 + 159,600) ÷ 6] = 5.0314465

Chapter 19: The Use of Statistical Techniques in Business

1.

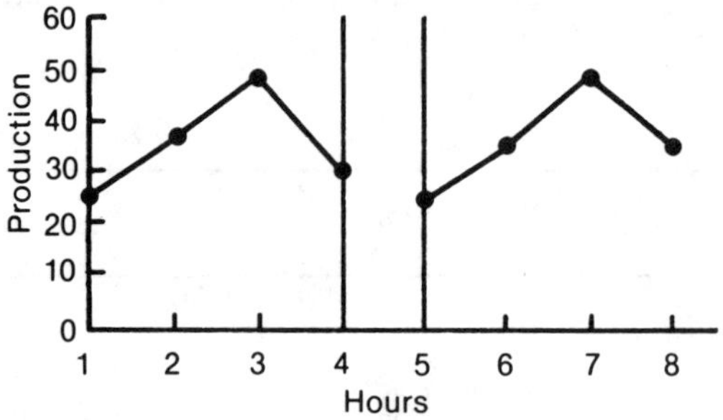

2.

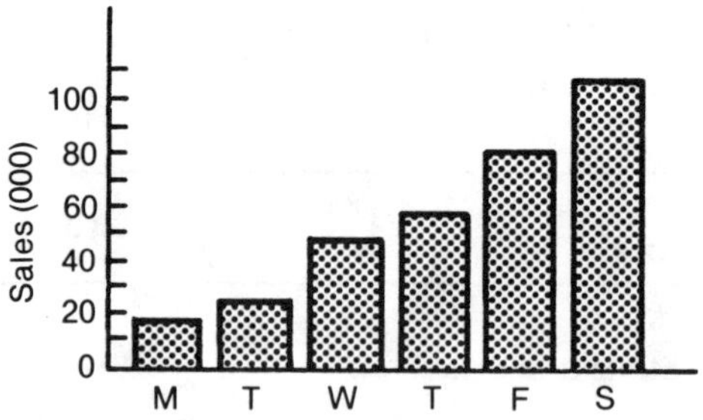

3. 60%, found by
$12 \div 20 = 0.6$
30%, found by
$6 \div 20 = 0.3$
10%, found by
$2 \div 20 = 0.1$

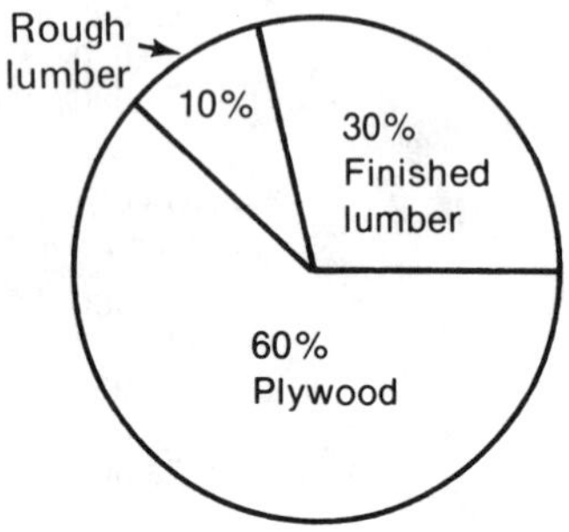

4.

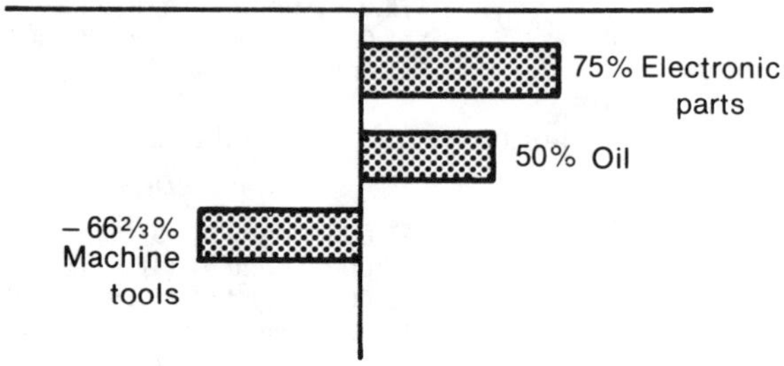

5. A.

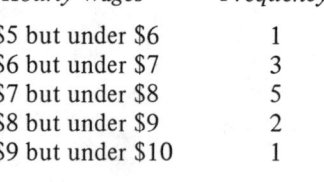

Hourly Wages	*Frequency*
$5 but under $6	1
$6 but under $7	3
$7 but under $8	5
$8 but under $9	2
$9 but under $10	1

B. Histogram and frequency polygon shown at right

C. $\overline{X}$ = $7.325, found by $87.90 ÷ 12

D. Median = $7.425, found by ($7.20 + $7.65) ÷ 2

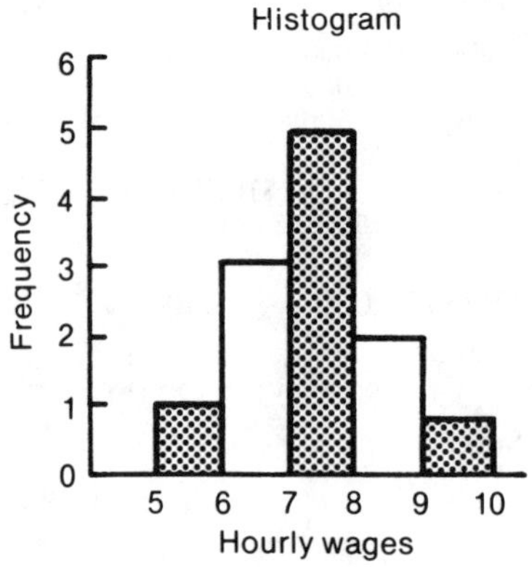

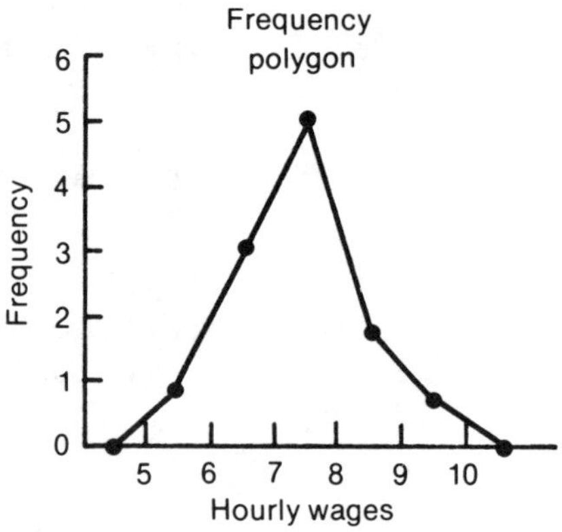

Chapter 20: The Metric System

1. T
2. T
3. F
4. T
5. F, it would be closer to 2 meters
6. T
7. T
8. T
9. F
10. F
11. T
12. F
13. T
14. T
15. F, kilometer
16. T
17. T
18. T
19. T
20. T
21. T
22. F
23. T
24. F
25. F

Index

This book has been set IBM Composer, in 11 and 10 point Press Roman, leaded 1 point. Chapter numbers are Avant Garde Bold and chapter titles are 30 point Avant Garde Extra Light. Section numbers and titles are 11 point Univers Bold. The size of the maximum type area is 42 by 56 picas.